Dionysiac Poetics
and Euripides' *Bacchae*

EXPANDED EDITION

Dionysiac Poetics and Euripides' *Bacchae*

EXPANDED EDITION

CHARLES SEGAL

Princeton University
Press
Princeton, New Jersey

Library of Congress Cataloging-in-Publication Data

Segal, Charles, 1936-
Dionysiac poetics and Euripides' *Bacchae*. Expanded edition.
Bibliography: p.
Includes index.
1. Euripides. *Bacchae*. I. Title.
PA3973.B2S56   882'.01   82-47612
ISBN 0-691-01597-X   AACR2

This book has been composed in Electra

Princeton University Press books are printed on acid-free paper and
meet the guidelines for permanence and durability of the Committee on
Production Guidelines for Book Longevity of the Council on
Library Resources

First printing of the Expanded Edition, 1997

http://pup.princeton.edu

Printed in the United States of America

1 3 5 7 9 10 8 6 4 2

For
Richard, Susan, Cindy, and Michael
and
Jimmy, Mauricio, Alesia

Contents

Preface to the Expanded Edition

The *Bacchae* remains ever new, exciting, and so controversial. "Every reader gets the *Bacchae* he deserves. No two scholars agree on the meaning of the play, let alone on the intention of the author." So writes H. S. Versnel, surveying the state of the scholarship in 1990 (Versnel 1990, 96; also Fitzgerald 1992/93, 13: I refer to the Bibliographical Addenda at the end of this volume). But if the controversy over the meaning of the *Bacchae* has not diminished in the fifteen years since *Dionysiac Poetics* first appeared, there has been a major shift of emphasis in the interpretation of Dionysus. The view of Dionysus primarily or solely as the dissolver of order and of boundaries, which has it roots in Nietzsche and was fostered by the influential work of Walter H. Otto, has been balanced by a broader recognition of Dionysus' place within the polis. The *Bacchae*, as Albert Henrichs has rightly emphasized, presents a very partial and limited view of the god; and the attempts of Henrichs and others over the last two decades to distinguish Dionysus from the "Dionysiac" and to recover a sense of the god's "personality" as it appeared to a wide range of his ancient worshipers offer an important corrective to the Nietzschean approach. In his fine synthesis of research on Dionysus in the third edition of the *Oxford Classical Dictionary* (1996, 479), Henrichs describes Dionysus as "the most versatile and elusive of all the Greek gods," and "elusive" was also the word I chose to introduce the god in my first chapter. It is a pleasure also to note the ever-growing concern with "metatragedy" as a wider phenomenon of Greek culture and to see the interest in investigating Dionysiac patterns, with something like a "Dionysiac poetics," across the whole corpus of Greek tragedy.

Were I writing the book today, although I would not change my view of the play as a whole or of Dionysus' role in it, I would put even greater stress on Euripides' *construction* of Dionysus from the cultic and political background of the god (pp. 68–77; for such an approach to the "palace miracle," see Fisher 1992); and I would strengthen my discussions of Dionysus' place in the polis (see pp. 10, 16, 247, 328–29). On the other hand, reading the play solely in terms of the social and civic functions of the Dionysiac cult goes too far toward the opposite extreme, for the Dionysus of the play cannot be equated with the Dionysus of cult in any simple, one-to-one relation, nor can one reduce the play to a black-and-white attack or defense of the god, or assume that Euripides' intention was to bolster Athenian civic religion or civic identity. In fact, the civic functions of Dionysus in Athens, Thebes, and other parts of Greece make his destructive role in the play even more striking.

In addition to the intensive reexamination of Dionysus over the past fifteen years (including at least three major international conferences between 1984 and 1990), there have been a number of new books and articles devoted wholly or in part to the *Bacchae*; many new studies of Greek tragedy; James Diggle's new Oxford Classical Text, with accompanying notes in his *Euripidea*; a recent commentary by Richard Seaford, also with a text; significant new work on the iconography of Dionysus; and the publication of several important new Dionysiac inscriptions. All of this puts some issues in the play into new perspective, and I try to take account of these in my Afterword. I have myself returned to the *Bacchae* in two recent studies, Segal 1994 and 1997. The 1994 essay developed from recent work on female lament in ancient Greece (see Segal 1993), which led me to appreciate more fully the play's use of mourning ritual. In my 1997 essay I reexamine some of the problematic relations between the chorus and the polis. I have summarized some of the main points of both essays in the Afterword, but for more detail I refer the reader to the respective publications. Although it was not possible to make changes to the original text, the Press has kindly permitted me a few minor corrections.

I warmly thank my Harvard colleague Albert Henrichs for generously reading a draft of the Afterword and for making many valuable suggestions, and also for much stimulating conversation on Dionysus and tragedy over the past years. As is inevitably the case with Dionysus and with the *Bacchae*, there are many points on which he would not necessarily agree. No one but myself is responsible for the mistakes and shortcomings that remain. I am also grateful to Brigitta van Rheinberg of Princeton University Press for her initiative, encouragement, and patience in the production of this volume, and to

Joy Abellana for efficiently overseeing the new edition. I renew my thanks to the friends and colleagues named in the original Preface and particularly to Jean-Pierre Vernant, whose friendship, kindness, and wisdom over the years have remained an inspiration. I would like to express my loving appreciation to my wife, Nancy Jones, to Josh, Tad, Amy, and Cora, to the other family members to whom I originally dedicated the book, and, last but not least, to Frank and Geraldine Jones, for many years of encouragement and support.

Cambridge, Massachusetts
February 1997

Preface

Euripides' *Bacchae* continues to be one of the most read, produced, and discussed of the ancient Greek plays. As it also continues to be one of the most puzzling and disturbing, a detailed reexamination of its meaning needs no apology. Its implications, reverberating from Nietzsche to Marcuse, are still very much with us.

In a stimulating passage of *Violence and the Sacred*, René Girard suggests, "To resolve the problem of the *Bacchae*, we would need to establish a system of differentiation that did not dissolve under scrutiny and that permitted us to affirm the play's literary, psychological, and moral coherence. Such a system would be based, once again, on recourse to *arbitrary* violence" (p. 138). In the *Bacchae*, I would argue, Euripides inscribes that arbitrary violence figuratively into the civic, ritual, and aesthetic forms designed to contain it. This play brings into the Apollonian limits of the tragic form and literary conventions the god who dissolves limits. My interpretation, then, seeks to define a "Dionysiac poetics" not so much of arbitrary violence as of a world-view and an art-form that can admit logical contradictions and hold them in suspension. By choosing as his central figure the god in whom opposites coalesce and differences collapse, Euripides explores what in tragedy is able to reach beyond the social, ritual, and historical context from which tragedy itself arises. The *Bacchae* is not only about the god of ecstatic religion, wine, and madness; it is also about the god of tragedy and about the "Dionysiac" in its relation to artistic illusion and artistic truth. To reach this point, however, it is necessary first to traverse the ritual, social, and psychological domains of the play. The argument, therefore, forms a progression, as logical as Dionysus permits, which culminates in the long Chapters 7 and 8 and the generalizations of Chapter 9.

I wish to thank Jean-Pierre Vernant, Marcel Detienne, Nicole Loraux, and Pierre Vidal-Naquet for making possible a term at the École des Hautes Études, VIᵉ Section, Paris, in 1975-76, when the first stages of this work were begun. Their stimulating company and warm hospitality made a good beginning. Thanks to a Summer Stipend for Research from the National Endowment on the Humanities in 1977, I was able to devote several months of uninterrupted study to the play. A term at the University of Melbourne in the summer of 1978 under the auspices of the Fulbright program and the Australian-American Educational Exchange Foundation furthered my work. I owe special thanks to Graeme Clarke, George Gellie, Robin Jackson, and Harriet Edquist of Melbourne and to A. J. Boyle and Gerald Fitzgerald of Monash University. Last but not least, a Fellowship from the John Simon Guggenheim Memorial Foundation in 1981-82 provided the leisure for the final polishing and rethinking. To all of these individuals and institutions I am deeply grateful.

Albert Cook and William Wyatt of Brown University and Eva Stigers of Wheaton College generously read through the entire manuscript and made numerous suggestions and improvements. I thank them all with great appreciation for a very considerable sacrifice of time and effort. Froma Zeitlin of Princeton University read portions of an earlier draft and offered much useful advice. I also thank Kenneth J. Reckford and Peter Burian, who read the manuscript for Princeton University Press, for careful criticism. Brown University, through the good offices of Provost Maurice Glicksman and Associate Provost Frank Durand, supported this project with a leave of absence in 1975 and various forms of clerical assistance. Mrs. Frances Eisenhauer of Brown University once more typed the entire work with a devotion, concern, and critical sense of style and logic that weeded out many an infelicity. My thanks go also to Joanna Hitchcock, Executive Editor of Princeton University Press, for her patience, interest, and sound advice on numerous details. For whatever errors or defects remain I alone am responsible.

I have tried to make the book accessible to the Greekless reader. I have therefore consigned most of the technical details to the notes and translated or closely paraphrased all quotations from the Greek. Unless otherwise indicated, these translations are my own. Their aim is reasonable fidelity to the original rather than literary elegance. I have transliterated individual words and short phrases when the result was not hopelessly exotic or annoyingly obscure; I have left Greek font if transliteration seemed confusing. The apparent lack of consistency has behind it the criteria of clarity and intelligibility for both the general reader and the classicist. Some books and articles published in late 1980 and in 1981—particularly those of Coche de la Ferté, Foley, Loraux, and Seaford—arrived too late for me to consider them as fully as they deserve.

In a few places I have incorporated in revised form material that I have published in *Ramus* 6 (1977) 103-120, *Arethusa* 11 (1978) 185-202, and *Classical World* 72 (1978/79) 129-148 (see Bibliography). I wish to thank the editors of these journals for kind permission to make use of material from these publications. I presented the kernel of Chapter 7 at the Duke University Conference, "New Directions in Euripidean Criticism," in March 1977. I am indebted to the organizer of the conference, Peter Burian, and to the participants for helpful responses and comments.

Dionysus is truly, as Sophocles says, a god "of many names," inspiring his interpreters with visions almost as ecstatic as those of his worshipers of old. This book is an interpretation of the play and not of the god or his cult. Like all interpreters of the *Bacchae*, however, I have had to draw on the labors of historians of religion and make up my mind about Dionysus. Sorting out the probable from the possible in the heady pages of Otto and Kerényi or in the darker visions of Green and Slater has not always been easy. Apollo, I hope, has at least sometimes been my guide and enabled me, as "Longinus" advises, "to keep sobriety amid the Bacchic revels."

Providence, Rhode Island
February 1982

Abbreviations

AC   *L'Antiquité Classique*

AJP   *American Journal of Philology*

BICS   *Bulletin of the Institute of Classical Studies,* University of London

Burkert,   Burkert, Walter, *Griechische Religion der archaischen*
Gr. Rel.   *und klassischen Epochen* (Stuttgart 1977)

CJ   *Classical Journal*

C&M   *Classica et Mediaevalia*

CP   *Classical Philology*

CQ   *Classical Quarterly*

CR   *Classical Review*

CW   *Classical World*

D   Diehl, Ernestus, ed., *Anthologia Lyrica Graeca* (Leipzig 1925), 2 vols.

DK   Diels, Hermann, and Walter Kranz, eds., *Die Fragmente der Vorsokratiker*, ed. 6 (Berlin 1952), 3 vols.

Entretiens,   *Entretiens sur l'antiquité classique*, VI, *Euripide,*
Euripide   ed. O. Reverdin, Fondation Hardt (Vandoeuvres, Geneva 1960)

G&R   *Greece and Rome*

GRBS   *Greek, Roman and Byzantine Studies*

HSCP   *Harvard Studies in Classical Philology*

HThR   *Harvard Theological Review*

ICS   *Illinois Classical Studies*

JHS   *Journal of Hellenic Studies*

Lesky, TDH   Lesky, Albin, *Die tragische Dichtung der Hellenen*, ed. 3 (Göttingen 1972)

LSJ   Liddell-Scott-Jones-McKenzie, eds., *A Greek-English Lexicon*, ed. 9 (Oxford 1940), with Supplement (1968)

Mette   Mette, H. J., *Die Fragmente der Tragödien des Aischylos* (Berlin 1959)

MH   *Museum Helveticum*

N   Nauck, Augustus, ed., *Tragicorum Graecorum Fragmenta*, ed. 2 (Leipzig 1889); Supplement, ed. B. Snell (Hildesheim 1964)

NJbb   *Neue Jahrbücher für das klassische Altertum*

Nilsson, GGR   Nilsson, Martin P., *Geschichte der griechischen Religion*, I, ed. 2 (Munich 1955)

OCT   Oxford Classical Texts

P   Page, Denys, ed., *Poetae Melici Graeci* (Oxford 1962)

PCPS   *Proceedings of the Cambridge Philological Society*

QUCC   *Quaderni Urbinati di Cultura Classica*

RE   Pauly-Wissowa-Kroll, eds., *Realencyclopädie der classischen Altertumswissenschaft* (Stuttgart 1894ff.)

REG   *Revue des Études Grecques*

RhM   *Rheinisches Museum*

RPh   *Revue de Philologie*

SMSR   *Studi e Materiali di Storia delle Religioni*

SO   *Symbolae Osloenses*

TAPA   *Transactions of the American Philological Association*

WI   Winnington-Ingram, R. P., *Euripides and Dionysus* (Cambridge 1948)

WS   *Wiener Studien*

YCS   *Yale Classical Studies*

ZPE   *Zeitschrift für Papyrologie und Epigraphik*

The Greek text is generally cited from the Oxford Classical Text of Gilbert Murray, *Euripidis Fabulae*, ed. 2, vol. 3 (Oxford 1913), with deviations indicated in the notes. Secondary literature is cited by short title, by author's name alone, or by one of the above abbreviations. Full bibliographical information will be found in the Selected Bibliography.

Dionysiac Poetics
and Euripides' *Bacchae*

EXPANDED EDITION

It is not easy to recognize that the city should
be mixed like a wine-bowl, wherein the wine
as it is poured forth seethes in its madness,
but if checked by the other god, sober, a god
by a god, receives thereby a graceful and
beautiful companionship and fashions a good
and healthily balanced beverage.

Plato, *Laws* 6.773 c-d and
Plutarch, *Moralia* 15 e.

Nah ist,
und schwer zu fassen der Gott.
Wo aber Gefahr ist, wächst
das Rettende auch.

Hölderlin, "Patmos"

Introduction

Every literary critic in some way addresses the question: what vision of life is the work under consideration seeking to represent? As every critic has roots in his own time, he cannot but emerge with a reading that is in some sense contemporary as well as historical. In this continual adjustment between the historical uniqueness of an ancient work and the inevitable contemporaneity of subsequent interpretation lie the incessant changes in our understanding of the past and our constant need for the reinterpretation of the past.

In the case of the *Bacchae* the problem is especially acute, for this play is deeply rooted in the intellectual, artistic, and religious life of the late fifth century, yet also speaks to our time with an extraordinarily clear and powerful voice. It remains one of the most contemporary of ancient Greek texts. Its concern with the dissolution of order and boundaries—the boundaries between divinity and bestiality in man, reality and imagination, reason and madness, self and other, art and life—makes it unusually accessible and particularly important to the closing decades of the twentieth century. Because of its self-conscious correlation of the order of language with the order of personality, art, city, and world, it is also important to the concerns of current literary scholarship.

Our awareness of the symbol-making and order-imposing work of all aesthetic and indeed all cultural forms, beginning with language, is probably heightened at periods of the disintegration of old systems and the nascent development of new ones. The *Bacchae* was composed at such a transitional moment—an historical moment not unlike our own. Both geographically and spiritually exiled, the poet looks back from the fringes of the Hellenic world to the collapse of the Athenian Empire whose power and confidence fostered the development of tragedy. Writing at the end of this great age of tragedy, he also reflects, indirectly, on the inner logic and spirit of the tragic form, in whose development he had played no small role. Through the multiple meanings and ambiguities of Dionysus he explores the mythopoeic imagination and the constructive energies that underlie tragedy, and also their reversals, the arbitrariness and instability of tragic and theatrical illusion, the affinities of tragedy and its god with limit and order on the one hand and with madness and chaos on the other.

More than any other single work, the *Bacchae* is responsible for that complex of associations that the Romantics extolled as "the Dionysiac." This quality of released emotion must probably appear to our own chaos-ridden time in a more subdued light. The Dionysiac includes the dissolution of limits, the spanning of logical contradictions, the suspension of logically imposed categories, and the exploration of in-between-ness and reversibility in a spirit that may veer abruptly from play and wonder to unrestrained savagery. It remains as fascinating and bewildering to us as to the fifth century. Implicit in these processes is the "Dionysiac poetics" that the *Bacchae* both enacts and examines.

The *Bacchae* is a play about primordial beginnings, primitive forces, the clash of different cultures and different modes of constructing reality. Because it is also a distillation of Euripides' tragic art and because its divinity is so closely linked to the origin and form of tragedy itself, an interpretation of the *Bacchae* becomes, at least in part, a reflection on all of Euripides' work, on the nature of classical tragedy, and indeed on the tragic in general.

My reading of the play also situates itself firmly in the context of twentieth-century interpretation. I discuss the play thematically from several different critical stances, utilizing a number of complementary methodologies. After a largely (though not exclusively) structuralist analysis in Chapters 2 through 5, I move to a more psychological approach in Chapter 6 and then to the poststructuralist concerns associated with writers like Barthes and Derrida in Chapters 7, 8, and 9. All these methods, however, interpenetrate throughout; beneath them all runs a dominant concern for Euripides' language and dramatic structure. The newer approaches, I believe, help us pose some new questions to this rich text and, I hope, gain some new answers. At the same time the careful philological and interpretive work of Winnington-Ingram, Dodds, Roux, and many others, the numerous studies of Greek ritual and religion over the past decade, and particularly the reexamination of Dionysus in relation to cult and tragedy by Detienne, Girard, Henrichs, and Kerényi, to mention only a few, have laid a valuable foundation for a critical reevaluation of the *Bacchae*.

My primary concern is with the play as a work of literary art. I rely on a close reading of the text, but I also utilize the social, cultic, and literary context of which the play formed a part. Despite all that has been written on the *Bacchae*, much remains to be said about the poetry, structure, and dramaturgy. The language of the play in particular can be taken even more seriously and probed more deeply than has generally been done. On any reading, however, ritual, myth, theatrical illusion, and language itself are central issues, and these are also in the foreground of this study.

My premise is that a literary masterpiece like the *Bacchae* does not have one single, definitive meaning, but rather is an endlessly shifting constellation of possibilities, multiple relations and interactions, fixities and indeterminacies that are constantly rearranging themselves with each reading and each reader. This is not to say that such a work can mean anything one wants it to mean. There is a text which prescribes definite limits and directs us to its principal concerns. But this text is an open network rather than a closed field. Any interpretation is an intervention in the text and a re-creation of the text. There is no escaping the rearrangement of relations or the shifting of emphases among details that any interpretation brings. Or, as Heidegger put it, there is no avoiding the hermeneutic circle: the problem is to come into it in the right way.

The *Bacchae* is itself about the process of constituting these symbolic relations, that is, about the relations between art and illusion, imagination and truth, and about the nature of artistic truth. For that reason viewing it through a variety of critical optics may help us better clarify its peculiar polysemicity and its relation to the changing shapes of the god who stands at its center.

This method makes for an inevitable overlap between chapters. I have tried to keep this to a minimum. The details of the early chapters will, I hope, be justified by the cumulative effect of the whole. In the case of so multifaceted a work it is necessary to disentangle the separate strands before trying to weave them together again into the syntheses of the last chapters. The reader eager to reach the intoxicating realms of masking, illusion, and the Dionysiac in tragedy in the last chapters will, I hope, bear with me through the elucidation of detail from which the larger interpretation is built up.

Winnington-Ingram's deservedly influential *Euripides and Dionysus* is the only recent book-length interpretive study of the *Bacchae* in English, and a word about its differences from my approach may be helpful. Like all students of the play, I owe a great deal to this sensible and sensitive work. Completed in 1939 (though not published until 1948), it is remarkable for its time not only in the author's grasp of Dodds' work on the irrationalist strains in Greek culture but also because of its awareness of verbal echoes and repetitions, the associative patterns of Euripides' poetry, multiple levels of meaning. Yet these insights need to be supplemented by what we have learned in recent years about Dionysus, sacrificial ritual, the role of madness in Greek literature and cult, the sexual tensions of fifth-century Athens, and about Euripides' language, dramaturgy, theology, characterization, and so on. Recent approaches like structuralism, symbolic anthropology, and semiotic and psychoanalytic criticism, together with the awareness of the literary work's reflexive consciousness of its own strategies and mimetic devices, its own fictionality and peculiar kind of truth, are, as I try to show, particularly illuminating for the *Bacchae*.

Though Winnington-Ingram is not avowedly (and certainly not consciously) a "New Critic," his study shares a great deal with the text-immanent approach of the New Criticism. Abandoning his scene-by-scene approach, I am more concerned with the areas where the literary structure of the text intersects the social, ritual, and aesthetic structures in and around Dionysus in his various meanings and manifestations. Winnington-Ingram is chiefly concerned with the nature of the Dionysiac religion (in a broad sense) and with Euripides' attitudes for and against it, whereas I am concerned, especially in the last three chapters, with the role of art, illusion, and fiction in Dionysiac drama. It is a mark of the depth and richness of the *Bacchae* that it invites and sustains such diverse readings.

 1

The Elusive God

It is the function of the creative individual not only to represent the highest transpersonal values of his culture, thereby becoming the honored spokesman of his age, but also to give shape to the compensatory values and contents of which it is unconscious.

Erich Neumann,
The Archetypal World of Henry Moore

• I •

Nietzsche's basic insight about Greek tragedy, despite exaggeration, contains much truth. One of the destroyers of tragedy, in the Nietzschean view, was Socrates, a Socrates whose logical rigor, insistence on reason, and principle of noncontradiction both fascinated and repelled Nietzsche's other destroyer of tragedy, the author of the *Bacchae*.[1]

In the *Hippolytus* Phaedra utters the famous lines, "We understand what is right and proper, and know it, but do not work it out in acts" (380-81). The passage has often been regarded, probably rightly, as a polemic against the rationalism of Socrates:[2] the problem of moral action and happiness is a matter of intellectual understanding (*epi-*

---

[1] Nietzsche, *Birth of Tragedy*, chaps. 12-16.

[2] Bruno Snell, "Das frühste Zeugnis über Sokrates," *Philologus* 97 (1948) 125-34. Though the polemic against Socrates has sometimes been doubted (e.g., W. S. Barrett, *Euripides, Hippolytos* [Oxford 1964] 229), it is widely accepted among recent scholars: see Dodds, *The Greeks and the Irrational*, pp. 186f. with note 47; Conacher 37-38; Di Benedetto 8ff. For a full discussion and bibliography see Bernd Mannwald, "Phaidras tragischer Irrtum," *RhM* 122 (1977) 134-48, supporting Snell.

stēmē, Phaedra's word above); if men know the good, they will follow it. Whether or not Euripides has Socrates specifically in mind, this passage, like many others, reveals a poet who exploits sophistic intellectualism and also explores the contradictions within the human heart, the mysterious crossings-over between logic and illogic in feelings and behavior.

This tension between the extremes of reason and emotion is one of the most characteristic features of Euripides' art and one of the most difficult to grasp fully. It takes many forms. The scientific and rationalistic procedures associated with the Sophists, Anaxagoras, Socrates, and Thucydides contrast with the violence and instability of the passions that blaze forth on nearly every page of Euripides' works. Debates of logical exactitude are juxtaposed with lyrics of wistful longing; nostalgia for an orderly world of just gods with relentless undercutting of the traditional Olympian theology; delicate romanticism with unsparing realism; intense patriotism with bitter disillusion about contemporary politics. In no ancient poet are the contradictions both so marked and so central to the art itself. They are deeply stamped on the traditions about his life, a life already mythicized by the time of the poet's death.[3]

The spirit of contradiction that seems so indispensable a condition of Euripides' creativity is also the spirit of Dionysus, god of ecstasy, wine, madness, but also god of tragedy and comedy. It is probably not coincidental that the play that comes at the end of the grand creative tradition of dramatic performances in the fifth century brings on the stage the god of those performances. The *Bacchae*, I shall argue, is not only about the god of maenadic rituals and all that they imply, but about the god of the tragic drama and all that it implies: the paradoxes and the peculiar logic of the unreal and the illusionary that are Dionysus' realm.

The poetics of the form that belongs to this god differs radically from the poetics of his opposite, the god of epic and lyric, Apollo, the god of the golden lyre that leads the bands of Muses and Graces in the brilliant festivities of Olympus, counterpart to the lyre of the mortal poet who leads the choral performances in the cities of men (Pindar, *Pythian* 1.1-12). Both gods' presence assures the transfigur-

---

[3] See Mary R. Lefkowitz, "The Euripides Vita," *GRBS* 20 (1979) 187-210, esp. 208f.

ing joy of art that illuminates the moment of the performance with the immortality of divine radiance. But the pleasure of Dionysiac song, like the pleasure of Dionysiac wine and ecstasy, is full of contradictions, surrounded by dangers. It offers no simple validation, through the microcosm of art, of the established harmony, moral as well as musical, of Olympian Zeus. Rather, it opens into the unknown, the boundless, the wild realms beyond the ordered framework of the city-state, the places where the individual, surrendering too much to that joy, may lose himself entirely.

Let us listen for a moment to a celebrated modern critic on the ambiguities of aesthetic pleasure:

> Fiction of an individual . . . who would abolish in himself the barriers, the classes, the exclusions, not by syncretism, but by simply getting rid of this old specter: *logical contradiction*; who would mingle all the languages, even were they considered as incompatible; who would endure, in silence, all the accusations of illogicality, of infidelity; who would remain impassive before Socratic irony (bring the other to the supreme disgrace: *self-contradiction*) and the fear of the law (how many juridical proofs founded on a psychology of unity!). This man would be the outcast of our society: the courts, the schools, the asylum would treat him as a stranger: who without shame would endure contradiction? Now this anti-hero exists: he is the reader of a text, at the moment when he takes his pleasure. Then the old biblical myth returns: the confusion of tongues is no longer a punishment; the subject reaches enjoyment by the cohabitation of languages, *which work side by side*: the text of pleasure is Babel, happy.

Roland Barthes, the writer of these lines in the opening pages of *Le plaisir du texte*, is concerned principally with modern literature;[4] but much of what he says is directly applicable to Dionysus. He is intimating what we may call a "Dionysiac poetics," a poetics that is a major theme (albeit not the only theme) of the *Bacchae*.

The *Bacchae* is about pleasure, and about resistance to pleasure. It is about man's urgent need and drive for pleasure, raised by Freud into a universal "principle," which, like everything in the realm of pleasure, necessarily coexists with that which denies, obstructs, and

---

[4] Barthes 9-10 (my translation).

destroys it. That drive for pleasure excites in the self, in the society, and in the authority-figures of the society a paradoxical resistance to pleasure. The paradoxes of pleasure are a theme of Socrates too, as we recall from the *Phaedo*. In the Dionysiac poetics of the *Bacchae* these paradoxes form a series of expanding concentric circles reaching from the conflicts within the state and the divided impulses of its rulers to the nature of drama, dramatic illusion, and ultimately all art.

• II •

Dionysus is an Olympian god, but he has chthonic attributes. Divine, he appears in the bestial form of bull, snake, or lion. He has a place at the center of the civic religion. The Greater Dionysia of Athens, where tragedies and comedies were performed, is the most familiar example. Yet his worship also involves ecstatic flaming torches on the mountains. He is a male god, but he has the softness, sensuality, and emotionality that the Greeks generally associate with women. He has the force and energy of a vigorous young man, but the grace, charm, and beauty of a girl. He is Greek, but he comes from barbarian Asia, escorted by a band of wild Asian women. He is a local Theban divinity, but he is also a universal "god of many names," whose power, as Sophocles says in the last ode of the *Antigone*, extends from Italy to the East. As he crosses the geographical division between Hellene and barbarian, so he crosses the class division within society, offering his gift of wine as an "equal joy" to both rich and poor (421-23). Both a native by birth and a violently resisted intruder, he honors Thebes and threatens its destruction. He is neither child nor man, but, eternal adolescent, occupies a place somewhere between the two. He has the residual functions of both a fertility daimon and a chthonic deity.[5]

[5] See Plutarch, *Isis and Osiris* 35.365a; Farnell, *Cults* 5.118-25; Ramnoux 198-99; Kerényi chaps. 2 and 3; Guthrie, *The Greeks and Their Gods* 156, 164; Nilsson, *GGR* 579; Coche de la Ferté 128ff. and 161ff. For later uses of this aspect of Dionysus see Philipp Fehl, *Studies in the History of Art* (National Gallery of Art, Washington D.C.) 6 (1974) 74-78, à propos of Titian's *Andrians* in the Prado Museum and Philostratus, *Imag.* 1.25.1.

The opening of the play places his birth from Semele next to Zeus's lightning-fire (3). The "memorial" of a vegetation-god's birth is the smoking debris of a ruined house and a mother's cruel death (6-9)—intimations of what Euripides has in store for us in the rest of the play.

The opening lines also stress the process of mortal birth by which immortal Dionysus came into being (2f.). He has come to Thebes "having taken mortal shape in exchange for divine." The collocation of "mortal" and "divine" is common enough in Greek literature and recurs elsewhere in this play (e.g., 42, 635f.). Not so common is the collocation of "beast" and "god" that characterizes Dionysus. He is "the bull-horned god" (ταυρόκερων θεόν, 100) and will make his epiphany in bestial as well as in divine shape. In 42 he will compel Thebes to admit that "he was revealed a god to mortals" (φανέντα θνητοῖς δαίμονα); but in 1017f. his followers pray, "Appear a bull . . . or serpent or lion for us to behold."

Dionysus can leap the boundaries between the three major categories of sentient life, but the mortals on whom he impinges have trouble. Semele, he says early in the prologue, encountered Hera's "immortal violence" (athanaton hybrin, 9). Cadmus eventually attains a godlike bliss in the "Isles of the Blest" (1339), but only after a painful metamorphosis into the "savage form" of a serpent (1338), a beast-god collocation as problematical as that of Dionysus. His wife, Harmonia, is the child of a god (cf. 1332, 1357), but also is forced to assume this bestial shape (1357f.). Like Semele and Agave, she is a woman who becomes an innocent victim of divine wrath.

Pentheus sees Dionysus as a horned bull (920-22)—how different an apparition from the soft and seductive adolescent of the first encounter!—but only then begins to perceive the god-man in the splendor and terror of his animal nature, full of a sharp, intoxicating beauty, but also impervious to human sensibilities, pity, mercy.

God of the new vegetative life that burgeons from the soil in the abundant clustering of the grapes (12f., 107-108, 874-76), Dionysus can also use the destructive power of earth against men, shaking the king's palace (585ff.). Those curling green shoots that attest his presence take on a different meaning near the end when the bloody head of his human victim is carried to the palace as a "newly cut tendril" (helix, 1170).

The thyrsus or narthex that his devotees bear reveals the essential ambiguity of the god. Covered with ivy (25, 709, 1055), able to open channels of life-sustaining fluids from the earth (702-11), it is yet a dangerous weapon, a "missile" (*belos*, 25) that can inflict wounds (761-63).[6] In a later ode the chorus calls it "a trusty pledge of Hades" (1157f.).

The Dionysiac "joy in the eating of raw flesh" in the parode (*ōmophagos charis*, 139) paradoxically has a place beside the spiritual purity of the soul's mystic initiation into the Dionysiac *thiasos* or holy band (73-82). Annihilating the frontiers between god and beast, man and god, savagery and civilization, peace and frenzy, the god's rite is both sacrament and pollution.[7] From the opening ode on purification we move to the most horrible of all defilements, a mother reeking with the blood of the son she has torn apart, fleeing the mountain of her "pure" ecstasies as cursed with uncleanness (*miaros*, 1383).

• III •

What the Dionysus of the tragic performance and the Dionysus of the maenads' ecstasy most fundamentally share is the experience of what lies *beyond* familiar limits, the limits of civic space, social norms, the familiar boundaries of personality, energy, perception. As Apollo imposes limits and reinforces boundaries, Dionysus, his opposite and complement, dissolves them. From the *Iliad* on, Apollo embodies the distance between god and man. Dionysus closes that distance. His worshipers identify themselves with the god, and in the ecstasy of his cult they experience something like the divine joy and power. Dionysus and the Dionysiac bridge the gap that Apollo so threateningly guards. Often placed in close association with other gods—Zeus, Poseidon, Demeter, Aphrodite—Dionysus can serve as a principle of unification among diverse aspects of other divinities, able to join their energies to his in the heightened intensity of life that accompanies

[6] Cf. also the "golden faced thyrsus" invoked in a context of vengeful divinity in 553 and the god's "golden wings" in a context of holiness and ritual purity in 372. Note, too, the aggressive use of the thyrsus by maenads against attacking satyrs in red-figure vase-painting, on which see McNally, passim.

[7] Dodds, "Maenadism," 165.

him. But he can also appear as a principle of encroachment on others' prerogatives.[8]

Where Dionysus stands, limit gives way to what Victor Turner and others have called "liminality," an in-between state where fluidity challenges stability, where fusion replaces boundary.[9] In this "space between," order and disorder lose their familiar clarity of definition and energies are released to combine in new ways, often with a thin edge between creation and destruction. Hence fruitful and imaginative possibilities can be engendered, but the risk of disorder stands close. It is the spirit of the carnival, also closely akin to the Dionysiac; and here too normal relations and normal inhibitions are suspended in a quasi-magical interlude characterized by joyful play, imaginative exuberance, and free energy.[10] In the maenadic cult of Dionysus, however, that carnivalesque freedom has a more deeply and seriously religious dimension, and greater danger, in the mystical union with the god celebrated in the parode of the *Bacchae*.

In the Dionysiac performance, as in the Dionysiac ritual, the individuality of personal identity gives way to fusion. The actor, wearing the mask that has close associations with the Dionysiac cult from early times, fuses to some extent with the personage whom he represents in the theater. The spectator, watching the performance, at some point loses his separateness and identifies with the masked figure before him. Whether or not the sufferings of that masked actor also symbolically represent the sufferings of the god is a controversial point

---

[8] Sale, *Existentialism* 85.

[9] Turner (1973, 1974, 1974b) passim; Leach 71-75. For Dionysus and the "in between" see Gernet (1953) 390-93; Otto 110ff., 120ff.; Girard 181ff. (Eng. trans. 127ff.).

[10] For the "carnivalesque" see Kristeva 99-107 and Toporov 334, drawing on the work of Bakhtin; also Jean Claude Carrière, *Le carnaval et la politique* (Paris 1979). For a good statement of the dynamic of the carnivalesque at the festivals of Dionysus, particularly the Greater Dionysia where the dramas were performed, see Angelo Brelich, "Aristofane: Commedie e Religione" (1969) in Marcel Detienne, ed., *Il mito: Guida storica e critica* (Rome-Bari 1975) 17f.: "Dionysos è il dio che rompe (o scoglie) l'ordine prestabilito, per reintegrarlo su un nuovo livello. La tragedia e la commedia che portano lo spettatore attraverso i due opposti rischi che minacciano l'ordine umano, per farglieli superare, sono perciò in linea con quanto il culto di Dionysos doveva rappresentare nella struttura della religione dell' Atene classica." For sociological and psychological approaches to this same area see below, Chap. 8, n. 75.

in the history of the Greek theater. Whatever the historical situation
may be, this process of symbolic identification and dissolution of self
into other is an important point of connection between the maenadic
and theatrical aspects of Dionysus and will be explored more fully in
Chapter 7. Though the point cannot be discussed here, this theatricality of Dionysus extends to comedy as well as tragedy. Indeed, as a
number of recent interpreters have shown, there is a curious fusion
of comic and satyric with tragic elements in the *Bacchae*, another
aspect of the crossing of boundaries and fusion of opposites characteristic of this god.[11]

The tragic performance itself exists in a kind of contradiction. In a
sense, tragedy is the meeting point between the civic Dionysus worshiped by the citizen choruses within the walls of the city and the
ecstatic Dionysus worshiped by the maddened women exulting in the
mountains. As part of the civic ritual of Athens, the performances in
the theater of Dionysus affirm the social order at a state-sponsored
occasion in a public and holy place. Tragedy also endorses that order
through its lofty poetic language, traditional and dignified, through
the elaborateness of the state-financed costumes and the discipline of
the dancers, and through the choral odes, which often celebrate the
city or the moral and heroic values of the city or comment upon the
action from the point of view of ordinary citizens. Yet the narrative
material of the myths that tragedy dramatizes shockingly violates this
order with the most feared and abominated pollutions: matricide, incest, patricide, fratricide, madness. The actual *content* of these works
denies what their ritual *context* affirms.[12]

Sophocles gives us an imagistic representation of this contradiction
in the last ode of the *Antigone*, an ode to Dionysus, a god of the city
and a god of the wild. At this point when the rationality of the civic
leader is engulfed by the irrational demonic energies both within man
and in the world as a whole, the chorus invokes Dionysus as "chorus-
leader of the fire-breathing stars, you who watch over the voices of
the night, child born of Zeus"

[11] Sansone, passim; Seidensticker (1978) passim: see below, Chap. 7, section 8.

[12] For a development of this point see my *Tragedy and Civilization* 50ff., and also
my "Griechische Tragödie und Gesellschaft," Propyläen Geschichte der Literatur I
(Berlin, 1981) 198-217.

ἰὼ πῦρ πνειόντων
χοράγ᾽ ἄστρων, νυχίων
φθεγμάτων ἐπίσκοπε,
παῖ Διὸς γένεθλον. . . .
    (Antigone 1146-49)

Here the "chorus leader" of stars in the mysterious, remote spaces of
the nocturnal sky fuses with the civic god who watches over those
civic choruses being performed at that very moment in the orchestra
before the eyes of the spectator-citizens, the god celebrated as "lord
of Thebes" in the first ode (Antigone 153-54). The civic space of the
theater and its chorus is thus opened to the superimposed vastness
and uncontrollable mystery of the "orchestra" of the night and its
"chorus" of flaming stars.[13]

In this dissolution of the familiar, we lose old bearings and also old
preconceptions. The Dionysiac performance and the Dionysiac gift
of the vine are parallel and analogous means of access to the border-
land of the self in the new "psychic geography" that Dionysus opens.[14]
Both the illusion of the drama and the intoxication of the wine bestow
a fresh vision of a hitherto concealed reality, a vision that may either
be enlightenment or (as in Pentheus' case) delusion. Here we may
meet an as yet untapped creative potential of the self, as of nature,
but also a destructive darkness, like the Jungian "shadow," in which
we may be engulfed and lost. Dionysus' realm blurs the clear line
between conscious and unconscious, sanity and madness, exalted purity and wild abandonment, strength and weakness. The vision opened
by Dionysus, whether through his wine and cult or through the illusion of the drama, makes us see in simultaneous perspective things
otherwise kept apart.

By his very nature, then, such a god must exist in a framework of
tension, ambiguity, paradox. Euripides expresses the profound truth
of the god in insisting on his destructive force as the necessary and
inevitable partner of his creative energies and life-fostering gifts. A
play about Dionysus, then, is almost inevitably a play about the relation between illusion and tragedy and about the relation between

[13] See my Tragedy and Civilization, 201-206.
[14] See Hillman 269ff., 275ff.; Otto 126ff. On the two sides of the Dionysiac madness see also Plato, Phdr. 244d-e.

tragedy and the social order. The problem of Pentheus' Thebes is, *mutatis mutandis*, also the problem of the dramatist: how to bring into the bounded realm of form this principle that dissolves boundaries, how to make Dionysus live within the civic and aesthetic confines of city, theater, and festival without annihilating that space.

Historically these issues formed part of the problem of Dionysus to the city, a problem resolved at Athens by establishing the sanctuaries of Dionysus in the city, by creating and permitting such festivals as the Anthesteria, Lenaea, and Dionysia, and by connecting the mimetic performances of comedy, tragedy, and satyr play with Dionysus at the City Dionysia. By their very nature the Dionysiac cult and the Dionysiac drama contain a potential for disorder. Hence the concern to keep them within limits. Wine, freedom to mimic, joke, and dance, the emotional power of drama, and music, ecstatic religion, a loosening of sexual restraints all indulge the irrational, the need for escape in all of us. If two or more of the above are combined at the same time, major disruptions may easily result. In the face of such phenomena the sober citizens, the older and more powerful members of the society, and particularly those responsible for the maintenance of public safety and morality, are likely to fear for the civic order. We may compare contemporary attitudes to rock concerts, banned by many a town council out of just such concerns.

Dionysus' role in the origins of drama is one of the most controversial questions in the history of Greek literature. Whatever the historical factors that led to the god's association with the dramatic festivals of Athens, Euripides' play has its own view of what Dionysus has to do with tragedy. The *Bacchae*, as I shall argue in Chapter 7, reflects on the parallelism between the ambiguity of Dionysus in the city (of Thebes) and the ambiguity, even the subversiveness, of tragedy in the city (of Athens).

To center a play on Dionysus is to bring into the city that which transcends the city. It is also to bring into the realm of Dionysus that which both includes and transcends Dionysus. Can one surrender to Dionysus and enjoy the benefits of his gifts without losing oneself irrevocably in his madness? In the compounded dialectics that form Euripides' answer to these questions lies the essence of the contradictory and difficult Dionysiac poetics of his play.

In this conjoined polarity of the creative and the destructive in

Dionysus stands the deeply rooted ancient recognition that nothing comes into being without the destruction of something else, without loss, sacrifice, violence. From Anaximander to the *isonomia* of Epicurus, this principle finds rationalized, philosophical expression in Greek thought. In Euripides it surfaces not only literally in the *Bacchae* but in one way or another in all of his plays. Elsewhere too in his work, as Pietro Pucci has suggested, it takes the form of sacrifice, the sacrifice that the poet makes in order to create, the "sacrifice to the Muses" (*HF* 1021-22)[15] and the violence done to the quiescent surface of life by the questions, the unsatisfied yearnings, the dreams of impossibilities raised by art.

This aspect of the Dionysiac *coniunctio oppositorum* is an essential constituent of all tragedy. In the waste of something inestimably precious there is a hopeless sadness but also the recognition that that essence cannot be confined and possessed within the familiar continuities and prosaic durability of the everyday, the predictable, the rationally known and knowable.

• IV •

In other areas of the myths of Dionysus, too, destruction and creativity coexist. On the one hand Dionysus appears as a culture-hero, bringing to men the boon of the cultivated wine.[16] On the other hand he comes as a threat to civilization, leading dangerous bands of raging women and strangers, exciting in civilized lands hostility and resistance.[17] In the stories of Lycurgus in Thrace, the daughters of Minyas

---

[15] See Pucci (1977) and *Violence of Pity*, chap. 4, esp. 133ff.

[16] For Dionysus as culture hero see Kerényi 141ff.; Henrichs (1979) 4; cf. Apollod. *Bibl.* 3.14.7. Paolo Scarpi, "Melampus e i 'miracoli' di Dionysos," *Perennitas: Studi in onore di Angelo Brelich* (Rome 1980) 431-44, esp. 442ff., would view Dionysus in early Greece as a god of institutionalized change and "cultural choice" of humanity over bestiality. The tragic Dionysus of the *Bacchae*, I would suggest, embodies rather a cultural ambivalence between the human and the bestial.

[17] See Otto 71ff.; Kerényi 179ff.; Jeanmaire 139, 142ff., 201ff.; Guépin 38-39; Guthrie, *Greeks and Their Gods* 165-73; Coche de la Ferté 190f.; G. A. Privitera, *Dioniso in Omero e nella poesia arcaica* (Rome 1970) 14-48; Park McGinty, "Dionysos's Revenge and the Validation of the Hellenic World-View," *HThR* 71 (1978)

in Boeotia, the daughters of Proetus in the Argolid, his arrival not only excites opposition, but causes suffering for the royal house, a suffering which, as in the *Bacchae*, involves change or confusion between man and beast.

In the *Antigone*, where Dionysus has a small, but important role, Creon makes his appearance just at the moment when the chorus celebrates its Dionysiac dance. Dionysiac exultation thus stands in immediate contrast with the most un-Dionysian of men, a confident, platitudinous rationalist who has many traits in common with Pentheus. The Dionysiac joy of the end of that ode, moreover, contrasts with the dangerous violence of one of Thebes' attackers, also characterized as Dionysiac, Capaneus' unbridled bacchantic delight in war (*Antig.* 135-37). And the civic Dionysus of that ode has a further contrast with the expansive, universal Dionysus of the fifth stasimon, where the god fuses with the vast stellar spaces far beyond the limits of the city (*Antig.* 1146-49).

In Euripides' *Heracles* too, Dionysiac emotionality spans the two poles of triumphant joy and wild sorrow. The song of Heracles' victory is connected with the ecstatic happiness of "Bromios, giver of wine" (*HF* 680-82); but the hero's murderous insanity, with its crazed, out-of-tune music, is also Dionysiac (*HF* 893, 899, 966, 1085, 1122); and the hero himself moves from the songful joy of the Olympian god's benefactions to his chthonic madness as "Hades' bacchant" (*HF* 1119). Everything involved with Dionysus partakes of the precarious, unstable quality of his gifts. Like his bacchants, Dionysus himself embodies the volatility of emotion, that within us which lies beyond our full control and, if released from the usual discipline and restraint, may suddenly rush to its diametrical opposite.

In so often connecting the music of tragedy with Dionysus, Euripides may be intimating his own art's place at the crossing-over between the extremes of emotion. The poet, like every artist, has always been more exposed and more open to the extreme ranges of feeling in his own, and all men's, natures, to the outer limits of horror and beauty. But instead of repressing these contradictions, he forces them into the open in the form of symbols and images. The *Bacchae* itself forms a "liminal" space where the creative potential in ourselves can

---

77-94, esp. 78ff., 89ff. Aeschylus treated the resistance to Dionysus in his *Edoni*, *Lycourgeia*, and his own Pentheus trilogy: see Dodds, *Bacchae* xxxi-xxxiii.

reach its closest proximity to the destructive. The god's and the human protagonist's changes of dress and form visually enact this momentarily fluid state of the new, suspended reality opened up by the tragic moment. We take from the god what we bring to him. He reflects back upon us the destructiveness or the creativeness hidden deep in our own natures, our capacity both for ecstasy and for annihilation of self and others, both joyful self-affirmation and tragic disintegration.

What the poet brings forth in his Dionysiac vision, what he sees and makes us see, partakes necessarily of both the sublime and the terrible. Through the play Euripides enters deeply into both the Pentheus and the Dionysus in himself, and leads each of us on the same inner journey. The risks of Pentheus are, in a sense, also the risks of the poet who has experienced the truth of Dionysus in his own soul, and the risks of the spectator as well who surrenders fully to the magic of the poet's vision. As Walter Otto remarks, "He who begets something which is alive must dive down into the primeval depths in which the forces of life dwell. And when he rises to the surface, there is a gleam of madness in his eyes because in those depths death lives cheek by jowl with life."[18]

• V •

Does Euripides approve or disapprove of Dionysus? Does he view his worship as a blessing that leads to an experience of a world otherwise closed to us by the limits and definitions that we allow society to impose upon us? Or does he regard Dionysus with the fascinated horror of a humane intelligence confronting the frightening violence of untamed instincts, better left unsatisfied and even unrecognized, which lurk beneath the ordered regularity of civilized life? Interpretations have ranged from notions of "a heartfelt glorification of Dionysus" (Gilbert Murray)[19] to the idea of "the sweeping horror of Dio-

---

[18] Otto 136-37; see also Kerényi 133-34. Roberts 39, adapting a phrase of D. H. Lawrence, calls Dionysus " 'the something not ourselves that makes for life' and for death also."

[19] Murray, 88.

nysus' triumph" (Grube), a god "at least as devilish as he is divine."[20]
More recent critics have stressed Euripides' demonstration of "the
inexorable interdependence of the cruelty and the beauty" in the god
and his cult (Winnington-Ingram)[21] or the "divine inscrutability" which,
as in the case of the Aphrodite of the *Hippolytus*, makes it hard to
take any final position for or against Dionysus (Kirk).[22]

Winnington-Ingram and Kirk are, I believe, basically right, though
I would formulate the answer in another way, namely that Euripides
dramatizes the fundamental ambiguity of Dionysus' nature and that
therefore the problem can have no resolution and is meant to have
no resolution. To pose an alternative of praise or blame, attraction or
horror, is to dissolve that mysterious and perhaps ultimately unfor-
mulable coexistence of opposites that is the essence of Dionysus and
of the realm of mythic and symbolic representation to which the
Dionysiac stands so close, in music, mask, and drama.

What Euripides gives us in the *Bacchae* is not a choice between
one side or another, but an experience, an experience that involves
the doublings, ambiguities, crossing of opposites into one another that
form the essence of Dionysus himself. The play forces us to live not
just the "unresolvable antithesis of two worlds," in Lesky's phrase
("unausgleichbaren Gegensatz zweier Welten"),[23] but the melting of
those worlds into one another in an experience that questions the
very thought-processes that make reality intelligible and therefore

---

[20] Grube, *Drama* 398, though he also admits the joyous and peaceful side of the
god in his cult (p. 402 with n. 2). Simon 121 finds Dionysus "revealed as cruel and
vengeful beyond measure; gods should be more understanding and forgiving than
men. The *Bacchae* is far from a piece in praise of madness." For a similar view see
A. C. Coolidge, Jr., *Beyond the Tragic Flaw* (Lake Macbridge 1980) 75-78.

[21] WI 178.

[22] Kirk 9 and in general 8-11. Good surveys of the "problem of the *Bacchae*" and
the complexity of Euripides' attitude toward the god will be found in WI 6ff.; Lesky,
TDH 498-99; Rohdich 162-67; Parry 146-48; Carrière 136-39; Cantarella (1974) 305ff.;
Bremer 2-7; Oranje 1-17.

[23] Lesky, *TDH* 499. On the two-sidedness of the Dionysiac experience, see also
WI 31-39; Dyer 19-20; Wassermann (1953) 562-63; Detienne, *Dionysos*, chap. 4;
Henrichs (1979) 2ff. Festugière (1957) appreciates the tension between savagery and
serenity in the maenadic cult, but stresses Euripides' ability to make the gentler side
of the god a symbol of inner peace in the soul's identification with a pure, quasi-
bucolic realm of nature—a reading that gives too much weight to the early odes in
comparison to the later.

manageable. Euripides brings us to the verge of what, next to death, is the most terrifying experience of human life, madness, the loss of our hold on the clarity of those relations on which we depend for that boundary between fusion and otherness that we call sanity.

The play shows major clashes of opinion about the god: Pentheus and Teiresias disagree violently in the first episode, Pentheus and Messenger near the middle of the play, Pentheus and Chorus throughout. This multiplicity and reversibility pervade even quite small details of language. In his first bitter attack on Dionysiac rites, for example, Pentheus denounces the presence of the god's "sheen of the vine at the banquet" (ὅπου βότρυος ἐν δαιτὶ γίγνεται γάνος, 261) as a sure source of debauchery. Some hundred lines later the identical phrase recurs in a choral ode to mark the joyous song, laughter, and release from anxiety that the god brings (ὁπόταν βότρυος ἔλθῃ / γάνος ἐν δαιτὶ θεῶν, "when the vine's sheen comes at the banquet of the gods," 382f.). The studied repetition brings out two antithetical perspectives on Dionysus' gifts and their effects. As Dionysus himself puts it at the peripety,

Pentheus will come to know Zeus's son, Dionysus,
By nature a god in full perfection, god
Most terrible and to men most mild.

> γνώσεται δὲ τὸν Διὸς
> Διόνυσον, ὃς πέφυκεν ἐν τέλει θεός,
> δεινότατος, ἀνθρώποισι δ' ἠπιώτατος.
> (859-61)

The dissolution of boundaries in the Dionysiac cult represented in the play occurs on two planes, the psychological and the cultural. On the psychological plane Dionysus signifies the free flow of the emotional life, untrammeled by the restrictions of family, society, traditional religion, or personal morality. Though Euripides makes it clear that we cannot associate Dionysus simply with *physis*, wild nature, he is, in the terms of fifth-century thought, closer to *physis* than to its opposite, *nomos*, the imposed, "artificial" conventions of the social order. As a god close to the free passage of instincts and the open expression of emotions, Dionysus becomes for Pentheus, who has blocked that expression, the "return of the repressed." In a metaphor which recurs throughout the play, he is "Dionysus the looser"

(*Lysios*), he who "unbinds" what Pentheus has "bound up"; he releases what Pentheus has held constrained and tight. Psychologically he lets loose in Pentheus his own interior bestiality and sexuality. On the cultural plane he confuses distinctions between city and wild, mortal and immortal, man and beast, male and female, Greek and barbarian, heavens and earth. For those who accept him, this dissolution of oppositions is liberating, energizing. For those who resist, it throws city, house, and psyche into chaos.

For Aristotle and the Greeks generally, the city is the necessary locus of human life, placed between the gods who are above the human condition and the beasts below it (*Politics* 1. 1253a 28-30). The city walls demarcate the wild from the tame; the family regulates the potential violence of the sexual instinct, civilizing the quasi-"savagery" of the children and the "untamed" virgins; agriculture brings the vital forces of the earth into the service of man; ritual makes the supernatural less terrifying and provides a means of regular access to the gods.

In compensation for the collapse of the usual barriers that man érects between himself and nature, Dionysus creates a new relation. As Winnington-Ingram remarks à propos of Aristotle's definition of the city, "When Aristotle remarked that the solitary man must be either a beast or a god, he forgot perhaps that there were social groups which make a man both at once."[24] Here man loses some of his distinctively human capacities in the ease with which he blends into the world of nature; but he also surpasses his normal human capacities in a sudden, almost divine access of strength, speed, or supernatural powers.[25] The long account of the Theban maenads in the center of the play shows their subhuman bestiality as they tear apart cattle and stain themselves with the gore (734-47) or swoop down on cultivated fields and carry off children (748-51). Yet a mysterious fire blazes harmlessly around their hair (757f.), an attribute of divinity that recalls the Olympian fire of Zeus in the prologue. The snakes that licked their faces as a sign of a harmonious accord between man and wild nature at the beginning lick off the drops of blood, traces of the maenads' murderous violence against animals, at the end (cf. 697 and 768).

[24] WI 176. See also my *Tragedy and Civilization* 13.
[25] See Diller (1955) 473.

• VI •

As Vernant, Detienne, and others have pointed out, sacrifice and the myths about sacrifice are entwined into a complex coding system, linking together marriage, agriculture, limit, and moderation as the privileged values of civilization, over against promiscuity or rape, hunting, excess, and violence.[26] The word that describes the rite of ōmophagia in the parode, charis, "delight" (ὠμοφάγον χάριν, "the delight of raw-eating," 139) is the very word that elsewhere denotes the favorable mediations established between mortal men and the distant Olympian gods by the burnt offering of normal sacrifice.[27]

This passage, with its deliberate destruction of the mediatory function of sacrifice, begins with the language of mystical beatitude, "Sweet in the mountains, when from the running bands (thiasoi) he falls to the ground" (πέσῃ πεδόσε . . . , 135). It is symmetrical with the beatitude of the first strophe, "Blessedly happy he who . . . hallows his life and joins his soul with the holy band (thiaseuetai psychan), reveling as a bacchant on the mountains (ἐν ὄρεσσι βακχεύων, 76; cf. 115) amid holy purifications" (73-77). What follows the second passage is not serene "purity" (hosioi katharmoi, 77), but the god himself or his worshiper (the subject of 135ff. is ambiguous, but probably the god is meant) as he "hunts down" his quarry. The purity of blood spilled in sacrifice is here rendered even more ambiguous by the details of the bloody hunt. This meat is devoured raw, not burnt in the fire of sacrifice. The victim, a goat, might be the domestic animal led to the altar in the solemn procession of normal sacrifice, but here it doubles with a wild animal caught after desperate running in a hunt on the mountains. The rite takes place not in the well-defined space of city or sacred precinct, but on the exposed mountainside, where a more terrible and still more bloody rite of sacrificial ōmophagia will take place later. Then he who "leaps to the ground" (πέσῃ πεδόσε, 136) will not be the god-hunter who devours, but the hunted human victim who is devoured (cf. ὑψόθεν χαμαιριφὴς / πίπτει πρὸς οὖδας,

---

[26] See Detienne, Dionysos 139ff., 164-207, and Jardins 71-113; Vernant and Detienne, Cuisine, passim; Vernant, Mythe et société 141ff. See also my Tragedy and Civilization 29-35 with the further references there cited.

[27] E.g., Aeschyl. Ag. 371, 1387; cf. Detienne, Jardins 169 and Dionysos 197ff.

"falls flung to the ground," 1111f.), not with shouts of joy, but with "myriad groanings" (1112).

By numerous turns of phrase and verbal echoes throughout the play Euripides calls attention to this deliberate breakdown of normal sacrifice and its mediatory, hierarchical functions. To take one small example, Dionysus warns Pentheus, just before the latter's discomfiture, that if he engages the maenads in battle, he will "cause bloodshed" ($α\check{ι}μα\ \vartheta\acute{η}σεις$, 837). This shedding of blood proves to be the blood of Pentheus himself, the king sacrificed as beast-victim; and the chief celebrant, his own mother, is left "bloodied all over" ($π\hat{α}σα\ δ'$ $\acute{η}ματωμέν\eta$, 1135). That phrase of Dionysus in 837, $α\check{ι}μα\ \vartheta\acute{η}σεις$, has no exact parallel in Greek.[28] Its closest analogues denote ritual pollution of an altar or sanctuary, as in Euripides' *Ion* 1225 and 1259, where bloodshed between mother and son is also in question.

This ritual, then, rather than clarifying the limits between the sacred and the profane, the pure and the impure, is, as Dodds remarks, both "holy and horrible."[29] The status of victim, celebrant, and deity becomes confused and problematical. The victim is torn by hand, not killed with a sacred cult implement. The remains are eaten raw rather than cooked by the civilizing fire which separates what is mortal from what is immortal, what is bestial from what is lawful for humans to consume. The mood is one of orgiastic passion rather than of stately ceremony. Our reactions are, as Dodds says, "a mixture of supreme exaltation and supreme repulsion . . . , the same violent conflict of emotional attitudes that runs all through the *Bacchae* and lies at the root of all religions of the Dionysiac type."[30]

Sacrifice is important in itself as an example of the special kind of religiosity that Euripides is exploring in the *Bacchae*. It can also be regarded as part of a code, one "language" among several that give implicit definitions of civilization as opposed to savagery, normality as opposed to the abnormal. It is a microcosmic reflection of the total order, parallel to other microcosms—family, space, architecture, food. Each of these elements is a strand in the total bundle that comprises

[28] Dodds, *Bacchae* ad 837. Broadhead 117f. judges the phrase corrupt, wrongly in my opinion.

[29] Dodds, "Maenadism," 165. Of the movement between the *ōmophagia* and the following description of honey, milk, and wine, WI 38 remarks, "The clash is staggering."

[30] Dodds, "Maenadism," 165; see Detienne, *Dionysos* 149-50.

the value system of the society. Each area forms a coherent semantic system, a code, congruent with every other code, each defining the limits and modes of behavior acceptable in its area.[31]

When we turn from such a structuralist view of the society to a work of literature like the *Bacchae*, we move into a more complex situation. The literary work utilizes the precoded patterns of the social norms; but it also imposes its own secondary structures of meanings, its own internal system of signs, metaphors, and symbols, upon those given by the society. It thereby rearranges, transforms, distorts, or interweaves the codes in new and unpredictable ways. The familiar relation between signifier and signified in the semantic system of ritual or spatial definition or dress becomes part of a new internal coding within the work. Here the relation between overt and latent meaning, between word and act, between literal and figurative, changes from familiar expectations to fluidity, questioning, more or less violent derangement. In all of literature, but especially in tragedy, the "message" of the specific text may bring out something that was not in the code and may actually threaten to destroy the code itself.

One of the most characteristic and powerful effects of Greek tragedy lies in its specific and systematic interweaving of all the codes of the civilized order through metaphor and other forms of analogy in language and action. The *Oresteia* brings together language, ritual, sexuality, family in a continually expanding representation of the entire cosmic order at a precarious and threatened moment. Sophocles' *Oedipus Tyrannus* operates with an elaborate parallelism between the doublings in the area of language and those in the area of kinship (incest) and ritual (coincidence of king and scapegoat, purifying savior and polluted outcast).[32] The mind is forced to reach beyond the familiar demarcations in a painful questioning of the given principles of order or the admission that no such order exists. Here we are forced beyond normal definitions of men and actions to the unclassifiable, the interstitial, the unique.

Such an approach does not deny the psychological interpretations that have dominated the criticism of the play. It rather attempts to restore to the play an area of significance that the psychological ap-

[31] See my *Tragedy and Civilization* 14ff.; Jonathan Culler, *Structuralist Poetics* (London 1975) 43-54.
[32] Segal, *Tragedy and Civilization* 16, 55-58, 241-45.

proach has obscured, that is, the relationship of the action to the kind
of language that constitutes that action, the play's implicit definitions
of civic values and social norms, and the relationship of the Dionysus
of the maenads to the Dionysus of tragedy.

Even the madness of Pentheus has its cultural as well as its psychological dimension. Madness in Greek literature is a social as well
as a purely individual and interior phenomenon. It manifests a violent disturbance of all the civilized codes, an imbalance in the relations between man and nature. The madman belongs to the raw and
the wild, rather than the "cooked" and the civilized.[33] He is more
akin to the beasts than to men. He cannot use speech properly, is
ritually impure, has no settled abode, but "wanders" in place as in
mind, beyond the familiar limits of civilized men, often in the mountains. Pentheus' neurosis, however interesting, has blocked our vision
of the totality of the social order, including language, ritual, and art,
which is equally a victim of Euripides' tragic action.

[33] Ibid. 35-38, with the references there cited. On the destruction of normal social
classifications in Pentheus' madness see also Rosenmeyer 149.

2

Forms of Dionysus:
Doubling, Hunting, Rituals

Πολλαὶ μορφαὶ τῶν δαιμονίων
Many the shapes of what belongs to divinity

• I •

Euripides' "feeling for the tragic antinomies of life,"[1] perhaps more pronounced in the *Bacchae* than in any of his earlier plays, finds its clearest expression in doubling, the pairing of opposites, and the sliding of opposites into one another. As the previous chapter suggested, Euripides found in Dionysus an extraordinarily rich symbolic and mythical focus for these inversions. A later chapter will show how Euripides used these themes and devices of the plot and the mythical background to present a microcosmic condensation of all the tragic reversals (*peripeteiai*) that Dionysus had ever seen at his dramatic festivals in Athens.

The *Bacchae* creates a continually deepening split of normal reality into two. There are two worlds of experience: the supposedly rational civic world of Pentheus and the irrational, emotional, ecstatic worldview of Dionysus. Each world has its own set of moral and intellectual values, its own "wisdom" or "intelligence" (*sophia*, *phronēsis*), its own form of "sensible" or "sound" thinking (*sōphrosynē*), justice (*dikē*), violence (*hybris*), happiness (*eudaimonia*), holiness (*hosia*), and so on.[2]

---

[1] The phrase is Wassermann's (1953) 563.

[2] The ambiguities and inversions of the ethical terms have been much discussed: see De Romilly, passim, esp. 372ff.; WI 19f.; Diller (1955) 482; Arrowsmith (1959) 53-56 and "Euripides' Theater of Ideas" (1964) in Erich Segal, ed., *Euripides, A Collection of Critical Essays* (Englewood Cliffs, N.J. 1968) 24-27; Arthur (1972) 176-

There are two sets of maenads, the voluntary Asian maenads who follow the Phrygian Stranger, and the constrained maenads of Thebes. To complicate matters, the Asiatic maenads often espouse the commonplaces of "normal" Greek ethical values.[3] The paradox of traditional gnomic wisdom in the mouths of figures who are extraneous, if not actually hostile, to the polis throws us off balance and leaves us without a secure ethical center, a single clear focus of values.

At the center of this doubling of value-systems stands not one Dionysus, but two: the god disguised as the Stranger and the god who asserts his power over Thebes in his own person in the prologue and epilogue. There are also two scenes of maenads in the grip of Dionysiac ecstasy, each described by a messenger from the mountains. The first begins benignly, and even at its peak of violence involves no loss of human life. The second is murderous. The mystical joy in the Asian *thiasos* in the first three odes of the play is doubled by the destructive and bloody madness of Agave's maenads near the end. Pentheus' hunt for the maenads at the beginning becomes the maenads' dreadful "hunting" of Pentheus at the end. A son's attempt to establish his mother's honor at the beginning (Dionysus and Semele) is answered by a mother's claim to honor in having killed a son at the end (Agave in 1233ff.).

Of the two Dionysuses one is concealed, disguised as the Stranger, and the other is made manifest to his worshipers. To the two Dionysuses correspond two Pentheuses: a Pentheus in control of his realm as ruler and guardian of civilization, and a Pentheus who is violent, "savage," destructive of civilization, an enemy of the Olympian gods (45, 537-44, 995f. = 1015f.). The revelation of the hidden identity of the Dionysiac Stranger accompanies and parallels the revelation of the hidden identity of his opponent.

Opposites cross here in still another way, for the "youthful" king doubles with his "youthful" antagonist, as he gives himself over into the Stranger's power to become the very thing he abominated, an ecstatic woman, a maenad in the dress and service of the Asian god. The excitability of "young" Pentheus (*neanias*, 274) at the "new/young" god (*neos*, 272) shifts from its repressed emotionality to full "ecstasy"

79; McDonald 252-71. Dyer 24 and Scott 333, 343f. also have good observations on the doublings of the play.

   [3] See Arthur (1972) 146, 165, 177; Norwood, *Essays* 67.

(cf. 850) in Dionysiac madness.[4] The opponent of the god then becomes the sacrificial victim of the god. In the fusions that occur in
Dionysiac ritual, he is also identified with the god. The same bestial
imagery of serpents, lions, and bulls describes both figures.[5] The god's
enemy becomes the god's bestial double, the god in his animal shape,
to be torn apart by his worshipers in a rite where logical distinction
and differentiation are left far behind.[6]

Conversely, if Pentheus can appear as the bestial surrogate for the
god, the god is also Pentheus' other self, his double, the repressed
alter ego of the young king. Dionysus is the side of Pentheus that
Pentheus can become only at the cost of losing, by sacrifice, his
rational identity.

Pentheus' tragic task is to reveal the hidden identity of Dionysus by
obstructing the god. He follows the common pattern of resistance to
the god's arrival. Correspondingly, it is Dionysus' task to reveal Pentheus' hidden identity by converting him into his apparent opposite,
revealing the concealed sameness of identity beneath apparent polarity. Hence Pentheus becomes not only a crypto-maenad, but also a
crypto-Dionysus. An androgynous figure at the center of a band of
Dionysiac women, he is duped by the god but simultaneously represents the god; he impersonates a maenad and also impersonates Dionysus (the etymology of *persona* as "mask," though not Greek, is not
irrelevant, as we shall see in Chapter 7).

Dionysus enters Thebes as a stranger, disguised and nameless. Pentheus leaves Thebes as a stranger, disguised, his name the ambiguous
token of his fate (367, 508).[7] Dionysus would establish his mother's
contact with divinity as a mark of her place *above* the normal level
of humanity. Pentheus by his death at Agave's hands establishes his
mother's contact with divinity in just the opposite way: the death, not
the birth, of a son sets her apart, but at a place *below* the level of
human norms, as a huntress polluted with the blood of her own
child, a child proven not a god, but a beast. Dionysus confers "honor"
on Semele in Thebes (cf. 335f.); Pentheus becomes the reason for
Agave's "misery" (cf. 1324) and exile from Thebes (1368ff.).

[4] See Diller (1955) 486; Seidensticker (1971) 51-52.
[5] E.g., 100f., 618, 920-22, 1017-19 for Dionysus; 539, 1174, 1185 for Pentheus.
[6] See Girard 182-83 (Eng. trans. 128f.).
[7] On the Stranger's lack of name as a mark of the Dionysiac fluidity of identity
see Rosenmeyer 109 and Kott 192.

When Dionysus' ecstatic madness meets resistance, it takes the form of violence rather than joyful release. Hence the difference between the happy Asian maenads of the first half of the play and the raging Theban maenads at the end. Dionysus not only mediates contradictions, but exists in the midst of contradictions.[8] He releases a denied or untried capacity for ecstasy, a source of uninhibited joy obstructed by the conventional trappings of ordinariness and prosaic routine. The bright face of this release is playfulness, art, the joy of mystical communion with divinity and with nature; its dark face is homicidal madness.

Doubling and reversal work together to reinforce the ambiguity of identity in the realm of Dionysus. At the peripety, when Pentheus, thanks to Dionysus' magic, sees two suns and two cities of Thebes (918f.), he is also acting out a hitherto hidden side of himself. His is not a vision that can contain the hidden doubleness of the world and survive. He stands there on the stage in a grotesque combination of king and maenad, a visual representation of contradictions that he cannot harmonize. The element of the grotesque gives the scene a comic touch, suggesting still another bifurcation of meanings.[9] But the tragic aspect of this bizarre collocation of opposites lies just in the fact that doubleness and reversal coincide, that the protagonist sees only one side of reality at a time (one thinks of Creon in the *Antigone*). When he swings to the opposite pole, it is not for integration, but for destruction, dismemberment. Moving from the darkness of the palace interior (cf. 549, 611) to the light of his "twin suns," Pentheus still cannot "see" clearly.

The palace itself, we realize in retrospect, has also fused with its "bestial double," as it were: instead of being the seat of regal power and authoritarian domination over Dionysus and his followers, it becomes the dark labyrinth where the hero, far from defeating the bestial monster, is ultimately overcome by the unacknowledged animal side of his own being. Lost in his own interior darkness, he is overcome by his own hidden monstrosity (536ff.). Whereas Athena presides over the hero's conquest of the labyrinth and its monster in the legend of Theseus, Dionysus presides over Pentheus' defeat by his

---

[8] See Otto, 100ff. and 120ff.; Gernet (1953) 390-93; Girard 181ff.

[9] See Dodds, *Bacchae* ad 912-76 (p. 192); Seidensticker (1978).

labyrinth and the monster/double it contains.[10] The one divinity is an *anima*-figure of psychic reintegration and the successful crossing of boundaries; the other god holds the threat of psychic disintegration and the danger implicit in abandoning boundaries.

• II •

The general tendency in the art, literature, and philosophy of the fifth century is to assert man's independence from nature, a tendency since then stamped on all of Western thought. In Sophocles' *Antigone* man's domestication of animals and victory over earth, sea, and air are a point of proud assertion (*Antig.* 332-52). In the Hippocratic *Ancient Medicine* truly human life begins as man leaves behind the "raw" food of the beasts for the "tamed" diet of civilized man. Elsewhere in Euripides and in other writers separation from "the beastlike life" is virtually the definition for civilization.[11] The *Bacchae* and its god, however, reverse that process and call into question the ostensibly upward progress away from the animal and natural roots of our being. In this respect the play, as so much in Euripides, is the voice of a countercultural, counterrational longing in which Western man has repeatedly sought an alternative to his attitude of domination and control: the Golden-Age fantasies and pastoral poetry of the Greeks from Homer to the Cynic Diogenes, the writings of Rousseau, the songs and communes of the hippies. For this reason, too, the *Bacchae* lacks a true heroic spirit, but like much of Greek tragedy permits the surfacing of themes, needs, desires that are repressed by the dominant trends of the culture.

The blurring of the basic division between man and beast is evident in all the main themes of the play, the hunt, rituals, male-female relations, relations between the generations, landscape and setting. Already in the *Homeric Hymn to Dionysus* the god assumes the shape of wild beasts to terrify his victims before changing them into dolphins. Through a bestial (or piscine) metamorphosis, he destroys his opponents' hold on a stable reality and a stable human identity.

[10] See Calame, *Choeurs* 1.228ff.; Kerényi 89ff.
[11] See Segal (1973/74) 296-98 and *Tragedy and Civilization* 34f.; Turato 23-33.

One of the primary forms of this reversal in the play is the hunt, regarded by some as the "key metaphor" of the play.[12] Whereas Pentheus moves from man to hunted beast, Dionysus can remain both god and beast simultaneously. He can maintain a polarization of identities that for Pentheus is disastrous. Whereas the Sophoclean hero can in some way contain his nature's contradiction between the two extremes, Euripides' hero disintegrates. Oedipus moves from king to outlaw, from wise ruler to "bull of the rocks" who haunts "savage forest and caves" (OT 477ff.), but still retains the inner greatness of his powerful, if difficult, nature. When Pentheus moves from male to female, from angry opponent of the maenads to pseudo-bacchant, his name and royal genealogy are ineffectual and pathetic (cf. 1118-19).

The Dionysus of cult often takes the form of bull, fawn, calf, lion—animals to which Pentheus is also likened.[13] The bull, creature of proverbial sexuality, is the appropriate form for the epiphany of a god who will effect Pentheus' ruin, for the bull symbolizes just those parts of himself that he cannot accept.[14] When Dionysus seems to "lead" Pentheus "as a bull" (920) and also "accompanies as a god" (923), he creates onstage that fluidity between heightened perception and madness characteristic of his cult. In the rite celebrated onstage the tauriform god is present as a religious event; but he is also present symbolically within Pentheus, as he was earlier within his palace buildings (618, 622-24), as the animal sexuality which, when released, "leads" him to his "doom" (1159).

"I followed my master," the Messenger will say, introducing the account of Pentheus' death (1046). But the "master is at this point the victim who himself follows the bull which "leads" (1159). He is, furthermore, the "young calf" (neos moschos, 1185) caught at the center of a "murderous maenad-herd" (thanasimon agelan, 1022).[15]

---

[12] WI 12; Kirk 13-14; Dyer 20-21; Otto 108-109; Rosenmeyer 132ff.; Diller (1955) 491.

[13] See Farnell Cults 5.126ff., 166f., 250ff., 284f.; Dodds, Bacchae ad 920-22, Roux ad 99-100.

[14] WI 84 and his remark in Entretiens, Euripide (1960) 196; Sale (1972) 69f., 72f. For the latent erotic element in Pentheus' desire to see the maenads, see Green 204f., 207f.; also Roberts 46f.

[15] Dodds, Bacchae ad 1020-23 takes thanasimon with brochon ("noose"); word order and colometry suggest that it might be taken with both words: both the "noose" and the "herd" are "murderous."

As Pentheus is "led" away, his position as *despotēs* becomes horribly ironical. The analogous title, *anax*, "lord," was given Pentheus by the first Messenger (666, 721; also *despotēs*, 769); but that title is now conferred on the god: ἄναξ ἀγρεύς (1192). This "lord" is a "hunter" in a truer and more literal sense than Pentheus ever was.[16]

Another hunter turned into hunted quarry occurs at the major junctions of the action: Actaeon.[17] His "raw-eating" dogs (*ōmositoi*, 338) recall the "raw-eating" of the Dionysiac cult (cf. *ōmophagos*, 139). "Raw-eating," *ōmadios*, is in fact a cult name of Dionysus who appears to his worshipers in the form of a stag (like Actaeon), killed and eaten, presumably raw.[18] In the dissolved hierarchies of Dionysiac ritual, the god is both the devoured and the devourer.[19] As the maenads' "fellow hunter" (1146; cf. 1189), he is at once god and beast. When he appears in beast-form, it is a sign of his mysterious power. When Pentheus tries to hunt men as beasts, he loses all of his power. Actaeon is destroyed by the very dogs (female) "which he nurtured" (*ethrepsato*, 338). Pentheus, in the inversion of his "hunting," also experiences a reversal of "nurture" from females, death instead of life; and his mother and aunts momentarily appear as "dogs" that hunt him down (731; cf. 977, 872).

As the myth of Actaeon implies, the hunter walks a thin line between the civilized and the wild.[20] Pentheus does his "hunting" ostensibly in the service of the civic order, with "nets of iron" (230; cf. 451). The maenads catch their prey without nets (1172, 1206), just as they dislodge their "climbing beast" with "levers not of iron" (*asidēroi mochloi*, 1104). Yet in the fluctuation between the human and wild savagery characteristic of this anomalous hunting, Dionysus, the beast-huntsman, is also a crafty human hunter who carefully leads his prey into the "net" (848, 1021). With his "smiling visage" in this

[16] Line 1192, "The lord is a hunter," sounds like a ritual formula. Cf. Agave's call to the god as "fellow hunter," 1146. At the end of the play Agave, describing the destruction of her house, gives him the title *Dionysos anax* (1375). Note also the Chorus's repeated *despota, despota* ("master") at 582. See Podlecki, 161f.

[17] For Actaeon see 229, 337, 1227, 1291, 1371; see below, Chap. 4, n. 54 and Chap. 6, nn. 15-16.

[18] For the rites of Dionysus *Ōmadios* see Picard in *BCH* 70 (1946) 455f. = Calame, *Rito* 165f.; Roux 1.65f.; Farnell, *Cults* 5.164ff., 302, 304. Nilsson, *GGR* 572f.; Detienne, *Dionysos* 149-50; Burkert, *Gr. Rel.* 256; Henrichs (1978) 150ff., with some qualifications about the cultic practice of omophagy.

[19] See Dodds, "Maenadism," 166.

[20] See below, Chap. 6, section 2.

latter passage (γελῶντι προσώπῳ, 1021), he is also the god in his epiphany, calm and unreachable in the midst of the violence around him.[21]

In this fluid passage between god and beast, man and nature, his followers are both dangerous beasts of prey and innocuous domestic animals, young fillies or fawns. In the parode the maenad rejoices on the mountain "like a foal with its mother at pasture" (πῶλος ὅπως ἅμα ματέρι / φορβάδι . . . , 166f.); but that image turns out to have a very different significance for Pentheus at the end: when he finds union with his mother on the mountain, he is the "calf" ripped to pieces (1185) or the lion cub hunted down (1174). The eating there, too, is grimly different from the horses' vegetarian "pasture" (cf. *phorbadi*, 168).

The foal simile of the parode is echoed later, as this shift of mood is imminent, when the maenads are helpless fawns skipping joyfully among rivers, shady thickets, and forest meadows, having escaped the "dogs' running" (δράμημα κυνῶν, 872) of the cruel huntsman Pentheus.[22] Yet in the prologue it was the god himself and his bands that did the "running" (cf. θιάσων δρομαίων, 135f., "runnings bands") as they hunted down the goat for the bloody raw-eating (*ōmophagia*, 135-37). Here the fawns are the victims not of the god's hunter-antagonist, but of the god himself, who wears the skin of fawns (137). When Pentheus is about to join the god and his followers as devotee/victim on those mountains, he too wears the "dappled hide of a fawn" (835), a change indicative of the sudden movements from the idyllic to the dangerous side of the wild and the Dionysiac rites that take place there. The hunting in the parode has a mirror-image in the fourth stasimon where Pentheus is the "tracker" (*mastēr*) of the "mountain-running" maenads (ὀρειδρόμων, 984). In the next scene in fact they catch him with their own burst of intense effort in running (συντόνοις δραμήμασι, 1091; cf. συντείνῃ δράμημα κυνῶν, 872; δρομαίων, 136).[23]

---

[21] Note the similar effect of the god's smile and calm in the midst of his miracles in *Hom. Hymn* 7.14f. The paradoxical coincidence of god and beast would be even greater if one accepted Tyrrell's θὴρ θηραγρέτᾳ in 1020, "The beast [Dionysus] with smiling visage cast his net about the maenads' beast-hunter."

[22] See WI 106f. and 122.

[23] For the problem of the text at 1091 see Dodds, *Bacchae*, ad loc. The echo of 872 seems to me not an argument for deleting the line as an interpolation but a self-

The "deserted paths" (*hodoi erēmoi*, 841) where Pentheus will change from hunter to hunted will hold not joy like those of 875 (*erēmiai*), but fearful carnage. Earlier Pentheus had imagined the "shade" and "deserted places" of the maenads as the setting for orgiastic sex (218, 458, 688). But in this Dionysiac landscape, veering between bucolic innocence (as in 873-76) and savage wilderness, he finds an orgy not of sex, but bloody of death (1052, 1138, 1176, 1221). The maenads' characteristic dance-gesture of flinging back the head in the third stasimon, "throwing the neck into the dewy aether" (866), recurs here with a more sinister meaning for both the aether and the throwing (1072, 1096-1100). We may compare also the "dewy dripping of water" in the Golden-Age setting before they are disturbed (705).[24]

In this unstable and anomalous shift between human and bestial in the "hunt," the maenads are not only wild fawns but also a herd of cattle helplessly driven by the "gadfly-sting" (*oistros*) of the Dionysiac goad (32, 119, 665, 1229). From their passive role as fillies, cows, or fawns they move to an aggressive role as hunting dogs (732). Themselves driven like cattle by the *oistros* to the mountain, they invoke the "dogs of Madness" to sting their prey, Pentheus, with the Dionysiac *oistros* (979). The "herded flocks" in the pastoral serenity at the beginning of the Messenger's speech (677-79) soon become the bloody, hunted prey torn apart in the maenadic frenzy (737-58).[25]

Pentheus himself is both a tame young calf (1185) and a wild lion (1141, 1196), his hair both a curling tendril and a bloody mane (1170, 1187). Even when he gave regal orders to "track down" the enemies of the city (352), he is, figuratively, an animal that will "bite" his opponent (δήξομαι, 351). The metaphor is fairly common and might not have any further significance were it not for the extraordinary violence of the threat which precedes it. In the name of civic order Pentheus would destroy the seer's holy place of augury and scatter the

---

conscious echo, of the sort not infrequent in Euripides, as the "hunter" becomes the "hunted."

[24] Cf. also *chlōros* (*chloē*) in 12 and 38 as well as 866. We recall Dionysus' connection with fertilizing and vitalizing moisture: see above, Chap. 1, n. 5.

[25] The phrase *sarkos endyta* in 746 suggests the vulnerable "envelope of flesh" that the maenads will tear away to lay bare the skeleton. As Roux ad 746-47 remarks, "Tuer, écorcher et dépecer un taureau est un travail de force . . . ," all the more powerful a reversal when undertaken by these sheltered women of Thebes' royal house. Here the poetry of violence parallels the poetry of pastoral and mystical beauty in the previous description. The two stand side by side in the Dionysiac realm.

sacred fillets to the wind (346-51). Ten lines after that, he is explicitly called *agrios*, "savage" (361), an epithet that recurs in an ode soon after (542). Pentheus would punish madness, but he is mad himself (cf. 326, 359). When he finally confronts his "hunted prey" (*agra*, 436), the "beast" turns out to be "tame" (436). Similarly in the next scene the allegedly riotous stranger is "quiet" (622, 636, 647), while Pentheus rushes about in beast-like rage (620f.). When he confronts the "bull," he "pastures" emptily on "hopes" (ἐλπίσιν δ' ἐβόσκετο, 617). If Dionysus embodies a capacity for mystical serenity in the midst of wild ecstasy, Pentheus exemplifies, at times, a destructive savagery in the guise of ordered civility and discipline.

In the midst of the grim hunting imagery of the fourth stasimon (977, 986, 1017-22) the Chorus sings of their joy in "hunting after wisdom" (χαίρω θηρεύουσα [sc. τὸ σοφόν], 1006). In the previous ode too, as they praise the power of the divine (881-96), they hymn the inexorable justice of the gods who "hunt down" the irreverent man (890). In both cases the metaphorical "hunt" stands at the furthest possible remove from the bestial hunting in which the Theban maenads and Pentheus are now immersed. Conceiving of the maenads in their mountain solitude as only "hunting after sex [*Kypris*], isolated in the forest" (θηρᾶν καθ' ὕλην Κύπριν ἠρημωμένας, 688), Pentheus cannot grasp this higher aspect of their "hunt," just as he cannot admit the "wisdom" (*sophia*) which is its object (1006).

· III ·

Among the functions of ritual are the assertion and maintenance of order within the various categories of experience. The demarcation of the sacred from the profane by establishing physical, tangible limits is itself a fundamental part of the ritual act.[26] The rites involved in the *Bacchae*, however, confuse rather than establish limits.[27] Com-

[26] For the establishment of boundaries for religious ritual see Leach 85-93, esp. 85f.; Segal, *Tragedy and Civilization* 65f., à propos of Soph. *Trach.* 753ff.

[27] For the reversals and ambiguities of normal ritual in the Dionysiac rites see Daraki, passim; Detienne, *Cuisine* 202f.; Guépin 31; Henrichs (1978) 147f. On the *Bacchae* see now Seidensticker (1979) 186-87, who, however, does not carry his analysis of the essential perversion of normal sacrifice far enough. For a salutary

mentators have noted an archaic, ritualistic formality about the play. "It is like a return to the hieratic stiffness of the *Seven Against Thebes*," one critic remarks.[28]

This ritualized style is particularly prominent in three scenes: (1) the catechism-like question-and-answer between Dionysus and Pentheus (810ff.); (2) the robing of Pentheus as a maenad (912-76), which is itself symmetrical to Pentheus' threatened disrobing of the Stranger (492ff.);[29] (3) the account of his death (1064-1136), with (a) its ritual procession (1047), (b) the elaborate bending down of the tree (1064-74), (c) the dislodging of Pentheus (1095-1113), and (d) the *sparagmos* or rending (1122-36). A similar mood of ritual stylization may well have characterized the now lost description of the piecing together of the body (cf. 1298ff.).

At one time it was fashionable to discern in the play an underlying ritual pattern of the *Eniautos Daimōn*, the old "year-king" slaughtered to make way for the new, or a representation of the "misrule" of the Saturnalian festival, the mimed disorder from which a new order, fresh and purified, would be reborn, or the model of sacral kingship wherein the king's spilled blood and dismembered body were cast into the soil to replenish the earth.[30] Whatever validity there may be to such mythic patterns, Euripides' play itself offers but the most fitful glimmers of any rebirth or renewal of order after chaos. Virtually all the ritual actions of the play are ambiguous. They serve only to underline the fundamentally ambiguous nature of the Dionysiac religion, its problematical relation to civilized life, its precarious suspension between individual ecstasy and collective violence.

More recent critics see in the ritual action the city's successful passage through its "sacrificial crisis," choosing the correct victim by

---

warning against excessive emphasis on the ritual character of the drama see Taplin 161f.

[28] Rosenmeyer 125; see also Roux 1.8; Dodds, *Bacchae* xxvii-xxviii. This effect is enhanced by studied repetitions like those between 973 and 1092 or between 1199 and 1243f.

[29] In more detail cf. 493-94 with 928; the thyrsus in 495-96 with 941; enclosure in 497-98 with freedom on Cithaeron in 949ff.; the invisibility of Dionysus in 500-502 with his mysterious visibility as a bull in 920-22.

[30] See A. G. Bather, "The Problem of the *Bacchae*," *JHS* 14 (1894) 244-63; Murray (1913) 181ff.; with a different emphasis Gallini 215 with the bibliography there cited; Conacher 56-58. The search for primitive elements and archaic rituals is revived by Coche de la Ferté, passim: see esp. 208-21 and 249f.

a random process that expels violence, resacralizing it and giving it back to the gods,[31] or else the city's fulfilment of an "old dispensation of human sacrifice" as it progresses to that "milder version of his cult that the Asiatic Bacchants had described."[32] Yet the text offers little basis for such optimistic views. What we see is a king terribly (if, in part, justly) killed, the sanctities of kinship horribly outraged (note the stress on kinship in 1092 and 1323f.), and the innocent grievously afflicted. The progression, if such it is, seems rather from the benign serenity of the early odes to increasingly bloody rites, marked, as we have seen, by a shift in the imagery from the maenads as frolicsome fillies or fawns (165f., 863ff.) to savage hunters. The "limbs" that move in happy "leaps" in the parode (169) change to the martial "shooting forth" of "limbs" like "javelins" in the first rampage (665) and then to the "javelin-throwing" of deadly rocks against the cornered "beast" in 1098.[33] The maenads in the third stasimon, having escaped their "hunter," throw their necks "into the dewy aether" (863-70), but that aether proves far from "dewy" when Pentheus is about to hurtle through it (1072); and what is "thrown" are missiles that bring down the prey to the carnivorous hunters waiting below (1096ff.).

The play makes a division between the maenads by choice and the maenads by constraint, the one benign, the other dangerous. Yet the voluntary Asiatic maenads have their "delight in raw-eating" (139) and their narthexes of violence and Death (1114, 1157).[34] The Athenians who may have thought of the Dionysiac cult in terms of the "old-fashioned country gaiety" and "pious and cheerful drunkenness" that characterized the god in their native city and villages must have experienced profound disturbance at this encounter with a god who so radically challenges the civic order.[35] His "dances" are not the citizen choruses of the polis, but barbarian "orgies" (*orgia*, 482) where

[31] Girard, passim, esp. 190-97 (Eng. trans. 134-39).

[32] Burnett (1970) 29. For a more interiorizing view of the milder side of the Dionysiac cult of the *Bacchae* see Festugière (1957).

[33] κῶλον ἄγει ταχύπουν σκιρτήμασι βάκχα (169); οἴστροισι λευκὸν κῶλον ἐξηκόντισαν (665); ὄζοισί τ᾽ ἐλατίνοισιν ἠκοντίζετο (1098).

[34] See WI 154; De Romilly 377. Although there is possibly a corruption in 1157, the association with Hades, confirmed by the Antinoe Papyrus fragment, seems fairly firm: see Dodds, *Bacchae*, ad loc.; for attempts at emendation see Willink 241.

[35] See Dodds, "Maenadism," 168.

cries of triumph ring out at the brutal death of a legitimate king (1153-55).

The *kōmos* or revel here is no joyful feast (cf. 1167, 1172), but a scene of mourning to be attended by "cries of lamentation and wailing" (1162). What would be eaten at the "feast" to which all Thebes has been invited (cf. 1242, 1247) in celebration of a "fortunate hunting" (1183) is a human "victim" (*thyma*, 1246), focus of multiple pollutions. "Lovely the victim that you strike down before the gods, inviting Thebes here and me to the feast," Cadmus grimly exclaims at Agave's return from her "hunt" (1246-47). The "priestess" (*hierea*, 1114) in the ritual "slaughter"—*phonos*, a word which also means "murder"—foams at the mouth (1122) and like her companions in the ritual is spattered with blood rather than being pure (1163; cf. 1135f.).

In his very first speech Pentheus, questioning the religious seriousness of the maenads, alleges that "as maenad-sacrificers" (ὡς δὴ μαινάδας θυοσκόους, 224) they but pretend to worship and in fact pursue illicit sex in the woods. His scornful word here, *thyoskoos*, literally means "sacrificial priest" or "priestess." The authenticity of their worship and the sacrifice that goes with it is proven only too true at the end in the act of the "priestess of murder" who officiates at Pentheus' ritual death (1114).

Pentheus returns to the motif of sacrifice in his second encounter with the Dionysiac cult. Now face to face with the Stranger, he asks about the form (*idea*) of the rites (*orgia*, 471) and when confronted with the prohibition against divulging that knowledge to the uninitiated (472) asks, "What help then do they bring for those who do sacrifice?" (ἔχει δ᾽ ὄνησιν τοῖσι θύουσιν τίνα, 473). Unknowingly he has touched on the part of the ritual that will concern him most. The Stranger's reply, "To hear is not lawful, but they are worth knowing" (474), foreshadows that intimate experience of the sacrificial ritual that awaits Pentheus. Euripides has carefully introduced the theme of sacrifice early in the play and interwoven it with Pentheus' interest in the maenadic cult from the very first.

The culmination of the worship brings into the protected interior realm the deeds and sensations that belong only outside, in the "raw" world of the beasts. The sacrificial banquet contains the horror of filicide and at least the intimation of cannibalism.

In normal sacrifice the skull of the animal was often set up in a prominent place as a mark of piety.[36] Here, however, the torn head of the king himself, carried by his priestess-murderess-mother, is to be hung from the rafters of the palace (1212ff., 1239f.). Into that symbolical center of civilized values it brings chaos rather than order, desecration rather than sanctification.

Throughout Greek tragedy the confusion of hunt with sacrifice and of hunted beast with human being operates as a focal point for major inversions in all the civilized codes. Orestes in the *Choephoroe* and *Eumenides*, polluted with a stain of matricide that places him beyond the pale of the civilized world, is hunted down by the "dog-like" Furies and in fact compared to Pentheus torn apart as a hare (*Eumen.* 25-26).[37] In Sophocles' *Ajax* the hero's madness and confusion of men with beasts, of cattle with wild animals, are interwoven with an anomalous tracking and hunting down of a man as if he were a beast (cf. *Ajax* 1-8, 60, 64, 93, 297, etc.). Within Euripides the *Iphigeneia in Tauris* provides a good example. The Taurian herdsmen initially take Orestes and Pylades for gods (*daimones*, 267ff.), but soon decide to "hunt" them as "sacrificial victims" (*sphagia*) for the goddess (278-80). In this "savage" place at the fringes of civilization the practice of human sacrifice introduces a total confusion between god, man, and beast. The wild setting is the appropriate place for a madness that removes Orestes from godlike beauty (cf. 267ff.) to bestial savagery (284, 291ff., especially 297). The "hunting" of men as beasts in the biological code exactly parallels the sacrifice of men as beast-victims in the ritual code. Thus Iphigeneia complains to the barbarian king, "Not pure are the *victims* that you have *hunted*, lord" (οὐ καθαρά μοι τὰ θύματ' ἠγρεύσασθ', ἄναξ (*IT* 1163; cf. 77, 1324, 1426). The interwoven inversions in the *Bacchae* draw on the same homologies.

[36] Seidensticker (1979) 187 notes the relevance of this rite to 1238-40, but does not pursue its significance.

[37] For this and similar perversions of sacrifice see Vidal-Naquet (1972) 135-58; Froma Zeitlin, "The Motif of Corrupted Sacrifice in Aeschylus' *Oresteia*," *TAPA* 96 (1965) 463-508. Orestes also alternates between being sacrificed and hunted: see Aeschyl. *Eum.* 264-68, 304f., 325-27, and Zeitlin 485f. On Sophocles' *Ajax* see my *Tragedy and Civilization* 138-42. On the combination of hunt and sacrifice at the Dionysiac festival of the Agrionia and related myths see Daraki 139ff.; Burkert, *Homo Necans* 191-200; Roux 1.66-68.

What leads the "victim" to that confused sacrifice is a ritual procession (cf. *pompos theōrias*, 1047), which shifts from openness to stealth (840f., 961). Instead of the shouting of a festive crowd, there is covert silence (1049-50), soon to be followed by a stranger silence, not of the holy *euphēmia*, but of the woods and beasts (1084-87). The "escort" (*pompos*) in this sacrificial march is not a member of the city, but a "stranger" (*xenos*, 1047), who, as we know, calls into question the dividing line between human and bestial, sacrifice and hunting, foreign and familiar. Previously called "an escort of salvation" (*pompos sōterios*, 965),[38] he is in fact an escort to death. Instead of the human celebrant leading the animal victim, it is the god, in the form of a bull, who leads the man (cf. 922f.). When the rite is consummated, it is labeled "a misfortune," and a bull is its "leader" (ταῦρον προηγητῆρα συμφορᾶς, 1159). This "procession" has a pendant at the end, where the "priestess" of that sacrifice bids a final farewell to its locale on the mountain (1381-85):

> Agave. Come, my escorting companions [*pompoi*], lead me where we may find my poor sisters, fellow exiles, and may I come where accursed Cithaeron may not look on me, nor I on Cithaeron.

This procession, like the first, is centrifugal: it leads outward, from the city to the wild, from home to exile. It thus marks a confusion or destruction, not a reaffirmation, of the limits that constitute civilization.

Agave goes on here (1386f.):

> μήθ' ὅθι θύρσου μνῆμ' ἀνάκειται·
> Βάκχαις δ' ἄλλαισι μέλοιεν.

> [And may I go] where no reminder of the thyrsus lies stored up,
> but may these be a care to other maenads.

Her language completes the inversion of the socio-religious order. The verb ἀνάκειται, "is stored up," could also mean "dedicated" in the way spoils or a victim may be "dedicated" to the god.[39] It is in

---

[38] Seidensticker (1979) 183 notes the echo between 965 and 1047. For the ritual connotations of the language see also Roux ad 963-65 and 1046f.

[39] See Dodds, *Bacchae* on 934; WI 118, n. 3; Seidensticker (1979) 182f. For the ritual usage in a playful Dionysiac context see Plato *Smp.* 197e and cf. also Soph.

fact the very word that Pentheus, not suspecting the *double entendre*, uses when he is about to become a sacrificial victim to the god (934):

ἰδού, σὺ κόσμει· σοὶ γὰρ ἀνακείμεσθα δή.

Do you adorn us, for we are in your hands [i.e., dedicated to you].

Used here at the end, ἀνακεῖσθαι recalls both the inverted sacrifice and the totally unheroic "contest" (cf. *agōn*, cf. 975) in which this youthful would-be warrior-king meets his end. He leaves behind no glorious "memorial" (another meaning of *mnēma*) set up to commemorate a victory, but in fact nearly becomes a grim and unholy trophy through the madness of the woman who speaks these last lines (cf. 1212-15, 1239-41).

· IV ·

The confusion of hierarchy by perverted sacrifice operates also in another ritual pattern underlying the action, that of the expulsion of the scapegoat or *pharmakos*. This symbolical bearer of all the ills and pollutions of the society was ceremonially driven out of the city at the Athenian festival of the Thargelia. Whether or not the mock whipping and expulsion in classical times were a survival of a more primitive ritual of human sacrifice, the *pharmakos* ritual left important traces in fifth-century Athens, most clearly perhaps in the *Oedipus Tyrannus* of Sophocles.[40]

Like Oedipus in the *Tyrannus*, Pentheus ultimately succeeds in removing the dangerous and disruptive element from the city; like Oedipus he does so by expelling himself as that source of disruption. Early in the play Pentheus threatens Dionysus with death by stoning,

---

Ajax 1214. As Girard 186 notes, it is anomalously not the celebrant, but the god himself who prepares this "victim" (Eng. trans. 131).

[40] See Vernant, *Mythe et Tragédie* 114ff.; Guépin 89-91; Roux 1.16f. and 2.567 (ad 1058-62). See also F. M. Cornford, *The Origin of Attic Comedy* (1914), ed. T. H. Gaster (Garden City, N.Y., 1961) 129-33; Burkert, *Structure*, chap. 3 and *Gr. Rel.* 139-42. For the *Bacchae* see Coche de la Ferté 165-74, who concentrates on the sisters of the royal house rather than Pentheus.

the *leusimos dikē* usually reserved for the bearer of the pollution, the *pharmakos*.[41] But, in the doubling of savior and destroyer in the role of the ambiguous god (cf. 806, 965) and the ambiguous king, the victim of death by stoning proves to be Pentheus, not the Stranger (1096ff.). At the end, as Cadmus admits, Pentheus receives the "punishment that he deserved" (*dikēn axian*, 1312). In terms of his own view of the city, Pentheus is correct to perceive Dionysus as a threat to its existence (cf. 215-25). But in the course of action he adopts he becomes a figure who can save his city neither as king nor as pharmakos.

Changed from regal to bacchantic dress in carefully enumerated stages (827f., 832ff., 852f., 924ff.), Pentheus is the surrogate for the maenadic element that he is expelling from the city. In thus expelling the Dionysiac madness in his own person, he enacts that madness, to return to the palace as the torn prey of the maenadic *ōmophagia* (cf. 1212ff.). Pentheus submits to being paraded, thus garbed, "through the middle of the Theban land" (961); like the *pharmakos*, "conspicuous to all" (*episēmos pasin*, 967), alone (*monos*), he bears the suffering of the whole community (962-63):

Πε. μόνος γὰρ αὐτῶν εἰμ' ἀνὴρ τολμῶν τόδε.
Δι. μόνος σὺ πόλεως τῆσδ' ὑπερκάμνεις, μόνος.

Penth. For I am the only man of these to dare this thing.
Dionys. Only you alone toil in behalf of this city, alone.

The hieratic effect of the repeated *monos*, "alone," stresses the isolation of the king as scapegoat. The *Christus Patiens*, the early Byzantine drama which adapted the *Bacchae* to the story of Christ's passion, uses 963 to describe the Savior's redemption of mankind (*Chr. Pat.* 1525). But nothing could be further from the Christian spirit of divine mercy and forgiveness than the way in which Pentheus' suffering in-

---

[41] See Rudolf Hirzel, "Die Strafe der Steinigung," *Abhandlungen der Sächsische Akademie der Wissenschaften zu Leipzig*, Phil.-Hist. Klasse 27 (1909) 238; Roux ad 356-57. The ritual dressing scene may also contain traces of a *pharmakos* rite: see Louis Gernet, *Anthropologie de la Grèce antique*, ed. J.-P. Vernant (Paris 1968) 166, on Sudas' *estolismenos*. Likewise the procession (840, 855, 961, 965, 1047) and the "luxurious" treatment of 968-70 may also belong to the ritual of expelling the *pharmakos*: see the new survey of the evidence by Jan Bremmer, "Scapegoat Rituals in Ancient Greece," *HSCP* 87 (1983).

volves the destruction rather than the salvation of the city.[42] "There-fore the god joined together all into one disaster" (συνῆψε πάντας ἐς μίαν βλάβην, 1303), Cadmus says at the end, implying that this sacrifice of "one" for "all" has just the opposite effect. The house too, which Pentheus should have "held together" (συνεῖχες, 1308), he in fact destroys.

That repeated *monos*, "alone," echoes an earlier scene of Dionysiac initiation. Teiresias and Cadmus, eager to worship the god on the mountain, have the following exchange (194-96):

Τε.   ὁ θεὸς ἀμοχθὶ κεῖσε νῶν ἡγήσεται.
Κα.   μόνοι δὲ πόλεως Βακχίῳ χορεύσομεν;
Τε.   μόνοι γὰρ εὖ φρονοῦμεν, οἱ δ᾽ ἄλλοι κακῶς.

Teires. The god will lead us there without toil.
Cadmus. Alone, then, of the city will we dance to the Bacchic god?
Teires. Yes, alone, for only we have good sense, the others bad.

This isolation of the "only" worshipers of the citizen body has its pendant in the isolation of Pentheus as the other side of the Dionysiac power. Now the "freedom from toil" (*amochthi*) becomes "toil for the whole city" (*hyperkamnein*, 963); and the "leader" is not "the god" (*ho theos*, 194), but the beast (1159). Here, as throughout the play, the dark face of Dionysus is always present, the "destroyer" just behind the "savior."

The confusion of king and scapegoat in the *Oedipus Tyrannus* throws together the "highest" and the "lowest." Oedipus, "the one best nur-tured man in Thebes" (*OT* 1380), is proven the source of the pollu-tion by the very stroke that makes him the legitimate king, thanks to the combination of incestuous birth and the patricide that led to his

[42] See Dodds, *Bacchae*, and Roux ad 962f. I cannot agree with Burnett (1970) 28 on the positive significance of this *pharmakos* pattern: "Pentheus' free decision had been to destroy the city that he ruled; his unfree action in going to the women destroys himself but saves Thebes and his subjects." The exodos, with the exile of the remnants of the Theban royal house, hardly suggests the salvation of Thebes. Arrowsmith (1959) 54 rightly remarks that the folly or insensitivity (*amathia*) of a man "is less heinous than that of a god."

kingship. Yet this fusion, along with that of savior and pollution, actually does save Thebes and culminates in the king's eventual reintegration of the two poles of his problematic identity (cf. *OT* 1414-15, 1455ff.). Pentheus, collapsing the two poles, both literally and metaphorically undergoes a disintegration of self and contributes to the destruction of Thebes. Unlike Oedipus, he cannot ultimately come to terms with the violence within himself or in his city.

In his first encounter with the god he disregards the warning that he might suffer the dismemberment of Actaeon (ὃ μὴ πάθῃς σύ, 341, "Do not suffer this") and answers with insults about Teiresias' not "wiping off" his foolishness and with threats to destroy the prophet's place of augury (343-51). Later, led off as the sole bearer of Thebes' suffering (962f., supra), he likewise threatens widespread destruction to the sacred places of nature: he would destroy the abodes of nymphs and Pan on the mountain (945-52). The syntactical inversions in the language of this scene (e.g., 912f., 924, 955, 960) are similar to the inversions that occur in the ironical *pharmakos* motif of the *Tyrannus* (e.g., *OT* 138-41). In the *Oedipus* Apollo in his remote and mysterious way can be a "savior" (80f., 149f.) and lead Oedipus to his painful destiny as the "pollution/savior" of Thebes. Dionysus' role as *sōtēr*, "savior," works in only one direction. Where he would lead Pentheus off to "save" him (*sōtērios*, 965; cf. 806), "another will lead him back" (966)—dismembered, not reintegrated.

• V •

Not only are the normal civic sacrifices perverted, but some relatively innocuous aspects of the Dionysiac religion take on sinister meanings when they are resisted. One of these is libation. In his long speech urging the acceptance of Dionysus, Teiresias urges (312f.):

τὸν θεὸν δ' ἐς γῆν δέχου
καὶ σπένδε καὶ βάκχευε καὶ στέφου κάρα.

But receive the god into the land
And pour libations and revel and crown your head.

Both the "libations" and the "crowning" recur as parts of the terrible sacrificial rite where Pentheus is the victim. "The god accompanies, reconciled by our libations (*enspondos*)," the Stranger tells Pentheus, now robed as a maenad and nearly ready for sacrifice, "previously not propitious" (923f.). It is that very "propitious accompanying" of the god that means the doom of Pentheus, transformed from antagonist to celebrant-victim at the center of the ritual. In the prologue Dionysus had narrated how Pentheus had "fought against the god" (*theomachei*) and driven him "away from his libations" (*spondai*, 45f.). He had paid no heed to Teiresias' explanation of Dionysus as the very substance of libation, the god who "is poured out as libation to gods" (οὗτος θεοῖσι σπένδεται θεὸς γεγώς, 284). In the maenads' worship, however, it is not the mortals who pour forth wine or honey or milk to the god, but the god who pours it forth for them, not from cups or goblets, but from the very earth (707). The formal libations of normal civic ritual not only become dangerous in the realm of the god (923f.), but in fact prove totally irrelevant, at least in their familiar form.

"Crown your head," Teiresias had said in his instructions of 313 (στέφου κάρα). Pentheus soon violently pushes Cadmus away when the latter tries to put a wreath on his head in honor of the god (341-44):

> Cadmus. Do you not suffer [Actaeon's] fate. Here, I shall crown your head with ivy [σου στέψω κάρα / κισσῷ]. With us give honor to the god.
> Penth. Keep your hand away. Won't you go off to do your reveling and not wipe off your silliness on me?

Throughout the play the garland of ivy recurs as a regular feature of the Dionysiac cult (e.g., κισσῷ στεφανωθείς, "garlanded with ivy," 81; στεφανηφόρους θιάσους, "garland-bearing holy bands," 531; κισσίνους στεφάνους, "ivy garlands," 702f.). The first Theban worshiper of Dionysus to appear onstage, Teiresias, makes a point of mentioning his garland of ivy and defends his dignity in joining the dance "garlanding my head with ivy" (χορεύειν κρᾶτα κισσώσας ἐμόν, 205). When Pentheus wears the Dionysiac wig and headband (*mitra*) as a pseudo-maenad (cf. 830-33, 928f., 1115), his headdress takes the place of the garland worn by the celebrant in a normal ritual sacrifice.[43] So "garlanded," he is as much the maenads' victim as their companion.

This normal concomitant of the sacrifice of the domestic animal in the city, in allusive form, grimly accompanies the wild beast/human victim offered to Dionysus. Just before their attack on Pentheus the maenads "wreathe the thyrsus with ivy" (ϑύρσον . . . / κισσῶ ἐξανέστεφον, 1054-55), an ironic echo of Cadmus' act in 341f. The reconciliation implied in that earlier action has now turned to violence as the god shows his destructive other side. The wreathing both here and in the dressing scene of 928ff. contrasts with the joyful wreaths of the ecstatic chorus in the parode (81, 101-102, 106-13).

The outlandish "garlands" worn by the god's followers in the second passage clearly mark the distance between these rituals and civic cult (99-104):

ἔτεκεν δ᾽, ἁνίκα Μοῖραι
τέλεσαν, ταυρόκερων ϑεὸν
στεφάνωσέν τε δρακόντων
στεφάνοις, ἔνϑεν ἄγραν ϑη-
ροτρόφον μαινάδες ἀμφι-
βάλλονται πλοκάμοις.

And when the Fates accomplished their fulfilment, Zeus brought [Dionysus] to birth, a bull-horned god, and *with garlands of snakes garlanded him*, whence the maenads place about their hair this wild-nurtured prey of the hunt.

This strange garlanding harks back to a moment of felicitous creation of new life, a time of fruitful "origins" (in Mircea Eliade's sense) of the god's birth. At that moment polar opposites come together in an even more strongly condensed form: the paradox of male birth substituted for female, of god and beast, of ritual garlanding and wild beasts. These serpentine garlands not only conjoin divinity and bestiality, Olympian and chthonic, but reinforce the collocation of mor-

---

[43] See Paul Stengel, *Die griechischen Kultusaltertümer*[3] (Munich 1920) 108f. For the inversions in this part of the sacrificial ritual in tragedy see Segal, *Tragedy and Civilization* 72, à propos of Soph. *Trach.* 781ff.; Burkert, *Homo Necans.* 10, n. 6, 63f.

tal birth and immortal life, the serpent being an ancient symbol for what Kerényi calls "the indestructible life."[44]

The garlanding of Pentheus, however, points not to life but to death. "Crown your head" (kara), Teiresias had urged (177, 313). But in the rite where Pentheus is "wreathed," particularly grisly horror attaches to the hair (1170, 1186) and the head (kara, 1139-42, 1214, 1284, etc.; cf. 241).[45]

The Stranger had offered the change of garb as a means of "saving" Pentheus (sōzein, sōtērios: 805f., 965f.). But the potentially saving effect of the ruse merges with a ritual of the king's destruction. Changing dress can serve as a symbolic token of passage between life and death as well as between different stages of life or facets of identity. The motif is deeply rooted in ancient epic. Gilgamesh strips himself of his clothes for the passage across the waters of death. Odysseus casts off his clothing on the perilous crossing between Calypso's island and the Phaeacians. Achilles loses his armor, lent to his companion, Patroclus, who dies in his place. Closer to the Bacchae is the disguising of Menelaus by his faithful wife, Helen, to make possible the crossing back from Egypt, a land of symbolic death, to Sparta (Helen, 1049ff., 1296ff., 1382ff.).[46] The saving power symbolized in the change of dress and a clever ruse by a figure on the side of survival, life, and beauty in the Helen contrasts markedly with the destructive force of the similar "ruse" (dolos, 805, 956) of the ambiguous god of the Bacchae. Annihilation of identity here, unlike Menelaus' situation in the Helen, does not bring renewal of a lost self.

Within the Dionysiac cult and its Orphic adaptation the sparagmos of the victim leads ultimately to a symbolic rebirth of the god. Torn apart in the form of a beast and eaten by his worshipers in a symbolical reenactment of his sparagmos by the Titans, the Orphic Dionysus is renewed from the portions which remain uneaten and the ashes.[47]

[44] Kerényi, chap. 3. For chthonic aspects of the serpents here see Kirk ad 102-104 (p. 37).

[45] Cf. Soph. Trach. 781ff. and the grim kallipaida stephanon of Eur. HF 839, which is followed by an inverted libation of blood instead of Dionysus' wine (894-95).

[46] Webster 273 suggests a parallel with the deception of Theoclemenus in Helen but does not elaborate on the idea nor exploit the much clearer parallel and contrast with Menelaus. On these patterns in Helen see Segal (1971) 569ff., 600ff.

[47] See Guépin 47ff., 52ff., 179f.; Coche de la Ferté 179ff. with the further literature there cited.

Although there is no explicit allusion to this part of the cult, the stress on the painful "searching out" and piecing together of Pentheus' torn body after the *sparagmos* (cf. *diasparakton*, 1220) may be intended to recall the piecing together of the torn body of Dionysus/Zagreus. Thus the Messenger calls that body "no easy object of search," *ou rhadion zētēma*, 1139). Cadmus enters with the body found (*heurōn*, 1219) "in a woods not easy to discover" (*dysheuretos*, 1221) and only after "myriad searchings" (*myria zētēmata*, 1218) and "difficult tracking" (μόλις τόδ᾽ ἐξερευνήσας, 1299). Pentheus, of course, is not the god, only a mortal victim.

In Orphic theology the *sparagmos* of the god confers a special purity.[48] Here the result is a terrible pollution. In ordinary sacrificial rituals, too, purity is a major concern.[49] Here the rite is impure in every way. As victim, Pentheus must be "pure" for the sacrifice; as madman and *pharmakos* he is at the opposite pole (cf. 1135, 1163f.). As Agave handles the bloody fragments of his body in the last rite of the play, she speaks of "taking her own defilement (*mysos*) into her hands" (ἴδιον ἔλαβον ἐς χέρας μύσος, frag. 1, quoted by the scholion on Aristophanes, *Plutus* 907).

These inversions of purity are all the more striking as Dionysus is also a god of purification (Sophocles, *Antigone* 1140-45).[50] The Asian maenads of the parode lay heavy emphasis on the "holy purifications" of their cult (*hosioi katharmoi*, 77; cf. 74). In the next ode they invoke Holiness herself (*Hosia*, 370f.).[51]

As they are beyond the normal mediations effected by civic rituals, so they stand outside the normal modes of purification. Whereas the stain of blood is normally cleansed by a god in the context of civic ritual, the blood shed by the maenads is purified by beasts on the wild mountainside: snakes lick off the gore of the rent cattle (cf. 741ff., 767f.).[52] Pentheus, having denied the blessings of the purity that the

[48] Guépin 235f.

[49] See Burkert, *Gr. Rel.* 129-42; Louis Moulinier, *Le pur et l'impur dans la pensée et la sensibilité des Grecs* (Paris 1952).

[50] See Vicaire 363 with n. 39.

[51] On this passage and its connections with notions of ritual purity see Roux ad 370; De Romilly 362-63. On the ambiguities see Deichgräber 338-39 and Musurillo 308-309.

[52] Note, too, the failure of the maenads' armed opponents to "draw blood" in 761. The violence of this intended shedding of human blood contrasts with the mysterious peace-in-violence of the shedding of animal blood in the first, more benign phase of the maenadic revel on Cithaeron.

maenadic ritual might convey (77ff.), sees the cult as only a source of polluting infection that might be "wiped off" on him (344) or a "disease" that "befouls" (*lymainetai*) the beds of women (352-54). But, as we have seen, Pentheus himself becomes the bearer of all the city's pollutions, the symbolical *pharmakos*, put to death by the very rite of stoning with which he threatens the allegedly polluting god (356f., 1095ff.).

In an archaic pattern reflected in early epic poetry, from *Gilgamesh* to the *Iliad*, the hero, "by losing his identification with a person or group and by identifying himself with a god who takes his life in the process, . . . effects a purification by transferring impurity." This process, as Gregory Nagy describes it, involves the hero's identification with the god who embodies the heroic qualities he seeks to realize and attain in his own life.[53] In the *Bacchae* the hero's identification is not with the god who embodies those qualities but with his opposite, the god of an outside group, despised and degraded as female, licentious, and soft. His ritual identification with and substitution for the god brings no purification, but a terrible *miasma* (1384), and throws heroic values into confusion.

• VI •

The inversions of the hierarchies among beast, man, and god through sacrifice are closely intertwined just before Pentheus falls under Dionysus' power. It is Dionysus' last attempt to dissuade him from his violent resistance (794-99):

> Δι.   θύοιμ᾿ ἂν αὐτῷ μᾶλλον ἢ θυμούμενος
>   πρὸς κέντρα λακτίζοιμι θνητὸς ὢν θεῷ.
> Πε.   θύσω, φόνον γε θῆλυν, ὥσπερ ἄξιαι,
>   πολὺν ταράξας ἐν Κιθαιρῶνος πτυχαῖς.
> Δι.   φεύξεσθε πάντες· καὶ τόδ᾿ αἰσχρόν, ἀσπίδας
>   θύρσοισι βακχῶν ἐκτρέπειν χαλκηλάτους.

> Dionys.   I would sacrifice to him rather than in spirited anger kick against the goads, mortal against god.

---

[53] Nagy, *The Best of the Achaeans*, chap. 18 (quotation from p. 307).

Penth. Sacrifice I will, and female blood aplenty, as they de-
        serve, routing them in Cithaeron's folds.
Dionys. You will all flee; and there is this shame too, to turn
        aside your shields of beaten bronze before the bacchants'
        wands.

The violent ruler who would "sacrifice" human blood (*phonos*) in
wrath (note the play on ϑύοιμι, "sacrifice," and ϑυμούμενος, "in
anger") himself meets death (*phonos*) as a "victim" (*thyma*, 1246) at
the hands of a female priestess-sacrificer (ἱερέα φόνου, 1114).

The hierarchy god-man-beast is implicit in the metaphor of 795:
the man controls the beasts by spurs or goads (*kentra*), as the god
receives from man the token of his superiority in the sacrifice.[54] But
Pentheus would make a sacrifice of human victims (796), as earlier
he would ritually slaughter (*sphazein*, 631) the god as a bull—a situation diametrically reversed when he takes the bull's place (1185),
led as victim by the God-bull (1159). The ritual action of the *Bacchae*
reflects in microcosm the precarious condition of the whole civilized
order. The technological weaponry of the male warriors yields to the
"natural" thyrsuses of the maddened women (731ff., 763f.). The king,
so insistent on boundaries and limits, becomes the living (and dead)
exemplar of their dissolution in the sphere of Dionysus. In ritual, as
in war and hunting, Dionysus releases in Pentheus his own interior
liminal space, where the opposites within his personality coalesce,
with terrible results.

The Dionysiac cult irked and fascinated Pentheus by its insistence
on its private and secret nature: the profane must stand apart (68-70),
and not everyone may "hear" and "see" (472ff.). Now grimly initiated
into the "hidden" and "deserted" places of his realm and of himself
(cf. 841, 875, 954f., 1176), Pentheus himself exhibits public fused
with private, openness with secrecy. In every way the king's person
becomes the field not for the maintenance of civic order but for the
Dionysiac coincidence of opposites.

Dionysus appears throughout as the hidden god, the object of search
and inquiry. Even in his first face-to-face encounter with Pentheus
he exercises his power over the king by the mysteries of which he
speaks. With the authority of a religious leader he uses words of sol-

---

[54] See the similar inversions in Soph. *Trach.* 839-40 and 1259-62; cf. Segal (1977)
136f. and *Tragedy and Civilization* 104f.

emn sacral value (*themis*, "lawful," in 474), and holds up before the examining magistrate the lure of the impenetrable and the ineffable, that which lies always "beyond" the institutional order (471-74):

> Penth.   These rites of yours [*orgia*], what shape do they have?
> Dionys. They are unspeakable, not for un-maenadic mortals to know.
> Penth.   What help do they have for those who do sacrifice?
> Dionys. It is not lawful [*themis*] for you to hear, but they are worthy to be known.[55]

In the ritualized stichomythy of the exchange, Pentheus continually confronts the limits of his own ability to understand the god, the limits of what he may hear, see, or know. He distorts, but cannot fully stifle, the longing for some knowledge that is beyond his ken, the yearning for an intensity of experience that is alien but fascinating. He replies, therefore, "Well have you counterfeited this, in order that I may wish to hear" (475). That unstifled and irrepressible part of the "wish to hear"—and to see—will be just the god's means of completing his power over his antagonist. Even in his resistance Pentheus already manifests his emotional attraction toward the god. Something in him wants to surrender to Dionysus. The god enters where he can. He uses this element of "wish" and "desire" (*boulesthai, erōs,* 811, 813), repressed as it is, to transform Pentheus from opponent to celebrant/victim, the god's own surrogate.

After describing Pentheus' horrible death and the procession through the mountain glades with the mother carrying her son's mutilated head, the Messenger sermonizes (1150-52):

> τὸ σωφρονεῖν δὲ καὶ σέβειν τὰ τῶν θεῶν
> κάλλιστον· οἶμαι δ' αὐτὸ καὶ σοφώτατον
> θνητοῖσιν εἶναι κτῆμα τοῖσι χρωμένοις.

> To have good sense and revere what is of the gods
> is loveliest. I think this, too, to be the wisest
> possession for mortals who use it.

[55] Compare Agave's defense of the god's "secret dances" (*chorous kryphaious*), which she vehemently guards against Pentheus' intrusion, 1108f. On this "mystic" aspect of the forbidden rites see Coche de la Ferté 236, 241 and now R. Seaford, *CQ* 31 (1981) 252-75.

No exhortation to "worship as most lovely what is of the gods" (*sebein ta tōn theōn / kalliston*, 1150f.) is more enigmatic, more disturbing. The Messenger quickly abandons an attempt at understanding for a frightened *credo quia absurdum*. But Euripides' suggestion that such "reverence" holds both beauty and wisdom probes more deeply into the *terra incognita* of religious ecstasy and mystical cult.

Set into the perspective of Euripides' total *œuvre*, these reversals and mysteries surrounding the god of the *Bacchae* are the culminating effort of the poet's relentless examination of "the many forms of divinity" (*Ba*. 1388 et al.). Euripides tests these forms against the demands of human justice. He is uncompromising in his exposure of the discrepancy between man's need for an orderly world and the disorder, both within and without, of which the gods are both the controllers and the symbolic projections.

As the *Bacchae* shows perhaps more powerfully than any of its predecessors, that painfully reached, problematical theodicy is not merely the result of displacing human passions onto the gods. The two-sidedness of Dionysus (861) represents in more sharply religious and specifically theological form the conflicts and ambiguities with which divinity appears everywhere in Euripides. The crossfire between conflicting gods takes a toll of innocent mortals, as in *Hippolytus*, or the action constitutes a bitter *reductio ad absurdum* of selfishly anthropomorphic or cruelly remote gods, as in *Trojan Women*, *Ion*, *Orestes*. Yet Euripides never entirely gives up hope for a purer, more ethical, more mystical conception of divinity. In the famous fragment of the lost *Bellerophon*, he states, "If the gods do something shameful, then they are not gods" (frag. 292.7 Nauck). Heracles courageously refuses to capitulate to a limiting and facile incrimination of divine cruelty (*Heracles Mad*). Theonoe in the *Helen* espouses a lofty philosophical religion of ethereal divine substance and celestial intelligence. Even the young heroine of the *Taurian Iphigeneia* rejects the gods' responsibility for the abomination of human sacrifices of which she is the priestess.[56]

[56] See respectively *Helen* 865ff., 998ff., 1013ff.; *HF* 1340ff.; *IT* 378-91, 1082ff. On Theonoe in the *Helen* see G. Zuntz, "On Euripides' *Helena*: Theology and Irony," in *Euripide, Entretiens* (1960) 213-16 and Segal (1971) 585ff. For recent views on Euripides and the gods see Whitman 120f., 147f.; Kjeld Matthiessen, "Euripides: Die Tragödien," in *Das griechische Drama* (Darmstadt 1979) 148-52, especially 149.

In all these passages an intensely searching spirit is at work that is in its own way also intensely religious. In these works, and most of all in the *Bacchae*, Euripides is trying to grasp the "multiple forms" of man's need for gods and for definitions of gods. He is asking what divinity is, how it manifests itself to men, and how men see it and comprehend it within the means and terms of human passion and understanding, moral consciousness, civic institutions, and language. In addition to the special traits of the maenadic cult, the Dionysus of the *Bacchae*, is also that in the divine which inspires yearning and fascination but always remains beyond our grasp.

Dionysus and Civilization: Tools, Agriculture, Music

Is there anything
To be serious about beyond this otherness
That gets included in the most ordinary
Forms of daily activity, changing everything
Slightly and profoundly . . . ,
. . . To install it on some monstrous, near
Peak . . . ?
John Ashbery,
"Self-Portrait in a Convex Mirror"

• I •

A god of the wild and of the autonomous, unpredictable surges of the life energies in nature and in man as part of nature, Dionysus has a necessarily ambiguous relationship to civilization. He is a force within man that the society can channel to creative purposes and a force that threatens and dissolves the bonds of the society. Both the acknowledgment and the repression of Dionysus are necessities for civilized life. For these reasons he can serve as a catalyst for the crises in the social order and the rifts between individual needs and the culture as a whole that preoccupied Euripides throughout his career.

In the last years of his life Euripides seemed particularly pessimistic about the ability of the polis to retain the balance between the contradictory needs and capacities of its citizens. Plays like the *Phoenician Women*, the *Orestes*, and the *Iphigeneia in Aulis*, composed, like the *Bacchae*, within the last decade of his life and near or after the time when he left Athens for Macedon, show the civilized order cracking apart. The male-centered polis is not merely threatened, as earlier, by a female figure of powerful and violent emotion like Medea or Phaedra, but is fundamentally unable to contain the emotional violence that is perceived as ready to burst forth in a sudden, widely destructive explosion of emotional energies. In these late plays there is little counterweight to that violence, nothing like the radiant ode on Athens in the *Medea*; the noble, if flawed, commitment to an ideal in *Hippolytus*; the heroic endurance and trust in the moral order in the face of crushing disaster in the *Heracles*. Instead they call into question the ability of the city to hold in equilibrium the conflicting forces within man and to restore the balance and harmony between them that constitutes *dikē*, the way of justice.

In the *Bacchae* the precariousness of the civic authority has both its cause and its symbol in the precariousness of regal authority and heroic identity. From the very first Pentheus exhibits the traits of the violent tyrant rather than the good ruler (cf. 215ff., 670f.).[1] He is aggressive, rigid, prone to narrow stereotyping, irascible, intemperate, and exaggerated in his reactions to people and events.[2] When at his first stage appearance he threatens to "cut [the Stranger's] neck apart from his body" (241), we know that this king cannot represent a valid civic order. The impression is confirmed a hundred lines later when he orders the obliteration of Teiresias' holy seat of augury (346-51), an act which, as we know from Aeschylus and Sophocles, can have only the most dangerous consequences for both king and community (*Agamemnon* 527ff.; *Antigone* 1033-1114). It is at this point that Teiresias calls him, for the first time, *agrios*, "savage" (361). The epithet questions his civic responsibility and places him in the bestial realm outside civilization.[3] The Chorus repeats his word and connects it with his chthonic (and for them bestial) origins as the son of Echion (542).

As Pentheus moves to the fringes of the civilized space, the Stran-

---

[1] See Seidensticker (1972) 39f.; Roux 1.25ff. and E. M. Blaiklock, *The Male Characters of Euripides* (Wellington, New Zealand 1952) 214ff., who overstress the positive side of Pentheus. Diller (1955) 475f. provides useful parallels with the "stage tyrant" of Greek tragedy like the Creon of *Antigone* and also an instructive contrast with the Oedipus of the *Tyrannus*.

[2] See Seidensticker (1972) passim, esp. 57-61, with a useful list of earlier studies. See also Oranje 145f.

[3] For these connotations of *agrios* see Segal (1973/74) 296-99 and *Tragedy and Civilization* 32f.

ger from the wild, barbarian realms takes the place of authority at the center of the polis. Gradually Dionysus usurps the titles of power: "lord," "master," "power" (*anax, despotēs, kratos*).[4]

The "master" of Thebes, refusing to "receive the god in the city" (769f.), would lock up the worshipers "in the prisons of the whole city" (*pandēmoi stegai*, 226; cf. *pandēmos stegē*, 443). But Dionysus becomes the god of "all the Thebans" (πᾶσιν Θηβαίοισιν, 48). "The whole city" at the end, as the ex-king Cadmus explains to the confused and fearful Agave, "fell under the Bacchic rage" (πᾶσά τ᾽ ἐξεβακχεύθη πόλις, 1295).[5] The verb *bakcheuein*, "to rage as a bacchant," is generally used with a personal subject in the play.[6] The Messenger used it, in a striking phrase, possibly influenced by Aeschylus, of the climax of the revel on Cithaeron, when "all the mountain and the beasts joined in the bacchic frenzy" (*symbakcheuein*, 726f.).[7] Applied to the city in line 1295, the word expresses a surprising collocation of opposites that signifies Dionysus' victory. This "Bacchic" city exists in a state of open "madness," whereas the madness that characterized Pentheus' legitimate rule is just beneath the surface (cf. 344-45 with 326, 359; also 298-301).

Pentheus's mother "will see him first," the chorus says (982-87), "spying from a smooth rock or from a stake [λευρᾶς ἀπὸ πέτρας / ἢ σκόλοπος ὄψεται / δοκεύοντα] and will cry out to the maenads, 'What hunter of the mountain-running Cadmeans has come to the mountain, to the mountain, O bacchants.' " The fir tree in the wild on which Pentheus is soon perched for his death (cf. 1070-1113) is here seen proleptically and anomalously as a "stake" or "pole" (σκόλοψ); the shaped artifact fuses with the natural growth on the mountain.[8]

---

[4] *Anax* (Pentheus): 666, 721: *anax* (Dionysus): 601, 1192, 1375. *Kratos* (Pentheus): 213, 660; *kratos* (Dionysus): 1037f. *Despotēs* (Pentheus): 769, 1046 and cf. 1033; *despotēs* (Dionysus): 582.

[5] For the theme of the "whole city" see Podlecki 148, 161-63.

[6] *Ba.* 76, 251, 313, 343, 807.

[7] See Aeschylus frag. 58 N (76 Mette): ἐνθουσιᾷ δὴ δῶμα· βακχεύει στέγη. See Dodds, *Bacchae* xxxii.

[8] Cf. the use of a stake (*skolops*) for the impalement of Aegisthus' head in Eur. *El.* 898. Nowhere else in classical Greek literature does *skolops* seem to mean a tree or other natural growth. Editors have consequently sought to emend the passage, but there is no consensus. The parallel with *IT* 1429-30, noted but not utilized for interpretation by Willink 223 with note 2, may shed some light on our passage. There the barbarian king Thoas threatens the fleeing Greeks with "hurling them

That fluctuation also foreshadows the impalement of the head of the hunted lion/young king on the battlements of the palace (1214f.). The smooth rock in 982, on the other hand, shows this pattern in reverse. In 982 the epithet "smooth" locates it within wild nature; later, when the "pole" or "stake" is clearly a tree, the rock is compared to a city's tower (*antipyrgos petra*, 1097). These small details enhance the nightmarish aspect of the Dionysiac slippage of boundaries between nature and culture.

The Theban maidens on the mountain are called "unyoked," *azyges* (694). The metaphor is mild; the term is relatively innocuous. Later it develops in a more sinister direction. In the Second Messenger's speech, the account of Pentheus' death, the maenads, excited to the pitch of homicidal fury, are compared to "fillies who have left their embroidered yokes," ἐκλιποῦσαι ποικίλ' ὡς πῶλοι ζυγά (1056). The adjective *poikilos*, "embroidered," "variegated," marks the elaborate, crafted, and hence especially civilized quality of this "yoke." Here, as in its two other occurrences in the play (249, 888), *poikilos* ironically points to a collapsing of the antitheses between culture and nature, divinity and savagery, which soon reaches a climax in the death of the king as a hunted wild beast.[9]

The description of the maenads as "unyoked fillies" in 1056 caps the progression from the happy foal-like leaping of the parode (165-69) to the happy fawn safe from the hunter in an idyllic forest-setting in 865-76—so different from the Theban maenads in the forest-world

---

from a rough rock or impaling their bodies on pikes" (ἢ κατὰ στύφλου πέτρας / ῥίψωμεν, ἢ σκόλοψι πήξωμεν δέμας). The parallel with *Ba.* 982-83 both in phrasing and in context suggests the further association of the Chorus's *skolops* with the punishment of impalement that the mad Agave seeks for the head of her prey at 1212ff. One might think also of the impalement of the head on the thyrsus, sometimes assumed by interpreters (e.g., Green 209; Steidle 38, Kott 205, Foley [1980] 131), but not in fact shown onstage: with 1139-42 cf. 1168-74, 1238, 1277, 1280, 1286 and compare 969. See also below, Chap. 6, n. 56. The impalement of 1211-15 is a different matter.

[9] In 249 Pentheus uses *poikilos* in a contumelious description of the fawn-skins worn by the maenads. In 889 *poikilōs* (the adverb) characterizes the gods' vengeful pursuit of the impious man: "With crafted skill they conceal the long foot of time and hunt down [*thērōsi*] the irreverent one" (888-90). Following upon the fawn-maenad's escape from a hunter's pursuit (866ff.), this passage implicitly brings together the bestial "hunting" of the maenads by Pentheus (and its reversal) and the gods' crafty hunting of the irreverent king.

that the erstwhile hunter is now entering. That movement, as we have noted, is part of a nexus of motifs that also involves a change from the "swift limb" of 169 to the "white limb" shot out as by a javelin in 665 to the "white foot" of the happy maenad in the joyous "all night dance" of 862-65 and then finally to the mysterious "foot of time" and divine "hunting" in 889-90. This last "foot" is that of neither man nor beast, just as the "hunt" here is of a different order from either Pentheus' or the maenads'. In both cases something remoter, less tangible, and therefore more terrifying is at work.

In the coded system of metaphors in classical Greek poetry, the "unyoked filly" or "heifer" has a specific social significance. It denotes the ambiguous position of the young girl who is ready to leave the shelter of the patriarchal *oikos*, but is not yet domesticated as the member of a new household. When she has made that transition to the status of wife and mother, she is a civilized member of society, the "plowed field" that bears a crop of legitimate children under the cultivation of the husband-farmer. The codes of animal husbandry, agriculture, and space all come together here in the classification of the legitimate wife as yoked, plowed, and enclosed in the safe, interior space of the house. The domestication of animals, agriculture, marriage and childbearing, and interiority are all homologous to one another in the codes that implicitly define woman's subordinate place in the civilized order.[10] The "unyoked" girl, however, is in a liminal stage, between nature and culture, the wild and the human. An anomaly, she is like a wild beast, subject to "wandering" in the savage places of forest and mountain, liable to fits of madness, unstable, potentially dangerous. Her sexuality, not yet brought within the bounds of marriage and the proper function of bearing legitimate children, adds its power to the danger of the irrational that the Greeks associate with the spirited, independent, and sexually aggressive female. More disturbingly still, the maenad-fawns or fillies of the *Bacchae* have actually left their "yokes" by abandoning the infants they have borne to their husbands in their Theban *oikoi* and taking up wild creatures

[10] On these forms of conceptualizing the female see Vernant, *Mythe et pensée* 1.140ff. and *Mythe et société* 191-93; Segal, *Tragedy and Civilization* 27ff., 61ff. On the associations of women, Dionysus, and the dangerous power of the irrational see Slater, Chaps. 7-10; Girard 197-200 (Eng. trans. 139-42); Segal (1978) passim; also below, Chap. 6, passim.

to which they offer the breast (699-702).[11] The married women have taken off the "yoke" that civilizes them; and the young "unyoked" girls have these "maddened" wild women, not settled, domestic wives and mothers, as their models.

Images of the bit (*chalinos*) and the spur or goad (*kentron, kentein*) correlate technological, ritual, and domestic order. Pentheus loses control of animals, sacrifice, women, and himself. In 794-97, as we have noted, he kicks against Dionysus' "spurs" (*kentra*) as a mortal trying to control a god, as a king committing human sacrifice, and as a male repressing unruly females. Earlier he would "prick" as with a goad (*kentein*) the Dionysiac phantom (*phasma*) in his palace (631). That gesture was as futile as his effort to keep the bull enclosed in its prison (618-22). The Stranger does not state the precise form of this phantom-image (629-31). In the light of Pentheus' later delusion (920-22) it is not impossible that there was something taurine about it.

Amid the festive joy of Dionysiac worship in the first stasimon the chorus warns against "unbridled mouths" and "lawless folly" (*achalina stomata, anomos aphrosyna*, 387f.). Lawlessness will later, paradoxically, appear as one of the attributes of this volatile king (995-1015). The man who cannot properly use the "spurs" (*kentra*, above) on other beasts is himself like a beast "without the bridle" (*chalinos*, cf. 387). At his end the god uses beasts to make good his warning about mortals contesting against gods. He not only reduces Pentheus to a beast-victim, but also makes him a rider who cannot keep his seat on the animal that he would ride (cf. 1070, 1072, 1074, 1076, 1095). Destroyed as the "climbing beast" (*ambatēs thēr*, 1107-1108), Pentheus is also the "riding beast" (another possible meaning of the phrase), an anomalous beast-passenger who cannot wield the spurs. He is himself "without the bridle" (387) and is hurled to his death from his supposedly lordly "seat" (cf. 1095) by wild women who become "passengers" on a mountain crag that takes the place of a tower (ἀντίπυργον ἐπιβᾶσαι πέτραν, 1097).[12]

---

[11] Cf. Bacchylides *Ode* 11, where King Proetus' "untamed" daughters are driven mad (in one version of the legend by Dionysus), flee to forest and mountain, and are restored to city and house by the father's sacrifice of "unyoked" cattle (104f.) in a kind of homeopathic ritual: cf. Segal (1976) 122-28 and *Tragedy and Civilization* 36f.

[12] Both *ambatēs* (*anabainō*) and *epibatēs* (*epibainō*) can refer to a "passenger" on a horse or chariot or, in the case of *epibatēs*, on a ship: see LSJ svv. The verb

• III •

In his anger at Teiresias' defense of the Dionysiac cult Pentheus orders his men to take levers (*mochloi*) to overturn the prophet's seat of augury (347). These levers recur to mark Pentheus' peculiar status, suspended between civilized and savage, as Dionysus leads him out to his ritual slaughter as beast-victim on Cithaeron (948f.): "Shall we bring levers" (*mochloi*), the king asks, "or with my hands shall I tear up the mountain, putting shoulder or arm beneath it?" The civilized use of tools subserves an insane distortion of the relation between man and nature. The distortion has even grimmer overtones, for the violence of "hands" here and the parts of the body involved, shoulder and arm, along with the act of "tearing" or "pulling" recur in the details of Pentheus' own death (cf. 1125-27).

In his suppression of maenadic violence in the name of civil order Pentheus is a hunter who uses "nets of iron" against his "wild" prey (σιδηραῖς ἁρμόσας ἐν ἄρκυσιν, "catching them in nets of iron," 231). In the play's reversals of tame and wild, not only do the maenads escape these "well-woven nets" (870) as they leave the "elaborately crafted yokes" (*poikila zyga*, 1056), but they finally corner and capture their huntsman-beast with "levers not of iron" (ἀσιδήροις μοχλοῖς, 1104). The oxymoron is a double negation of Pentheus' threat: it substitutes hunter for hunted and unworked branches for the products of metallurgy. It is a massive defeat of culture by nature that reaches its climax when Agave boasts that she and her companions have caught their grisly prey "not with thonged Thessalian missiles, not with nets, but with the white-armed points of hands" (1205-1207):

οὐκ ἀγκυλητοῖς Θεσσαλῶν στοχάσμασιν,
οὐ δικτύοισιν, ἀλλὰ λευκοπήχεσι
χειρῶν ἀκμαῖσιν.

The last phrase is a bold hypallage for "the fingernails of white-armed women," the "points" (*akmai*) at the end of "white-armed" women's "hands." These elaborate periphrases for both javelins and fingernails set off the negation of the technology of the hunt, and also virtually

---

anachaitizein in 1072 is also used of a horse throwing its rider: cf. *Hipp.* 1232 and Segal (1979) 156.

substitute nature for culture.[13] That tension between the stress on culture in the style and its negation in what is actually happening continues into the martial code as Agave continues her boast (1207-10): "After that should huntsmen brag while they needlessly procure the tools of the spear-makers" (λογχοποιῶν ὄργανα), while we with hand alone (αὐτῇ χειρί) captured this and tore asunder the limbs of the beast?"[14]

For the Greeks madness itself is a reduction of man to the status of a wild beast: the madman rejects the implements of culture and reverts to a state of feral nature. The madness/savagery of Agave is thus triply overdetermined: a mother kills a son, a hunter hunts down a human being as prey, and a user of tools reverts to the use of bare hands.

This fluctuation between implements and bare hands runs all through Dionysus' vengeance, for his "hunting down" of his human quarry shifts repeatedly between using nets and not using nets (848 and 1021 as against 736, 1104, 1173, 1206-10). In the god's characteristic movement between Golden Age and savagery, the shackles fall off the imprisoned maenads' feet "of their own accord" (*automata*) and "keys open the doors without a mortal hand" (447f.). Here we see the miraculous power of the god (cf. *thaumata*, "miracles," 449), a power magically protective of the god's devotees, not something fierce and aggressive. But what operates as beneficent liberation for the Asian maenads becomes insane violence for the women of Thebes, who are maenads only under the god's constraint. Forcibly cut loose from their civic frame, they occupy a dangerous limbo between Golden-Age mildness and uninhibited aggression. Their fluctuation between savage and civilized in the contrasts within the technological code (nets/no nets, tools/bare hands, iron/natural objects) is exactly ho-

[13] The phrase used for the Thessalian javelin is especially striking as both noun and adjective are extremely rare. *Stochasmata*, literally "aimings," occurs only here in extant Greek tragedy. The implicit logic of 1205-1207 actually involves a rather intricate relation of culture and nature: Agave first denies javelins, then asserts a possible parallelism of javelins and fingernails, and finally states the superiority of nails to javelins, with the implicit replacement of culture by nature.

[14] In rendering 1208-1209 I have borrowed the first part of the brilliant translation by Dodds, *Bacchae* ad loc., but changed the end ("the armourers' engines," Dodds) to bring out the military connotation of *lonchē*, "spear."

mologous with their ambiguity in the ritual code: hunt/sacrifice; wild lion/calf; regular sacrificial rite in the city/*sparagmos* on the mountain; sacrificial knife/bare hands; roasted meat/ raw and bleeding flesh of the *ōmophagia*.[15]

Elsewhere in Greek tragedy this oxymoron of tools that are not tools, like the "levers not of iron," expresses deep violations of civilized values. In the *Choephoroe*, for example, "fetters unbronzed" (πέδαις ἀχαλκεύτοισιν, 493) are the terrible net in which Clytaemnestra entrapped and murdered Agamemnon, another act with shocking familial, ritual, sexual, and man-animal inversions. In Sophocles' *Trachiniae* the centaur Nessus plies his trade as a ferryman "with hands, rowing not with propelling oars nor with a ship's sails" (χερσίν, οὔτε πομπίμοις / κώπαις ἐρέσσων οὔτε λαίφεσιν νεώς, *Trach.* 560f.). His ferrying *au naturel* parallels his other perversions of civilized activities, distorting marriage by rape, medicine by his poisonous "drug," and sacrifice by his conversion of Heracles to beast-victim.[16]

It is characteristic of this inversion of technology that the play's most complex image of tool-using, the lathe-figure of 1066, describes Dionysus' power over the king as the god bends to the earth the tree that shoots Pentheus into the air.[17] The context and the material— the remote setting of an ecstatic rite and "a branch of the mountain" (κλῶν' ὄρειον, 1068)—jar against the expected association of workshop or studio.

As the god's vengeance fluctuates between nets and bare hands, so his followers exercise a peculiar kind of magnetism upon metals, and are surrounded by a mysterious fire (755-58). This command over metals, however, paradoxically marks their distance from civilized normality, for they are carrying children off along with the bronze and iron.[18] Their power over iron (*sidēros*, 757) is perhaps another

[15] On the regressive savagery implied in tearing the victim apart with bare hands in the Orphic myth of Zagreus see Detienne, *Dionysos* 172f., 197ff. On the reversal of the usual "syntax" of the sacrificial ritual see Daraki, passim, esp. 143f., 152-57.

[16] See Segal (1975) 46 and *Tragedy and Civilization* 91f.

[17] For the problems of this difficult passage see Dodds, *Bacchae*, and Roux ad loc.; Willink 237-40; Broadhead 118-25.

[18] See Detienne, *Dionysos* 201; Jeanne Roux, "Pillage en Béotie," *REG* 76 (1963) 34-38, esp. 37.

reminder of the impotence of Pentheus' "iron nets" (231) and an anticipation of the fact that their uncanny strength is of an order not to be measured by familiar tools like iron levers (cf. 1104) or checked by familiar weapons (cf. 761).

The same collocation of contradictions marks Agave's elaborate periphrasis, "approaches of fastened ladders" (πηκτῶν . . . κλιμάκων προσαμβάσεις, 1213), when she gives instructions for attaching her gruesome prey to the house. The stylistic device and the effect are similar to that of the "thonged Thessalian missiles" discussed above (1205). Like the god, author of her madness, she is both artisan and wild hunter (cf. 1066f.), both above and below the human condition.

A different kind of inversion marks the series of commercial images that Pentheus employs. He would "sell" (diempolan) the maenads as slaves, making them possessions (ktēmata) of the palace, set to work at the loom instead of dancing and thumping in their rites (511-14). The Stranger, he accuses, is making "counterfeit coinage" (kibdē-leuein, 475) when he answers the king's questions about the Dionysiac worship. Four lines later Pentheus adds an image of channeling water (parōcheteuein, 479). The orderly activities of these metaphors contrasts with the vehemence of the feelings behind them.

When the Stranger's spell begins to exert its power over him, Pentheus' commercial language takes a different turn. Asked if he would like to see the maenads in their rites on the mountain, Pentheus replies, "Yes, enormously, and I would give a countless weight of gold" (μυρίον . . . χρυσοῦ σταθμόν, 812). The language implies the quantitatively calculating and accumulating economy of a well-settled state, just as its opposite begins to triumph. Gold, we recall, has a very different meaning elsewhere in the play. It is associated with Dionysus' exotic Eastern origins, the "lands of the Lydians, rich in abundant gold" (13) and the Tmolus "flowing with gold" (154). His worshipers call upon him as the brandisher of the "gold-visaged thyrsus" (χρυσῶπα θύρσον) when they ask him to descend from Olympus and punish Pentheus (553-55). Given these associations of gold with Dionysus' Asiatic luxury and divine power, it is perhaps appropriate that the maenad Chorus, invoking "Holiness queen of gods" on their side, should describe her "golden wing" (372). The attributes of oriental luxury and Olympian brilliance coincide in this ambiguous god who spans both the conventional "holiness" of the first stasimon and the mystical religious experience of the parode.

• IV •

Throughout the play, as elsewhere in Greek cult and myth, Dionysus is closely associated with agricultural fertility. Miraculously causing the earth to flow with milk, honey, and wine (141f., 704-11), he enacts for his worshipers the miracle of those ever-renewed energies of the life of nature to which he is so close. Just before the First Messenger's description of the maenads on Cithaeron, the Stranger describes the god as "the one who makes the many-clustered vine grow for mortals" (ὃς τὴν πολύβοτρυν ἄμπελον φύει βροτοῖς, 651). Yet the god's miracles for his devotees bypass the normal civilized work of tillage and harvest. The preceding ode stresses the god's associations with fertilizing liquids (565-75, especially *lipainein*, "make fat and rich"; cf. *karpizein*, 408); but here, as in the previous ode too (405ff.), the geography involved is on the fringes of the Greek world.

When the maenads "scrape at the earth," it is with bare hands, not agricultural implements: they cause streams of milk to flow from the ground by "scraping apart the earth with sharp fingers" (ἄκροισι δακτύλοισι διαμῶσαι χθόνα, 709). The produce is not a civilized crop but the mysterious divine gift in the Golden-Age paradise that their ecstatic worship temporarily creates. Yet the other side of that Golden-Age image is implicit in the violence of the language of 709. Less than thirty lines later the proud bulls that the maenads tear apart are "led by the myriad *hands* of the young women" (μυριάσι χειρῶν ἀγόμενοι νεανίδων, 745). The violence of those scraping hands of 709 is more explicit still in Agave's boast over the human equivalent of those bulls, hunted not with javelins or nets but with the sharp nails of their bare hands (λευκοπήχεσι / χειρῶν ἀκμαῖσιν, 1206-1207), literally "with the white-armed points of hands." The hinted threat of ἄκροισι δακτύλοισι in 709 is completely unveiled in the phrase of 1207.

The sharp contrasts between life and death at the equidistant extremes of pacific abundance and bloody savagery make the maenads' place in the city and their god's relation to civilized norms dangerously precarious. Dionysus can cause the "soil of the earth" to shake in his destructive vengeance against Pentheus' palace, just as he can cause the "soil of the earth" to send forth his life-sustaining liquids. Nearly the same phrase recurs for both actions, a little over a hundred lines apart (πέδον χθονός, 585; πέδον γῆς, 706; cf. also *pedion parapotamion*, "the flat earth beside the river" where the maenad-fawn rests in 873). When these maenads demonstrate the destructive side of the god's power, they swoop down on the carefully tilled slopes near the Asopus river with their "fertile ears of grain" (*eukarpon . . . stachyn*, 749f.).

The agricultural details here only set off the fact that the Theban women are attacking what is fruitful in their own land. Earlier the mothers among them offered the breast to the young of wild animals (699-702), but soon they tear apart a domesticated cow, "a heifer full of milk for nursing" (*euthēlon porin*, 737). Becoming "unyoked" themselves, they turn against the nurturing aspects of their own civilized condition and revert to its wild potential. Giving to wild beasts the breast that should be offered to the child in the secure interior of the house, they act out an inverted form of their creative life energies. They summon milk from the earth (708-10), but simultaneously destroy the milch-cows whose nurturant capacities are made tame and useful for civilization.

Veering between suckling the young of wild beasts and destroying the heifer, they act out, in the freedom of the Dionysiac frenzy, their repressed rage at their children and their socially unacceptable ambivalence toward their role as mothers and nurturers.[19] Carrying off children from houses (754) is a milder form of what Agave, with her companions' help, will do to her own child. In them, as in Pentheus, Dionysus liberates the repressed extremes of hatred and desire and disrupts the sometimes precarious balance, in the culture and in the psychology of the individual, between *thanatos* and *eros*. He releases in them, as in Pentheus, the dark mirror-image of their creative capacities. Their affinity as mothers with the life-giving power of the earth and with animal nature turns into an affinity with the boundless strength of the wild and the alien, reasonless frenzy of the beasts.

In spanning these two aspects of the powers in the earth Dionysus makes manifest the mysterious life of nature, its otherness, its forward drive that pays little attention to human needs or purposes. He is in this respect "the god of the unreachable quality in nature," that which defies or eludes conceptualization or verbalization. As one scholar

---

[19] See Slater 216-29; Simon 257; Green 202ff.; from a Kleinian point of view see Roberts 39ff.

remarked recently, he is the god whose "nature manifests itself in its own *mystery*."[20]

The shift from the life-giving to the destructive side of earth and agriculture in Dionysus has a parallel in Pentheus and Thebes. In the *Bacchae*, unlike the *Phoenissae*, the aggressive side of Cadmus' founding act is suspended. His civilizing task consists not in killing the serpent at Dirce's waters—the familiar exploit of the culture-hero, from Pythian Apollo to Saint George—but in planting or sowing the teeth.[21] The *Bacchae* never actually speaks of Cadmus as the serpent-slayer.

"Do you not feel shame and reverence (*aidōs*) for the gods and for Cadmus who sowed the earth-born crop?" the Chorus reprimands Pentheus after his opening tirade against Dionysus (263f.). Here they juxtapose Cadmus and his "sowing" with the "gods" as worthy of equal respect. Cadmus' "sowing" of the Theban race recurs impressively at other critical junctures of the action. "O house . . . of aged Cadmus, who sowed in the earth the earth-born harvest of the serpent Ophis . . . ," begins the messenger who will tell of Pentheus' death (1024-26). "I, Cadmus, the great, who sowed the Theban earth and reaped the loveliest harvest," the old king says of himself as he laments at the end the bitterness of exile from that earth he tamed and "sowed" (1314f.).

This "sowing," though of a remote and fantastic agriculture, yet symbolizes that domestication of wild nature that made the city possible. The presence of Dionysus serves as a catalyst for what is still violent and untempered in the earth and the earth-born descendants of Thebes.[22] "Seed" and "sowing" recur for the god's revenge upon the race of the Sown Men. In the prologue Dionysus describes how he has driven mad from their homes "the whole female *seed* of the Cadmeans" (πᾶν τὸ ϑῆλυ σπέρμα Καδμείων, 35): as wild animals on

---

[20] Sale, *Existentialism* 90. See also Kerényi 131 à propos of Plato, *Laws* 6.773d; Rosenmeyer 151 on the Dionysiac sense of the natural world that "engulfs man in its eternal rhythm of animal necessity."

[21] For the culture-hero's killing of the serpent or dragon see Fontenrose, *Python*, esp. chaps. 1, 3, 4, 11, 12; Theodore Gaster, *Thespis* (Garden City, N.Y., 1961.) 462ff. For other aspects of Cadmus' "sowing" of the dragon's teeth see below, Chap. 5, section 4.

[22] We may compare the function of Ares in the *Phoenissae*, who symbolizes the destructive heritage of Thebes: see Guépin 44-45 and 207-208; Arthur (1977) 176ff.

the mountainside, the women undo the civilizing work of Cadmus the Sower. The same root recurs twice more in contexts that stress the inversion of civilized norms among these descendants of the "earth-born." The Stranger predicts that "the daughters of Cadmus, of the same seed" (homosporoi), along with Agave, will destroy Pentheus" (973), a possible echo of 35. When that madness takes effect and the women rush like birds or beasts in pursuit of their kindred prey on Cithaeron, they are called, in a clear echo of 973, "Agave the mother and her kindred of the same seed (homosporoi) and all the maenads" (1092-93). The interweaving of violated kinship ties and inverted agriculture reaches its gruesome climax in Agave's mad boast to her father as she shows him the bloody head of her prey-victim: "Boast that you have sown (speirai) the best of daughters . . ." (1234). All the civilizing work implied in the "sowing" of the old culture-hero in both house and city is wiped out by the implications of Agave's word and its circumstances. As we now know from a papyrus fragment, the mangled body of Pentheus was described in another image of inverted agriculture: his limbs were "plowed as by furrows and spattered with blood."[23] These furrows bear not life but death. The activity that is the norm of stable civilization in classical Greece is here a violent and murderous disturbance of the social order.[24]

• V •

Euripides does not let us forget that Dionysus is also a civilizing god and a benefactor of culture. He has his nomima or "lawful insti-

[23] P. Antinoe 24, frag. 2a, confirms earlier scholars' conjecture that Christus Patiens 1471f., τὰ δ' αἱμόφυρτα καὶ κατηλοκισμένα / μέλη, "limbs plowed as by furrows and spattered with blood," in fact came from Euripides' text, almost certainly from the lacuna after 1300 or 1329 describing the piecing together of Pentheus' body or his death. The rare word katēlokismena, "plowed into furrows," in Chr. Pat. 1471 is, fortunately, one of the few nearly complete words visible on the papyrus scrap. For the text and restoration see Dodds, Bacchae, appendix, 243f. Willink's questioning of a compositio membrorum onstage, 44-49, is salutary, but probably unjustified. See also Seneca, Phaedra 1082-1114, and M. Patin, Études sur les tragiques grecs, Euripide (Paris 1879) 2.270; also Roux 2.614f.

[24] On agriculture as the model of civilized activity see M. I. Finley, The Ancient Economy (Berkeley and Los Angeles 1973) 123; Segal, Tragedy and Civilization 29-33.

tutions" (72, 895), a word that connotes the stable values of the city. Teiresias, who perhaps would assimilate the god too much to civilization, even seems to envisage this cult from the East as part of "the ancestral tradition (*patrioi paradochai*) which we possess coeval with time" (201f.).

Among the most important of Dionysus' civilizing activities in the play is his role as the "inventor" of wine. In a number of myths Dionysus appears as the *heuretēs* or "discoverer," not only of wine, but of agriculture in general.[25] Yet even this agricultural product shares in the ambiguous characteristics of the god. On the one hand wine, as a civilized product, contrasts with the "savage" life of Cyclopes or centaurs. Deprivation of wine constitutes one of the "savage" features of Philoctetes' desolate life on Lemnos in Sophocles' play (*Phil.* 712-15). On the other hand wine is the source of violent and unruly behavior, inciting the centaurs to rape in the myths of Pholus and the wedding of Peirithous. In an important Dionysiac legend about its invention the herdsmen who first taste it kill the inventor, Icarius, thinking that he has drugged or poisoned them.[26] Even as a creation of civilizing agriculture it has something dangerous and disruptive about it.

In the *Bacchae*, likewise, wine is an "invention" (*heurēma*, 279), as Teiresias optimistically points out; but Dionysus' other "inventions" include the wild tympanum and cymbals associated with foreign deities worshiped in orgiastic rites in remote, mountainous places (58-59, 120-25). When Dionysus himself, as the Stranger, alludes to the invention of wine, he uses not the verb of intellectual discovery, *heuriskein*, but *phyein*, a word that stresses the connections with the powers of nature, growth, vegetation (651): ὃς τὴν πολύβοτρυν ἄμπελον φύει βροτοῖς ("the god who makes the many-clustering vine to grow for mortals").

At the end of the play the civilized meaning of Dionysus as "inventor," *heuretēs* (cf. 279), undergoes further reversal. The *sparagmos* of his victim leads to a search for a body not easily "found" (*heurōn*, 1219, *dys-heuretos*, 1221).

The first stasimon (370-432) dwells on other civilizing gifts of Dio-

[25] See Diodorus 3.70.7-8 and now the newly discovered comic (?) fragment published by B. Kramer, *ZPE* 34 (1979) 7ff.

[26] Apollodorus, *Bibl.* 3.14.7, with Frazer's note ad loc. in the Loeb Classical Library edition. Also above, Chap. 1, n. 16.

nysus. The dance, flute, laughter, banquets all have their place in the daily life of a well-ordered city. The chorus goes on to praise a life of "calm" (*hēsychia*) and the "good sense that holds together houses" (389-92). In the final strophe Dionysus' "festal joy" (*thaliai*) accompanies his love for "Peace, giver of blessings, a goddess who nurtures children" (417-20). To both the rich and poor he brings "a joy that holds no pain" (*terpsis alypos*, 423; cf. 280-83). But at the end of the play he brings about a "banquet" that is far from festive (1242, 1247), a mother who destroys both her child and her house, and a deluded joy that contains the most anguished pain (cf. 1259-63).

Dionysus, as we have seen, has a place in the untamed wilderness among rugged mountains and savage beasts. But he can also appear as an overcivilized youth, lapped in his soft Lydian airs, as Pentheus sees him—or wants to see him—in the early part of the play (233ff., 453ff.). That overcivilized aspect also has its destructive side. The disguised god lures his victim out to his death on the mountain with the promise of "luxury" and "softness" (*tryphē*, *habrotēs*, 968-70). Indeed the repeated first word, *tryphan*, *tryphai*, "luxury" (969f.) may, in view of later events, be a play on the related verb *thryptō*, "break."[27] In any case the god's "softness," like his munificent gifts, coexist at every point with its concealed and destructive double: joy with pain, intoxication with madness, fertility with destruction, softness with cruelty, kindness with terror (861).

• VI •

Dionysus is the "inventor" not only of wine but also of music, not the ordered and harmonious music of the polis, but the intoxicating Phrygian song, accompanied by the flute (*aulos*) and the tambourine (*tympanon*). At the end of the prologue the god describes the latter as the "inventions" (*heurēmata*) of himself and mother Rhea (59). The ode that follows echoes his words ("Mother Rhea" in 128): the chorus sings of the birth of Zeus in Crete, where "the Corybantes invented this skin-stretched circle [of the drum] and in the tense ecstatic dance mingled it with the sweetly calling breath of Phrygian

---

[27] The two words are etymologically related: see below, Chap. 6, n. 66.

flutes, and put it into the hands of Mother Rhea to beat time for the joy-cries of her worshiping women" (126-29, Dodds' translation, in part). In the next strophe the chorus calls upon the bacchants to "sing (*melpete*) of Dionysus to the deep beat of the drums, giving joy to the god whose cry is Euoe, Euoe, in the Phrygian shouts and cries, when the sweet-sounding holy flute sounds its playful note, deep, holy, accompaniment to you in ritual march to mountain, to mountain . . ." (155-65). Both passages stress the sweetness, joy, playfulness of the "deep" sound of flute and drum (*barybromoi*, 156; *bremei*, 164). Yet the "sweetness" and joy of that "shouting" (*hadyboā(i)*, 127, *Phrygiaisi boais*, 159) will change to a very different quality in "shouts" that inspire terror or madness (cf. 1085).

As the Messenger describes their rites on Cithaeron, he assures Pentheus that they do not use the music of the flute for drunken orgies, as Pentheus had imagined (687, cf. 221-25, 458-59). Pentheus, appropriately enough, had made no mention of music in either passage, envisioning coarser pleasures. When the Messenger describes how Agave "gave the ritual cry of *ololygē* when she heard the "mooings from the horned cattle" (μυκήμαθ᾽ ὡς ἤκουσε κεροφόρων βοῶν, 691), the account takes on a note of something less reassuring. Agave's next utterance is a "shouting" that rouses her companions to a deadly hunting (*aneboēsen*, 731). The Theban maenads, like the Asiatic maenads of the parode, can produce the "songs" as a kind of natural music as they "shout back song in responsion to one another" (βακχεῖον ἀντέκλαζον ἀλλήλαις μέλος, 1057). The Asiatic maenads sing "barbarian songs of Euoe" in joy at the news of Pentheus' death (1034). But this "music" can turn into a wild shouting that not only defeats Pentheus' appeal to the "singing" of the bow-strings against them (*psallousi*, 784), but drowns out his hopeless appeal to reason and finally his groans of pain as he dies (1131-33):

> ἦν δὲ πᾶσ᾽ ὁμοῦ βοή,
> ὁ μὲν στενάζων ὅσον ἐτύγχαν᾽ ἐμπνέων,
> αἱ δ᾽ ἠλάλαζον.

> There was a single cry all together,
> he groaning as long as he had the breath of life,
> they raising the cry.

The ritualized language of the parode brilliantly and powerfully imitated the orgiastic effects of this Dionysiac music, but only for the mood of joy and play. Now we see the other pole of that "sweet-shouting" (*hadyboa*).

The two sides of the Dionysiac music are not static in the play, but form part of a dynamic progression. The earlier odes, on the whole, celebrate the god's festive and joyful aspect. With the mounting hostility of Pentheus and the vehemence of his attacks on the god, the later odes reveal and release the god's destructive power. These early odes, particularly the first and second stasima, show a potentially civilizing power in his cult. The first stasimon begins with an invocation to "Holiness, Lady goddess, Holiness who on golden wing soars over the earth . . ." (370-73). The antistrophe, however, juxtaposes warnings about "lawless" and "witless" behavior with the "calm" (*hēsychia*) of the god, a contrast that will be made specific in Pentheus' encounter with the bull (604-69; cf. "calm," *hēsychos*, 622, 636, 647; also 790).

The second strophe of this ode connects Dionysus with the positive "enchantment" (*thelxis*) of love and music. Drawing on an age-old association between Aphrodite and Dionysus, but in a far more positive way than Pentheus (see 225, 460), the Chorus wishfully calls upon their god to lead them to Aphrodite's island, Cyprus, a place of love and fertility (402-408).[28] From here they move to the "Pierian seat of the Muses, Olympus' holy slope" (410-11), where both the Graces and Desire, Charites and Pothos, are found. This, they say, is the lawful place for Dionysiac worship: "There is it right (*themis*) for bacchants to hold their revels" (*orgiazein*, 414-15). The Dionysiac music can unite the sexual charm of Aphrodite with the Pierian Muses of Olympus, Pothos, desire, with the Graces, spirits of refined beauty in art as in love.

This strophe suggests the radiant side of the god invisible to Pentheus, for whom the god's connections with *eros*, *pothos*, and Aphrodite are a matter for lewd thoughts or desires (225, 460, 686-88, 813). On Aphrodite's isle the Erotes are *thelxiphrones*, "spell-binders of the mind" (404); but Pentheus, who sees the god's representative

---

[28] For the associations of Aphrodite, Dionysus, and the Muses as a common source of the joyfulness of life (*euphrosynai*) see Solon frag. 20D = 26 West. Cf. also Eur. *Medea* 829-45. See Roux ad 402-403.

only as a charlatan, "a sorcerer and enchanter from the Lydian land" (234), experiences a different aspect of the god's "spell" and is "led" on another kind of journey by the god's eros (813; cf. "leading" in 412 and 820, 855, 974). The mountains and water here are very different from those of the second stasimon (cf. 1051-53, 1093-1100).

In the next strophe the Chorus invokes "Peace, who nurtures children" (*Eirēna kourotrophos*). Pentheus, who impulsively declares war (780-85), encounters a mother who destroys rather than "nurtures" her child. This sexually repressed king will not move upward to Olympus for the song of the Muses (409-12), but downward as a chthonic monster (cf. 537-44, 995-96), to the accompaniment of savage shrieks in the wild (1131-33). Instead of the joyful "spell" of the "mind-enchanting Erotes" on the island of Love (400-404), he falls victim to the spell of the god that turns his repressed eros (813) to madness.

Whereas Dionysus in this and the previous ode appears as a god of music and song, Pentheus, in his madness, would destroy the places where the Nymphs and Pan make their sylvan music (949-52):

> Penth. Shall we bring levers, or with my hands shall I tear up (Cithaeron's glens), heaving shoulder or arm beneath the peaks?
>
> Dionys. No, do not destroy the seat of the Nymphs and the abode of Pan, where he holds the playing of his pipe (*echei syrigmata*).

Sane, presumably, Pentheus would have destroyed the seat of Teiresias' augury (346-51). Mad, he acts out the same destructive impulses. The Dionysiac "spell" does not change the latent violence of his nature.

These contrasts are developed even more clearly in the second stasimon (519-75). Its first strophic system, which we shall consider in more detail in Chapters 5 and 6, contrasts the immortal birth of Dionysus with the chthonic origins of Pentheus. The second strophe enlarges upon the positive affinities among Dionysiac music, nature, and Olympian music in the first stasimon (556-74):

> Where on beast-nurturing Mt. Nysa, O Dionysus, do you lead the thyrsus with your bands, or where on the Corycian peaks? Soon [you will be] in the many-treed dells of Olympus, where once Or-

pheus, playing his lyre, led together the trees with the Muses, led together the beasts who dwell in the wild. O happy Pieria! There the Euian god reveres you, there he will come to dance with his bacchic revels. Crossing the swift-eddying Axios, he will lead his whirling maenads, crossing father Lydias, a river that gives wealth to mortals and happiness, who, as I hear, makes fat the land, rich in horses, with his loveliest waters.

The language and matter of this ode have close links with the previous stasimon: Olympus, Pieria, music, the fertility of rivers, beauty (409 and 575), nurture (420 and 556), the potential generosity and richness of nature, again a crucial point of difference between the maenads and Pentheus (cf. 142-44 and 705-11 with 1051-53, 1093-94). After the mention of Pentheus' monstrous violence in the previous strophe, however, this ode evokes not "the goddess Peace, nurturer of children" (419-20), but a remote mountain, "nurturer of beasts" (*thērotrophos*, 556; cf. *thēras agrōtas*, 564).

The Orphic lyre or cithara, a more stately instrument than the excited *aulos* or tympanum, can "lead wild beasts together" on the mountain (563-65), but the god's "spell" on wild nature, through his mysterious voice from the heavens, has an eerier, more ominous effect (1078-94). This Orphic music does more than fuse man and nature in the Dionysiac ecstasy, where "beasts and mountains join in the bacchic revel" (*sym-bakcheuein*, 726-27). Rather, it elicits from nature a sympathetic response wherein the power of human art is clearly marked as superior through the active compound of the verb "lead," *syn-agein*, "lead together" (562-64):

’Ορφεὺς κιθαρίζων
σύναγεν δένδρεα μούσαις,
σύναγεν θῆρας ἀγρώτας.

. . . where Orpheus playing his lyre
led the trees together by the Muses,
led together the wild beasts.

This beautiful, benign, nonaggressive side of the Dionysiac music has its counterpart in the previous ode, where the chorus longs for the "Pierian seat of the Muses," abode of the Graces and Desire and the "rightful" place for the Bacchic revel (410-15). In evoking Olympus and Pieria here, the Chorus eagerly asserts the Olympian heritage of Dionysus, and also connects his music with the Olympian and Orphic music of the poetic tradition that reaches back to Homer and Hesiod.

References to Orpheus are rare but significant in Euripides.[29] He invokes Orpheus here as a figure connected with Olympus and the Muses, a singer whose wondrous power of song elicits a potential sympathy between man and nature. The two parallel glyconic lines, each beginning with a compound of *syn-* "led together," σύναγεν (563-64), invite us to see Orpheus as a Dionysiac figure, for these *syn*-compounds, denoting nature's fusion with man, belong to the Dionysiac power (cf. 726-27).[30] Orpheus here seems to embody all the most beautiful, haunting remoteness of the maenads' god. There is a striking contrast with the monstrous violence of the Theban king in the previous strophe. This music is a potentially ordering, peace-bringing, and therefore civilizing force. We may compare the second stasimon of the *Phoenissae*, written not long before the *Bacchae*, which uses the grace and brilliance of Dionysiac festive song as a foil to the harsh notes of the bloody god of war (*Phoen.* 784-800).

Orpheus, however, has other associations with Dionysus. He is the doublet of the god in his terrible suffering. Torn apart by enraged women as Dionysus in "Orphic" mythology is torn apart by the Titans, he suffers a *sparagmos* that also corresponds to the dismemberment of Pentheus.[31] By a process frequent in mythical representation, Euripides splits the Dionysiac figure of the musician-enchanter into two. The positive side, the life-fostering, joy-bringing god of musical festivity dominates this and the previous stasimon; and it is reinforced by the association of Dionysiac orgiastic music with the Olympian Muses and with the Orphic lyre. The more dangerous side, hinted at in the parode, is developed in the wild shouting of the maenads on Cithaeron and perhaps alluded to in the reference to Dionysus' hypnotic "music arts" in the verb *ek-mousoō* in 825, an aspect of the Muses rather different from that of the first two stasima.[32]

[29] See Segal (1978b) 117f., 121ff.

[30] Cf. Simonides frag. 567P; Aeschyl. *Ag.* 1629f.; cf. Nilsson (1935) 187f.

[31] Ibid. 203-204; also W.K.C. Guthrie, *Orpheus and Greek Religion* (1952; reprint New York 1966) 42f.

[32] WI 81, n. 3, reminds us that the legend of Orpheus "had a less lovely pendant and that Orpheus was torn to pieces in the rites of Dionysus, like the beasts over which he had such power, or like Pentheus." See also Kott 195; Coche de la Ferté

As Pentheus fuses with the darker side of the god whom he resists, the god as beast-victim killed and devoured by his worshipers in the *ōmophagia*, so he also has associations with the suppressed side of the Orphic musician alluded to here in the second stasimon. Unlike Orpheus, he is a victim rather than a user of the music's spell (825; cf. 234); he is led as a beast rather than leading the beasts (cf. 563-64); and he would destroy the music in the mountains rather than elicit the musical responses of beasts and trees on the mountain (949-52 and 562-63). Yet, like the dismembered Orpheus, he is torn apart by a band of furious, raging women.

One might speculate on further similarities. Both Pentheus and Orpheus meet violent death because they resist basic laws of nature, life in the case of Pentheus, death in the case of Orpheus. But whereas Orpheus resists out of tragic love (at least in the version adumbrated in the *Alcestis* and developed, with a different ending, by Virgil and Ovid), Pentheus resists out of shallowness, narrowness, immaturity. Clearly, we should not push these parallels, for Orpheus' importance in the text seems to have more to do with Dionysus than with Pentheus. Had Euripides wished to develop them, he had ample opportunity to do so in other odes. Still, the three-way association, Dionysus-Orpheus-Pentheus merits, at the least, a brief mention. Orpheus is relevant to the play's main themes, for he mysteriously fuses man and nature, crosses the limits set by civilization, and possibly also crosses between life and death, between creative and destructive forces in himself and the world.[33] The two sides, Janus-like, are mythically united in the single god.

Old Cadmus, founder of the city, was perhaps too optimistic in incorporating Dionysus into it. In establishing the shrine of Semele he merits the god's praise (10-12); but in turning Dionysus' birth too simply to the advantage of the city (29-31) he, too, suffers the god's

---

184f. Lucian, *Piscator* 2 cites an iambic trimeter that joins together "Orpheus or Pentheus" who "found a doom of rending in the rocks" (καθάπερ τινὰ Πενθέα ἢ Ὀρφέα / λακιστὸν ἐν πέτραισιν εὑρέσθαι μόρον). Though there is no evidence for associating these lines with the *Bacchae* as Musgrave once did (cf. appendix to Murray's OCT), they at least demonstrate the existence of such an association in the classical poetic tradition.

[33] See Peter Dronke, "The Return of Eurydice," *C & M* 23 (1962) 205f.; Segal (1978b) 137f.

vengeance. For all his paradoxical role as a fountainhead of civilization, Dionysus does not lend himself so easily to human purposes.

Cadmus' limited attempt to incorporate the god into what he believes to be the civilized structure of the polis results in the complete
undoing of his own life's work. His "clever devices" (*sophismata*, 30)
would enhance the glory of Thebes and honor the female half of his
line; but the result is to call the entire civic order of Thebes into
question and drive the women of the city, mad, from city to mountain (32-36). Human "cleverness" (*sophismata, to sophon*) toward the
gods is not necessarily the "wisdom" (*sophia*) necessary for dealing
with things divine (395-96):

τὸ σοφὸν δ᾽ οὐ σοφία
τό τε μὴ θνητὰ φρονεῖν.

Cleverness is not wisdom, nor is having thoughts of what is not
mortal.[34]

Beyond both modes of receiving Dionysus into the city, Pentheus'
and Cadmus', is the reception accorded to the god by the tragedy
itself, as part of the Dionysiac festival and as a meditation on Dionysus' nature. In its unresolved fusion of the paradoxes and contradictions of the god, tragedy emerges as possibly the only way of incorporating Dionysus into the structures of civilization, bringing together
festive joy and horror, music, dance, and language. No wonder that
Nietzsche sought the birth of tragedy in the spirit of music.[35] Tragedy
gives us symbolically what we can rarely grasp clearly in the abstrac-
tive forms of language, the coincidence and simultaneity of the god's
hidden duality, the awareness that the two faces of existence, as of
the god, the creative and the destructive, the "terrible" and the "gentle"
(861), are one and the same.

[34] For *sophia* and *sophisma* cf. also 200, 427, 1005f. For the problems of the text
and interpretation of 395f. see Dodds, *Bacchae* and Roux ad loc.; Deichgräber 340.
See also below, Chap. 7, n. 15 and Chap. 8, n. 33.

[35] Nietzsche, *Birth of Tragedy* 46: "The cosmic symbolism of music resists any
adequate treatment by language, for the simple reason that music, in referring to
primordial contradiction and pain, symbolizes a sphere which is both earlier than
appearance and beyond it."

4

The Horizontal Axis:
House, City, Mountain

Οὐχ ὑπερβαίνουσι καὶ τείχη θεοί;
Do not gods pass over even walls?
Bacchae 654

• I •

In the *Bacchae*, as in much of Greek tragedy, the problem of defining what is proper to civic life and what is alien to it takes the form of spatial contrasts and tensions. In most of the extant Sophocles these questions focus on the ambiguous placement of a hero who is both outcast and savior, both polluted and close to divinity. In his earlier work Euripides uses heroic, or ambiguously heroic, figures to explore similar issues. Hippolytus, bastard son of a great king, prefers sport and quasi-mystical worship to martial exploits and political responsibility. In his marginal place in the wild, close to the goddess he honors, but also close to the beasts he hunts, he embodies a precarious union of opposites that the norms of civic life cannot sustain.[1] Phaedra, lustful and yet exhibiting "nobility in a certain way" (*Hipp.* 1300-1301), opens a parallel set of contradictions wherein the house is forced to confront the potentially destructive passions amid which human life exists.

In the *Medea*, a few years earlier, the dangerous power of sexuality, especially female sexuality, is combined with the ambiguity of an intelligence that both saves and destroys and a maternal capacity for both love and hatred that cherishes and sacrifices life. Euripides' her-

[1] For the marginal position of Hippolytus see Segal (1978/79) 133-39.

oine defies categorization just as she defies spatial definition: she is both the guardian of a house and a savage barbarian, an exemplar of both justice and monstrous cruelty, both heroic and ignoble.[2] Sophocles' *Trachiniae*, which shares the *Medea*'s concern with the ambiguous place of sexual violence in house and city, joins to the disruptive force of female passion the alien and bestial power of a beast-man whose seductive lie succeeds in lodging at the center of the house a monstrous poison that will destroy it.

The *Bacchae* introjects the destructive power of the unknown into the city in the person of the god who is both native and alien, both barbarian and Greek. Unlike Hippolytus, Dionysus cannot simply be reincorporated into the polis in a final act of commemorative adoption (*Hipp.* 1452, 1459-66). Unlike Medea, he cannot simply be expelled as the Other, the rejected violence of an alien way of being. Unlike the *Heracles Mad*, the *Bacchae* shows no reintegration of heroic values that could reabsorb the chaos let loose by insanity, violence, and divine injustice. Instead, Dionysus' arrival brings an ambiguous interchange between incorporation of the Other and expulsion of the familiar. The known becomes strange and the foreign becomes acknowledged as native. The estrangement of a mother from her own flesh and blood works on the level of private, domestic life as parallel to the psychological estrangement of madness and the civic derangement in which the female half of the city kills the king and replaces him by a new ruler who is also a "Stranger." This Stranger will lead a kind of sacred procession (*theōria*, 1047); though "born native to the house" (*oikeios*, 1250), he will do it terrible outrage (1374-75). The king who dies in the bloody "embrace" of his own mother (1163-64) is to consider his killer "the first of his dear ones" (*prōton philōn*, 939).

The tales of Actaeon and Cadmus form, in a sense, alternative myths for Thebes' relation to the otherness constituted by wild nature, the unknown and the uncanny in the world and in the self. The two myths mark opposite responses to the creative mystery of the earth and the wild. Actaeon loses power over the wild, as over himself; Cadmus harnesses that power to the needs of civilization. Ambiguously poised between the two stand both Dionysus and Pentheus. The

---

[2] These ambiguities of Medea are well set forth by B.M.W. Knox, "The *Medea* of Euripides," *YCS* 25 (1977) 193-225 = *Word and Action* 295-322, esp. 300ff.

former turns the king into an Actaeon-like hunter and changes the civilizing old ruler into his opposite, a monstrous destroyer of cities. The latter, if he could receive the god into himself and his city, might attain the civilizing reconciliation of Cadmus; failing, he obtains the fate of the adolescent savage hunter, extruded into wild places where he dies the death of a beast.

· II ·

On the horizontal axis of the play's spatial field the action passes back and forth between barbarians and Greeks on the one hand (13-20 and 1333ff., 1354ff.) and between city and wild on the other. A Messenger "from the mountain" (657f.) introduces the crucial scene at the center of the play; and the king's reaction to that account determines his decisive exodus from the city. The mountain is only background space, but the vivid narrative of what transpires there plays off foreground and background against one another.[3] The remote background takes on a spatial reality as gripping as any visually enacted stage setting.

In the first third of the play the king's action consists primarily in his attempt to re-enclose the Theban women within city and house and to confine the foreign Stranger within the prisons of the palace. Failed attempts at enclosure dominate Pentheus' encounter with the god, until at the god's victory Pentheus is led forth from city to mountain, himself now in the maenadic dress of a worshiper of Dionysus.

The Messenger who has come back from the mountain to Thebes reports the maenads' escape from the pursuers who would return them to the city. This failure prefigures the futility of Pentheus' later expedition from city to mountain. Pentheus is unable to grasp what the Messenger's tale might mean for himself. No open "reader," he encloses its message in his own narrow frame. He not only fails to check unruly Dionysiac exultation outside the city, but also exposes the powerlessness of the city's discipline against the alien god.

Through a number of verbal repetitions between the Messenger's speech and Pentheus' death Euripides reinforces the symmetry be-

---

[3] See Wassermann (1929) 278.

tween this first failure on the mountain and the total disintegration of the Theban kingship.[4] The now maddened Pentheus in the city desires to be "brought through the middle of the Theban land" (961); at the dénouement his decapitated head is carried as that of a "lion of the mountains" and borne "through the middle of Cithaeron" (1141f.). When Agave returns from mountain to city, she too has become a marginal figure who has lost the hold on the order of reality and the norms that entitle her to a place within the polis. Her journey back to the palace, the literal and symbolical center of the city (1202, 1212f.), only expresses the horrible inappropriateness of her presence there.

The rest of Pentheus' torn body, meanwhile, has been carried back from mountain to city (1216ff.), but that last movement from Cithaeron to Thebes is only the prelude to the exile of the remaining members of the royal house. Dionysus now has made good his triumphal entry into Thebes. He has proven himself a rightful inhabitant. In a grim symmetry, the former queen and original founder abandon the city, in one case by choice, in the other by force.

All the scenic action takes place before the royal house of Thebes. The prologue at once defines Dionysus in his ambiguous relation to that house. He is returning to Thebes to claim the honor due him as a member of Cadmus' house through his descent from Cadmus' daughter, Semele. The first clear spatial point of reference of the play is the smoking ruins where she died at his birth. This holy place, set apart as tabooed by Cadmus, embodies the mixture of creative and destructive potential in this god. The language, as befits divinity, is richly poetical, elevated, and at the end deliberately lush. The following translation tries to preserve a little of this flavor (1-12):

Ἥκω Διὸς παῖς τήνδε Θηβαίων χθόνα
Διόνυσος, ὃν τίκτει ποθ᾽ ἡ Κάδμου κόρη
Σεμέλη λοχευθεῖσ᾽ ἀστραπηφόρῳ πυρί·
μορφὴν δ᾽ ἀμείψας ἐκ θεοῦ βροτησίαν
πάρειμι Δίρκης νάματ᾽ Ἰσμηνοῦ θ᾽ ὕδωρ.
ὁρῶ δὲ μητρὸς μνῆμα τῆς κεραυνίας
τόδ᾽ ἐγγὺς οἴκων καὶ δόμων ἐρείπια
τυφόμενα Δίου πυρὸς ἔτι ζῶσαν φλόγα,

[4] Cf. 742f. and 1135f.; 744 and 1112; 745 and 974, 1080, 1109; 746 and 1130, 1136; 748 and 957; 749 and 1044; 750 and 1115.

ἀθάνατον Ἥρας μητέρ᾽ εἰς ἐμὴν ὕβριν.
αἰνῶ δὲ Κάδμον, ἄβατον ὃς πέδον τόδε
τίθησι, θυγατρὸς σηκόν· ἀμπέλου δέ νιν
πέριξ ἐγὼ᾽κάλυψα βοτρυώδει χλόῃ.

The son of Zeus, I have come to this Theban earth,
Dionysus, whom the daughter of Cadmus bore,
Semele, brought to the bed of birth by lightning-carried fire.
Changing my shape to mortal from a god
I am present here at Dirce's streams, Ismenus' water.
I see my mother's memorial, her the thunder-stricken,
Here near the house, and of those halls the ruins
Smouldering even now with the living flame of Zeus's fire,
Hera's immortal violence against my mother.
For Cadmus I speak praise, who made this place
Not to be trod upon, the precinct of his daughter.
This with the vine's grape-clustering growth
Entwined around I have concealed.

The vertical axis, to be discussed further in the next chapter, is established in the opening lines: a son of Zeus comes to the "earth" (*chthōn*) of Thebes, an immortal "born" in a mortal woman's travail (2), a god who takes on "mortal shape." The god's presence among men involves a meeting of celestial fire and the earth where mortals dwell (1, 3). The juxtaposition of earth-mortality-birth on the one hand and sky-divinity-fire on the other is powerfully represented in the language of line 3, with its dense cluster of four key words: Σε-μέλη λοχευθεῖσ᾽ ἀστραπηφόρῳ πυρί ("Semele brought-to-the-bed-of-birth by lightning-carried fire"). *Locheutheisa*, with its connotations of the pain, risk, and uncertainty of a woman's mortality, stands in immediate proximity to the sign of indifferent divine power, the beautiful but deadly fire of the sky-god. A few lines later "immortal outrage" (*athanaton . . . hybrin*) frames "mother" in the center of the line in such a way that the two words "immortal" and "mother" seem to pull in opposite directions. "Immortal" might, at first glance, seem to modify "mother," but of course it is precisely Semele's status as mother that marks her as mortal and subject to immortal Hera's "outrage" (ἀθάνατον Ἥρας . . . ὕβριν).

These contrasts prepare for the paradoxes in Dionysus: water and fire, smoking ruins and budding plant life, sacred foundation and fiery desolation from the gods. Dionysus' presence "near the smouldering ruins of the house" (7) prefigures what will happen when he makes good his claim to the house of Pentheus. The birth of a son of divine lineage in a royal house destroys rather than ennobles it. The honor that thereby accrues to the mother proves a mixed blessing to all concerned.

The foundation that honors Dionysus within the civic space similarly partakes of the god's ambiguous contact with nature's uncontrollable life-forces. The "monument" to Semele is called *mnēma* (9), a word that could suggest a memorial of cut stone; but "compassed around with the clustering growth" of Dionysus' vine (12) it has a form of enclosure (cf. *kalypsa*, "covered") appropriate to his place between crafted artifact and unformed nature, static form and growth. The phrasing foreshadows the conflicts around that house, prize of a tug of war between king and Stranger. As palace, it is under the rule of the king; as house, it belongs to the woman as mother and nurturer (cf. 1118f.) and hence has some affinities with the vital energies associated with Dionysus. Pentheus undergoes a trial of converting house to palace. In his extreme reaction he overshoots the civilized space of the house, experiences his birth in that house as the cause of his death (1119), and ends in the wild, the savage hunter-hunted instead of the king.

His death in Dionysus' realm outside the city involves another spatial opposition, for here the man-made towered height of the walls that Pentheus defends as king doubles with the rough crag where Pentheus dies, trapped as hunted beast. To stone Pentheus, the maenads climb "a rock like a tower" (*antipyrgon petran* (1097), or possibly, with Dodds, "towering opposite". The maenads scale a kind of "anti-tower," just as they make use of "anti-tools," "levers not of iron" (*asidēroi mochloi*, 1104).

The parode offers a remote paradigm of Dionysus' ambiguous relation to birth. The chorus invokes the "secret chamber" (*thalameuma*, 120) in Crete where Idaean Zeus was born. They then link the Couretes, who guarded the infant with the bacchants who follow Dionysus (129), with the wild creatures, "the maddened satyrs" in his train, and with the dances of the festivals "in which Dionysus rejoices" (134).[5] In the realm of Dionysus the dwelling or interior spaces (*thalameuma*, 120; *enauloi*, 122) where a child might be sheltered fuse with the wild spaces of remote mountains, a cave (*antrois*, 123) where divinities of nature celebrate with outlandish music a birth that signifies a renewal of cosmic vitality.

The word for "chamber" in this passage, *thalameuma* (120), identifies the interior space of Idaean Zeus' cave/house with the interiority of the womb.[6] Some twenty lines earlier the word *thalamē*, from which *thalameuma* is derived, describes the "birth-chambers" of Zeus' thigh that "received Dionysus" (94-98):

λοχίοις δ' αὐτίκα νιν δέ-
ξατο θαλάμαις Κρονίδας Ζεύς,
κατὰ μηρῷ δὲ καλύψας
χρυσέαισιν συνερείδει
περόναις κρυπτὸν ἀφ' Ἥρας.

And at once Zeus son of Cronos received him in the chambers of birth [*lochiois . . . thalamais*] and covering him in his thigh drew [the opening] together with pins of gold, [keeping] him hidden from Hera.

As in Dionysus' opening lines, "birth" is joined to "concealing," preserving the precarious new life amid the fiery death of the mother. We may note the recurrence of *loch-*, "birth," in 3 and 94 and of *kalyptein*, "conceal," in 12 and 96. Both passages bring together the god's fused polarities, life and its destruction.

The description in the next strophe of his birth as a "bull-horned god" whom the maenads garlanded with snakes fuses divinity and animal nature and also links Dionysus' birth in the enclosure of Zeus' thigh with the birth of infant Zeus, attended by satyrs who are "mad" (*mainomenoi*, 130; *mainades*, 103) in the cave. At Zeus' birth there

---

[5] See Dodds, *Bacchae* ad 126-29: "βακχεία and Βακχᾶν have troubled editors, since the worship described is that of Rhea, not of Dionysus," and he cites Eur. frag. 472.13ff. N (*Cretans*).

[6] Dodds, *Bacchae* ad 120 points out that *thalameuma* is a "poetic variant for *thalamē*, which was a *vox propria* for a sacred cave." In *Ion* 393f. Euripides uses the latter word for the oracular cavern of Trophonius. In *Suppl.* 980f. *thalamai* denotes the grave of Capaneus where Euadna immolates herself for the good of Thebes. In both cases Euripides associates these *thalamai* with passage between upper and lower worlds, mortal and supernatural power. See also Roux ad loc. and Soph. *Antig.* 947.

is a dance of wild satyrs (132); in Dionysus' revel there is a dance of "all the earth" (*ga pasa choreusei*, 114). In both cases a word suggestive of a house (*thalamos* recurs often in the play in that meaning exclusively) where a child is born into a human family describes an anomalous "chamber" of birth at the two extremes of the hierarchy between beast and god. On the one side is a wild cave on the fringes of civilization in a pre-Olympian world (120ff.) where the vulnerable infant Zeus is threatened by a cruel, devouring father (note Zeus' patronymic, "son of Cronus," 95); on the other is the thigh of the Olympian ruler with its "golden pins" that protects the new god as a surrogate womb.

The same word, *thalamē*, recurs in the second stasimon to describe the "many-treed coverts of Olympus" (ταῖς πολυδένδρεσσιν Ὀλύμπου θαλάμαις) where Orpheus, playing his music in the mountain forest, "brought together the trees and the wild beasts" (560-64). As the Dionysiac music moves from city to wild, from men to beasts, so the enclosure or "chamber" shifts its significance from the safe interiority of the house to exposed places outside the city, a border-place between Greeks and barbarians. This is the appropriate setting for a singer who practises one of the chief civilizing arts on the one hand but on the other, like the god with whom he is here associated, has a marginal relation to civilization.

In the *Phoenissae* an important prophecy concerns such *thalamai* (*Phoenissae* 931-41). To make recompense for the killing of the earthborn serpent at Thebes' founding, a member of the royal house must be sacrificed and pour a libation of his blood into the chambers of the earth. Here again the word denotes the sheltering hollows of earth that are both part of the city and yet elude the city's control, a mysterious chthonic power potentially hostile to the city.

These "chamber/hollows," then, swing between shelter and destruction, civilization and savagery, life and death. They are associated with rites of purification, where the polluted and abominated objects (*aporrhēta*) are cast out into the potters' fields.[7] Men preserve the civilized quality of their territory, the dominated surface of the earth, by burying and concealing pollution in its mysterious hollows underneath. "The things beneath the earth" are virtually synonymous

[7] Schol. ad *Phoen.* 931, the passage that describes the *thalamai* where the "earthborn Serpent was the guardian over Dirce's streams."

with the unknown. In Aristophanes' *Clouds* Socrates' pupils in the Thinkery are engaged in "searching out what is below the earth" (*Clouds* 188-92). In an earlier play of Euripides "what shines beneath the earth" is a source of human delusion, a source of mysteries that may entice men to their doom (*Hippolytus* 193-97).[8]

• III •

Near the end of the play Cadmus complains, "The god, Lord Bromius, justly, with more than justice, destroyed us, born a member of our house" (*oikeios gegōs*, 1249f.). The proximity of Dionysus as *oikeios*, a member of the "household" (*oikos*), shatters the protective security that the house provides for mother and child. In the first stasimon the maenads praised the "life of calm peace," *hēsychia*, which "holds together houses" (*synechei dōmata*, 388-92). At the end Cadmus sees his "house destroyed" with the death of his last surviving male heir: the god has "ruined the house" and left dead the one "to whom the house looked up—O you who held together [*syneiches*] my house, O my dear son" (1304-1309). Commiserating with Cadmus, Agave repeats the lament in her dirge-like lyrics at the end (1374-76): "For terribly did Lord Dionysus bring this disfigurement upon your house" (*oikoi*). The shelter offered young gods in mythical "chambers" of remote caves or divine thigh contrasts bitterly with a mortal mother's "ill-fortune" as "an exile from her chambers" at the end (ἐπὶ δυστυχίᾳ / φυγὰς ἐκ θαλάμων, 1369f.).

Teiresias had warned Pentheus that his present course of action would bring *penthos*, grief, within Cadmus' house (367f.). As Agave returns, still insane, she is carrying the head "of a lion of the mountain," as she believes (1141f.), "inside the walls" (1145). She would affix it as a trophy to the outer wall of the palace itself (1212-15). At this point Cadmus is arranging the rest of Pentheus' remains "before the house" (*domōn paros*, 1217) and is literally holding the "grief" (*penthos*) that Pentheus-*penthos* has become (1244; cf. 367, 508). When

---

[8] See Segal (1979) 154. For what lies below the earth as the dark mystery of the irrational that eludes human control and domination cf. *Antig.* 338ff. and 361 and see Seth Benardete, "A Reading of Sophocles' *Antigone*," *Interpretation: A Journal of Political Philosophy* 4 (1975) 189-91.

Pentheus comes back to the palace, where the regal trophies of valor are prominently displayed for all the citizens to admire, he is the displayed trophy, not its proud possessor (cf. 1239f.).

Dionysus' invasion of the house serves as the objective correlative of his invasion of the boundaries of the personality in the crisis of identity that his arrival provokes. In 827, as Pentheus falls under Dionysus' power to release his own repressed attraction toward the maenads, Dionysus tells him, "I will go within the house and deck you out" (ἐγὼ στελῶ σε δωμάτων ἔσω μολών). That movement within initiates the confusion of the hero's inner space both of dwelling and of self. When Pentheus emerges from that inner space, his relation to the secure identity affirmed and solidified by his house is at its most fragile point. He goes through the town in secret, a spy, not a warrior-king, disguised as a woman, taking "deserted paths" out to the mountains (cf. 841). The next scene begins with Dionysus calling Pentheus "forth from the house" (914). Now everything in the house is askew. The male heir looks like one of the daughters (917). Singleness of definition yields to to doubleness, unity to ambiguity (917ff.).

Dionysus' centripetal movement from the outside as a Stranger to reclaim his Theban house sets off a centrifugal movement away from the house for the inhabitants. The bacchantic madness of Dionysus drives the women of Thebes, gadfly-stung like cattle or horses, "from their houses" (32) to "unroofed rocks beneath green firs" (36-38). At the end the surviving human characters reenact this movement in a more permanent and catastrophic way as Cadmus, condemned to exile, sees his house destroyed (1303-1309) and Agave bids her house and city a last farewell (1368-70).

Dionysus' centrifugal effect on the houses of those who resist him is prominent in other myths of the god. The daughters of Proetus at Argos and Minyas' daughters at Orchomenos leave the house for the wild and in the latter case destroy their own children. In the myth of King Lycurgus of Thrace, too, the god's vengeance brings about the destruction of a house through a father's killing of a son.[9]

In the first episode, as in the prologue, the house is a major focus of attention. As the Chorus concludes the beautiful parode with its images of distant Lydia and Crete, Golden-Age abundance, the intoxicating music of foreign rituals and excited dances on the moun-

---

[9] See Dodds, *Bacchae* xxixf.; Kerényi 175-88.

tains, the aged Teiresias, prophet of doom rooted in the native traditions of Thebes, enters "at the gates," blind and faltering, to "call
Cadmus from the house" (170). Cadmus makes his entrance from the
palace: "I came," he says, "when in the house I heard your voice,
wise from a wise man" (178f.). The contrasts between lithe maenads
and feeble elders, mountains and house, the joyful ecstasy of Dionysus and the traditional "wisdom" (*sophia*, 189) of the city of which
the old men are the repository, are all aspects of the larger antithesis
between the far and the near. The emotional freedom and thrilling
risk of surrender to the Asian newcomer contrast with the familiar
traditions and the power of the house from which Cadmus enters the
stage.

The old men soon agree on leaving city and house for "the mountain," echoing in their deliberative iambics the Asian Chorus's lyrical
cry, "to the mountain, to the mountain" (191 and 165). Teiresias'
philosophical speculations would reconcile Dionysus with the "traditions of their fathers" (*patrious paradochas*, 201), but he is cut short
by the arrival of Pentheus, excited and in haste. Arriving "at the
house" (212) from "outside the land" (*ekdēmos chthonos*, 215), he has
heard of "the new troubles in the city" (216): "The women have left
our houses" (δώματ' ἐκλελοιπέναι, 217), he explodes, for "the wooded
thickets of the mountains" (218f.). There, as he fancies, they drink
wine and serve men's lusts (223). For him the alternative to the wom-
en's enclosure in houses is their total abandon and license in the
woods of the mountain. His remedy is confinement within house or
prison: "All those whom I have caught my servants keep, their hands
bound, in the enclosing prisons of the city" (226f.; cf. 514). His
expression for prisons, *pandēmoi stegai*, uses the general noun *stegē*,
which refers to any built enclosure, including private houses. Pentheus' phrase, repeated and used with the motif of "binding" (*desmoi*)
again at 443, reflects his view of himself as the guardian of both
private and public interior space. That conjunction is to prove fatal:
he dies at the hands of a mother who has lost touch with the domestic
aspect of her house (cf. 1118f.; cf. 1211-15). His utter failure in blocking
the leaving of houses in 217 is marked by the recurrence of that verb
in Agave's lament at the end, where "leaving" the house is in a very
different spirit (ἐκλείπω, 217 and 1369).

As Pentheus works himself up to a pitch of frenzy in his first scene

(233-36), "house" signifies more than domestic space or means of punishment. It is also a symbol of his authority. It implies the carefully demarcated limits of his world, now invaded by this sensual, barbarian, disturbingly good-looking youth. These limits he must defend at all costs. Here, as throughout the play, Dionysus serves as a screen on which the human characters project their own visions, idealized or distorted, of their own personalities and their world.

At the peak of his violent outburst Pentheus illogically regards Dionysus as an interloper in the containing space (*stegē*) of house or palace (239-41): "If I ever catch him within this house [*stegē*], I'll stop him from beating his thyrsus and tossing his hair, for I'll cut his head from his body."[10] The presence of a figure so fundamentally alien to Pentheus' closed world defies his rigid control over his house. The first episode thus ends as it began: Teiresias speaks of Cadmus and his house, but now prophesies the "grief" (*penthos*) that Pentheus will bring upon it (367f.; cf. 170, 178f.). The symmetry is reinforced by the contrast between Cadmus' "wise voice from a wise man," which he hears "in the house" (179), and Teiresias' closing warnings, as he exits to his original destination (363ff. and 174ff.), about "a fool [who] speaks foolish things" (369).

The forcible enclosure of the maenads in the *stegē* of the public jail (444) opens the third episode, but Dionysus' threat to Pentheus' authority is already framed in a paradox of spatial terms. These bound prisoners are in fact in their "mountain glades" (*orgades*), "loosed" and "skipping about" (445f.). The Servant's repetition of Pentheus' earlier commands only underlines total failure (cf. 227 and 444). The characteristically Dionysiac verb, "skipping" (*skirtōsi*, 446), harks back to the maenads' joyful "skipping" on the mountain (*skirtēmata*, 169).[11]

Pentheus would use decapitation to "stop" (*pausō*, 240) the Stranger's free movements of Dionysiac worship. Later, with a similar hy-

---

[10] Dodds, *Bacchae* ad loc. notes that the word *stegē* is "a little odd: Pentheus objects to the Stranger's activities not merely in the Castle but in the country at large, and orders his men to arrest him *ana polin*." Norwood's emendation, aside from introducing a clash of singular and plural verbs (not necessarily impossible), is hardly necessary; and it is difficult to see how such a phrase would be corrupted into the present text.

[11] For the word *skirtân* of spontaneous joy and freedom from authoritarian restraint see Antiphon the Sophist 87 B 49 DK ad fin.; Plato *Repub.* 9.571c; Aristoph. *Clouds* 1078 with Dover's note ad loc.

perbole, he would "stop" (*pausas*, 514) the maenads' dancing and drumming by "selling" them into slavery or making them his "possessions" as palace servants who work the looms (511-14).[12] Both threats, as we have seen, turn the characteristic activities of civilized life, commerce and manufacture, into instruments of repression. This transformation parallels the shift of Pentheus' kingship between discipline and chaos, order and savagery. With this threat of enslavement we may compare his later indignation at 803, "What shall I do, be a slave to women who are slaves to me?" He can conceive of civic or domestic authority only in terms of the relation of master to slave, but now the collapse of that authority is imminent.

Dionysus, the Chorus sang in the parode, freed the women from the "looms" (*aph' histōn*, 117-19); Pentheus would enslave those women as "possessions" set to work inside, "at the looms" (*eph' histois*, 514). The motif comes full circle in the grim scene that makes clear the precariousness of Pentheus' various forms of enclosure and exclusion. As Agave enters holding her son's severed head, she boasts of the special honor that she has brought to the house (1234), "having left the shuttles at the looms" (*par' histois*, 1236) for a demonstration of prowess in the hunt (1237-39).[13]

• III •

"When the many stand at the gates," Teiresias tells Pentheus, "and the city magnifies the name of Pentheus, you take joy; so he too [Dionysus], I think, delights in being honored" (319-21). The association of the king's name (*onoma*, 320) with the gates in this little parable suggests Pentheus' tendency to define his identity in terms of boundaries, exclusion, and the public fortifications of the city. It is akin to his hierarchical ranking of his people (so here "the many," *polloi*, over against the king) and contrasts with the god's deliberately nonhierarchical society of worshipers made equal in the ecstatic *thia-*

---

[12] See Dodds, *Bacchae* ad 513: "The proposal to enslave them is drastic and could hardly be put in the mouth of a character intended to be sympathetic."

[13] For leaving the looms and the house as both a physical and emotional liberation for women see Slater 225. Cf. Bacchyl. 11.38 and Jacob Stern, "Bestial Imagery in Bacchylides' *Ode 11*," *GRBS* 6 (1965) 276-77.

sos. "Whatever the meaner multitude [*to plēthos* . . . *to phauloteron*] practises and holds as customary [*nomizein*], that would I receive," sings the Chorus at the end of the next ode (430-32). "Dwell [*oikei*] with us, not outside of the customary practises" (*nomoi*), advises Cadmus, endorsing Teiresias' words (330f.). But Pentheus' dwelling remains hierarchically defined and rigidly exclusive. What he will bring "into his dwelling" (*domoi*) as Teiresias prophesies at the end of the scene is not the "magnified name" of Pentheus (320; cf. 508), but the etymology of the name "Pentheus" as *penthos*, grief (367f.).

It is characteristic of Pentheus that he should punish the wandering Stranger from remote Asia with confinement in the darkness of the palace-buildings, near the subdued animality of beasts of burden (509f.):

καθεῖρξατ' αὐτὸν ἱππικαῖς πέλας
φάτναισιν, ὡς ἂν σκότιον εἰσορᾷ κνέφας.

Shut him up near the stables of the horses
so that he may see the dark gloom.

But the prisoner will soon overcome the darkness with his destructive fire and a blaze of "greatest light" (594-97, 608). In those very stables where Pentheus would "contain" the Stranger (509), Pentheus will find a bull, symbol of the god's irrepressible animal power (618), a creature against whom Pentheus fails in a struggle whose violence suggests the release of the latent bestial and erotic forces in himself (618-21).[14]

The root *herk-*, "enclose," "constrain," recurs throughout the play, not only for Pentheus' enclosing of others, but also for his enclosure within himself and his tightly bounded space of walled city and palace. The opposite of the *herk-* compounds are the various forms of *lyein*, "to loosen," "to release."[15] Unable to acknowledge and let loose the Dionysiac in himself, Pentheus must insist on ever more massive forms of enclosure and containment.

Under Dionysus' spell, Pentheus imagines the maenads as "birds in a thicket, caught in the dearest enclosures [*herkē*] of their beds" (957f.). His madness reveals his own ambivalence toward the mae-

[14] See WI 84.
[15] For a possible figurative use of *lyein* see Dorothea Wender, "Letting Go: Imagery and Symbolic Naming in Plato's *Lysis*," *Ramus* 7 (1978) 40ff. For Dionysus and the dissolution of emotional boundaries see Slater 267f., Roberts 43ff.

nads between repulsion and desire. Trapped in the "toils" of their beds, they are once more safely enclosed in the male-dominated civic and domestic world, like the captured maenads at the looms in the threat of 511-14. That image of netting them in the "dearest enclosures of beds" (958) shows Pentheus' salacious thoughts breaking through repression, "unloosed" from their constriction (cf. also 216-25). Ironically, nothing could be further from helpless birds on the ground than these maenads who have just swooped down like birds soaring on the wing to attack the outlying fields of Thebes (748f.). The contrasting directions of the image reveal the instability of the forms of enclosure that Pentheus exerts, both on others and on himself.

The "palace miracle" signifies not only the triumph of Dionysiac energies over Pentheus' repression but also the initial dissolution of Pentheus' authoritarian personality as Dionysus gets inside. When Dionysus is "within the halls" (589) and Bromios shouts the ritual cry "within the house" (ἀλαλάζεται στέγας ἔσω, 592f.), Pentheus' inner defenses, infiltrated, begin to crumble. The "public enclosure" (226, 444) cannot hold a god so refractory to the guarded spaces of Pentheus' domain, in both the psychological and political sense. The palace scene and its immediate sequel, Pentheus' encounter with the bull, prefigure the literal surrender of Pentheus to the Stranger in 810ff. Having defeated attempts to constrain his free movement, Dionysus invades Pentheus' palace and then Pentheus' mind.

In his futile attempt to enclose the maenads, the Messenger from Cithaeron reports, Pentheus would not only "hem them in" (εἶρξας, 443) but "carry them all off together" (syn-harpazein) and "bind them in the bonds of the all-citied enclosure" (443f.): ἃς δ᾽ αὖ σὺ βάκχας εἶρξας ἃς συνήρπασας / κἄδησας ἐν δεσμοῖσι πανδήμου στέγης. When we see the maenads "loosed" on the mountain, however, not only are the men of the city routed in their attempt to do the "carrying off" (syn-harpazein, 729, as in 443), but the maenads "carry off" with a violence of supernatural energy (harpazein, 754). This scene, too, has a precursor in Pentheus' frustration when he rushes madly into the palace "carrying off" a sword (harpasas, 628).

The self-conscious play on the root dē-, "bind," and dēmos, "city," in 444 suggests that for Pentheus the city is enclosure.[16] In the sti-

---

[16] The various terms for binding, imprisoning, constriction (e.g., desmos, anankē, brochos) recur frequently and significantly throughout the play, e.g., 355, 545, 548f.,

chomythy shortly afterward Pentheus, identifying Thebes with himself, virtually defines his "authority" as the power to bind (*dein*) (503-506):

Penth.   Take him. He scorns me and Thebes.
Dionys.   I say do not bind me [μὴ δεῖν], speaking as one sane to
            those who are not.
Penth.   Bind him [*dein*], I say, being of greater authority than
            you [*kyriōteros*].

His failure to "bind" or "close in" the god in the next scene reveals, among other things, that this conception of self, sanity (504), and name (507f.) rests on the most precarious foundation. The next scene poses the challenge precisely whether Pentheus or the Stranger has "greater authority."

· IV ·

Pentheus uses his palace, as he uses his city, to imprison what is free, to keep out what may cross the boundaries he needs to maintain. Making the palace-dungeons the prison of the Lydian Stranger, he reveals the palace's double meaning: an image of his rule over Thebes and a symbol of his own emotional state.

The equation of the king-hero with the royal palace is a frequent motif in Greek literature and myth.[17] Euripides' *Heracles* offers a close parallel. The hero's self-disintegration in madness operates in close conjunction with the literal disintegration of his palace (e.g., *HF* 864, 919ff., 943ff., 1006-12). Dionysus' enclosure within the palace visually enacts the meaning of events onstage, that the god has entered and taken possession of Pentheus. Possibly following a motif from Aeschylus' play about Dionysus, the *Edoni*, Euripides shows Pen-

552, 611, 615f., 618, 642f., 755, 1020f. For walls and towers see Scott 340ff. For the association of "binding" and *ananke* in early Greek literature generally see Heinz Schreckenberg, *Ananke: Untersuchungen zur Geschichte des Wortegebrauchs*, Zetemata 36 (Munich 1964) 2-11, 40-42, esp. p. 42 on *Ba.* 552 and 642. For further details see Segal (1982) (forthcoming).

[17] Wohlberg 149-55, who, however, touches only briefly on the meaning of the motif for the character of Pentheus and its psychological implications (152, 154).

theus' palace as transformed from a would-be prison of the god to a vehicle for the god's expression of his power.[18] Dionysus causes the palace, caught in his web of illusion, to tremble as he makes the earth tremble. He subjects it, too, to the "fall" (*pesēmata*, 588) that will soon afflict its ruler. Fashioning the false image of "bright air" (631) to elude the king and his "dark sword" (628), he reveals the darkness hidden in the interior of the ruler's guarded palace and guarded soul. In contrast to that darkness at the center of Pentheus' fortress-prison, bright flashes of fire demonstrate the god's power to his worshipers (594-99). We recall too the bright "sheen of the vine's cluster" in his joyful gifts outside in the open air (cf. *botryos ganos*, 261, 382-86).

The god not only "shakes," "burns," and "turns upside down" the palace of Pentheus (cf. 594f., 603f., 606, 623, 633f.), but also confuses the inner and outer space of Pentheus' perceptions and orientation. By invading his stronghold, Dionysus begins the process of calling into question those rigid divisions between male and female, master and servant, Greek and barbarian that comprise the king's compartmentalized view of his world. To Pentheus' dismay, the Stranger steps freely and calmly "outside the house" (636f., 646, 648). "Thinking that he sees his house ablaze" (624) and then dashing wildly "inside the house" (628), Pentheus shows that he has lost his battle to preserve his kind of order over his inner space. His defeat is sealed as the Stranger calmly announces his sandal's noise "inside the house." The last phrase, *domōn esō* (638), echoes his furious entrance ten lines before (628).

• V •

The long Messenger's speech is the transition from the symbolical shattering of the psycho-spatial security of Pentheus' "house" to his total surrender to the god. It removes the action abruptly from the

[18] Aeschyl. frag. 58 N = 76 Mette; see above, Chap. 3, n. 7; also Wohlberg 152. On the Aeschylean trilogy see now T. N. Gantz, "The Aeschylean Tetralogy: Attested and Conjectured Groups," *AJP* 101 (1980) 154-56.

house to its symbolic antithesis in the play, the wild mountainside. The economic activities here are not commerce or weaving, with which Pentheus threateningly ended the preceding scene (cf. 511-14), but herding and hunting at the fringes of urban life.[19]

The married women in this setting are wives now "unyoked" (694), outside the civilized space that should define them.[20] As they destroy tame cattle, bull and heifer (736ff.), and threaten the cultivated fields (748ff.), they become as ambiguous to the tamed earth as to the tamed beasts. In the plains (*pedion*) they threaten these "rich-fruited ears of grain" (εὔκαρπον στάχυν, 748-50), whereas it was from "the plains of the earth" on the mountain that they drew forth the mysteriously nurturing milk, wine, and honey (πέδον γῆς, 706). The phallic imagery of thrusting the thyrsus into the ground to obtain this magical food is an inversion of agriculture, the female earth penetrated and plowed by the traditionally male act of plowing. This shift from the male-governed plow to the female-wielded, untooled pine-wand is exactly homologous with the movement from the interior space of the house to the open mountains, from cattle to wild beasts, from marriage to virago-like independence. Their maternity, too, becomes an impersonal fusion with the wild, "the magic of a motherliness that has no bounds."[21] It can reach out to all of nature, but can also swing precipitously to its opposite, a bloodthirsty violence that destroys the young and can "carry off children from their houses" (*ek domōn*, 754). Later Agave literally and metaphorically brings the wild into the domestic space of the house, individualizing what was a collective manifestation on Cithaeron.[22]

Pentheus' "conversion" completes the interchange of inner and outer space. Dionysus' promise, "I shall go within the house (*dōmatōn esō*)

[19] For the marginality of the hunter see Detienne, *Dionysos* 75ff.; Vidal-Naquet (1972) 137ff.; Schnapp 39ff.; Fontenrose, *Orion* 58ff., 79, 94f., Chaps. 7-8, 252ff.

[20] See above, Chap. 3, n. 11.

[21] Otto 109.

[22] Although this movement from the shelter of an infant in the house to murderous savagery in the wild occurs in other myths of maenadic women like the Daughters of Minyas, Euripides may be the first to apply the pattern so forcefully to the story of Pentheus. Webster 269, with note 41, points out that Euripides is the first known poet to have had Pentheus torn apart by his own mother. On a psykter in Boston the maenad who bears his head is called Galene.

and deck you out" (827), climaxes his recurrent threat to that defended interior (cf. 367, 628, 638, etc.). In the next scene, the Stranger, far from being shut away in the dark prison inside, controls the
king's movements both within and without. He summons him "forth
before the house" (ἔξιθι πάροιθε δωμάτων, 914) and leads him to
the deserted places outside the city (cf. 945). He thus reverses the
movement from outside (ekdēmos, 215) to "the house" (pros oikous,
212) at Pentheus' entrance. Pentheus' "eager haste" to enter the interior civic space under his control is matched by the unseemly "eager
haste" to leave it (dia spoudēs, 212; speudonta t' aspoudasta, "in eager
haste for what one should not be eager about," 913).

Pentheus' death in the Second Messenger's speech is introduced
with an address to a house "once happy" (1024f.). The messenger
exits, his fearful story told, in haste "before Agave comes to the house"
(1149). The ensuing lyrics stress the abrupt shift from the wild to the
house (domoi, 1165; melathra, 1170) where Agave is now "rushing"
(hormōmenē, 1165) with the spoils of her "happy" hunting (1180).

Addressing the "towered town of Thebes" (1202), Agave declares
her intention to have the head fastened to the triglyphs of the royal
house, showplace of the city's power (1212-15):

>   αἱρέσθω λαβὼν
> πηκτῶν πρὸς οἴκους κλιμάκων προσαμβάσεις,
> ὡς πασσαλεύσῃ κρᾶτα τριγλύφοις τόδε
> λέοντος ὃν πάρειμι θηράσασ' ἐγώ.

Let him take to the house the approaches of fastened ladders and
raise them up so that he may peg to the triglyphs this head of a
lion with which I have come from my hunting.

Just when she is a maddened huntress polluted with filicidal murder
she speaks with the dignity of a queen. The language of raising ladders here evokes the theme of attacking a city, as other parallels in
tragedy suggest,[23] so that the affirmation of secure civilized space conceals its multiple disintegration.

Cadmus will gradually recall Agave to sanity by reminding her of
the ties of the house, the locus of her real personality not as maenad
but as the nurturing woman inside that she once was (1273-76):

[23] Cf. Aeschyl. Sept. 466 and Eur. Phoen. 489, 1173. See below, Chap. 6, section 9.

Cadmus.   To whose house [*oikos*] did you come with marriage rites?

Agave.   You gave me to one of the Sown Men, they say, to Echion.

Cadmus.   What child was then born for your husband in the house [*oikois*]?

Agave.   Pentheus, by the union [*koinōnia*] of the father and myself.

Returning to herself, she asks, still half stunned, "Where was he killed, in the house [*kat' oikon*]—or in what places?" (1290). In the innocence of the question lies the irony that Pentheus' death is intimately bound up with the negation of the house and all that it implies. Cadmus may invoke his daughter's past domesticity to recall her to the identity by which she has defined herself for most of her life, but their closing exchanges stress the destruction of the house in the death of its last surviving male heir and the bleak exodus from house and city (1304-10, 1368-71, 1374-76).

• VI •

As Dionysus invades and destroys the sheltered space of the house, so even more radically does he open the bounded limits of the city to the forces of the wild alien to it. Throughout the poetry of his descriptions of nature Euripides evokes the otherness that the city must exclude. That exclusion involves a struggle between "man- and polis-centered rationalism and god- and nature-centered emotionalism," between acculturation and instinct, *nomos* and *physis*. [24]

Whereas Dionysus' followers come "from Phrygia's mountains to the roads of Greece, broad for dancing" (86-88), all of the human characters move away from the city. Pentheus enters from the country outside (215), but soon makes that journey in reverse as the god leads him "through the town" (855) or "through the midst of the Theban land" (961) into its "deserted places" (cf. 841) where he "alone suffers in behalf of the city" (963). Cadmus, like Dionysus, has come from

[24] The quotation is from Wassermann (1953) 563; see also Barlow 34.

barbarian Asia to Greece, but at the end will lead barbarian bands against Greeks. Agave will march "through the middle of Cithaeron" (1142) to within the walls and palace of Thebes (cf. 1145, 1202), but at the end will be "cast forth from her native land" (πατρίδος ἐκβεβλημένη, 1366), as Cadmus is "cast forth honorless from the house" (ἐκ δόμων ἄτιμος ἐκβεβλήσομαι, 1313). In the totality of her destruction she laments her exile from both "native land" (patris, patria polis, 1366, 1369f.) and her "house" (melathron, 1368).

Dionysus has shrines in both city and country, although small sanctuaries in the country are more common than formal temples in the city.[25] We have already noted in Chapter 1 the myths about resistance to his adoption in civic cult. In another Theban legend, he is said to have sent the Sphinx, half-human, half-bestial creature located sometimes at the center of the city, sometimes outside, preying on the citizens.[26] In the spatial movements of the play, the attempts both to receive him into the city (by Cadmus and Teiresias) and to keep him out (by Pentheus) fail.

Invaded by Dionysus, the well-defined space of the polis loses its monolithic unity and veers between symbolizing psychological states of personality and embodying political order. "Space itself," as one interpreter remarks, "laden with superhuman energies, has become a kind of hypostasis of the god."[27] By locating major events on the mountain, out of sight of the spectators, Euripides causes the action to unroll on two spatial planes at once, one visible, the other imagined. Any play that draws on the audience's knowledge of significant events offstage, of course, uses such a division. It is especially sharp here, however, for the clash between the values implicit in the two spatial fields is so strong.[28] The old men who embody "the ancestral heritage" (201) leave the city for Dionysiac dances on the mountainside. The young king becomes increasingly unreliable. The gnomic wisdom of the choral odes, which often in Greek tragedy serve as a stable, if prosaic, reference point for the values of the city, is now the ambiguous "wisdom" (sophia) of a foreign cult.

[25] See Farnell, Cults 5.133ff.; Jeanmaire 20; Gernet (1953) 392; Roux 1.63.
[26] Schol. ad Hesiod Theog. 326 and ad Eur. Phoen. 1031. See Otto 114.
[27] Wassermann (1929) 277.
[28] Ibid. 278; also Rudberg 46f.

• VII •

From the beginning Pentheus responds to the Dionysiac experience in narrowly political and military terms, and he is paid back in kind. When the Messenger from Cithaeron urges that the miracles on the mountains should inspire "prayers" (*euchai*), not "insults" (712f.), Pentheus responds with "arms," *hopla* (759, 789, 809, 845). His "insults" soon reach the point of viewing the maenads' rites as themselves an "outrage" (*hybrisma*) and "a great insult to the Hellenes" (779).

His reaction, anticipated by Dionysus, plays exactly into his hands, for the god had warned in the prologue (50-52): "If the city of Thebans [*Thēbaiōn polis*] in anger seeks with arms [*hopla*] to drive the maenads from the mountains, I shall give them battle, leading a Bacchant army." When the god announces his arrival in his opening lines and stresses his maternal connection with Thebes, he calls the city "this earth of the Thebans" (1). As he describes the city in terms of its life-giving natural features, "the streams of Dirce and Ismenus' water" (5), he creates an affinity between the city and the god's own attributes of life-giving liquids (cf. Teiresias' exposition, 274-85). But in the rest of the prologue, envisaging resistance from Thebes, he regards it solely as a political entity: "Thebes" (23), "this city" (39), "all the Thebans" (48), "the city of Thebans" (50), "Cadmus' city" (61).[29]

The Messenger from Cithaeron apparently fulfils the god's prophetic warning. First "the whole mountain" joins in the bacchic revel: πᾶν δὲ συνεβάκχευ' ὄρος (726); at the end "the whole city has been made bacchic": πᾶσά τ' ἐξεβακχεύϑη πόλις (1295).

The contrast between Pentheus' and the Messenger's response to events on the mountain (712ff.) confirms an earlier pattern. At the first confrontation of king and Stranger a guard or servant approaches with a tale of "wonders" (*thaumata*, 449f.). Pentheus replies by treating the captive not as a thaumaturge who is therefore close to the gods but as a beast caught in "nets" (451) from which he will not be able to "escape" (*ekphygein*, 452), a butt of insults and ironical remarks (453-59). Later the "beast" will indeed "have escaped" (*diapepheuge*, 642) and proven himself close to the gods through "wonders"

[29] On the terms for Thebes see Podlecki 148.

that will have their full scope in routing Pentheus' men on the mountain (*thaumata*, "wonders," in 667, 693, 716).

As the play goes on, it becomes clear that Pentheus, like Creon in Sophocles' *Antigone*, identifies the city with his own person.[30] "He scorns me and Thebes," he says angrily of the Stranger in 503, as he bids his guards take him away. "I come to tell you and the city," the Messenger says at 666. "Receiving the god into this city," as the Messenger pleads at 770, is a matter of Pentheus' receiving the god into himself. This is exactly what happens in Pentheus' sudden "conversion" some forty lines later (810ff.).

When Pentheus tries to confine the maenads, his "binding" is negated by a "spontaneous loosing" in the bonds themselves, as if they have a mysterious life of their own, not obedient to human purposes (445-47):

φροῦδαί γ᾽ ἐκεῖναι λελυμέναι πρὸς ὀργάδας
σκιρτῶσι Βρόμιον ἀνακαλούμεναι θεόν·
αὐτόματα δ᾽ αὐταῖς δεσμὰ διελύθη ποδῶν.

They are gone, set loose, skipping to the mountain glades, calling on the god Bromios; and of their own accord the bonds were loosed from their feet.

That "spontaneity" takes another form when the Theban maenads on Cithaeron, the women now set loose from the authority of husbands and fathers, "loose the confining bonds of their clothing" (*syndesm' elelyto*, 697) to put on the wild fawnskins. When their Golden-Age benignity reveals its more savage side, they carry off bronze implements without the need for *desmoi* ("bonds") to hold them (755). If Pentheus is the binder, the constrictor, then Dionysus is the looser, the freer; and in the background stands the cult-figure of Dionysos Lysios, "Dionysus Looser."[31] Yet this god can also bind those who

---

[30] Seidensticker (1972) 46 speaks of Pentheus' "Selbstidentifikation mit der Stadt, die Überzeugung, als Vertreter von Recht und Ordnung im Interesse des Staates zu handeln."

[31] Dionysus Lysios had a temple near the theater of Thebes: Pausanias 9.16.6; and the cult of Dionysus Lysios at Sicyon also had Theban connections: Paus. 2.7.5f. Rohde p. 287 with n. 21, p. 308, remarks on this aspect of the god as stilling and calming the madness he inspired. See also Ramnoux 200ff., who remarks of myths like those of Pentheus, "L'homme a voulu lier le dieu qui délie" (201). Further references in Roux ad 447.

oppose him. Later the maenads will sing of a destructive "noose" (*brochos*) constraining and killing Pentheus (1021), the foil to the "nooses" with which he would have caught the maenads (545) or their leader (619). The shift of the "noose" from pursued to pursuer is an indication of the reversals characteristic of this ambiguous god.

• VIII •

Constriction has a psychological dimension too. Pentheus ends his first violent tirade against the Stranger (including the threat of decapitation) with a metaphor of strangulation (246-47):

ταῦτ᾽ οὐχὶ δεινῆς ἀγχόνης ἔστ᾽ ἄξια,
ὕβρεις ὑβρίζειν, ὅστις ἔστιν ὁ ξένος.

Is this not worthy of terrible *strangling*, that this stranger, whoever he is, should commit such outrages?

The metaphor may be a tragic commonplace, as Dodds notes; but that does not make it any less relevant to a theme prominent in the play. Pentheus fires his anger with the image of the Stranger "tossing his hair up and down" (ἀνασείοντα . . . κόμας, 240f.). In the next scene Pentheus describes that long hair, "full of desire" (*pothos*) as "flowing loose" (κεχυμένος), the exact opposite of the constriction that characterizes his own person and attitudes.

Just as Pentheus conceives of his palace as an enclosing prison (cf. 239ff., 443f.), so he views the city as an enclosure on a large scale, a fortress against everything embodied in the god's revels on the mountain. The "unloosing" of Pentheus can take place only through his enclosure in the very nets with which he would have encircled the maenads.

The motif of enclosure is prominent in compounds of *peri* and *amphi*, "around," and especially in the verbs *periballein* and *amphiballein*, "to cast around," "encircle," "embrace." In the play's opening lines Dionysus does his "encircling" with the budding grape-clusters (note *perix*, "all around," 12); Cadmus, on the other hand, establishes a closed precinct (*sēkos*) of forbidden entry (*abaton*, 10f.). Where the mortal ex-ruler uses separation and prohibition (*a-baton*,

"not to be trodden"), the god uses the intertwining and uniting vegetative embrace of his plant, whose fruit also joins men together in
other ways. In Dionysus' view cities are encircled not only by walls
(cf. 15, 19), but also by "flowery" mountains, a far softer form of
enclosure. The exchange between the Stranger and King Pentheus is
significant (462-63):

Δι.   τὸν ἀνθεμώδη Τμῶλον οἶσθά που κλύων.
Πε.   οἶδ', ὃς τὸ Σάρδεων ἄστυ περιβάλλει κύκλῳ.

Dion.   You know by hearsay of the flowery Tmolus.
Penth. Yes, the mountain which embraces [periballei] the town
        of Sardis in a circle [kyklos].

The pattern is that of the prologue: where the rulers of Thebes speak
of enclosure and encirclement, the god (in or out of disguise) speaks
of the unconfined growth of nature, vine-shoots or flowers (11f., 462).[32]
Just before the Tmolus passage the Chorus sang of the very different
mode of Dionysiac encirclement: the ivy worn around the mixing
bowl "casts around [us] the embrace of sleep" (hypnon amphiballein,
385f.).

In like manner the parode of the play celebrates the "circle of the
stretched hide" of the drum that accompanies the joyful freedom of
the corybantic dances on the Cretan mountains (byrsotonon kyklōma,
124). Here the satyrs "join together" (συνῆψαν) in dances that bring
delight to Dionysus (132-35). Pentheus' "joining together," on the
other hand, is an act of coercion. "He will fasten me [synapsei],
Bromios' devotee, in knotted bonds" (brochoi, 545f.), says the Chorus. "Did he not join together [synēpse] your hands in binding knots?"
they ask their leader, astonished to see him walking free (615). Resisted, the god's "joining together" becomes punitive. The maenads
scattered the bull's torn flesh "faster than you could fit together [syn-
apsai] your lids upon your royal eyes," the Messenger reports with
unwitting foreboding (747). The god has finally "joined together" all
the members of the house "in single ruin," as Cadmus laments at the
end (synēpse, 1303).

A different kind of enclosure marks Teiresias' relation to the god.

---

[32] The fact that Tmolus was celebrated in antiquity for its vines and crocuses (cf.
Virg. G. 1.56 and Roux ad 462f.) does not make the epithet at 462 any less dramatically effective in Euripides' context.

When he rationalizes his nature and his name in terms of "aether encircling the earth" (τοῦ χϑόν' ἐγκυκλουμένου αἰϑέρος, 292f.), he is trying to imprison Dionysus not in prison walls or chains, but in the subtle nets of his own allegories. The god's own use of "aether" soon after (631) shows how little power both physical and intellectual enclosures have over him.

The coercive enclosure attempted by Pentheus dominates most of the action. Countering the god's power to loosen or dissolve, Pentheus summons up his full authority as king and general. The pattern will by now be familiar. Dionysus (as Stranger) describes his power to "make grow the much-clustering vine for mortals" (τὴν πολύβο-τρυν ἄμπελον φύει βροτοῖς, 651), to which Pentheus soon replies, κλῄειν κελεύω πάντα πύργον ἐν κύκλῳ ("I give the command to close up every tower in a circle," 653). The sound of the line reinforces the sense of enclosure: the k/kl sounds of "command" and "close" enframe the p's of "every tower" in the center (klē . . . kel . . . / p . . . p / . . . ky-kl . . .).[33]

Pentheus' attempt to close in the god and his worshipers meets its defeat in an enclosure of a different kind. Initially a grassy pleasance (1048), this setting soon appears as a place enclosed by crags (amphi-krēmnon, 1051) and shut in by the enfolding shade of its fir trees (πεύκαισι συσκιάζον, 1052).[34] The compounding prepositions, amphi- and syn-, which had a positive meaning in the "embracing" and "to-

---

[33] Note also the alliterative effects of 306-308 to describe the freer, open movement of Dionysus as he "leaps with pine torches over the twin-peaked plateau in Delphi's crags, brandishing and shaking the Bacchic branch," κἀπὶ Δελφίσιν πέτραις / πηδῶντα σὺν πεύκαισι δικόρυφον πλάκα, / πάλλοντα καὶ σείοντα βακχεῖον κλάδον. . . . Cf. also the word-play and alliteration to describe Pentheus' biting his lips with his teeth in 621 χείλεσιν διδοὺς ὀδόντας. For the language of emphatic enclosure and locking up, cf. the description of the siege of Olympus, Aristoph. Birds 1158-59: "And now everything there is be-gated with gates [pepylōtai pylais] and set with bolts and guarded in a circle [phylattetai kyklō(i)]."

[34] For the topography of 1048ff. and the sense of syskiazon see Dodds, Bacchae and Sandys ad loc. For the motif of shade see Scott 343f. Winfried Elliger, Die Darstellung der Landschaft in der griechischen Dichtung (Berlin 1975) 254, is surely mistaken to view 1050f. as a "typical locus amoenus" in which "peaceful nature corresponds to the peaceful impulse of the Bacchants." The passage must be read in its dramatic context, the grim news of Pentheus' death with which the Messenger opens his speech (1024-30), which alerts us to the tensions between idyllic scenery and gruesome events. Cf. Theocr. Id. 26.5ff.

getherness" of the Dionysiac celebrations, here take on ominous associations.

Diabrochos, another compound adjective, describes this place: ὕδασι διάβροχον, "with watery streams flowing through it" (1051). The word derives from the verb *brechein*, "to wet," but it is a homonym of *brochos*, "noose."[35] In the potentially life-giving trait of the god of vitalizing fluids, then, we hear also an echo of the strangling enclosure or binding with which Pentheus tried to repress this Dionysiac power (cf. *brochos*, "noose," in 545, 615, 619, and the strangling image in 246f., above). In the open country of the god's loosed energies Pentheus finds the very constriction that he would have imposed.

That it is not fanciful to hear this echo in *diabrochon* (which, with different accentuation, could mean "on account of the noose") is confirmed by the "poetic justice" in the return of the "noose" in the multiple inversions envisaged by the Chorus just some thirty lines before: they ask Dionysus to "embrace" Pentheus in "a noose of death" (*peribale brochon / thanasimon*, 1021f.). In the landscape of 1048ff. Pentheus the imprisoner is himself entrapped in an enclosure, not the man-made walls and gates under his authority as king and general, but features of wild nature. These obey the god's mysterious voice, not the king's martial orders (compare 1084ff with 1118ff., 1131f.).

The exact place of his death is "near a rock like a tower" (*antipyr-*

---

[35] Etymologically *brechein*, "to wet," and *brochos*, "noose," may be from the same root, if the original sense of *brechein* is "to smother": see T. G. Rosenmeyer, "On Snow and Stones," *Cal. Studies in Class. Antiquity* 11 (1978) 217, citing Hermann Fränkel, *Glotta* 14 (1925) 1-2. Thus the gap between *diabrochos* in 1051 and *brochos*, "noose," may be linguistically much less for a fifth-century Greek speaker than it seems to us. Cf. also Pindar *Ol.* 6.55. *Ankos*, "glade," in 1052 continues the root *ank-*, which comes to express the god's reply to Pentheus' constricting *ananke*: cf. 246, 552, 642f., 969 and *ankalai* in 699f. and 1277. The "softness" (968) of embracing *ankalai* proves to be the harsh *ananke*, or "necessity," of the god (969, 1351) punishing the king for his attempt to apply the *ananke* of *desmoi* or *brochoi* (552, 642). See above, n. 16. From another point of view, the "binding" of Pentheus in his constrictive "noose" may reflect an ancient notion of fate as the immobility imposed on a mortal by a god: see R. B. Onians, *The Origins of European Thought*, 2nd ed. (Cambridge 1954) 326ff., esp. 331: "The 'binding' of the gods is no mere trick of language but a literal description of an actual process, their mode of imposing fate upon mortals, a religious belief and not a metaphor." This notion of fate as a "binding" is also the subject of a forthcoming study of Sophocles' *Oedipus Tyrannus* by Jules Brody.

gon petran, 1097), surrounded by maenads who hem him in "standing about him in a circle" (*peristasai kyklōi*, 1106). The encircling embrace here is that of a mother's hand dripping with the blood of a child (*chera . . . peribalein*, 1163-64).[36] Having failed to encircle (*peri . . . eballe*) the bull he has "enclosed" (*katheirxe*) in his palace (618-19), Pentheus is himself "encircled in a net of death" (*peribale brochon / thanasimon*, 1020-22). He is a wild beast anomalously defeated by a herd, an animal in the wild caught paradoxically both in a noose (1021) and "without nets" (1173). In the parallelism of cultural and psychological meanings, he is also a child stifled in the murderous embrace of an all-powerful mother (1163-64). Destruction of personal identity parallels destruction of house and city. At the end old Cadmus asks Agave, "Why do you embrace me with your hands, unhappy child?" (*amphiballeis chersin*, 1364). Those hands are still stained with blood from their earlier "embrace" (1163-64; cf. 1135-36). The embrace of father and daughter cannot completely efface the earlier embrace of mother and son. Here the daughter is exiled from her "fatherland," and the "father" is but a "small ally" to the daughter (1366-67).

The complex simile that initiates the final stage of Pentheus' death describes a fir tree bent into the circular form of bow or lathe (*kyklouto*, 1066). The enclosed circle of interior space thus formed obliterates rather than delineates the boundary between city and wild, man and beast. It points to an area just the reverse of the discipline of war or the civilized tool-using in the content (vehicle) of the simile itself.

A "command" about enclosure is the prelude to the account of the maenads who are "loosed" and running free on Cithaeron (653). Another command about enclosure ends the episode. When the Messenger finishes his tale, Pentheus responds (780-85):

[36] Reading, with the MSS, χέρ' αἵματι στάζουσαν / περιβαλεῖν τέκνου (1163-64), which Dodds, *Bacchae* ad loc. translates, "to clothe a dripping hand in the blood of one's child." Many editors, however, prefer Kirchhoff's τέκνῳ, which would mean, "to throw her hand, dripping with blood, around her child"; cf. also 1135. With the compounds of *ballein* in *peri* and *amphi* here, denoting union, we may compare Pentheus' *hyper-ballei*, "surpass," in his violent reaction to the notion of men being defeated by women. He closes his orders for a muster at the "Electran Gates" with the general remark, "But this surpasses [shoots above, *hyperballei*] [all measure] if what we suffer we suffer from women" (785f.).

Go to the Electran gates [*pylas*]; order all the shield-bearing hoplites to meet there, and the riders of the swift-footed steeds and
those who brandish javelins and who make the strings of the bow
sing in their hands; for we shall lead an army against the bacchants.

As in 653, "gates" and military force go together in Pentheus' mind;
they are his characteristic mode of opposing the god's revels. As he
replied to the "outrage" (*hybris*) of the god with a metaphor of constriction (the "strangulation" of 246f.), so here he replies to the "outrage" (*hybrisma*, 779) of the bacchants with a defense of those enclosures that he now sees threatened. The flurry of martial details in
780-86 betrays the insecurity he would deny in the face of the threat
posed by the maenads.

Dionysus' impact on Thebes is first dramatized with a call "at the
gates," as Teiresias summons the old king "who gave Thebes its towers" (*epyrgōse*, 170-72). At the end this king's daughter addresses these
very towers when the god's vengeance is nearly complete (1202f.).
Pentheus' abrupt initiative in "closing up" the city in defense against
the god (653) now recurs, transformed to total passivity as his torn
body is "closed up" (i.e., pieced together) after the *sparagmos* ($\pi \hat{\alpha} \nu$
. . . $\sigma \nu \gamma \kappa \epsilon \kappa \lambda \eta \mu \acute{\epsilon} \nu o \nu \ \kappa a \lambda \hat{\omega} s$, 1300). The identification between the king
and his palace or city reaches its grim and final elaboration as the
desiderated invulnerability of the city "closed in" by its towers (653)
turns into the extreme vulnerability of the king outside the defenses
of his wall. The correlation between the king's body and the body
politic, between city and individual psyche, is central to Sophocles'
Oedipus Tyrannus and is "writ large" in Plato's *Republic*; it is already
implicit in the imagery and scenic action of this play.

· IX ·

As the city of the *Bacchae* is both a political and a psychological
entity, so is the natural world outside the city. It is a landscape of the
soul as well as a landscape of realistic nature. In its blissful, Golden-
Age features we can recognize the joy, spontaneity, and purity of
response that belong to the lost innocence of childhood. At the same
time we also recognize here a demonic violence in ourselves that we

cannot always keep "locked up," and yet can let loose only at a certain risk. [37]

From the very first Dionysus' landscape is a landscape of extremes. The god's account of his wanderings in the prologue includes both "sun-struck plains" and "harsh-wintered earth" (13-16). The long account of the maenads on Cithaeron begins with mountain peaks "where white snow's glistening falls never lose their grip" (662, Dodds' translation), but soon moves to the upland pasturage "where the sun shoots forth its rays as it warms the earth" (677-79).

The god's opponents in Thebes see nature in relation to the enclosures of the city. Teiresias introduces Cadmus in terms of gates, towers, citadel (170-72). The only adjective is the geographically precise toponym, "Sidonian" (171). The cities named by the god appear in a wide landscape of "golden fields," "sun-smitten plains," "wintry earth," "salt sea" (13-20). With a god's perspective he takes in "all of Asia." He envisages the human world against the elements of earth, sky, and sea, amid the changes on the face of the land in seasonal alternation, from summer to winter (cf. 14-15). Even when he describes cities they are teaming with life and possessed of an aesthetic aspect ("full," "lovely-towered," 19).

Later Dionysus can call Tmolus a "fortress of Lydia" (ἔρυμα Λυδίας, 55), but soon his maenads give Tmolos the epithet "sacred," *hieros* (65). He describes its luxury in "flowing gold" (*chrysorhoos*, 154), perceiving even its metallic wealth as part of the movements of natural forces, the rivers coursing down the mountain with their precious metals (cf. also the god's stress on Lydian gold in 13). In the Dionysiac Stranger's encounter with Pentheus Tmolus is "flowery" for the Lydian, an "enclosure" for the Theban king (462f.; contrast also 651 and 653, above).

Even the sympathizer Teiresias describes Dionysus' invention of wine abstractly as "the liquid drink of the grape" (βότρυος ὑγρὸν πῶμα, 279), whereas to the Stranger Dionysus is the god "who makes the grape-clustering vine *grow* [*phyei*] for mortals" (651). Mortals, says Teiresias, "fill themselves with the flowing of the grape" (*ampelou*

[37] Rudberg 42 speaks of Euripides' creation of a "psychological landscape" that favors the recognition or surfacing of repressed or hidden needs, a landscape from which the soul "gains joy or strength, often also a landscape which the soul believes it recognizes again—from childhood, from important hours of life, perhaps also from pre-existence."

rhoē, 281) to ease their minds of cares, but for Dionysus these liquid movements of the earth are not always adapted to the needs of civilized men: we may recall the miracles of liquids gushing from the earth for the maenads on Cithaeron, the streams of the fugitive deer in the third stasimon (873ff.), or the mountain torrents near Pentheus' place of death (1051f.).

The "hybristic narthexes" of the parode (νάρθηκας ὑβριστάς, 113) evoke that luxuriant exuberance of unchecked vegetation that overwhelms man's attempt at control.[38] There is a hint of danger in the wild vegetation of the parode (cf. 109f.) or on Cithaeron (684f.) that develops into concrete reality in the setting of Pentheus' dismemberment (cf. 1061, 1064, 1098, 1104). Here the tall firs, oaks, and deep shade mark the invincible otherness of nature. The body is "no easy object of search" because it is "in the wood's deep foliage" (ὕλης ἐν βαθυξύλῳ φόβῃ, 1138).

Even as a would-be follower of Dionysus, Pentheus is instinctively a destroyer of nature. Led out as a pseudo-maenad, he would overturn the mountain or obliterate the haunts of Pan and the Nymphs (948-52). Earlier, too, he colors the "deserted places" (*erēmiai*) of the maenads' rites with his own lewd imaginings (218-25, cf. 688). Whereas the maenad Chorus see those "deserted places" as a green world of joyful retreat, a refuge from man's aggression against creatures of the wild (873-76), Pentheus can find there only the death that comes from unleashing their destructive potential (cf. the "deserted places," *erēmiai*, in 841 and 1177).

Here the now aroused maenads "leap maddened by the god's breath" (1094). This "leaping" (*pēdan*, 1094) is no longer the frisking of the earlier maenad Chorus (cf. 167, 873) or the god's ecstatic "leaping" on Delphi's twin peaks (307) or the gush of refreshing water from the earth (705). At the end the word loses its literal meaning almost entirely and becomes the metaphorical leaping of Agave's heart in dread as Cadmus calls her back from Dionysiac madness to sanity: ὡς τὸ μέλλον καρδία πήδημ' ἔχει, "How my heart has a leaping for what is to come" (1288). The free, ecstatic movement of limbs joyfully in

---

[38] For the association of *hybris* with the unchecked growth of nature, vegetation out of human control, see the important article of Ann Michelini, "Hybris and Plants," *HSCP* 82 (1978) 35-44, esp. 39, 43f.; also Grube, *Drama* 402, n. 2; WI 34f.; Dyer 19.

air and sunshine now becomes something inward, anxious, constricted.[39] The maenadic rite that Pentheus would "secretly" share only closes him more darkly in that repressed, interior world that he opens to the god at the price of his own destruction (cf. 953-58).

· X ·

The sympathetic responsiveness between man and nature is a recurrent feature of the magic of the Dionysiac *thiasos*: "All the land will dance whenever Bromios leads the sacred bands" (114f.); "All the mountain and the beasts joined in the bacchic revel" (726f.); "The air became silent, in silence the wooded vale held its leaves; the beasts' cry you would not hear" (1084f.). This fusion with nature, like the Dionysiac leaping, has a darker face.

As Agave returns to sanity and her Theban identity after the ecstasy on the mountain, Cadmus explains (1295), "You were mad, and all the city was caught up in the Bacchic revel" ($\pi \hat{a} \sigma \acute{a} \ \tau' \ \grave{\epsilon} \xi \epsilon \beta \alpha \kappa \chi \epsilon \acute{v} \vartheta \eta$ $\pi \acute{o} \lambda \iota s$). His verb is no longer a compound of *syn-*, "together with," that has characterized the Dionysiac fusion throughout the play. The maenads are the god's "fellow travelers" (*synemporoi*, 57), "fellow hunters," "fellow revelers," and so on (*synkynagos, synergatēs*, 1146; *synkōmos*, 1172). Dionysus' last word in the prologue is a promise to "join and share with (*sym-metaschēsō*) the maenads in their dances" (63). In the remote mythic past the satyrs "join together" (*synaptein*) their music for the god (133).[40] But at the end Agave's "joining" will be in the sad fellowship of exile (*symphygades*, "fellow exiles," 1382).

[39] This joyful "leaping" of the maenads in 167 and 873 also contrasts with the aggressive "leap" of Pentheus' followers as the Messenger describes how he "lept forth" (*exepedēsa* 729) to seize Agave. Comparing Cadmus' description of Pentheus in 1321 as protecting him from whoever "troubled [his] heart" (*tis sēn tarassei kardian*, 1321) with Agave's "leaping" of the heart in 1288, one wonders if the contrast is another reminder of the cruel destruction of the reciprocity between parent and child, that between quasi-father and quasi-son in 1321 setting off the violation of that reciprocity between son and mother in 1288.

[40] Note also $\sigma \acute{v} \nu o \chi \alpha$, 161, of the Phrygian music that "joins with" the worshipers on the mountain. When a "joining together" occurs for Pentheus on that mountain, it has the associations of ominous and vengeful constriction, as in the "joining shade" of $\sigma v \sigma \kappa \iota \acute{a} \zeta o \nu$ in the locale of his death, 1052.

Cadmus and Teiresias have some inkling of the "joining with" demanded by the Dionysiac cult, as indicated in their *syn*-compounds at 197 and 324. Pentheus' threat to enslave the maenads, whom he calls the Stranger's "coworkers in evil" (*kakōn synergoi*, 512), exemplifies the contrast between his subordinating authority and the god's "togetherness."[41] When his followers would "come together" (*synelthein*) to gain his favor by suppressing the maenads, the result is only "a strife of words in common" (κοινῶν λόγων ἔριν, 714f.). How different is the "common mouth" (*athroon stoma*) with which the maenads shout out the name of their god, bringing animate and inanimate nature together in the revel (726f.).

The Stranger lures Pentheus into the wild with the promise of seeing the maenads "sitting together" (*syn-kathēmenai*) on the mountain (811). When Pentheus, a few lines later, envisages himself as "sitting in silence beneath the firs," the *syn-* is dropped (*kathēmenos*, 816), a change faithful both to his personality and to his actual fate when he is the isolated victim, all alone (*monos*, 962f.). In the striking phrase of the parode, ϑιασεύεται ψυχάν, (75), the individual "mingles his spirit with the sacred band" (Kirk) or feels "an inward unity with the *thiasos* and through it with the god" (Dodds).[42] But the civic frame of Pentheus, with its hierarchies of inferior and superior, can bring together individual and collectivity only in a relation of fear, the subordination and self-effacement of the individual in the city-directed violence of the soldiery (780ff.).

Pentheus is always alone, always isolated.[43] When he does break through to fusion with others, it is in a grim parody of the Dionysiac ecstasy, where he is both participant and maenad, the bacchant and the hostile spy from outside. His aloneness as king fuses with his

[41] Note too the difference between Pentheus' *di-empolan* here in 512 of selling the maenads "apart" into slavery to break up their *thiasos* and their union as *syn-emporoi* of the god in 57, a word that could also have commercial associations.

[42] See also Roux 1.70f.; Harrison, *Themis* 48; Festugière (1956) 81-86, who stresses the spiritual, mystical side of Euripides reflected in this passage and its affinity with figures like Theonoe in the *Helen* or passages like frags. 897 N or 388 N.

[43] Note, too, the effect of the word-order of 59-61 in isolating Pentheus: Dionysus will go to rejoin his maenad bands in order "that the city of Cadmus may behold"; but "Pentheus" in the genitive case and separated from its noun, *dōmata*, is left hanging as if in an exposed position between the dancing maenads and the city (60-61): βασίλειά τ' ἀμφὶ δώματ' ἐλθοῦσαι τάδε / κτυπεῖτε Πενθέως, ὡς ὁρᾷ Κάδμου πόλις.

apartness as the victim. Consecrated to the god, he is set off from all others as *sacer* (961-63). His deluded image of himself as united with his mother in a kind of infantile posture (969f.) turns into the most extreme alienation: the woman who bore him destroys him as a total stranger (1115ff.). In that perverted sacrifice the ritual isolation of the victim comes together with the psychological isolation of this now loneliest of men.

Like the compounds of *syn-*, the word *pas*, "all," contrasts Pentheus' isolation with the universalism of the god. Dionysus' worship embraces "all" of Asia (14), "all the earth" (114), "all the mountain" (726). It reaches "all the race of women" at Thebes (35f.), "every barbarian" (482), and finally, vindictively, "all the city" (1295).

The pattern is very different when the god meets not welcome and union but resistance. Opposition results in the collapse of "all the palace," συντεθράνωται δ' ἄπαν (633, where the *syn-* compound has a destructive force), and "all the city" (1295). Pentheus uses the adjective once, as he musters "all" his infantry in aggressive military resistance to the god (781). The result is a fusion of all with all in the violence that Dionysus can also release. At his death "it was *all* a confused cry," ἦν δὲ πᾶσ' ὁμοῦ βοή (1131), a line of powerfully understated horror. "*Every* [maenad] has blood on her hands" as she throws around Pentheus' torn flesh (πᾶσα δ' ᾑμασωμένη / χεῖρας διεσφαίριζε σάρκα Πενθέως, 1135f.) that at the end will have to be "all closed up" for burial (*pan*, 1300).

· XI ·

In the spatial axis that runs from the controlled interior of the city to the joyful but potentially dangerous realm of Dionysus, mountains play an especially important role. The first detail of Dionysus' vengeance includes the movement of the women from their houses (*domoi*) to the mountain (*oros*), where they now "have their *oikos*" (*oikousi*, 32f.). Later in the prologue he threatens dire consequences if Thebes "in anger seeks to drive the bacchants from the mountain" (*ex orous*, 50-52). This first tentative sounding of the inversion of man and beast in "driving" (*agein*) brings together "city," "anger," "arms" (*hopla*) in a constellation of motifs that defines Pentheus' precarious civic order. It recurs when the king himself is about to leave the city for the mountains and the Stranger advises not taking up "arms" but keeping "calm" (*hēsychazein*, 789f.; cf. 670ff.), for Dionysus will not permit him to drive the bacchants "from the mountain" (*orōn apo*, 791).

That attempt to remove the bacchants "from the mountain" proves increasingly futile against the rising impulse "to the mountain" (*es oros*). This phrase echoes as ritual cry throughout the play, until it finally engulfs Pentheus himself.[44] The first news of the maenads' triumph comes "from the mountain" (658), to be answered, after Pentheus' death, by Cadmus' bleak return "to the mountain" to gather the torn remains (1225)—a procession "to the mountain" different from his joyful journey earlier (191; cf. also 1224 with 186, 193).

If the mountains contain the sweet but fearful joy of the *ōmophagia* (135-40) and the awful *sparagmos*, they also show the miraculous transformations of wild nature into a beneficent Golden-Age landscape (cf. 141f., 704-11).[45] The mountain glades (*orgades*) may be the site of the dreadful punishment of Actaeon, whose fate parallels Pentheus' (370), but they are also the place of release and liberation from Pentheus' dark prison. The maenads are "released to glades," *lelymenai pros orgadas* (445), where *orgades* is perhaps chosen for its resemblances to the *orgia* ("orgiastic rites") of the god (cf. 470f., 476, 482). The unleashing of Dionysus' dangerous power follows a progression from the lowland plain and river valley of the third stasimon (873-76) to the upland hills of the fourth ("mountain-running Cadmean women," *oreidromoi*, 985; cf. 977, 986) to the craggy setting of the *sparagmos* (1048ff., 1093ff.).

Yet as the parode implies (72-77), there may be more calm in the mountains, for all its rushing maenads, than in the city with its pent up, seething emotions of the king. Mountains are both the location and the symbol for the mysterious otherness of the god, the place

---

[44] For the repeated "on the mountains" or "to the mountains" see 76, 116, 135, 140, 165, 191, 977, 986, 1225, etc.; Arthur (1972) 166f. Such repetition may also be intended to recall the ecstasy-producing or self-hypnotic techniques of the chanted repetition of a single word or phrase common in shamanistic practices such as Euripides may have observed in Macedonia.

[45] Diller (1960) 103f. well describes the setting of the Dionysiac spell as permitting the "Verwandlung der Natur durch das dionysische Wunder. Symbolik und Realität sind in der Szenerie untrennbar verschmolzen" (104). See also De Romilly 364f.

where the god has unchecked power to bring ecstasy or madness, happiness or pain.

Like other remote settings in Euripides, mountains are a refuge from the conflicts and complexities of life.[46] They are also a place where man confronts the ultimate reality of self, his most hidden desires and impulses. Hence they become instinct with the power of the god: the mountain itself "joins in the bacchic revel" (726) and partakes of the god's ecstasy (cf. 791, "the mountains that cry *euoi*," εὐίων ὀρῶν). The woods of these mountains seem to answer the god's command, keeping their leaves from rustling when he calls for silence (1084f.). In this mysterious affinity with the god's power they are associated not only with the rite of *oreibasia*, the women's mid-winter revel on Parnassus and other mountains,[47] but also with the remote and awesome Great Mother of the Gods, Rhea or Cybele (59f., 79ff., 125ff.), whose intimate fusion with nature's energies, cosmic fertility, and power of renewal seems to have fascinated Euripides.[48]

Pentheus can see in this landscape only the darkness of his own repressed impulses. To him the "shade" of the mountain's "thickets" (*skia*, 458f.; *daskia orea*, 218f.) only conceals illicit sex. In maddening him, Dionysus releases his desire to trap the maenads in their thickets as if in the beds and nets of love (957f.). For the maenads those forests are a place of joyful freedom and "happy toils" (874-76, 1051-53); to Pentheus the enclosing shade becomes a trap (1051f.). The same polarity holds true for other aspects of the woods: forest glades, branches, rocks.[49]

[46] For mountains and the theme of "escape" see Barlow 38ff., esp. 40-41; Helen Padel, " 'Imagery of the Elsewhere': Two Choral Odes of Euripides," *CQ* 34 (1974) 227ff., esp. 234.

[47] See Paus. 10.32.5; Plutarch *De Primo Frigido* 18.953d; in general Dodds, "Maenadism," 156; Henrichs (1978).

[48] Compare the landscape of *Helen* 1301-69 and *Cretans*, frag. 472 N; see Dodds, "Maenadism," 170f. We may recall too the reverence for mountains in ancient Sumeria and Minoan Crete, as well as such Greek holy mountains as Parnassus, Helicon, Cyllene, Lycaeon, Atabyrion, Aetna, etc.

[49] We may note the following contrasts between Pentheus and the maenads in their relation to landscape: 873ff., 1084 vs. 1093ff., 1137 (glades); 110, 685 vs. 1098, 1103, 1221 (branches and foliage); 677, 703 vs. 751, 982, 1045, 1093-98 (rocks and crags). The *antipyrgos petra* of 1097, the "rock towering opposite" or "rock like a tower," condenses this contrast into a single image and brings with it the transmutation of Pentheus' fortified boundaries against the wild into the destructiveness of the wild against him; on 1097 and the contrast of city and wild see Scott 341ff.

What is a setting of purest beauty of unspoiled nature in the one case becomes a landscape of horrible carnage in the other. Dionysus' "green firs and roofless rocks" where his maenads sit in the prologue (χλωραῖς ὑπ' ἐλάταις ἀνορόφοις ἧνται πέτραις, 38) have a very different aspect at the *sparagmos*. Likewise the copses and thickets of the maenads' repose take on a grisly aspect in our last view of the maenads after Pentheus' death (1227-29): "I saw Autonoe . . . and Ino still together *in the thickets*, gadfly-driven in frenzy, miserable" (ἔτ' ἀμφὶ δρυμοὺς οἰστροπλῆγας ἀθλίας, 1229; cf. 32). The thyrsus or narthex, similarly, can be a growing plant, like the god's vine or ivy, expressive of his contact with nature's free-flowing life (141-51, 702-11), or a weapon (*kissinon belos*, "ivy missile," 25), capable of "outrage" (*narthēkes hybristai*, 114), a match for the warrior's spear (761-64), a thing of death, associated with Hades (1157).[50]

• XII •

The central section of the play, the long account of the maenads' revel on Cithaeron, makes these contrasting values of city and mountain especially vivid. The Messenger, as Dionysus says, arrives "from the mountain" (*ex orous parestin*, 658). He addresses Pentheus in terms of his civic authority, "You who rule this Theban earth" (660); but his next words describe the haunting beauty of Cithaeron, "where glittering falls of the brilliant snow never fail" (ἵν' οὔποτε / λευκῆς χιόνος ἀνεῖσαν εὐαγεῖς βολαί, 661f.). The lines are more than just a purple patch that transports us "into the domain of pure literature," as a recent commentator suggests.[51] Rather, they evoke the mystery and remoteness of a purified nature. The brightness of this snow, emphasized by two adjectives, *leukos* and *enargēs*, contrasts with the dark enclosures of the preceding scene (cf. "dark enclosures," *skoteinai horkanai*, 611). It suggests also the radiance of life and light connected with the god (cf. *ganos* in 261, 383). The glittering snowfalls amid which the maenads now range freely provide another foil

[50] Reading νάρθηκά τε πιστὸν "Αιδα in 1157 with P. Ant. 1.73. Kirk translates "Hades' pledge in its thyrsus shape." Similarly Verdenius (1962) 361.

[51] Roux ad loc. (2.454). On the poetic values of snow see Rosenmeyer (above, n. 35) 209-225.

to Pentheus' attempt to constrain. But whiteness in this setting has connotations of purity that soon contrast with the blood, both human and animal, that will stain these woods.[52]

The peaceful rhythms of bucolic life introduce the details of the maenads' activities (677-80):

ἀγελαῖα μὲν βοσκήματ᾽ ἄρτι πρὸς λέπας
μόσχων ὑπεξήκριζον, ἡνίχ᾽ ἥλιος
ἀκτῖνας ἐξίησι θερμαίνων χθόνα.
ὁρῶ δὲ θιάσους τρεῖς γυναικείων χορῶν. . . .

Pasturing herds of young cattle were just climbing toward the steep heights, as the sun was shooting forth its rays to warm the earth. Then I saw three sacred bands of women's dances. . . .

Against the peaceful and productive regularity of pastoral life the mention of dances must irk Pentheus (cf. 509-11). To the audience it recalls the god's predictions in the prologue (choreusas, 21; choroi, 63), now fulfilled. The combination of sun and snow may also remind us of Dionysus' connection with the seasonal rhythms, also prominent in his prologue (14f.). Set within a framework of nature's processes, the scene intimates a cooperation between man and nature remote from Pentheus' dichotomizing. But the words "shoot forth," "herds," and "calves," innocent here, have ominous meanings later (cf. 762, 1022, 1185).

This place of shepherds is a liminal area, at the frontier between civilization and wild nature. It is the appropriate place for the uncanny to enter human life, with its terrible reversals from ecstasy to savagery. With this bucolic calm as a prelude to horror we may compare the Corinthian's account of his herding on Cithaeron in the *Oedipus Tyrannus*, the introduction to the tale that reveals the truth of Oedipus' incestuous birth (*OT* 1133-39).

In contrast to the miraculous spouting forth of milk, honey, and wine from the maenads' wands (704-11) stands the prosaic argument of Pentheus' sympathizer, a man of the town in every sense, "one who wanders around the town well practised in speeches" (716). Divine "wonders" (*thaumata*, 667, 693, 716) contrast with everyday quarrel, enclosed city wanderings with ecstatic freedom on the moun-

[52] Cf. *Ba.* 741f., 1135f., 1163f., 1221.

tain (cf. *planēs* in 717 and *planētēs*, of "Dionysus the wanderer," in 148). This townsman seeks to curry favor with his "lord" (*anax*, 721) in the city. His address to his rustic companions seems to show irony and scorn for their mountain habitat (718-21): "Dwellers in the mountains' awesome valleys [*semnas plakas / oreōn*], shall we hunt Agave, Pentheus' mother, from her bacchic revels and lay up grateful thanks from our lord?"[53] The mountain folk, who might have known better, accept the suggestion, conceal themselves in ambush in the thickets (*thamnōn . . . phobais*, 722), foreshadowing the disastrous procedure of Pentheus himself later, and predictably detonate the concealed violence that lies just on the other side of this secluded tranquillity. From this remote setting of "Cithaeron's crag" (*Kithai-rōnos lepas*, 751; cf. 677) the sheltered fields near "Asopos' streams" are exposed to violent attack. The same collocation in reverse—"Aso-pos' streams" and "Cithaeron's crag"—recurs as Pentheus, in the Second Messenger's speech, leaves the shelter of the city to expose himself to the violence that awaits him on the mountain ('Ασωποῦ ῥοάς / λέπας Κιθαιρώνειον, 1044f.).

As an embodiment of the mysterious otherness and allure of Dionysus, the mountain comes to hold a special fascination for Pentheus. At the crucial moment of his conversion this attraction of opposites leads him to his doom. His response to the question, "Do you wish to see them sitting together *on the mountains*" (811), gives Dionysus his strange hypnotic power over him. The spatial contrast expands to its psychological dimension as Dionysus follows up his question about the mountains with the sexual language of 813: "Why then have you fallen into great lust [*eros*] for this?"

The mountain, naturally enough, plays a prominent part in Dionysus' revenge. The branch that he uses to shoot his victim into position is compared to "a mountain sprig" (*klōn' oreion*, 1068). It is as "a lion of the mountains," (*oresteros leōn*) that Pentheus appears to Agave, who carries her prey proudly "from the mountains" (*ex oreōn*) to the "halls" of the palace (*melathra*, 1169-71). Cadmus enters from

[53] Dodds, *Bacchae* ad 717 seems to me correct in taking these lines as the "advice of an irreverent *agoraios anēr*," a figure akin to the "town-bred demagogue" whom Euripides elsewhere "portrays with little sympathy." His description of the mountains in 718 needs to be viewed in that light. See also Barlow 76 and Roux ad loc. For a rather more sympathetic view of the speaker see WI 93 with n. 1. See below, Chap. 8, n. 14.

those same mountains, having painfully searched out the dismembered limbs "in Cithaeron's folds" (1219). His tragic reversal from joy to sorrow takes the spatial form of a double journey from house to mountain, first to honor the god in bacchic dances (191), then to collect his grandson's remains. He explicitly calls attention to that double journey (1222-26): "From someone did I hear of my daughters' deeds of daring when I had *already returned* from the maenads to the town within the shelter of its walls [*kat' asty teicheōn esō*, 1223] in the company of aged Teiresias. But now, turning back again to the mountain [*palin kampsas eis oros*, 1225], I fetch my son, killed by the maenads." On the first journey he had suggested traveling on a chariot (*ochoi*), a mark of age and status appropriate to the ex-king but not to the "honor" that this god demands (192f.). The chariot recurs to mark a Dionysiac dissolution of differences as the god foretells his last journey, "driving a chariot of young bulls" to lead barbarian ravagers of Greek cities (1333f.).

The accumulating references to Mt. Cithaeron throughout the play show, in effect, the gradual encroachment of the wild upon the city. At the end of his prologue the god combines the corybantic drummings of Phrygia, soon heard again in the parode, with the dances of the maddened Theban women that he will soon join on Cithaeron (58-63). "Going to Cithaeron's folds, where they are, I shall join and share their dances" (62f.). "Cithaeron's folds" recurs three times: first in the full rage of Pentheus' martial suppression of the maenads (796f.); then when the god's madness deludes him into thinking that he can carry "Cithaeron's folds, maenads and all," on his shoulders (945f.); and finally when Cadmus returns from mountain to palace with the body "found in Cithaeron's folds, torn apart in the *sparagmos*" (1219f.). Cithaeron has also been associated with the parallel death of Actaeon (338), kept in our minds throughout (229, 337, 1227, 1291; cf. 1371). The penultimate reference localizes Pentheus' dismemberment "in the very place where earlier Actaeon's dogs tore him apart" (1291).[54]

---

[54] The first reference to Actaeon came from Pentheus himself as he threatened to "hunt from the mountain Ino and Agave who bore me to Echion, and Actaeon's mother, I mean Autonoe" (228-30). The triad comes back not as women "hunted from the mountain" but as the leaders of an invincible maenad band (681f.) and finally as the murderers of the king (1225-28). Agave is conspicuous by her absence from 1228, for at this moment she is carrying Pentheus' head to the palace. Cadmus' description in 1228 closely echoes Pentheus' words in 229:

The mountain changes from snowy and radiant purity to pollution (662, 1384), but it also has another side.[55] In the first stasimon Mt. Olympus is the seat of the Muses and the Graces (410-15). The second stasimon expands that vision to include Mt. Nysa, sacred to Dionysus and "nurturer of animals" (*thērotrophos*, 556f.), the Corycian cave high on the slopes of Parnassus, and Olympus "where Orpheus playing on the lyre drew together the trees by his music arts, drew together the beasts of the wild" (560ff.).[56] We hear again of Pieria (565; cf. 410f.), called "blessed" (*makar*), the epithet of the Dionysiac worshiper in the parode (73). Dionysus himself "reveres" Pieria and will bring his bacchants there to dance (565-68).

• XIII •

On the spatial axis of the conflicts between Dionysus and Pentheus the dichotomy of Greek and barbarian parallels that of city and mountain. Dionysus is emphatic about his and his followers' barbarian origins (13-22). Thebes is the first Hellenic city that they have reached in their journey from Asia (21f.). At the end of the prologue Pentheus' city (61) is framed by two elaborate descriptions of the god's Lydian home: "Tmolus, defence of Lydia" comes just before (55); "from Asia's land, departing sacred Tmolus" in the parode comes just after (65f.). The details of Phrygian Rhea's drums and timbrels both at the end of the prologue and in the parode (58f., 120ff.) reinforce this framing effect.[57]

Ἰνώ τ' Ἀγαύην θ', ἥ μ' ἔτικτ' Ἐχίονι (229)
καὶ τὴν μὲν Ἀκτέων' Ἀρισταίῳ ποτε
τεκοῦσαν εἶδον Αὐτονόην Ἰνώ θ' ἅμα (1227-28).

The two mothers are both described with the more vivid and (in the context) more pathetic term, "she who gave birth" (*tiktein*). Some editors delete 229-30, but with no good reason, and the lines are successfully defended by Dodds, *Bacchae* and Roux ad loc. and by Verdenius (1962) 342. Kirk omits them without comment.

[55] To the references to Cithaeron cited in the text, we may add 661, 1045, 1142, 1176. Note the emphasis on the pollution of Cithaeron by the strong word *miaros* in 1384.

[56] For Orpheus see above, Chap. 3, section 6.

[57] On the Greek-barbarian contrast see WI 31. One need hardly stress how familiar a *topos* that contrast is in the fifth century. Note the recurrence of the Asian place-names in 18-24, 55-66, 85-88.

Pentheus' resistance to Dionysus takes the form of championing Hellenic discipline against Asian sensuality, reason against fanaticism, logic against thaumaturgy and magical spells. He himself poses the issue in these terms in his initial denunciation of the "magician and charlatan from the Lydian land," perfumed, soft, and seductive to women (232-41). His face-to-face confrontation with the Stranger repeats many of these terms (451ff.), including the contrast of "flowery Tmolus" with the Hellenic feeling for the polis as enclosure and limit (462-65).

Teiresias defends Dionysus as "great in Hellas" (309); but Pentheus, mustering military forces to resist, regards the maenads' victory as "a great insult to Greeks," a verbal echo of Teiresias' phrase (ψόγος ἐς Ἕλληνας μέγας, 779; μέγαν τ' ἀν' Ἑλλάδα, 309). Cadmus' entrance had stressed the migration of the civilizing hero from Asia to Greece (170-72); but the god's devastating triumph undoes that journey (1330-36, 1354-56; cf. 1024-26).[58] These prophecies at the end give the action a larger historical and geographical dimension. Not only is the house of Cadmus involved, but the whole history of a civilization, his whole life's work as a culture-hero. Was Euripides, composing this play at the northern limits of Greece, particularly aware of the conflicting points of view between Greek and non-Greek and particularly sensitive to the potential of introducing this ambiguous god to explore that division?

Dionysus' presence in Thebes certainly has the effect of calling that division into question. By infecting the ladies of Thebes' royal house with that Asiatic frenzy and then extending it to the elders and eventually to the ruler of Thebes, he breaks down the exclusive, dichotomous view of the world so deeply rooted in Pentheus. Geographical dichotomizing is only one form of the narrow compartmentalization of thought and values that characterizes the ruling establishment of Thebes. As elsewhere in his work—one thinks of Medea, Taurian Iphigeneia, Helen—Euripides reaches across the localism of the Greek city and at least suggests the possibility that a broader view might reveal traditional Hellenic values as less absolute than they seem.[59]

Over against the particular laws and institutions of a single city-

---

[58] Cf. WI 147.

[59] Compare the Taurian King Thoas' reaction to his Greek prisoner's matricide, "By Apollo, not even among barbarians would one venture such a thing," IT 1174. On Euripides' cosmopolitanism see Nestle, Euripides 361-68, esp. 367f. For late fifth-century cosmopolitanism see Guthrie, Hist. of Greek Philos. 3. 160-63.

state Dionysus champions a universal law of nature (cf. 890-96), or at least a perspective in which the different institutions of different cities can be appreciated and respected.[60] When Pentheus scornfully remarks that "barbarians" are "much inferior to Hellenes in intelligence," Dionysus calmly replies that at least in their acceptance of Dionysus they are better, "but they have different customs" (*hoi nomoi de diaphoroi*, 484).

The blurring of distinctions between Greek and barbarian in Dionysus has a visual counterpart in an important detail of the stage action: the Chorus that sings the odes is not the familiar citizen-band of most plays, but a group of barbarian women, ecstatic Asian maenads. The citizen Chorus, the women of Thebes, are described, but never seen in action on the stage.[61] This doubling of the Chorus, the seen by the unseen, the barbarian by the Greek, is especially strong at the end. When the king is dead and a grimly ambiguous "revel" (*kōmos*) and "banquet" (*thoina*, 1184) celebrate the triumph of the orgiastic, Lydian god, the Chorus of Asiatic maenads addresses the Theban women as "Cadmean bacchants," and the leader of the Theban citizen Chorus, Agave, replies, "Asian bacchants" (*bakchai Kadmeiai*, 1160; *Asiades bakchai*, 1168). Here, in these responsive addresses, the two groups of maenads seem almost to blend into one another, the women of Thebes who have a legitimate place within the polis and the women of Asia who stand outside by virtue both of their origin and their cult. As Pentheus' restrictive view of the polis order collapses, the Theban bacchants prove even more destructive and more inimical to civilization than their Asiatic counterparts.

In attempting to expel the bacchic element from Thebes, Pentheus turns the Theban women into "enemies" (*polemioi*, 752) who ravage the city's outlying fields as if they were foreign territory. In Pentheus' hierarchical view women, beasts, barbarians, maenads are analogous: all require repression by the discipline of the polis. But in Dionysus'

---

[60] On the text and interpretation of the much vexed lines 890-96 see Dodds, *Bacchae* and Roux ad loc.; Verdenius (1962) 355f.; Willink 231f.; Conacher 77; Gold 13; R. D. Dawe, "A Note on Euripides Bacchae 896," *RhM* 123 (1980) 223f., who gives a brief critique of earlier interpretations and suggests emendation.

[61] In 1381 Agave addresses "followers" (*pompoi*), but her sisters (and the other women of Thebes?) are elsewhere (1382). When Agave enters at 1168, the maenad Chorus addresses her in the singular. Her first-person plural forms in 1204 and 1209f. need not imply a Theban chorus: she uses the singular in 1215.

confusion of basic distinctions, the maenads are both women and beasts, both on the mountain and in the polis, both citizens and enemies, both insiders and aliens. The god's fusion of imagination and reality turns the figurative category horribly into the literal. The Theban women, as wild females, do in fact hunt down Pentheus and rend him as one beast does another. They become actual, not metaphorical, "enemies" of the state, defeating its armed forces, killing its king, and causing the exile of the founder and his family.

As the Theban women change their status from civilized ladies to maenads on Cithaeron, they also change their dress. They let their hair down, free and loose (695), like the Stranger's (240f., 455f.), unbind their Theban dress with its belts or brooches (696f.) and put on in its place the fawnskins, which they tie with living snakes that lick their cheeks (696-98). Their dress not only marks the shift from city to wild, Greek to barbarian, but also, in the manner characteristic of Dionysus, blurs the distinction between animate and inanimate (cf. 726f.), living creature and artifact, nature and culture. The word that describes their "girding on" of the snakes stresses this bizarrely animate form of "belt" (κατεζώσαντο, 698). The element of dress, one of the distinguishing marks between man and animal, as (in a different way) between Greek and barbarian, loses its distinctive meaning in the code of signifiers that makes up the value-system of the society.

In Pentheus' case this confusion is more drastic still, for in putting on the maenads' "female garb" (827) he moves from male to female (cf. 822). By putting on the "robe of Eastern linen" (byssinoi peploi, 821) he becomes barbarian instead of Greek. In wearing the "fawn's dappled skin" (835, echoing 697), he confirms his place in the wild rather than the city, moving toward beasts rather than men. All three of these shifts, from male to female, Greek to barbarian, man to beast, in turn are parallel to and causally derived from the spatial shift from polis to mountain, from the realm of the city to the realm of Dionysus.

For Pentheus Thebes is a bastion of Hellenic discipline against Asian riot. His mission as its king is to "put down / all Asiatic vague immensities."[62] But Dionysus' presence evokes another aspect of Thebes, revealing it as a meeting-place of civilizations, a place where Greek and barbarian, both literal and figurative, cross and mingle. The first

[62] W. B. Yeats, "The Statues," in Collected Poems (New York 1956) 322.

ode of the play, although stressing the Lydian and Phrygian origins of the god, still suggests that Thebes, "nurse of Semele" (105), is the point of transition between Asia and Hellas in the god's passage (cf. 83-88). Through the links between Dictaean Zeus in Crete and the rites of the Phrygian Cybele, already established in the prologue (58f., 120-34), the ode also evokes a remote, mythical past, a time of creative origins. We are back *in illo tempore*, when the god, present among men, transcends the division between Greek and barbarian.

The next ode, the first stasimon (402ff.), describes other islands at the crossroads of Greece and Asia, Cyprus, island of Aphrodite, and Paphos (or Pharos), made fertile by the "hundred mouths of a barbarian river" (406-408), which seems vaguely identified with the Nile.[63] In the second stasimon Dionysus' realm embraces the three holy mountains of Nysa (usually located in Asia), Parnassus, and Olympus (556-64) and then extends further north across the Axios and Lydias rivers to barbarian Thrace (568-75). The Lydias river is probably chosen with a view to Dionysus' Lydian origins and marks another linking of Asia and Europe. As commentators suggest, these lines may be a compliment to the northern kingdom of Archelaus where Euripides wrote the play.[64]

Dionysus' account of his travels in the prologue (13-22) includes not only parched desert and snowy wastes—that is, the scarcely habitable parts of Asia at the fringes of the civilized world (14f.)—but also "all Asia," with its "populous lovely-towered cities by the salty sea which the mingled [population of] Greeks and barbarians have in common" (17-19):

> Ἀσίαν τε πᾶσαν, ἣ παρ' ἁλμυρὰν ἅλα
> κεῖται μιγάσιν Ἕλλησι βαρβάροις θ' ὁμοῦ
> πλήρεις ἔχουσα καλλιπυργώτους πόλεις.

The spatial features of the Hellenic city founded by Cadmus and defended by Pentheus are not restricted solely to Greeks. The barbar-

---

[63] Dodds, *Bacchae* ad 406-408 vigorously defends the MSS reading *Paphon*; also Verdenius (1962) 346. Roux ad loc. hesitantly concludes in favor of Reiske's emendation, *Pharon*. Willink 222f. and Musurillo 303 with n. 8 prefer *Pharon*; that reading would perhaps also join the east-west contrast of Greece and Asia with a north-south contrast of Greece and Egypt, but the latter is implicit in any case in the references to the Nile. Probably we should not insist too much on the literal exactness of Euripides' geography in a lyrical ode of this nature.

[64] Dodds, *Bacchae* ad 568-75; McDonald 256.

ians, like the Greeks, inhabit towns with lovely towers (cf. 19 and 1202), walls (cf. 15 and 653), fortifications and citadels like Cadmus' Thebes (cf. 55, 58, 462f. with 171f.). As lines 171-72 remind us, Thebes owes its origin to a barbarian migration from Asia (also 1024f.). Just as Dionysus paradoxically has attributes of civilized technology, so even in the barbarian Asia from which he leads his ecstatic, mountain-loving worshipers he appreciates civic structure and political order.

Cadmus' exile at the end of the play involves a future war between the two peoples (cf. 1334, 1354-56). The "mingled" (population) of Greek and barbarian in the prologue (18) becomes "a mingled barbarian horde" led on an incursion "into Greece" in the exodos (1356). The verbal echo is significant:

18: κεῖται μιγάσιν Ἕλλησι βαρβάροις θ᾽ ὁμοῦ

1356: ἐς Ἑλλάδ᾽ ἀγαγεῖν μιγάδα βάρβαρον στρατόν.

Far from being an anachronistic error,[65] Euripides' representation of Asia Minor as already colonized by Greeks evokes the quasi-mythical time of Dionysus' remoter origins when Greeks and barbarians are not clearly differentiated. The first Greek resistance to Dionysus at Thebes marks the advent of an aggressive relation between the two races. The catastrophe there brings an end to the Golden-Age coexistence that was possible in Asia when the god was unopposed and triumphant. Cadmus' new incursion into Greece will not repeat the benign character of his earlier migration. Here too Thebes functions as a symbolic meeting-place of civilizations and cultural crisis. In its fate is inscribed a movement from myth to history, from a vague and remote age of peace to a present reality characterized by hostility and war.

Addressing Cadmus, Teiresias mentioned the founding of Thebes' towers (ἐπύργωσ᾽ ἄστυ Θηβαίων τόδε, 172). Pentheus, establishing the Stranger's origins, identifies Sardis by the circuit of Mount Tmolus that surrounds it (ὃς τὸ Σάρδεων ἄστυ περιβάλλει κύκλῳ, "Tmolus, which encloses the town of Sardis in a circle," 463). Later he falls back on the closed and towered circuit-wall of Thebes (653). Only Dionysus in the prologue and Agave in her Dionysiac madness near the end acknowledge the *beauty* of cities' towered appearance. He speaks of "lovely-towered cities" (*kallipyrgōtoi poleis*, 19), she of

[65] Dodds, *Bacchae* ad 17.

"the lovely-towered citadel of Theban land" (*kallipyrgon asty*, 1202). The Tmolus that Pentheus knows only as a defending circuit (463) for Dionysus not only fortifies (cf. *eryma*, 55), but also possesses sacredness, gold-flowing streams, and flowers (65, 154, 462).

Is Pentheus then punished, in part, for cutting himself off from the beauty around him, for erecting the barriers that impose aesthetic as well as moral and emotional blinders on his vision of the world? This aspect of Dionysus' meaning concerns us too. The damaging, denying, or sullying of any life-supporting element is not without retribution (*dikē*). In the limited area of Dionysus' revenge and justice, we also contemplate the larger implications of polluting the "bright joy" of life's potential purity and self-renewing energy in our environment and in ourselves.

5

The Vertical Axis:
Earth, Air, Water, Fire

If one strains his view towards far-off things,
he is too small to reach the bronze-floored
seat of the gods.
                                        Pindar

Shedding white rings of tumult, building high
Over the chained bay waters Liberty. . . .
                                        Hart Crane

• I •

In a celebrated fragment Heraclitus identifies Hades and Dionysus
as "the same" (22 B15 DK). Dionysus' mother, Semele, is probably
an old Anatolian earth-goddess.[1] The parode connects him with Rhea-
Cybele, whose maternal caverns sheltered the infant Zeus on Crete
(120-34).[2] Teiresias pairs him with Demeter-Ge, goddess of the fertile
earth (274ff.), and like her he is a god of the vegetative life that springs
from the earth.[3] In Pindar he shares with Demeter a role as one of
the main divinities of Thebes (*Isthmian* 7.3), and in our play he can
call on the subterranean divinity of earthquake in his behalf (585).

As the child of Olympian Zeus, however, he has his birth from

[1] See Otto 66-73 with the references in notes 23-27, p. 215; Farnell, *Cults* 5.95f.
with the note; Nilsson, *GGR* 568; Guthrie, *Greeks and Their Gods* 154; Dodds,
Bacchae ad 6-12.

[2] For the close identification of Rhea-Cybele and Ge or Gaia in this period cf.
Soph. *Phil.* 391ff.; U. von Wilamowitz-Moellendorff, *Der Glaube der Hellenen* (1931-
32, reprint Darmstadt 1959) 1.198ff.

[3] E.g. 11f., 382f., 534f., 651; cf. above, Chap. 1, n. 5.

the celestial fire and thunder (3-9), signs also of his victorious power (597-99, 1082-83). Yet this token of his status as an Olympian god also means death and an earthly tomb for the mortal woman who gave him birth (1-9, 523-29, 597-99).[4] The "ever-living flame" that legitimizes the god's place in Thebes (8) foreshadows the fiery destruction later of the city's symbolical center (590-603). Cadmus, founder of the city, wins the god's praise for erecting that shrine (10-11), but is censured for the rationalizing cleverness (*sophismata*) that would too easily stabilize the precarious union of mortality and divinity, earth and sky, that the shrine embodies (26-31). Pentheus dissolves that precarious combination in a different way: to him Dionysus' birth is a conflagration only, and the god is the one "set ablaze [*ekpyroutai*] by the thunderous flames with his mother" (243-44). By contrast, both the god and his worshipers associate that celestial fire with "birth" or "life" (3, 8, 88-95).[5]

Dionysus' association with snakes expresses his proximity to the ever-renewed energies of the earth (cf. 101, 698, 704-11, 766-68, 1019). But the serpentine associations that might have linked him to the origins of Thebes also show his ambiguous relation to the city in which he claims a place. His vengeance on the city reverses the old founding act of killing the serpent and sowing its teeth in the ground (1025-27; cf. 1331 and 1358).

Insofar as Dionysus is Olympian, he is above the changeful processes of earth. Insofar as he is a god of vegetation, he participates in them. What coexists in the mysteries of the god is fraught with danger for men. As in the *Phoenissae*, Thebes holds a precarious balance between the nurturing powers of earth and the potential destructiveness of its own chthonic origins.

The choral odes focus these tensions in the mythical background on moral conduct and values. In the first stasimon Holiness, "who bears its golden *wing over* the earth," is to witness Pentheus' violence against the god (370-75). The antistrophe stresses the celestial location of "the heaven-dwellers" (*ouranidai*), who "inhabit the aether" and

[4] For the ambiguity of Dionysus' Olympian nature in the play see Sale, *Existentialism* 90f. with note 4, p. 138. In *Hipp.* 559-64 Euripides also touches on the theme of celestial fire as the destructive agent of mortal Semele's death: see Segal (1979) 156f.

[5] Note, too, the pointed contrast between the destructive fire of the prologue and the joyful flame of the parode: *pyros eti zōsan phloga* (8); *pyrsōdē phloga* (146).

see mortal acts from afar (392-94). Gnomic generalizations follow: "Cleverness is not wisdom [*sophia*], nor [is it wisdom] to think thoughts not mortal; life is brief; this being so, whoever pursues great things, would not win what is here at hand" (395-99). These apophthegms fix an absolute distance between earth and heavens, men and gods, and prescribe the limits for human action. This commonplace "wisdom" (*sophia*) recurs in slightly more complex vertical metaphors in the third stasimon, at Pentheus' transition from high to low (877-81 = 897-901):

τί τὸ σοφόν; ἢ τί τὸ κάλλιον
παρὰ θεῶν γέρας ἐν βροτοῖς
ἢ χεῖρ' ὑπὲρ κορυφᾶς
τῶν ἐχθρῶν κρείσσω κατέχειν;
ὅ τι καλὸν φίλον ἀεί.

What is cleverness [wisdom, *to sophon*]? Or what lovelier prize from the gods among mortals than to hold one's hand in superior strength *above* the head of one's enemies? Dear always is what is lovely [noble, admired, *kalon*].

The play circles about the problem of "wisdom," *sophia*, which here takes the form of the precarious height for mortals. "Happy he who has come to be *above* toils," the last strophe says (904f.), calling attention to another of the play's ambiguous key words (*eudaimōn*, "happy," also 911). But the Chorus's exultation in being so raised up confuses our emotions, sympathies, and sense of justice. Pentheus, the object now of their vengeance and their god's chastisement, here becomes an object of pity as he himself is prepared for his own great fall from quasi-Olympian heights to the earth (cf. 974, 1070ff., 1111-12). His madness, soon after, echoes the Chorus's moralizing in distorted form: "Or with my hands shall I pull up (the mountain), putting arm or shoulder beneath its peaks?" (949-50):

μοχλοὺς φέρωμεν; ἢ χεροῖν ἀνασπάσω
κορυφαῖς ὑποβαλὼν ὦμον ἢ βραχίονα; . . .

The Chorus rejoiced in having their "hand . . . *above* the head" (*koryphas*) of their enemies; Pentheus exults in putting his "hand *beneath* the peaks" (*koryphais*) of his. Whose is the greater madness? The question cannot be answered, but the verbal echo casts even more doubt on the moral validity of the Chorus's trite apophthegms about the limits between high and low.[6] The dramatic context renders ambiguous even that most fundamental of all moral principles, the division between earth and heavens. With it crumbles also any clear distinction between order and chaos, just vengeance and cruel affliction, sanity and madness. The king's insane plunge as a hunted maenadvictim from heavens to earth in the next scene enacts that confusion of spatial order as a confusion of moral and emotional order.

• II •

The political implications of that ambiguity center in part on the ambiguous value of autochthony in the play.[7] To be born of the earth marks the unity of the citizens as brothers of a common parent and the long habitation of citizens who have never been expelled from their own land. This positive side of autochthony recommends itself to the fourth-century Attic orators, who use it as a *topos* that asserts the solidarity of the citizen body proud of their inviolate earth. This aspect of autochthony also characterizes the Golden-Age bliss that precedes the necessity of sexual union for reproduction. On the other hand, autochthony characterizes monsters and Giants. It is a concomitant of chaos and resistance to the Olympian order, as in the myth of Typhon in the Homeric Hymn to Pythian Apollo.[8]

Cadmus' "sowing the earth-born harvest of the serpent Ophis in the earth" (1025-26) embodies the mediate position of the city between the chthonic violence of rude nature and the paradisiacal ease of a Golden Age untouched by the complexities of civilization. The

[6] On 879ff. = 899ff. Winnington-Ingram (1966) 35f. observes that the traditional *sophia* praised by the Chorus here includes also the traditional valuing of revenge on one's enemies. On the vertical imagery in the play Simon 114 remarks, "No other play with which I am familiar is so replete with the imagery of dislocation, of the ground and the house giving way, of sudden shifts from vertical to horizontal, and vice versa."

[7] On the ambiguous value of autochthony in relation to the concept of civilization see Loraux (1979) passim and now *L'invention d'Athènes* (Paris and The Hague 1981) 150f. and *Les enfants d' Athéna* (Paris 1981) 35ff., 119ff., 197ff.; Arthur (1977) 172ff. on the *Phoenissae*; Whitman (1974) 97-99.

[8] See my *Tragedy and Civilization* 26f.

former marks the life of brutes below man, the latter the life of gods above man.[9]

Dionysus' veering between chthonic and Olympian confuses this division both for his worshipers and for Thebes. His presence involves Pentheus in an abrupt swing between the potential savagery of his chthonic father (the name Echion is a masculine form of the serpentine monster Echidna) and the civilizing meaning of his grandfather's foundation of Thebes by sowing the serpent's teeth, thereby making earth's potentially monstrous fertility usable for civilized life.[10]

In Pentheus' death fusion with the god-beast-victim aloft in the tree to which Dionysus lifts him is followed by a downward plunge as a savage earth-born monster. He bypasses negatively from below the mediate position of the city between chthonic and Olympian, bestial and divine, which Dionysus bypasses positively from above. In proving himself the son of Olympian Zeus, Dionysus makes a successful passage, figuratively speaking, from earth to heavens; in experiencing the contradictions in his own parents, Pentheus undergoes a literal plunge from high to low.

The encounter between Pentheus and Dionysus is not merely a necessarily unequal battle between mortal and god but also a clash between chthonic and Olympian wherein each figure embodies the threatening opposite that his antagonist struggles to reject. Dionysus would separate himself from the imputation of birth from a mortal woman and earth-born or chthonic mortal, like his cousin Pentheus. Dionysus' Olympian divinity lures Pentheus to overreaching power and dangerous exaltation.

The play repeatedly stresses the chthonic ancestry of Pentheus as the god's bestial adversary. He is the *theomachos*, the enemy of the

[9] I am drawing here on my earlier study of Cadmus' sowing: Segal (1977) 114-16.

[10] Note the collocation of Pentheus' identification as the "son of Echion" in 1030 with Cadmus as the "sower" of the Serpent's teeth in 1026. On the associations of Echion with chaos and violence see Fontenrose, *Python* 311f., 316. The feminine original behind Echion is Echidna, "a monster unmasterable, in no way resembling mortal men or immortal gods, . . . terrible, huge, glittering, raw-eating" (Hesiod *Theog.* 295-303), closely associated with the dangerous Typhon (304ff.). Guépin 208 would view Echion as "the typical adversary of Dionysus" in a harvest ritual centering on saving the crops from destructive violence; but in Euripides' play Pentheus himself assumes much of that adversary role. Ovid *Met.* 10.686f., on the other hand, mentions a *clarus Echion* who functions as a kind of culture-hero, setting up a temple to the Mother of the Gods. In Paus. 9.5.3 Echion also has a more positive civic aspect.

gods (45, 325; cf. 795-96, 1255).[11] As the son of earth-born Echion he is explicitly compared to a "blood-thirsty Giant, hostile to the gods" (544-45).[12] The Chorus's opening exclamation (if genuine) and the densely woven syntax of the whole passage depict the Chorus's emotional intensity (537-44):

οἵαν οἵαν ὀργὰν
   ἀναφαίνει χθόνιον
γένος ἐκφύς τε δράκοντός
ποτε Πενθεύς, ὃν Ἐχίων
   ἐφύτευσε χθόνιος,
   ἀγριωπὸν τέρας, οὐ φῶ-
τα βρότειον, φόνιον δ' ὥστε γίγαντ' ἀντίπαλον θεοῖς.

What anger Pentheus shows, the breed of earth and born of serpent, Pentheus whom Echion, of the earth, sired, a savage-faced monster, not a mortal man, and like a giant murderous, antagonist to the gods.

In Euripides, as in other Greek authors, the Giants, chaotic destroyers of the civilized and the Olympian order, are earth-born, *gēgeneis*. They threaten the gods' serene celestial seat from their murky abode beneath the earth. On the Siphnian frieze at Delphi Dionysus himself probably had a role in battling their invasion.[13]

The chthonic aspect of Pentheus resembles the figure of Capaneus in the *Phoenissae*, "fearful to look upon, like an earth-born Giant, not resembling a tame creature" (*Phoen.* 127-30):

ὡς φοβερὸς εἰσιδεῖν,
γίγαντι γηγενέτᾳ προσόμοιος
 . . . οὐχὶ πρόσφορος
   ἀμερίῳ γέννᾳ.

[11] Cf. also Aeschyl. *Sept.* 424f.; see Kamerbeek (1948) 280ff.; Verdenius (1980) 11; cf. also Burnett (1970) 18ff.; WI 79; Sale, *Existentialism* 118.

[12] See Aristoph.Clouds 853 with Dover's note ad loc. for the disorderly associations of the *gēgeneis*; also Fontenrose, *Python* 316f.; Turato 119ff.; Whitman (1974) 98f. See, inter alia, Homer *Od.* 7.59; Pindar *Nem.* 1.67f., *Bacchyl.* 15. 59-63; Eur. *HF* 178ff., 906ff., 1193f.

[13] See Francis Vian, *La guerre des géants* (Paris 1952) 206f.

The Chorus's view of Pentheus, would-be protector of Thebes, assimilates him to the "savage" prototypes who would destroy it (539-44). Dionysus' movement from god to tauriform beast in punishing him answers Pentheus' own inward oscillation between ruler and chthonic savage.

The maenads' vision of Pentheus' monstrosity is partly a projection of their own anger and savagery. Yet Pentheus' own exaggerated hostility to Dionysus and the resultant unloosing of the dark side of the Dionysus in himself also unleash the hidden monstrosity of his own being. A generation later Plato will develop this image of serpentine monstrosity lurking in the depths of the incontinent tyrannical soul (*Republic* 9. 588c ff.). Like the Giants who would pile Pelion on Ossa, Pentheus will uproot mountains and destroy with bare hands the shrines of Pan and the Nymphs (945f., 949f.), an intensification of the violence of his orders to uproot with tools Teiresias' place of augury (346-51).[14] He then becomes a monster of another sort to the Theban maenads, and particularly to his mother, as he fluctuates between "calf," "lion," or unspecified "beast" (1173-75, 1185-87, 1196, 1203f., 1214f., 1278).

The Chorus, however, also knows of another side to the city's origins. The second stasimon opens with Dirce, a maiden goddess (*potni' euparthene*, 520), divinity of the place and symbol of the peaceful and life-giving aspect of the city. Receiver of the young god from "Zeus' immortal fire" in its "streams" (*pagai*, 521-25), Dirce can accommodate the god's celestial origins to human habitation. She counters remote and dangerous fire with the waters of life and birth.[15]

In the Dirce ode's opening description of Dionysus' birth, Zeus "snatched him from the immortal fire" and placed him in his "male womb" (*arsēn nēdys*, 526-27). Here celestial fire, immortality, Olympus, and birth from the male contrast implicitly with earth, mortality,

---

[14] Conacher 65 has an excellent observation on the implicit monstrosity in Pentheus' acts of 945-50. For similarities between Pentheus' chthonic aspect and the Giant-like figures of earlier myths see also *Phoen.* 1130-33, Aeschyl. *Sept.* 424, Paus. 9.5.4. For the ominous significance of the "earth-born" origin of Thebes see also Vian (preceding note) 151 and Arthur (1977) 172ff.

[15] In other legends Dirce has more ominous chthonic associations as the lair of the serpent that Cadmus has to slay before human settlement can take place: cf. schol. on Soph. *Antig.* 126 and on Eur. *Phoen.* 931, 935. See in general Fontenrose, *Python* 307ff., 548f.; Vian, *Origines*, chap. 4, esp. 106-109.

the chthonic regions, and birth from the female womb in sexual reproduction. That contrast creates the greatest possible distance between Dionysus and his antagonist, for the antistrophe stresses the
"savagery" of Pentheus' chthonic origins (538-44).[16]

To the maenad Chorus, who associate the potential gentleness of
Thebes with its natural features rather than with its human trans-
formers, with nature rather than culture, Theban Dirce becomes a
remote, suprahuman *unio oppositorum*, a mythic place of the coincidence of fire and water. Life in this city is left polarized between
hopeless contradictions. Echion's chthonic monstrosity subverts the
norm from below; Zeus's "male womb" and Dionysus' fiery birth
subvert it from above. Earth-born monstrosity is no more appropriate
an image of paternity than celestial incineration of the mother by a
thunder-god father. Pentheus' position outside the norm of the human *oikos* through his chthonic origins culminates in death in the
wild at the hands of a crazed mother. Dionysus' anomalous parentage
is ironically made good in Thebes; he successfully stakes his claim to
a place within it by totally destroying three generations of the royal
house.

Both of Pentheus' parents turn into nightmare fantasies: the father
is associated with serpentine monstrosity, the mother with murderous
savagery. But whereas Dionysus separates himself from his terrestrial
mother thanks to his Olympian father's "immortal fire" and "male
womb," Pentheus' origins leave him exposed to the most destructive
aspect of father and mother both. To his mother the fantastic image
of the son as a "savage-faced monster" (*agriōpon teras*, 542) becomes
a reality as she bears that "face" (*prosōpon*, 1277) as that of the savage
lion she has made her prey.

Pentheus begins in close, if tense, proximity to his cultural father,
the city-founder, Cadmus.[17] Cadmus is actually his grandfather, but
clearly a surrogate father figure. In the course of the play Pentheus

---

[16] The phrase *agriōpon teras*, "savage-visaged monster," in 542 is so placed that it
can refer either to Echion or to Pentheus. Taken in parallel construction with *ou
phōta broteion*, "not a mortal creature," it must grammatically refer to Pentheus but
there may be an intentional ambiguity. For more details see Segal (1977) 107ff.
Contrast 263-65, where the Chorus cites Pentheus' "earth-born" ancestry as a positive
foil to his present violence.

[17] Cadmus, suggests Vian, *Origines* 123, is perhaps "l'aspect bénéfice du dragon
qui retient les eaux de la source sacrée de Thèbes."

moves rapidly from his cultural to his natural father, from founding hero to chthonic "savage." That movement coincides with his removal from a secure place within polis and *oikos* to an endangered and untenable existence outside as a beast in the wild. Dionysus, on the other hand, begins with a mortal father (cf. 26-31, 331-36), but moves to his rightful position as son of the sky-god, Zeus, thereby exchanging his status as a Stranger outside Thebes for a position of awe and honor within, but at the price of destroying his mother's house much as Zeus destroyed his mother's body.

After the second stasimon Echion and Pentheus' earth-born ancestry evoke images of violence and savagery. The implicitly "pious" Echion of 263-65 becomes the father of a "godless lawless unjust earth-born son" (995f. = 1005f.). The son is even placed beneath the normal human level of birth from woman (987-90):

> τίς ἄρα νιν ἔτεκεν;
> οὐ γὰρ ἐξ αἵματος
> γυναικῶν ἔφυ, λεαίνας δέ τινος
> ὅδ᾽ ἢ Γοργόνων Λιβυσσᾶν γένος.

Who then gave him birth? For he was born not of the blood of women, but from some lioness or the Libyan Gorgons in race.

The reference to the Gorgons harks back to the cosmic struggle in the Greek myths of the origins of the world and of the city, from Hesiod's *Theogony* to Aeschylus' *Oresteia*. It is a conflict between pre-Olympian female divinities of the chaos of the deep and of night, of water and swamp, and the patriarchal order of Zeus and the Olympians.[18] Here, too, cosmic and psychological order interpenetrate, for the Chorus is making Pentheus the child of the Evil Mother in her most monstrous, nightmarish form.[19]

---

[18] In Hesiod *Theog.* 270-79 the Gorgons are the daughters of Phorkys and Keto, primordial divinities of the waters, and dwell "beyond glorious Ocean at the extreme limit towards night" (274f.). For their grim snaky form see ps.-Hesiod *Aspis* 230ff.; for the type of female monster of the deep see Gilbert Durand, *Les structures anthropologiques de l'imaginaire* (Paris 1969) 105ff.

[19] The psychological symbolism of the Gorgon has been much discussed. There are divergent views, ranging from Freud's symbolism of the female genitalia to Slater's of the phallic mother and the dissolution of personal boundaries: see Sigmund Freud, "Medusa's Head" (1922) in *Collected Papers*, ed. James Strachey (New York 1959) 5. 105f.; Slater 18f., 319ff.; Feldman, passim, esp. 485-88, 492f.; Michael

These Gorgons, a mythical foreshadowing of Agave herself in the next scene, represent the maternal "uroboros," in Erich Neumann's terminology, the archetype of the Great Mother who pulls the son back into the orbit of her devouring power.[20] Ironically the Gorgonic qualities of which the maenads accuse their victim in 987-90 often characterize murderous female insanity, associated with or sent by other Gorgon figures like the chthonic Erinyes (e.g., *Heracles Mad* 868-70, 880-84, 990). The maenads here project upon Pentheus the destructive madness of their own dangerous counterpart, the murderous Theban mother figures. From another perspective they can be seen as embodying Pentheus' fantasy of the evil side of the mother, or the fantasy of those members of the audience who identify with Pentheus.

On the play's vertical axis Pentheus is strung between impossible celestial aspirations and roots in the earthly violence of his human nature. He resembles other adolescent heroes like Phaethon, Icarus, Hippolytus—youths who would escape their mortal nature and the demands of adult sexuality by flight to the sky but end by crashing disastrously to earth.[21] More successful models are Ganymede, who escapes to Olympus fixed in the role of beautiful and seductive adolescent, or Perseus, who succeeds in a winged journey, kills the female monster, marries the princess, wins the kingdom, and liberates an imprisoned mother.

Pentheus, like Hippolytus, does not soar in triumph over the land, bearing the insignia of triumph over threatening maternal sexuality. He is drawn back toward darkness and earth, reabsorbed into the Gorgonic aspect of himself and his earthy uroboric progenitors, both male and female, whom he can neither accept nor overcome. Hippolytus is doomed by his denial of the full sexuality of both paternal

Simpson, *The Library of Apollodorus* (Amherst, Mass. 1976) 82-88, ad Apollod. 2.4. Perseus, whose successful dealings with monsters and maternal figures place him at the opposite pole from Pentheus, triumphs over these monstrous projections of the Evil Mother: see Ps.-Hesiod *Aspis*, 216ff.; Pindar *Pyth.* 10 and 12; Aeschyl. *Cho.* 831-37 and in general Slater 71f. and 308-33.

[20] See Erich Neumann, *The Origins and History of Consciousness*, tr. R.F.C. Hull (Princeton 1954), chap. 2

[21] On these images of adolescent flight for the evasion of sexual maturity see Segal (1979) passim; K. J. Reckford, "Phaethon, Hippolytus, and Aphrodite," *TAPA* 103 (1972) 405-32.

and maternal figures (Theseus-Poseidon and Phaedra-Aphrodite). He meets his end through the manifestations of violence on both sides.[22] Pentheus, as the son of the violent earth-born Echion, is killed by the Evil Mother in her terrible, incomprehensible fury (1114-20); but his death has behind it also a failed encounter with the paternal uroboric symbols associated with his own male sexuality and its roots in male generation, the bull and the serpent.

Taken together, the two antagonists, Pentheus and Dionysus, create a double polarization of the parental figures: a brilliant celestial father and a dark chthonic monster; a mother totally subordinated to (and in fact destroyed by) patriarchal male power able to dispense with the female womb, and a mother invincible in her conflict with the agents of the patriarchal house and city, murderous toward the representative of that authority. The latter maternal image is further polarized between Golden-Age fertility and the destructive fury of wild savagery. In all cases the hero is strung between oppositions too great to be mediated. Each alternative is equally unrealistic, equally remote from a viable civic, domestic, or psychological balance, and equally destructive in its implications.

The ode on Pentheus' Gorgonic birth and chthonic savagery occurs just between the ritual dressing of the king and the news of his death on the mountain. It solemnizes the reversal that leads to his death; he does not return to the stage alive. Defined now as both chthonic monster and wild beast, he is no longer protected by the political or religious enclosures of his city. As the Messenger ends the next scene with the grim tale of his death, the maenad chorus utters their lyrical cry: "Let us dance the Bacchic one; let us shout out the doom of Pentheus, the one born from the serpent. . . . O Cadmean bacchants, you have brought the glorious victory-song to its completion in groans, in tears. Lovely the contest . . ." (1153-55, 1161-63).[23] The opposite of a true epinician hymn, which reaffirms the hero's connection with the traditions of his family and his polis, this song celebrates the displacement of king from city as he is redefined as both chthonic monster and hunted beast. "Glorious victory-song," *kallinikon klei-*

---

[22] See Segal (1978/79) 135-37.

[23] Lines 1160-63 contain a number of double meanings: *kallinikos* can refer to the victory-song or to the victorious king, now defeated; *ekprattein*, "to bring to an end," "accomplish," can also mean "exact vengeance."

non, can also mean "the [youth] who won the glorious victory." In that case the difference between handsome athlete and monstrous serpent-brood is another measure of Pentheus' reversal from king to victim/scapegoat, from civic space to wild forest.

• III •

All these descriptions of Pentheus as chthonic or serpent-born come from the maenads, barbarian women who may be expected to see only the negative side of Theban autochthony. Winnington-Ingram aptly asks, "Can those whose contacts with the animal world are so close rightly bring a charge of sub-humanity? Are they not in fact abusing Pentheus for the possession of Dionysiac traits of character?"[24] Winnington-Ingram is surely right to question whether the maenad chorus's pronouncements are to be taken at face value. Yet their vision of Pentheus, for all the anger behind it, does hit home at several points. As noted above, the maenads can also recognize the positive side of the Theban legend of the dragon-sown men (263-65).

The *Phoenician Women*, performed a few years before the *Bacchae*, provides independent confirmation of the sinister overtones that Euripides felt in this Theban myth of origins. In that play a member of the royal line must be sacrificed and must pour a libation of his blood to the earth in retribution for the killing of the "earth-born serpent" (*drakōn gēgenēs, Phoen.* 931-41). This done, Ares will become an ally instead of an enemy; and the earth, which once "sent forth the golden-helmeted crop of Sown Men," will be propitious if it receives fruit for fruit and blood for blood (939-40). The ambiguity of earth parallels the ambiguity of Ares. Both have a bloodthirsty and vengeful as well as a benign side. In a later ode the destructive Sphinx, with her "raw-eating talons" (1025), appears as an offspring of earth and the chthonic monster Echidna (*Phoen.* 1019-20). In the *Bacchae* Ares will eventually rescue Cadmus and Harmonia from their serpentine metamorphosis and transport them to the Blessed Isles (*Ba.* 1338-39). But Ares does not intervene sooner to save his descendants from

[24] WI 80. For the danger of identifying Euripides' view of Pentheus with the maenads' see also Parry, *Lyrics* 148.

Dionysus' wrath. In Dionysus, too, there is "a certain portion of Ares": so Teiresias warns (302-304), and so the Theban followers of Pentheus learn to their cost (cf. 751-64 and 50-52).[25]

In both *Phoenissae* and *Bacchae* autochthony, Earth, and Ares express in mythical terms the precarious balance of mankind between order and savagery, culture and nature, reason and madness. Dionysus' radical shift from beast to god, chthonic to Olympian, releases the chthonic violence latent in Pentheus' own dragon-born, chthonic ancestry. Possibly because Dionysus' chthonic origins are on the maternal side, his assertion of power and masculine identity follows a less problematical course. When he proves himself the son of Zeus, he is successfully distancing himself from the female and chthonic parent. When Pentheus moves toward his male parent, he is associating himself with his chthonic and serpentine ancestry, which also, paradoxically, draws him back to the threatening, all-devouring, monstrous aspect of the mother.

As Dionysus finally makes good his claim to Olympian immortality, Pentheus comes to embody the dark, chaotic side of Thebes' earth-born race. Yet the two poles never remain fixed. The tellurian aspect of the god as an ancient daimon of life and fertility crosses over into his uranian role as a son of the remote, fire-hurling ruler of Olympus.

Pentheus' aspiration to divine immortality fluctuates much more precipitously between sky and earth, heroism and savagery, mystical initiation and bloody dismemberment. Dionysus, on the other hand, can claim his sky-father and yet retain his associations with the fertility and liquid vegetative life of the earth that were once in the power of his mother. Zeus's thunder has freed him of bondage to the Great Mother and left the smouldering ashes as a reminder of the victory, fire over earth. Pentheus' tragedy is just the reverse.

• IV •

Over against the emerging chthonic violence of Pentheus stands the founding hero, Cadmus. He reenacts his role as a civilizing hero

[25] On the association of Ares and Dionysus see Dodds, *Bacchae* ad 302-304; WI 51.

early in the play by establishing a cult (10), albeit imperfectly (30-31). Teiresias' opening address to Cadmus stresses his role as culture-hero (170-172), "Cadmus . . . who left the Sidonian city and built this towered town of Thebes." In the reversals acted out in the play Cadmus' achievement gets its most elaborate expression just at the point when the civic order embodied in the new king collapses: the Messenger addresses Cadmus as the sower of the earth-born serpent crop as he prepares to relate the king's death (1024-28).

Nowhere does the play refer to Cadmus' actual killing of the serpent. The three full descriptions of Cadmus' deed mention only "sowing" the serpent's teeth to create the new "crop" (*stachys*) or "harvest" (*theros*) of new Thebans (264, 1024-27, 1274, 1314-15). The omission is significant. In Cadmus, the true civilizer, the violence of Theban autochthony is suppressed. He is a farmer, a "sower," not a killer (*speirein*, "sow," recurs in 264, 1026, 1315; cf. 1274). His foundation of the city is a deed not of war but of agriculture, which for the Greeks is the privileged model for the settled, stable quality of civilized life. True, Cadmus' yield is of a fantastic and unpromising sort; yet its positive associations remain. The same word, "crop," *stachys*, describes the plowed and fruitful fields in the Theban territory that the maenads' depredations threaten (750-52). When Agave regains sanity, her recollection that Cadmus gave her to "the Sown Man, Echion" (*Spartos*, 1274) extends the civilizing force of his foundation from city to house and reestablishes the homology of city, marriage, and agriculture at the point when Dionysus' power has turned the system inside out.[26]

In another version of the founding legend the earth sends up the Sown Men to avenge the death of the serpent. Cadmus, however, is able to unite the survivors in a more positive form of association.[27] He separates them from the chthonic and bestial and makes them

[26] On the homologies of agriculture, marriage, and civilized life see Segal, *Tragedy and Civilization* 61f., 90f.; also above, Chap. 3, section 4.

[27] See Eur. *Phoen.* 933-35. The scholion ad 934 remarks, "Earth [Ge] sent up the Sown Men to punish the death of the Serpent; but they [the Thebans] didn't exact the punishment, but rather joined in association [*ekoinōnēsan*] with the Thebans; for Echion, one of the Sown Men, even married Agave, Cadmus' daughter." This, says the scholion, was regarded as "treason" (*prodosia*) to the race of Earth and was to be expiated by the sacrifice of one of that race, as Teiresias prophesies in *Phoen.* 931-34.

truly human, the future race of a walled and towered city (cf. 170-72).

The line of Theban succession, Cadmus-Echion-Pentheus, follows a pattern common in Greek myth. A just king wins or inherits the throne from a violent predecessor. The succession Ouranos-Cronos-Zeus is the most familiar example, but there is an interesting parallel too in the Arcadian kingship: Pelasgus-Lycaon-Arcas. Pelasgus, the first king of Arcadia, is autochthonous; his reign is virtually a Golden Age. Lycaon, bestial and savage, practises cannibalism and provokes a god-sent deluge that destroys humanity. Arcas, the founder of "cultural Arcadia," introduces agriculture, restores civilization, and gives his name to the country.[28]

In Thebes Cadmus' foundation through a nonviolent planting of earth-sprung men corresponds to a remote, Golden-Age past. It is followed by the savage autochthon, Echion, who is never explicitly said to rule (cf. 213), but corresponds to the intermediate violent kingship. Pentheus, the third in succession, should establish a stable state of civilization, a balance between the Golden-Age autochthony suggested by Cadmus' rule and the savage autochthony of Echion.[29] But the reconciliation that should result from the union of the founder's daughter with the "sown" crop of the serpent has the opposite result. The god's presence triggers Pentheus' "savage" inheritance and calls forth from Thebes' mythical origins only the primordial violence of the king's chthonic progenitor. The distinction between Golden-Age and savage autochthony through the separation between Cadmus and Echion is now collapsed and condensed into the single figure of Pentheus. He himself soon experiences the swing from Golden Age to savagery on the wild mountain outside of Thebes.

Tragedy—and particularly Euripidean tragedy—characteristically calls up these mysterious forces at the hidden origins of the city and of culture generally, the forces that lie close to their sources of energy, both destructive and creative. We may compare the legend of Erichthonius that Euripides explores in the *Ion*, where the mysterious

[28] See Philippe Borgeaud, "The Open Entrance to the Closed Palace of the King: The Greek Labyrinth in Context," *History of Religions* 14 (1974) 1-27, esp. 6-13; also the discussion of Hesiod's myths of sovereignty in J.-P. Vernant and Marcel Detienne, *Les ruses de l'intelligence* (Paris 1974) 99-103.

[29] See Bourgeaud (preceding note) 12.

drops of Gorgon's blood in Creusa's possession symbolize the double potential of Athens' autochthonous origins.[30]

· V ·

These oscillations between high and low in the mythical background take on concrete form in the language of the play. At his first appearance Pentheus' status as "the son of Echion" who possesses the "power over the earth" (*kratos . . . gēs*) forms part of a contrast with a vertical "fluttering" of emotion (212-14):

Κα.   Πενθεὺς πρὸς οἴκους ὅδε διὰ σπουδῆς περᾶ,
       'Εχίονος παῖς, ᾧ κράτος δίδωμι γῆς.
       ὡς ἐπτόηται· τί ποτ' ἐρεῖ νεώτερον;

Cadmus. Here Pentheus strides to the house with zeal, the son of Echion, to whom I give the power to rule this earth. How he is aflutter. What new, what violent word will he speak.

The detail of "fluttering," *eptoētai*, mark of an excited temperament, is the first hint of this instability between high and low.

The image of flight recurs near the end of this scene as Cadmus attempts to support Teiresias in restraining the impetuous young king (331-32): "Dwell with us [*oikei*], not outside the laws; for you are flying aloft [*petē(i)*] in your excitement, and your thinking is non-thinking." In this figurative movement "above" the level of calm intelligence, Pentheus is already moving outside the safe norms of house and laws. It is just through this incipient imbalance that Dionysus gains control of his mind. One of the effects of Dionysiac madness, as Teiresias explains shortly before, is the "flutter" of panic fear in an army (*phobos dieptoēse*, 304).

For Dionysus and his worshipers flying has a very different significance. In the parode the Chorus described how the god was born

---

[30] On the symbolism of the Gorgon's blood in Eur. *Ion* 1003-17 see Anne Burnett, *Catastrophe Survived* (Oxford 1971) 115ff. and Loraux, *Les enfants d'Athéna* 239ff.

when Zeus's thunderbolt "flew down" (*ptamenas*, 90), after which
the yet unborn god was carried up to Olympus (94-95). Now Teiresias
repeats the tale, answering Pentheus' mockery. He relates how "Zeus
snatched him from the lightning-fire and brought him, an infant, up
to Olympus as a god," thereby baffling Hera's attempt to "cast him
out of the heavens" (287-90). The imagery of birds and flying that
conveys Pentheus' irreverence soon expresses his own precarious position between beast and god, high and low, king and *pharmakos*, a
suspension that is a dark mirror-image of the embryonic Dionysus'
"flight."

The imagery of flying grimly echoes throughout the maenads' excitement and especially Agave's "fluttering" state (*to ptoēthen*, 1268).[31]
This is the word that Cadmus uses to sum up the madness in her
soul. The language of flying, like the language of madness (cf. 326,
359; also 399, 887, 999), expresses that combination of affinity and
resistance to the power of the god that enables Dionysus so fully to
take possession of Pentheus. That inward disposition to the Dionysiac
"flutter" of madness is then acted out with fearful consequences at
the end.

In contrast to Dionysus' upward flight in the parode, the second
stasimon brings Pentheus down to earth as the child of chthonic Echion
(541). Here the "golden-faced" Dionysus (553), in contrast to the
"savage-faced" Pentheus (542), is to "come down from Olympus"
(553-55).[32] We may contrast also the maenads' "Holiness," Hosia, in
the preceding ode, who "plies her golden wing over the earth" (370-
72). The implicit warning has even more direct vertical imagery in
the antistrophe, where "the heavenly gods [*ouranidai*] who dwell in
the aether see the deeds of mortals" (393-94). Though not uncommon in gnomic poetry of this type, these images form a pattern that
receives vivid and detailed description at the climax of the action.

Pentheus prefers to think of the maenads as close to earth, crouch-
ing or slinking in the bushes (218-23), caught "in their closest toils
of love" (957-58). Yet the First Messenger's speech has shown us

---

[31] For the imagery of flight in which the earth-born origins of Pentheus move
toward their opposite see Diller (1955) 486.

[32] Reading *kat' Olympou* in 554, with Kirchhoff, accepted by Dodds, *Bacchae* ad
loc. and by Kirk; contra, Roux ad loc.

another view of the maenads: birds lifted high in flight (*artheisai dromō[i]*, 748) as they swoop down "like enemies" on the vulnerable Theban fields stretched below them (*pediōn hypotaseis*, 749). When the maenads later swoop down on Pentheus himself in the Second Messenger's speech, they have the swiftness of doves (1090). Here they are no longer passive and helpless birds on the ground, but attackers with the role of hunter and prey reversed. A transitive form of the verb *airein*, "raise up" (cf. *artheisai* of the maenad birds "raised aloft" in 748) will then describe the triumphant gesture with which Agave would have the severed head of the lion/victim "lifted" to the topmost part of the palace wall (1212-14): "Where is my son, Pentheus? Let him take and lift [*airesthō*] the climbings of fastened ladders to the house, that he may peg this head upon the triglyphs. . . ." Her word for the "civilized" climbing of the ladders, *pros-ambaseis*, repeats the vertical imagery of Pentheus' disastrous upward climb (*ambas*, 1061, 1107), as beast in the wild, not king in the palace. The king who should occupy the high places at the center of the city has fallen to its lowest place, as expelled *pharmakos*, as hunted beast in the wild, and as young male hurled down from high phallic pride to infantile helplessness before the Evil Mother. The reversals in the spatial, biological, familial, political, and sexual codes are all homologous and are closely interwoven by the poetic imagery.

The fate of the hero is also the fate of his palace. Even before it is sealed with the trophy of the maenads' victory (1212ff., above), it "falls" or is hurled down "to earth" (*pesēmata*, 587; *chamaze*, 633). Dionysus is now "on the roof" (*ana melathra*, 589) and comforts the maenads who have "fallen" to the ground in terror at his appearance (605). Earlier Cadmus and Teiresias tried to help one another from "falling" as they make for Cithaeron to serve the god (365-66), but now the god himself intervenes with that reversal of strong and weak characteristic of his cult.

The palace miracle turns the building literally "upside down" (*anō katō*, 601-603), an ironical echo of Pentheus' earlier threat to Teiresias (349). Pentheus' fury in that passage again takes the form of instability between "up and down"; and the echo in 602 once more juxtaposes Pentheus' violence and Dionysus' power, only to show the futility of the former. The same phrase, *anō te kai katō*, "up and down," recurs to describe the next phase of the god's vengeance, the maenads' irresistible rampage on the mountain (741, 753).[33] In the latter passage they "fall upon" and ravage the villages (*epespesousai*, 753). When Pentheus, in the scene after the palace miracle, attacks the "radiant aether" that Dionysus has formed into his shape to baffle and humiliate his enemy (630-31), we are reminded of the chthonic antagonists who oppose the gods (543-44) or, further back, of the moral power of the "aether-dwelling celestial gods" (393-94). In relying on gates or towers as defenses against Dionysus, Pentheus forgets that an Olympian god can leap or fly "over" walls (*hyper-bainousi*, 654). The psychological and dramatic climax of this movement is Pentheus' "fall" into "great desire" of seeing the maenads in the mountain (*eis erōta . . . peptōkas*, 813).

Sure of victory, Dionysus promises his antagonist an exalted flight into the "aether" in heroic glory (972), a promise grimly fulfilled when he shoots Pentheus literally "upright into the upright aether" (1073). Soon after this the maenads shoot their thyrsuses "through the aether" (1099), as earlier, in the joy of anticipated victory, they flung "their necks into the dewy aether" (864-65). Pentheus' "flight," however, is not the achievement of godlike glory, the immortal fame (*kleos*) that reaches "to the heavens" (972), but a downward plunge to an infamous and inglorious death, torn apart like a beast.

When the maenads aim at the aether in 1073, they have a very different mood from that into which they toss their heads in the joyous freedom of 863. It is not "dewy," *droseros*, but "straight upright," *orthos*, a word suggestive of the stark remoteness of the heavens and the steepness of Pentheus' fatal fall.[34] By looking up at that distant aether Agave will be made to recognize the horrible reality of what she has done (1264-65), brought back to a recognition of human limits and the distance between earth and heavens.

[33] The echoes between 741 and 753 are noted by WI 97, n. 1; see also 55 with n. 4.

[34] Note also the recurrence of *orthos* in *idoim' an orthōs* 1062 and *estēsan orthai* of the maenads' standing "bolt upright" in 1087. The latter is probably an intentional echo of the first scene on Cithaeron, ἀνῇξαν ὀρθαί (693: "rushed straight up") on which see Barlow 66. For the importance of the aether in Dionysus' relation with mortals cf. also 150, 293, 631. In the first passage the maenads throw their "rich lock toward the aether," and this "richness" (*tryphē*) is akin to the repressed sensual side of Pentheus by which the god enters and destroys him: cf. 493, 455f., and esp. 979f. (*tryphan . . . tryphas*).

Whereas Pentheus' death marks both the literal and figurative disjunction between heavens and earth, Dionysus' final miracle in the play is to bring together high and low (1063-65):

τοὐντεῦθεν ἤδη τοῦ ξένου ⟨τὸ⟩ θαῦμ' ὁρῶ·
λαβὼν γὰρ ἐλάτης οὐράνιον ἄκρον κλάδον
κατῆγεν, ἦγεν, ἦγεν ἐς μέλαν πέδον.

And then I see this miracle of the stranger:
seizing the heaven-high topmost branch of the fir
down he led it, led it to the black soil.

When the god lets the tree go, it shoots "upright up to the upright aether" (1073): ὀρθὴ δ' ἐς ὀρθὸν αἰθέρ' ἐστηρίζετο. The verb translated "shoot," *stērizein*, occurs also in 972, of the promised "glory reaching to the heavens." *Stērizein* occurs only once outside the *Bacchae* in Euripides' extant œuvre, to describe the disastrous fall of a hero very similar to Pentheus, namely Hippolytus at the point when his passage beyond the limits of Troezen to adult maturity is cut short by the bull and the monstrous wave from the sea that "reaches to the heavens" (*kym' ouranō[i] stērizon, Hipp.* 1207).[35] In both cases a young hero's aspirations beyond mortal limits and his denial of a basic aspect of emotional reality result in this inversion of high and low.

The god's miraculous spanning of earth and heavens seems to reaffirm the limits of mortality. When he bends the tree down to earth, the Stranger is "performing acts no longer mortal" (1068). The mysterious voice that stretches between earth and sky and spurs the maenads to the final frenzy of vengeance marks the increasing distance between god and beast (1082-83):

καὶ ταῦθ' ἅμ' ἠγόρευε καὶ πρὸς οὐρανὸν
καὶ γαῖαν ἐστήριξε φῶς σεμνοῦ πυρός.

These things he spoke, and to the heavens
and the earth he set fast the light of solemn fire.

This is the third occurrence of the uncommon verb *stērizein* (cf. 972, 1073), all within a little over a hundred lines. The word suggests the firmness of the *axis mundi*, the celestial Pillar of the Heavens that symbolizes the order of the cosmos. Yet here it also marks the re-

[35] On the significance of the image see Segal (1965) 142-47.

moteness and ambiguity of any such cosmic order in the terrible reversals of the divine vengeance.[36] The vast outreach of the image
dwarfs Pentheus into a helpless victim, but in so doing suggests the
massive cruelty of this divine overkill.

Soon after Pentheus is fully abased (1111-13):

ὑψοῦ δὲ θάσσων ὑψόθεν χαμαιριφὴς
πίπτει πρὸς οὐδας μυρίοις οἰμώγμασιν
Πενθεύς· κακοῦ γὰρ ἐγγὺς ὢν ἐμάνθανεν.

Seated on high from his height earth-plummeting
he falls to the ground with myriad shoutings,
Pentheus. For he learned that he was near the woe.

We may recall the fall of the celebrant in the parode: as he "hunts
the blood of the slain goat, the joy of the raw-eating, wearing the
holy garb of the fawnskin, . . . in the mountains rushing forth from
the running bands [thiasoi] he falls to the ground" (pesē[i] pedose,
135-39). In this fall the worshiper is ecstatically united with the god
and the distance between man and god is bridged over.[37] Pentheus
falls as victim, not as celebrant, and that distance is enlarged to an
impassable chasm. Now his own mother "falls upon him" (prospitnei,
1114-15), as a priestess of a murderous sacrifice.

As the distance between god and man increases on the upward part
of the vertical axis, that between man and beast is effaced on the
lower part. The anomalous "climbing beast," ambatēs thēr (1108-
1109), Pentheus is assimilated to the chthonic origins of Thebes,
identified with a subhuman race of monsters.[38] In his last words he

[36] On the axis mundi see Mircea Eliade, Patterns in Comparative Religion (New
York 1958) 265ff.; Segal (1978/79) 143f. and Tragedy and Civilization 22f. on the
image in Pindar Pyth. 1; Hdt. 4.184; Hesiod Theog. 778f., where the verb stērizein
also occurs in the imagery of the cosmic pillar.

[37] The "fall to the ground" in 136 is variously explained. Dodds is probably correct
in suspecting "that the words describe a moment when the celebrant falls unconscious and the god enters into him": Bacchae ad 136. For a review of the problems
of text and interpretation see Oranje 155ff. The tree from which Pentheus "falls to
the ground" in 1111ff. may also have associations with Dionysiac cult: Paus. 2.2.6-
8 reports seeing at Corinth two images of Dionysus, Lysios and Baccheios respectively, carved from the wood of the tree from which Pentheus plunged to his death:
see Roux ad 1058-62.

[38] WI 130 suggests that the ambatēs thēr evokes "some panther or wild-cat crouch-
ing on a branch," but more is probably involved.

claims normal human birth in "Echion's house" (1119), treating Echion as a civilized father in a secure domestic *oikos*. But the maenads, when the killing is accomplished, exult over "the doom of Pentheus sprung from the serpent" (*symphoran / tan tou drakontos Pentheos ekgeneta*, 1154-55). Only as Agave returns to sanity does she combine the notion of Echion as a Sown Man or *Spartos* with the civilized institution of marriage and house (1273-74):

> Cadmus.   To what *house* [*oikōs*] did you come with the hymns of marriage rites?
> Agave.   To the *Sown Man* [*Spartō(i)*], Echion, you gave me, as they say.

Ironically, the higher Pentheus ascends in physical space, the lower he "falls" on the scale of civilized values. When he occupies the summit of the actual height that he attains in the play, he is "a poor wretch" (*tlēmōn*) and a "beast" whose "climbing up" (*ambatēs thēr*, 1107-1108) is singularly unsuccessful. This is a climber soon caught by his lack of a "path" forward (*aporia*) as the maenads hurl their thyrsuses "through the aether" at him (1101-1102):

κρεῖσσον γὰρ ὕψος τῆς προθυμίας ἔχων
καθῆσθ' ὁ τλήμων, ἀπορίᾳ λελημμένος.

[They could not hit him], for having a height greater than their [his?] zeal, he sat [down], the poor wretch, caught in helplessness [literally, "pathlessness," *a-poria*].

The Greek is ambiguous enough to suggest that Pentheus is "higher than he wishes" as well as "higher than the maenads' eagerness" to hit him. One should perhaps not lay too much stress on the prefix, *kath'*, "down," in *kathēsto*, "sat down" in 1102, but the verb may also stress the paradoxical mixture of exaltation and abasement in his precarious perch. "Sitting under the fir trees" (*hyp' elatais kathēmenos*, 816), he would see the maenads "sitting down all together on the mountains" (*synkathēmenas*, 811), as the god described them in the prologue (*hyp' elatais*, 38). Pentheus has obtained his desire, but the vagueness of that "seat under the firs" in 816 is grimly clarified. The god has bent *down* (*kat-ēgen*) to earth "the fir tree's heavenly, topmost branch" (*elatēs ouranion akron kladon*, 1064-65) and seated Pentheus "on the fir-tree limbs" (*elatinōn ozōn epi*, 1070). Now Pentheus, seen, not seeing, "sits upon the fir tree" (*elatē[i]* . . . *ephēme-non*, 1095) a "climber" caught with "no place to go" (*aporia*, 1102), his scattered remains soon "lying" (*keitai*, 1137) in the low places of the mountain, "beneath" the rocks (*hypo*), "in" the foliage of the forest bushes (*en*, 1136-37). When his head is to be affixed to the high place of the palace with ladders for "climbing" (cf. *prosambaseis*, 1213; *ambatēs*, 1107), he has reached his lowest point as ruler, son, and hero.

When they kill Pentheus, the maenads assume something of their god's ambiguous position between high and low. The verb that describes their uprooting of the fir tree with their "levers not of iron" is *synkeraunousai* (1103), from *keraunos*, "thunder," and means "shattering (as) by a thunderbolt." The verb is rare, but occurs elsewhere in connection with wine and its effects as the manifestation of the celestial power of the wine god on earth.[39] In their vengeance the maenads seem to assume the celestial power that Dionysus has himself been claiming as a son of Olympian Zeus (1103-1104):

τέλος δὲ δρυῖνους συγκεραυνοῦσαι κλάδους
ῥίζας ἀνεσπάρασσον ἀσιδήροις μοχλοῖς.

Finally striking the branches of the oak as with thunderbolts they tore up its roots with levers not of iron.

The verb *synkeraunein* recalls other attributes of Dionysus' Olympian powers among men. The oak tree, whose branches the maenads wield as thunder (another implication of 1103), is sacred to Zeus. With thunder Dionysus apparently destroys Pentheus' house in the palace miracle: "Kindle the thunderous blazing torch" (*keraunion*), the Stranger cries out to his followers (594). The fire that blazed up anew around Semele's tomb also has its connections with the "thun-

[39] Dodds, *Bacchae* ad 1103 comments, "The Maenads, like their master (594), command the magic of the lightning." As Dodds, Kirk, and Roux ad loc. point out, the verb connotes the intoxicating effects of the god's wine, a sense in which it is used by Archilochus frag. 77 D = 96 Lasserre-Bonnard; Cratinus frag. 188.4 Edmonds = 187 Kock. Hence it suggests the triumph of the god's power of emotional excitement over the repressive king and also implies a transformation of the hidden, internal power of the god into visible, physical action. Green 204-205 suggests a parallel with Dionysus' assuming the power of his father's lightning to destroy Pentheus' palace (cf. 594) and elaborates on the symbolism of the maenads' phallic power.

der" that struck her, "the thunder-smitten one," *keraunobolos* (598). In both the prologue and the parode Semele is described as "she of the thunder" (*keraunia*, 6) or smitten by "thunder's blow" (*kerauniō[i] plēgā[i]*, 93). Theban Pentheus and Teiresias, though with differing points of view, refer to "thunder's fire" for Dionysus' birth (*lampasin kerauniais*, 244; *pyr keraunion*, 288).

From the very beginning of the play the thunderbolt marks the distance that separates Olympian Zeus from mortals. In the maenads' *synkeraunein* of 1103 that male, phallic weapon becomes a metaphor for the female power that converts a mortal into a beast. The thunderbolt thus becomes another expression of the polarity between Dionysus and Pentheus. It established Dionysus' divinity by separating him from a human mother and marking his descent from a celestial and immortal father. Here it asserts Pentheus' status below the human as he is absorbed into and destroyed by a band of female hunter-warriors led by his mother.

The negation of civilized tools, stressed by the oxymoron "levers not of iron" in 1104, parallels the coincidence of divinity and savagery in the maenads' action: wild female hunters who yet possess the attribute of the sky-father (1103).[40] As the god's cry that inspires them to the last murderous furor binds together earth and heavens (1082-83), so their bloody triumph unites both bestiality and divinity. The savage nonmetal weapons of 1104 accompany the power of Zeus's celestial fire (*synkeraunein*) in 1103; but in the lyrics that follow some fifty lines later those same weapons are the "trusty pledge of Hades," while Pentheus has moved from "climbing beast" to chthonic serpent (1155-57).

The smoke that streams from the torches of the god's narthex or pine-wand, like the smoke of incense, establishes communication between gods and men (144-50). Yet this rite takes place in a context that subverts all the normal mediations of sacrifice. The "light of awesome fire" that binds heaven and earth creates not the Heavenly Pillar that symbolizes a firm cosmic order but a paradoxical and unstable coincidence of oppositions. In like manner the fire that the maenads carry around their hair (757-58) could be a sign of divinity;

---

[40] Roux's suggestion about *asidēros* in 1104, that "l'épithète explique l'échec de la séconde tentative des bacchantes," seems to me to miss the point, especially as the preceding verse stresses the supernatural violence of this second attempt.

but at that moment they are carrying off children from their homes (754-55). The fire that marks the "immortality" of Zeus (cf. *athana-ton pyr*, 523-25) and separates the infant god from his mortal mother's womb (90, 597-99) recurs for Dionysus' appearance as a "fire-blazing lion" (*pyriphlegōn leōn*, 1018).

The fire associated with Dionysus throughout the play is not the Promethean fire of technology nor the sheltered fire of house and hearth but the elemental fire of lightning that flashes suddenly and destructively from the sky. This fire destroys houses (cf. 594, 623-24). Real or imaginary, Pentheus tries to quench it with water (625), but only prefigures his helplessness before the maenads' violence, which he describes as "blazing up like fire" (778). Pentheus who scornfully denied Dionysus' birth from the "blaze of lightning fire" (244) and spoke insultingly of Teiresias' "burnt offerings" (*empyra*, 258) responds only to the illusory fire in his palace (624-25) or rants against the metaphorical "fire" of the maenads' "outrage" (778-79):

ἤδη τόδ᾽ ἐγγὺς ὥστε πῦρ ὑφάπτεται
ὕβρισμα βακχῶν, ψόγος ἐς Ἕλληνας μέγας.

Already this outrageous violence of the maenads blazes up close at hand, like fire, a great insult to the Hellenes.

Yet from the opening scene the reality of fire has already been blazing around Thebes as a sign of Dionysus' power and celestial origins. The fires that smoulder around the ruins of Semele's tomb in the prologue have the ambiguity typical of all facets of the god: they designate both the special honor and the special suffering for which Thebes has been singled out.

• VI •

Dionysus' cult associations include not only fire—particularly the flaming torches carried in the *oreibasia*, the roaming on the mountain[41]—but also water, the moisture of plants, the sap that nurtures and constitutes the vegetative life of growing things. "Lord of

[41] For the flash of fire on the mountains in the trieteric procession see Soph. *Antig.* 1146; Eur. *Ion* 1125f.; Aristoph. *Clouds* 603-606.

the moist growth" Plutarch calls him (*Isis and Osiris* 364d).[42] Words for Dionysus' liquid growth and fertility, like *droseros*, "dewy," or *anthemōdēs*, "flowery," recur throughout the play.[43] With that characteristic feeling for live nature that Euripides attributes to him, the god in the prologue calls the fir trees under which the Theban maenads sit *chlōrai*, "of pale green color" (38; cf. *chloē*, 11f., 107), whereas the fir trees at the end, involved in death, not life, have no epithet.[44] Both fire and water belong to the contrasting effects of Dionysus' miracles: life-giving liquids spring from the earth (141-42, 704-11), and the mysterious fire blazes in the palace or among the maenads (594-99, 624-25, 757-58, 1018).

In the first third of the play "streams" are associated with the god's Eastern luxury ("the luxury of gold-flowing Tmolus," 154), with love and art (the enclosed garden-like enclosure of Aphrodite's island, 403-15), or with the freedom and fertility of the remote Northern rivers of Axios and Lydias (568-75). The safely enclosed garden of the Muses in the first stasimon (403-15), the scene of the miracles on Cithaeron (704-11), and the fawns' grove of the third stasimon resemble the secluded "meadow of Modesty" in *Hippolytus* or the idealized image of Athens as a land of the Muses in *Medea*, and like them hold the sources of their own destruction.[45] The abundant springs of wine, milk, and honey soon become the setting for a life-fluid of another kind, the blood shed by the raging maenads (cf. 704-11 and 765-68). In contrast to the exotic aqueous scenery of Asiatic wealth, art, and love in the first three odes stand the "streams of Asopus," the setting for a progressively bloody exhibition of Dionysiac ecstasy, marked by the verbal echo of *Asōpou rhoai* in both the maenads' rout on Cithaeron and the dismemberment of Pentheus (749 and 1044).[46] One

[42] See Farnell, *Cults* 5.123f., 284; Ramnoux 128f. Cf. *Ba.* 274-83, where another philosopher of religion draws a parallel between the "wet" and the "dry." For this contrast and its antecedents see Dodds, *Bacchae* ad 274-85.

[43] E.g., 11f., 107f., 462, 534f., 651, 705, 865.

[44] See 1064, 1070, 1095, 1098; cf. also 742 and 816.

[45] See *Hipp.* 73-87; *Medea* 824-45. For the symbolism of "holy gardens" and their destruction see Pucci, *Violence of Pity* 116ff.

[46] Cf. also the "vine's flowings," *ampelou rhoai*, in 281, part of Teiresias' defense of Dionysus' useful and creative gifts. We may also compare the view of the sea as a place of peaceful communication between cultures in the prologue (17) and the sea as a threatening place of storms that one escapes with gratitude in the third stasimon (902f.), in contrast to the peaceful inland river-setting of the first strophe of the ode (872ff.).

of the most powerful contrasts in the play is that between the forest
streams flowing through fertile woodland plains where the maenad-
fawns gambol in a green pleasance (873-76) and the mountain torrents where Pentheus approaches his bloody end (1093f.), a landscape
of sheer crags (982f.), steep ravines, and harsh rocks.[47] Indeed, the
landscape contains the instruments of his death (1096ff.).

The erotic and creative aspects of Dionysus also have figurative
connections with liquid imagery. The Stranger's "flowing" hair (*ke-
chymenos*, 456, literally "poured forth") attracts Pentheus' attention
and forms the butt of his insults. A few lines afterwards he uses an
image of controlled water to accuse the Stranger of evading his questions (479): "Cleverly did you channel this aside [*parōcheteusas*] and
say nothing at all." But the opposite of this controlled water marks
Pentheus' death: fire (1082-83), rushing torrents (1051, 1093-94), and
the hard, dry rocks where the parts of his body are found (*styphlai
petrai*, 1137-38).

• VII •

The second stasimon, which we must now examine in more detail,
contains the maximum polarity between Dionysus' celestial and Pentheus' chthonic origins. This ode also combines the watery and fiery
attributes of Dionysus with the greatest density (519-27):

Daughter of Achelous, virginal Lady Dirce,
For once in your streams
You received the infant of Zeus,
When Zeus, his sire, from the immortal fire
Snatched him to his thigh, shouting,
"Dithyrambus, hither come
To this male womb of mine. . . ."

The waters of Dirce receive the divine child either because they ex-
tinguish the lightning fire of his celestial father or else because they
serve to wash the newborn in anticipated normal birth from the

[47] See Lesky, *TDH* 495: ". . . Mit dem Attribut *cheimarrhous*, von wilden Wassern
durchtobt, nimmt es (das Tal) nun an der Wildheit der Szene teil."

mother.[48] The city, in any case, potentially mediates between the creative and destructive aspects of the god. When the Chorus turns back to the civic meaning of Dirce, they identify the spring with the city and complain of the city's refusal of the god. Even as they do so, however, they evoke briefly a happy communion between the watery setting and the worshipers of Dionysus who gather on the banks (530-33):

σὺ δέ μ', ὦ μάκαιρα Δίρκα,
στεφανηφόρους ἀπωθῇ
θιάσους ἔχουσαν ἐν σοί.
τί μ' ἀναίνῃ; τί με φεύγεις;

Do you then, O blessed Dirce, drive me away as I hold my garland-bearing *thiasoi* on your banks. Why do you reject me? Why do you flee me?

The tone is of sorrowful reproach and disappointment rather than anger.[49] The last lines of the strophe, "Yes, by the clustering grapes of Dionysus' vine, Bromios will still be a care to you" (534-36) implies a threat, perhaps, but simultaneously evokes the life-giving side of Dionysus, the side associated with nurture, moisture, and growth.

The antistrophe, on the "savagery" of Pentheus, sprung from earthborn Echion, pictures the Theban earth not as a place of civilized settlement and agriculture but a fertile source of monstrous beings who throw the universe into disorder (538-44). Linked to the life-giving properties of Thebes' waters, Dionysus then appears as an opponent of the destructive forces that the locale of Thebes also contains. In some versions of the Theban legend the spring of Dirce is the home of the serpent. In the *Phoenissae* the "earth-born serpent" is the "guardian of Dirce's streams" (930-31): as founding hero, Cadmus kills the serpent and makes the waters of the spring available for creative and civilized human use.[50] The associations of Dionysus with fertile liquids and the life-giving capacities of earth throughout the play suggest a paradoxical affinity between Asian Dionysus and Theban Dirce. In one legend, in fact, it is Dionysus who transforms

---

[48] See Dodds, *Bacchae* xxixf.; Roux ad 521.
[49] For the nuances of 530-32 see Dodds, *Bacchae* and Roux ad loc.
[50] See Eur. *Phoen.* 931-35; Fontenrose, *Python* 307ff., esp. 311; above, n. 15.

Dirce into a spring.[51] Pentheus, drawn back to the violent aspect of earth and to the dangers of Thebes' chthonic origins, is blind to this aspect of Dionysus.

The end of the antistrophe polarizes the god and the Theban king even further (553-55):

μόλε, χρυσῶπα τινάσσων,
ἄνα, θύρσον κατ' Ὀλύμπου,
φονίου δ' ἀνδρὸς ὕβριν κατάσχες.

Come, Lord, brandishing your golden-visaged thyrsus down Olympus, and check a murderous man's outrageous violence.

Given the celestial attributes of Olympian dwelling and gold, Dionysus seems to reenact the battle between gods and Giants alluded to a few lines before (543-44; note the echo of *phonios*, "murderous," in 543 and 555). Attacking his violent foe from above, Dionysus here prefigures his later defeat of Pentheus, hurled down from his overreaching height to the earth. Archaic myths of conflict between order and chaos define the action in terms that extend beyond Pentheus' Thebes.

The closing epode of the stasimon (556-75) suggests that Pentheus' hierarchical rule of Thebes in fact excludes other modes of order. Dionysus may dwell, the Chorus suggests, "in the many-treed hollows of Olympus, where once Orpheus playing his lyre drew together the trees with his Muses, drew together the beasts of the wild" (560-64). As in the first stasimon (403-15) the Dionysiac fusion of man and nature creates a magic garden of song and fertility. "O blessed Pieria," the Chorus continues, echoing the beatitude of Dirce from the first strophe ("O blessed Dirce," 530), "Dionysus reveres you and will come to dance with his revelings. Across the swift-flowing Axios will he lead his whirling bacchants, across father Lydias, giver of wealth and happiness to mortals, who, as I hear, makes the well-horsed land rich with his loveliest waters" (565-75). The paradisiacal garden of the Muses that Dionysus would create lies not in Thebes but in the remote north, at the fringes of the civilized world. The

---

[51] Fontenrose, *Python* 315. The waters of Dirce play an important part in Pindar's imagery describing the city of Thebes, where the spring is associated with the creative energy of the poetry and the living traditions that the city shelters and continues: cf. *Isth.* 6.74f.; cf. also *Isth.* 8.19f. and 6.63ff.

choruses are not citizens, but wild beasts and maenads (564, 566-70). The "whirling" of the latter (*heilissomenai*, 569) in the dance in fact seems to share sympathetically in the whirling of the "swift-flowing" waters (568). Dionysus has a special affinity with fertilizing waters (cf. 575); but the rivers at the end of the ode are in the wild terrain of Macedonia, not the Theban homeland of central Greece. By contrast the Theban territory comes increasingly to contain the threatening torrents of the wild (749, 1044, 1051, 1093-94).

Directly after the second stasimon Dionysus brings fire and earth together to overthrow Pentheus' palace (594-99). Against the god's mysterious fire he brings "Acheloan water" (625), a token of his pathetic helplessness before elemental divine power. "Achelous," one of the major rivers of Greece, can serve by metonomy for water in general.[52] Yet some hundred lines before, Dirce was named "Achelous' daughter" (519), and the word recurs nowhere else in the play. Even in resisting Dionysus, then, Pentheus unwittingly evokes an aspect of Thebes that has a close association with the god in a life-giving and nurturing way.

Dionysus' victory over the chthonic, Giant-like Pentheus in the second stasimon takes the metaphorical form of a victory of light over darkness. The epiphany of the god whom the maenads "show forth" (*anaphainō*, 528) contrasts with the "chthonic birth" that Pentheus "shows forth" (*anaphainei*, 538-39). The worshipers assert their god's origins from the heavens and its "immortal fire" (523-24), while they "show" their adversary as sprung from the earth. Whereas the strophe describes the Dionysiac *thiasos* roaming free on the banks of Dirce (530-32), the antistrophe describes the leader of the *thiasos* as imprisoned in dark places (547-49):

τὸν ἐμὸν δ᾽ ἐντὸς ἔχει δώ-
ματος ἤδη θιασώταν
σκοτίαις κρυπτὸν ἐν εἰρκταῖς.

But the companion of my *thiasos* he holds within the house, hidden in dark enclosures.

---

[52] "Achelous" as a metonomy for "water" is fairly common in the fifth century, but there are only two other examples in the extant Euripides: *Andromache* 167 and *Hypsipyle* frag. 753 N. It occurs once in Sophocles (frag. 5 Pearson) and not at all in Aeschylus. See in general G. W. Bond, *Euripides, Hypsipyle* (Oxford 1963) 86.

That conflict of light and dark continues into the next scene, where the brilliance of the fire in the palace miracle contrasts with the "dark enclosures" *skoteinai horkanai* (611) of the dungeons where Pentheus would imprison the Stranger and his followers. In their joy of deliverance the maenads call out to the "greatest light" (*phaos megiston*, 608-609). The difference between this fire and light of the faithful and the fire to which Pentheus compares the Bacchic "outrage" in 778 corresponds to the difference between the life-giving and the destructive side of Dionysus. Pentheus' distance from that creative aspect of the god is already implicit in the extreme polarization between Olympian birth and chthonic origins in strophe and antistrophe of the second stasimon. Hence his "dark enclosures" of 549 would imprison and constrain; but for Dionysus, defending his nocturnal rites shortly before, "darkness holds a holy awe" (487). Dionysus' affinities with both darkness and light, and with the positive as well as the dangerous sides of both, point once more to the place between opposites that he can maintain.

Dionysus' rebirth from the dark concealment of Pentheus' prison (549, 611) is a figurative rebirth of the god in his triumph over his "chthonic" adversary; it also metaphorically reenacts his birth from the thigh where he was "hidden away" (*krypton*, 97) from another enemy, Hera. This line, describing his movement from concealment to the light, verbally and metrically echoes his concealment in Pentheus' dungeon (549):

98:    περόναις κρυπτὸν ἀφ' Ἥρας.

With pins hidden from Hera

549:    σκοτίαις κρυπτὸν ἐν εἰρκταῖς.

Hidden in dark prison.[53]

[53] The echo is all the more conspicuous because, as Dodds, *Bacchae* notes ad 549, "Here and here only in the play a 'straight' Ionic dimeter corresponds to an 'anaclastic' (530)." Dodds' explanation, however, is different from mine. The notion of rebirth in this passage is reinforced if there is an etymological play on *dithyrambos* in 526 as "coming twice to the doors" (*dis thyraze*), as some ancient writers understood the word (*Etymol. Magnum* s.v.): see Van Looy 362f. with n. 71. For the possible association of the passage between dark and light with the Dionysiac mysteries see Seaford (1981) 256-58.

In both cases the "enclosed" god is about to be released into "light." In the first ode it is from birth to life; in the later ode, it is from apparent helplessness to destructive vengeance upon the oppressor who has pent him up.

That echo is another form of the extreme polarization between Olympian birth and chthonic darkness involved in Pentheus' rejection of Dionysus. In both contexts gold is present as an attribute of the god's Olympian origins ("golden pins," 97-98; "golden-visaged thyrsus," 553). Gold will later attend another sort of rebirth and another kind of epiphany as Pentheus, falling under the Stranger's spell, offers "gold in myriad measure" to see the maenads (812). Here, however, the god's emergence from concealment into the light is psychological and figurative rather than actual and religious. Elsewhere in the play the flowing gold of distant Tmolus establishes another link between flowing water, light, and Dionysus' attributes of exuberance and generosity (13, 154). We recall, too, the "sheen" or "radiance" of the grape clusters in the joy of the god's gift (382-85; cf. 261) and the "shining falls of white snow" for his rites on Cithaeron (662). Yet that brightness also characterizes the "brilliant aether" (*phaennon aithera*) that he devises to mock Pentheus (632) and the rending hands of the maenads who tear him in the *sparagmos* (*leukopēcheis cheirōn akmai*, "white-armed points [nails] of hands," 1206-1207).

• VIII •

These contrasts between sky and earth, fire and water, light and darkness evoke myths of an all-embracing cosmic order—the gods' victory over the Giants, the Pillar of the Heavens—only to call into question both Dionysus' and Pentheus' role as a defender of order.

At the arrival of the god whose birth retraces and inverts the origins of Thebes, the king is drawn back to his chthonic ancestry. Dionysus, though born in a blaze of remote and perilous Olympian fire, retains a potentially benign relation with the life-sustaining waters of the city, akin, in his case, to the fostering waters of birth (519-25) and the moisture of nature's growth (cf. 569-75). The movement from the watery imagery of the second stasimon to the fiery events of the palace miracle is the climax of these contrasts, but they are implicit in the entire text, from the prologue on (3-12).

In proving his Olympian birth and defeating his chaotic chthonic foe, Dionysus musters his own chthonic power as a shaker of the earth. Invocations to the "Olympian" and "chthonic" Dionysus stand side by side in 553-55 and 583-85 respectively. The light from the sky that flashes into the dark subterranean enclosures of the palace at his triumph is a renewal of his mysterious birth (cf. 88-90), but also an act of destruction. The light that binds heaven and earth in the final stage of his victory (1082-83) brings the two sides of Dionysus together. As an image of cosmic harmony, the Pillar of the Heavens or *axis mundi*, it offers a momentary glimmer of the Olympian order in the obscure mortal world. But that column-like union of earth and heavens as a symbol of the divine order brought to earth also recalls the king's deluded and fatal ascent from earth to sky (972, 1073). Euripides characteristically depicts the human world as shifting between heroism and pathos, radiant beauty and helpless subjection to its own inner darkness and destructive passions. Here the joining of earth and sky that validates the cosmic order in the divine perspective brings a disastrous reversal in the human. The adumbration of cosmic order at the epiphany of Dionysus in 1082-83 marks no final stability but the precarious conjunction of opposites that takes place whenever this god is present among men in the full force of his mystery and his power.

6

Arms and the Man:
Sex Roles and Rites of Passage

His grief is that his mother should feed on him,
himself and what he saw,
In a distant chamber, a bearded queen,
wicked in her dead light.
Wallace Stevens,
"Madame La Fleurie"

· I ·

In the *Birth of Tragedy* Nietzsche brilliantly analyzed the dichotomy between the Dionysian and the Apollonian, the principle of emotional fusion and the principle of differentiation and individuation. The point was epoch-making for the understanding of Greek tragedy and Greek culture. But what is missing from Nietzsche's discussion, otherwise fruitful for the study of the *Bacchae*, is a consideration of the feminine in relation to both Dionysus and Apollo. The vehemence of Pentheus' resistance to Dionysus and the close association of Dionysus with women in the play together constitute a remarkable insight into the weaknesses of that Apollonian view of self and world that has come to dominate Western consciousness. "This structure of consciousness," to quote James Hillman, "has never known what to do with the dark, material, and passionate part of itself, except to cast it off and call it Eve. What we have come to mean by the word 'conscious' is 'light'; this light is inconceivable for this consciousness without a distaff side of something else opposed to it that is inferior and which has been called—in Greek, Jewish, and Christian contexts—female."[1]

Dionysus' cult gives to women a power and an importance that were denied them, on the whole, in fifth-century Athens. Yet it does so in a complex and ambiguous way. Dionysus releases the emotional violence associated with women and gives it a formalized place in ritual, a ritual not in the polis but in the wild, particularly in the *oreibasia*, the revel on the mountains where those emotional energies, repressed in the city, can have full play.[2]

If divinities like Demeter, Hera, Hestia, and Athena belong to the fully civilized aspect of women and embody their contribution to the orderly life of house and city, other divinities, like Dionysus, Artemis, and sometimes Aphrodite, reveal women's potentially subversive side. In tragedy these latter divinities combine with women to bring the city's desire for independence from process and change back into contact with the realities of man's place in time and change and the power of the irrational. In setting women and Dionysus together against the king and his rigid definition of the city, the *Bacchae* forms a kind of quintessential tragedy, a distillation of the conflict between human power and human impotence and of the contradictory movements between reason and the irrational in our ability to understand ourselves.

Dionysus is felt to have a special affinity with women not only because he symbolizes the repressed emotionality associated with the female but also because he himself spans male and female. In appearance, as Pentheus is quick to observe, he has the long hair, softness, protected complexion of a young girl (451-59). Representations of the god in the latter half of the fifth century favored this androgynous quality by shifting from the virile, bearded Dionysus of black-

[1] Hillman 8. See also L. E. Shiner, "The Darker Side of Hellas: Sexuality and Violence in Ancient Greece," *Psychohistory Review* 9 (1980) 111-35; and M. S. Silk and J. P. Stern, *Nietzsche on Tragedy* (Cambridge 1981) 173f.

[2] For the Dionysiac release of the emotional life of women and Dionysus' association with women see Slater 294ff., with the further refinements of Simon 251-57; Otto 126 and chap. 15; Girard 197-200 (Eng. trans. 139-42); Calame, *Choeurs* 1.241ff.; J. T. Sanders, "Dionysus, Cybele, and the 'Madness' of Women," in R. M. Grass, ed., *Beyond Androcentrism: New Essays on Women and Religion* (Missoula, Montana 1977) 125-33; McNally, passim. On the violence of women released in the Dionysiac group sacrifice see Daraki (1980) 142-44, 150, and Detienne, *Cuisine* 183-214, esp. 188ff.; Coche de la Ferté 204f.

figure vases to a more youthful and seductive figure.[3] Within the
Bacchae, Dionysus is an adolescent, closely attached to women, concerned with his own *rite de passage* by proving his identity as the son
of Zeus, free of responsibilities. But he has the martial force capable
of defeating the adult male warriors of Thebes.

Dionysus dissolves generational as well as sexual boundaries. Defending his participation in Dionysiac revelry as not "disgraceful" to
his "old age" (*to gēras ouk aischynomai*, 204), Teiresias remarks early
in the play (206-209):

οὐ γὰρ διῄρηχ᾽ ὁ θεός, οὔτε τὸν νέον
εἰ χρὴ χορεύειν οὔτε τὸν γεραίτερον,
ἀλλ᾽ ἐξ ἁπάντων βούλεται τιμὰς ἔχειν
κοινάς. . . .

The god has made no distinctions as to whether young or old should
dance; he wishes to have honor in common from all.

The principle is put into practice when we hear of the Theban maenads on the mountain, "young women and old and maidens still
unwed" (νέαι παλαιαὶ παρθένοι τ᾽ ἔτ᾽ ἄζυγες, 694). For Pentheus, however, it is not a question of old or young as a class behaving
in a way inappropriate to their age-group, but of a personal inability
to progress at a critical moment from one stage of life and psychic
development to another.

The play enacts a kind of double initiation rite. Two young men
are each separated from the women with whom they have been associated. Both are tested by a trial of strength that involves passage
through a no-man's-land where identity dissolves. Both are defined
in terms of a father hitherto remote or in some sense unknown. Separation from women and initiation into the father's world constitute
the major step of generational passage for young men in Athenian as
in other society. The play not only holds a mirror to this ritualized
passage, but also explores its psychological dimensions and its connections with other areas of social action and behavior, other "codes"
of the social order: sexual, political, ritual, spatial.

Both Pentheus and Dionysus have a remote and obscure father
figure in the background, chthonic Echion in the one case, Olym-

[3] See Jeanmaire 155; Philippart (1930) 33f.; Burkert, *Gr. Rel.* 259 with n. 48;
Diodorus Siculus 4.5.2.

pian Zeus in the other. Dionysus' chthonic origins are linked to his mother, Semele, Pentheus' to his father, the "earth-born" Echion. Rather than escaping the pull of parental power, Pentheus is drawn back into their most nightmarish manifestations, the destructive, uroboric images of both father and mother.[4] Pentheus' death, then, is a failed rite of passage, although this explanation by no means exhausts its other meanings.

Like Dionysus, Pentheus stands ambiguously between youth and manhood, between the excitability and unreliability of adolescence and the firmness of adult manhood. Like Dionysus he is described as "young" (neos) or a "young man" (neanias): 274, 974, 1174, 1185. At his first appearance he is called the "child," or pais, of Echion (213); and old Cadmus calls him pais again at his death ("the dead child," 1226). In their first ode the Chorus also calls Dionysus pais: "Bromion god, child of a god" (Bromion paida theon theou, 85). Like Dionysus too, Pentheus has his status in Thebes as the son of Cadmus' daughter (cf. 181 and 250, 254); it is through the female rather than the male line that he wears his city's crown (43-44, 213).

In the tragedy of Pentheus Euripides has brilliantly interwoven cultural norms with psychological insight. He brings together the adolescent's problem of defining his identity against that of both male and female models and the adolescent's marginal status between civic responsibility and the wildness symbolized by forest and mountain.

Pentheus not only has to separate himself from the maternal women of his household but also has to deal with his sexual desires for women. Euripides here touches on the family's and society's problem of recognizing and channeling the sexual drives of its young adults. The Bacchae, however, takes this issue further by interweaving the sexual issue with religion and with the tension between city and wild, ordered social existence and the released instincts of Dionysiac ecstasy.

Euripides characteristically delineates the extremes of the psychological situations. Here, as in the case of Medea, Hippolytus, Heracles, Electra, and Orestes (in both Electra and Orestes), the boundaries between normality and neurosis, between individual psychology and pathology, are unclear. As in the other plays, too, Euripides is particularly concerned with the disintegration of personality, perhaps

[4] Neumann, chap. 2, passim, especially 58, 72, 81. For infantile fantasies in the Bacchae see the suggestive, though brief, remarks of Simon 114; also Roberts, passim.

nowhere more graphically represented than in the physical dismemberment of Pentheus in the *Bacchae*.

Dionysus embodies, among other things, a force that Pentheus can neither integrate nor confront. Yet it would be an oversimplification to regard Dionysus as a symbol only of the Freudian Id.[5] The crisis that Dionysus provokes in Pentheus includes but also transcends a crisis of the individual alone. Pentheus fulfils the office of sacral kingship: he stands at the exposed point where the supernatural enters the human world, and he bears the brunt of that confrontation. Like character generally in Greek tragedy, Pentheus is not only an idiosyncratic individual but the bearer of a larger, transpersonal meaning for the society as a whole.

The crisis provoked by Dionysus' arrival in Thebes and by his challenge to Pentheus' world-order and personal order has the look of inevitability, and in that sense of inevitability lies the universal tragic power of the play. It is not, of course, inevitable that Pentheus should confront a Dionysus, any more than it is that Hippolytus should encounter a Phaedra. What is inevitable is that the condition of alienation from the self, from one's real emotional needs, instincts, and life energies, leads to disintegration and self-destruction.[6]

Pentheus' distance from emotional reality centers on sexuality and women. Women in the *Bacchae*, however, are not only sexual objects for Pentheus but also symbols of otherness, of the unknown. More closely connected than the male members of the polis to the biological processes of natural life, to birth, growth, and change, they are more closely associated with Dionysus as a god of vital energies and also more closely associated with the release of repressed emotionality that he embodies.[7] In their direct participation in the creation of life,

[5] On the limits of a narrowly Freudian approach see Sale, *Existentialism* 100f. For a well-balanced psychoanalytic approach to Pentheus' character see Simon 113-21. Coche de la Ferté 158, on the other hand, goes too far in subordinating psychological meaning to alleged traces of prehistoric ritual.

[6] In Sale's Heideggerian terminology, Dionysus symbolizes one of the "existentials," something in his life that Pentheus can deny or neglect only at the cost of self-mutilation: see Sale, *Existentialism* 78 and 110ff.

[7] See Sigmund Freud, *Civilization and Its Discontents* (1930) tr. Joan Riviere (Garden City, N.Y. 1958) 50f.: "Women represent the interests of the family and sexual life; the work of civilization has become more and more men's business. . . . Woman finds herself thus forced into the background by the claims of culture and she adopts an inimical attitude towards it." Whatever the limitations of Freud's no-

they not only are closer to nature, but they also challenge the yearning for autonomy, for the timeless, for immortality and transcendence that characterizes male creations in the polis, the ageless works of plastic or verbal art, the deathless fame of the great heroes. Embodying the otherness of nature in its closest proximity to human life, women stand between culture and nature. They are part of the city, but they also have a closeness to something beyond the city and potentially destructive of it. They are worshipers of the Asian god of ecstasy, wandering huntresses in the wild, and destroyers and devourers of the king.

In taking us back to a remote point of crisis when the mysteries of Asiatic emotionalism penetrated the defenses of Hellenic rationalism and discipline, the play also constitutes a myth of origins that applies as much to the origins of art and imagination as to those of Dionysiac cult. It explores the roots of art and of myth, which also lie in the Dionysiac free passage between consciousness and the unconscious. This myth of origins may be viewed psychoanalytically as reconstituting the time when the boundaries of selfhood were still fluid, a time just anterior to "that mythical moment when the symbiotic presubjective universe gives way to the differentiation of self and other; that is, that point at which the biological existence of the human being is complicated by the introduction of a historical dimension."[8] The "historical dimension" of the mythical time reconstituted by the play, then, may be taken as the history of the city in its separation from nature and the wild. It may also be viewed as the history of the

---

toriously inadequate view of the feminine for contemporary society, his remarks have some interest for earlier periods of Western history. On Baudelaire's remark, "Woman is *natural*, that is to say abominable," Leo Bersani comments, "The 'abominable' feature of women is that they are 'natural,' and the examples of their closeness to nature all have to do with their appetite to absorb (food, drink, and the penis). They would seem to be characterized by an animal ecstasy very much like that ecstatic openness which . . . Baudelaire finds in children and in artists": *Baudelaire and Freud* (Berkeley and Los Angeles 1977) 12. The less flattering side of this description is not too far from the Hesiodic view of women (e.g., *Theog.* 590-602, *Works and Days* 77f., 373-75).

   [8] R. S. Caldwell, "The Psychoanalysis of Desire: Speculations on 'Symbolic Exchange,' 'Nature/Culture,' and Lacan's Phallocentric Signification," unpublished paper; cf. idem, "Primal Identity," *International Review of Psycho-Analysis* 3 (1976) 417-34, esp. 426f., 431. I am indebted to Professor Caldwell for making the first of these papers available to me in advance of publication.

self in its drawing of the limits between self and world, rational and irrational. Both city and self are thrown back into that primal moment when those energies are free, unbounded, available for noncivic, nonrational ends.

• II •

Far from idealizing childhood as a kind of lost paradise like the Romantics and some moderns, the ancient Greeks regarded it often as an incompletely civilized state, akin to the bestial, something between culture and nature, like the women themselves who have the primary responsibility for tending and nurturing the small child.[9] In the *Bacchae* the Theban maenads on the mountain can equally well suckle wild beasts as the human infants they have left at home (699-702). Close to the animal world of nature, unrestrained in satisfying his animal needs, the child himself is "a beast," as Orestes' nurse says in the *Choephoroe* (753-54). For Plato the child is "the most violent of beasts" (*hybristōtaton thērion*), in need of many forms of reining in. His humanizing, as it were, begins when he leaves nurse and mother for the *paidagōgos* (*Laws* 7. 808d-e). Only when the male separates himself from the woman's realm of the *oikos*, associated with birth and nurture, does he enter upon fully civilized status, achieved and celebrated with the son's full recognition by male citizens consequent upon adoption into his father's tribe.

The in-between state of adolescence receives special attention in Greek cult; and the passage from it to full manhood, as in many other societies, is marked by initiatory practices and other special institutions. One of the latter, the status of the ephebe, or youth in the years just before maturity (the years between sixteen and twenty), is especially relevant to the *Bacchae*. It has been brilliantly analyzed by Pierre Vidal-Naquet, on whose work I draw heavily here.[10]

[9] See Pierre Vidal-Naquet, "Les jeunes: Le cru, l'enfant grec et le cuit," in J. Le Goff and P. Nora, eds., *Faire de l'histoire* (Paris 1974) 3.137-68 and now *Le chasseur noir* 177-207. There are, of course, exceptions, but the very self-conscious, nostalgic mood of such passages proves the rule, e.g., Soph. *Trach.* 144-50, *Ajax* 552-59.

[10] Vidal-Naquet (1968) passim; also his remarks in *Problèmes de la guerre en Grèce ancienne*, ed. J.-P. Vernant (Paris and The Hague 1968) 177-81 with the bibliog-

The initiatory character of the ephebe's passage between adolescence and maturity is marked by a two-year transitional period in which the young warrior acts out the reverse of hoplite values. Instead of fighting on the plain in full armor, the ephebe does his military service in the mountains or forests at the frontiers of the city. He uses trickery, cunning, and deception (*apatē*) rather than open confrontation. His activities are associated with night, with the hunt, with the dagger rather than with spear and shield.[11] These features of the ephebate place it on the side of the "raw" and "savage" rather than the fully civilized realm of the city.

Given the marginality of the ephebe, association with Dionysus is not surprising. It is explicit and prominent in the mythical conflict between Melanthus ("the black one") aided by Dionysus Melanaigis, ("of the Black Goatskin"), and Xanthos ("the fair one") in the frontier territory of Eleutherae. At the Greater Dionysia ephebes carried a statue of Dionysus Eleuthereus from the outskirts into Athens.[12] The battle between Melanthus and Xanthus formed the aetiological myth for the festival of the Apatouria (traditionally derived from *apatē*, "deceit"), the festival in which the male child, both at birth and at puberty, was registered in the phratry, or clan, of his father.[13] It also involved an opposition of darkness and light, the terms in which part of the conflict between Pentheus and Dionysus is framed.

In the myth Dionysus of the Black Goatskin appears suddenly and mysteriously to aid the Athenian Melanthus against his Boeotian adversary, Xanthus, in their battle at Eleutherae. In the suddenness of the apparition and in the apparent doubling (Melanthus-Melanaigis) we may recognize characteristics of Dionysus in the *Bacchae*. The

---

raphy there cited; see also Ridley, passim, especially the discussion of the controversies on pp. 533f. Brelich (1969) 223-38 has reservations about inferring origins from ephebic practices in classical Athens, but these do not seriously affect their initiatory character. See also P. Pucci, "Lévi-Strauss and Classical Culture," *Arethusa* 4 (1971) 117, n. 15.

[11] See also Calame, *Choeurs* 1.259f.; compare the description of the hoplitic relation of "man standing beside man, with shield, with spear . . . ," Aristoph. *Wasps* 1081-83.

[12] For the documentation see Farnell, *Cults* 5.321; Arthur Pickard-Cambridge, *The Dramatic Festivals of Athens*, rev. J. Gould and D. M. Lewis (Oxford 1968) 60f.

[13] See Parke, *Festivals of the Athenians* 89-90; Vidal-Naquet (1968) 52ff.; Farnell, *Cults* 5.130, with number 69 on p. 299.

motif of the double recurs throughout Western literature in connection with loss and recovery of identity. Separation from the double, as Heracles from Nessus in the *Trachiniae* or the narrator from Leggatt in Conrad's *Secret Sharer*, generally marks a successful reintegration of personality.

Pentheus, however, fails to save himself from his darker self or "bestial double."[14] His rigid but precarious self-image is unable to sustain the surfacing of the submerged sides of himself embodied in Dionysus. His contact with this figure releases the savage aspect of his adolescent personality, that part of the not yet civilized self that belongs to the raw and the wild. In the spatial code, he cannot negotiate the crucial passage back from the mountainous frontier characteristic of the ephebe's initiatory trial period to the sheltered space of the polis. He thereby loses his right to male citizenship and instead remains grimly attached to the mother, subject to the preponderance of female power in infancy and early childhood.

Several times Pentheus is compared to Actaeon, another youthful hunter who fails to cross from the wild to the realm of civic life.[15] In one version of the myth, which seems to go back to the sixth century, Actaeon incurs Zeus's anger for wooing Semele, his maternal aunt, a female relative of his mother's generation.[16] That motif closely parallels Pentheus' fascination with the sexual activities of the maenads,

[14] For the doublings see Simon 155ff.; Girard 187; and, more gingerly, Kirk 14-16. Barlow 87f. notes in 233ff. and in 453ff. "an apparently gratuitous sensuousness" in Pentheus' language that is "appropriate to his own repressed nature" (p. 88). Note, too, that the role of the hair as a sign of Dionysiac license (150, 235, 454ff.) later returns for Pentheus himself (928ff.), as does the language of "luxury" (150 and 968-70).

[15] For Actaeon see Chap. 2, section 2; also WI 26f. with n. 4, and 138; Dodds, *Bacchae* ad 337-40; Roux ad 337-42.

[16] See Stesichorus 236 P (Paus. 9.2.3). For discussion see H. J. Rose, *Mnemosyne*, ser. 2, vol. 59 (1931) 431f.; Joseph Fontenrose, *Calif. Stud. in Class. Antiqu.* 1 (1968) 84f. and *Orion* 39f., 259f., pointing out a number of links between Actaeon and Dionysus. Aeschylus may have treated Actaeon's amorous interest in Semele in his lost *Toxotides*: see T. Gantz *AJP* 101 (1980) 156-58 with n. 85; T. Renner, *HSCP* 82 (1978) 282-87. The more familiar story of Actaeon's death as a result of seeing Artemis bathing in the nude (as opposed to the boast over hunting in *Ba.* 337-41) cannot be traced with certainty earlier than Callimachus *Hymn* 5.110-16; still, the motif of voyeuristic sexuality here shows affinity felt between the two youthful heroes who perish in the wild. We cannot, of course, exclude the possibility that Callimachus adapted the sexual motif of Pentheus' end to the tale of Actaeon.

his mother and two aunts prominent among them, in the wild forests of Mt. Cithaeron (217-25, 957-58).

Pentheus' situation may be compared with that of Hippolytus in Euripides' earlier play and with that of Hylas in Theocritus' *Idyll* 13.[17] Hippolytus is destroyed by his seductive stepmother and remains in the wild, fixated at a point of adolescent marginality. Hylas is lured away from his heroic mentor and male lover, Heracles, and is trapped by seductive and rather maternal nymphs in a forest pool. In all three cases the wild that would seduce, imprison, or devour the youth is closely associated with female figures of ambiguous sexuality and/or maternity. Successful alternatives, on the other hand, contain a successful passage through the wild, as in Odysseus' hunting expedition in *Odyssey* 19, or the ability to pull away from clinging maternal figures, like Telemachus in *Odyssey* 1, or to defeat them, like Orestes in the *Oresteia*, or to find them helpful and generous, like Theseus in Bacchylides' Seventeenth Ode.[18]

Orestes in particular is instructive as virtually the mirror-image of Pentheus. "Hunted" by devouring, blood-drinking female avengers emanating from the power of the mother, he escapes the vengeance of the female-dominated house to the patriarchal realm of the city. The *Eumenides* explicitly compares Pentheus, the "hare" torn by the maddened women or maenads, with Orestes, pursued by the Furies (*Eum.* 26), who are themselves called "maenads" (*Eum.* 500). Were Orestes to fail, he would end up, like Pentheus, the devoured hunted beast in the wild, caught and eaten by powerful and dangerous female figures no longer confined to the limited area of the *oikos*. Foil to Pentheus, too, is Perseus, defender of his mother, slayer of the Gorgon, snaky-headed imago of the Evil Mother, and winner of bride and kingdom. We have already noted the maenad Chorus's definition of Pentheus as the "offspring of Libyan Gorgons" (990), which implicitly puts him back in the power of this monstrous maternal horror.

Euripides seems to be drawing on a widespread cultural representation of the passage to male adulthood, wherein being hunted, de-

[17] See Segal, "Death by Water: A Narrative Pattern in Theocritus," *Hermes* 102 (1974) 20-38, reprinted in *Poetry and Myth in Ancient Pastoral* (Princeton 1981) 47-65.

[18] For these and other initiatory forms in Greek culture see Henri Jeanmaire, *Couroi et Courètes* (Lille 1939); Brelich (1969); Bremmer (1978); Calame, *Choeurs*, vol. 1, chap. 3.

voured, caught in the wild, trapped by a powerful maternal figure, and resorting to guile rather than force are all homologous expressions of failed passage. Some of these elements seem to have universal psychological significance; others are culture-specific and have parallels in ritual or social institutions (like the ephebeia, Apatouria, or the myths of the young hunter).[19] Some express social realities in mythical terms, e.g., the fact that the transition to male adulthood implies a movement from the private realm of the house to the less personal, collective warrior code of the city, where performance rather than blood ties determines status.[20]

• III •

The *Bacchae* is striking for the way in which these elements are interwoven in parallel *rites de passage* of the two protagonists, the doubles, Pentheus and Dionysus. Each, in a different way, seeks an affirmation of identity that involves separation from definition by the mother and affirmation by a male-governed body. Dionysus, having a hereditary right to Thebes through the maternal line as the son of Semele, is principally concerned, as he says repeatedly, with proving himself the son of Zeus. Pentheus, who has obtained his kingship through his maternal grandfather, Cadmus, father of Agave (as also of Semele, of course), is concerned to defend the authority and prestige of the male warrior class, the hoplites, with whom he identifies. The two figures mysteriously exchange roles. The effeminate, languid prophet suddenly becomes the vigorous, energetic, controlling master of the situation. The threatening, vociferous, fear-inspiring king (cf. 668-71) suddenly becomes pliant, confused, vulnerable.[21]

At the peripety, when Dionysus takes command and gains full con-

[19] For the initiatory significance of the hunt see Schnapp (1979) esp. 38-40; Detienne, *Dionysos* 64-77, esp. 75ff. For ethnographic parallels see Brelich (1969) 175 and p. 77, n. 75. The positive side of the pattern appears in the youthful hunting of Achilles, Jason, Peleus as described, e.g., in Pindar *Pyth.* 9 and *Nem.* 3.

[20] See Sven Armens, *Archetypes of the Family in Literature* (Seattle and London 1966) 4ff., citing Baldwin Spencer and F. J. Fillen, *The Arunta* (London 1927) 1.201-3; Joseph Campbell, *The Hero with a Thousand Faces* (New York 1956) 136ff.

[21] For this double reversal see Burnett (1970) 23; Roux 1.24ff.

trol over Pentheus, the latter's failure in the symbolical passage to male adulthood is heavily overdetermined: it is represented simultaneously in the several homologous codes of the cultural order. He goes from king to maenad, from male armor to female dress, from the city to the wild, from honor to dishonor, from human to bestial, from adult to child. The robing scene seems to be a fantastic inversion of the arming scene that precedes the epic warrior's entrance into battle. Instead of proceeding to martial conflict after the call to arms in 780-86, he dons a woman's dress, not hoplite armor, and exits, never to be seen again, as his undone bestial double. Instead of marching off proudly to save his city, he sneaks out, under the orders of the adversary, to destroy his city.

The robing scene has particular importance in this failed passage, for it is one of the most graphic and most memorable visual experiences of the classical Greek theater. In its carefully graduated procedure in 913-44, it imitates ritual action. It in fact resembles a number of initiatory rites in classical Greece and elsewhere where the male initiand temporarily wears the clothing of the opposite sex, entering the liminal or in-between period in which he has no identity, or rather has both male and female identities at the same time, before the definitive passage to the male side.[22] The process is not dissimilar to that of the ephebe, who passes to full hoplite status by taking on the very opposite qualities, light-armed, rapid, tricky movements in frontier places and uninhabited mountains.

In this interim space the initiand's temporary loss of identity, as his past self is negated, is often symbolically represented as a death and rebirth. This imagery plays some part in the *Bacchae*, though with a characteristic inversion. When Pentheus encounters Dionysus in the apparition of a bull in the darkness of the palace, another initiatory passage, he strains to throw the noose about the beast and "breathes out his spirit," *thymon ekpneōn* (620), as if he were dying. The next scene, the robing scene, opens with Pentheus seeing the light of the sun (918-19), a symbolical rebirth from darkness to light, except that

[22] See Victor Turner, *The Forest of Symbols* (Ithaca, N.Y. 1967) 98: ". . . in liminal situations (in kinship-dominated societies) neophytes are sometimes treated or symbolically represented as being neither male nor female. Alternatively, they may be symbolically assigned characteristics of both sexes, irrespective of their biological sex. . . . They are symbolically either sexless or bisexual and may be regarded as a kind of human *prima materia*—as undifferentiated raw material."

the light is anomalously doubled, just as the initiatory process is presided over by his monstrous double. The bull-shaped youth whom he now sees before him is a symbolical projection of his own unintegrated animality (920-22). The scene ends with hints of his being handed over to his mother to be carried as an infant (966-70). But this potential rebirth also ends in disaster and disintegration when that mother takes the lead in tearing him apart as a beast hunted in the wild (1114-47). We may contrast the birth and mystic "rebirth" of Dionysus and his followers (98, 549, 597ff., 608).

Pentheus' dressing as a female maenad may well reflect initiatory rituals still familiar to Euripides and his audience. At the ritual of the Oschophoria two young men called *paides* put on girls' dress and led a procession from the sanctuary of Dionysus in Athens to a shrine of Athena in Phaleron.[23] A somewhat similar ephebic change of dress seems to have taken place at the Dionysiac celebration of the Anthesteria.[24] Dionysus' own shifting between male and female garb in both cultic and literary presentations suggests his role in such initiatory practices.[25] The initiatory meaning of such acts in Greek myth is also clear from the story of Achilles hidden as a girl among the maidens on Scyros.[26] In the case of Pentheus this cultic significance fuses with religious meaning (the acceptance of the female emotionality of the Dionysiac cult) and psychological meaning (the youth's coming to terms with his own feminine side and with the problem of behavior toward women).[27]

This ritual, like the others in the play, undergoes a massive inver-

[23] On the Oschophoria see Parke, *Festivals* 77f.; Vidal-Naquet (1968) 58f.; Vernant, *Mythe et société* 39; Brelich (1969) 445 and 72, n. 60 for ethnographic parallels.

[24] See Gallini 216. We may compare also the transvestite procedures of the Hybristika at Argos, on which see Harrison, *Themis* 505-508.

[25] Cf. *Ba.* 455 and Dodds, *Bacchae* ad 453-57; Aristoph. *Thesm.* 134ff., *Frogs* 46; Apollod. *Bibl.* 3.4.3 with Frazer's note ad loc.; Jeanmaire, *Dionysos* 138-56, 201f., 263-67, 340-44; Bérard 109f.; Roux ad 1172; Slater 288.

[26] See Roux 1.22f.; Gallini 220ff. In many initiatory rituals the young man is said to cease being a woman and to be "reborn" from the society of women into that of men: see Slater 114, 288f. Kirk ad 857-60 is unnecessarily skeptical in considering the transvestite motif here as without "much relevance"; for other ritual implications, see Dodds, *Bacchae* ad 854-55.

[27] See Jeanmaire, *Dionysos* 143; Sale (1972) 71. Coche de la Ferté 123-26 suggests a ritual transvestism reflecting Bacchic mysteries.

sion. The initiand takes on the very attributes of his alter ego that he most scorns: hunted beast instead of hunter, barbarian instead of Greek, female instead of male. He loses rather than gains a place in the city and its political life. He acts out the opposite of the values of his male peer group: effeminacy instead of masculinity; emotionality instead of rationality; illusion, magic, and trickery instead of realistic clarity, forthrightness, and martial discipline.

Pentheus' failure in the male virtues of the adult citizen appears from his very first appearance. He is characterized, as old Cadmus says, by a youthful violence of speech, by excessive "zeal" (spoudē), and by a "fluttering" of mind (212-14):

Πενθεὺς πρὸς οἴκους ὅδε διὰ σπουδῆς περᾷ,
Ἐχίονος παῖς, ᾧ κράτος δίδωμι γῆς.
ὡς ἐπτόηται. τί ποτ᾽ ἐρεῖ νεώτερον.

Here comes Pentheus to the house in eager zeal, the child of
Echion to whom I give the rule over the land. How aflutter he
is. What strange new [young] thing will he say?

This is the first of several subsequent places in the play where *neos*, which means both "young" and "new," carries similar associations of violence, instability, menace, in keeping with "young" Pentheus' failure to behave as an adult ruler rather than a moody and unpredictable adolescent.[28] The "zeal" or "haste" (*spoudē*, 212) with which he makes his entrance might seem at first to be the energy of a concerned monarch; instead, it proves to be the dangerous impetuosity of the "bad citizen" (cf. 271), lacking in "good sense." When Pentheus makes his last entrance, the god calls him *out* of the house, as one who "was zealous for what deserved no such zeal" (*speudonta aspoudasta*, 913).

The emphasis conferred on the patronymic, "Echion's son," by the

[28] While the elders attempt to integrate the "new" gods into the "ancestral traditions" (201f.) Pentheus scorns the "new" god (216, 219, 272) and ignores the warning to "do nothing new" about this divinity (362), a threat that finally rebounds on himself (1029). Note also the importance of Dionysus' union of both young and old (206-209, 694) and the motif of time (895, 888ff.). On these themes see H. L. Levy, "Euripides Bacchae 204-209," *Hermes* 103 (1975) 378-79; on the social and political implications, particularly the concern about the violence of the *neoi* in political affairs in the late fifth century, see W. G. Forrest, "An Athenian Generation Gap," *YCS* 24 (1975) 37-52, esp. 45-48, citing Eur. *Suppl.* 160ff., 190f., 250ff.

enjambment and hyperbaton of 212-13 calls attention to a theme of increasing importance in the play. Pentheus will show himself too much Echion's son in his heritage of chthonic, serpent-born "savagery" (537-44); yet he will prove himself too little the son of his father as he falls back into the infantile posture of helplessness before an all-powerful mother (1114-28).

In four places in the play Pentheus has his full name in formal address:

Πενθεὺς . . . / 'Εχίονος παῖς.

"Pentheus, Echion's boy." (212-13)

Πενθεύς, 'Αγαύης παῖς, πατρὸς δ' 'Εχίονος.

Pentheus, Agave's boy [son] of Echion the father. (507)

Πενθεὺς ὄλωλεν, παῖς 'Εχίονος πατρός.

Pentheus is dead, Echion's boy, the father. (1030)

'Εγώ τοι, μῆτερ, εἰμί, παῖς σέθεν
Πενθεύς, ὃν ἔτεκες ἐν δόμοις 'Εχίονος.

I am your boy, mother,
Pentheus, whom you bore in
Echion's house. (1118-19)

In almost formulaic regularity lines 507, 1030, 1119 all begin with "Pentheus" and end with "Echion." In the only two places where he himself pronounces his formal appellation he gives the matronymic particular emphasis (507, 1118f.). At his death his status as Agave's "child" (*pais*, repeated in 1118 and 1121) far outweighs Echion's paternity. Here he mentions his father not as part of his name but only as the possessor of the house where Agave bore him (1119). He has the full patronymic, "son of Echion, his father," only when his death is being announced (1030)—a death that insures that he will never become a patronym to a future "son of Pentheus" (cf. 1305). [29]

[29] 'Cadmus' questioning of Agave to bring her back from sanity rings another change on this pattern, 1275-76: "To the Sown Man, as they say, you gave me to Echion.— What child was born in the house to your husband?—Pentheus, in the union of myself and his father." As the focus here is on Agave, not Pentheus, the formal

At his last mention in the play Pentheus has no patronymic at all. Lamenting his loss of male heirs, Cadmus names him only in terms of his mother, "the offspring of your womb," he says to Agave (*sēs ernos nēdyos*, 1306). In Pentheus' failure to achieve manly status and effectiveness, birth from his mother and death from his mother are drawn together. The word *nēdys*, "womb," in 1306 reduces him to the ultimate biological dependence of male on female. Deprived of both heroic death and continuation of his line through children, Pentheus is totally absorbed into "nature." Instead of being a support to house and city (1308-10), he is a "sprig," "shoot," or young branch (*ernos*), broken off before its time. This word also contrasts his fate with the ever-renewed vegetative life of which Dionysus is the god.

Lacking the adult male citizen's virtues of reasonableness, steadiness, and moderation, Pentheus overreacts to the opposite traits in his hidden double, the Lydian Stranger. Thus in his first speech, shortly after Cadmus' introduction, he stresses the Stranger's magical arts (*goēs*, 234; *epō(i)dos*, 234); his sexual attractiveness, long hair, and looks that radiate the grace or charm (*charis*) of Aphrodite (235-36). The Stranger consorts with "young women" (*neanides*) rather than young men and does this "night and day" (237-38). Pentheus echoes his last phrase with even more explicit sexual innuendoes in the next scene (see 469, 485-87). The Stranger's fair complexion, he says, suggests the deliberate avoidance of sunlight in order to participate in other activities "in the shade," or "in shadow" (*hypo skias*), "hunting Aphrodite with his beauty" (457-59). Pentheus' concern with night and shade has obvious erotic overtones.[30] It also recalls the

pattern of appellation for the latter is broken, but the echo of 1118f. is clear and expressive. Herodotus 1.173.4-5 remarks on the Lycian peculiarity of calling sons by their mother's name. Dionysus, on the other hand, will establish himself as "son of Zeus" (1, 27, 466, 550f., 859, 1340f.) See Dodds, *Bacchae* on line 1. On the special significance of the matronymic in Euripides see Valentina Mabilia, "Il metronimico in Euripide," *Atti del Ist. Veneto di Scienze, Lettere ed Arti* 137 (1978-79) 439-50, with an interesting collection of data and a good comment on 1305ff. (p. 446). She argues convincingly that whenever the matronymic is used it is for a special purpose or effect. See also M. L. West, ed., *Hesiod: Theogony* (Oxford 1966) p. 431, ad *Theog.* 1002.

[30] See *Hipp.* 106, where the chaste young hero proclaims, "No god whose wonders are by night pleases me." Dionysus, however, has another explanation for the use of night: 485f., and see Roux ad loc. On the other hand, Devereux (1974) 42ff. suggests, on comparative and psychological grounds, that Pentheus' erotic suspicions may not be unfounded. For the nocturnal cults of Dionysus see Soph. *Antig.* 1146ff.;

initiatory significance of night and darkness in the lore around the ephebe and the contest of Xanthus and Melanthus, the Fair One and the Dark One, the bright and the shadow side of the self at this crisis of identity.

Another initiatory motif appears in the stress on hair. "If I ever get him inside this palace I'll stop him from shaking his thyrsus and tossing his hair; I'll cut his head from his body" (239-41). This is the first of several outbursts where Pentheus loses the control and reasonableness that a mature citizen and ruler should possess. He is particularly irritated (and attracted) by the free-flowing and luxuriously soft hair of the Stranger (455-56; *habros bostrychos*, 493).

Hair, as a magically charged substance, can have sexual overtones, but it may also have an initiatory function (not, of course, separated from its sexual connotations).[31] Both young men and women cut off and dedicated a lock of hair upon entering maturity. That ritual occurs prominently in an initiatory context at the end of the *Hippolytus* (1425-27). The connection of hair with generational passage is reinforced by its prominence for a kind of reversed initiation shortly before where old Cadmus is ready "to shake his hoary head" (185) in the Dionysiac revel. Here he will be led "an old man by an old" (185-86), but will also serve as a kind of anomalous *paidagogus*, an old man to an old, in leading Teiresias to the mountain (γέρων γέροντα παιδαγωγήσω σ' ἐγώ, 193). They will forget their old age (188-89) and regain "youth," *hēbē* ("I too am in youth, *hēbō*, and shall try the dances," says Teiresias in 190). The entire context, then, places Pentheus' first appearance into the framework of generational passage; and his extreme violence in his response to Dionysus is a clear hint of his failure.

Pentheus' personal crisis in crossing generational boundaries may also reflect the greater discrepancy between generations at a time of rapidly changing values.[32] Ironically the young king proves more conservative than his elders. He violently resists the "new," whereas old

---

Farnell, *Cults* 5.285f. It is part of Pentheus' limited understanding of the god that his worship is also associated with sun and light: 90-93, 244f., 596, 608f., 679: see above, Chap. 5, section 7.

[31] For cross-cultural data see Brelich (1969) 71, n. 59; Edmund Leach, "Magical Hair" (1958), repr. in John Middleton, ed., *Myth and Cosmos* (Austin, Texas and London 1967) 77-108. For its initiatory significance in Greece see Calame, *Choeurs* 1.197-99 with the literature there cited; for the *Bacchae* see Roux 1.23f.

[32] See Simon 151-54; also above, n. 28

Cadmus and Teiresias exemplify perhaps too facile a transition. They do not recognize the radical otherness of this "new" god and would incorporate him too easily and superficially into the city. Pentheus would obstruct him entirely. The mixing of old and young indiscriminately in the Dionysiac cult here takes place in a curiously and characteristically inverted form.

The significance of hair in Pentheus' failed *rite de passage* is even more marked when he has fallen victim to the destructive mother figure in the forest. Agave, bearing her grim prey, describes him thus (1185-87):

νέος ὁ μόσχος ἄρ-
τι γένυν ὑπὸ κόρυθ' ἁπαλότριχα
κατάκομον θάλλει.

The calf, young, has its cheek freshly blooming with down beneath the soft-haired crest.

Fused with his chaotic adversary in his bestial form, Pentheus simultaneously is in the wild, is pulled back entirely into the power of the mother, and has the distinctive quality of soft hair that he despised in the Stranger (γένυν παρ' αὐτὴν κεχυμένος, "flowing loose by the cheek," (456). This Stranger's cheek is "wine-faced," *oinōpon genyn* (438), the same quality that Pentheus earlier attributed to his Aphroditic "charms," with their fragrance of perfumed hair (εὐοσμῶν κόμην / οἰνῶπας . . . χάριτας, 235-36).

The luxuriance and freedom of hair has another meaning for the god and his followers intimated in the parode where he is said to "throw his luxurious locks into the aether" (τρυφερόν [τε] πλόκαμον εἰς αἰθέρα ῥίπτων, 150). In the maenadic rite luxuriant softness joins with the mysterious freedom of their wild state. The first thing that the Theban maenads do on the mountain is to "let their hair down to their shoulders" (*katheisan eis ōmous komas*, 695; cf. 455-56). Their "locks" (*bostrychoi*) bear an uncanny fire (757-58; cf. 235). Their "cheeks" are licked clean of blood by snakes (*genys*, 698; cf. 1186). In their murderous mood they bear the thyrsus "wreathed with the hair of ivy" (*komētēs*, 1055), and the word for "hair" used of Pentheus in 1187 can also mean the "foliage" of the shaded forest where he dies, a wild thing, not a civilized man.[33]

[33] For *komē* and its compounds as "foliage" with relevance to the place of Pen-

Dionysus can hold together the two polarities of sensuality and savagery, but Pentheus cannot. His derision about the Stranger's hair in the earlier passages reveals, in fact, a hidden "savage" self. It is as if Pentheus' refusal to accept the erotic, sensual side of his own youth leads to this bizarre vision of himself as the downy young beast, its decapitated head cradled and fondled in his mother's arms. His failed generational passage leaves him split in half, the two unintegrable sides projected as the seductive, long-haired Lydian Stranger and the wild beast. In this doubling Pentheus' intended punishment for the Stranger—hunting, confinement, and beheading (239-41)—is fulfilled for himself.

As in the robing scene, this failure in 1185-87 is overdetermined in the collocation of soft hair, bestiality, object of the hunt, and destruction by the mother. Pentheus "seems like a wild beast with his hair," the Chorus answers Agave in 1188 (πρέπει γ' ὥστε θὴρ ἄγραυλος φόβῃ), and the word for "hair" in this line, phobē, is also used for the dense foliage of the wild (cf. 684, 722). Far from defending the city, Pentheus becomes virtually part of the forest.

The initiatory meaning of hair in Pentheus' death emerges even more clearly on closer examination of the phrase that describes "the downy cheek beneath the soft hair" in 1186-87. The last phrase, ὑπὸ κόρυθ' ἁπαλότριχα, is virtually an oxymoron, expressing the anomalous fusion of opposites in this ritualized action. The word korys should mean "helmet," the sign of the mature warrior, like Hector, whose frequent epithet in Homer is "of the shining helmet" (note its prominence where Hector's status as a mature man is strongly marked, *Iliad* 6.494). Pentheus, however, can bear neither the flowing mass of hair of the androgynous bacchantic leader, his repressed other self, nor the helmet of the warrior. What he wears on his head is the *mitra*, the Lydian cap, and the wig. And when he tries to break through the madness around him and reclaim his identity as ruler of Thebes, he throws the *mitra* "from his hair" (komēs apo, 1115), but to no avail.

The word *korys* occurs one other time in the play in the meaning "helmet" and in an interesting initiatory context. In the parode the maenads balance their invocation to Thebes, "nurse of Semele" (105f.), with a strophe about "the chamber of the Couretes" on Crete "where

---

theus' death see 1051f., 1138f.; cf. also the significantly contrasted pastoral locale of 875f., *skiarokomoio t' ernesin hylas* ("saplings of shady-leafed woods").

the triple-helmeted [*trikorythes*] corybantes in their caves invented the drum of stretched rawhide" (118-25). The entire strophic system has to do with the birth and nurture of children. Since Jane Harrison, scholars have recognized the corybantic clash of cymbals as the survival of an ancient *rite de passage*, marking the boy's entrance into warrior society.[34] What is a joyous song of Dionysus' successful claim to adult status and honor in Thebes, however, points back to the wild and to a mother who will destroy her son. For Pentheus the Chorus of "mad" dancers (cf. *mainomenoi*, 130) and a "mother" (129, 131) will bring not the "joy" of Dionysus (*chairei*, 134), but the "sorrow" of his own name.

The strophic system, moving from "Thebes, nurse of Semele" (105), to a chorus of bacchantic warrior figures in a cave on the fringes of the Greek world (120-34), sets up a radical alternative to the social and familial values of Pentheus' Thebes. Thebes, too, seen through the eyes of Dionysus' followers, is revealed as its "monstrous double," as it were: not the city of disciplined male warriors ready to defend gates and towers but the "nurse" of a Stranger from the East. It is drawn into analogy with a cave of the Great Mother from Phrygia and Crete whose son is an ancient vegetation god. The participants in this rite are antithetical to the polis in every way: they are a "female mob," wearing the skins of beasts, moving toward the mountain as they evoke an ecstatic following of wild singers and prancing satyrs who make loud, foreign music in honor of an archaic mother goddess and her womb-like cavernous earth. The mirror-image of a valid initiatory rite for a young man in a Greek polis, it yet foreshadows the kind of *rite de passage* that Pentheus will have.

· IV ·

As we have already implied, Pentheus' failure in initiatory crossing to full maturity contrasts with Dionysus' success. Both young men have a double ancestry and a remote or mysterious father. For Pentheus, the son of Echion, the visible father figure is old Cadmus, his

---

[34] Harrison, *Themis* 16ff.; Bremmer (1978) 23-29. For other functions of the Couretes passage see WI 36f. and 120ff. Harrison 34-42 also points out a number of initiatory themes in the second stasimon.

maternal grandfather. He is Pentheus' surrogate father, and he in fact calls Cadmus "father" (*patēr*, 251, 1322; cf. 254), as Cadmus calls him "child" (*pais*, 330; *teknon*, 1317). It is from Cadmus, in fact, not his own father Echion, that he has inherited the royal power or *kratos* of Thebes (44-45, 213). "Pentheus, Echion's boy [*pais*], to whom I give the power over the land" is the way in which Cadmus introduces him at his first stage appearance (213). Whereas Pentheus has his *kratos* from his mother's line, Dionysus has, and asserts, his from his father's, Zeus. Whereas Dionysus vindicates his authority as his father's son, Pentheus is absorbed entirely into his mother's power.

In a successful initiatory passage Pentheus would affirm his identity from his male parent and with it his right to the *kratos*. At his first appearance his youthful vehemence undercuts his ability to hold the *kratos* (213-14). Some hundred lines later, Teiresias, warning him about his lack of "good sense" (*phronein*, 312), cautions him "not to boast that his *kratos* has power [*dynamis*] over men."

Dionysus and the women challenge this *kratos* in their rampage on the mountain. The Messenger begins his account with a deferential address to "Pentheus who has the power over this Theban land" (*kratynōn*, 660). At the end of that conflict the Chorus exults, "Dionysus, Dionysus, not Thebes, has power [*kratos*] over me" (1037-38). These lines follow the Second Messenger's news, "Pentheus, son of Echion, his father, is dead" (1031). In the ode just before, as they likened his violence and injustice to that of his father, they accused him of madness in his attempt "to gain power over the invincible by force" (τἀ-νίκατον ὡς κρατήσων βίᾳ, 1001). Here heroic "victory" (*nikē*) through martial "force" (*bia*) has turned into a defeat for Pentheus' claims to *kratos*. The defeat is all the more ironical as Dionysus in the scene just preceding has lured him into attempting "victory" (*nikē*, 953) by trickery and concealment rather than "force" (953-56), a motif that leads us back to the contrast of ephebe and hoplite discussed above.

The anomaly of Pentheus' *kratos* has much to do with his mysterious father, Echion, conspicuous by his absence. The absence of a positive father figure behind this *kratos* complements the role of the raging women followers of Dionysus, led by Pentheus' mother, in uncovering his inadequacy for that *kratos*.

Echion, though absent, is not a cipher, but has an important role in the thematics of initiation, maturation, sexuality.[35] Pentheus' psy-

---

[35] For Echion see Arthur (1971) 171-75; Segal (1977) 108f. and (1978/79) 141.

chological instability takes the form of a contradictory pull between the chthonic violence of his "earth-born" father (537-44, 995-96 = 1015-16) and a metaphorical "fluttering" or "flightiness" (304, 789). As a child of Echion, he has an ambiguous claim to the *kratos* in Thebes, and also lacks *dikē* and *nomos*, the "justice" and "law" that a righteous ruler should have (995-1003). According to the maenad Chorus "Justice" herself will execute him (*dikē*, 991 = 1001).

From the point of view of the relation between Dionysiac cult and the city, it is significant that the maenad Chorus sees in Thebes' origins only the violence of chthonic monsters. Yet Pentheus is not, in fact, earth-born, chthonic, or monstrous; he is an all-too-human figure with a mortal mother who suffers terrible agony for what she does.

In a psychological perspective the allegedly monstrous father complements the destructive, devouring Evil Mother. The very remoteness of Echion makes it possible to project upon him a fantasy of a savage figure. The power of Dionysus releases in Agave an actual, not imagined, savagery. The maenads attribute this monstrous savagery to Pentheus' father, whereas their own god instills an actual and more present savagery in Pentheus' mother. On both sides of Pentheus' origins, nevertheless, reality gives way to nightmarish projection of destructive uroboric figures. For Dionysus, too, there are hints of the savage father and hostile Evil Mother: the Chorus alludes to the hiding of the infant Zeus from Cronos who would devour him (120-34, and note the epithet *Kronidas*, "Zeus, son of Cronus," in 95), and Hera recurs as the jealous foe of Semele and her son (9, 94, 294-97). The ambiguous side of Dionysus' maternal origins is not developed psychologically, although it is important for another dimension of the play's meaning, as we shall see in Chapter 8.

The tragic humanity of the mortal characters eventually reclaims the emotional realities of ties between parents and children. The Messenger, Pentheus, and Cadmus all treat Echion, remote though he is, as a real father (1030, 1119, 1273-76), even if it is too late to provide a positive male model to counter the destructiveness of the maternal imago. When she regains sanity, Agave feels all of a moth-

---

Slater 299 briefly notes the role of Echion as evidence of a weak marital bond; Sale, *Existentialism* 110 observes the enigmatic nature of Pentheus' parentage and Cadmus' assumption of the paternal role, but seems to me to underestimate the importance of Echion in the background (p. 77). Both in his absence and in his "savagery" Echion leaves Pentheus without an adequate male model.

er's grief for her dead son; and there is the scene of consolation and pity between Cadmus and Agave, father and daughter, at the very end. By contrast, Dionysus, triumphant in his proven identity as the son of Zeus, seems shallow, petty, and vindictive (1344-51). As in the finale of the *Hippolytus*, genuine tenderness between parent and child is one of the few things to survive the wreckage of the god's revenge.

Before this point is reached, Pentheus and Dionysus are locked together in a diametrical contrast of utter defeat and total victory. Dionysus enters as a nameless stranger and exits as a proven god. Pentheus begins as the firmly ensconced king of Thebes and exits deprived of every facet of his human identity. The one validates his right to the greatest of fathers, his Olympian patronymic as "son of Zeus" firmly established (1, 1341, 1343, 1349).[36] The other is subdued by the mother in her terrible power (1118-21) and defined as the son of a monstrous, chthonic father (537-44, 990-91, 1015-16).

• V •

Viewed in psychosocial terms, the contrasts and similarities between the two youthful protagonists reflect opposite but complementary solutions to the ambivalence felt toward sexual reproduction and particularly to the maternal figure. Dionysus, as the son of Olympian Zeus and his "male womb" (526-27), is somewhat (though not entirely) removed from the full cycle of birth. Pentheus is destroyed in the total immanence of his tie to his mother, offered a quasi-infantile fondling in the "luxury" of being carried in his mother's arms (966-70):

Dionys.   . . . and from there another will lead you back.
Penth.   She who gave me birth.
Dionys.   As one marked out among all [*episēmos*].
Penth.   To this I go.

[36] See above, n. 29. Dionysus' appeal to Zeus in 1349 is also, as WI 146 suggests, "an appeal to ultimate mystery, to a world-structure in which the forces Dionysus represents are an inescapable element," but there is also a psychosocial dimension that Winnington-Ingram neglects.

Dionys.   Carried you will go.
Penth.   My soft delight [habrotēs] you are speaking.
Dionys.   In your mother's hands.
Penth.   You will compel me to be luxurious [tryphan].
Dionys.   Such luxuries indeed.
Penth.   I lay hold of what I deserve.

The parallelism of the two youthful protagonists is even sharper as Pentheus is called "the offspring of [Agave's] womb" (nēdys, 1306) at the point when she is revealed as his killer, stained with her son's blood. On the male side Dionysus' "revelation" as the Bacchic lord of Thebes and the offspring of Zeus's "male womb" by "immortal fire" (523-29) in the second stasimon contrasts with Pentheus' identification as the son of the chthonic and monstrous Echion in the corresponding antistrophe (537-44).

In a broader view, birth from the father by the purifying celestial fire stands at the farthest possible remove from death from the mother amid the bloody pollution of filicide. If Pentheus' death carries the connotations of a metaphorical and paradoxical "second birth," not into the new state of adult manhood but into infantile death, then his end is a nightmarish reenactment of the pollutions that are felt to attend childbirth. Dionysus, in his birth from Zeus's "immortal fire" and "male womb," acts out a fantasy of the male's independence from the female cycles of menstruation and birth, with their attendant uncleanness, and achieves that independence from the female which recurs wishfully throughout early Greek literature. [37]

At the critical decision between the rights of the father and the rights of the mother in Aeschylus' Eumenides, Apollo calls Athena as his witness because she is born without a mother, "daughter of Olympian Zeus, not nurtured in the darknesses of the womb" (οὐδ' ἐν σκότοισι νηδύος τεθραμμένη, Eum. 665-66). In the Bacchae Dionysus' birth begins with the womb's "travails of necessity," ἐν ὠδίνων / λοχίαις ἀνάγκαις (88-89), but then moves to celestial imagery of flight, brilliance, fire associated with Zeus, the father (cf. 90, 93, 523-27). In the Hippolytus the young hero, threatened by the sexual aggressiveness of a woman in a maternal role, cries out to Zeus for a

[37] E.g., Eur. Hipp. 618-24; Hes. Theog. 600-12; see Nicole Loraux, "Sur la race des femmes et quelques-unes de ses tribus," Arethusa 11 (1968) 43-87 (Les enfants d'Athéna 75-117) for further references and bibliography.

way of having children "not from woman" but by depositing precious metals in temples in accordance with masculine economic values, "each according to his worth" (*Hipp.* 616-24). Pentheus, on the other hand, acts out the reverse fantasy, the terror of reabsorption into the mother in a bloody mess, utterly helpless before her irresistible demonic power.

The autochthonous generation of the Sown Men, sprung from earth without sexual reproduction, implies an intermediate stage: denial of birth from woman without confronting the issue of heterosexual union. Yet the violence of these "earth-born men" (only males are mentioned) suggests that this solution is not, after all, viable. The solution fantasied in Dionysus' birth, the superiority of male nurture and the celestial and pure element of the sky-god, would seem preferable, simply because Dionysus is a god and wins. The price of this victory, however, is the cold and remote cruelty of the Olympian justice. The end of the play brings Agave back as a feeling, agonized mother, overcome with horror at killing her son. Pentheus, sane in his last moments, gasps out his double parentage, male and female both (1118-19). Our humanity, Euripides seems to be suggesting, is for good or ill bound up with accepting the sexual origins of our life and the conflicts they entail.

Euripides is here dealing with a larger mythical structure that we touched on briefly in the previous chapter. It holds the multiple contrasts of mortal father/immortal mother and immortal father/mortal mother, Olympian and chthonic birth, autochthony as a reflection of Golden-Age bliss, uncomplicated by sexual reproduction, and autochthony as a precivilized savage state. The mortal/immortal union between Cadmus and Harmonia, alluded to only at the end of the play after the family of Cadmus is totally destroyed (1332; cf. 1338), contrasts with the union between Zeus and Semele.

Autochthony is a form of denying sexual reproduction: babies come from the earth, from one, not from two.[38] Yet such a solution to the problem of birth and sexuality involves contrasting attitudes toward the realities of civilized life. On the one hand, autochthony can signify the savage, primitive quality of precivilized life; on the other

---

[38] See Claude Lévi-Strauss, "The Structural Study of Myth," *Structural Anthropology* (1958), tr. C. Jacobson and B. G. Schoepf (Garden City, N.Y., 1967) 226f.; see also Segal (1977) 114-16, on which I am elaborating here.

hand, it can point back to a Golden-Age happiness. Cadmus' sowing of the serpent's teeth suggests man's mastery of nature and also integrates autochthony into civic life in one of the Greeks' strongest metaphors for civilized stability, agriculture. Here the autochthonous origins of Thebes form a bond among the citizens as "brothers" of a common mother.[39] The two different attitudes toward autochthony reflect two different views of civilization: Cadmus and the Thebans regard the city's autochthonous origins as a founding act, parallel to agriculture and the demarcation of civic space (cf. 171-72); their perspective is from within "culture," *nomos*. The Asian maenads see Theban autochthony as the inverse of their own Golden-Age freedom in the wild; their perspective is from "nature," *physis*. Perhaps because they so precariously occupy the divide between culture and nature, they impute to Thebes' chthonic origins only the monstrous savagery and violence into which they may all too easily slip themselves.

Pentheus' place in this complex of relationships is complementary to Cadmus'. Cadmus' civilizing act constitutes a positive, communal definition of autochthony, an optimistic reconciliation between nature and culture in the city's fruitful incorporation of its ties to its earth and the creative energies of that earth. Pentheus' violence, released by the maenads whose balance between nature and culture is just the opposite of his, reveals the latent violence in those chthonic origins. On the plane of culture, he will not be another Cadmus, integrating autochthony and the generative forces of the earth into the needs of the city. On the plane of personal and psychological integration, his resistance to or denial of sexuality is symmetrical with the violence of his autochthonous origins. It releases the savage rather than the Golden-Age aspect of autochthony, just as it detonates the savage rather than the Golden-Age aspect of Dionysus and his wor-

[39] See Isocr. *Paneg.* 24; Lycurg. *Leocr.* 48; Demosth. *Epitaph.* 4 and in general Loraux (1979) 17ff. See also Bérard 34f. The Athenians seem to have emphasized the more benign side of autochthony in their own origins from Erichthonius, while they view the autochthonous origins of Thebes as more sinister. Loraux (1979) 9 notes, "Pour être des hommes, les Spartes et les *Gégeneis* n'ont guère figure humaine; tout au contraire, la naissance d'Erichthonios se situe d'emblée dans un univers éminemment socialisé. . . ." But as Euripides' *Ion* shows, even Athenian autochthony has its darker side: see Loraux 8f.; Walter Burkert, "Kekropidensage und Arrhephoria," *Hermes* 94 (1966) 1-25, esp. 20ff.; Whitman (1974) 98.

shipers. His repression of sexuality proves to be as incompatible with civilization as the recourse to autochthony to account for birth.

This negative autochthony, attempting to bypass the problem of sexuality from *below* (earth and underground), only releases the violence and monstrosity which that subterranean realm contains, a violence parallel to the emotional violence pent up in Pentheus himself. Dionysus' second birth from the thigh of Olympian Zeus bypasses sexual reproduction from *above*. His birth is thereby celestial, fiery, and solely paternal rather than earthy, impure, and maternal. Yet this solution is possible only for a god; it is as remote from the reality of mortal life as Olympus is from earth. Some of these relationships may be presented schematically in the following table:[40]

Wild	*City*	*Olympus*
beast	man	god
hunt	agriculture	blissful life without toil; Golden Age
Echion (chthonic as violent)	Cadmus (earth, mastered and nurturing)	Dionysus (sky, leaves mortal Semele for Zeus via "immortal fire")
autochthony as negative (serpent; denial of heterosexual reproduction from "below"; earth as dangerous)	autochthony as bond between citizens	sky; immortality; bypassing of sexual reproduction from "above" ("male womb" of Zeus, eternal adolescence of Dionysus)
Daughters of Cadmus and Harmonia as wild women ("maenads") who destroy house and city	Birth and nurture of children from mortal mother and father in the house	Divine son with eternal youth, born from mortal mother, incinerated by "immortal fire," and Olympian father.

[40] This is an expansion of the diagram in Segal (1977) 115.

Not all of the relations in this structure are fully elaborated in the play. Yet they form an armature of elements in the mythical material with which Euripides had to work. Many of them, as suggested above, appear figuratively in the imagery surrounding the birth of Dionysus, the ancestry of Pentheus, the origin of Thebes. They connect legends of the remote past with the specific action, in that quasi-historical coherence to which Greek myth tends. They also link the cultural with the psychological significance of the events recounted in the drama. Pentheus' destruction is not just a tale of individual psychic collapse but involves the entire history of a great house and a great city, indeed implicitly the entire history of civilization through the founding act of Cadmus so prominent in Euripides' version of the story. Here, as elsewhere, myth, imagery, and symbol enable Euripides to condense complex and wide-reaching meanings into the relatively short compass of a single play.

• VI •

In Philip Slater's interesting analysis the myth of Dionysus embodies an attitude of fusion or identification with the mother.[41] The god's action in the play takes the form of rehabilitating his mother's honor. Pentheus' attitude is one of hostility to the mother and her collective representatives, the maenads. Both reactions are equally excessive and equally impossible as solutions to the problem of sexual differentiation and hence generational passage confronting young males on their road to adulthood. Slater's approach, however, neglects the element of repressed fascination with the mother and her sexuality. It also does not recognize fully enough the importance of each youth's relationship to his *father* in his success or failure in the *rite de passage* to adult status.

The problem of rivaling and overtaking the father is doubtless, as Freud maintains, a fairly universal crisis for the young male. In a democratic society like that of late fifth-century Athens the problem is particularly acute, for the sources of authority, clearly visible in a

[41] Slater 279ff.

traditional monarchy like those represented in most of the tragedies, are diffused over the whole society, in the assemblies, law courts, and magistracies. The gripping power of father-son conflict is well attested by tragedies like Aeschylus' *Seven Against Thebes*, Sophocles' two Oedipus plays, Euripides' *Hippolytus* or *Ion*, and by comedies like Aristophanes' *Clouds* and *Wasps*.[42]

Greek myth in general and Euripides in particular often operate with a doubling of the father, one mortal, one divine, like Zeus and Amphitryon in the *Heracles*, or Apollo and Xuthus in the *Ion*. In the latter play, too, the hero's divine ancestry on the paternal side is balanced by a chthonic ancestry on the maternal, through the Erechtheid Creusa. Ion's situation has some analogies with Dionysus': an initiatory movement from chthonic origins on the mother's side to celestial status on the father's.[43] This pattern may be explained psychologically, as Otto Rank does, by a discrepancy between the boy's idealized and actual parents, fantasy and reality.[44] In the *Bacchae*, however, it is complicated by the contrasting patterns of two youthful figures, the one vindicating his celestial father, the other increasingly identified with his chthonic, monstrous father.

Pentheus' succession to the Theban kingship is also a fantasy solution to the problem of his Oedipal rivalry with the father.[45] The actual, biological father is kept in the background; the gentler, cultural father has the foreground, and he has given his "son" the kingdom without struggle or Oedipal confrontation. Echion, the biological father, is seen (admittedly through the maenad Chorus's eyes only) as violent, lawless, monstrous. This potentially threatening figure is absent, presumably dead. Instead, the father figure who is present is old, almost on the verge of senility (cf. 184ff.), capable of being bullied and intimidated by the vehement, energetic "son."

[42] See above, n. 29; also Stephen Bertman, ed., *The Conflict of Generations in Ancient Greece and Rome* (Amsterdam 1976); Laura L. Nash, "Concepts of Existence: Greek Origins of Generational Thought," *Daedalus* (Fall 1978) 1-21, esp. 9-12.

[43] See Carl Ruck, "On the Sacred Names of Iamos and Ion: Ethnobotanical Referents in the Hero's Parentage," *CJ* 71 (1976) 235-52, esp. 249.

[44] Otto Rank, *The Myth of the Birth of the Hero and Other Writings*, ed. Philip Freund (New York 1959) 69ff.

[45] For more detail see Segal (1978/79) 140-44. On Pentheus' repressed incestuous wishes see Devereux (1974) 40, 44, and Green 208: "Or, derrière chacune des Bacchantes, c'est Agavé qu'il cherche comme objet de son désir."

This pattern is almost the reverse of that in the *Hippolytus*, where the "cultural" father, also the maternal grandfather, Pittheus, the educator of Hippolytus (11), is remote, and the aggressive, irascible, potentially murderous Theseus holds the foreground. Hippolytus abjures any desire to rival this father and succeed him either to the throne or to the bed (*Hipp.* 1010-15). Indeed, it would take a bolder son than Hippolytus to challenge so powerful and dangerous a father figure, and it is not without reason that Hippolytus has chosen so radically different a mode of life. If Hippolytus avoids Oedipal conflict by opting out of succeeding his father and thereby remains in the marginal, politically powerless status of adolescent athlete, hunter, and mystic, Pentheus' solution is equally unreal: bypassing conflict with his real father in generational passage and having the *kratos* as a free gift from an enfeebled father figure whom he himself has protected and looked after in time past (1310-22).

Gaining the prerogatives of his "father" without the strains involved in taking over his power, Pentheus also has exclusive claim on the mother. In the absence of the real father, Echion, the mother is free to devote herself entirely to him. Under the influence of Dionysus, who releases (makes conscious) his hidden erotic interest in the mother and her followers (810ff.), Pentheus envisions a situation of infantile dependence, amid tactile "luxury" (966-70; note *haptomai*, "lay hold of," 970) as she lavishes all her care on him, holding him softly in her arms ("hands," Dionysus actually says, with ominous foreshadowing: cf. 969 and 1207). What his mother finally cradles "in her arms' embrace" (*en ankalais echeis*, 1277, a phrase that Euripides uses often for a mother carrying her baby) is the decapitated head of the "lion." The scene is a grim transformation of our first news of the Theban maenads on the mountain who have literally put away their babies to hold and nurse fawns or wolfcubs "in their arms' embrace" (*ankalaisi echousai*, 699-700). This promiscuous mothering of the first bacchantic revel is the Golden-Age side of the savage mother figure that Pentheus discovers in his own figurative return to infancy on the mountain.

Pentheus' evasion of the reality principle on both sides of the Oedipal conflict, victory over the father and possession of the mother, veers abruptly to its nightmare opposite: powerlessness before the Evil Mother who glowers over the son in murderous fury (1122-24), tears him limb from limb (1125-36), and then takes his body back into herself in a monstrous "feast" (*dais*, 1242, 1247).[46] Unlike Hippolytus, who, though dying, compels his father's recognition of his legitimacy and nobility (*Hipp.* 1446-55),[47] Pentheus has only a moment of lucidity, and even this is swallowed up in the homicidal insanity of his mother (1115-21). At that point he evokes, weakly and too late, the biological fact of the father's role and presence: "I am your son, mother, Pentheus, to whom you gave birth in Echion's house" (1118-19).

The absence of Echion may also reflect, at some level, the psychological difficulties that the absent father posed for the male development in Athenian society.[48] Agamemnon in the three tragedians' versions of Orestes' boyhood, Heracles in Sophocles' *Trachiniae* and Euripides' *Heracles*, Theseus in the latter's *Hippolytus* are familiar examples. We may add the unfathered boyhoods of Euripides' Ion and Phaethon, Sophocles' Neoptolemus, Homer's Telemachus, or Pindar's Iamus. Pentheus' family life seems dominated by women, his mother and two aunts. Though he is old enough to be king, nothing is said or implied about a wife or fiancée. The absence of his biological father seems to reflect something of Pentheus' incomplete or immature grasp of heterosexual union, symbolized perhaps by the Theban autochthony in his background.

Dionysus, his repressed alter ego, takes over the task of initiating him into the secrets of his own sexuality. Their first face-to-face encounter at one moment seems to focus on the issue of sexual reproduction. When the Stranger names Dionysus as "son of Zeus" (466), Pentheus asks cynically, "Is there then a Zeus there who begets [*tiktei*] new gods?" to which Dionysus replies, "No, but [he begot Dionysus] yoking Semele here in marriage" (467-68):

Πε.   Ζεὺς δ' ἔστ' ἐκεῖ τις, ὃς νέους τίκτει θεούς;
Δι.   οὔκ, ἀλλ' ὁ Σεμέλην ἐνθάδε ζεύξας γάμοις.

---

[46] The repeated references to Pentheus as "victim" and to "banquets" at the end of the play at least raise the possibility that Agave and company may have eaten some portion of the body in the ritual omophagy, whether or not they actually have: see 1184, 1220ff., 1246f., 1292; Dodds, *Bacchae* on 1184; Guépin 37f. with n. 14; Devereux (1970) 44f.; Coche de la Ferté 137-39.

[47] For this scene see B.M.W. Knox, "The *Hippolytus* of Euripides" (1952) in *Word and Action* 228f.; Segal (1970) 152-54.

[48] For another view of the effects of the absent father in classical Greek culture see George Devereux, "Greek Pseudo-Homosexuality," *SO* 42 (1967) 69-92.

It is almost as if the Dionysiac Stranger is offering the kind of initiatory lesson that the absent Echion should have provided. Zeus does not bring forth new gods as a woman does in birth (*tiktei*), but needs a woman partner in marriage.

Even before he actually meets the Stranger, Pentheus is fascinated by his sexual attractiveness (235-38). When he does meet him, he opens the conversation with a remark on his good looks. Later his wrestling and panting with the god-bull in the darkness of his palace (620-61) may have overtones of a homosexual encounter. Dionysus, it would seem, takes Pentheus gradually through an early adolescent stage of nascent or latent homosexual eroticism in the first encounter and then leads him on a little further to interest in women, albeit still the immature stage of maternal women.[49]

Viewed psychologically, Pentheus' death in a failed generational passage proves the impossibility of the regression to infantilism and shows the triumph of the Freudian reality principle. The necessities of the life-cycle forbid banishing the virile father and lording it over an impotent and decrepit father figure or being held again as a little child in his mother's arms after viewing her secret, allegedly sexual activities in a context suggestive of phallic power (cf. 1063-74, 1101). The mother's murder of the son, thus infantilized, acts out the opposite fantasy; but in the play's interchange between reality and illusion this nightmare vision becomes actual fact. The play throws up the wildest subconscious terrors as the enacted deed that we witness at but one remove when Agave reenters the stage with her son's severed head.

• VII •

Dionysus' threat to Pentheus' integration of adult personality takes specific form in three exclusively male prerogatives, the hunt, military action, and athletics. These three areas form a part of the cultural

[49] For homosexual elements in initiatory rituals see Calame, *Choeurs* 1.423-27 with the bibliography there cited; Jan Bremmer, "An Enigmatic Indo-European Rite: Paederasty," *Arethusa* 13 (1980) 279-98. Sale, *Existentialism* 112 recognizes the sexual overtones of Pentheus' encounter with the bull in the palace, but while noting the movement to a "deeper layer of Pentheus' world" stresses the aggressive rather than the strictly sexual aspect.

code for distinguishing male and female. All three codes pervade the vocabulary of Pentheus' failed *rite de passage*. Of the hunt enough has been said in Chapter 2. We shall turn first to warfare and related areas.

Pentheus' idealized image of himself rests on his image of the social order that he sees himself as leading and upholding: a warrior society of obedient, disciplined male citizens ready to form hoplite ranks and protect the enclosed, walled space of the city in which the women are safely shut in and secured.[50] Dionysus' arrival with his maenad band poses an immediate threat to this conception. At the end of the prologue the god warns (50-52):

> ἢν δὲ Θηβαίων πόλις
> ὀργῇ σὺν ὅπλοις ἐξ ὄρους βάκχας ἄγειν
> ζητῇ, ξυνάψω μαινάσι στρατηλατῶν.

But if the city of the Thebans in anger with arms seeks to drive the bacchants from the mountain, I shall join battle, leading my maenad army.

The juxtaposition of "anger" with "arms" (*orgē, hopla*) and of "maenads" with "lead an army" (*mainasi, stratēlatōn*) creates two parallel collocations of opposites. The first discordantly conjoins the steadiness implicit in hoplite "arms" with unruly passion; the second conjoins disorderly "mad women" with the discipline of soldiers under their general.[51] Pentheus proves to have the emotional violence and instability that should characterize women rather than hoplite warriors. Just before the Messenger's news of the confrontation on Cithaeron the Stranger tells him to check his "anger" (*orgē*) with "calm" (*hēsychia*, 647).[52] The Messenger himself begins his narrative with

---

[50] See in general Girard 181 (Eng. trans. 127f.) and Slater 297. For other parallels to these inversions in the Dionysiac literature see Roux ad 761-64.

[51] See Ridley 543ff.; Rosenmeyer 144 on the hoplite arms and "the panoply of embattled civic life." The contrast between the hoplite armor and the exotic Eastern garb and fawnskins of the maenads would be a powerful visual effect on the stage: see Roux 1.31f. Note, too, the contrasts of war with women and with hunting in Aeschyl. *Eum.* 25f., where Dionysus "is a general over maenads" in rending Pentheus "like a hare."

[52] Note the *hēsychia* of Dionysus in 623 and 636, in contrast to Pentheus' hasty anger feared by the Messenger at 670. The maenad Chorus gives this anger still darker tones when they describe it as *paranomos orgē*, "lawless wrath," 997.

concern about the king's sudden changes of mood (*to tachos sou tōn phrenōn*) and irascibility (*to oxythymon*, 670-71).

In the Messenger's account of the battle the traditional values are dramatically reversed as the men of Thebes respond with the passion of "anger," *orgē*, as they rush to "arms." The collocation of "arms" and "anger" echoes the prologue (757-58). The women, too, initially have the "moderation" (*sōphrosynē*, cf. 686) that is problematical for Pentheus (504). They also have the "good order" (*eukosmia*, 693) of an army and are able to follow "orders" (cf. *tēn tetagmenēn hōran*, "the time ordered," 723; cf. 303), synchronizing their Bacchic shout (724-26).[53] The male pursuers on the mountain behave in a very un-hoplite fashion, "hiding" (*kryptein*, 723, 730) in the bushes. The women, on the other hand, obeying their leader, follow "under arms" (*hōplismenai*, 733), thereby fulfilling Dionysus' threat about a maenad army in the prologue (50-52).[54] In the ensuing battle the hoplite spear or lance, *lonchōton belos* (761), proves futile, as Teiresias, warning about Dionysus' prowess "in arms" (*hopla*), predicted it would be (303-304).[55] The women have the phallic power of the warrior, "shooting forth the thyrsus" ($\vartheta\acute{v}\rho\sigma o\upsilon\varsigma\ \grave{\epsilon}\xi\alpha\nu\iota\epsilon\tilde{\iota}\sigma\alpha\iota$, 762), wounding and putting to flight the men (761-64).[56] The juxtaposition, "women

[53] On the military and political virtues associated with *eukosmia* see Gold 5 and 11f.; on the hoplite virtues of *sōphrosynē*, *eutaxia*, *peitharchia*, see Vidal-Naquet in *Problèmes de la guerre* (above, n. 10) 171. On the military order of the maenads in 680-82 see Roux ad loc. Note too the verb *kyrein*, "have authority," used of Agave in 728. Pentheus had used the same word to assert his authority over the Stranger in 505 (*kyriōteros sethen*): see Roux 1.26.

[54] On the echoes of 50-52 here see Roux ad 761-64; Hamilton 142ff.; Verdenius (1980) 13; cf. also Aeschyl. *Eum.* 25, *Bakchais estratēgēsen theos* ("a god was general over maenads"), of Dionysus'victory over Pentheus.

[55] Roux ad 302 has a valuable note pointing out the rarity of Dionysus' association with war and with Ares. When he does fight, as against the Giants, he is seldom armed, and he fights not with the conventional arms of spear, sword, shield, etc., but "with staffs of ivy not suited to war" (*apolemoisi kissinoisi baktrois*, Eur. *Ion* 216f.). See the further literature cited by Roux.

[56] See Slater 298f.; Green 204. Compare the scenes of maenads defending themselves against satyrs with the thyrsus illustrated by McNally (1978). Green's notion of an inversion of phallic power in a triumphant procession with Pentheus' head held aloft on the thyrsus (209) needs qualification, for neither onstage nor in pictorial representations is the head so carried: see Philippart 66-71. F. T. Van Straten, "Ar-cheologische bijdrage tot de bestudering van Euripides' Bacchae," *Lampas* 9 (1976) 72f. But see 1139-42 and supra, Chap. 3, n. 8.

[defeating] men," *gynaikes andras,* enjambed at the beginning of 764, makes explicit this reversal of traditional sexual power.

The preceding scene shows the psychological dimensions of that reversal in Pentheus' complementary realm of power, the interior of his palace buildings. Seeking to trap Dionysus there, he "rushes forth" with drawn sword (*xiphos,* 628), but, exhausted by his vain efforts, soon "slackens from the toil and gives up the sword" (κόπου δ᾽ ὕπο / διαμεθεὶς ξίφος παρεῖται, 634-35). The failure of the sword here not only intimates the futility of his supposed martial valor but also, in the double compounds of *hiēmi,* "send forth," the verb that described the maenads' victorious thyrsus in the vivid compound of 762, *exanhieisai,* interlocks the martial with a symbolical sexual failure ("sword" as phallus).[57] Later he is totally helpless and without sword as he falls down from his lofty perch on the fir tree, uprooted by the potent maenads (1103-13). That scene began with another show of phallic power on the part of the maenads as they "shoot the thyrsus through the aether" (θύρσους ἵεσαν δι᾽ αἰθέρος, 1099; cf. 762).

The defeat of hoplite values by the women parallels their usurpation of the hunt. Agave brings war and the hunt together when she boasts that they have caught their "beast" with hands, not nets or javelins (1203-1207), and that therefore the arms of the "spear-makers" (*lonchopoioi,* 1208) are unnecessary. Her word recalls the traditional hoplite weapon, the spear, termed *lonchē* in the two earlier passages when its defeat in war, not hunt, is imminent (304, 761). The hands that rend Pentheus, however, could also send forth the life-giving liquids from the earth (cf. 709 and 1207).

Pentheus' defeat in this central section of the play is not only martial and sexual but also ethical, for hoplite prowess also constitutes a code of civic virtues. In the scene just before the news of the battle

---

[57] The "jets" of milk that the maenads cause to spurt forth from the earth in 710, *hesmoi,* is from the same root of *hiēmi.* Compare also the thyrsus' blow causing the "dewy moisture of water" to "leap forth" in 705: *drosōdēs hydatos ekpēda(i) notis. Drosos* tends to be associated with the male generative force, as Deborah Boedeker will show in a forthcoming study; so here the maenads seem to have taken over the sexual as well as the martial components of the masculine phallic power. Compare also the death of Actaeon on the vase by the Pan Painter in the Boston Museum of Fine Arts (10.185), where Artemis points her phallic arrows at the doomed youth while his sword, sheathed, remains inert at his side, its phallic shape pointed downward to the earth.

on Cithaeron it is the Dionysiac Stranger who is "calm" (*hēsychos*, 622, 636) and advises the king to keep "calm" (647). The "daring" (*tolmē*) admired in a warrior is here the excessive and dangerous "boldness" of a "man" (*anēr*) not really adult, ready to fight against a god (635-36). This would-be warrior, unable to bear the *xiphos* or "sword" properly, has an immature *tolmē*. The Asian Stranger, not the Theban king, is the one to give advice about "practising the well-tempered moderation of anger," *sōphrōn euorgēsia* (641). Pentheus' "anger" is not moderate. Ambiguous in both his sexual and moral capacity to bear the "sword," he will be punished, the Chorus hopes, as a savage, "unjust" monster by "Justice who wields the sword" (*dikē xiphēphoros*, 992).[58]

From his first appearance Pentheus mocks the Stranger's effeminate, unmanly appearance. But here, after the encounter in the palace, he calls him *anēr*, "the man" ("here is the man," 645). Paradoxically, the Stranger exhibits the hoplite virtue of steadfastness: "We shall await you; we shall not run away," he says, introducing the Messenger (659). In the first encounter, too, he has the vocabulary of hoplite virtue on his side: he does not "run away" (436-37) or "change" his looks with fear (438) but holds his ground, "waiting" (*menein*, 440, 659).[59] Pentheus is not only to undergo a radical "change" of form to that of a woman (*gynaikomorphos*, 855) but is disturbingly unstable in his "flightiness" (*eptoētai*, 214; *petē[i]*, 332). The word recurs for the total antithesis of warrior stability, the insane maenad (*to ptoēthen*, 1268). The metaphor becomes reality when he is lifted up in the air in his own madness. Dionysiac panic, Teiresias had warned, can set an army "aflutter" in terror (*dieptoēse*, 304): the clearly martial context confirms the implication of military discipline, or rather its lack, in Pentheus' case.

Not an *anēr*, a mature man of the tempered character that would befit a hoplite warrior, Pentheus is generally defined by others or

---

[58] On 992 see Hamilton 144, n. 17.

[59] *Menein* is the regular Homeric verb for "standing fast" in battle; and note such epithets as *meneptolemos* and *menecharmos* for that steadfastness. It is part of the ironic reversals of martial values that those who once pursued the "fleeing" maenads (*pheugein* in 437, 452; cf. 642) are now themselves put to flight (*pheugein*, 734, 763; cf. 792, 798). The image of the deer "in flight" in 868 will soon be reversed for Pentheus, hunted instead of hunter.

himself as a "youth" (*neos, neanias*) or a "child" (*teknon, pais*).[60] A "young calf" (*neos moschos*), he is led to his death by an adult "bull" (cf. 1185 and 1159). Pentheus had described the androgynous, un-martial Stranger as *anēr* in 645; and a hundred lines later the *andres* are defeated by women (764). When Pentheus is himself called *anēr*, it is with bitter irony: first when he is dressed as his opposite, a bac-chant led out to the wild (962), and second when he is already killed as a hunted wild beast and termed "dearest of men," *philtatos andrōn*, by Cadmus, who also calls him "child," *teknon*, in the next line (1316-17). When that death is first announced, the Messenger calls him the "boy of Echion," *pais Echionos patros* (1030), and a few lines later cries that his death has made Thebes "bereft of men," *anandroi* (1036). In failing to defend the male, hoplite identity of his city and himself, Pentheus causes Thebes to resemble Clytaemnestra's Mycenae, where only old men and children are left and there is "no Ares in the land" (Aeschylus, *Agamemnon* 73-82).

Pentheus' physical defeat is the visible expression of his failure to learn and grow. Early in the play Teiresias warns him that his lack of "good sense" (*phrenes*) may make him a "bad citizen" (*kakos po-litēs*, 269-71). Soon afterwards the king drastically reverses the normal relations between youth and age when he responds to the aged Cad-mus' admonition with a charge of infectious madness acquired from the latter's "teacher," *didaskalos*, Teiresias (345). He then flies into a furious rage against both the "teacher" (346-51) and the "woman-appearing Stranger" (*ton thēlymorphon xenon*, 353). Dionysus can invert age and youth as Pentheus cannot. Pentheus' anger at the "teacher" recalls Cadmus' voluntary role as *paidagogos* to an aged prophet (193). The young grandson proves less educable. After the defeat by the maenads, Dionysus will soon turn Pentheus' insult, "woman-appearing," against the king himself (*gynaikomorphos*, 855; cf. 353, 980).

Pentheus' response to the threat of the maenads is not only a re-inforcement of gates, towers, and enclosure (cf. 653 and 780-81, just before and just after the Messenger's speech) but also a flurry of mar-tial orders (780-86):

[60] *Neanias*: 274, 974; cf. 1254; *pais*: 213, 330, 507, 1030, 1118, 1121, 1226, 1252; *neos*: 1174, 1185; beardless: 1185-88; see Roux 1.22f.; Sale (1972) 81 remarks, "We started out by detesting the *man*; we pass to pity for a grotesque invalid; we end by weeping for a little boy."

στεῖχ’ ἐπ’ Ἠλέκτρας ἰὼν
πύλας· κέλευε πάντας ἀσπιδηφόρους
ἵππων τ’ ἀπαντᾶν ταχυπόδων ἐπεμβάτας
πέλτας θ’ ὅσοι πάλλουσι καὶ τόξων χερὶ
ψάλλουσι νευράς, ὡς ἐπιστρατεύσομεν
βάκχαισιν· οὐ γὰρ ἀλλ’ ὑπερβάλλει τάδε,
εἰ πρὸς γυναικῶν πεισόμεσθ’ ἃ πάσχομεν.

Go to the Electran gates. Order all the shield-bearing men and the riders of swift-footed steeds to come, and those who brandish the shields and make the bow-strings sing in their hands, so that we may lead our campaign against the bacchants. For this surpasses all bounds, if what we suffer we suffer from women.

His extreme sexual differentiation sets war and women at opposite poles and makes defeat by woman the greatest "outrage" (*hybrisma*) and "insult" (*psogos*) not just for Thebes but for Greeks (*Hellēnas*, 779-80). He sees himself as the self-appointed champion not only of males against females but of Greeks against barbarians. His language in 780-86 is full of the rhetoric of battle, but it ironically echoes the bacchantic rhetoric describing maenads on the mountain (699ff., 737ff.). Pentheus' verb of military action, *epistrateuein*, "march against," recalls Dionysus' word in the prologue (*stratēlatein*, 52). But when Pentheus does lead the march against maenads, he will bear not the hoplite "arms" (*hopla*, 845) but the dress of a woman and a bacchant, with Dionysus himself as "leader" (cf. 841). Pentheus' term for "brandishing" shields (*pallein*, 783) is a maenadic word (149) and recurs in Agave's cry of victory as she describes how the "Bacchic hunter" in his mysterious "wisdom" drove them forth (*anapallein*) to hunt their beast (1189-91):

ὁ Βάκχιος κυναγέτας
σοφὸς σοφῶς ἀνέπηλ’ ἐπὶ θῆρα
τόνδε μαινάδας.

The passage forms another collocation of war, hunting, wisdom, and victory on the side of women rather than men.[61]

The turnabout in the action, as the Stranger begins to take control,

---

[61] Pentheus' *peltas* . . . *pallousi* in 783 is probably to be regarded as a *figura etymologica* that emphasizes the martial gesture. See Segal (1982).

focuses on the martial values that Pentheus espouses so vehemently. He uses the strong value-word *aischron*, "shameful," in another juxtaposition of male arms and the female thyrsus (798-99):

φεύξεσθε πάντες· καὶ τόδ᾽ αἰσχρόν, ἀσπίδας
θύρσοισι βακχῶν ἐκτρέπειν χαλκηλάτους.

You will all be put to flight. Is this not shameful [*aischron*] to turn shields of beaten bronze back from maenads' thyrsuses?

Dionysus echoes the inflated epic language of Pentheus himself a few lines before (cf. 781-84 and 799), perhaps mockingly. But the sharp contrast of "bronze-beaten shield" and the thyrsus not only opposes male and female, hoplite discipline and maenadic revel, but also culture and nature, Greek and barbarian. Dionysus captures Pentheus at his own game. He seems to enter into his opponent's vision of the conflict, the civic values of the polis embattled against savagery and license. Cunningly he hits at the issue of arms, *hopla*, with its connotation of hoplite arms. "I tell you that you should not take up *arms* against the god but remain calm" (*hēsychazein*, 789-90).[62] "I shall bring the women here without *arms*" (804). In presenting Pentheus with an alternative to military action, he also demonstrates tacitly the irrelevance of hoplite armor and all that it symbolizes. This is not a contest of weapon against weapon; the enemy is within.

This crucial scene between the Messenger's speech and Pentheus' exit under Dionysus' power (778-861) marks the transition from Pentheus' armed resistance to his submission to the god. It also focuses on hoplite arms as the crucial element in Pentheus' failed *rite de passage*. "Arms," *hopla*, recur three times (789, 809, 845). They contrast with the "arts" (*technai*) or guile (*dolos*) of the youthful Stranger, attributes of the ephebe in his marginal place on the frontiers.

As Dionysus undermines Pentheus' identity as a hoplite warrior, he also subverts his authoritarian, hierarchical view of personal and social relations. After Pentheus' excited military commands and vehement outburst on sacrificing female blood (796-97), Dionysus plays on his sharp dichotomization of male and female and his notion of "shame," as noted above (798-99). He then adopts a new tactic (802-806):

---

[62] For the play upon the Dionysiac meanings of *hēsychia* see above, n. 52.

Dionys. My friend, it is still possible to settle these matters well.
Penth. How? By serving those who are my slaves [*douleuonta douleiais emais*]?
Dionys. I shall lead the women here without arms [*hopla*].
Penth. Alas, this is a trick of guile [*dolion*] that you are devising [*mēchanā(i)*] against me.
Dionys. What trick, if I wish to save you by my arts [*technais emais*]?

Pentheus keeps the god at bay a moment longer with suspicion of conspiracy, using the political term *syntithēmi*, "agreement," almost "collusion" (808-809). Weakening under the god's "arts," however, he makes a final effort, calling to his men for arms and asking the Stranger to keep silent as he had done just before (801). Dionysus' reply, an apparent concession to Pentheus' demand for silence, is a very ambiguous concession. His single syllable, "Ah," outside the meter, brings the discourse to a level beyond Pentheus' control, indeed beyond the rationalized, authoritarian discourse between ruler and subject, general and soldier. Dionysus' speech probes Pentheus' hidden desires as he moves from the combatants to the man himself, from external to internal, from armed resistance to desire, from impersonal command to guarded wish (809-11):

Πε. ἐκφέρετέ μοι δεῦρ' ὅπλα, σὺ δὲ παῦσαι λέγων.
Δι. ἆ.
βούλῃ σφ' ἐν ὄρεσι συγκαθημένας ἰδεῖν;

Penth. Bring me my arms here. And do you stop talking.
Dionys. Ah.
Do you wish to see them on the mountains sitting together?

At this point Pentheus relinquishes the adult warrior's "arms" for the childish desire to "see." Dionysus lays bare and exploits his opponent's repressed, voyeuristic (and thus immature) sexuality, made more explicit in his next line, "Why have you fallen into great desire [*erōs*] of this?" (813).

As he moves now from city to wild, authority to childlike obedience, he also changes his dress from male to female. At the first hint of this, Pentheus balks and sharply opposes "man" to "women" (822):

"What is this? Will I then pass from man to women" (ἐς γυναῖκας
ἐξ ἀνδρὸς τελῶ; 822). Dionysus' reply, "Yes, lest they kill you, if
you are seen there as a man" (anēr, 823), hints at the truth that
Pentheus will become an *anēr* only in death, that is, not at all. Line
822 also implies that in "completing" (*telein*) his role as *anēr* he
becomes not a "man" but a beast, for the line carries the ritual connotation, "pass as perfect victim from man to women."[63]

Instead of armor, spear, and helmet Pentheus will now wear a
trailing robe, long hair, the cap or *mitra*, fawnskin, and thyrsus (828-
35). The phrase *thēlys stolē*, "female dress," recurs three times (828,
836, 852), in a steadily decreasing resistance on Pentheus' part. The
first obstacle in his "shame" or "modesty," *aidōs* (828), analogous to
the "shame" (*aischron*) that Dionysus exploited a little earlier (798-
99). Then, after the enumeration of the items of bacchantic dress, he
flatly refuses: "I would not be able to put on female dress" (836).
Dionysus quickly wins him over by pointing out the impossibility of
joining battle (*machē*) with the maenads (837), completely reversing
Pentheus' readiness for all-out war and shedding blood fifty lines before (780-86). The blood he will now shed in gory sacrifice will be
not the maenads', as he threatened (796-97), but his own (837).

The third occurrence of "female dress" follows closely upon another juxtaposition of "man" and "women": "Women, the man is
placed for the net . . ." (848). When Pentheus wears the "female
dress" now (852), he is fully converted from male warrior to beast-
victim. Instead of drawing up forces outside to defend the gates (653,
780-81), he is "dressed inside the house" (827). Instead of commanding the civic territory where the hoplites muster, he is "led" (*agomenos*) to the wild mountains (811) on "deserted roads" (841) "in woman's shape" (*gynaikomorphos*, 855). Instead of embodying reasonableness
and discipline, he is "out of his wits" (851-53); and his military "orders" (*keleuein*, 653, 781) are cancelled out as empty "threats" ("the
threats before, with which he was fearful" (ἐκ τῶν ἀπειλῶν τῶν πρίν,
αἷσι δεινὸς ἦν, 856).

Before these closing remarks by Dionysus, Pentheus has a last ap-

---

[63] For the ritual meaning of *telein* see Eduard Fraenkel, *Aeschylus, Agamemnon*
(Oxford 1950) ad 105, 931-34, 973, 1202; also J. H. Kells, *Sophocles, Electra* (Cam-
bridge 1973) ad 1508ff. This meaning is reinforced by the implicit "dedication" of
Pentheus to his death, 856-59, 934.

peal to "arms" (hopla), the last words he speaks in this scene (845-46): "I would set forth. For either I shall go bearing arms [hopl' echōn] or I shall obey your counsels." He still thinks that he has the military authority and the emotional and intellectual capacity to make a free choice. In fact, he has no real alternative, as Dionysus' next words show (848): "Women, the man is prepared for the net." Pentheus had hesitated momentarily at the "guile" and "arts" with which Dionysus proposed to bring the women "without arms" (804-806). Now, dressed as a woman himself, he becomes a part of that guile. He gives up open battle (machē, 837) for "spying" (kataskopē, 838). In terms of the elaborately coded differentiation between hoplite and ephebe discussed earlier, he has moved backward rather than forward in his initiatory ritual: he emerges from the symbolic change of dress as ephebe spying in the mountains rather than as hoplite bearing arms at the city gates.

This initiatory reversal accompanies another reversal of ethical values. Aischron in 798, aidos in 828, and "insult to the Hellenes" in 779 are all characteristic of the "shame-culture" from which Pentheus comes. In this society to be "laughed at," gelasthai, is the most intolerable of insults.[64] "Anything is better than the maenads' laughing at me" (en-gelan, 841-42), Pentheus says in his penultimate utterance of the scene. But a few lines later, when Dionysus describes the completion of his humiliation "in woman's form," he makes clear the reality of the laughter (gelōs) he will get, not from the maenads (who do far worse than laugh), but, more shameful still, from his own Theban subjects (Thēbaiois, 854).

In his first scene onstage Pentheus had laughed at the god (250, 272, 286, 322). Later the Stranger himself, when he appeared, was the one to laugh, making light of the king's power (439). This laughing god inverts the traditional heroic values. With "laughing visage" (gelōnti prosōpō[i], 1021), he brings his victim to an end that is the total reverse of the noble death extolled by the poets as appropriate to the heroic warrior.

In the next scene (912ff.) Pentheus enters in "the garb of a woman, maenad, bacchant" (σκευὴν γυναικὸς μαινάδος βάκχης ἔχων, 915). Dionysus' striking collocation of the three nouns makes clear the ex-

[64] E.g., Soph. Ajax 367; see Gustav Grossmann, "Das Lachen des Aias," MH 25 (1968) 65-85.

tent of the reversal. His form of address in the next line, "spy of your mother and her company" (μητρός τε τῆς σῆς καὶ λόχου κατάσκο-πος, 916), reiterates the shift from hoplite force to ephebic "guile" and also lends military status to the "mother's" maenad band, now a *lochos*, "company."

The parallelism between these reversals in the areas of sex and war with the other reversals has been suggested by the preceding ode, the third stasimon (862-911), which shifts between hunter and hunted and fuses *nomos* and *physis*, culture and nature (895-96). Pentheus now looks like "one of Cadmus' daughters" (917), confuses the reality of the physical world in his vision of "two suns" and "two Thebes" (918-19), and mixes up man, beast, and god (920-22). He not only wears the long hair that he scorned in the Dionysiac Stranger (928 and 831; cf. 235, 455-56, 695), but even tosses it to and fro in Bacchic ecstasy (930-31), just like the Asiatic bacchants in the parode (cf. 149-50). More pointedly still, his description of himself tossing his hair in 930 closely echoes his fury at the Stranger for doing exactly that in 240-41. As the maenads previously confronted the warriors of the city with "a miracle of good order" (*eukosmia*, 693), so here, Dionysus promises, Pentheus will see "bacchants of unexpected moderation and good sense" (*para logon sōphronas bakchas*, 940).

Pentheus, now himself involved in a paradoxical interchange of "unsound mind" and "good sense" (947-48), would direct his newly released physical energy against wild nature (945-52). Dionysus' new madness in fact only makes clear Pentheus' latent madness earlier, in his violence against the other holy places of the wild, Teiresias' seat of augury (346-51). The Chorus's identification of *nomos* and *physis* in the preceding ode (893-96) is realized here with a far from conventional significance as he would bring his newly gained physical force and changed mind (*phrenes*, 944) from the city to wild nature. His threat to tear up Cithaeron (945-52) soon rebounds on himself (1103ff.) and reveals the impotence, psychological as well as physical, in those earlier threats against divinity in nature (346-51).

Dionysus, however, succeeds in instilling a rudimentary piety in the king that was lacking before (951-56):

> *Dionys.*   Do not, however, destroy the Nymphs' abodes and the seat of Pan, where he holds his flute-playing.

Penth. You have spoken well. Not by strength [*sthenei*] must we conquer the women. I shall hide myself in the fir trees.

Dionys. Yes, you shall hide yourself with the hiding in which you deserve to be hidden, going as a crafty spy of the maenads.

These women are "unconquerable by force" not because "guile" (*dolos*) is the answer but because Pentheus' illusion of strength, as of sanity, masks his underlying weakness, much as his authoritarian exterior masks an uncertain and unstable identity that the god can easily swing from warrior to woman, from claims of hypermasculinity to feminization. The change from hoplite commander to ephebic "crafty spy" adumbrated at the beginning of the scene (916) is now complete (*dolion kataskopon*, 956). The "guile toward women" (*es gynaikas dolion*, 487), which Pentheus previously insulted in Dionysus, now applies to himself.

"Bring me through the middle of the land of Thebes," Pentheus then cries, "for I am the only man [*anēr*] with the daring [*tolmē*] to do this" (961). Manhood and courageous "daring" now fuse with their opposite for Pentheus. "The contests that you deserve await you," Dionysus reassures him (964), but these contests (*agōnes*) are to be those of neither warriors nor athletes. On first meeting the Stranger, Pentheus remarked jeeringly on the long hair that suggested pursuits other than wrestling (455-56), but he fell afoul of the Lydian in a contest of sorts where he could not get a hold (800).[65] Able to "trip up" violent bulls, the maenads prove no mean wrestlers themselves (743-44), and indeed they soon win their "lovely contest" over Pentheus (*kalos agōn*, 1162). Immediately after the "contests" announced in 964 the would-be athlete and warrior regresses to the infantile softness and luxury (*habrotēs, tryphē*) of being carried in a mother's arms (964-69).

The word "luxury," *tryphē*, occurs in the *Ion* explicitly of the passive joy of the infant cuddled in the mother's embrace. The young hero there reflects regretfully, "During that time that I should have spent in luxury [*tryphan*] in my mother's arms and in the pleasure of

[65] On the wrestling metaphor in 800 see Dodds, *Bacchae* ad loc. Cf. also *antipalon* in 544. On such inversions of athletics see Froma I. Zeitlin, "The Argive Festival of Hera and Euripides' *Electra*," TAPA 101 (1970) 656f.

life [*terpsis*], I was deprived of my dearest mother's nurture" (*trophē*, *Ion* 1375-77).

The *Bacchae*'s ominous oxymoron-like collocation of the two antithetical verbs, "You will *compel* me *to be luxurious*" (*tryphan m'anankaseis*, 969) exposes the paradox of the hard power that lies in Dionysus' "softness" (*habrotēs*, 968). The strange juxtaposition plays on the etymological meaning of *tryphē* as "breaking" (*thryptein*), "being dis-solute."[66] Pentheus is now wearing that "soft" or "luxurious" hair (*habros*) that he scorned in Dionysus and his followers (493; cf. 150). Working upon his opponent by eliciting his concealed other self, the god exposes the rift between disciplined warrior and needy infant, hoplite sternness and sensuality. The impact of the Dionysiac release of emotion and letting down of barriers is one of "compulsion" (*anankē*, 969): Pentheus can no longer defend himself against the infantile self that a part of him still wants to be, passively enjoying the physical attention lavished on him by an adoring mother. But this change from active to passive works in a very different way as the god makes him the one who "suffers" (cf. *pathē*, 971; cf. 643, 786) instead of the one who "acts," and the mother's attentions with her "hands" are far from "soft" (cf. 969 with 973, 1136, 1207).

This scene, like the preceding one, closes with a monologue by Dionysus after rapid dialogue or stichomythia (971-76; cf. 849-61). This little speech, too, confirms the reversal of heroic values for Pentheus (971-76):

δεινὸς σὺ δεινὸς κἀπὶ δείν' ἔρχῃ πάθη,
ὥστ' οὐρανῷ στηρίζον εὑρήσεις κλέος.
    ἔκτειν', Ἀγαύη, χεῖρας αἵ θ' ὁμόσποροι
Κάδμου θυγατέρες· τὸν νεανίαν ἄγω
τόνδ' εἰς ἀγῶνα μέγαν, ὁ νικήσων δ' ἐγὼ
καὶ Βρόμιος ἔσται. τἄλλα δ' αὐτὸ σημανεῖ.

Terrible you are, terrible, and to terrible sufferings do you come, so that you will find glory reaching to the heavens. Stretch forth, Agave, your hands, and you too, daughters of Cadmus, of the same seed. This young man here [*neanias*] I am leading to a great contest [*agōn*], but the conqueror will be Bromios and I myself. The thing itself will show the rest.

[66] On the etymological play on *tryphē* and *thryptein* ("to break") and related words see Laurence J. Kepple, "The Broken Victim: Euripides *Bacchae* 969-970," *HSCP* (1976) 107-9; Segal (1982).

Defined here as a "young man," Pentheus enters upon an agonistic trial where his defeat will be total. Instead of the "glory that reaches to the heavens" that marks the Homeric warrior (*Odyssey* 9.20), he plunges downward to an inglorious death (where the verb *stērizein*, 972, again recurs: 1073, 1083) on the "black earth" (1065; cf. 1112).

At the beginning of the next ode the Chorus spurs on the Theban maenads and the "swift hounds of Madness" (ϑοαὶ Λύσσας κύνες) to attack Pentheus, "the one in woman-miming garb, maddened spy of the maenads" (980-81):

ἐπὶ τὸν ἐν γυναικομίμῳ στολᾷ
λυσσώδη κατάσκοπον μαινάδων.

Pentheus' female dress, described in language that recalls the earlier scene (cf. *gynaikomorphon*, 855), now accompanies his status as "spy" rather than hoplite warrior. "Maddened spy of the maenads" (981) closely echoes Dionysus' description of Pentheus as "crafty spy of the maenads" less than twenty-five lines before (956):

δόλιον μαινάδων κατάσκοπον (956)
λυσσώδη κατάσκοπον μαινάδων (981).

The change from "crafty" to "maddened" reflects the total disintegration now about to befall Pentheus. "Maddened," *lyssōdēs*, he is assimilated to the maenads' own state, driven by the "hounds of Madness" (*Lyssa*, 977). Now seen as a monstrous offspring of a "lioness or the race of Libyan Gorgons" (989-90), he is "not of woman's blood born" (988-89). This means not bypassing mortal generation, as Dionysus does, through his father's "male womb" and "immortal fire," but the diametrical opposite, assimilation to his subhuman origins. The sword of justice that, in the maenads' view, will punish his evil ways (*dika . . . xiphēphoros*, 991 = 1011) recalls his own failure with the *xiphos* as he encounters the bull in the depths of the palace buildings. The ode's closing lines depict his destructive "fall" (*pesonti*) as a hunted beast beneath the anomalous "herd" of destructive maenads (1022-23).

The Messenger who enters to announce the now anticipated death calls Dionysus, not Pentheus, *anax*, "lord" (1031). Dionysus now has the Theban *kratos* (cf. 213) as the maenads cry triumphantly (1037-38): "Dionysus, Dionysus, not Thebes, has the power [*kratos*] over me." The old "masters" or "rulers" (*despotai*) "fare ill" (1033). Cadmus' house, addressed in the opening lines of this scene as "happy

once in Greece" (*an' Hellada*, 1024) marks Pentheus' failure to check
the maenads' rampage as "a great insult to the Hellenes" (779). Now
the Asiatic "strangers" celebrate their victory "in barbarian song" (*eu-
azō xena melesi barbarois*, 1034).

Pentheus' "march" against the maenads in the next lines reflects
that disintegration into polarized opposites that marks his defeat. His
disguised exit has the character of a public procession (*pompos theōrias*, 1045, "escort of the sacred procession"), a peacetime activity,
not a warlike act. The "great contest" where he would win the open
recognition of "glory" (*kleos*, 971-76) veers ambiguously between secrecy and public movement. Ostensibly alone, Pentheus is yet accompanied by a host of followers (1043ff.), who now behave more
like the "crafty spy" that Pentheus has himself become, going in "silence" to avoid being seen (1049-50; cf. 816, 954-56) as they follow
their "lord" (*despotēs*, 1046). The holy silence on the mountain after
the mysterious "voice" addressing the "young women" (*neanides*, 1078-
79) is of a different order from the careful "silence" that Pentheus
and his men would observe (1084-85).[67]

War and sex again pull against one another: intrusion into a moist,
grassy hollow, well shaded (1051-52), carries sexual innuendoes. Here
the maenads sit, "with hands in pleasurable efforts" (*cheiras in ter-
pnois ponois*, 1053). But the "efforts" in which the maenads will soon
use their "hands" will be far from "pleasurable" (cf. 1128, 1136). The
alternation between inviting gentleness and dangerous harshness already noted in this, as in other, maenadic landscapes in the play,
may reflect Pentheus' ambivalence toward a sexual freedom that he
desires but finds terrifying and alien.

• VIII •

By plummeting from tall tree to the earth at his death (1110-14),
Pentheus not only undergoes physical rending (*sparagmos*), but also
disintegrates psychologically in an unresolved ambivalence between

---

[67] The alternation of noise and silence is all the more striking in the light of the
shouts of the maenads in 688 and 731, the noise of Pentheus' army in 780ff., the
ritualized shouting of the maenad Chorus at his death in 1131-33.

delusions of phallic potency on the one hand and rejection of his masculinity in submission to the mother (dressing as a maenad) on the other. Elevation in the high tree may symbolize the precarious delusion of phallic power. The fall to earth after the tree's uprooting by the maenads and the consequent dismemberment enact a nightmarish scene of failure and castration.[68]

The defeat of male phallic power by the female, already implicit in the victory of maenad's thyrsus over hoplite's spear (758-64) and in Pentheus' dropping of his sword in the palace (634-35; cf. 626-28), is developed and refined in the scene of Pentheus' death. In the previous scene he plotted with Dionysus (953-54), "We must not conquer the women by force [sthenei]; but I shall conceal my body in the fir trees." When Dionysus replies, "You will be concealed with that concealment with which you deserve to be concealed" (955), his language calls attention to the hidden meanings soon to be clarified: the inversion of active and passive, observer and participant, maenad and victim of maenads. From a psychoanalytic perspective Pentheus' inability to confront and accept his full male sexuality takes the form of a sexually regressive voyeurism that also involves refusing to confront the women directly by "force" (sthenei, 953, where a sexual meaning may also be latent). Pentheus here would use the phallic visibility of the fir tree for concealment. Unable still to accept his phallic sexuality, he regards the tree as a means of self-concealment, not self-revelation: it serves as an instrument in the substitute sexuality of looking rather than the overt sexual act of doing, which would require exposure rather than hiding. Dionysus, however, will use the tree, as he uses the bull, for just the opposite purpose, namely to reveal the libidinal energies that Pentheus cannot consciously admit.

The death itself is the last stage in Pentheus' movement back from adult male heroism to infancy. He reverts to the position of the small child, lying on his back, having "fallen to the earth" (1112) and facing the "mother" (1118, 1120) who has "fallen upon him" (1115), a stranger who glowers at him with an enraged, terrifying face that gives no sign of recognition. She responds neither to his touch (1117f.) nor to the words in which he attempts to identify himself: "It is I, mother, your son, Pentheus, whom you bore in Echion's house (1118f.). In-

[68] See Sale (1972) 67, 73ff.; Slater 298-300; Green 204ff.; Segal (1978/79) 145f. See also Roberts 50f.

stead of the maternal look, there is the fearful glare of the maniac, with rolling eyes and foaming mouth (1122f.), the Evil Mother in her most horrific aspect. Instead of the soft touch, there is the furious attack that tears the arm from the socket with more than human force (1125-27), a "force" (*sthenos*) more potent than that which he, in his submissive feminine disguise, could not bring himself to use against women (953).

In the extreme agony of this dismemberment Pentheus gains a certain degree of self-recognition. He throws off the *mitra* or cap that symbolizes his bondage to Dionysiac delusion (1115; cf. 833, 929). He asks for "recognition" (*gnōrisasa*, 1116) and declares his identity, giving both mother and father. But the recognition only intensifies the pathos. What Dionysus has released in him might have proven the means of an ultimate integration of personality, but it can now lead only to dismemberment or *sparagmos*.

There is just the glimmer of growth in Pentheus' willingness to acknowledge "errors" or "faults" (*hamartiai*, 1121), the word used of his mother's and aunts' accusations of Semele in the prologue (29). But this dropping of defense mechanisms comes too late for Pentheus and too soon for Agave. He does not possess the integrity and strength through which Hippolytus survives his *sparagmos* and reaches new self-understanding and heroic endurance (*Hipp.* 1446-66). As Pentheus also fulfills the symbolical role of sacral kingship, bearing the responsibility for integrating the supernatural into the social order, his death simultaneously reflects this city's inability to integrate rational and irrational, public and private needs, social order and personal fulfillment.

• IX •

The lyrical dialogue, or kommos, between Agave and the Chorus after Pentheus' death (1153-99) brings together the multiple inversions of generational passage. The "contest" announced by Dionysus at the end of the earlier scene (964, 971-76) is now, from the maenads' point of view, "a lovely contest" in which "the Cadmean bacchants accomplished as groans, as tears, the glorious hymn of victory" (1161-62):

τὸν καλλίνικον κλεινὸν ἐξεπράξατε
ἐς στόνον, ἐς δάκρυα.

The adjective *kleinos*, "glorious," recalls Dionysus' ironical offer of "glory reaching to the heavens" (*kleos*, 972). *Kallinikos* implies Pentheus' loss of "victory" (*nikē*, 953 and 975) as young athlete as well as general and king. In another inversion of his military efforts, the bull that "led" him to disaster is the "general," or "commander," *proēgētēr*, in the preceding line (1159).[69] That specifically military dimension of his failure also appears, as noted earlier, in the ambiguous description of the calf-victim's soft hair with the usual word for "helmet" (*korys*, 1185-87).

At the end of the kommos Agave and the Chorus exchange the cries, "Do you praise [*epaineis*]? / I praise. / Soon the Cadmeans / And your child Pentheus / Will praise his mother, winner of this lion-sprung prey" (1193-96). The opposite of this "praise" (*epainos*) is the insult (*psogos*) incurred by barbarian women's defeat of men (779).[70] Generally the son wins "praise" from his parents; but in this scene the "mother" wants "praise" from her son, now definitively fixed not only as "child" (*pais ge Pentheus*, "Pentheus the child," 1195), but as wild beast, excluded from the civilized order (cf. 989-90). She, too, wins the "prize of honor" (*geras*, 1179) and the *kleos* or "glory" (*klē[i]zometha*, 1180) and "rejoices in the great, great, and visible deeds" (1197-99).

When Agave turns from lyrical utterance to her first iambic speech in the play, she continues the coincidence of personal and political failure implied in Pentheus' death (1200-1204):

Chorus.   Show now, poor woman, to the citizens the victorious prey of your hunting that you have come bearing.

Agave.   O you who dwell in the lovely-towered town of Theban land, come, that you may behold this prey that we, Cadmus' daughters, have hunted down. . . .

Addressing the "citizens" (*astoi*, masculine, 1201; *asty . . . naiontes*, 1202-1203), she calls attention to those very familial and civic boundaries that she has violated by the mad "hunting" of her son. Pentheus'

---

[69] For the military vocabulary see Hamilton 144, with nn. 16-17.

[70] For the antithesis of "praise" and "blame" in early Greek poetics and values see Detienne, *Maîtres* 20-27; Nagy, *Best of Achaeans*, chap. 12.

attempt as warrior and king to defend his gates and towers (653, 780-81) is totally negated when the Theban women return from wild to city as "conquerors" (cf. *nikēphoros*, 1200). Praising bare hands over nets or spears (1205-1208), Agave uses a compound of the word *lonchē*, "spear," that was prominent in the Bacchic defeat of hoplite arms earlier (1208; cf. 304, 762). Her phrase "white-armed points of hands" in 1206-1207, λευκοπήχεσι χειρῶν ἀκμαῖσιν, completes the sexual reversal in "white" and "black" earlier (cf. 438, 457-58, 628, 665, cf. 863); but the brilliant hypallage also transfers to destruction the epithet of female sexual attractiveness (cf. "white-armed" in Homer). These "white arms" are tipped with "points," like spears. Pentheus had made fun of the Stranger's seductive "white complexion" (*leukēn chroian*, 457-59), but these "white-armed points" of fingernails have vindicated the god. Agave is using language in a Dionysiac way, fusing the seductive with the deadly, the soft with the violent.

Wishing to attach her grim trophy as an adornment to the palace walls (1211-15), Agave in fact sets the seal on her destruction of the *oikos* that she should nurture and sustain. Her instructions, "Let him take the fastened steps of ladders and bring them to the house" (1212-13), use the martial language of an attack upon a city.[71] In usurping the weapons of male warrior and hunter, she also assumes the male role of besieger. She thus symbolically completes the maenad women's invasion of gates and towers that Pentheus had tried to defend.

Entering with attendants who carry Pentheus' torn body, Cadmus "comes within the walls of the town [*asty*] from the bacchants" where he "heard of [his] daughters' deeds of daring" (1222-24). *Tolmē*, the "daring" of male warriors, was Pentheus' boast when he was about to leave Thebes for the maenads' valley in the wild (961-62). Reversing that journey with the grim result of Pentheus' failure, the torn body, Cadmus now attributes this masculine courage to his daughters, victorious "warriors" as well as "hunters." Agave had already usurped the male warrior's right to "boast" (*kompazein*) over his fallen enemy (1207; cf. 1233). The Stranger, confronting Pentheus for the first time, denied any need for martial "boasting" (*kompos*, 461).

Agave's first words to her father take these inversions of male and female roles even farther (1233-43):

---

[71] See above, Chap. 5, n. 23.

Father, you can now make the greatest boast, that you have sown
by far the best daughter of all mortals. I mean all your daughters,
but me supremely, who have left the shuttles at the loom and come
to greater things, the hunt of beasts with my hands. And I bring
this now in my arms, as you see, taking this prize of excellence
[*aristeia*], to be hung up in your halls. Blessed you are, blessed,
since we have accomplished such feats.

The *aristeia*, the prize of excellence that the young warrior would
bring back to his father as proof of his manhood, is here the decapitated head of the son, hunted as beast, destroyed as helpless infant by
his mother, and presented by the daughter, not the son, to her father.[72]
Such are the "feats" or "deeds" (*exeirgasmena*, 1245) in which the
father should feel "blessed" (*makarios*, 1242-43, one of the key words
in the play). But the great "deeds," as Cadmus cries out two lines
later, are "deeds of murder" that the women have committed "with
miserable hands" (φόνον ταλαίναις χερσὶν ἐξειργασμένων, 1245;
cf. 1197-99). Parallel to these inversions in martial prowess and generational passage is the spatial and technological inversion, the woman's abandonment of the looms and shuttles in the interior of the
house (cf. 118-19, 519) for hunting with bare hands on the wild
mountains. The "infant" whom she there "carried in her arms" is
now her murdered prey, as Dionysus had hinted earlier (cf. 1238 and
968-69).

"You are *like* one of Cadmus' daughters in form," Dionysus told
the transvestite Pentheus at his point of passage from city to wild
(917). "Would that my son were good at hunting, *resembling* his
mother's ways, when he would go searching for beasts with the Theban youths," Agave wishes here as Cadmus utters a cry of grief (1252-
55). In the warrior ethic of early Greek society the son shows his *aretē*
when he proves himself like his father. Resemblance of son to father
is what Homer's Hector wishes for Astyanax and what Sophocles' Ajax
prays for Eurysaces (*Iliad* 6.476-81; *Ajax* 545-51). In the total inver-

[72] For the traditional notion of the son's following the *tropoi* or character of the
father see Soph. *Ajax* 434-40, 545-57. Agave's *exochōs* in 1235 may also carry connotations of heroic values, as the word regularly denotes martial "excellence" in
heroic contexts: e.g., Hom. *Il.* 2.183, 483, 9.638, 18.56, *Od.* 4.629; Pindar *Pyth.*
5.26 and *Nem.* 3.71.

sion of this pattern here, Agave wishes that her son resembled the "character" of his mother (*mētros eikastheis tropois*, 1253).

Agave's allusion here to her son's hunting forays with the "young men" (*neaniai*) of Thebes (1254-55) not only calls attention to his adolescent status but also alludes to the traditional use of the hunt to represent the *rite de passage* to manhood (see above). Now the hunter has himself been hunted down as the prey; and the successful hunter is the mother, leader of "young women" (*neanides*, 1079) against men on the mountain.[73] Her word *euthēros*, "good at hunting" (1252), carries a grim ambiguity, for it can also mean "good for hunting," "good to be hunted," in a passive rather than an active sense.[74] She asks Cadmus to call the friends and family (*philoi*) to a banquet (1242), and Cadmus repeats her words with a groan of sorrow (1245-46). A banquet might well celebrate some act of youthful prowess by a son or the boy's inscription into the fratry or male confraternity by his father, like Xuthus' celebration for his supposedly new-found son in the *Ion* (651ff., 1122ff.). But Agave's "banquet" to celebrate this hunt is a perverted rite where the "victim" (*thyma*, 1246) and quarry are the youth himself.

Cadmus recalls Agave to her ties with "house," "husband," and "child" (1273-76):

> *Cadmus.* To what house did you go in marriage?
> *Agave.* You gave me to one of the Sown Men, as they say, Echion.
> *Cadmus.* What child was then born to your husband in the house?
> *Agave.* Pentheus, in the union of his father and myself.

He thereby reconstitutes the boundaries between house and wild, civilization and savagery, that she has lost.[75] The father evokes the patriarchal world against which the woman has so utterly revolted, a world where the "son" belongs to his father, her husband (τίς οὖν ἐν οἴκοις παῖς ἐγένετο σῷ πόσει, 1275). The name "Pentheus" in 1276 now replaces her nameless "lion" of the hunt, although Cadmus' cry, o *penthos*, "O grief," shortly before (1244) reminds us of

---

[73] Cf. Pentheus as *neanias* in 274, 974, and his scornful suspicion of Dionysiac initiation of "young girls," *neanides*, in 238; cf. also 1254. See above, n. 60.

[74] *Euthēros* in the passive sense, "good to be hunted," is attested at least as early as the third century B.C.: Mnasalcas, *Anth. Pal.* 6.268; see LSJ s.v., 2.

[75] For the psychological dimension of the scene see Devereux (1970).

the total loss of name that Pentheus suffered in the wild, another inversion of the "glory" he hoped to attain (*kleos*, 972). When Cadmus locates Pentheus' *sparagmos* in the same place "where the dogs once rent apart Actaeon" (1291), he clinches the significance of Pentheus' death as a failure to cross from youth to manhood through the marginal ground of hunt and wild. Like Actaeon, Hippolytus, Adonis, Hylas, Narcissus, Hyacinthus, Pentheus does not make his way through the shadowy forest of adolescent trials (cf. 1051-52).[76]

Cadmus' lamentation places Pentheus' failure in the larger context of the "destruction of the house" (1304, 1308). Surveying his family's survival in his patriarchal role, Cadmus sees himself "deprived of male children" (*ateknos arsenōn paidōn*, 1305). The old man calls his dead grandson *anēr*, mature man, as he recalls how he once protected the house and was a bulwark for the city (1309-10).[77] Pentheus has his manhood validated, but posthumously and ambiguously. His death, as Cadmus says, was not the noble death of a hero, but took place "in the most shameful and basest way" (*aischista kai kakista katthanonta*, 1307), a complete reversal of Pentheus' hope to keep "shame" from his gates (cf. 779, 798). He protected the old man from outrage and injustice (*hybris, adikia*), but these terms also figure in the maenads' and Dionysus' accusation of Pentheus (991ff., 1347); and line 1312, though complimentary in intent, can also mean that Pentheus "received just punishment" (*dikēn axian*).

Cadmus is not only childless in his male line but also deprived of

---

[76] Pentheus' entrapment in the deep shade of a forest forms part of a clear progression, from the maenads' joy in the shady woods in 875f. to his entrance there in 1051f., then the dismemberment in 1138, and finally the search for the body among the foliage in 1220f. We may compare the following:

874-76:   ἡδομένα
βροτῶν ἐρημίαις σκιαρο-
κόμοιό τ' ἔρνεσιν ὕλας.

1051f.:   ἦν δ' ἄγκος ἀμφίκρημνον, ὕδασι διάβροχον,
πεύκαισι συσκιάζον.

1138:   τὸ δ' ὕλης ἐν βαθυξύλῳ φόβῃ . . . .

1220f.:   κοὐδὲν ἐν ταὐτῷ πέδῳ
λαβών, ἐν ὕλῃ κείμενον δυσευρέτῳ.

[77] "You were a source of fear [*tarbos*] to your city," 1310, is surely ambiguous, though Roux ad loc. denies that *tarbos* is "un trait péjoratif." There seems, however, to be a similar ambiguity in 1312, "You used to exact just punishment" and "you received your just punishment."

the rights and honors of a full citizen, *atimos* (1313; cf. 1320). Viewed in the larger succession of generations characteristic of the Greek household, Pentheus' death and Cadmus' end are just the opposite of the situation described by old Laertes in the *Odyssey*, the patriarch's joyful sight of the three generations of male warriors, grandfather, son, and grandson, standing together in full armor against their foes (*Od.* 24.513-15).

In the last moments of the action Pentheus' failure as an adult warrior contrasts with Dionysus' triumphant flaunting of his paternity from Zeus (1340-42, 1349). The final martial deed mentioned in the play, Cadmus' leadership of barbarian hordes against Greeks, the former armed with the characteristic weapon of hoplite warriors in the play, "spears" (*lonchai*, 1360), is another reminder of Pentheus' inability to muster hoplite arms against his barbarian invaders.

Agave is left no better off than Cadmus. She is bereft of all the defining and sustaining structures of her life. Like Cadmus she is deprived of country, city, and house (1366-70). She has no place in the wild, either; for Cithaeron and her revels there she feels only disgust and remorse (1382-87). As all the defining boundaries of civilized life dissolve, Agave, not unlike Phaedra in *Hippolytus*, is seen as both the god's instrument of vengeance and his victim.

If the play shows the failure of the younger generation, it is equally unsparing about the moral and intellectual bankruptcy of the adults. Cadmus, cynically serving dynastic advantage, verges on silliness and senility. Teiresias fluctuates between empty Polonian rhetoric and discredited sophistic rationalism. Echion, dead and remote, is hardly a model for adult behavior. Agave succumbs to an even more unstable and destructive emotionality than Pentheus. There is little in Thebes that brings comfort to those who would hope for a new and more secure political order. Cadmus' house deserves and wins our pity for its sufferings, but it is not clear whether it deserves our respect. Nothing is said about a prospective ruler after Cadmus' exile. This city cannot resist the irruption of the irrational. Leadership is virtually destroyed, and Cadmus will betray the Greek cause, a "leader" (*hē-goumenos*, 1360) of barbarians against his adopted country.

The other late plays—*Phoenissae, Orestes, Iphigeneia in Aulis*—offer parallel situations of incompetent or corrupt leadership. By the time Euripides came to write these works, he had already left Athens in self-imposed exile or was on the verge of doing so. Does the situation of ancient Thebes, Mycenae, and Sparta in these works reflect the old poet's view of his own city, the hollowness of ideals, the corruption and cynicism among the old, the violence, instability, and poor judgment among the young?

From a psychological rather than a historical point of view, Slater has suggested that one of the functions of the cult of Dionysus was to offer "the ultimate fantasy solution to the torment which sex antagonism occasioned in Greek life by eliminating the exaggerated differentiation imposed by culturally defined sex roles."[78] The *Bacchae*, however, seems to reinforce rather than eliminate that sexual differentiation. What the tragedy gives us is not the solution to these tensions but their dramatic representation in the most extreme and uncompromising terms. The social function of myth and cult may be to mediate polarities, as Lévi-Strauss thinks, or to provide a solution to deeply felt emotional conflicts, as Slater suggests. But the function of myth as recast in tragedy is to strip away the mediations and expose the conflict in its most absolute form. The "problem of the *Bacchae*," then, has no resolution; and the power of the tragedy lies in the vehemence with which the two sides clash and in the unmitigated horror of the wreckage that emerges from that encounter. Neither young nor old, neither men nor women, neither the yielding nor the recalcitrant are spared.

However useful Slater's formulation may be for understanding the social and psychological function of the cult of Dionysus, it does not do justice to the suffering and violence that Euripides' presents in his play.[79] Here equilibrium is not restored; we are left with total disorientation: exile, suffering meted out far beyond the offense, cruel and distant gods who liberate men and women from the constraints of their ordinary consciousness and familiar values, but at the price of releasing also their most destructive impulses.

In Bacchylides' account of the maddened daughters of King Proetus of Tiryns, a myth of female generational passage, the paternal figure can appease the angry goddess with sacrifice and temples and the girls

[78] Slater 283f.

[79] See the fruitful formulation of Girard 196: "La tragédie ne parvient à trouver son équilibre nulle part, elle n'a pas de lieu où elle puisse s'installer. De là son incohérence féconde, face à la coherence stérile de tant de schèmes intellectuels et esthétiques irréprochables" (Eng. trans. 138f.).

can be brought back within the framework of house and city not much the worse for their wanderings in the Arcadian wilderness (*Ode* 11.95-112).[80] But in the tragedy even the paternal figure is exiled and brutalized, and the mother's relation to both marriage and child is left open to the bitter memory of its destructive reversal.[81]

The play provides a powerful closing image of Dionysus' destruction of the house. The two survivors, both past the age of childrearing, bend over the torn body of a figure who has been in fantasy the little boy of Agave's childbearing years. The man and the woman before us cannot regenerate new life, but only commemorate a death as they piece together the body for the last rites and lament the sterility of the house.[82]

[80] For the Proetides see Calame, *Choeurs* 1.214-20; Segal, *Tragedy and Civilization* 35-37; above, Chap. 3, n. 11.

[81] On Dionysus' negation of women's roles in the house see Calame, *Choeurs* 1.241ff.

[82] See Green 209: "Imaginons ce père et cette fille agenouillés devant ce qui n'est même plus un corps, un amas de restes morcelés, auxquels ils essayent à deux de redonner apparence humaine comme s'ils procedaient à la fabrication d'une nouvelle naissance." On the level of the mythic structure note also the contrast between the murderous Agave's talk of "sowing" daughters (1234) and Cadmus' "sowing" of the male Spartoi in the founding of Thebes (1274, and above, p. 182).

Metatragedy:
Art, Illusion, Imitation

Is it not monstrous that this player here,
But in a fiction, in a dream of passion,
Could force his soul so to his own conceit
That from her working all his visage wan'd;
Tears in his eyes, distraction in's aspect,
A broken voice, and his whole function suiting,
With forms to his conceit? And all for nothing!
Hamlet, II.ii

• I •

Dionysus is the god not only of wine, madness, and religious ecstasy, but also of the drama, of the mask. His worship breaks down
the barriers not only between god and beast and between man and
wild nature, but also between reality and illusion. In the tragic theater, as in the Bacchic ecstasy, the participant "stands outside" of himself: he temporarily relinquishes the safe limits of personal identity in
order to extend himself sympathetically to other dimensions of experience.

The audience's identification with the mythic persona on the stage
is a very different thing from the bacchants' fusion with their god in
the dancing and leaping on the mountainside in torchlight processions. Yet the little evidence we have suggests that the ancient spectator knew very well the joy of full surrender to the illusion of the
dramatic mask. The anecdote in the ancient *Life of Aeschylus* that at
the entrance of the Furies in the *Eumenides* children fainted and
women miscarried, though doubtless exaggerated, nevertheless indi-

cates how powerfully the audience could be thought to respond to the theatrical spectacle.

In the *Bacchae*, I suggest, Euripides uses the figure of Dionysus as god of the tragic mask to reflect on the paradoxical nature of tragedy itself—paradoxical, because by creating illusion tragedy seeks to convey truth; by causing us to lose ourselves it gives us a deeper sense of ourselves; and by representing events filled with the most intense pain it gives us pleasure. The paradoxes of Dionysus, therefore, his liminal status, his place *between*—between truth and delusion, sanity and madness, divinity and bestiality, civilization and the wild, order and chaos—are in part also the paradoxes of tragedy. This self-conscious reflection by the dramatist on the theatricality and illusion-inducing power of his own work, on the range and the limits of the truth that the dramatic fiction can convey, I call the metatragic dimension of the play.[1]

Arguably the play embodies a *fin-de-siècle* self-awareness about a literary form that was now nearing the end of its creative life. Similar preoccupations occur in Aristophanes' *Frogs*, where Dionysus is also a major figure, and Sophocles' *Oedipus at Colonus*.[2] On the other

[1] See James L. Calderwood, *Shakespearean Metadrama* (Minneapolis 1971), with his useful bibliography and discussion of the origins of the terms "metadrama" and "metatheater," p. 4, n. 1 (the latter apparently due to Lionel Abel's *Metatheatre: A New View of Dramatic Form*, 1963). Calderwood defines "metadrama" as a form of drama "in which the boundaries between the play as a work of self-contained art and life are dissolved" (p. 4). Metadrama, he goes on, is concerned with "exploring the nature of contextual form and the function of aesthetic distancing," with "not just 'the idea of the play,' . . . but dramatic art itself—its materials, its media of language and theater, its generic forms and conventions, its relationship to truth and the social order . . ." (p. 5). He has continued this approach more recently in *Metadrama in Shakespeare's Henriad* (Berkeley and Los Angeles 1979). On dramatic language as reflecting a species of metatragedy see Cook, *Enactment* 35f.; also Segal (1980/81) 136f. and *Tragedy and Civilization* 287-90 on the urn in Sophocles' *Electra* as a "metatragic" symbol. On the play's concern with theatrical illusion see also Simon 146-51. Helene Foley's Harvard dissertation (1975), "Ritual Irony in the *Bacchae* and Other Late Euripidean Plays," which came to my attention only after I had written this chapter, also explores the relation of reality and illusion, but her emphasis is on the ritual and cultic background, mine on the language of the play itself. The chapter on the *Bacchae* is now published in *TAPA* (Foley 1980).

[2] See Segal (1961) 211f., 225-30 for the *Frogs*; *Tragedy and Civilization* 406ff. for the *OC*. The metatragic dimension of the *Orestes* is well studied by Zeitlin (1980) 69-70.

hand concern with illusion and reality in art is nothing new in Euripides: it is a major issue in the *Helen*, written less than a decade earlier.
That such problems concerned Euripides and his contemporaries is
also attested by the *Helen* of Gorgias.[3]

Viewed in this perspective, the problem of Dionysus in the *Bacchae*
is, in part, the problem of the relation between imagination and reality in both art and life. By bringing Dionysus himself on the stage
and symbolically enacting the power of Dionysiac illusion, Euripides
raises and explores the question of how the falsehood of (dramatic)
fiction can bring us truth, how by surrendering ourselves and losing
ourselves to the power of imagination we can in some measure find
ourselves, discover or recover some hidden, unfamiliar part of our
identity.

The "most terrible" Dionysus (861) brings wild joy or wild madness; the tamed Dionysus is the patron of the tragic performance. The
play shows Dionysus moving from ecstatic rites in the wild to the
center of Thebes, from Asia to the springs of Theban Dirce (519-36).
Yet there is no simple conversion of Dionysus from barbarian to Greek,
from god of wild cults of the mountain to god of the dancing places
within the polis. In the parode the Chorus describes its movement
from "Asia's land" and "Phrygia's mountains" to the squares and streets
of Greek cities, with their "broad dancing places" (64-88; cf. *eurycho-
roi agyiai*, 85-87). Yet their god retains his alien, inassimilable quality. The play reflects upon tragedy itself as the necessary, perhaps the
only, mediation between the remoteness and the local emplacement
of Dionysus, between the god of the civic festivals and the god of the
oreibasia, *sparagmos*, and *ōmophagia*. Like its god, tragedy comes
into being at the point where man's creative and destructive impulses
cross. Like its god, too, tragedy makes visible the contradictions beneath the surface of civilized life. The paradox of tragedy (as of the
Bacchae) is the paradox of the Dionysiac space at the heart of the
polis.

Dionysus enters the civic of Thebes as a "man full of many wonders" (*thaumatōn pleōs*, 449), wonders that both literally and figuratively take us outside the boundaries of the city and its logic. Wonder

---

[3] See Segal (1962) 112ff., 125ff., 130ff. and (1971) 610-12; Winnington-Ingram
(1969) 130-32; J. de Romilly, "Gorgias et le pouvoir de la poésie," *JHS* 93 (1973)
155-62.

also characterizes the god in his earlier literary representation, the Homeric Hymn to Dionysus.[4] The word recurs three times in the play's first long narration of his power, the account of the maenads' rampage on Cithaeron (667, 693, 715). That thaumaturgic power is also the spell of the god's theatrical illusion, which can make us see vivid events through mere words and feel wild exultation, deep sorrow, and intense concern for "unreal" people and nonexistent events. The capacity to evoke miracles of joy is carefully counterbalanced by a miracle of another kind when, in the second long narration, he shoots Pentheus high into the air, "a wonder to behold" (1063). The "marvel" or "enchantment" of the narrator's words to persuade us of the reality of the god is both the literary equivalent and the prelude to the cultic epiphany that soon follows (cf. 1077-89).

The play gives the participants in the dramatic spectacle, the audience seated in the god's theater, the opportunity to experience the epiphany and the ecstasy of Dionysus without having to suffer what Pentheus, Agave, and Cadmus suffer. Just as the scapegoat-king within the play is a surrogate victim for the entire community in its contact with the wild ecstasy of the god, so the play as a whole is a surrogate for the real violence and chaos that the Dionysiac frenzy brings to the ordered structures of civilization. In witnessing the represented rite, the city is spared the potential destructiveness of the actual rite. By sacrificing the mythical representative of order, the poet makes it easier for the city and the citizens to surrender something of their own need for order and to confront their own Dionysiac impulses without the violent and bloody rendings of a literal or an emotional *sparagmos.*

• II •

Two scenes are more or less explicitly concerned with the boundaries between imagination and reality and hence with the illusion-creating power of the dramatic spectacle. These are the so-called palace miracle and the robing of Pentheus.

The palace miracle takes place shortly after Pentheus orders the imprisonment of the Lydian Stranger, the god in disguise. The youth

---

[4] On the importance of "wonder" in the play see now Parry, *Lyrics* 151f.

is led off in chains, the Chorus sings the second stasimon, and immediately Dionysus' voice is heard off stage. "Goddess Earthquake,
shake the earth," he cries, and the Chorus replies that the Theban
palace will collapse. "Do you see the stone beams here gaping [with
cracks] upon their columns?" they ask. Bring fire and burn the palace,
the god's voice says. "Don't you see, don't you behold, the holy fire
around Semele's tomb," the Chorus answers.

How realistically was this scene presented? A production at Cambridge in England in 1930 developed one possibility. "The miracle,"
according to Dodds, "was indicated by the partial collapse of an ar-
chitrave of the castle and a burst of flame from the smouldering fire. [5]
At the other extreme Verrall and the early Norwood, with a rationalism that Euripides himself anticipates and parodies in the sophistries
of the prophet Teiresias, suggested that the whole miracle was a hoax
perpetrated on the Thebans by the Stranger, who is not Dionysus at
all, but a charlatan possessed of hypnotic powers. [6]

Even if there was some visual indication of the destruction of the
palace, [7] there remains a discrepancy between what could probably be
shown on the stage and the Stranger/Dionysus' remark at 633, "He

[5] Dodds, *Bacchae*, p. 148.

[6] Norwood (1908); Verrall (1910). For criticisms see WI 182-85, stressing the pre-
dominance of dramatic and symbolic function over stage effects; Castellani 63-67
with notes 2-11; Dodds, *Bacchae* xlviii-l; Conacher 66 with n. 14.

[7] See A. M. Dale, "Seen and Unseen on the Greek Stage," WS 69 (1956) 96-
106, reprinted in *Collected Papers* (Cambridge 1969) 119-29, esp. 124f.; Grube (1935)
44-47 and *Drama* 408-11; Murray, *Euripides* 186f.; Steidle 37 with n. 23 thinks that
the scene could not be entirely left to the imagination, but has no specific suggestions. Jeanne Roux, "A propos du décor dans les tragédies d'Euripide," *REG* 74
(1961) 30f. thinks that the effects were conveyed by noises out of sight of the spectators. WI 182 stresses the "vagueness" and "phantasmagoric quality about the whole
episode." Castellani 68 believes that there was some visual representation of the
destruction, perhaps a wooden facade showing a displacement of the entablature
corresponding to 591f.; but his attempt to reconcile this with 633f. is not successful,
nor does his emendation of 633 (68f. with n. 16) commend itself. Oranje 114 stresses
the epiphanic aspect of the scene and would allow for some stage effects. Thomson
434 suggests the influence of cultic representations from the Mysteries and the use
of a deliberate illusionism to suggest the religious atmosphere: "At the call of their
god the terror-stricken maenads are thrown into a trance, in which they are unable
to distinguish between illusion and reality. The result is that we, too, are carried
away by what is indeed a mystery, and do not pause to reflect." But may we not be
equally struck by the contrast between the "trance-like" enthusiasm (if such it is) of
the Chorus and the inflexible boundaries of the severe architectural structures? Coche
de la Ferté 207 would abandon scenic necessities entirely.

[the god] has broken the palace down to the ground; it has collapsed entirely." This discrepancy between what is said and what is seen forces us to recognize the symbolic nature of what is enacted onstage.[8] Euripides thereby brings home to us the power of dramatic illusion, the power of his art—which is also in part the power of Dionysus—to create a fictive and yet convincing world. This clash not only makes manifest the invisible, inner workings of Dionysus but enacts the realm of symbol itself as the only means of representing that hidden but nonetheless very evident power of the god.

Is the power of Dionysus, Euripides implicitly asks, something that can hypnotize us, the audience, into thinking that we can see something occur that has not in fact occurred (the collapse of the palace), or is it really a means of revealing the presence of divinity among men, or is it both together, that is, the power of illusionistic tragedy and of illusionistic (mimetic) art generally to reveal divinity? I would suggest the last alternative. Dionysus' show of force is a religious

---

[8] Note that the syntactical construction of 633f. defines the action of the second verb, *syntethranōtai*, in terms of the subjectivity of Pentheus, his perception under the influence of the madness, sent by the god: συντεθράνωται δ' ἅπαν / πικροτά-τους ἰδόντι δεσμοὺς τοὺς ἐμούς. For the meaning of *syntethranōtai* see Dodds, *Bacchae* ad loc. and Castellani 68f. with n. 16. Castellani's idea that 633f. is "symbolic utterance" while 591f. is performed action (68f., 75ff.) in fact supports my view of a tension between the two kinds of representation. Rohdich 132-37 also stresses the radical contradiction between what is imagined and what is seen, but he interprets this only in the light of the intellectual and religious crisis of the fifth century, as reflecting Euripides' continued concern with the clash of mythical and rational thought, "den Zwiespalt zwischen sophistischem und mythischem Weltverständnis, mit dem er die unüberwindliche Tragik als notwendiges Resultat ihrer Auseinander-setzung aus dem Theater mit sich fortnahm." Through this very contradiction, Roh-dich suggests, this scene reenacts and renews on stage the power of Dionysiac inspi-ration (135f.). The contradiction brings out the mysterious, invisible, and inward power of Dionysus that transcends or defies rational explanation: "Erst dadurch, dass das behauptete Wunder nicht geschieht, zeigt sich das Dionysische als ein Phäno-men der menschliche Seele, das auch den religiösen Skeptiker betrifft" (p. 136). Norwood, *Essays* 61-63, appreciates the reference of the palace miracle to the theme of "stage-illusion" (p. 61), but pulls back from the logical conclusion of his argument: "In precisely the same way the Athenian choristers pretend to be mastered by glam-our, and so to believe that the house falls; the spectator believes them thus possessed, but does not believe that it falls. He cannot, for he sees that it is unchanged, just as he sees that the head is in fact the king's. The miracle, in short, is effected, but not the downfall: it is the divinely induced belief in the downfall; and Euripides shows the method by which glamour may be created—that and nothing more" (p. 62).

epiphany. It is also the force of the tragic spectacle, the capacity of a fiction to embody truth through symbolic meaning, and the actor's (and spectator's) ability to lose himself in fusion with an alien personality. This power is also "Dionysus," and it is akin to the other powers associated with the god: the religious ecstasy of the maenads, the sudden epiphany, and the intoxicating effect of wine as a *pharmakon*, a drug that can bring joy and forgetfulness of sorrows.[9]

The repeated verbs for "seeing" in the so-called miracle call attention to dramatic illusion per se and the possible discrepancy between what is actually there and what appears to be there but may not be. "Did you *see* these stone lintels upon the columns spread apart?" the Chorus asked excitedly. Do you not *behold* the fire, do you not *see* it around Semele's holy tomb?" (591-97). "Did you *perceive*, as is *likely*, the Bacchic god shake the palace . . . ?" is the Stranger's first utterance after his mysterious escape from Pentheus' dark prison (604-605). The physical reality of the miracle is not denied, but the phrasing stresses the subjective side of the event. Then immediately after the miracle the Stranger interprets what has just happened in terms of the illusionistic power of the god (624-31). Pentheus "thought he bound him"; he "thought the palace was burning"; he "seemed" to be stabbing his enemy, and was puzzled that the prisoner "appears" before him outside. Expressions like *dokein*, "seems," *phainesthai*, "appears," *phasma*, the "seeming image," *hōs eoike*, "as seems likely," all keep in the foreground this concern with the power of Dionysiac illusion (605, 616, 629-30, 638, 646).

The god is exercising his power of theatrical as much as of hypnotic illusion when, as the Stranger, he fashions an image or *phasma* that Pentheus takes to be corporeal reality: "He rushed forth and dashed upon it and kept stabbing the bright air, as if [sacrificially] killing me"

[9] See Norwood, *Essays* 62: "Through Dionysus he [Euripides] casts on his Maenads the spell that every competent playwright casts on his audience." On the relation between the theatrical and the ecstatic aspects of Dionysiac cult Rohde, *Psyche* 285, remarks, "Now the art of the actor consists in entering into a strange personality, and in speaking and acting out of a character not his own. At bottom it retains a profound and ultimate connexion with its most primary source—that strange power of transfusing the self into another being which the really inspired participator in the Dionysiac revels achieved in his *ekstasis*." For the theater and ecstatic or shamanlike possession see David Cole, *The Theatrical Event* (Middletown, Conn. 1975) chaps. 2 and 3. On the theatrical and the ecstatic in the *Bacchae* see WI 164f. and Glover 84ff.

(*sphazōn eme*, 629-30).But Pentheus' illusion is only part of the larger illusion of the ritual and the performance in which Dionysus "ritually kills" Pentheus (*katasphageis*, 858).

When the raging Pentheus actually enters at 642, he says nothing about fire, earthquake, or damage to the palace. Instead he demands in puzzlement how the Stranger got out of the prison and "appears" (*phainesthai*) before him (645-46). Both the palace miracle and its immediate sequel are thus made to stand on the same plane of fantasy and imagination. If we cannot know reality directly, if all reality is, on one view, a function of our way of viewing it, and if perception shades into illusion and illusion into madness, then the poet's task is to provide a stage for the simultaneous projection of the multiple planes of reality. "Dionysus" is both the power that enables the poet to do this and at the same time the screen on which each of us can project his own world-views, his different selves, his own interpretation of the vision.

The poet who deals with his material at this level of complexity cannot do so naively. He becomes involved in exploring his own symbolic system. His concern is not just to depict a coherent reality but to question the symbolic discourse and the aesthetic means that enable him to create the world his characters inhabit. Openly or implicitly, he asks,

> Can this cockpit hold
> The vasty fields of France? Or may we cram
> Within this wooden O the very casques
> That did affright the air at Agincourt?
> O pardon! since a crooked figure may
> Attest in little place a million;
> And let us, ciphers to this great accompt,
> On your imaginary forces work. . . .
> For 'tis your thoughts that now must deck our kings,
> Turning the accomplishment of many years
> Into an hour-glass.[10]

The miraculous power of Dionysus to elude Pentheus' bonds and emerge from the enclosed darkness into the "light" (cf. the Chorus's

---

[10] Shakespeare, *Henry V*, prologue. For a lucid discussion of a theatrical image of this sort see Richard A. Lanham, *The Motives of Eloquence* (New Haven 1976) 219-23.

cry, "O greatest light," *phaos megiston*, 608) contains the kernel of
the entire play. The audience that responds to the religious thrill of
the god's saving light from darkness is also submitting to the magic of
the poet's fiction acted out before them, the fiction that is encapsu-
lated and reflected back to them later in Pentheus' submission to the
Stranger's hypnotic spell. Within the play, as within the audience's
reaction to the play, the real and the imagined event, the act and the
emotion, are strangely, inextricably blended.

• III •

The robing scene, some two hundred lines later, clarifies this parallelism between the religious and specifically theatrical aspects of the
power of Dionysus. As a symbol of religious ritual acted on the stage,
the robing transforms Pentheus from king to scapegoat, male to female, human to beast-victim. As a metatragic symbol, it enacts the
power of the tragic mask to reveal a truth hidden beneath surface
appearance and to disclose an identity of opposites beneath apparent
differentiation.[11] By putting on a foreign garb, as the actor puts on a
foreign mask, Pentheus lays bare a truth about himself hidden beneath the regal robes he wears. Dionysus' mask is a mirror for Pentheus, a mirror where the significant thing is what he does *not* recognize.

As a religious symbol Dionysus' mask is, in Walter Otto's phrase,
the god's "strongest symbol of presence,"[12] the means of the most

[11] See Girard 225ff., 232-34, esp. 234 (Eng. trans. 162ff., 166-68, 168): "Le masque
se situe à la frontière équivoque entre l'humain et le 'divin,' entre l'ordre différencié
en train de se désagréger et son au-delà indifférencié qui est aussi le réservoir de
toute différence, la totalité monstrueuse d'où va sortir un ordre rénové."

[12] See Otto 90f.; Versényi 125. Jeanmaire 310f. also has suggestive remarks on the
god's mask as a means by which the divine takes possession of the individual and
transforms him into god, creating a fusion with the god. See also Foley (1980) 128ff.
For the cult significance of the Dionysiac mask see also Nilsson, GGR 571f.; Burkert,
Gr. Rel. 259 with nn. 45-47; M. Bieber, s.v. "Maske," RE 14.2 (1930) 2113; for the
masks and the connection with the theater in the late fifth century see E. B. Bell,
"Two Krokotos Mask Cups at San Simeon," *Calif. Studies in Class. Antiquity* 10
(1978) 1-15, esp. 9-11. Further references in Farnell, *Cults* 5.241-43 and cf. 5.210f.
For the fusion of face and mask in the Greek representation of stage character see
John Jones, *On Aristotle and Greek Tragedy* (London 1962) 44-46.

immediate confrontation with the terrifying otherness of deity in tangible and physical form. But the mask is also a man-made artefact that embodies the human power to create and use symbols. As a deformation or exaggeration of human features, it stands between culture and nature. As both an implement of cult and a covering that hides the wearer's face, it stands between community and isolation, between the accessibility and the alienation of the person in his relation to others and to reality. Its artificiality aids in the performance's validation of the social norms; and the theatrical acting out of taboos and the ritualized violation of the norms in the magical space of the anti-world, the carnivalesque, the ludic, demonstrate the necessity of those norms.[13] Yet that very artificiality of the mask and the theatricality of which it is the tool mark the constructed, arbitrary nature of all the symbol-systems, including those that create the models and roles of acceptable behavior. That artificiality or theatricality opens up a suspended, privileged space within the society where the familiar laws and the familiar logic do not apply, where the spectator confronts a hidden, coexisting chaos within the ordered frame of the art-work, the society, and his own personality. While opening that gap for socially useful ends (e.g., cathartic, apotropaic, or monitory), the mask's freedom from reality also prevents complete reclosure.

The stage action of the *Bacchae*, in which the doubly masked (because disguised) god is now masking (but also unmasking) his spellbound human victim, dramatizes how precariously the symbolic, represented world can shift from being under control, a mechanism of the society's symbolic construction of order, to being itself a controlling force, autonomous and therefore ambiguous. The imagination, once set into motion, does not necessarily stop at the boundaries of the social norms. Fantasy, make-believe, symbol-making, mythopoiesis are, in a mysterious way, allied to madness. Illusion, if carried

[13] I am developing here some remarks by Ogibenin 1-9, especially 6ff. He cites some interesting anthropological work on the "societies of contraries" created by ritual clowning: "Symbolically incarnating an asocial model of behavior, the ritual clown, by consistent perversion of the accepted and allowed models of behavior, shows what the accepted standard should be. In this fashion he becomes the preserver of the important social norms, ruling in the community . . ." (p. 6). But to this preservative function should also be added the other side, the suspended quality of the "carnivalesque" as analyzed by Kristeva, Bakhtin, and others: see above, Chap. 1, n. 10.

far enough, becomes delusion. The capacity of the human mind to enter and identify with a fictional reality holds its darker potential, as Agave and the Theban maenads demonstrate.

The realm of the symbol is one of power. Like all such power for the Greeks, it is bound up with divinity and therefore dangerous as well as useful, as is Dionysus himself (861). A microcosm of the illusion-creating effects of the drama itself, the robing scene invites us to view the working of the dramatic fiction in a series of mirrors. As an actor among actors, Dionysus stands on the same level as the other characters in the orchestra. But he is also the director, dressing and instructing his "actors" for the role they will have to play. Like the ancient tragedian, he is also the poet-director, for in the same gesture he masks his characters and casts over them, his audience, the spell of his magical power to transform illusion into reality and to question whether reality may not be illusion.

As master of theatrical illusion Dionysus also involves Pentheus in another kind of theatrical doubling. Pentheus is a "spectator," *theatēs* (829), who would "look upon" the Dionysiac rites (811-15) "seated in silence" in a secure vantage-point where he is not seen (816). But this spectator becomes a participant against his will. That participation, furthermore, will prove necessary to the full performance of the rite that he would witness. Symbolically effacing the distance between spectator and actor, the robing scene is a sinister mirror-image of the play's effect upon its audience, its *theatai*. In order for the "sacrifice" at the center of the rite-spectacle to work for them, they too must relinquish some of their distance; they must become participants, at least partially, if the *penthos*, the pain or grief of this spectacle, is to be fruitful as cathartic sympathy.[14]

There is much in the language of this scene that suggests the art of the theater: not only the word *theatēs*, "spectator," and the recur-

---

[14] On the crossing of the border between self and other, illusion and reality, in the theatrical experience see above, n. 9; also Versényi 126; Simon 115; Sale, *Existentialism* 114, stressing also the sexual dimension of Pentheus' avoidance of "coming together." For interesting remarks on audience resistance to such participatory fusion see Cole, *Theatrical Event* (above, n. 9) 78ff. On *theatēs* in a "theatrical" sense see Aristoph. *Knights* 536 (which perhaps hints humorously at Dionysus' presence in the theater); also Thuc. 3.38.4, where Creon's phrase about being "spectators of the words," *theatai tōn logōn*, contains the notion of the gap between word and deed brought by the deliberate distancing of the agonistic setting.

rent *sophia*, "skill or wisdom," which may also refer to the poet's "craft," but also the rare verb *ekmousoō* that specifies the nature of that craft in 825: Διόνυσος ἡμᾶς ἐξεμούσωσεν τάδε. "Yes, I am wise [*sophos*]," we may translate, "for Dionysus gave me this music instruction."[15] The irony of Pentheus' "How wise [*sophos*] you have been of old" (*palai*, 824) extends the time-scale from the immediate present to the perspectives of an immortal god, a god whose *sophia* has accompanied every performance in the theater of Dionysus.

With this "musical" power Dionysus makes Pentheus "see with pleasure things that are painful" or "bitter" (ὅμως δ᾽ ἴδοις ἂν ἡδέως ἅ σοι πικρά, 815). The line can refer to the paradox of tragedy as well as to the paradoxes of identity within Pentheus that Dionysus' robing serves to unmask. Theatrical illusion, wine, and the religious ecstasy of the *thiasos* all belong to Dionysus' power to release the impulses of "desire" (*erōs* is Dionysus' word in 813) governed by what we usually conceive to be our real selves.

In the Dionysiac performance of which Pentheus would be a spectator (829) the reversal will be double. Not only will the spectator move from his secure periphery to the exposed and violent center, but Dionysus' initial proposal of the theatrical situation also implies an analogous reversal for the audience: "Do you want to see them sitting together [*synkathēmenas*] on the mountains?" the Stranger asks Pentheus at the crucial point (811). The participants are here described with a verb more appropriate for an audience in the theater. The fact that the same verb is applied to Pentheus as spectator five lines later (*kathēmenos*, 816) indicates this interchanging of the two roles. This spectacle will take place not in the enclosed civic space of a theater but on the exposed wild mountainside.

Pentheus, the participant who hopes to remain the spectator (829), is to be punished by becoming the impersonator of the god. He thereby loses the separate identity that he so vigorously defends until line 811. From that point on, he exists in the ambiguous state of an actor whose mimetic role is exposed by doubling, by a mask placed upon a mask. The actor playing the god's antagonist in a remote form of obeisance to Dionysus (the play at the Dionysiac festival) is made in turn to play the worshiper-victim of the god in the more intense

[15] For the verb *mousoō* in a literary context see Aristoph. *Lys.* 1127. For the double reference of *sophia* to both poetry and religion see WI 62f.

obeisance of the maenadic cult. The pretense of the actor who plays the part of a character whom he knows to be fictitious gives way to the madness of the newly masked king whose disguise confuses appearance and reality. Beneath the conscious and intentional fiction of the dramatic performance, wherein we willingly and indeed eagerly submit to a domination of reality by appearance, runs a less controllable and more dangerous power of delusion, the hypnotic power of the god that completely takes over this actor's mind.

The boundaries between poetic illusion and madness, imagination and intoxication, are not always clear. The drug of the work of art may be as much an escape from reality as the drug of wine (cf. 280-83). DeQuincey, Poe, and Castaneda are not the only writers to have blurred the division between the metaphorical opiate of fiction and the dreams stimulated by the real opium. "Everything is a drug for the man who chooses to live on the other side," writes Gaston Bachelard. "And what is a beautiful poem," he goes on, "if not a touched up madness? A little poetic order imposed upon aberrant images? The maintenance of an intelligent sobriety in the utilization—intensive all the same—of imaginary drugs. Reveries, mad reveries lead life."[16] Or, still closer to our own time, is this reflection by Saul Bellow:

> To perform higher actions, to serve the imagination with special distinction, it seems essential to be histrionic. This, too, is a brand of madness. Madness has always been a favorite choice of the civilized man who prepares himself for a noble achievement. It is often the simplest state of availability to ideals. Most of us are satisfied with that: signifying by a kind of madness devotion to, availability for, higher purposes.[17]

The paradoxes of Dionysus parallel the paradoxes of all art: created to counter madness, ennui, neurosis, it needs to contain a bit of that madness.[18]

The robing of Pentheus is such an effective representation of this proximity of art and madness precisely because the potency of the god's hypnotic spell draws near to the power of the poet's fiction,

[16] Gaston Bachelard, *The Poetics of Reverie* (1960), tr. Daniel Russell (Boston 1971) 169f.

[17] Saul Bellow, *Mr. Sammler's Planet* (Harmondsworth and New York 1977) 136.

[18] See Barthes 13.

ritual to theatrical spectacle. The power of illusion veers between representing divine epiphany and representing bestial metamorphosis. Pentheus' earlier attempt to disrobe the Stranger and remove the god's signs of power is now answered by the god's ritual robing of his antagonist. As the director of the miniature play acted out before us, the god makes the un-Dionysian king the vehicle of the major manifestations of his power: madness, religious ecstasy, and dramatic illusion.

Pentheus will take off the god's *mitra* and resume his civic, non-theatrical identity for a moment of recognition or anagnorisis as he cries out, "Mother, I am yours, your son Pentheus," (1118-19). But this return to reality finds him at the center of the spectacle/ritual where his identity is totally dissolved: figuratively in the fusion of human king and bestial victim, literally in the rending and scattering of his body.

For all its stress on the power of illusion, the play also gives us a return to reality, albeit painfully, in the anagnorisis of Agave at the end. Early in the scene she asks, "Of these things what is not well? What then is painful?" (τί δ' οὐ καλῶς τῶνδ' ἢ τί λυπηρῶς ἔχει, 1263). This line echoes and acts out Dionysus' paradox about "seeing with pleasure that which gives you pain" in the first robing scene (815). For the spectators who remain spectators—that is, for us, the audience—the anagnorisis functions as part of this paradoxical pleasure that tragedy confers. For Agave the anagnorisis may signal a deeper knowledge of the god, but it is a "hard and painful truth" that she acquires (paraphrasing δύστην' ἀλήθεια in 1287). For Pentheus, who remains trapped in the fusion of spectator's and actor's roles, the moment of anagnorisis coincides with the moment of his death.

Viewed in the context of Euripides' earlier dramatic work, this anagnorisis is a horrible parody of the recognition scenes composed a decade before in the *Ion*, *Helen*, and *Taurian Iphigeneia*.[19] In the *Bacchae*'s recognition the mother recovers only the mangled body, not the beautiful, longed-for person. The recognition of long-lost loved ones in the earlier plays expressed some intuition of hidden harmonies in the world and an intimation of ultimate generosity and kind-

---

[19] See Diller (1955) 488f., who describes the *Ion* as "das untragische Gegenstück zu den *Bakchen*" (488); also Wassermann (1929) 283 on the *Bacchae* and the intrigue plays; Oranje 65-67.

ness among the remote, unpredictable Olympians. Agave's anagnorisis is a hard lesson in the intransigence of a moral order governed
by cruel, dangerous, and irascible divinities.

"I have come, the son of Zeus, Dionysus, to this Theban earth,"
the god proclaims in the opening lines of the play. His purpose, he
explains twenty lines later, is to reveal himself "a divinity clearly shown
to mortals, a god manifest" (ἵν' εἴην ἐμφανὴς δαίμων βροτοῖς, 22).
Throughout the prologue he repeats expressions of revealing himself
as a god (phanenta thnētois daimona, 42) or showing his divine birth
(ϑεὸς γεγὼς ἐνδείξομαι, 47; δεικνὺς ἐμαυτόν, 50). At the simplest
level, then, he gives his action the ritual structure of a hieros logos,
the demonstration of the truth of a sacred text. We may compare the
Homeric Hymn, where the god, initially disguised, "appears" [ephanto]
as a mortal (Hom. Hymns 7.3-11) and then causes miraculous events
to "appear" (34, 46) or be "seen" (42, 52), as a prelude to the god's
formal declaration of his identity (56-57; cf. Ba. 1340-41).[20] Yet how
he "reveals himself" and becomes "visible" to each character, and
also to each spectator in the audience, depends on each one's predis-
position to the god. This god's epiphany reveals as much about the
one who receives the vision as about the god himself. The recipient
may lose or find himself in the god. Those who accept him freely
experience him differently from those who do so under coercion.

Like Teiresias in the Oedipus Tyrannus, the Stranger, as the god's
prophet, claims access to a world beyond the physical sight of Pentheus. Like Sophocles' Teiresias confronting Oedipus (the verbal echo
suggests direct imitation or subconscious reminiscence), the Stranger
reveals to the king that he "knows not in what respect he is alive or
what he does or who he is" (Ba. 506; OT 367, 411-12). The blind
prophet of the Tyrannus knows the dark truth about the riddle of
existence to which Sophocles' remote gods hold the answer; the vision
of Euripides' disguised prophet (cf. 298) is more subjective, for illusion itself is a fundamental part of his world and not even this prophet
is what he seems.

Pentheus' first face-to-face encounter with the prophet/god makes

---

[20] With the Homeric Hymn one may compare the stress on appearance and reality
and the recurrent verbs of sense-perception in Ba. 470-78 and the stress on seeing
the god or his effects in 811, 940, 1279f., etc. On the language of sight, understanding, and epiphany see WI 163-65. For connections with the Dionysiac mysteries see
Seaford (1981) 253f., 256f.

much of how he "sees" the god and how the god "appears" to him
and to others (cf. 469, 470, 485). "The god—you say you see him
clearly—what was he like?" Pentheus asks the Stranger (477). "He
was as he wished," comes the reply; "I gave no instructions on the
point." This ambiguous answer is also an ironical echo of Pentheus'
military authority (*etasson*, "gave instructions"), so totally helpless now.
The fluidity and multiplicity of this god's shape, as of his religion, so
foreign to this authoritarian literalist, cannot but frustrate him (479).
The god gives that frustration the form of the mental and visual subjectivity appropriate to his nature but increasingly impenetrable to
Pentheus (500-503):

> Dionys.   Present nearby he *sees* what I am suffering.
> Penth.   Where is he then? For he is not visible to *my* eyes.
> Dionys.   Here with me. You, being irreverent, do not look upon
>   him.

At the same time Dionysus makes capital of Pentheus' hidden wish
to "hear" and "see" the god (475)—an anticipation of his later success
in undermining his sanity through the very intensity of repressed "desire" (*erōs*, 811) to see. Operating like the poet, the god leads us on
into the plot that he has created, using our own complicity, our own
"desire," to "see" and to experience the outcome, however well we
know it in advance, however confident we are about the vision and
its meaning.

The ensuing ode, the second stasimon, calls upon Dionysus to
"reveal himself as Thebes' Bacchic god" (*anaphainō*, 528-29). But
the result of this epiphany is Dionysus' revelation of Pentheus' hidden
self. In a kind of inverted epiphany Pentheus will reveal (*anaphainei*,
538) his chthonic birth as the monstrous son of Echion. In the next
scene the maenads see the god's celestial fire (596ff.). Pentheus'
equivalent vision is the bull (618-21), and against this he sweats and
struggles (618-21). It is not clear whether the "apparition" (*phasma*)
that he attacks with a sword is also tauriform (629-31), but it is appropriately in his bestial form that he receives the god who robes him
as a sacrificial victim (922) and leads him out to his death (1159).

When Dionysus becomes visible to the true believers, he spreads
an atmosphere of light, joy, and power. He is a "great light" (609-10;
cf. 594ff.), and he is "revealed" to them as "a great god" (1031). But

to Pentheus his epiphany will be "Justice . . . carrying a sword, made manifest" (*Dika phaneros*, 991, 1013; cf. 501). The sun that Pentheus sees is not the dawn that warms a mountain landscape, with its bright patches of snow (661-62, 677-80), nor even the level glare of the arid Persian plateau (14), but a symptom of delusion. Instead of the heightened perception and power of the worshiper, he is helpless before the hallucinogenic god who makes him "see what he should see" (924; cf. 918); and a sense of power alternates with passivity (cf. 948-52 and 966-69). For Pentheus, as for Semele, the brilliance that attends the complete epiphany of a god means destruction for the mortal onlooker. But instead of the physical fire of Zeus' lightning-bolt, Dionysus destroys by the madness in his victim's own mind.

The revelation of the palace miracle and the second stasimon deepens in meaning at the Chorus's call for the god's "epiphany" (*phanēthi*, "appear," 1017) just before the news of Pentheus' death. This epiphany takes the form of bull, snake, or lion, the bestial shapes that correspond to the inverse revelation of Pentheus' savagery in the second stasimon and his reduction to the status of beast-victim for the *sparagmos* later.

Pentheus' explicit motive for the climb that leads immediately to his death is "rightly to *see* the maenads' shameful doings" (ἴδοιμ᾽ ἂν ὀρθῶς μαινάδων αἰσχρουργίαν, 1062; cf. 815). In defining in advance the object of his sight as *aischrourgia*, "shameful doings," he shows that his vision manifests his own inner distortion of the god. He has lost the power of true seeing and, as in the previous scene, can behold only mirages, the projections of his own desires.[21] At the end Agave "rejoices at the great deeds revealed plain [*phanera*] accomplished by the hunt" (φανερὰ τᾷδ᾽ ἄγρᾳ κατειργασμένα, 1199). Yet the visible clarity of those deeds masks their reality as an act of an unheroic and polluting madness.

The last part of the action restores the clarity of human vision, at a price. Agave's "joy" at the visibility of her great deeds contrasts with Cadmus' recognition that her return with the all-too-visible trophy and sign of those "deeds" is "a vision not happy" (*opsin ouk eudai-*

---

[21] See Wohlberg (1968) 155: Pentheus' double vision is not due to intoxication but to the "pathologically simultaneous duality within Pentheus that has now come out into the open, but which has lain suppressed within him through all the previous scenes of the play."

mona, 1232). Cadmus' task is to undo the effects of the god's epiphany. He would recall her from an "appearance" (*opsis*) where she imagines herself "happy" (*eudaimōn*, 1257-58) and would demonstrate that what she sees is not the maenads' "greatest light" but her own "greatest grief" (1281-84):

Κα. ἄθρησον αὐτὸ καὶ σαφέστερον μάθε.
Αγ. ὁρῶ μέγιστον ἄλγος ἡ τάλαιν᾽ ἐγώ.
Κα. μῶν σοι λέοντι φαίνεται προσεικέναι;
Αγ. οὔκ, ἀλλὰ Πενθέως ἡ τάλαιν᾽ ἔχω κάρα.

Cadmus. Look at this and learn more clearly.
Agave. I see the greatest grief—alas, miserable that I am.
Cadmus. Does he then still appear to you to be like a lion?
Agave. No, but I miserable hold the head of Pentheus.

The syntactical change from the periphrasis "appear to be like" a lion (λέοντι φαίνεται προσεικέναι, 1283) to the concrete and direct, "I hold the head of Pentheus" (Πενθέως . . . ἔχω κάρα, 1284) expresses this shift from the realm of subjectivity and illusion to the tangible solidity (*echō*, "I bear") of the object and the facts to be deduced from it. Cadmus had made that change earlier as he reentered carrying the remnants of the torn body and addressing his servants who "carry the sad weight of Pentheus" (φέροντες ἄθλιον βάρος, 1216), his first words of the scene. "I bear his body . . . ," he repeats a few lines later (οὗ σῶμα . . . φέρω τόδε, 1218-19). Totally under the god's delusive power, however, Pentheus, in his last words on stage, claimed to "lay hold of " his reward as something tangible (ἀξίων μὲν ἅπτομαι, 970).

· IV ·

The truth that tragedy brings through its fiction contains and transcends the truth of the ecstatic Dionysus. The Dionysiac ritual brings a total subjection to the power of the god; the tragedy imitates that experience, but through its symbolic structure holds it at a distance and reflects upon its meaning. The "drugs" or *pharmaka* of Dionysus the enchanter (*goēs*, 234) can take away pain, but they can also bring the degrading madness of Pentheus and the murderous delusion of Agave. The Asian maenads have beatific visions but also invoke the god in his terrifying beast-shapes.

As the patron god of the theater, Dionysus is the culture's symbol for the power of fictional representation and illusionistic drama, the power that makes us believe that a masked actor is Pentheus or that a stage-front is the royal palace at Thebes. By making the god Dionysus himself a masked actor, Euripides forces Dionysus the patron of tragedy to become the subject of tragedy. He thereby suggests a view of his play as an infinite regress of illusions. But by calling attention to the aesthetic frame of the play, he also draws the distinction between the illusion of Dionysiac art and the delusion of Dionysiac madness. Pentheus encounters Dionysus as the god of illusion, and the result is madness; Euripides encounters Dionysus as the inspirer of tragedy and creates art. His tragedy, derived from Dionysus' power, may share a common boundary with madness; but the poet contains and controls the madness as his creation, Pentheus, cannot.

Dionysus thus exists both as a character among characters and as a symbol of the very process that makes the dramatic fiction possible at all. The privileged status of this double role is marked by his shifts between divine and human roles within the play. He is both an object of the process of symbol-making and the process itself, both a signifying term in the symbolic representation of reality and a principle of the convertibility of objects into symbols. In the language of Saussure he is both signifier and signified, both the source and the goal of the referential process.

The verb of "signifying," *sēmainein*, at the peripety, is literally Dionysus' last word as he leads the disguised/masked king/victim out of the city to the mountain: *ta alla d'auto sēmanei*, "The thing itself will show [signify] the rest" (976). With its *double entendres* the verb illustrates the god's double role, within the fiction and controlling the fiction, in contrast to Pentheus who is totally immersed in the fiction and in the god's delusion. A few lines before, using the same root, *sēma* ("sign"), Dionysus declares Pentheus "clearly marked out for all," *episēmon onta pasin* (967). The rapid half-line dialogue or stichomythy of that phrase is itself part of the net of delusion in which Pentheus is caught. In his last phrase of 976 the god speaks in his own person (*egō*, "I," 975), not as the Stranger; he has a privileged

knowledge of the whole, the full meaning of the events that the present will signify or reveal. Both prophet and god, he uses oracular
futures with the irony of his double role. Marching Pentheus off the
stage like the playwright-director, he addresses Agave by name ("Stretch
forth your hands, Agave . . . ," 973), as if he were giving a cue to
the actor who will change from Pentheus' role to Agave's. He prepares
for that new role at the same time as he announces the next movement of the plot.[22]

· V ·

The loss of the capacity to distinguish truth from illusion on the
epistemological level coincides with the loss of the ability to distinguish self from other on the psychological level, or man from beast
and beast from god on the political and theological levels. In all these
areas Dionysus operates as the principle that destroys differences, particularly (in this context) the difference between symbol and referent,
vehicle and tenor. He confuses the ecstatically imagined and the solid
reality. The fire that the worshipers may see as part of their religious
revelation blurs with the fire that can destroy a king's palace; the
hallucinated bull in the palace parallels the bull torn apart in a bloody
ritual madness (cf. 743-48), as Pentheus or Dionysus or both.

Dionysus' very nature converts the figurative into the literal. In this
play the trope becomes the reality. The fictive illusion of art may at
any point become the "unmediated vision" of trance and ecstasy, and
vice versa. The Dionysiac poetics over which the god presides affirms
the simultaneous existence of conditions that the binomial, dichotomizing logic of our normal mental operations disallows. The ambiguity of the god's presence throughout, in both symbolic form and
in three-dimensional solidity on the stage, leaves us unsure which
level of reality—or illusion—we are confronting, epiphany or imagination, divine presence or insanity, or even (for the Verrallians) god

---

[22] It may be more than coincidence that Dionysus' verb in 973, "stretch forth"
(ektein') sounds like "kill" (ktein')—which is what Agave's hands, soon to be bloodied,
will do: 858, 1135f., 1207, 1240, 1245. In 1286 Agave brings together kteinein,
"kill," and cheires, "hands," in her dawning recognition: "Who killed him? How did
he come to my hands?" (τίς ἔκτανέν νιν;—πῶς ἐμὰς ἦλθεν χέρας;).

or charlatan-hypnotist. Our very construction of reality through perception, thought, and language is called into question.

Language ceases to function as a clear means of distinguishing between subjective and objective experience. Thus there is a relative sparseness of metaphor and simile in the play. When the Asian maenads sing of their god or when the god addresses his maenads there is no word for "likeness" or "resemblance," no *hōs* or *hōsper* ("as," "as if"; cf. 100, 618, 1017, 1159). Pentheus may be "like a Giant" (543), but to the Chorus he actually is a "savage monster" (542). Pentheus' language is quite different: for him the outrage of the maenads "blazes up *like* fire" (778), and that simile only marks his own distance from Dionysus' fusion of appearance and reality in the miraculous fire that burns at the palace or around the maenads' hair (597ff., 757f.; cf. 1083). The dressing of Pentheus as a maenad involves the language of likeness and resemblance (*prepeis*, "you resemble," 917; *eikasthēsomai*, "I shall be made like," 942). But Dionysus who "seems" to lead him as a bull (*dokein*, 920) is actually "present as one made a bull" in the verb *tetaurōsai* in 922 (cf. 1017, 1159). Pentheus compares the maenads to birds with a simile in 957, echoing the messenger's simile of 748; but when they are fully caught up in their Dionysiac ecstasy they are simply "hunting dogs," with no "as" or "like" (731; cf. 977). When Pentheus is totally drawn into his likeness to a human maenad, he actually becomes the beast of the maenadic *sparagmos*, the beast that he not merely resembles but "is," just as in the likeness of his disguise he is already dedicated as an offering to the god (*anakeimestha*, 934).[23]

As part of these interchanges between reality and appearance Agave, returning with Pentheus' head in her grasp, prays (1252-53), "I wish that my son were a skillful hunter [*euthēros*], made like his mother's ways" (*eikastheis . . . tropois*). Yet that confusion of likeness and reality, of external form and inward "character" (*tropoi*), has indeed made Pentheus hunted instead of hunter, beast instead of man.

That verbal play on the language of "likeness" and "character" also has a metatragic dimension, for the actor who plays Agave is now (we may plausibly conjecture) carrying the mask he wore in the previous scene when he played the role of Pentheus. Thus the relation of "likeness" or physical "resemblance" conveyed in the participle *ei-*

---

[23] See Sale, *Existentialism* 100f.; WI 118 with n. 3.

kastheis ("formed in the likeness of") to "character" or "personality" (*tropoi*) can be extrapolated to the work of the actor, who must change inner "character" or "personality" when he takes over the physical "likeness" of the personage whose mask he wears. Euripides was fond of speculating about the veil that conceals inner thoughts and feelings from the face we show to others or see in others. It is not hard, then, to recognize the implication that the stage mirrors life. All of us wear masks to conceal, and sometimes to reveal, the *tropoi* of what we are.

Euripides takes us to the next level in the recognition scene between Agave and Cadmus. Now, as Cadmus brings her to recognize her "vision" (*opsis*, 1232, 1257-58; cf. 1280-85), she distinguishes between "being" and "likeness" (1282-83):

> Agave.   I *see* the greatest grief, alas miserable.
> Cadmus.   Does he then *appear* to you to *be like* a lion [*phainetai proseikenai*]?

What Cadmus does for Agave the poet in a sense does for us his audience. By reflecting on the status of his work as fiction, illusion, image, symbol, and a form of truth, he invites us toward "greater clarity" (*saphesteron*, 1281) in distinguishing truth and illusion, depth and surface, in ourselves; and he also convinces us of the vital importance of that distinction.

The end of the play returns to the theological framework of likeness and reality. Cadmus confronts the actual god, now in his last and (epistemologically, at least) most certain epiphany as he stands above the actor-participants on the *theologeion*, in his real Olympian shape. The old Theban king makes a futile protest against the carnage wrought upon his house (1348): ὀργὰς πρέπει θεοὺς οὐχ ὁμοιοῦσθαι βροτοῖς ("It is not seemly that gods *should be made like* to mortals in their wrath"). "It is seemly," *prepei*, is the word elsewhere in the play for the power of Dionysiac illusion that makes sane men "like" wild maenads or human "like" wild beasts (917, 1188). The logical and ethical reasoning of Cadmus in 1348 would seek to reintroduce distinctions between gods and men, at least in moral sensibilities. But the effort rings discordantly against the divinity who confuses god and beasts in his epiphanies and proves his power by making men see one another in the likeness of beasts.

Through his metatragic criss-crossing between actor and audience, participant and spectator, fiction and reality, Euripides also opens the distance between what can be lived and what can be said, what can be grasped by the symbolic fictions of poetic representation and what can be communicated in everyday language. How much of what we experience in the theater (of Dionysus) can we bring into the rest of our lives? Does the self that surrenders to the power of the Dionysiac illusion overlap with the self that performs the daily responsibilities of worker, citizen, spouse, parent, friend? Pentheus and Agave's experience does not leave us sanguine. The *Bacchae* refuses fully to close this gap between the power of illusion within the fiction and the power of the fiction to convey truth.

The question of how much truth or what kind of truth the represented "falsehood" of the play conveys is itself the question of the value of Dionysus' "drug" or *pharmakon*. Teiresias' eulogy of the god includes praise for this "drug against toils" (*pharmakon ponōn*) that "brings wretched mortals cessation from pain when they are filled with the flowing [juice] of the vine and gives them sleep and forgetfulness of the woes of the day" (280-83). He ends this long speech with an admonition to Pentheus, whose painful madness and disease are beyond cure by any "drugs" (*pharmaka*, 328-29).

The spell of Dionysus' "drug" would then be the power of art to evoke "presence," an intuitive feeling of the reality of experience and the reality of the god. Yet the play's self-conscious representation of that illusionistic power (what I have called its metatragic aspect) as sorcery and as the hypnotic fascination of the Stranger, not necessarily the god (cf. 234), also shows us the god as absence, in Derrida's terminology as the "trace" of an experience that never can be fully (re)captured. To make himself felt fully among men, Dionysus manifests himself in human shape and in the human form of language. But by virtue of those very human manifestations, he becomes only a trace of his divine reality. His "presence" in Thebes as the Stranger is the "absence" of his divinity; and the fate of Semele reminds us of what happens when divinity comes to men with full presence.[24] The

---

[24] In Derrida's critique of the "metaphysics of presence" that has dominated Western philosophy since Plato, language and the thought inscribed in language through the "writing" (*écriture*) and "proto-writing" of language can be only the mark of an absence, the "trace" of an ultimate truth or "presence" never fully recuperable, for it manifests itself to us only in its separation from an origin that eludes us by the very fact that origin is at once devoured and displaced by what follows it.

mirroring, self-reflective undercurrent in the play erodes the presence of the god; the illusionism that is the god's very nature undermines the truth of all that he presents. The gap between the Stranger of ambiguous status among mortals and the god who speaks in the prologue and epilogue remains open. Theatrically the two figures are different personae. Though undoubtedly different manifestations of a single divine power, the one wears human clothing and moves, speaks, and acts on the same level, in the same space as the mortal characters, whereas the other appears, at the end, above the action, with the sacral garb and features of the god worshiped at the Dionysiac festival itself.

We have presumed throughout that the Stranger is the god; any other view involves Verrallian oversubtlety. Yet however close Euripides comes to absolute closure of the distance at the end of the two central scenes (849-61, 973-76), he does not make it final. Unlike the epiphany of Heracles at the end of Sophocles' *Philoctetes*, only a few years before the *Bacchae*, Dionysus' reality is in constant tension with the very means he uses to demonstrate that reality. In this way, too, the ambiguous power of the god parallels the ambiguous power of the poet. The failure of the illusion, the fiction, is built into the illusion itself. In demonstrating its capacity to exercise magical enchantment over us (what the Greeks called *thelxis*), language itself reminds us that all its "cloud-capped towers" and "gorgeous palaces" are but a "baseless fabric," an "insubstantial pageant" that will melt "into air, into thin air," once the revels are ended.[25]

Dionysus' mask, even more than the magician Prospero's wand, is the implement of a fiction that, willingly or not, also demonstrates its own fictionality and therefore the absence of the god. The play, which can give us the illusion of epiphany, also emerges as the epiphany of illusion. The mask is a symbol both of the "pure presence" of Dionysus and of the elusiveness of that presence, as of any divine presence in the time-bound mortal world. In this respect the mask is also a symbol of the mystery attaching to the process by which the divine can be made manifest in human life. In primitive ritual the act of putting on the mask, felt as a sacred object, transforms a man

---

[25] Shakespeare, *The Tempest*, IV.ii. By explicitly calling attention to his act of taking on a human "shape" or "form" in the prologue (53f.), Dionysus also reminds us of the artificiality and fragility of his "cloud-capped towers" too. See Steidle 32.

into a god. In the *Bacchae*, the sacral disguising of the king transforms him into a beast and fuses celebrant and victim.

The play's reduction of the god to the status of a symbol within a construct of symbols, a piece of mimetic representation, is half of the double dialectic that runs between the play and the rite, between religion and art, between ritual and literature, here and elsewhere in Greek tragedy. On the one hand the tragedy transcends the god it contains and depicts, for the play is not a ritual and holds ritual at a distance. On the other hand the Dionysus of the *Bacchae* has an existence that transcends Euripides' fiction. Unlike Pentheus or Agave or Cadmus, he is not *only* a character in a play or a figure in a myth. He also has a sacral existence as a god of the civic religion, one manifestation of which is the festival at which the play is performed. The masks in that performance have no power outside of the theater. But the masks of Dionysus are also a part of his cult, from early times hung on trees and placed in temples as objects of worship.

When the god enters the human world depicted in the play, he has to demonstrate his power through the dismemberment of the king, who is as literally deconstructed by the *sparagmos* as he is figuratively by the action, which reveals him finally as but an empty mask.[26] The theatrical or metatragic image of carrying the severed head/mask of the king as a sign of the god's power itself unmasks the fragility of that power. It shows the precariousness of the capacity of language and of the illusion created through language to reach reality and reveal the god. The stage business calls attention to the sign-systems, the conventions of illusion, of the theater itself, and thereby calls them into question. Once we are made to feel that a mask is a mask, that a character before us is an actor, not "Pentheus," "Agave," or "Dionysus," we exchange the sense of pure presence for a double vision.

As a result of Dionysus' presence as a manifestation of a divine reality in human life, the king's body, found only with difficulty, loses the heroic commemoration and claim to an eternal memorial of fame

[26] For the "deconstruction" of character in tragedy see David McDonald, "Forms of Absence: Derrida and the Trace of Tragedy," *Helios*, vol. 7, no. 2 (1979-80) 75-95. Writing on the *Orestes*, Zeitlin (1980) 66ff. speaks of Euripides as a rummager in "a closet of masks" that the poet has created "for the actors to raid at will, characters in search of an identity, a part to play" (69). There is much in this stimulating study that is applicable to the *Bacchae*.

that poetic language, in the Greek tradition, is supposed to be able to confer (cf. 972). The revelation of Dionysus not only shakes the coherence of the ritual, civic, and psychological order but implies a further *sparagmos*, symbolically, of language and of the art of symbolical representation itself.

The Dionysiac mask is an overdetermined symbol of the power of (dramatic) illusion. The god's presence is divided between a doubly masked character on the stage (that is, the god disguised as Stranger) and a divinity who has a privileged place and voice in prologue and epilogue. His mask, too, is divided: when Dionysus speaks in character, *in propria persona* in the literal sense, it probably resembles and certainly represents the cult-images of the god both inside and outside the theater; but in the middle portion of the play, the mask that the Dionysiac Stranger wears is a mask among masks. Dionysus is then not only a participant in the illusion but also a mirror within a mirror, the symbol of an ambiguous, ever-receding reality.

• V •

The problem of dramatic illusion and truth, of uncovering hidden depths by disguising and covering the surface, is but one of several areas in which the *Bacchae* reconstitutes symbolically the basic elements of tragedy only to stress their most ambiguous aspects. The first of these has already been discussed, the mask. The robing scene, as we have suggested, reflects in various ways on the paradoxical relation between imagination and reality. It is a symbolical condensation of the mimetic art of drama, in which the actor steps out of his own personality and with the mask literally puts on another. The other elements involved in the play's metatragic deconstruction of its own illusionistic power are its spatial field, the chorus, the hero, comedy and tragedy, tragic reversal, and recognition.

Space

The play designates the privileged and ambiguous quality of the space circumscribed by tragedy in two senses. First, its action and setting isolate and intensify one of the essential symbolic properties of tragic space as the field where order and chaos, city and wild, protected and exposed areas intersect and overlap. What in fact initially motivates the protagonist is the attempt to keep out of the city foreigners, barbarians from Asia who come with exotic rites. Enclosure or imprisonment, the protection of walls and gates, the destruction, real or imagined, of the palace, and the movement between city and mountain delineate the basic stages of the action. At the climax of that action the death of the king in the wilds of Cithaeron symbolically negates the interior space of the city.[27] The Messenger from the mountain narrates the catastrophe before the palace front that makes tangible for us the civic space of Thebes.

The second aspect of the problematical quality of theatrical space focused by this play consists in the relation between seen and unseen, which, as we have already noted, is another facet of the relation between reality and imagination, truth and fiction. The plot structure heightens the tension between the tangible theatrical space and the imagined but more vivid space behind the *skēnē* where in fact the most exciting action occurs, the events on Cithaeron narrated in the two long Messenger speeches. Likewise when Dionysus describes the "visions" inside the palace, invisible to the audience (604-41), these are the all-important confrontations between the two chief protagonists. Such effects heighten our sense of the conventional, arbitrary nature of the space that we actually see before us. That real physically present three-dimensional spatial field becomes an increasingly marginal locus from which we are distracted by other more vivid events evoked only by the power of words, not acted out in gesture and movement. We are pulled away emotionally either to the dark interior of the palace or the remote mysterious wild of Mt. Cithaeron, until at the end the entire action, cast and all, follows this movement in the massive exile of the house of Cadmus.

By making us particularly aware of the two spatial fields, seen and

[27] Steidle 35 remarks that Pentheus' disappearance from the stage in the fourth episode is the spatial symbol of his doom, "raumsymbolisch seine Niederlage sichtbar macht"; but he does not explore the paradoxical implications of this "negative" space. On the staging see also Roux 1.94-97. For the spatial dimensions of the conflicts in the play see Castellani 72f.; Diller (1960) 103f.; Scott 342f.; Tschiedel 67-70; Steidle 35-37. See also Hourmouziades 35ff., 109ff., esp. 125. Klaus Joerden, "Zur Bedeutung des Ausser- und Hinterszenischen," in Walter Jens, ed., *Die Bauformen der Tragödie* (Munich 1971) 394ff. observes Euripides' tendency to frame conflicts or tensions in terms of spatial contrasts, but does not deal with the *Bacchae*. Oranje 116-26 also stresses the importance of the spatial contrasts.

unseen, the play self-consciously delineates the symbolic and mimetic dimension of theatrical representation. In a manner analogous to the robing scene, it calls attention to the conventionality of its own orchestral space as a stage for illusion and thereby provides another form of double vision. Through perceiving in a sense, two "stages" for the action, the seen and the unseen, we participate in the illusion that the *skēnē* represents the Theban palace, but we are also drawn to recognize the spell of words that can make us "see" the events on unseen Cithaeron as vividly as those before us in the theater of Dionysus. Euripides is less explicit than Shakespeare, but he is equally aware that the "O" of his theater holds the "vasty fields" that imagination must supply.

• VI •

Chorus

The *Bacchae* calls into question the familiar role of the chorus as a voice of the community and a representative of ethical and political norms. This is one of the very few Greek plays in which the chorus does not represent such values. Instead of being citizens or confidantes of the chief protagonists, this chorus of Asian bacchants has its proper place in the wild, is hostile to Thebes and its king, and embodies the very antithesis of everything for which the Greek polis stands. Their "barbarian" or "Bacchic" cry of exultant song (*melos*, 1034, 1057) celebrates the misfortune, not the success, of the city's rulers (1032-39).

True, the Persian chorus of Aeschylus' *Persae* and the chorus of Phoenician women on their way to serve Delphic Apollo in the *Phoenissae* offer some parallel; but even those choruses have the moral values and sentiments with which civilized men, that is, Greeks, can identify. Not so in the *Bacchae*, whose choruses violently challenge these values, are emotional, ecstatic, devoted to no human city and no human house, and free of male control. The chorus of Aeschylus' *Eumenides* is certainly difficult and ambiguous in its relation to the male protagonist of the play, but it also has some clearly recognized claim to justice and at the end is incorporated into the polis. In the

Philoctetes the chorus can participate in a scheme to deceive and make statements that we are probably not to take at face value (e.g., 507-18). Though moral values are involved, lying versus honesty, the chorus does not have the major role in creating this rift. When the *Bacchae*'s chorus praises wisdom, moderation, the right attitude toward the gods, justice, a calm and peaceful life devoted to beauty and serenity, we are left far more deeply puzzled. The discrepancy between the traditional gnomic wisdom of these utterances and the character of those who speak them widens as the play goes on.

This tension, in turn, is part of a deeper disharmony and disequilibrium between form and content throughout the choral odes generally. Like the Dionysiac music that they both describe and recreate, the choral lyrics veer between hauntingly beautiful poetry full of the beauty of nature and violent cries for vengeance and bloodshed.[28] The second stasimon, for example (509-75), moves from the evocations of Pentheus' chthonic savagery to Orphic song in a landscape of remote mountains and verdant river valleys. Later, within the hundred lines between the third and fourth stasima (862-911 and 977-1016), the Chorus's song changes from gnomic reflectiveness in a lovely sylvan setting to a fierce hunting cry, spitting rage and hatred. From the pastoral lyricism and gnomic reflections on piety, the justice of the gods, a quietistic freedom from toils in the third stasimon, where there is little that would trouble the morality of a Greek audience, they change abruptly in stasimon four to calling forth Cadmus' daughters as driven by the "hounds of Madness." The slow fulfillment of the gods' punishment and obedience to law in the antistrophe of the previous ode (888-92) become a demand for a blood-thirsty sword-bearing Justice that slits throats with a violence as great as any Pentheus had mustered in his most tyrannical outburst. Indeed, if we compare their utterance in lyrics on Justice "cutting through the throat, slaughtering the godless, lawless, son of Echion, earth-born" with Pentheus' threat to "cut and sever [the Stranger's] throat from body" (991-96 and 239-41), we seem to reach a lowest common denomi-

[28] See Kamerbeek (1960) 8: "Tout le charme enivrant du plus cruel mythe hellénique s'exhale de leur poésie en contrepoint avec l'horreur provoquée par le spectacle de la ruine des humains." On the ambiguity of the Chorus see also Arthur (1972) passim; Norwood, *Essays* 67; Kranz 235; Bogner 242f.; Diller (1955) 472; Carrière 135f.; Parry, *Lyrics* 148-52. WI 2 remarks, "In no other extant Greek play since Aeschylus . . . is the Chorus so prominent."

nator of violence: the once mystical worshipers now stand on the same level as the homicidal young tyrant. And yet it is not the Asian maenads who do the killing, but the Theban women of the house of Cadmus. Bystanders and instigators, they yet retain their distance and, at least technically, the purity that they extol in their first lovely lyrics (77).

At times the maenad Chorus speaks in the more or less conventional role of moderate citizens advising against the excess and irrational haste of a foolish ruler. As the Messenger finishes his long account of events on Cithaeron, for example, they interpose (775-77): "I fear to speak my words in freedom [logous eleutherous] to the ruler, yet it shall be said: Dionysus is inferior to none of the gods." Just as their leader Dionysus can for a moment offer to save his victim (806), so they legitimately hold out in their odes an alternative to Theban authoritarianism. For a moment, early in the play, they can see in Thebes' past and in the civilizing work of Cadmus as "sower of the earth-born crop" of the Spartoi something that could inspire "piety" and "reverence" (263-65). But once Pentheus definitively rejects them and pursues his aggressive path, they regard the "earth-born" origins of Thebes as a source of monstrosity, injustice, violence (537-44, 995-96 = 1015-16) and are totally blind to its other side.

The status of the Chorus becomes even more uncertain near the end. Even as they participate in Agave's madness and aggravate it with words of praise (e.g., 1172, 1193), they seem to show compassion, calling her tlamōn and talaina, "poor woman," "suffering" (1184, 1200). Their last utterance in our preserved text (excluding the five-line tag that closes this, like several other plays) is a statement of pity for Cadmus (1327-28): "I grieve for your part, Cadmus; but your son has his punishment, deserved, to be sure, but still grievous to you." Their words, in fact, echo Cadmus' own statements of compassion for his daughter and grief for his grandson (cf. 1260, 1312).

This split within the choral lyrics is the most extreme development of the freer relation of chorus to action with which Euripides experimented in his later plays.[29] Yet this split has a special significance for the Bacchae. It corresponds to that polarity between horror and

---

[29] By "freer" I do not mean to imply that there is no relation or that these odes are merely decorative. On the alleged irrelevance of the Euripidean ode see Parry, Lyrics, chap. 6, especially his conclusion, 203-205.

beauty, revulsion and fascination, that Euripides perceived in the Dionysiac cult; and it has its counterpart in the movement from Golden-Age bliss to the bloody rending of living creatures in the First Messenger's speech. On the metatragic reading this gap marks Euripides' awareness of tragedy's complex relation to the established moral values of the city. Given the Chorus's ambiguous relation to traditional wisdom, *sophia*, the play lacks a firm, clear voice of civic reason, restraint, authority. Instead we are at every moment pulled in different directions, pulled beyond the civic *sophia* to the beauty or the horror of the wild.

Besides being an actor in the play, the Chorus itself is a theme of the action, a motif that focuses the paradoxes and problems of the Dionysiac worship. In the opening ode this Chorus describes its own music, which includes the "sweet toil" and the "effort that is sweet effort" (*ponon hēdyn, kamaton eukamaton*, 66-67). But *ponos* and *kamatos* recur in their bitterest meaning as the results of the Chorus's presence. "Pain," "grief," and "misfortune" (*penthos, algos, dystychia*) dominate the closing movement of the play. At the peripety Pentheus is the exact inverse of the Chorus in the parode: they have a collective joy in their *kamatos*; he suffers it alone (*kamnei monos*, 963).

In the parode the Chorus will "lead Dionysus down from the Phrygian mountains to Greece's streets of the wide dancing-places" (*Hellados eurychorous agyias*, 85-88). But, as we have noted in Chapter 4, this movement is reversed by the action of the play. Dionysus leads his double and victim from the center of a Greek city up into the mountains, and the survivors of Cadmus' house will lead barbarians against Greek temples (1333-36, 1354-60). Instead of affirming the civilized identity of the polis like the choruses of the city, this Dionysiac Chorus blurs the division between Greek and barbarian and between man and nature. "All the earth will dance in chorus" (*choreusei*, 114). An outlandish dancing of corybantes, joined with mad, reveling satyrs (*mainomenoi Satyroi*, 131), add the wild flutes and drums to their "dancings" (*choreumata*, 132) at the feasts that give delight to Dionysus (123-34). The bizarre effects produced by the Dionysiac Chorus, though less picturesque, are no less strong when old Cadmus and Teiresias picture themselves soon after as joining the Bacchic dance (*choreuein*, 184), shaking their white hair. They constitute a strange "chorus" not of all the citizens but of two men alone (195-96):

> *Cadmus.* Alone of the city shall we two alone dance to the Bacchic god?
>
> *Teires.* Alone, for alone do we have good sense, the others bad.

For Pentheus the maenads' "honoring Dionysus with dances" (*chorois*, 220) is inseparable from lewd imaginings of promiscuous embraces. But he is killed by his mother who shouts for this death "lest he bring back news of the god's secret choruses" (*chorous kryphaious*, 1108-1109). The fusion of the worshipers with one another and with nature separates these Choruses from those of the city. Furthermore, these Choruses are "secret" rather than public. When imitated by men and women of the city, they produce horrible reversals or an anomalous chorus of two old men.

The Chorus and the choral worship of Dionysus per se focus the problem of Dionysus' presence in the polis; hence the play is called "Bacchae" rather than "Dionysus" or "Pentheus." Sophocles' son Iophon wrote a "Bacchae or Pentheus," Aeschylus a "Pentheus" and possibly a "Bacchae" as well.[30] In the absence of a single firm center of values, the vacuum is filled by the maenad Chorus in their ambiguous way.

These tensions in the role and theme of the Chorus reflect an awareness in the late Euripides that his art contains a deep ambivalence between reason and human sensibilities on the one hand and the untrammeled, potentially beautiful, but also potentially destructive, life of the instincts on the other. The ecstatic music of the maenad Chorus is the shadow side of both the civilized women in Thebes and of the emotional freedom of Euripides' own lyricism.[31] The ambiguous position of the Chorus's moralizing about "wisdom," "piety," and the divine justice undermines confidence in the traditional rationalism and humanism of the polis. Values traditionally expressed by the communal utterance of the chorus are shown to be no longer adequate to the individual citizen's experience and understanding of life. Reason and civic authority seem to corrupt and block a more

---

[30] See Dodds, *Bacchae* xxviii-xxix.
[31] See Bogner, 241-43; Parry, *Lyrics* 149.

spontaneous, natural access to the sources of joy and fulfilment. Yet the instincts and the unchecked emotions also seem to leave the human actors stranded in a strange, bare, and fearful place. This Chorus, confronting the poet's fellow citizens in the circle of the orchestra, is transmitting the words of a poet writing in the distant frontierland of a not too securely civilized country. He has to tell them no longer of the well-defined civic spaces and heroic traditions of their past, but of the mingled joy and horror of the unknown, the exotic, the unbounded. The choruses of the *Helen* or *Taurian Iphigeneia* less than a decade before belong to that unfamiliar world at the fringes of Hellenic civilization. But the Chorus of the *Bacchae,* unlike those of the earlier plays, pulls us across to the other side, across the frontier of civilized life, rather than back to the stable life of Greek society and Greek values. A full generation earlier, the Dionysus ode of Sophocles' *Antigone* had juxtaposed the infinite reaches of the circle of stars, led by the god in his fiery "chorus," with the secure, geometric space of the theater (*Antigone* 1146-54). But in Sophocles the Dionysus who leads the chorus of "fire-breathing stars" complements the civic Dionysus of the parode who leads the all-night choruses of celebration for the city's salvation (*Antigone* 150-54). In the *Bacchae* the wild music of an ambiguously foreign Dionysus and his Asian Chorus expands to fill the entire play. For all the personal suffering of the *Antigone,* the civic frame remains secure; the king is not killed or exiled. In the *Bacchae* there is no point that is not under the most violent stress.

• VII •

Hero, Action, Tragic Pattern

The erosion of clear civic values, the fluctuation in the nature of the chorus, and the radical change in the relation between Pentheus and Dionysus in the play also call into question the role of the hero. The play contains no single center of heroic action whose strength of spirit is somehow tested, discovered, or affirmed through suffering. The play, again, is called "Bacchae," not "Pentheus." The tragic suffering, though centered upon Pentheus, is distributed among the three main figures, a device that recalls plays like the *Trojan Women* and *Hecuba*.[32]

From the illusionistic role of hero whose intransigent will brings him into conflict with the gods and the realities of life they embody, Pentheus slips into the metatragic role of the actor playing roles. He tries on different roles, different masks and costumes, until his final role is to become only the mask, the empty *prosōpon*, carried by one of those figures whom he was impersonating, the maenad Agave. The logical consequence of Pentheus' taking on the role and garb of the maenads is that he is present onstage in the last portion of the play only as the severed head with which Agave enters at 1168. Her grisly trophy could well have been the mask that Pentheus wore, now daubed with red. When Cadmus asks Agave, "Whose *prosōpon* do you hold in your arms?" (1277) the word may connote "mask" as well as "face," although the former meaning is not clearly attested until Demosthenes and Aristotle.[33] Agave's reply, "A lion's, as these hunting women say" (1278), calls attention once more to the illusionistic convention of the stage.

The play-within-the-play effect of "masking" Pentheus is now answered by this scene of unmasking, where Agave's delusion that the *prosōpon* she carries is that of a lion mirrors the theatrical illusion itself, that the masked actor is Pentheus. This movement from the costume of king to that of bacchant and then to the mask alone parallels Pentheus' movement in the plot from king to sacrificial victim. Psychologically, the multiplicity of roles/costumes/masks also parallels the multiplicity of unintegrated character-traits in his fragmented and conflicted personality. Torn apart emotionally as well as literally, he

[32] Arrowsmith (1959) 44 observes that the *Bacchae* has "protagonists but no heroes."

[33] The notion of "mask" may also be present in *Cycl.* 227 and *Orestes* 224. Cf. also the *phobera prosōpa* of Aeschyl. *Eum.* 990; cf. Aristoph. *Ach.* 990, *Peace* 524, *Frogs* 912. On 1277 Roux remarks, "Plus frappant que *kephalē* parce que le visage implique à la fois une expression humaine et une identité. Le mot contient aussi l'indication d'un jeu de scène: jusque là, Agavé tenait la tête par la chevelure et ne pouvait voir le visage que Cadmos l'invite ici à examiner." See also Taplin, *Greek Tragedy* 98-100; Foley (1980) 131; Kott 206; Jones, *On Aristotle* (above, n. 12) 270. In *El.* 855ff. and 894ff. Orestes enters carrying, probably, the mask/head of Aegisthus: see David Sider, "Two Stage Directions in Euripides," *AJP* 98 (1977) 17. For representations of Agave carrying the head in Greek vases and sculpture see Philippart (1930) 66-71, with plates 11, 14, and figs. 11, 12.

is also torn apart metatragically, dismembered into a sequence of costumes that ends up as the empty mask, the disembodied *prosōpon*
(1277). He is not even "Pentheus" any longer, only "the head of
Pentheus" (1284; cf. 1139).

The revelation of truth by the severed mask/head, however, also
serves to unmask the maenads and their god in another sense, for it
shows the homicidal potential in their ecstasy and delusion. Like his
double and opposite, Dionysus, too, plays roles. But when he changes
the mask of the Stranger for that of the powerful *deus ex machina* at
the end, it is to demonstrate the helplessness of the human actors and
to introduce another myth of men changing shape and losing identity
(1330-39).

The bloody visage/mask revealed as Pentheus' head in 1277 contrasts with the "laughing visage" with which Dionysus, once the hunted
beast, will now ensnare the hunter, Pentheus (1020-23): "Come, beast
Bacchus, over the beast-hunter of the bacchanals cast with smiling
countenance [γελῶντι προσώπῳ] the noose of death when he has fallen
among the herd of maenads."[34] The *prosōpon* in this choral prayer is
possibly a reference to the "mask" as well as the "visage" of the smiling Stranger in the early scenes of the play. The reversals of hunter
and hunted, king and beast, agent and victim, therefore, are bound
up with the reversals in the maenads and their god and visually enacted in the change from the smiling *prosōpon* of the Stranger in the
first half of the play to the grisly, blood-flecked *prosōpon* of Pentheus
carried onstage at the end.[35]

Like the *Oedipus Tyrannus*, the *Bacchae* calls attention to the basic
syntax of both language and action that underlies the tragic experi-

[34] For the text and translation of these lines see Dodds, *Bacchae*, and Roux ad
loc.; WI 126f.

[35] Georges Méautis, "L'expression des masques dans quelques tragédies d'Euripide," *REG* 36 (1923) 181f., stresses the visual effect of the contrast between the
masks of the two protagonists, Pentheus' expressing vehemence, passion, energy,
anger, Dionysus' having a feminine, sensual, calm and smiling aspect. See also Foley
(1980) 127-29. On the other hand if Pentheus in his last stage appearance is made
up really to resemble Dionysus, Agave's entrance with the *prosōpon* makes the audience see double in a number of ways, and effects a visual fusion of god/victim/king.
The fusion of god and victim is all the greater as masks of Dionysus, hung on trees
or pillars, were daubed with red in cult practice: see Farnell, *Cults* 5.242f; Paus.
2.2.6 and 8.39.6.

ence.[36] The massive reversals between king and scapegoat, ruler and helpless child, celebrant and victim, god and beast are part of that precarious state of things that tragedy reveals beneath the apparently firm surroundings of our life. This unpredictable reversibility is also part of the double vision, appearance and reality, central to tragedy and prominent in the *Bacchae*.

The convertibility of agent into victim, active to passive in tragedy, is also central to the *Bacchae*; and in this sense, too, the play defines a model of sorts for the nature of tragic action. There are no winners in the game of violence; and the strongest, most confident agent is or soon becomes a victim himself.

Pentheus and Dionysus are locked together in a reversible violence where "doer" and "sufferer," *drōn* and *paschōn*, become paradoxically interchangeable. At the moment of central reversal in the play, when Pentheus seems to be exercising his greatest violence as doer, he finds himself confronted by an antagonist both active and passive, frustratingly active in and through his passivity: "Neither suffering nor doing will he be silent" (801).

In his desperation and helplessness here Pentheus unknowingly expresses the mystery of the god's power as both victim and agent together. Earlier he complained of the hybris done him and his city (247), a complaint that he repeats in the central scene discussed above (cf. 779, 785-86). But at the end this is just the complaint that Dionysus, in his own person, makes against Pentheus: "Born a god I suffered hybris [*hybrizomēn*] from you" (1347). Pentheus' threat to sever the Stranger's head from his body (241) is turned, with grim exactitude, against himself.[37] By doing nothing, remaining "calm" (*hēsychos*), Dionysus defeats the frenetically energetic king (616-41). Hence perhaps the ambiguity in the word *aporos*, "helpless" and "not to be circumvented," in Pentheus' line shortly before his "conversion" (800): ἀπόρῳ γε τῷδε συμπεπλέγμεθα ξένῳ ("We are at grips with this stranger who is *aporos*"). The athletic metaphor reflects the change from the apparent passivity of the soft-looking youth (455-56). The word *aporos* also contains a spatial metaphor, "allowing of no path or road." Pentheus soon believes that he is taking a decisive step

---

[36] For the logical structure of this king of reversal from king to scapegoat, the "principle of oxymoron," see Kenneth Burke, A *Rhetoric of Motives* (New York 1950) 328.

[37] For a different view of these systematic reversals see Sansone 41.

out of his blocked path of helplessness or *aporia* in moving on the "road" (cf. 819, 841) to the mountains. His next line combines "doing" and "suffering" to characterize the god who frustrates him (801). Only a little later, insulted, mocked, and manipulated, he will ask, "And now what else besides all this will you fit on me?" (834). Now totally in the power of his erstwhile victim, he becomes the "led" instead of the "leader" (cf. 841, 845, 855).

In the absolute clarity and yet almost phantasmagoric exaggeration of the reversal of antagonist and protagonist, king and god, we seem to be moving back to somewhere near the origins of drama itself, the "doing" (*drama* from *dran*, "to do") involving the helplessness of a once powerful hero and/or death of a god. But lest we lose sight of the play in a primitivist haze of remote origins, we must recall the careful formalism of the structure that Euripides has designed for these reversals. There is something characteristic of classical Greek art in the massive, almost sculptural simplicity with which the two sides, mortal and divine, confront one another and then change places. As in the great temples of the fifth century, the balanced antithesis of the form is taut with a significance, an integrated dynamic totality, that no static conceptual formulation can exhaust.

These inversions, Euripides suggests, are rooted in the name, and therefore in the essence, of the agent/victim himself. When the Stranger asks for and elicits from Pentheus a full, formal statement of his name, he tells him, "In your name you are suited for ill-fortune" (*endysty-chēsai*, 508), thereby anticipating the later appellation, "Pentheus the wretched" (*Pentheus ho tlēmōn*, 1058), the "ill-fated" (*ho dysdaimōn*, 1126 and 1292; cf. 1100, 1139). Teiresias had made the prophetic connection of "Pentheus" with *penthos*, "grief" (367), and Cadmus echoes it when the prophecy seems fulfilled: "O grief unmeasurable" (*penthos*, 1244). The etymological plays on Pentheus' name, however, also include *pathos*, "suffering," as well as *penthos*, "grief." This persecutor of the god will come to "suffer" (*paschein*, *pathos*, and related words) the "grief" (*penthos*) contained in his name. "Tell me what must be *suffered*; what terrible thing will you *do* to me?" Dionysus, disguised as the Stranger, asks in his first interview with Pentheus (εἴφ' ὅ τι παθεῖν δεῖ· τί με τὸ δεινὸν ἐργάσῃ, 492). But in the next scene it is Pentheus who complains, *pepontha deina*, "I have had terrible things done to me." Ironically his own hyperactivity betrays his helplessness before the apparent passivity of the god's "calm" (cf. *hēsychos* in 623 and 636; also 647). In the long Messenger's speech the women "do terrible deeds" (*deina drōsi*, 667, 717), whereas Pentheus exclaims soon after, "This exceeds all limit if what we suffer [*paschomen*] we suffer from women" (*peisomestha*, 785f.).

The god continues with one of his rare addresses to Pentheus by name (787-90):

πείθῃ μὲν οὐδέν, τῶν ἐμῶν λόγων κλύων,
Πενθεῦ· κακῶς δὲ πρὸς σέθεν πάσχων ὅμως
οὔ φημι χρῆναί σ' ὅπλ' ἐπαίρεσθαι θεῷ,
ἀλλ' ἡσυχάζειν.

In no way are you persuaded, heeding my words, Pentheus. Yet, though I suffer evil from you, I say you should not take up arms against the god, but remain quiet.

Dionysus is exploiting a three-way play on *Pentheus, penthos*, and *paschō/peithō/peisomai*. The last form may be the future of both *paschō*, "suffer," and *peithō*, "persuade" (in the middle voice, "obey"). Thus when Pentheus says, at the end of the previous line, "Nothing surpasses this, if what we suffer we suffer from women" (*πεισόμεσθ' ἃ πάσχομεν*, 786), there is also a play on the verb *peisomestha*, "we shall obey," particularly as the next line opens with Dionysus' *peithē(i)*, "you obey." "Pentheus," *Pentheu* (vocative), comes in the same metrical position in the line after that (788). Rather than "obeying" Dionysus and remaining "calm" (*hēsychazein*), Pentheus has consistently shown that vehemence of willful, arrogant speech that leads to his *pathos* (cf. 216, 266-70).[38] Some sixty lines later his apparent alternative of "obeying the counsels" of Dionysus (846, ἢ τοῖσι σοῖσι πείσομαι βουλεύμασιν) actually conceals the destruction of free choice and holds the passivity of his inevitable doom by the god's "necessity" (cf. *anankē* in 969), for Pentheus' phrase in 846 may equally mean "I shall *suffer* [πείσομαι] through your counsels."

Dionysus completes these inversions when he sends Pentheus out to his death in the garb of his total opposite: woman, maenad, *pharmakos*, and beast-victim. He pronounces over his victim, "Terrible you are, terrible, and to terrible sufferings [*pathē*] do you go" (971):

[38] On the etymological connections of *penthos* and *pathos* see Gregory Nagy, *Comparative Studies in Greek and Indic Meter* (Cambridge, Mass. 1974) 259 with n. 27; Segal (1982). On the ambiguities of Pentheus as a tragic hero generally see WI 160f.; Deichgräber 348; Carrière 128ff.

δεινὸς σὺ δεινὸς κἀπὶ δείν' ἔρχῃ πάθη. The line climaxes the previous ambiguous references to "doing" or "suffering" terrible things (492 and 642, cited above). This inversion is then turned back upon itself in the ceaseless reversibility of the tragic movement when Agave proclaims herself the victim of the god's "terrible" revenge. The god's defense, "Yes, for I suffered terrible things from you" (1377), echoes Pentheus' words (642, 786), but now appears almost ludicrous in its arbitrary cruelty as he and Pentheus, formerly victim and agent, have completely changed places (1374-78):

Αγ. δεινῶς γὰρ τάνδ' αἰκείαν
     Διόνυσος ἄναξ τοὺς σοὺς εἰς
     οἴκους ἔφερεν.
Δι. καὶ γὰρ ἔπασχον δεινὰ πρὸς ὑμῶν,
     ἀγέραστον ἔχων ὄνομ' ἐν Θήβαις.

Agave.   Terribly did lord Dionysus bring this destructive outrage upon your house.
Dionys. Yes, for I suffered terrible things from you, having my name without the prize of honor in Thebes.

The inversion of "doer and sufferer" extend to a whole series of juxtapositions of active and passive forms of the same verb. The "leader" is the "one led" (agomenos, cf. 439, 518, 618 with 855; pheromenos and pheromen, 968, 1169; also 1216, 1280, 1299). The one who hopes to "see" is "seen" (cf. 1050 and 1075). The one who takes or captures (lambanein) is the one "taken" (cf. 239 and 355 with 960).[39] Just before Pentheus' "conversion" there is a variation on this syntactical inversion that cuts to the center of his transformation from aggressor to victim. As Pentheus threatens and blusters, Dionysus admonishes (794-95):

θύοιμ' ἂν αὐτῷ μᾶλλον ἢ θυμούμενος
πρὸς κέντρα λακτίζοιμι θνητὸς ὢν θεῷ.

I would sacrifice to him rather than, being angry, kick against the pricks, mortal against god.

[39] 954-55: —ἐλάταισιν δ' ἐμὸν κρύψω δέμας.
       —κρύψῃ σὺ κρύψιν ἥν σε κρυφθῆναι χρεών . . .
      960: λήψῃ δ' ἴσως σφᾶς, ἢν σὺ μὴ ληφθῇς πάρος.
      1050: ὡς ὁρῶμεν οὐχ ὁρώμενοι.
      1075: ὤφθη δὲ μᾶλλον ἢ κατεῖδε μαινάδας.

The active form, "I would sacrifice," *thyoimi* at the beginning of the line, is answered by a near homonym of its passive, *thyomenos*, "being sacrificed," in the word *thymoumenos*, "being angry." Pentheus' "being angry," the opposite of the "calm" that the god suggests (790), leads to his "being sacrificed." This alternation of active and passive dominates the sentence structure at the decisive point of inversion from king to sacrificial victim (1075):

ὤφθη δὲ μᾶλλον ἢ κατεῖδε μαινάδας.

He was the one seen rather than the one seeing the maenads.

On a metatragic reading these syntactical inversions are analogous to the splitting of the heroic role, and the heroic personality, between two characters who are doublets but also stand in an ambiguous relation to one another, as both opposites and the same, both similar and hostile. The god of ecstatic rites is the authoritarian king's repressed alter ego; as the bull he is the bestial double of Dionysus' own Olympian divinity. As the hero-king becomes the surrogate for the god and changes places with the beast-victim who really is the god, the symbolic substitutions of sacrificial (and by extension) of theatrical violence move terrifyingly close to actuality. Euripides plays with effacing the perilous boundary between the enactment of violence and the substitutes for violence provided by ritual and art. Instead of a beast symbolically replacing the god in the quasi-theatrical "performance" of the sacrificial rite, we come near to witnessing a human sacrifice, and we certainly see its after-effects acted out on the stage where illusion and imagination become the visible and visual "reality." Placing Dionysus himself and Dionysiac masking at the center of the action, the play reveals not the grandeur of a human king who could emerge as the bearer of the god's *pathos* but the confusing identification of the king with a helpless victim who has lost touch with both reality and divinity and is either child or beast.

• VIII •

Genre: Comedy and Tragedy

Dionysus is the god of the theatricality of both comedy and tragedy. The metatragic aspect of the play takes in both forms of the god's power of dramatic illusion. In the *Frogs* Dionysus appears as a comic god who is yet suitable to choose the best tragedian.[40] In the *Symposium* Socrates' last words, addressed to somnolent representatives of comedy and tragedy, assert the connection of the two genres, insofar as the same poet should be able to write in both forms (*Smp.* 223 d).

The *Bacchae*, though profoundly serious, contains scenes that appear distinctly comic: old Teiresias and Cadmus offering to dance with hoary locks on the mountain or Pentheus dressed as a maenad asking for advice about how to wear the wig or carry the thyrsus. Recently Bernd Seidensticker has explored these comic elements at length, and there is no need to repeat his observations here.[41] In·the same year (1978) David Sansone published an essay calling attention to certain elements of the satyr play in the *Bacchae*, principally in the plot, centering upon the theme of defeating and killing a monster.[42]

What is particularly curious about the *Bacchae*'s relation to both comedy and satyr play is its deliberate distance and ironic treatment of genres to which it seems to come so close. If the *Bacchae* is viewed as quasi-satyr play, its "monster," triumphantly killed, proves to be the king; and the "hero" of this endeavor is a god who appears in bestial shape. The play thus shifts ambiguously between hero and monster, and we are not fully sure who is the more monstrous. Likewise, rather than developing a full-blown comic mood in the grotesque scenes of the bacchantic elders or the king dressed as maenad, Euripides gives us a problematical and elusive shifting of tone. We do not know for certain whether we should laugh or grieve.

Euripides here not only calls attention to the ambivalence of Dionysus, as Seidensticker suggests,[43] but also depicts the ambiguity of illusionistic representation in the theater, the paradox that the same mimetic art may give us both pleasure and pain. This god, as Dionysus himself says, can make us "see with pleasure things that are painful" (815). Or, as Aristophanes implies in the *Frogs*, his realm includes both the "serious" and the "laughable" (*spoudaion, geloion*). The Dionysus of the *Bacchae* occupies a kind of liminality of genre,

---

[40] On the *Frogs* and the *Bacchae* see below, Chap. 8, section 11.

[41] Seidensticker (1978) 303-20. See also Cook, *Enactment* 132f. on the play's pushing at the traditional limits between comic and tragic form. For various "serious" readings of the old men dressed as maenads see Deichgräber 328; Nestle, *Euripides* 83-86; Steidle 33f

[42] Sansone 40-46, esp. 41f.

[43] Seidensticker (1978) 319f.

able to reflect on the illusionistic power of both of the theatrical forms under the aegis of the god. By bringing the god and the illusionistic power of the god upon the stage, Euripides situates his play both within and beyond the conventional form of both genres, a place where his text can explore the power and the limitations of its own mimetic mode.[44]

· IX ·

Reversibility and Change

The *Bacchae* not only enacts a situation of massive reversal, but also calls attention to the logical structures overturned in that reversal. This aspect of the play has been sufficiently described above in connection with the ambiguity of the tragic hero. It has another dimension in the play's concern with the instability, uncertainty, and deceptiveness of external form. Through its language and action the play calls attention to that shift between appearance and reality that is so fundamental a theme of all Greek tragedy.

The play presents a change of dress and appearance on the stage as striking as any that takes place in Greek drama. It also deliberately stresses the multiplicity and fluidity of forms that belong to the god who controls the power of illusion. Literal changes of shape or form occur on the stage (Pentheus from king to maenad to severed head; Dionysus from Lydian Stranger to Olympian god). The language, too, insistently dwells on terms for "change" and "shape."[45] Of the five times that Euripides uses the choral tag "many the *shapes* of the

[44] Dionysus' affinity to what Victor Turner calls the "liminal" could perhaps be rephrased, in a "metatragic" direction, toward something like Kristeva's "carnivalesque": see Kristeva 100: "Sur la scène generalisée du carnaval le langage se parodie et se relativise, répudiant son rôle de représentation (ce qui provoque le rire), sans arriver pourtant à s'en dégager. . . . Vicieuse (j'entends ambivalente), à la fois représentative et antireprésentative, la structure carnavalesque est antichrétienne et antirationaliste."

[45] *Morphē*: 4, 453, 855, 917; "change" (compounds of *meta-*): 296, 302, 944, 1269f., 1329f.; cf. also 477f., 607, 618f. On the former see Roux ad 4; on the latter, B.M.W. Knox, "Second Thoughts in Greek Tragedy," *GRBS* 7 (1966) 229 = *Word and Action* 243; also Wassermann (1929) 274, Foley (1980) 126f.

things of the gods" to end a play, nowhere perhaps is it more literally appropriate than here (1388-92; also *Alcestis, Medea, Andromache, Helen*).

The very "form" or "shape" (*morphē*) of the god is an active element in the plot, as it is in the character and cult of Dionysus himself. The fluid reality to which he leads his worshipers is that of Bacchic ecstasy, and also that of tragedy. The god appears in a multiplicity of shapes whose fluctuation between reality and imagination or delusion is a central theme of the play. He transforms the human characters into new "shapes," physically on stage in the case of Pentheus, mythically in the future of Cadmus that he prophesies at the end, and figuratively in the changed mental states that release suppressed desires or the hidden dark side of personality in the case of Pentheus and Agave.

In this role the god mirrors the metamorphic power of the poet himself. The poet holds in himself and reveals to others through his art the kaleidoscopic "many shapes of things divine" (1388) and, we may add, of things human as well. Dionysus is both the agent of sudden reversal and the principle of change, of that sudden and revealing *metabolē* that Euripides elsewhere identifies with the gods' intervention in human life. That sudden changefulness is essential to Euripides' tragic vision of life. In the *Iphigeneia among the Taurians* Pylades, trying to defend Apollo against Orestes' accusation of betrayal, expounds:

It is indeed misfortune in excess
That gives us changes in excess [*lian didousa metabolas*]
When it befalls. (*IT* 721-22)

On first hearing of the Stranger, Pentheus accuses him of being an enchanter, *goēs* (234), a word that implies a sorcerer capable of changing his shape.[46] The word may well have its origins in one of the shamanistic religions on the fringes of the Greek world (Herodotus 4.105) to which the Dionysiac cult is itself akin. But behind it stands the deeper meaning of the god's change of shape, his ability to manipulate the external appearance of things and give access to other forms that reality may take.

When Pentheus and the Stranger actually meet in person, how-

46 See Roux ad 234.

ever, the god shows an alarming steadfastness of both form and attitude: he did not blanch or "change [*ēllaxen*] his wine-faced cheek"
(438), but stood his ground, "waiting" (*emene*, 440). Pentheus turns
to the god confident that, for all his "swiftness," he is held fast in the
"nets" so that he "cannot escape from me" (451-52). His first words
of address hint at the god's paradox of form: "In body you are not
without form [*ouk amorphos*], Stranger, for women, no doubt, since
for that you are here in Thebes" (453-54). "Not without shape," *ouk
amorphos*: Pentheus' litotes says more than he knows. In one sense
Dionysus is "without shape," or rather he has the "many shapes" of
divinity (1388), the open shape upon which the beholder projects the
hidden forms of his own repressed desires, be it for sexual love (cf.
eros, 813) or for insane murder.

Upon the god's "shape" here Pentheus projects his own hidden
lust. In his first words about the god and his cult he voices suspicion
of illicit sexual activities (216-25); when he sees the god face to face
that "form" elicits at once those same thoughts, and almost the same
words (453-59; cf. "Aphrodite" in 459 and 225). The motive that
Pentheus attributes to Dionysus, "present here in Thebes" (454), is
his own in more than one sense.

Like the poet and stage director, Dionysus makes Pentheus appear
in many "shapes," his own shapes of snake, bull, and lion. He does
this figuratively (cf. 539) or through the suggestive effects of his illusionistic power (1174, 1185, 1214-15, 1238-39). Like a director, too,
he can make his actor-victim appear in a spectacularly theatrical change
of sex, "in the form of a woman" (*gynaikomorphos*, 855) or in the
"form" (*morphē*) of one of Cadmus' daughters (917). When in the
following ode the maenad Chorus incites the Theban women against
Pentheus "in woman-miming dress" (*gynaikomimos stolē*, 981), "dress
that imitates a woman," the language calls attention especially to the
"mimetic" power involved in this changing of "form." Dionysus' power
can change the "king" back into an actor whose role in the play-
within-a-play of the robing scene "mimics" a more serious and grimmer action than its surrounding, potentially comic frame. In Aristophanes' *Thesmophoriazusae* a male actor plays a sex-change for laughs.
In the *Bacchae* when Pentheus acts out the stage convention of a male
actor taking the part of a woman, putting on "woman-miming dress,"
the mixture of the laughable and the tragic is characteristic of the

dangerous fluidity of reality in Dionysiac representation. Its darker side is the figurative sex-change of the female bacchants discussed in Chapter 6 and Agave's new role as male warrior/hunter who brings back the slain prey triumphantly from the wild.

By bringing the disguised Dionysus onstage as god both of the maenadic ecstasy and the tragic mask, Euripides combines two characteristics of his tragic art: the precariousness of identity and the abrupt reversibility of circumstances. In the fusion of contrary roles through which Dionysus appears as the hidden alter ego of Pentheus, the play reveals the possible coexistence of opposites in our subconscious mental life. It also isolates the mysterious principle of conversion, of reversibility, that lies at the heart of our symbol-making and myth-making capacities. By these capacities the drama can explore the fluidity of reality that we experience once we leave the secure moorings of our everyday logic of noncontradictions, the safe, fortified, heavily defended walls of whatever Thebes each of us inhabits. With its 180-degree reversals in syntax, physical appearance, personal identity, and action, the play provides a model of the inversions of tragedy and focuses on Dionysus as the active force behind them.

In Teiresias' sophistic lecture on Dionysus, the "change of name," *onoma metastēsantes* (296), serves as a rationalistic instrument for purging the Dionysiac religion of some of its illogical, irrational elements, in this case the "myth" that Dionysus was born from the thigh of Zeus. But the change of name that the play *enacts* shows a very different level of Dionysiac transformation and takes place not in "words" but in bloody deeds, as Pentheus becomes a female bacchant and lives out the hidden meaning of his name, *penthos* (cf. 367).

· X ·

Recognition (Anagnorisis)

The inward dimension of transformation is recognition or anagnorisis. As in other plays (notably the *Heracles Mad* but also *Medea, Ion, Helen*), Euripides highlights the internal, spiritual meaning of the tragic action by contrasting it with remote, fabulous elements in the mythic narrative.[47] The result is a characteristically Euripidean tension between the mythic and the tragic elements of the play. Here the mythical metamorphosis of Cadmus and Harmonia into serpents in the remote future contrasts with the change in inner life, in feelings, perceptions, attitudes, enacted in the present on the stage. Agave's change of circumstances (*metestraphē*, 1329) contrasts with Cadmus' "change" (*metabalōn*) into a serpent shortly after (because of the lacuna after 1329 it is uncertain how much after).

The theme of recognition gains double force from at least two other aspects of the play. First, the stage business itself involves the masking and unmasking of actors and thus gives anagnorisis a visual counterpart onstage. Second, delusion and recognition are doubled in the parallel experiences of Pentheus and Agave.

The first aspect of recognition has already been sufficiently discussed above in connection with the mask. Some additional points need to be made in this context. Pentheus progresses (or, from another point of view, regresses) from seeing the god in the human guise of the Stranger to a hallucinatory vision of a bull in the palace (618-22) to a vision of the Stranger as the bull (920-22). His movement then is from human to animal to a strange fusion of god/human/animal in that fusion of categories that comprises the essence of Dionysus. Agave has a corresponding experience of Pentheus, but in reverse. She begins by seeing him as an unspecified hybrid of beast and man ("a climbing beast" that yet might reveal their "secret dances," 1107-1109). Then she sees him entirely as a wild beast, whether calf or lion (1173-99). Finally she recognizes the real human form in the head she bears.

At the same time Cadmus' question, "Whose *prosōpon* do you bear in your arms?" (1277), shows the multiple progression of "masking": the mask/face of Pentheus, overlaid by the disguise of a maenad, in which Agave saw the shape of a lion (1278). At his attempt to break through Agave's madness and bring her to "recognition" (*gnōrizein*,

---

[47] E.g., see Parry, *Lyrics* 157f. on *Alcestis*; William Arrowsmith's introduction to *Heracles* in *The Complete Greek Drama*, eds. David Greene and Richmond Lattimore, 3 (Chicago 1959) 272ff.; C. Segal, "Curse and Oath in Euripides' *Hippolytus*," *Ramus* 1 (1972) 165-80. Within the *Bacchae* we may note the shift in the motif of anagnorisis from the remote "mythical" level of Semele's birth of Dionysus and her "error of the bed" (*hamartia lechous*, 29) to the ethical meaning of Pentheus' recognition of "errors," *hamartiai*, in 1121.

1116), Pentheus threw off the *mitra*, the maenadic cap. That was not enough. Agave's recognition goes to the "mask/face" itself, the ambiguous *prosōpon*. Pentheus, having failed to break the spell of the Dionysiac illusion upon Agave, is now only a mask. Paradoxically, even as Agave does break through that spell and "recognizes" the *prosōpon* as the head of her son, *prosōpon* in 1277 reminds us that what she carries and now stares at with horror is still a "mask," that the entire "recognition," in other words, is still a theatrical event and therefore still under the power of Dionysus, albeit another aspect of Dionysus.

Yet it is not only by the stage object of the *prosōpon* that Agave reaches her recognition; it is also through the power of words and through the compassionate but steady reasoning of Cadmus. Cadmus can do what Pentheus could not. Not gesture alone, but the verbal medium of the tragedy, the carefully developed and articulated dialogue, brings the true recognition.

The "change" that Pentheus and Agave undergo in their "thoughts" presents the two ends of the Dionysiac ecstasy, entrance into it and emergence from it. "I praise you because you have changed your thoughts" (*methestēkas phrenōn*, 944) Dionysus tells Pentheus in the robing scene. "I am somehow coming to my senses [*ennous*], changing from my previous thoughts" (*metastatheisa tōn paros phrenōn*, 1269-70), Agave says as she returns to sanity. Pentheus awakens from the madness only long enough to see his possible "errors" (*hamartiai*, 1121), but not long enough to undo what he has done or to integrate the past experience into a complete identity. Tragedy may bring second thoughts, but it gives no second chances.

Agave, on the other hand, is led through a complex process of reawakening that has been likened to the medical treatment of a psychotic episode.[48] So convincing is the scene that one scholar has conjectured that Euripides actually witnessed maenads or shamans being brought out of their trance or quasi-hypnotic state. In any event, neither the victim nor the agent remains in the Dionysiac ecstasy. Both must return to a normal state of consciousness. The verbal echo between the two scenes brings out the complementary relation between the two sides of the experience. It suggests also the price paid for the exhilaration of entering a new state of consciousness, and the

[48] Devereux (1970).

necessity for resuming the normalcy of reason, speech, and feeling, with all the responsibility, pain, and guilt that they bring.

• XI •

Early in the robing scene Dionysus tempts Pentheus with the question, "Would you see with pleasure things bitter to you?" (815). Near the end, as Cadmus is about to bring Agave out from the spell of the Dionysiac illusion, he says (1259-62): "Alas, when you become sensible [*phronēsasai*] of what you have done you will suffer a fearful suffering. But if you continue to remain in this state in which you now find yourself, though not happy you will not think that you are miserable." Sanity in this situation does not bring happiness, but then neither does delusion. What this scene illustrates, however, is the paradoxical process by which the illusion created by tragedy can bring self-recognition and clarification. Tragedy immerses us in illusion only to break through that illusion by a "recognition" or anagnorisis of the underlying horror and cruelty of existence. That recognition requires both insight and courage. The madness of the Dionysiac illusion is not allowed to triumph or persist to the end, even though, as Cadmus says, Agave might be happier thus.

If the Dionysiac ritual gives the intoxicating ecstasy that unites man with nature, the tragic performance gives the recognition-through-illusion wherein man discerns the painful reality of his life and can confront his own suffering and the suffering he has inflicted. As in other Euripidean tragedies—one thinks especially of the *Hippolytus* and *Heracles*—a purely human encounter and human dialogue between *philoi* contrast with the mythical machinery of remote and cruel divinities.[49]

Agave, "priestess of the murder" (1114), is liberated from the collective emotion of the Dionysiac band, the *thiasos*, to suffer for herself as an individual. Pentheus, absorbed back into his identification with the god as victim-surrogate, never breaks free of the rite. Agave at the end definitively rejects the Dionysiac experience. In her insistence on lamentation (1368ff.), she affirms her right to suffer, which

---

[49] See Knox, *Word and Action* 227-29; Winnington-Ingram (1960) 190f.

is all that she has left. But she suffers not as a "priestess" or victim of a god, but as an individual human being in a world of arbitrary gods. She enacts the power of suffering in tragedy, such suffering as cannot be closed in ritual or moral orthodoxy.

The confusion of spectator and participant in Pentheus' "theatrical" experience exactly complements that in Agave's. He would be a spectator, *theatēs* (829), but not as a member of an audience in a *theatron*. Instead, he is a voyeur, isolated in his private neurotic world (and that despite the followers who accompany him to the "spectacle" on Cithaeron). He is shut out of the participatory community established by true theater or true belief in Dionysus. The audience's participation in the tragic action effects, for its members, the release of emotion that Aristotle labels catharsis. The voyeur's observation of the acts that he desires to see (cf. 813) creates no such positive identification with the experience. For the voyeur the observed acts are those of the Other, from whom he remains hopelessly alienated by his own repression. Instead of the shared theatrical participation in the mixed pain and pleasure of the enacted events (cf. 814f.), the voyeur would take his private pleasure in seeing real, not imitated, experience. Here there can be no healing catharsis, only the self-conscious distance and concealment of the spy (cf. 954-56).

Agave's isolation from the spectacle at the end works in just the opposite direction. On a metatragic reading her awakening from the Dionysiac delusion symbolizes the process by which drama frees itself from the bondage of ritual.[50] The play thus condenses into a single action the long and complex process by which the Dionysiac ritual no longer merely breaks down the barriers separating man and nature, human and bestial, but in the form of tragic art restores man to himself as the bearer of his human self-awareness even as it threatens him with the loss of his humanness or his firm personal identity.

In the distance between ritual and play, enacted rite and imagined event, literature comes into being. Tragedy puts to its own uses the seriousness and ordering power of the ritual, while it simultaneously insists on its own freedom in commenting on and distancing itself from the ritual. Pentheus' fictional death is the imagined sacrifice,

---

[50] Kott 207 quotes from Brecht's *Little Organon*, "Theater may be said to be derived from ritual, but that is only to say that it becomes theater once the two have separated."

the release of the mind's violence without real bloodshed, that maintains the separation between ritual and art. In order for the full tension between real and imagined violence to work, as Albert Cook suggests, the relation between actuality and imagination must be problematical.[51] The *Bacchae*, so much a play of origins and primordial beginnings, draws us back to the undefined ground where the distinction is as yet blurred, where the individual sufferer and the art form of which he (or she) is the center fight for their freedom and struggle for an existence apart from the god. In Greek tragedy the freedom can never be complete, for the god is also part of the hero, his double and his sacrificer. The tragic hero (and the tragic poet) can establish his autonomy from the god in the autonomy of the play as fiction. But he draws at least some measure of his significance and power from his role as the surrogate victim of the god and from the play as substitution for the rite of the god.

Far from being merely a humanistic revulsion against Dionysiac ecstasy, then, the last scene is a symbolic representation of the painful way in which tragedy itself comes into being. As the agent of this process, Cadmus reverses his own earlier superficial adherence to Dionysiac ecstasy. Thus he paradoxically lives up to his original role as a culture-hero, though in a way very different from the past. The facile joyfulness of his initial enthusiasm for the god (178-89) is now answered by his knowledge of the price that this Dionysiac ecstasy may entail. His earlier willingness to accede to useful lies (30f., 333-36) gives way to a courageous lucidity before the terrible truth that he is called upon to unmask, despite the happiness offered by remaining under the spell of the illusion (1259-62, above).[52] Ironically he performs these civilizing and humanizing functions only as he is about to lose his human shape, revert to the form of the dragon he once conquered, and like Agave leave his native Thebes for exile in the wild.

Beyond the illusion-creating power of Dionysus, therefore, the *Bacchae* places the tragedy itself that dramatizes the process of surren-

[51] Cook, *Enactment* 34; see Jacques Derrida, "White Mythology: Metaphor in the Text of Philosophy," trans. F.C.T. Moore, *New Literary History* 6 (1974) 39f.: "Mimesis brings pleasure only if it allows us to see in action what is nevertheless not given in action itself, but only in its very similar double, its mimeme. Let us leave open the question of this energy-carrying absence, this mysterious break, that is, this gap which creates stories and scenes."

[52] See in general De Romilly 361-80 and McDonald 252-71.

der to the power of the god's mask and madness, yet also can contain that power within its own frame, reflect upon it as an element in the dramatic fiction, and reject delusion for reality in the anagnorisis with which it ends.

Agave's gradual return to sanity (1264ff.) might be viewed as a "psychotherapy scene," as Devereux suggests. It is also a representation of the inner anagnorisis that takes place within each spectator as he attempts to integrate the fiction now ending into the reality of his own experience and self-understanding. This is what every spectator does as he leaves the theater and returns from the characters with whom he sympathizes or identifies to his own self.

Agave's successful return from delusion to reality completes and makes good the failed *anagnorisis* of Pentheus. Pentheus, as we have noted, becomes only the illusionistic role, only the mask or *prosōpon*. Agave comes to see the illusion behind the *prosōpon*, recognizes that the *prosōpon* she carries is not a lion's but her son's (1277-84). At that point she breaks through the illusionistic spell of the Dionysiac symbol to a "recognition" of the terrible reality, "the greatest pain," that it contains (1282).

Pentheus, "luxuriating" (968f.) in the robes of illusion/delusion, will "unmask" himself ("he flung from his hair the god's *mitra*," 1115f.) to the horror of his death as the god's victim, not his worshiper. Agave, who entered with cries of joy in the insanity of her infanticidal "hunting," will cry out to "truth, unhappy" that she unmasks, thanks to Cadmus' guidance, in giving up the illusion behind the *prosōpon* she carries. Under the spell of Dionysus, Pentheus "would see with pleasure what is painful" (815). But Agave's rejection of Dionysus' delusion within the frame of Dionysiac illusion is the other half of the tragic paradox reflected in the play: we willingly, even eagerly, submit to an illusion that will leave us with searing pain, the *algos deinon* or *megiston algos* of which Cadmus speaks repeatedly in this scene (1260, 1282).

Unlike the Dionysiac ritual, the Dionysiac art form enacts the power of the god but also reflects on the limits of that power. The play both is and gives us the *pharmakon*, the drug that like wine, makes us forget our pain in the *terpsis*, "delight," of its fiction.[53] Yet this power of illusion, be it through wine, religious ecstasy, or illusionistic art,

---

[53] For the ambiguity of the play as *pharmakon* see Pucci (1977), passim, esp. 167f., 178; also below, Chap. 8, section 7.

brings pain along with its pleasure; *algos*, *ponos*, or *penthos* along with *terpsis* or *hēdonē*.

Unlike the other manifestations of Dionysiac power, the "drug" of the theatrical illusion is its own antidote, for it contains the process of awakening from illusion to reality. Unlike the god whose rites it so vividly represents, the play proffers both madness and sanity. Dionysus' rites have their "wisdom" too, of course, and perhaps the play is saying that tragedy is the appropriate form, probably the only form, that can hold these contradictions in solution, the wisdom and the folly, the "pleasurable" and the "painful" spectacle that are one and the same (815; cf. 861).

• XII •

The mirroring, masking-unmasking effect of the play's metatragic aspect allows no meaning to be final. The Dionysiac poetics opens every meaning to its countermeaning. Meaning emerges as process rather than crystalline structure, as "dialogical: a process of writing that squanders the security of a stable meaning."[54] The multiple inversions and contradictions of Dionysus and of Dionysiac ritual are central to this dialogical quality. As the symbolic imitation of ritual, the play contains but also extends beyond the ritual. The very existence of the play, with all its masking and unmasking, is the triumph of consciousness and reason over the homicidal insanity that the rite can excite.

Yet the openness to explore that freedom also comes from the god. Dionysiac ritual is marked by "play," *paizein*. The "holy playings" of music join man and god (*hiera paigmata*, 161). The joyful release of energy in all-night song and dance also join man and beast, for the maenad Chorus describes these celebrations as a youthful frisking in which it is as "a fawn playing [*empaizousa*] in the green pleasures of a meadow" (866-67). This *ludic* dimension of the Dionysiac ritual creates the suspension, the liminal situation, of an anti-order wherein the poet can represent and imaginatively recreate experiences and

---

[54] John Brenkman, "Narcissus in the Text," *Georgia Review* 3 (1976) 327. Brenkman's essay (pp. 293-327) is about Ovid's *Metamorphoses*, but his formulation of this feature of style can also be extrapolated to the *Bacchae*.

states of mind that are accessible to very few but are nonetheless within the limits of reality.

Dionysiac play introduces something subversive into the world of Pentheus, a contrast of styles of life, language, behavior that fragments the rigidly unitary surface of the authoritarian city and the authoritarian personality. It is a contrast, in part, of politics and art, of the ethical and the aesthetic attitude, to adopt Kierkegaard's dichotomy. Instead of the constancy, directness, univocal language of the heroic and hoplite ideal to which Pentheus adheres, Dionysus' playfulness embodies shifting and change, guile, deviousness. Instead of robust masculine health he has a pallid delicacy and ambiguous androgyny. Instead of social utility he exemplifies marginality, amorality, irresponsibility.

Even as this god destroys Pentheus, he does so in the aesthetic mode of his own "Dionysiac poetics," smiling, seducing, changing shapes and appearances, using ambiguous language. The very manner of his revenge is itself ludic: he *plays* with Pentheus, deceives him, involves him in his own realm of disguise and deception, leads him on, exploits *double entendres*. He allows Pentheus to destroy himself by his own seriousness, self-righteousness, vehemence of concern for order and hierarchy. Pentheus' armor, both figurative and literal, is not made to keep out this kind of enemy; and the god's elusive playfulness slips past his guard into house, city, and self.

The seductiveness of Dionysus is also the seductiveness of his poet's text and of this text's subversion of the heroic tradition. Its way is not the way of directness that Pentheus and the heroic, martial values behind him endorse. Euripides' text works, like the god himself, by obliquity rather than direct attack, by delicate innuendo rather than open statement, by paradox rather than mutually exclusive decisions. It reveals the secret that the most serious, traditional heroic text still rests on play, pretense, delight. In unmasking the pleasure principle (*terpsis*) at the heart of every literary fiction, whether Homeric epic or ironic drama, this text also lays bare the paradoxical aesthetic of its own "Dionysiac poetics." To cite Roland Barthes once more, "Le plaisir du texte n'est pas forcément de type triomphant, héroïque, musclé. Pas besoin de se cambrer."[55]

The monolithic values and language on which Pentheus relies prove

---

[55] Barthes 32; cf. also 50: "Le plaisir du texte (la jouissance du texte) est au contraire comme un effacement brusque de la valeur guerrière. . . ."

no match for Dionysiac play. The god can incorporate the language of martial epic (cf. 50-52) and yet completely reverse its content (cf. 761-64, 1202-15). This text, like its god, exists in one sense not in its own right but as the negative of its opposite: its play is meaningless without the seriousness of its antagonist. Viewed historically, the ludic aspect of the *Bacchae* is both a recognition of and a subversive commentary on tragedy's dependence upon heroic epic. Aristotle, too, observed the dependence, but with the seriousness appropriate to his attitude toward both genres (*Poetics* 4.1448b 34ff., 5.1449b 14ff.).

The intensity of Pentheus' resistance to Dionysus owes something to his suppression of the play element in himself. We recall the stress on his *spoudē*, "zealous seriousness," the antithesis to *paidia*, "play," at two of his entrances (212, 913). In presenting the young god's victory over the Theban king, Euripides may be reflecting not only on the city's necessary incorporation of something as "unserious" as play, mimicry, and illusion but also on the passing of an age more in touch with its playful, creative, experimental energies. At such times the fine balance between rational and irrational, the serious and the playful in civilization, becomes more taut, more precarious. What Johan Huizinga wrote in 1938—a time when an historian of culture might well be particularly attuned to the break-up of an older order and the surfacing of the darker side of the play impulse—is suggestive for the *Bacchae*:

> During the growth of a civilization the agonistic function attains its most beautiful form, as well as its most conspicuous, in the archaic phase. As a civilization becomes more complex, more variegated and more overladen, and as the technique of production and social life itself become more finely organized, the old cultural soil is gradually smothered under a rank layer of ideas, systems of thought and knowledge, doctrines, rules and regulations, moralities and conventions which have all lost touch with play. Civilization, we then say, has grown more serious; it assigns only a secondary place to playing. The heroic period is over, and the agonistic phase, too, seems a thing of the past.[56]

The latter part of the fifth century saw the increasing importance of conceptual thought, logical definition, prose. In Athens the pro-

[56] Huizinga, *Homo Ludens* 75.

longed attrition of the Peloponnesian War took its toll. The last two
great tragedians died within a year of one another. The exuberant
playfulness of Old Comedy also came to an end about the same time
with Aristophanes' *Frogs*, roughly contemporary with the *Bacchae*.
Indeed the *Bacchae*, Sophocles' *Oedipus at Colonus*, and the *Frogs*,
all among the last works of their genre and all written around the
same time, have the same retrospective cast, the same sense of the
passing of an era.

In the victory of Dionysiac *paidia* over Pentheus' *spoudē*, however,
also lurks the danger of releasing the "deadly earnest" that this play
element may also contain: "play may be deadly yet still remain play,"
Huizinga wrote elsewhere,[57] and one thinks of the relentlessly "smiling countenance" of the god in the murderous frenzy of 1021. The
more the play element in culture is repressed, the greater the risk that
its creative energies will reemerge as destructive abandon, madness,
or in our time as the meticulously rationalized game theories of MAD
("Mutual Assured Destruction") in the calculus of nuclear war.

In representing something as foreign and perhaps as inimical to the
spirit of the polis as Dionysiac ecstasy, Euripides is stating the freedom of his art form: tragedy is itself a liminal space within the enclosure of the polis where conventional norms, judgments, and sympathies are suspended. By the very intensity and involving power of its
fiction, the play also creates that space, the magical circle of art where
we bracket our daily preoccupations, and even at times our values,
by play and imagination. At the same time, by focusing on the god
whose power makes possible this suspension, the play reflects upon
the capacity in art and in us to produce this suspension, to let the
play of mimed deeds and artificial words at a festal occasion tell us
about the most serious questions of life.

Play, as well as "the play," in this sense holds the same paradoxes
as Dionysus: poised between the trivial and the serious, childishness
and importance, entertainment and religious value. The *Bacchae* is
also a reflection on the nature of the Greek theater and its paradoxical
place between sacred performance and increasingly secularized spirit.
Here again Huizinga's thoughts on the play element in art and ritual
can help us:

[57] Ibid. 41.

The sacred performance is more than an actualization in appearance only, a sham reality; it is also more than a symbolical actualization—it is a mystical one. In it, something invisible and inactual takes beautiful, actual, holy form. The participants in the rite are convinced that the action actualizes and effects a definite beatification, brings about an order of things higher than that in which they customarily live. All the same this "actualization by representation" still retains the formal characteristics of play in every respect. It is played or performed within a playground that is literally "staked out," and played moreover as a feast, i.e., in mirth and freedom. A sacred space, a temporarily real world of its own, has been expressly hedged off for it. But with the end of the play its effect is not lost; rather it continues to shed its radiance on the ordinary world outside, a wholesome influence working security, order and prosperity for the whole community until the sacred play-season comes round again.[58]

As metatheater, the *Bacchae* calls into question that process of "hedging off" a sacred space for play separate from reality. It allows the one to break through into the other. In the contrast between the parode and the later odes it also shows the other side of the firm belief that "the action actualizes and effects a definite beatification, brings about an order of things higher than that in which [the participants] customarily live," for that conviction of being in a heightened state, a higher order or beatification, can equally characterize homicidal psychosis.

As fifth-century drama moves farther away from its origins in sacral performance and incorporates, perforce, more of the rationalistic questioning raised by thinkers like Protagoras, Socrates, or Democritus, the efficacy of the play as a healing reunion of man and God, of society and the cosmic order, becomes increasingly problematical. More than any other late fifth-century drama, the *Bacchae* resembles a sacred performance. But here more than anywhere else we feel precisely the lack of that radiant aura of well-being that should be among the aftereffects of successful ritual. Rather than leaving us with the glow of "a wholesome influence working security, order and prosperity for the whole community until the sacred play-season comes round again," the *Bacchae* explores the freedom of art raised to the

[58] Ibid. 14.

second degree: not only the removal of performance from actuality but the even more ambiguous removal of tragic performance from the religious and communal order wherein it has its origins and of which it is a part.

All art, insofar as it purports to present reality through illusion, contains these paradoxes, but the *Bacchae* and its god bring them particularly close to the surface. Euripides here is playing, seriously, with paradoxes that are echoed in a different mood in a not entirely frivolous *paignion* of his contemporary, Gorgias, who remarked à propos of tragic illusion ("deception"): "By its myths and passions tragedy creates that deception in respect to which he who deceives is more just than he who does not deceive, and he who is deceived is wiser than he who is not deceived" (82 B 23 DK). Euripides' metatragedy, like Gorgias' dictum, is reflecting on the fact that art, in some essential respects, lies outside morality. But, to quote Huizinga once more, "The human mind can only disengage itself from the magic circle of play by turning towards the ultimate."[59] That process, too, is the subject of the *Bacchae*.

[59] Ibid. 212.

The Crisis of Symbols:
Language, Myth, Tragedy

Wo jetzt nur, wie unsre Weisen sagen,
seelenlos ein Feuerball sich dreht,
lenkte damals seinen goldnen Wagen
Helios in stiller Majestät.
Diese Höhen füllten Oreaden,
eine Dryas lebt' in jenem Baum,
aus den Urnen lieblicher Najaden
sprang der Ströme Silberschaum.
Schiller,
Die Götter Griechenlands

Symbols are the poiesis of human possibilities.
Husserl, *Hermeneutics*

• I •

The *Bacchae* is strikingly modern not only because it invites reading contemporary concerns into the fifth century B.C. or fifth-century
concerns into the twentieth but because Euripides was confronting a
crisis of belief and of language, indeed a crisis of all symbolic expression, that *mutatis mutandis* resembles our own. His moment is one
of the junctures when the validity accorded to poetry and myth passes
over to philosophy and conceptual thought. In the myth of Dionysus
at Thebes he found the perfect vehicle for dramatizing that conflict.
In depicting the struggle over the reception of this ecstasy-provoking
god he could do justice to the irreducible, enigmatic quality of the
great, powerful symbols of myth while also recognizing the threatened, precarious status of those symbols.

In the *Bacchae* two major currents of Euripidean drama, rationalism and irrationalism, meet at their sharpest and most disturbing pitch. Euripides' powerful feeling for the sacred crosses with what André Rivier calls his "destructuration of the sacred."[1] This clash, the kernel of the "riddle" of the *Bacchae*, reflects in part the poet's effort to reconcile warring factions in himself. It also reflects a conflict between *mythos* and *logos*, mythical and conceptual modes of thought, written deep into the intellectual history of the late fifth century.

As Thucydides 1.22 makes clear, the conflict is sharpened by the increasing importance of literacy in the organization, presentation, and transmission of knowledge. The "delight" (*terpsis*) afforded by the "competition for the present moment" in the context of oral recitation gives way to the "effortful" (*epiponos*) sifting and analysis of truth, superficially less attractive and less pleasurable but in solid fact more reliable as a "possession forever." Plato's banishment of mythic poetry from his ideal state rests on a similar attempt to replace symbolic with analytical means of reaching and communicating truth about the human condition.[2]

With the growth of analytical thought comes the increasing importance of prose, already well developed in the last quarter of the fifth century and soon virtually to supplant poetry as the primary

[1] Rivier commenting on Kamerbeek (1960) 47; see Kamerbeek (1960) 23: "Il pouvait paraître un peu paradoxal que la matière la plus mythique (au sens précis), la plus religieuse, la plus traditionnelle, la plus rebutant aussi pour un esprit éclairé . . . ait inspiré à Euripide la tragédie la plus émouvante, la plus parfaite qu'il ait composée."

[2] See E. A. Havelock, *Preface to Plato* (Cambridge, Mass. 1963), passim, and *The Greek Conception of Justice* (Cambridge, Mass. 1978), chap. 18. For tragedy arising at a point of crisis in the political, moral, and social discourse of a community and reflecting, indeed creating, a shift from one mode of discourse about social order to another see Timothy J. Reiss, *Tragedy and Truth* (New Haven 1980), chap. 12, esp. 282-87. He remarks (p. 284), "In Western history tragedy seems to have appeared at moments that, retrospectively, are marked by a kind of 'hole' in the passage from one dominant discourse to another. . . . Tragedy brings about rationality by showing what can be termed the irrational within that rationality. That is no doubt why all tragedy is thoroughly embroiled in the political, and why to grasp and enclose the tragic, the inexpressible of the discourse being created, is at once an ideological and an anti-ideological activity: the first, to the degree that it hides what is unspoken in the law that is the order of discourse, the second, to the extent that it shows it." See also my essay, "Tragedy, Orality, Literacy," forthcoming in the Proceedings of the Conference, "Oralité: culture, littérature, discours, Urbino, 21-25 juillet 1980" (Rome, 1982 or 1983) and (in French) in *Poétique* 50 (April, 1982) 131-54.

medium of artistic expression and the main vehicle of cultural values. The fourth century is an age of prose, with the philosophers in the lead. These developments stretch gradually over the two centuries from Xenophanes and Heraclitus to Euripides and Plato. As the function of literary expression changes from transmitting traditional norms to exploring new ideas and opening new intellectual territories, there is an inevitable shift from verse, with its convenient mnemonic devices of rhythm and meter in an oral culture, to prose, which, as the ancient stylists called it, is "loosed" or "released" from the constraints of a traditional form, totally free for new methods of inquiry, new ideas, new material, new ways of conceiving of human nature and the nature of the physical world.

In this situation the poet no longer regards himself as the transmitter of stable cultural values, a master of truth, but rather as a creator of his own fictions, a self-conscious maker of plots, a fashioner of "deceptions" (*apatai*), aware of his craft, his cleverness, inventiveness, and skillful techniques of illusion.[3] Aristophanes' image of Euripides in the *Acharnians*, surrounded by the paraphernalia of his plots and the trappings of his distinctively original, bizarre-looking characters, brilliantly caught the poet in this light.

The previous chapter showed how the power of the enacted tragic myth to evoke the god's presence becomes ambiguous through the self-conscious artificiality of the mask, reminder of the fact that that presence is but an illusion. This new critical awareness of myth as something apart from truth creates the category of the fictional as such. The poet knows that he is dealing with a form of discourse that has an ambiguous or paradoxical relation to truth. Although the seeds of this idea are already in Hesiod, whose Muses know how to "speak true things" when they wish and also "lies that are like true things" (*Theogony* 26-28), the place of myth and poetry between truth and fiction is much more problematical by the end of the fifth century.[4]

---

[3] See Gorgias 82B23 DK; Segal (1962) 110ff.; De Romilly *JHS* 93 (1973) 160f. On Euripides see Winnington-Ingram (1969), passim, and also (1960) 34 à propos of the double perspective of *Phoen.* 88ff.; Zeitlin (1980).

[4] On Hesiod see Pietro Pucci, *Hesiod and the Language of Poetry* (Baltimore 1977), chap. 1. An interesting paper on the development of the notion of the fictional by W. Rösler will appear in the Proceedings of the Urbino Conference on Orality (above, n. 2). See now his article, "Die Entdeckung der Fiktionalität in der Antike," *Poetica* 12 (1980) 283-319, esp. 308ff. See also J.-P. Vernant, "Naissance d'images," *Religions, histoires, raisons* (Paris 1979) 105-37, esp. 111f., 124-30.

In the *Bacchae* Euripides explores his art's common boundaries with deception, illusion, hallucination, drunkenness, madness, and divine revelation. In Sophocles' *Philoctetes*, produced a few years before the writing of the *Bacchae*, the descent of Heracles from Olympus brings the brilliance of absolutes and the strength of direct heroic speech into the dark, tangled maze of human misconception, lies, and intrigue.[5] The *Bacchae's deus ex machina* can produce no such effect, for the god of this play is himself the central problem in the question of the truth-value of myth and dramatic art.

The beauty with which Euripides depicts the Dionysiac ecstasy in the first three choral odes also suggests an awareness that something in the culture has been lost, "an immediacy of belief" or "primitive naiveté," to use Paul Ricoeur's terms,[6] that cannot be recaptured in an age of abstract reasoning and analytical scepticism. Euripides is aware that there can be no return to the simpler religious attitude of the past. For his age Pan, if not already dead, is beginning to become moribund. The "great symbolisms of the sacred" (Ricoeur's phrase) begin to be seriously threatened.

By choosing as his subject a god whose worship consists in a fully emotional involvement and fusion and whose nature is itself bound up with the process of symbolification, Euripides poses the question of how much of the symbolic systems of the past can be retained. In order to answer the question he must explore the nature of the symbol itself. This Dionysus allows him to do. The very elusiveness of the god raises the question of the validity of the various means in which the characters of the play try to define him and understand him. To assimilate the otherness of Dionysus into the city requires a symbolic reformulation and therefore distortion of his essence, or conversely may involve the potential dissolution of all the mediating structures of the society: myth, ritual, language. The unmediated vision belongs to the wild maenads on the mountain but has no place within the walls of the city. In this respect Dionysus' conflict with the Theban *nomoi* (cf. 201-203) invites comparison with Jesus' conflict with the Mosaic law.

The concern with the truth-value of myth is hardly new to Euripides. Both *Medea* and *Hippolytus* view their central myth in the retrospective light of a ritual of which the dramatic action then becomes

[5] See Segal, *Tragedy and Civilization* 337ff.
[6] Ricoeur, *Symbolism of Evil*, 351.

the *aition*, the historical explanation (*Med.* 1378-83; *Hipp.* 1423-30). In the *Heracles* the mythical motif of the descent to Hades is juxtaposed to and in a sense superseded by a figurative descent into the hero's personal underworld of madness and murderous violence and then a reascent through friendship and compassion out of those subterranean depths of the soul to a new acceptance of self and of the gods.[7] The *Iphigeneia in Tauris* shows the poet's interest not only in the aetiological function of myth but also in the primitive myths of human sacrifice in remote and barbarous lands. A number of plays use the device of a myth within a myth: Orpheus in the *Alcestis*, Phaethon in the *Hippolytus*, Erichthonius and the founding myths of Athens in the *Ion*, Odysseus in the *Helen*. The *Phoenissae* plays on the contrast between the present situation of Thebes and its distant and sinister antiquity: the Serpent's teeth, the Sphinx.[8] In the *Helen* a self-conscious dialectic between reality and illusion about the central figure explores the problem of appearance and reality and the truth-value of myth and art.[9]

These concerns implicate not only myth but language as well. The philosophical debates about whether language exists purely by social "convention" (*thesei*) or through some "natural" affinity (*physei*) between the word and the object find several resonances in the play (cf. 297). The shifting meanings of the basic moral vocabulary—"wisdom," "good sense," "intelligence" (*sophia, sōphrosynē, phronēsis*)— reflect the parallel between the intellectual and the social crisis that Thucydides depicts in his account of the Corcyrean revolt (Thuc. 3.82) and Plato in dialogues like *Gorgias, Protagoras, Republic*.

• II •

In the plot of the *Bacchae* myth and language have a special place. The god from the East comes to Thebes to prove Dionysus truly "the

---

[7] See above, Chap. 7, n. 47.

[8] See Arthur (1977) 176ff.; Parry, *Lyrics* 171-73.

[9] Segal (1971). For the myth-within-a-myth device in Euripides see Zeitlin (1980); Parry, *Lyrics*, chap. 6; Reckford (1972); Anne Burnett, "*Trojan Women* and the Ganymede Ode," YCS 25 (1977) 291-316; Robert Eisner, "Euripides' Use of Myth," *Arethusa* 12 (1979) 153-74.

son of Zeus," *Dios hyios* (1, 1341; cf. 47) and to reveal the hidden meaning of Pentheus' name as *penthos*, "grief" (367, 508). The first part of the play, particularly the palace miracle and its immediate sequel, raises the problem of how to "name" this god (cf. 529) who appears in the guise of a nameless stranger, assuming many forms or shapes (53-54). "God of many names" is his epithet in the great Dionysus ode of the *Antigone* (1115). The action turns, in part, on the status accorded to his "name" (320, 529, 1377). The right understanding of his "name" is among the play's chief issues (cf. 276, 296). As the unnamed Eastern stranger gains his true name, the Theban king, so sure of his, loses it and becomes himself a disguised, nameless stranger in the wild, his rediscovery and proclamation of his name of no avail in warding off his death (1118-19). The stage action closely follows the fate of naming and speaking true names. The etymologies of the names are acted out. The revelation of Dionysus' origins and power takes the form of juxtaposing logical discourse and divine epiphany (cf. 47-50), conceptual abstraction and myth, "word" and "deed" (*logos, ergon*), veracity in language and its capacity for falsehood and deception (cf. 26-31).

All the characters define their relation to Dionysus, and therefore also their relation to their own identity and personality, through the kind of speech they use toward or about the god. The Chorus sings in reverent hymnic language. Cadmus begins with prudent utilitarian compromises. Teiresias practices philosophical and sophistic rationalism. Pentheus utters violent insults, authoritarian decrees, and martial bombast. Agave, who becomes the fullest bearer of the consciousness of tragic suffering, moves from lyrical ecstasy to the clarity-inducing sharpness of tight stichomythy and then back to emotional lyrics in her closing lines, a bleak anti-hymn that answers the ecstasy and joyful serenity of the parode.

Cadmus too, bearer of the mythic history of Thebes, comes finally to take over Teiresias' function of clarifying reality by the language of logic and reason. He does so, however, not to weave a philosophical prose hymn as a substitute for lyrical maenadic ecstasy, as Teiresias did in his sophistic encomium (272-313), but rather to reconquer a ground of solid human truth. After so much illusion the actors (and the audience) can evaluate the meaning of the god for their lives and take responsibility for those parts of themselves—the murderous fury as well as the sublime joy of fusion—that Dionysus releases. The language of his last speeches (1302-26, 1352-62) holds the knowledge of tragic suffering that Agave will modulate into the intenser, emotional utterance of her closing lyrics.

These speeches are also the vehicle for the continuity of Thebes as a human community with a past and a future, with that self-consciousness of change and durability in time that belongs to man's distinctive sense of history (cf. 1354-62). Cadmus' discourse, finally, is worthy of a founder of cities and a king. He speaks a language that leads from mad, homicidal delusion to tragic "recognition" (1285) and painful truth (1287), a language vibrant with his own pain and endurance but also encompassing the large vistas of time, the rise and fall of states, the succession of order and chaos in history and in his personal life. His last speeches concern man's struggle against his own barbarism and his own bestial violence in a perspective that spans many generations and many peoples. In direct contact with the god, he looks beyond the ruined city to the otherworldly places, the Isles of the Blest, the river of Acheron (1361-62; cf. 1339).

The change from Cadmus' indecorous opening invitation to dancing (178ff.) to his closing narrative of quasi-mythic migrations parallels the change from Agave's initially joyful lyrics to her final dirge-like song. This shift in the mode of discourse reflects the tragic form's struggle to test and purify language. Tragedy pushes language to its limits, but also brings language from superficial to authentic utterance. The experience of tragic suffering compels men to abandon the delusive, self-serving, or concealing speech of compromise and half-truth in which they imbed their lives. The god and his followers, with their "mouths of holy speech and silence" (69-70), seem initially to possess a purity, intensity, and authenticity of utterance. That heightened clarity of speech recurs in the Messenger's account of the maenads in the mountains, as if the closer contact with the Dionysiac experience affected the speech of the beholders. The other characters, caught in considerations of their own status or false images of themselves, forcibly confront these overlays upon the reality of self and world, so that their speech can become, for a good or ill, a truer expression of what they really are.

This process, however, involves an ironic contrast between the human characters and Dionysus. Whereas at the beginning and near the end Dionysus speaks the language of prophecy and history (13-22, 50-54, 1330-43), his last utterances show him engaged in line-by-line dialogue, defending his violent revenge (1344-51). In the prologue he had explained that this revenge stems from the refusal of Semele's sisters to *speak* the truth about his birth and from their gloating speech of mean delight at her end (24, 27). Yet his last words in the play are about himself, not Semele. They are less like the words of a lofty Olympian than the pique of an insecure mortal. Agave speaks to her father about the god in the third person as ruining her house, and Dionysus replies in sharp self-defense (1374-78):

Agave.   For terribly did Lord Dionysus bring this destruction upon your house.

Dionys.   Yes, for I suffered terrible things from you, bearing a name unhonored in Thebes [*ageraston . . . onoma*].

This unsolicited response seems to confirm Teiresias' purely anthropomorphic view of the god's "delight in being honored" (319-21). More grimly, Dionysus' closing defense about the lack of "honor" (*geras*) invites comparison with his actual punishment of Agave, her deluded joy in the "first prize of honor" (*prōton . . . geras*, 1179) in her inverted "hunt."

The discrepancy between the god, aloft on the *theologeion*, literally as well as figuratively above the mortal characters, and the all too human echoes of his speech (as well as his unexpected reversion to dialogic speech and debate) is itself a visual enactment of the sophistic rift between *mythos* and *logos*, mythical and scientific truth. We have seen this rift earlier in the contrast between Teiresias' rational view of divinity and the irrational violence of the mythic action dramatized in the play.[10] The ironies around divine speech are even greater here, for the god's last, petulant-sounding self-defense is either unheard or disregarded by Agave. Just when he has done his worst, Dionysus seems to matter least. The next exchange is entirely between father and daughter ("Farewell, my father." / "Farewell, poor daughter," 1379-80). The god's words either pass over the heads of the human interlocutors or are no longer relevant to them.

Although Pentheus' clash with Dionysus involves deeds as well as

[10] On the sophistic influences that result in a "distrust in the mediation of *logos*" see Di Benedetto 71-102.

words (initially refusal of libations and prayers, 45-46; later harassment of his worshipers), the nature of that conflict is prefigured first in the manner of Pentheus' speech ("What strange new thing will he say," 215). To Pentheus' rejection of the god's "saying that he is a god" (242) Dionysus will oppose the acts of divine epiphany ("showing," 47 and 50) and martial force answering force (50-54).

Teiresias' long justification of Dionysus (to which we shall return later) opens with a brief homily on the proper use of speech (266-71) and ends the scene (the first episode) with an allusion to his power of prophetic speech and a warning about foolish words (368-69): "I am speaking not through prophecy [*mantikē*], but in accord with the facts [*pragmata*]. A fool says foolish things." Yet Teiresias' "wisdom" (*sophia*), which Cadmus praised at their first meeting (178-79), also has its folly. His antithesis of *mantikē* and *pragmata*, which rather paradoxically evokes the sophistic critique of supernatural, nonhuman knowledge in a manner analogous to Thucydides' contrast of *mythos* and *logos* (Thuc. 1.22), betrays that same complacent, unexamined rationalism with which he expounds the nature of Dionysus. Like the Polonian Cadmus, he is equally removed from the hard "wisdom" of this god and will prove no more adequate to grasp or interpret it.

These three men of authority in Thebes are all characterized by how they speak about Dionysus. The ecstatic lyrics of the parode have shown another way of encompassing the god in mortal discourse and thereby incorporating him into the city. The ode that immediately precedes Dionysus' entrance warns against "unrestrained speech" (387-92): "Of mouths unbridled and of lawless witlessness the end is misfortune. But the life of serenity [*hēsychia*] and good sense [*to phronein*] remains without turbulence and holds houses together." The servant who conducts the Stranger, bound, tells his king of the prisoner's gentleness and compliance, which in turn elicited his own "reverence of speech" (*aidōs*, 441), exactly opposite to Pentheus' aggressive vehemence.

The god's first exchange with mortals carefully disclaims that "boastful" inflated speech against which Cadmus had warned his grandson (460-61; cf. 270-71, 310). In marked contrast to his antagonist's violent and self-assertive speech, the Dionysiac Stranger stresses the "ease" of speaking (*rhadion*, 462). The clash between the two young men is framed in terms as much of language as of personality.

Blind to the areas of which the Stranger speaks, Pentheus cannot in fact understand what his interlocutor is saying. They speak virtually different languages. Pentheus is literal and matter-of-fact where Dionysus is metaphorical, prosaic where the other is lyrical.[11] Yet by the end of the scene the Stranger can also give commands and face down Pentheus' assertions of "authority" with his mysterious knowledge of the emptiness that lies beneath the "mask" or role of king (504-506):

Dionys.   I declare [audō] that you not bind me, I who am sane [speaking] to those not sane [sōphronōn ou sōphrosin].
Penth.   And I say bind, being of more authority than you [ky-riōteros]).
Dionys.   You know not what your life is, nor what you do nor who you are.

In Dionysus' sphere the norms of language bend toward paradox, the coexistence of illusion and reality.

The god's rituals are not open, public affirmations, congruent with the communal openness of language, but closed to speech, arrhēta, "not to be spoken," as the Stranger tells the king (472). The ensuing stichomythy dissolves clarity of syntax and unity of reference in the play of illusion about the double identity of the Stranger:

The god will free me when I wish (498)
Even now, standing near, he sees what I suffer (500)

The last line of the scene is also the most ambiguous syntactically, for the pronouns are so placed that "us" and "him," present Stranger and invisible god, are interchangeable: ἡμᾶς γὰρ ἀδικῶν κεῖνον εἰς δεσμοὺς ἄγεις (518). The line can be translated "In doing us injustice, you cast him into chains," or "You are doing him injustice in leading us into chains."[12] Pentheus' accusation shortly before, that the Stranger is "saying nothing," i.e., talking nonsense (479), is at once turned against himself in the rejoinder, "To a foolish man one who speaks wise things [sopha] will seem to have no sense" (ouk eu phronein, 480). That line, echoing Teiresias' warning about "foolish speech" at the end of the previous scene (369), also calls attention to

[11] E.g., 498-508, esp. 506f.; see Wohlberg 154.
[12] On 518 see Roux ad loc. and Rosenmeyer 109f.

the fundamental ambiguities of good sense, sanity, and intelligence that underlie the ambiguities of language.

In his "ignorance" (*amathia*, 490) Pentheus fails to understand even plain words. The Messenger reported that the Stranger refused to flee (436-37); yet Pentheus still gloats over the "nets" that will hold his supposedly fearful prey from "flight" (*ekphygein*, 451-52). The king accuses the Stranger of "sophistries," *sophismata*, as one "not unpracticed in words" (*ouk agymnastos logōn*, 491). But suddenly, almost unobtrusively, the god becomes the questioner instead of the respondent and answers "words" with "deeds" (492): "Say what must be suffered, what is the terrible thing [*to deinon*] that you will *do* to me" (*ergasē[i]*, 492).

Pentheus becomes a kind of second Oedipus (506-508):

> *Dionys.* You know not what your life is nor what you do nor who you are.
> *Penth.* Pentheus, Agave's son, Echion my father.
> *Dionys.* Suited for misfortune in your name.

It is not fortuitous that the Stranger's pronouncement of this ignorance (506) closely echoes Teiresias' pronouncement to Oedipus in the *Tyrannus* (OT 367, 413-15). The god's answer to Pentheus' certain affirmation about himself in 506-508 is the revelation (not yet understood) of his ignorance about his real self. Like Oedipus, Pentheus cannot hear the true meaning of the most definite word of his life, his name. We may recall once more that the Stranger's role at the end of this scene is exactly parallel to Teiresias' in the previous scene (cf. 480 and 369, 508 and 367).

The visual and verbal deception consequent on the double identity of the Stranger and the doubled masking of his antagonist in the disguise scene brings out into the open the ambiguous function of language in poetry, theater, fiction: it signifies both what is there and what is not there, what is visible and what is invisible, often with a paradoxical interchange of the terms. The Stranger/god's disguise is itself the power of language, as of scenic representation, to serve as symbol, to be more than it seems to be.

Pentheus is the spectator who refuses to enter into the terms of the fiction, the reader who refuses to play, the opponent of the ludic who can, therefore, derive no benefit from the games of the god or the fiction. It is literalism as much as anger that destroys Pentheus. His *amathia*, "ignorance," stiff "ineducability" (490), includes both. With just a little more madness he might be able to "see" the god in the form of a graceful youth (cf. 470, 477). Instead, he will see him only as a beast (618-22) or a beast-man (920-22), never as a god or a human. His stubborn resistance both to what is shown and what is said throws him into the greater madness where he loses himself totally.

The great central section of the play—the Stranger's second encounter with Pentheus, the Messenger's account of the Theban maenads on Cithaeron, and Pentheus' "conversion"—also contrasts modes of discourse. Just before the Messenger's entrance Pentheus and the Stranger have a brief exchange (647-50):

Δι. στῆσον πόδ', ὀργῇ δ' ὑπόθες ἥσυχον πόδα.
Πε. πόθεν σὺ δεσμὰ διαφυγὼν ἔξω περᾷς;
Δι. οὐκ εἶπον—ἢ οὐκ ἤκουσας—ὅτι λύσει μέ τις;
Πε. τίς; τοὺς λόγους γὰρ ἐσφέρεις καινοὺς ἀεί.

Dionys. Stand still and beneath your wrath put a calm foot.
Penth. How did you flee the bonds and get outside?
Dionys. Did I not say—or did you not hear—that some one will release me?
Penth. Who? You are always bringing forth new sayings [*kainous logous*].

From the sharp commands of his first line (647) Dionysus seems to be in charge, and Pentheus confesses himself puzzled by the "new" or "strange" words of his interlocutor.

In the ensuing conversation with the Messenger from Cithaeron, the hierarchically structured discourse of civic authority—the king giving "orders" (e.g., 653) and the subjects obeying—contrasts with the voices that call from the other side of reality and the realm outside of Thebes, the wild bacchantic cries and the language of "miracles," *thaumata* (667, 693, 716).

Pentheus loses control over speech as over himself, for the Stranger, not the king, introduces the Messenger from the mountain (657). Only after the Messenger announces that he has arrived from Cithaeron does Pentheus inquire about his "urgent zeal for speech" (*spoudēn logou*, 662), a phrase that elsewhere characterizes his own unstable vehemence of speech or behavior (212, 913). The Messenger makes a tentative preliminary report of the miracles he has seen, but breaks off in fear of the king's irascibility that checks "free speech" (*parrhēsia*, 668-71). "Speak with impunity," Pentheus reassures him, "for the more terrible [*deinotera*] the things you say about the bacchants, the more we shall punish the one who suggests these arts to the women" (672-76). But Pentheus, already suffering, not doing *deina*, "terrible things" (646; cf. 667), himself falls victim to the "arts" of one whom he cannot silence (801, 806). His scornful and insinuating verb for the Stranger who "suggests" those arts (τὸν ὑποθέντα τὰς τέχνας / γυναιξί . . . , 675-76) is also the Stranger's verb commanding "calm" for his anger in 647 (ὀργῇ δ᾽ ὑπόθες ἥσυχον πόδα). In the echo his authority is again undercut by the essential nature of the god, power without force, passion without anger, "calmness" without loss of strength or effectiveness.

Pentheus' reply to the Messenger twice mentions "justice." His word for "punish" is to "give over to justice" (*dikē*, 676), and his gesture of magnanimity in allowing "free speech" at all is couched in the posture of the wise ruler uttering an apophthegm: "For toward the just [*dikaiois*] one should not feel wrath" (674). Yet Pentheus' use of the language of the "just" king is misleading; his relation to justice is one of his most ambiguous attributes in the play.

Dionysus' little parenthesis in 649, "Or did you not hear?" exposes a truth about Pentheus' mode of communication. His primary form of speech is command, and he does not hear. He is deaf to the Messenger's suggestion, a little later, that if he had himself witnessed the events on Cithaeron his "blaming" (*psegein*) of the god would change to "prayers" (*euchai*, 712-13). He is already immune to a *logos* that might change his view of the maenads. Far from the openness to both sides that constitutes the true "justice" of an impartial king, he is only seeking from the Messenger's *logos* more fuel for his anger and vengefulness. Hence the shift of the meaning of the root *dik-* in these lines from "justice" to "punishment" (673, 676) only brings out the real sense of Pentheus' "justice."

The Messenger's account itself provides a striking contrast between Agave's wild cries of *ololygē* and bacchantic hunting (689, 731-33) and the men's "strife of words" and calculation of gain (714-22). The speech of the male, civic institutions is discordant, selfishly demagogic, or ineffective.[13] Pentheus' followers on Cithaeron constitute a miniature assembly (cf. *synēlthomen*, "we came together," 714). The townsman, "experienced in words," like an ambitious politician, gives ill-fated advice that the group accepts with the formula of approval in the assembly or lawcourt, *eu legein edoxe*, "He seemed to speak well" (721f.). Agave's shout, "Follow me . . . follow me" (731-33), is far more successful in creating leadership and unifying her community. While the men who oppose them quarrel (715) and the king obstructs the task of his Messenger with his anger (670-71), the maenads obey commands about the "appointed time" (*tetagmenē hōra*, 723-24), call upon their god "with single voice" (*athroon stoma*, 725), and join in a larger community of nature that embraces "all the mountain and the beasts" (726-27).

The content of the Messenger's speech has an effect on the Asian bacchants still kept in Thebes before Pentheus. They, too, now overcome their fear of speaking freely (775-77): "To the ruler I hesitate to speak words that are free [*eipein tous logous eleutherous*], but even so it shall be spoken: Dionysus is inferior to none of the gods." The Chorus's pronouncement, taking the side of the "enemy" against the city and its king, deliberately reverses the conventions of the dramatic form. The catastrophe announced from outside brings not condolence and the cries of shared woe, but exultation.

Pentheus responds with a flurry of elaborate martial commands in an excited and high-flown style that reflects his anger and his authoritarian rigidity (780-86).[14] Repeating an earlier point, the Stranger replies that Pentheus is incapable of "being persuaded" or of "hearing [his] words" (787; cf. 649). The contest between them remains a contest of opposing forms of discourse, bluster versus calm, as Pentheus again confirms his inability to enforce silence upon his prisoner (800-801).

Pentheus' last fully sane words are commands: "Bring my arms here; but you—stop speaking" (809). Regal and martial authority again takes the form of a futile attempt to impose silence (cf. 801). Just after

---

[13] Thus the speaker is described as "a wanderer around the town, one fully experienced in words" (πλάνης κατ' ἄστυ καὶ τρίβων λόγων, 717); see above, Chap. 4, n. 53.

[14] Note, too, Pentheus' concern with dishonor or "reproach" (*psogos*) in the hyperbole of 779, an escalation of the Messenger's mild description of his "reproaching" the god in 712 (*psegeis*).

this question/command about arms and silence, Dionysus' language and action move to a new, mysterious level in the single syllable "ah," outside the meter, as he asks the fatal question, "Do you want to see them sitting on the mountains?" (810-11).[15] This violation of the restrictions of the iambic trimeter line marks the possibility of a new, unaccustomed kind of language, one conformable to emotion rather than reason, interjection rather than grammatical sequence. It also opens the realm of human speech to a new dimension of the situation, a different perception of the meaning of events. This question, as Dodds says, "releases the flood."[16] Now the "logical" structure of discourse and reason gives way to the Dionysiac fusion of opposites. The king who tried to silence the Stranger (801, 809) now finds him "speaking well" (*kalōs exeipas*, 818). The proud general who called out the army in his refusal to "obey" and "heed" the god (787) now exits with the coordination of terms that were previously his sharpest antitheses (845-46): "I shall go. For either I shall make my journey with arms [*hopla*], or I shall obey [*peisomai*] your counsels" (or, equally, "I shall suffer by your counsels").

Here again the god of the *Bacchae* distills into symbolic form what is probably a universal quality of tragic drama, the presentation of experiences that go beyond the realm of language or wrench language out of its familiar normative structures.[17] To force the individual to a new vision of himself one must also force his language to a new form. Language in tragedy loses its one-dimensional clarity and is made to enter the Dionysiac space where opposites and logical contradictions coexist. So Pentheus' exit lines bring together the hidden contradictions in his attitude toward the god: resistance and acquiescence, "arms" and "obeying," "obeying" and "suffering" (in the play on *peisomai*). The Dionysiac *logos* brings the contradictory pair out into the open not to harmonize them or to resolve the contradiction, as the Socratic

[15] On the exclamation "ah" in 810 see WI 102; Taplin 120f.; Steidle 37; also Donald J. Mastronarde, *Contact and Discontinuity: Some Conventions of Speech and Action on the Greek Tragic Stage*, U. Calif. Publ. in Class. Stud. 21 (Berkeley and Los Angeles 1979) 109.

[16] Dodds, *Bacchae* ad 781-86 (p. 173); also ad 810-12: "The question has touched a hidden spring in Pentheus' mind, and his self-mastery vanishes."

[17] See Emil Staiger, *Grundbegriffe der Poetik* (1946), ed. 8 (Zürich and Freiburg i. Br. 1968) 190; Segal, *Tragedy and Civilization* 52ff. On the double meaning of line 846 see above, Chap. 7, p. 252, with n. 38.

philosophic *logos* would do, but to reveal the coexistence of essential opposites in ourselves and the world, to open a window on a view of the world hitherto excluded, dismissed as unworthy, undignified, illogical.

Our sense of self is inextricably and mysteriously bound up with our speech. When one changes, the other does also. Psychoanalysis, it is sometimes thought, cures the patient of neurosis by teaching him a different language, a fresh way of describing himself and of telling, to himself or to others, his life-plot. The new language, like the "new" self, has both elements of the old and a strange novelty. Instead of serving as the vehicle of the king's conscious will, language here becomes the mark of his alienation from an essential aspect of himself, a self that he cannot know except as a "Discourse of the Other," to quote Jacques Lacan's definition of the unconscious.[18]

By his characteristic attitude of play—play on and with words— Dionysus creates a mirror for language that reflects the hidden Other. Through the god's presence Pentheus' words no longer constitute a solid sheet of referents, as it were, but become transparent to another set of meanings and another shape of identity. The uttering of words that contain a meaning hidden from the speaker is not merely a dramatic device, but, as Freud and Lacan imply, a fundamental means by which the unconscious finds its paradoxical expression: "The unconscious is knowledge," says Lacan; "but it is a knowledge one cannot know one knows, a knowledge which cannot tolerate knowing it knows."[19] Pentheus' *double entendres* are the devious form that his knowledge of the unconscious necessarily takes; they are the strategies of a language that both reveals and masks what he is saying about himself, a language that simultaneously expresses what he knows and what he refuses to know. In the "Discourse of the Other" that Dionysus constitutes for him, language is not merely a signifier of a con-

[18] See Roy Schafer, "Narration in the Psychoanalytic Dialogue," *Critical Inquiry*, vol. 7, no. 1 (1980) 29-53, esp. 35ff., 49-51. For Lacan's "Discourse of the Other" see Jacques Lacan, *The Language of the Self: The Function of Language in Psychoanalysis*, trans. with notes and commentary by Anthony Wilden (1968; repr. New York 1974) 27, with Wilden's note and discussion, 106-108, 159ff.

[19] Jacques Lacan, unpublished 1974 seminar, cited in Shoshana Felman, "Turning the Screw of Interpretation," *Yale French Studies* 55/56 (1977) 166. The whole of Felman's essay (pp. 94-207) is valuable for the application of Lacan's theory of the unconscious to literary criticism.

crete signified outside the self; it becomes the signifier of a signifier whose signified remains hidden from the speaker.

This entire scene between Pentheus and Dionysus reflects the capacity of tragic drama to make visible the bonds between our language and our sense of personal identity. The experience by which Pentheus loses control of familiar language to discover an unfamiliar part of himself also mirrors the capacity of all poetic language to take us beyond ourselves, to break through the structures into which we are locked by the "prosaic" language of practical life, utility, the surface of being. In Dionysus' "ah" and in the illogic of Pentheus' exit lines language is jolted out of the worn grooves of the familiar; and with that jolt comes a new view of the world and of the self—a self that, like the Dionysiac language, is both familiar and alien.

• III •

After this point language, like Pentheus, never quite returns to its original limits. The scene that follows (912-76) pushes language beyond even the ironies and *double entendres* of Pentheus' two previous encounters with Dionysus. The coherence of the physical world now gives way entirely to the duality and illusion of the god's spell. Virtually every line of this densely written scene shows language struggling to represent an experience that goes beyond its logical structures.

Pentheus' unusual verb *tetaurōsai*, "you have become be-bulled" (922), is followed by the Stranger's tragic ironies playing on the hidden presence of the god, the paradoxes of Pentheus as celebrant/victim, the double visions of truth and madness (923-24): "The god accompanies, previously not propitious, at truce with us [*enspondos*]; and now you see what you should see." The rational civic language of treaties implied in *enspondos* here stands in striking contrast to its use by the speaker, hovering between god, man, and beast, between apparition and reality.[20]

[20] The ironies of *enspondos hēmin*, "at truce with us," in 924 are not easily rendered into English. The phrase continues the martial language of the god from the prologue, as if he has declared a "truce," a truce that in fact leads to the next stage

The capacity for language to signify the opposite of its surface meaning, just as the Stranger is the opposite of his surface form, is adumbrated in the crucial word *tetaurōsai*, which here means "you have become a bull." In its other two occurrences in tragedy, however (*Medea* 92; Aeschylus, *Choephoroe* 275), the verb *tauroumai* means "cast savage [bull-like] glances" or "outrage," "treat savagely" (in the manner of a bull). Pentheus may be saying, "You have become a bull," but the audience also hears another truth, "You have done me outrage" or "have treated me with bull-like savagery"—an implication soon realized when Pentheus "has a bull as leader of his doom" (ταῦ-ρον προηγητῆρα συμφορᾶς, 1159; cf. 1017). The double meaning of the discourse in which the god involves Pentheus parallels the doubleness of the god's own appearance and the double meaning of the rite that Pentheus will soon enact as king and *pharmakos* (963), savior and sacrificed victim (965 and 934), epinician victor and helpless child (964-70).

In Pentheus' end the disguised god is no longer present as an interlocutor in two-level speech on the stage, but the mystery of his speech and his silence plays a prominent role and completely overwhelms ordinary human language. The "voice from the sky" (1078) emanates from the god in his immortal form and celestial abode, releasing the homicidal potential of the bacchantic madness. The sudden supernatural silence that falls upon sky, forests, and wild creatures (1084-85) finally brings to Pentheus that "silence" that he blusteringly enjoined upon the Stranger (801-802, 809). This silence of the natural world also contrasts with the cautious silence of the king's followers who prudently stay hidden in this sylvan setting (1048-49). The "grassy glen" is for them a place of silent concealment (1048-50):

πρῶτον μὲν οὖν ποιηρὸν ἵζομεν νάπος,
τά τ' ἐκ ποδῶν σιγηλὰ καὶ γλώσσης ἄπο
σῴζοντες, ὡς ὁρῶμεν οὐχ ὁρώμενοι.

---

of hostilities and his true mode of fighting. It also echoes the ritual themes of libation (*spondē*). Pentheus, who refused ritual "libation" to Dionysus earlier (284), now accepts the ostensible libation of the truce (*enspondos*), only to fall victim to a darker, nonmilitary aspect of the god's ritual. Roux ad loc. notes the irony of the truce ("en acceptant le sacrifice de Penthée comme bouc émissaire, Dionysos fait trêve à son courroux envers Thèbes," p. 531), but does not carry her analysis of the irony far enough.

First of all we settle into a grassy glen, keeping movements of foot
and all our tongues in silence, to see and not be seen.

But that glen holds a silence of another kind: not the shelter of men
spying on the rites, but the sign and instruments of the god's own
power, giving a strange, quasi-animate life to nature (1084-85):

σίγησε δ᾽ αἰθήρ, σῖγα δ᾽ ὕλιμος νάπη
φύλλ᾽ εἶχε, θηρῶν δ᾽ οὐκ ἂν ἤκουσας βοήν.

The aether grew silent, in silence the forest glen now held its
leaves, and cry of beasts you would not have heard.

The *napos* (glen) that is mere space and surrounding in 1048 is, in
the divine perspective, a *napē* with the near-human power to speak
or keep silent in 1084. The parallelism of thought and expression in
the two passages creates an uncanny resemblance between natural
objects and human intention, between the "body" of nature and the
bodies of men. The capacity for language (or the deliberate nonlan-
guage of silence) that should separate men and nature becomes, in
the Dionysiac realm, a disturbing fusion.

Like everything else in this god's power, the silence coexists with
its opposite, the wild, unbridled shouts of the furious maenads (1131-
35, 1144-47), whose mode of "hunting" here is so different from the
stealthy hunting of Pentheus and his men.[21] The polarities of Dionysiac celebration were already shown in the parode, where the sacred stillness of *euphēmia* at the beginning was answered by the corybantic music of the Couretes, Great Mother, and reveling satyrs at
the end (69-70, 120-34, 153-65). The joyful laughter of the flute in
the Asiatic worship of the god (380) and the Stranger's imperturbable
laughter at his captors (439) now change to the sinister "laughing" on
the face of the hunter-god-beast (1021).[22] Trapped in the rigidity of
his own heroic code, Pentheus could only protest, "Anything is better
than letting the bacchants *laugh* at me" (842). Even that remaining
scrap of Pentheus' regal identity is cut away as the supernatural shout

[21] See Roux ad 1084-85: "Un bel effet dramatique est produit par le contraste entre
le cri accompagné de lueur et le silence prodigieux qui pétrifie soudain la scène."
Otto 93 remarks, "A wild uproar and a numbed silence—these are only different
forms of the nameless, of that which shatters all composure."

[22] Rosenmeyer 106 observes, "The laughter is expressive of the gulf between god
and man." For other aspects of the laughter see above, Chap. 6, section 7.

and silence avenge his scornful "laughing" at Dionysus (1080-81; cf. 854).

Pentheus' last utterance brings his discourse back to sanity (1117-21), but in the form of a child's imploring whine rather than a king's authoritarian command. His stiff refusals to be persuaded (e.g., 787) now meet an inflexibility on the other side, more granitic and more terrible, in the uncomprehending madness of Agave (1123-24): "She was possessed by the Bacchic god, and [Pentheus] could not persuade her" (oud' epeithe nin, 1124). The god's "shouting" (aneboēse, 1079) had an immediate impact on sky, forest, and animals, all held by the supernatural stillness (1084-85; cf. boē, "shout," 1085). Pentheus' words to his own mother are unheard. He is then engulfed by a "shout all around" (pas' homou boē, 1131). Now he can only "groan" or "wail" (stenazōn) while the maenads raise the wild cry (1131-33):

$$\mathring{\eta}\nu\ \delta\grave{\epsilon}\ \pi\mathring{a}\sigma'\ \acute{o}\mu o\hat{v}\ \beta o\acute{\eta},$$
$$\mathring{o}\ \mu\grave{\epsilon}\nu\ \sigma\tau\epsilon\nu\acute{a}\zeta\omega\nu\ \mathring{o}\sigma o\nu\ \grave{\epsilon}\tau\acute{v}\gamma\chi a\nu'\ \grave{\epsilon}\mu\pi\nu\acute{\epsilon}\omega\nu,$$
$$a\ddot{\iota}\ \delta'\ \mathring{\eta}\lambda\acute{a}\lambda a\zeta o\nu.$$

There was a shouting all together, he groaning with as much breath as he chanced to have, they raising the ritual cry.

"Groaning with as much breath as he chanced to have": Pentheus' power to speak is reduced to the gasp of a dying man, from articulate word to the elemental life-function. The scene fulfills the intimations of death when he confronted the apparitional power of Dionysus inside the palace, for there, too, he kept a grim silence with clenched teeth (621), "breathing out his spirit" (thymon ekpneōn, 620) in his futile effort to tie up the bull.

The mad Agave's language of victory and war, as we have already seen, accompanies the play's bizarre reversals of sex roles and values.[23] Cadmus' question-and-answer technique—"Could you then hear and respond with clarity?" (1272)—brings her back to relatedness to others and to the self that the Dionysiac identity overwhelmed. She "forgets what [she] spoke before" (1272). The names of Pentheus and Echion, which had no effect on her earlier, now restore her to reality (cf. 1274-76, 1119) and to the agony that comes with a return from berserk fury to full consciousness. Coherent language and coherent

[23] Cf. especially the "boasting" in 461 with 1207, 1233; 780-86 with 1212-15. See above, Chap. 6, sections 2, 3, 7.

identity were both dissolved in the Dionysiac madness; both come back at the same time. The self fused with the sacred band or *thiasos* of maenads gives way to the former morally centered self of a person in society. Simultaneously the language of bacchantic group identity withdraws for the language of personal responsibility, guilt, individual suffering.

The Olympian speech of Zeus's oracle makes a brief appearance (1332ff.), but what it has to declare, through the mouth of the son of Zeus who has destroyed the Theban house, is the bestialization of old Cadmus. The last exchanges of speech enact a disruption of communication that cannot be restored after the vengeance of the god. Agave embraces her father "as the swan embraces the white-haired helpless [parent-bird]" (1365). The swan is famous for its song, but here is evoked not for its singing but for a last farewell by touch of hands (1364). Traditionally associated with the beauty of choral celebration in song,[24] the swan image also measures the gap between the joyful singing of the serene Dionysiac *thiasos* from Asia in the parode and the raucous destruction wrought by the Theban *thiasos* in this Greek city. After the mob violence of the maenads as a flock of birds grouped all together in attack or lust (cf. 748, 957-58), the image of a single bird stands in pathetic contrast. As individual responsibility and personal grief replace collective hallucination, as reflectiveness replaces ecstasy or fury, so the intense beauty and pure joy of community in the *thiasos* subside into solitary grief and the knowledge of loneliness soon to come.

• IV •

The play's most explicit reflection on myth and language is Teiresias' long speech (266-327), to which we must now turn in some detail. Modern audiences find the scene boring. Viewed in terms of dramaturgical effect only, it does interrupt the mounting excitement.

[24] See *inter alia* Alcman, *Parthen.* 1.100f.; Eur. *HF* 687-95; *IT* 1104f.; see J. Diggle, *Euripides, Phaethon* (Cambridge 1970) ad 74 and W. G. Arnott, "Swan Songs," *G & R*, ser. 2, vol. 24 (1977) 149-53. Musgrave's correction of P's *poliochrōs* to the accusative in 1365 is adopted by most modern editors. For other aspects of the swan image see below, section 10.

Yet it is vital to the meaning of the work, not only because the proph-et's exposition of Dionysus' nature builds up suspense for the actual encounter with the god or his avatar in the next scene, but also be-cause its intellectual focus, so characteristic of what Arrowsmith called "Euripides' theater of ideas," forces us to ask the moral, aesthetic, and intellectual questions raised by Dionysus' presence in the city.

To review the situation briefly, Pentheus enters, outraged and blus-tering, at 215. He quickly takes stock of events: the arrival of the Asian Stranger and his maenad followers, the Theban women on the mountain in Bacchic revelry, his own steps to repress the madness by imprisoning the maenads in Thebes and preparing to "hunt" those out on Cithaeron. The sight of Teiresias and Cadmus wearing fawn-skins and carrying the thyrsus is more fuel for his anger: he points out the laughability of the spectacle, insults and threatens Teiresias, and ends with a general denunciation of rites that suspiciously com-bine women and wine (248-62). The maenad Chorus appeals to rev-erence for the gods and for the venerable ancestry of Cadmus, and then Teiresias makes his speech.

In contrast to the young king's emotional outburst, old Teiresias speaks in tones of measured hauteur and conscious superiority. Whereas Pentheus began with a rapid jumble of details about outrageous goings-on (215-25), Teiresias, calm and aloof, speaks in the broad generali-ties and carefully structured syntax of an orator's proem (266-71): "Whenever a wise man takes good starting-points of words, it is no great task to speak well. But you have a glib and fluent tongue as if you had good sense, whereas in your utterances there is no sense at all. An able speaker who owes his power of speech to bold daring proves a bad citizen, for he has no sense."[25] This emphasis on the theme of language not only calls attention to Pentheus' irresponsible threats and insults just before (233-47). It also puts Pentheus in his place as a king whose words and thoughts are not really considerate of his people. The term "bad citizen," *kakos politēs*, in 271 may be, as Roux suggests, an anachronism, transferring the Athenian assem-

---

[25] In the text and interpretation of 270 I follow Dodds, *Bacchae* in accepting Mad-vig's emendation, *thrasei*. Roux defends the MS reading, but agrees essentially with Dodds on the basic meaning of the line. She also supplies some instructive parallels from the orators on the *topos* of dangerous "boldness" of speech. Cf. also Eur. *Orestes* 903.

bly to Bronze-Age Theban monarchy.[26] But it may equally well be the old prophet's reminder of the king's duty to his subjects, deliberately demoting him to the status of "citizen," and bad citizen at that.

Teiresias' argument is inspired by the rationalistic explanations of religion in Sophists like Protagoras, Prodicus, Democritus. The speech is "a minor masterpiece of satire" against this Sophistic allegorizing,[27] all the more ironical as Teiresias had said some sixty lines before that one does not practice Sophistry (*sophizomestha*, 200) where the gods are concerned. But interpreters in general have taken the speech too lightly; it is more than just a satire of Enlightenment rationalism.[28]

Teiresias knows his rhetorical handbooks. After the carefully marked proem there is an articulation of the argument into five distinct parts. Viewed as a personification of "the vine's moist drink" (279), Dionysus is reduced to a principle of nourishing nature complementary to "dry" Demeter and her grain (272-85, section 1 of the speech). Dionysus' birth from the thigh of Zeus (section 2) is explained away by a bit of etymological word-play that reminds one of Plato's *Cratylus*. Zeus gave Hera a deceptive cloud image of the god as a "hostage" (*homēros*) when she wished his expulsion from Olympus; so the story arose that he had hidden his son in his "thigh" (*mēros*). It is hard to see that this myth is any more edifying than the "true" story of Dionysus' birth; the jealousy of Hera and marital strife on Olympus remain. Teiresias' version seems a bit unworthy of his prophetic reputation. Is Euripides suggesting a trace of senility? Even if he is mildly satirizing the familiar stage figure of the old prophet, satiric effect is not incompatible with serious implications for the meaning of the play.

Teiresias next turns to the power of Dionysiac madness (section 3), with further etymological arguments. The god's "manic" power is also

[26] Roux ad loc.

[27] WI 48. See also Deichgräber 333-37; Lesky, *TDH* 488. Dodds, *Bacchae* 91 sees in Teiresian rationalism "the type of mind which would harness to the cause of doctrinal conservatism the spontaneous emotional forces generated by a religious revival." Conacher 62f. similarly views Teiresias as reflecting a philosophical mode of accepting Dionysus.

[28] So WI 47-54, who rather neglects its relation to the rest of the play and focuses its import too narrowly on the characterization of Teiresias and Pentheus. Nestle, *Euripides* 80-82 sees the speech as reflecting Euripides' attempt to develop a "Weltbildungstheorie" and present his own philosophical conception of the divine.

"mantic" (299); he can inspire armies with panic fear, and the god himself appears leading his bacchants in Delphi (298-304). After another appeal to Pentheus to receive the god's rites (309-13), he answers the charge of licentiousness (section 4), utilizing a further philosophical-sophistic point, a contrast of inborn nature and external necessity or compulsion (*physis* and *anankē*, 314-18). His last point (section 5) is the god's joy, like any mortal's, in the magnification of his name (319-21). His exordium (322-27) echoes his first section in the repeated phrase "whom you laugh to scorn" (322 and 272). He restates his determination to honor the god, but also takes a harder line toward Pentheus, whom he accuses of being insane and sick with a disease that no drugs (*pharmaka*) can cure (326-28).

Cadmus then reiterates Teiresias' advice about accepting Dionysus, adds the political expedience of a useful lie (333-36), and adduces the warning paradigm of Pentheus' cousin, Actaeon (337-42), although at this point the similarity is not yet very clear. To both defenses of Dionysus Pentheus reacts with predictable violence and redoubles his threats against the Stranger and the maenads (343-57). In the familiar posture of the tragic prophet scorned, Teiresias exits with dire warnings of the imminent fulfillment of the "pain" concealed in Pentheus' name (367).

The speeches of both Teiresias and Cadmus deal with the play's fundamental problem, Dionysus' relation to civic life and civilized institutions. Both men would admit Dionysus into the city, but both would do so on their own terms, not the god's. Neither the rationalizing sophistry of Teiresias nor the political utilitarianism of Cadmus is the proper vehicle for incorporating this god into the city. Teiresias' allegorizing interpretation of Dionysus would effect a mediation between culture and nature, *nomos* and *physis*. But Dionysus remains the god of nonmediated oppositions, and for this the proper expression is not rationalistic *logos* but tragedy itself, which embraces both *logos* and *mythos*.

Far from possessing a genuine sense of the mythical reality of the god, as a recent interpreter has claimed,[29] Teiresias severely misconceives the nature of Dionysus. Virtually every point he adduces in praise of Dionysus emerges in the subsequent action in just the opposite meaning: nurture of life, release from pain, the Bacchic mad-

---

[29] Rohdich 143ff.

ness, and so on. When Dionysus himself intervenes to vindicate Tei-resias' position in his own manner, he shatters the limited frame of rational understanding in which the prophet would enclose him.

Like Teiresias, Dionysus relies upon etymologies (cf. 508). But whereas Teiresias remains within the limits of intelligible discourse to demonstrate the meaning of Dionysus' name (295-97), Dionysus moves to the opposite end of the spectrum of language—ecstasy, wild cries, unintelligible speech—to demonstrate the truth that he sees in Pentheus and in Pentheus' name (cf. 508). Teiresias has a glimpse of the god's kind of etymologizing in his play on Pentheus and *penthos* ("grief," "pain") at the end of the scene (367), but the god's word-games have a grimmer and bloodier reality than the old prophet can imagine.[30] Dionysus takes Teiresias' etymologies much farther, and reveals in Pentheus' name both "suffering" (*pathos*) and "grief" (*pen-thos*) (cf. 367, 508, 1216; 784-86). On the other hand he makes good his own (not Teiresias') etymology of his own name as "son of Zeus" (*Dios hyios*: cf. 1, 859-61, 1340-41, 1349). For Dionysus, too, names are a source of magical power: he transforms Pentheus' name into an omen of his doom (507ff.).[31]

Teiresias' explanation of Dionysus' "change of name" (cf. *onoma metastēsantes*, 296) involves a hostile mother figure (294-97). When Pentheus "changes" his name, there is not only a hostile mother but a total loss of his human identity and a total rupture of speech and comprehension between mother and son (1115-24). The "holy mouth" of the gods' worshipers in the parode (69-70) suggests a divinity far less receptive to these subtle verbal explanations than Teiresias might suppose. The god had already denounced Cadmus' *sophismata* (30), and Teiresias had initially abjured the very practice in which he now indulges at such length (200). When Dionysus himself engages in prophecy, it is to predict a hard future. As *mantis* this god is less

---

[30] On Euripides' interest in modes of etymologizing and its historical background in fifth-century theories of language see Van Looy, passim, esp. 346f. with nn. 6-7. The sophistic-looking etymology of *meros-homēros-mēros* in 292ff. has a playfulness ("niet zonder ironie," says Van Looy 364) that contrasts with Dionysus' grimly plausible etymology of Pentheus-*penthos*.

[31] See Dodds, *Bacchae* ad 1; Van Looy 353; Verdenius (1980) 1. For the historical etymology (probably non-Greek) see Burkert, *Gr. Rel.* 253 with n. 10; Coche de la Ferté 222 with n. 342. On Dionysus' "name-magic" see Podlecki 157. On the name as power see also Van Looy 346.

helpful than Teiresias suggests (298); so too his "element of madness" contains much more dangerous effects than "mantic art" (299).

The contrast between Teiresias' and Dionysus' etymologizing also reflects on the special resources of drama. The tragedian's presentation of his myth in the theater acts out its hidden meaning not in the pallid allegories of *logos* but in visual images that assault our eyes and ears with a concrete shock-effect that we cannot fully explain away or refute. Thus Teiresias' remote myth to account for Dionysus' name, Zeus "breaking off a piece of the aether that encircles the earth" and giving it to Hera as "hostage" (292-93), is totally inadequate to the violence of Dionysus' birth described by the god himself in the prologue (2-9). That act of "breaking off" a portion of pure aether to save a child contrasts with the bloody "breaking" of a son's flesh by a hostile mother later ("breaking" occurs in the same metrical position, first in the verse: ῥήξας μέρος τι, 292; ῥηγνῦσα σάρκας, 1130). An audience familiar with the myth can be expected to detect in the verb "breaking" an intimation of an aspect of Dionysus that Teiresias' bland celestial mythologizing has screened out.

This rationalizing way of accounting for the god's "name" has another foil in the bacchantic Chorus's excited lyrics of religious epiphany to give the god his name (528-29): "To Thebes I reveal [*anaphainō*] you, O Bacchic one, to give you this name" (*onomazein*). This religious "revelation," moreover, directly leads into the Stranger's Dionysiac manner of demonstrating his "name" by the fires and earthquakes of the palace miracle (576-603).

The poetry of the dramatist functions as almost the opposite of the *logos* of the sophistic prophet. It opens language to a dimension of reality that Teiresias' speech cannot reach. The truly "Dionysiac" side of Teiresias' etymology is the poet's ability to make language reveal the primal power of its words, to recall it to the magic of its sound- and image-shaping capacity, and to renew our sense of the concrete particularities of its meanings, origins, textures, sounds, patterns. "In poetry the internal form of a name, that is, the semantic load of its constituents, regains its pertinence. The 'Cocktails' may resume their obliterated kinship with plumage."[32] The diverse forms of etymolo-

[32] Roman Jakobson, "Linguistics and Poetics," in Richard and Fernande De George, eds., *The Structuralists from Marx to Lévi-Strauss* (Garden City, N.Y., 1972) 119.

gizing in the play contain an insight into this essential function of poetic (and dramatic) language.

Euripides gives this point a characteristically Dionysian duality: to try to fix the essence of man or god in a name, a word, may also be to encase elusive flow in deceptively static forms. The "naming" of Pentheus, unlike the naming of Dionysus, brings "grief" not joy, mourning not ecstasy, death not life. The fourth stasimon is a nightmarish inversion of names: Dionysus is revealed not as the joyful Dithyrambus or Bromius of his first "epiphany" (526-29) but as bull, snake, or lion (1017-18). Pentheus' mother and aunts become closely identified with the "Hounds of Lyssa" (Madness; 977; cf. 731). Pentheus himself gains a new matronymic as "son of lioness or of Libyan Gorgons" (977-78, 988-90). The illusionistic power of Dionysus as the god of drama as well as the god of madness converts the purely verbal etymologies of Teiresias into the solidity of the "unhappy weight of Pentheus" that Cadmus "carries" (*pherontes athlion baros / Pentheōs*, 1215-16); the "pain [*penthos*] not to be *measured*, not to be *seen*," which consists of *deeds* of murder "done by hands most miserable" (*exeirgasmena*, 1244-45); and finally the "greatest grief" (*algos*) that Agave "sees" in the "head of Pentheus" that she "carries in her hands" (*pheromai en cheroin*), "sees" and "holds" (1280-84). In all of these passages the power of Dionysus, both as god of the maenads and as god of the theatrical representation, actualizes the *logos* of Pentheus' name in the grisly physical object on the stage. That object, the bloody *prosōpon* (cf. 1277 and 1021) of the mask/character, is actually seen, touched, and carried as the thing that Pentheus/*penthos* has now become. Uniting *logos* and *ergon*, signifier and signified, Dionysiac language converts verbal to disturbingly visual meaning.

V

Teiresias began his speech with "wisdom," *sophia* (266-67): "When a wise man [*sophos anēr*] takes a fair beginning of words, it is no great deed to speak well." But who is the "wise man"? In the complex ironies of this scene Teiresias' "wisdom," meant to contrast with Pentheus' "folly" and "ignorance" (269, 271), is hardly the *sophia* that can grasp and expound the mysterious nature of Dionysus. "That which is wise is not wisdom," *to sophon d'ou sophia*, the maenad Chorus sings soon after (395).[33]

Teiresias' first point couples Dionysus with Demeter, goddess of the nurturing earth (275-76). The image of earth as "nurturer of mortals" (277) evokes the Golden Age when earth supported life with spontaneous bounty (cf. Hesiod, *Works and Days*, 117-18). But we also see the mythical Golden Age in its potential savagery and uninhibited feral bloodshed (cf. 699-711, 734-68). In the next ode the Chorus depicts a world of fulfilled desires, grace, beauty, and art (403ff.), the "rightful place for Bacchic rites" (414-15). But neither Teiresias' rationalism (from which poetry and inspiration are notably absent)[34] nor Pentheus' authoritarian view of the city holds the possibility of envisaging or creating such a world.

Dionysus' drink, Teiresias says, is the "antithesis" or "foil" (*antipalon*, 278) to Demeter's "dry" nurture. He is drawing on a philosophical antinomy between "the dry" and "the wet" in pre-Socratic thought.[35] His rationalism creates sharp polarities that it is the essential nature of Dionysus to confound and dissolve. Dionysus, as we have seen, has his own associations with the earth that have nothing to do with the gentle, nourishing earth of Demeter (cf. 585, 1083). Teiresias praises Dionysus as an "inventor" (*heuretēs*) and a bestower of "drugs" (*pharmaka*) that take away pain and bring forgetfulness of woes (279-83). But the "finding" (*heuriskein*) at the end of the play will be that of Pentheus' body (1221), and the "drugs" of Dionysiac illusion bring a full measure of pain and sorrow. Teiresias himself attests to this other effect of the Dionysiac "drug" at the end of his speech when he warns Pentheus of a disease of madness that no "drugs" can cure (326-27). When those destructive "drugs" of madness have begun to take effect and Pentheus' doom is imminent, the promise

[33] This is not to say that 395 is an explicit criticism of Teiresias: see Dodds, *Bacchae* ad loc. But the paradoxes of *sophia* that the Chorus's words suggest would also include Teiresias' "wisdom." For the importance of *sophia* see 428, 877, 1005, 1150-52, and see WI 167ff.; Diller (1955) 482f.; Deichgräber 339-49 (Dionysus emerges as the only true *sophos*, p. 347); Arrowsmith (1959) 54-56; Winnington-Ingram (1966) 34-37; Conacher 73-75; Parry, *Lyrics* 147; Rohdich 157ff.; Oranje 129ff.

[34] A point well observed by Kirk 10.

[35] See Dodds, *Bacchae* ad 274-85 (p. 104) for discussion and parallels.

of freedom from pain has a very different meaning: "To behave as a mortal [brings] life without pain" (*alypos bios*, 1004).[36]

"Born a god," Teiresias goes on, Dionysus "is poured forth in libations [*spendetai*], so that because of him men have good things" (284-85). But when Dionysus is present to Pentheus, "propitious and reconciled through libations" (*enspondos*, 924, a play on the meaning of *spondai*, truce or treaty solemnized by libation, *spondē*), what is poured forth in the rite is blood, not wine. Teiresias' allegorization of Dionysus as wine hardly accounts for the anthropomorphic anger of the god who exacts a terrible price for the refusal to pour libations in his honor (45-46, 313). "Because of him men have good things," *ta agatha*, Teiresias said (285). But the enacted *mythos* shows as many "evils" as "goods" (cf. 1248); and the god's way of "establishing things well" (*themenos eu*, 49; *katastēsai eu*, 802) does not entirely harmonize with the optimism of his newly converted prophet.

Teiresias' rationalization of Dionysus' birth from Zeus's thigh has a counterpart in dramatic terms as the god, "hidden" in the dark enclosure of Pentheus' palace (611), bursts out of the darkness into the light with torches that flash on the mountain, the "greatest light" to his worshipers (608; cf. 549 and 98). However represented on the stage, this event also brings the god from remote Olympus to immediate presence in the scenic action, a problem and a mystery for participant and spectator alike.

Teiresias' story that Zeus broke off a piece of "the earth-encircling aether" as a "device" against Hera (291-93) also has a dramatic reality in the immediate present, with a characteristically Dionysian fusion of illusion and truth, for the Stranger tells a tale, itself hidden from sight, of how the god fashioned an image (*phasma*) in the palace and deluded the raging king so that he "stabbed the shining aether" (629-31). "Device" or "contrivance," *antimēchanasthai*, is Teiresias' word for Zeus's stratagem; but "device" or "craft" recurs as Dionysus' weapon against his enemy, the effects shown onstage (cf. *mēchanan, technai*, 805-6; also 675). In both parts of Teiresias' story the purified "myth" of Sophistic rationalism is set against the present mystery of the Dionysiac myth enacted in the play. Euripides uses Teiresias' *logos*, which

---

[36] The text and interpretation of 1002-1004 are much disputed: see Dodds, *Bacchae* and Roux ad loc; WI 124, n. 1. It is not certain whether 1004 is an independent clause or belongs with the previous line, but for the purpose of the contrast with the "release from pain" in 279-81 the sense is clear enough.

circumscribes and neutralizes Dionysus, as a foil to his own *mythos*, which can embrace the god in his full mystery, his awe-inspiring horror, and in the coexistent opposites of violence and gentleness, bestiality and divinity.

Teiresias' image of Olympus as a place of "quarrels" (*neikea*, 294), of anger, retaliation, devices and "counterdevices" (291) among the gods, is strangely at odds with the more enlightened allegorizing of the rest of his discourse. Zeus may have "devised things worthy of a god" (*hoia dē theos*, 291); but the picture of gods hurling one another out of Olympus, fighting, deceiving, plunges us back into the ancient anthropomorphism criticized from Xenophanes to Plato. The narrative that he creates to explain Dionysus' name, in fact, resembles several scenes in the *Iliad*'s comedy of the gods.[37]

For all his rationalism, then, Teiresias does not advance far beyond the limitations of traditional anthropomorphic myth. His view of divinity is certainly far below the spiritualizing theology of a figure like Theonoe in the *Helen* (865-72, 1013-16), or even the simpler piety that rejects "the poets' wretched tales" in the *Heracles* (1340-46). Teiresias concentrates on the material rather than the spiritual benefits of Dionysus: food and drink, sleep, wine, freedom from pain. As an exponent of religious thought he suffers from comparison with the maenad Chorus, whose praise of purity, holiness, the remote beauty and wisdom of the Olympians follows directly upon his exit (370-396; cf. 83-88).

The play offers a different qualification to Teiresias' next point, the power of Dionysiac madness in inspiring prophecy and producing panic among armies (298-305). The link between "prophecy" and "madness," "mantic" and "manic" power, rests upon another verbal sleight of hand (299); and in this case, too, Teiresias is closer to the letter than the spirit in more than one sense. We hardly need to be reminded of the other effects of the Dionysiac *mania* and the other activities into which the god leads "those who are raging mad . . . when he comes with full force into their bodies" (300-301). Later in the scene Teiresias will call Pentheus "mad" (326, 359), but the real madness that Dionysus will inflict is once more acted out on the stage in its full horror as we watch Pentheus go insane before our very eyes. There is an eerie effect as the Stranger, who has already shown himself to be the god, addresses "Dionysus" by name and prays (849-51),

[37] E.g., *Iliad* 1.511-600, 8.5-27, 14.159-360, 18.394-406.

"Dionysus, now the deed [ergon] is yours. For you are not far. Let us punish him. First stun him out of his wits and put the swift fury into him. . . ." Once more the mortal interpreter's "word" pales before the supernatural power of the god's "deed" (ergon) and the scenic action of putting on the maenad's robes (cf. 852-55). Teiresias speaks of "madness" as an abstraction, to maniōdes (299). Dionysus gives it specific, tangible attributes, "to make stand out of one's wits," ἔκστη-σον φρενῶν (850), "swift fury," ἐλαφρὰν λύσσαν (851). Soon that "fury" appears as a quasi-divinized power, akin to the Erinyes, whose "hunting dogs" are the maenads themselves (cf. 731). So Dionysus' attribute of speed (851) shifts from the madness itself (elaphran lyssan) closer to the women whom Madness inspires: "Come swift hounds of Lyssa," thoai Lyssas kynes (977).[38] At the other extreme, the prophet has little sense of the joyful madness of the satyrs whose mythical revelry in the entourage of Rhea and the corybantes is the prototype for the rapture of the thiasos (120-34).

Teiresias includes among Dionysus' powers the panic fear that routs an army (302-305). But when similar events occur in the dramatic action, they have a far more ominous atmosphere (cf. 731-33, 752-54, 760-64). The "flutter of fear" of which Teiresias speaks (phobos dieptoēse, 304) has a more terrible counterpart in the inward "flutter" in Agave's soul that led her to tear apart her son (to ptoēthen, 1268). "Still will you see him," Teiresias goes on enthusiastically, "upon Delphi's rocks, leaping with the pine trees along the twin-peaked upland vales, brandishing and shaking the Bacchic branch, great in Hellas" (306-309). But it is just this mad desire for a vision of the god's revels on the mountain that leads Pentheus to a vision of a very different kind.

Many of Teiresias' details of 306-309 recur in a more sinister vein closer to Thebes, on Cithaeron, not Parnassus. The maenads, assaulting Pentheus, "leap" among the crags (1093-94), use "rocks" as a vantage point for missiles (1097) and take "branches" as weapons (kladoi, 1103; cf. bakcheion kladon, 307). Although firs (elatai) replace the pines (peukai) of Teiresias' description, Dionysus extends his power over a branch (klados) in a more mysterious way than Teiresias imagines, bending down to the ground "the heaven-high top-

---

[38] For Lyssa cf. HF 822-74. See also Dodds, Bacchae and Roux ad 977; WI 183. Kirk ad loc. well remarks, "In a way the maenads, addressed by Agaue at 731 as 'my coursing hounds,' are to become the Furies' human embodiment."

most branch" (1064-65). The god's "leaping" mirrors the ecstasy of his followers (cf. 169, 446, 665), but has its miraculous side in the "leaping forth" of the "dewy water's stream" in the First Messenger's speech (705), as well as its dark pendant in the attack of 1094. Like the "flutter" of Dionysiac panic in 304 and 1268, the "leap" of the god on Parnassus in Teiresias' description has a painful inward meaning in the "leap of fear" in Agave's heart (*kardia pēdēm' echei*, 1288) as she steels herself to learn the truth from Cadmus. In the last words of his expository lecture before his direct advice to Pentheus to receive the god, Teiresias describes Dionysus as "great in Hellas." But Dionysus will defend his own greatness in Hellas as the phrase recurs to mark Pentheus' scorn: "an insult great to the Hellenes (*psogos es Hellēnas megas*, 779); a house "once happy in Hellas" (1024).

Teiresias' last point, that the god "takes pleasure in being honored," just as the king "rejoices when the city magnifies the name of Pentheus" (320-21), treats the anthropomorphism of the gods with an acceptant simplicity that is generally the first victim of Euripidean tragedy (e.g., *Hippolytus* 7-8). The action of the play shows this anthropomorphism in a very different light as we see the god's all too human anger about "his name unhonored" (*ageraston . . . onoma*, 1378; cf. 1297, 1347) as the cause of the catastrophe. Ironically Teiresias is proven correct in his assessment of the god's need for honor (320f.), but that correctness is itself qualified by the play's larger view of Dionysus. It is as if Teiresias is proven a poor reader of the tragedy, an inept moralizer of its message.

In linking Dionysus with other Olympian deities like Demeter, Ares, and Apollo, Teiresias would keep him within the limits of intelligible *logos* and publicly useful *mythos*. The action of the play proves him a failure on both counts. "You do not shame Phoebus Apollo in your words; and in honoring Bromian Dionysus, a great god, you show good sense," the Chorus optimistically reassures Teiresias at the end of his long speech (328-29). Historically, the cult of Delphic Apollo was careful to make a place for Dionysus. Yet the play shows how ill-founded that peaceful coexistence really is. The lyrical choruses of Asian maenads have already revealed aspects of Dionysus that the Apollonian prophet can grasp only in the most superficial way. [39]

[39] For Apollo and Delphi in relation to Dionysus see WI 51 with n. 2; Dodds, *Bacchae* ad 302-304 (p. 110).

As the god himself proves the more accurate etymologist, sophist, and prophet, so the tragic drama itself proves the truer and more appropriate vehicle for bringing Dionysus into the polis. That task, Euripides suggests, can be accomplished only by a form that is itself open to the chaos, the ecstasy, and the unmediated contradictions that are essential parts of the god's nature. The closer we come to Dionysus, the more we enter the realm of the "unspeakable," the god's own term for his rites (*arrhēta*, 472).

Cadmus seconds Teiresias (330-42) and is shown equally wanting in understanding of the god or the meaning of his arrival in Thebes. As he would have initially gone to the mountain in a chariot (*ochos*, 191)—the equivalent, perhaps, of a pilgrimage to the Scala Santa in a Rolls Royce—so he would convert the recent events into a useful bit of governmental propaganda (333-36; cf. 30-31). At the end, however, when his contact with the god has reversed both his civilizing role and his human form, he will drive a "chariot" (*ochos*) of another kind in a context far removed from his regal dignity at Thebes (1330-36).

He, too, experiences a radical change in his exposure to Dionysus and the wild places of his rites. Having returned to safety "inside the walls with old Teiresias from the bacchants" (1223-24), he "turns back to the mountain" (1225) and now reenters with the torn body of his grandson (cf. 1216-21). One does not return from that mountain quite the same person as one was in setting out (cf. 191). Unlike Teiresias, Cadmus moves beyond intellectualization or manipulation of the meaning of Dionysus to an experience of the god's terrible truth. He follows the tragic road of suffering. The pairing of him with Teiresias in 1223 reminds us of their earlier union in a limited grasp of the god and points up the divergent path that Cadmus takes in his subsequent knowledge of Dionysus.

In the Teiresias scene Cadmus advocated a politic "noble lie" (334) in incorporating Dionysus into Thebes. Teiresias' slightly earlier point about "honor" (*timē*, 319-21) is still the issue, but Cadmus' phrasing betrays the speciousness of his reasoning (334-36): "Lie nobly that Dionysus is a god, so that Semele may seem [*dokē(i)*] to have born a god and honor may accrue to our whole race." For him the birth drifts into the realm of "seeming," *dokein*, which at one level is far from the mysterious truth of Dionysiac myth and Dionysiac epiphany but at another level anticipates Dionysus' illusionism and fusion of god and beast. Semele's associations with Dionysus and the manner of her death have already distanced her from the civic and domestic realm with which Cadmus is familiar, and the birth has a sacred and lyrical vividness far from Cadmus' *dokein* (cf. 2-9, 88ff., 519ff.). Cadmus hopes that the tale of the birth will bring "honor to our whole race" (*panti tō[i] genei*, 336). At the end, however, the god makes Cadmus totally "without honor" (*atimos*, 1313; cf. 1320) and destroys his "race" in the ruin of his "house" and the death of his last surviving male descendant (1305-15). "Cadmus the great who sowed the race [*genos*] of Thebes" (1314-15) will soon become a serpentine monster leading barbarians against the holy shrines and tombs of Greece (1358-60).

Emergence from chaos in a founding myth on the one hand is answered by a return to chaos in a myth of metamorphosis on the other. Metamorphosis, the most arbitrary and unheroic of mythic forms, negates not only Cadmus' civilizing achievement as a dragon-slayer but also one of the most powerful impulses of heroic action, the preservation of personal identity in the timeless name or the "imperishable glory" (Homeric *kleos aphthiton*) that lives forever on the lips of men. Metamorphosis, particularly downward metamorphosis to a beast or serpent, dissolves that fixity of identity and returns aspiration for the eternal to the cyclical changes of nature.[40] Cadmus' end is a milder form of Pentheus': metamorphosis parallels *sparagmos* not only in violating physical identity but also in denying the immutability that heroic *kleos* or *timē* affirms. Dionysus replaces the sustaining heroic myths in the background of the polis with mythical narrations that question or disallow heroic independence from the changes, cycles, and mortality of nature.

• VI •

The chief mortal characters' reactions to Dionysus delineate a number of different levels and ways of accepting myth. Like Pentheus, Cadmus stands at a lower level of belief in the power of myth to convey

[40] See Florence Dupont, "Se reproduire ou se métamorphoser," *Topique: Revue Freudienne* 9-10 (1971) 139-60; Segal, *Landscape in Ovid's Metamorphoses*, Hermes Einzelschrift 23 (1969) 90ff.

truth, a kind of zero-grade of mythic signification. For both the ruler and ex-ruler of Thebes the tale of Dionysus' birth from Semele is a "lie" (*pseudos*, 245 and 334-36; cf. 31). Violent as he is and, misguided though he may be, Pentheus is the more honest, for he acts out of his own integrity of belief, rather than from ulterior motives. Cadmus is willing to exploit the political and dynastic advantages of the lie (334-36), whereas Pentheus rejects it outright.

With Teiresias Cadmus shares an attitude of rationalistic calculation toward Dionysus, in contrast to Pentheus' vehemence of emotional reaction. Cadmus' reaction constitutes *sophismata* (30), a word that suggests the rationalizing view of religion in the Sophistic Enlightenment. Teiresias is the clearer representative of the Sophistic movement, but he carefully abjures Sophistic practice (at least formally) in the belief that the new god can be reconciled with traditional cult and the established civic religion (cf. 200-202), an attitude that may well reflect the tendency of the older Sophists, like Protagoras, to endorse the *status quo*.[41] In any case, as we have noted, the initial pairing of Cadmus and Teiresias in their entrance and in their attempts to persuade Pentheus gives way to sharp divergence as Cadmus painfully learns the truth, not the convenient falsehood, of the god's origins and power.

Teiresias initially embodies a slightly higher level of acceptance of the mythical reality surrounding Dionysus. He accepts him as a god, but sees only one aspect of his nature, that part of him which is amenable to rationalized comprehension and optimistic intellectualization. In his world-view the gods are the benefactors of man and the source of "good things" (*agatha*, 285). Historically, this theology, which later developed into what is called Euhemerism, may reflect the thinking of Prodicus.[42] In terms of the play, it is revealed as woefully inadequate to the phenomenon of Dionysiac religion. The Chorus is temporarily willing to go along with Teiresias' reconciliation of Apollo and Dionysus (327-28). Pentheus takes a negative view of that association, lumping together in his threats both the new religion and the old, both the prophet and the maenads (255-60, 345-51).

[41] E.g., Protagoras apud Plato, *Theaet.* 161cff.; see Guthrie, *Hist. of Greek Philos.* 3.171ff., 3.187f.

[42] See Dodds, *Bacchae* ad 274-85; Nestle, *Vom Mythos zum Logos* 354f.; Guthrie, *Hist. of Greek Philos.* 3.241f.; Albert Henrichs, "Two Doxographical Notes: Democritus and Prodicus on Religion," *HSCP* 79 (1975) 107ff. with n. 64 on p. 110.

Myth and language are both polarized between the arid rationalism of Teiresias and the wild ecstasy of the Asian bacchants, between sterile logic and fanatical passion.[43] Stripped down to dry allegories in Sophistic discourse or exploded into incommunicable mysticism, myth loses its deeper meaning as a mode of reaching that realm of reality denoted as the divine. Thus we remain cut off from valid symbols that could give us access to that realm and to the energies and insights they contain. How can the experience to which the myths and the mythical gods point speak to us? This is the question that the *Bacchae* posed to its original audience, and poses to us still.

Rationalism, moreover, is not necessarily reasonableness. The individual and community that do not admit the creative expression of the emotional life in art, music, myth, and the other symbolic, imaginative forms fly apart through the explosive force of their own suppressed emotionality.

Dionysus himself is the focal point of this issue, both the problem and the solution. He stands above both his rationalizing and his ecstatic followers, above both his devotees and his antagonists. Yet above Dionysus stands another level of understanding. This is the elusive "wisdom" or *sophia* of the *Bacchae* as a whole, namely the wisdom of tragedy itself. The tragedy includes all of the points of view on Dionysus and all of the ways in which men try to grasp the god: rationalization, gesture, ritual, music, dance. Unlike the maenads' rites, the tragedy both encompasses and transcends Dionysus, for it places the rite and the myth within an aesthetic structure freer than either. It can hold contradictions without the need to impose resolution or mediation. In reflecting on its own status as a fiction that speaks truth, a mask that conceals the surface in order to reveal hidden depths, it spans the two poles of the Dionysiac spell or "drug," the destructive and the beneficent, the delusive madness and the cleansing intensity. It includes all the points of view, but in its dialectical structure prevents any single one from emerging as unambiguously correct or definitive. Each attitude stands in a relation of interaction and dialogue with the others.

Pentheus views the god as a harbinger of dangerous sexual license; Cadmus as an opportunity for the consolidation of political and dy-

---

[43] For the clash of *mythos* and *logos* in the *Bacchae* see Rohdich 139ff., 147f., 158f.

nastic prestige; Teiresias as a phenomenon open to regularizing, rationalizing interpretation, and so on. Dionysus is all of these, but also beyond them all. He is, as Winnington-Ingram has well said, what the beholder wants him to be.[44] But he is also the undefinable and mysterious in the world and in ourselves. We have intimations of this elusive essence, perhaps, in music, religious ecstasy, sexual passion—all linked to Dionysus in the play—but we grasp it, if at all, only through symbol and myth.

In the distant place of his exile Euripides could perhaps better contemplate this crisis of symbolic and mythic representation. In the play's ironical shifting between spectator and participant he could reflect on his own ambiguous relations to Hellenic culture. The changing attitudes to Dionysus within the play, veering from rationalistic distancing to impassioned identification, indicate something of that struggle for a hermeneutics of the symbol, as critical to our time as to Euripides'. We may cite Paul Ricoeur's analysis:

> The world of symbols is not a tranquil and reconciled world; every symbol is iconoclastic in comparison with some other symbol, just as every symbol, left to itself, tends to thicken, to become solidified in an idolatry. It is necessary, then, to participate in the struggle, in the dynamics, in which the symbolism itself becomes a prey to the spontaneous hermeneutics that seeks to transcend it. It is only by participating in this dynamics that comprehension can reach the strictly critical dimension of exegesis and become a hermeneutic; but then one must abandon the position—or rather, the exile—of the remote and disinterested spectator, in order to appropriate in each case a particular symbolism.[45]

The question of exile in the play, as perhaps also in Euripides' life, then, may have this other dimension: alienation from the meaning and intensity of existence, to which the Dionysiac myth offers (and symbolizes) a lost closeness.

In the city shown in the play there is little that would seem to welcome this kind of intensity. The old rulers are cynical or limited

---

[44] WI 49: "[Dionysus] is a god of all intoxication, and as such he appears to different persons in the aspect appropriate to them." On the different views of Dionysus and different degrees of understanding of him embodied in the various characters see also 166f.

[45] Ricoeur, *Symbolism of Evil* 354.

by doctrinaire commitments to rationalistic theories. The young are immature, impetuous, involved in images of their authority. The impingement of the truly Other, the outsiders and their god, is either neutralized by superficial incorporation or repressed, thrust into dark prisons, dungeons of the mind as of the palace, where they can be hidden away. If myth and symbol are to speak truth to us still, the play seems to say, they can do so only by confronting their obstacles, their antagonists, and their perils, and this is possible only through confronting also their own epistemological and experiential limitations.

There are, to recapitulate, four levels of mythic truth shown in the play: (1) Pentheus' total rejection of the tales about Dionysus (232ff.); (2) Cadmus' social utilitarianism; (3) Teiresias' rationalistic optimism and systematizing; (4) Dionysus' mysterious and ambiguous power, the embodiment of that in ourselves and the world which is not reducible to intellectualization or categorization. The tragedy itself occupies a fifth level, containing and reflecting on all the other points of view. Through its power to act out conflict and bring opposites into the sharpest possible confrontation without having to resolve the contradictions, it is free to open the issues to their fullest and most threatening implications: the possible bestiality of gods and the potentially chaotic violence behind the ordering, reasoning power of men. In the lucid order of its dance-movements, patterned language, harmonized gestures of Chorus and actor, it reveals the sinister shadow-side of existence both in the world and in our souls. The "Dionysus" of the play is the fictive covering that makes possible this brilliant play of illusion, but he is also the dark reality hidden behind the mask.

• VII •

In reflecting on the power of tragic myth to convey truth, the *Bacchae* employs not only the symbolism of masking and revealing but also another attribute of the god, the "drug" or *pharmakon* of Dionysus' intoxicating liquor. This is a particularly effective symbol for binding together the various meanings of Dionysus' gifts, for *pharmakon* means both "poison" and "cure" and thus unites the destruc-

tive and beneficent poles of the god's nature. Connected with medicine and disease, *pharmakon* also links the theme of the Dionysiac
joy to the questions of sanity and madness.

Only Teiresias uses the word to describe the power of Dionysus,
and it occurs twice in the important speech that we have already
studied in detail. First, in his optimistic allegorization of Dionysus,
Teiresias explains how wine "gives unhappy mortals surcease from
pain [*lypē*] when they are filled with the vine's flowing drink, and
gives them sleep, forgetfulness of daily woes [*kaka*], nor is there any
other drug against suffering [*pharmakon ponōn*]" (280-83).[46] Teiresias
ends his speech, however, with the other aspect of the Dionysiac
pharmakon. Defending his maenadic garb against the laughter of
Pentheus, he warns (326-27): "You are afflicted with the most painful
madness [*mainē(i) hōs algista*], and not even with drugs [*pharmaka*]
would you receive a cure, nor is it without drugs that you have your
sickness." The strained antithesis of these lines expresses the two sides
of the Dionysiac *pharmakon*.[47] Having refused the *pharmakon* that
might give "surcease from pain" (*lypē*), Pentheus receives the *pharmakon* that brings the "most grievous" (*algista*) madness and disease.

Is Dionysus' "drug" an anodyne that transports us into a realm
where we forget the pain of existence or a medicine that restores us
to a healthier, more whole attitude to reality? The question is fundamental to the status of art or any of the forms of symbolic representation. Does art give us an escape from reality or a clearer, more
sharply focused view of reality?[48]

[46] WI 48-50 has a good discussion of Teiresias' views on pain and wine as a *pharmakon*. On the latter see also McDonald 270, citing Alcaeus 158.3 and 346.3 Lobel-
Page. The "drugs" of the Dionysiac cult may have been real hallucinogens: see
Devereux (1974) 40-42 and Thomson 439ff. (drawing on the medical hypotheses of
Dr. Bernard Barnett); but that possibility does not exclude Euripides' figurative and
symbolic use of the term and the idea in his play. Indeed, the use of real drugs in
the cult would only enhance the ambiguity of the figurative *pharmaka* of the god's
theatrical illusions.

[47] See Dodds, *Bacchae* ad 326-27, who translates, "For you are mad, cruelly mad:
no drug can cure your sickness, but some drug has caused it."

[48] For art as relief from pain in the late fifth century see Gorgias, *Helen* 8 and my
remarks (1962) 104ff., 124-26; Eur. *Helen* 1338-52. Earlier cf. Homer, *Odyssey*
4.221-26 and see Linda L. Clader, *Helen: The Evolution from Divine to Heroic in
the Greek Epic Tradition*, Mnemosyne Suppl. 42 (Leiden 1976) 32f. See also Plutarch, *Quomodo Adolesc. Poet. Sent. Docendi* 15 C ff., where the notion of poetry
as a *pharmakon* is still vital.

Nietzsche, philosopher of the Dionysiac, made the famous remark, "We have art that we may not perish of life." Euripides takes a different and more complex view.

The notion of poetry as escape had been already formulated centuries before by Hesiod. His Muses speak both truth and falsehood and offer both memory and oblivion (*Theogony* 27-28, 54-55, 102-103); the poet both lies and performs a morally and personally useful function in society (*Theogony* 22-34, 88-103). Even in Homer the song that gives "pleasure," *terpsis*, reawakens grief and invites to weeping and lamentation.[49] Bringing forgetfulness of sorrows but also reviving old suffering, poetry stands between pleasure and pain and between oblivion and memory.

Though Teiresias alludes to the ambiguity of the Dionysiac *pharmakon*, he does not know the whole truth. The joyful side of the god's gift appears only in its negative terms, removal of pain (280-83), and in its purely physical aspect, a kind of food, parallel to Demeter's "dry" gifts, with which men "are filled" (*plēsthōsi*, 281). The guard, who echoes these words about the "gift" of the "vine that brings cessation to pain" (772), adds a more intense physical pleasure (773-74): "Without wine there is no Kypris nor any other pleasure [*terpnon*] for mortals." It is ironical that both the prophet who sees things hidden from physical vision and the messenger who has witnessed miracles that testify to the more than physical power of the god should limit the joy of his gifts to its tangible, physical effects.[50] The Asiatic maenads know of more spiritual pleasures (cf. 73ff., 165ff.), although they know too that the god hates the one who scorns his "painfree pleasure of wine" (*oinou terpsin alypon*, 421-26). Yet none of the pleasures offered by the god's intoxications are simple. The drunkenness caused by Dionysus' wine may seem merely physical pleasure, its dangers and advantages fairly clear; but the play shows the intoxication of his

[49] E.g., *Odyssey* 8.83ff., 521ff.; cf. 1.325ff. The paradoxes of pain and pleasure in art are also present in the Gorgon's wail as the source of the flute song in Pindar *Pyth.* 12, on which see Eilhard Schlesinger, "Pindar, Pyth. 12," *Hermes* 96 (1968) 280ff. Soph. *Ajax* 74ff. and 82ff. may also reflect the paradoxical pleasure of the tragic spectacle.

[50] Contrast for example the much deeper religious spirit of Theonoe in the *Helen*. On the life of intellectual and spiritual quest and purity cf. frags. 184-202 N (*Antiope*), 369, 388, 897, 910 and see Nestle, *Vom Mythos zum Logos* 502; Festugière (1956) 78-80, 86; McDonald 271.

religious ecstasy to be far more dangerous than the inebriation of wine.[51]

The tragedy further qualifies and complicates this relation between pleasure and pain in the Dionysiac experience. Like his *pharmakon*, Dionysus' "joy" is a paradox that contains its two extremes simultaneously. Whereas his worshipers initially celebrate the joy and freedom from pain that he brings, the action takes us progressively into deeper pain. The beatitudes of the parode, "Blessed he who in happiness, knowing the god's rites, hallows his life" (73ff.), are totally overturned in the grim beatitudes uttered by the insane Agave at the end.[52] The god "takes pleasure" (*terpetai*) in honor, Teiresias warned Pentheus (321), but "honor," as we have seen, is one of the motive forces in the god's infliction of pain and sorrow. The "painlessness" of the god's gift extolled in the first half of the play (280-83, 381, 423, 772) recurs in ominous contexts later (cf. *alypos bios*, 1004). The maenads' "joyful labors" (*terpnoi ponoi*, 1054) result in "toils" of a harsher sort (*mochthoi*, 1105; cf. 873, 904). "Happiness," "joy," and "good fortune" become insanely horrible (1180, 1183, 1198).

The same paradoxes play about the theme of escape.[53] As the god liberates from pain, so, his worshipers sing, he permits us to "escape" to a happier and simpler world. The first stasimon, coming at a point where we are still under the spell of the beatific mystical union with the god in the parode, envisages an escape to Cyprus, a distant isle where love, poetry, and beauty join to create an idealized world of sensual and aesthetic fulfilment, the "rightful place for Bacchic revels" (403-15). But later a voyage to death is the foil to another "Land of the Blessed" (cf. 1338-39 and 1361-62). When the escape theme sounds again, necessity is closing in on Pentheus. The pastoral imagery of the fawn's escape from its "hunter" in the third stasimon (863-76) is a prelude to the terrifying inversions of hunter and hunted as Pentheus moves from palace to wild. His experience of the natural world there will bring just the reverse of the Chorus's "pleasure" in 868 and 874. The stasimon closes with a formal echo of the beatitudes of the parode (902ff.): "Happy the man who has fled the sea's storms and has reached the harbor. . . . Whoever has a happy life, him I count blessed" (902f., 910f.). But in counterpoint to these lines

---

[51] See Versényi 121.

[52] *Ba.* 1242, 1258, 1262 and cf. 1260, 1328. See De Romilly (1963) 372ff.

[53] See Arthur (1972) 154; WI 114; Di Benedetto 273-80.

Dionysus enters leading Pentheus dressed as a maenad in the play's most powerful visual enactment of the reversal of "happiness." The beatitudes of these "escape" odes, then, as often in Euripides, only set off the impossibility of escape from the necessity that is the gods.

When Pentheus takes off the *mitra* that symbolizes the god's illusionistic power, he awakens to a terrible reality, as Agave does later. The stage action itself—the maddening of Pentheus and his and Agave's return to sanity—shows us the power of the Dionysiac "drug" to hold us and absorb us in a quasi-hypnotic, escapist trance, and also the process of awakening from the fiction to a lucid grasp of reality. The play dramatizes both the power of madness and the possibilities for sanity, both folly and wisdom. Dionysus is both the drug and the antidote, the poison and the cure, the pleasure and the pain. In the ambiguity of the god's *pharmakon* Pentheus becomes a "grief" to himself that he may be a *terpsis*, "delight," to others.

As an "enchanter" or "magician" with "the wine-faced charms of Aphrodite in his eyes" (234, 236), Dionysus reflects the hedonist, escapist streak in Greek culture, the passionate commitment to the vital energies of existence, to the full experience of the moment, and the tendency to lift music, dance, festivity into a timeless realm where men share in the radiant bliss of the Olympian gods, one of whose number appears on earth to bestow this intoxicating delight upon mortals.[54] Yet that same god presides over the festal form that most uncompromisingly questions the meaning of existence, raises the spectral image of its emptiness, sees life as suffering, and broods heavily on the fragility of happiness, the ineluctability of sorrow, the iron-clad necessity of old age and death.

While apparently consoling us for the painfulness of existence by his gifts of "joy without pain" (772), Dionysus also reminds us through his other function as a god of the tragic mask that this escape can be only momentary.[55] If we receive that gift rightly, the "wisdom" or *sophia* extolled by his worshipers may remain with us beyond the few

[54] See Jeanmaire, *Dionysos* 295.

[55] Rohdich 167f. seems to touch briefly on this point: "The functions of the cult, to affirm and simultaneously to overcome the tragic essence of the world in the religiously founded, shortlived flight from that world, are the functions of tragedy; the attack by alleged reason (*Vernunft*) on the cult is the attack on tragedy" (167). Yet I cannot agree with Rohdich, if I understand him rightly, that the play presents the failure of tragedy in its function of "overcoming the tragic," whatever that would be.

hours of the spectacle, the "drug" of the fiction that has for a while given us "forgetfulness of the woes of the day" (282).

• VIII •

The "wisdom" of Dionysus is no simple *fröhliche Wissenschaft* ("joyful science"), but something that holds both knowledge and deception, truth and illusion. The play takes us through the experience of joyful immersion in the Dionysiac frenzy, where there is nothing of the individual self left over and the psyche itself is "enthiasized" (*thiaseuetai psychan*, 75) in collective emotion. Yet by revealing the destructive side of this loss of self it also arms us against the madness even as it portrays and effects its sweeping, irresistible power. In the paradoxes of the Dionysiac poetics the dissolution of order renews our feeling for the preciousness, as well as the precariousness, of that order. The experience of this madness helps make us more sane. The acceptance of the god's remoteness and inhumanity deepens our own humanity.

The cumulative anagnorisis that takes place within the fictive framework of the tragedy in the successive "recognitions" of Pentheus and Agave mirrors the anagnorisis, the self-recognition, of the spectator who has experienced and understood the play. Like Pentheus and Agave, he does not remain immersed in the illusion of the fiction but, thanks to the poet's "wise deception" (Gorgias' term again), passes through it to a vision wider than any of the protagonists and wider than his own before the play.

When the god is no longer disguised, the human characters also return to reality, only to recognize what they have done in their delusion. The apparent triumph of the Dionysiac madness only confirms the human reality to which the play's ending decisively turns. The excited, broken lyrics of Dionysiac elation (1153-99) give way to calmer iambic dialogue and to the logical stichomythic question and response between father and daughter. Agave's stichomythy with Cadmus that brings her out of madness contrasts strikingly with the lyric stichomythy with the maenad Chorus that confirms her in madness (cf. 1168-99 and 1263-1300). The short lyrical passage that closes the play is subdued, solemn, heavy (1368-92).

Cadmus' question-and-answer technique is the foil to that of the Stranger at the center of the play (811-44): the one brought Pentheus under the spell of Dionysiac madness; the other frees his mother and killer from that spell. This formal symmetry mirrors the play's own process of intoxication and disintoxification, of playful illusion and serious meaning, *paidia* and *spoudē*, or in Gorgias' terms, "deception" and "wisdom." Having lost the truth in the double deceptions of the poet's mimesis and the god's maskings and disguises, just as Pentheus and Agave lost their identities in the god-sent delusions, we the audience recover self and reality at a deeper level. The Dionysiac madness provides the occasion for us to test our human knowledge, the test through which we find what "wisdom" we possess.

In order to bring Agave back to the truth of her human identity and the suffering it now contains, Cadmus draws upon a truth outside the Dionysiac madness. He has journeyed back "to the mountain" no longer as a bacchantic follower and he has come back to the city in full knowledge of the fearful carnage committed outside. To the aether that Dionysus used as part of his illusion-creating madness (630; cf. 293), he now opposes the bright aether of the clear sky that dispels the clouds of madness (1264). After the puzzling "changes" of the god, he effects a change back to sanity (*metabolas, metastatheisa*, 1266, 1270). To the double vision of Dionysus' two suns (918ff.), he opposes the cold light of a single vision that sees pain and suffering for what they are (cf. 1257-63, 1282-83).[56] After the god's fusion of opposites, he brings "clarity" (*saphes*) and "thoughts" (*phrenes, phronein*) that are no longer the expression or the instruments of the god's power (cf. 1257-63, 1281-83 with 944, 947-48, 1123-24) but an independent means of assessing the present horrors and assuming responsibility: "When you have conscious thought [*phronein*] of what you have done," he tells Agave, "you will grieve a terrible grief" (1259; cf. 1270).

Agave's awakening from the Dionysiac madness revives the human capacities for moral knowledge, responsibility, and above all memory: "Father, how have I forgotten what we said before?" she asks as Cadmus brings her back to the relationships that define her identity (1272-76). She must now pronounce for herself the names she could not

[56] See Dyer 21.

hear on Pentheus' lips in his futile attempt at "recognition" (cf. 1118-21 and 1274-76).

The shock of the discrepancy between her "hunting" (1278) and the parameters of her life in the enclosed spaces of house and city frees her occluded mind and enables her to "see." What she is "holding in her hands" is in fact the vision of "her greatest grief" (eisidein, "see," 1279; ti leussō, "what do I see?" 1280; athrēson, "look," 1281; horō megiston algos, "I see my greatest grief," 1282; phainetai, "appears," 1283).[57] As the clouds of madness disperse, the effortless effort or joyful toil of the Dionysiac frenzy (cf. 873, 1105, 1053; also 280, 381, 423) is replaced by the "small effort," brachys mochthos, of mental struggle (1279). Earlier the labor of following the god seemed "without effort," amochthi (194). His victim's body was recovered only "with the effort's myriad searchings" (mochthōn myriois zētēmasin, 1218). Now Agave's spiritual effort is far greater than the god-eased task of uprooting whole trees (cf. mochthōn termata, 1105).

The anagnorisis here is also recognition of the destructive side of the god. Agave's stark perception, "Dionysus destroyed us; I learn it only now" (arti manthanō, 1296), completes the circuit. This deeper recognition takes us back once more to the horrible visual symbol of anagnorisis, the "visage-mask" or prosōpon that she holds in her hands (1277). The token of recognition between separated mother and son is not the tapestry, cradle, or heirloom of the plays with a happy ending like the Ion or the Taurian Iphigeneia, but the severed head/mask that Agave has just now "recognized" as her "greatest grief," to be joined now to the mangled corpse that Cadmus has so carefully pieced together (1300).[58] That last, grim act of the recognition is lost in the lacuna after 1329, but it was undoubtedly one of the most gripping scenes of a play already taut with overwhelming visual effects. No wonder that Agave's closing cry is for escape from Dionysiac visions (1383-85): "May I go where Cithaeron may not see me, nor I look on Cithaeron with my eyes."

The play is called Bacchants, and its last scene lingers over the

[57] "In her hands" in 1280 also echoes Pentheus' fantasy of being held "in his mother's arms" ("hands") in 969 and the maenads' maternal embrace of the wild animals in 699.

[58] Cadmus' statement in 1285, that the body "is lamented over before you recognized it" (ᾠμωγμένον γε πρόσθεν ἢ σὲ γνωρίσαι) also stresses the visual horror of this "recognition."

experiences of the Theban bacchants' leader. However much we may pity Pentheus, the tragic element at the end belongs to those who become bacchants, those who surrender to the god, fall completely under his spell, but still have to return to the social, ethical, familial world in which they live, to their cities, husbands, fathers, children. They return with the knowledge of this other part of themselves fully awakened and with the responsibility for what the Dionysus in them has done and can do.

The tragic "learning" (1296) that the play both enacts and describes is not an intellectual act alone but belongs to that mixed, ambiguous zone of everything involved with Dionysus. Dionysus defends his vengeance on the grounds that mortals did not learn, or learned too late: "But if you learned how to have good sense [*sōphronein egnōte*], you would be happy in the possession of Zeus's son as an ally. . . . Late you learned of us, but when you should have, you did not know" (1340-42; 1345). Even when Cadmus protests, "So we gained knowledge; but you came too harshly down upon us" (1346), Dionysus' ultimate defense is to adduce to the will of Zeus (1349). At this Agave gives up with the pathetic cry, "Alas the decree is passed, old man: exile miserable" (1350);[59] and Dionysus buries any further questioning with a harsh demand for haste: "Hurry up. Necessity commands" (1351).

For all the emphasis on learning, knowledge is singularly ineffective in the play. Cadmus' last line of iambic dialogue (which is also the last iambic trimeter in the play) is a helpless confession of not knowing, moving in its bareness and futility (1367):

οὐκ οἶδα, τέκνον· μικρὸς ἐπίκουρος πατήρ.

I do not know, child; your father is a feeble ally.

In her last lines, too, Agave, whose "recognition" commenced with throwing off "forgetfulness" (1272), asks for oblivion, a place where "no memorial [*mnēma*] of the thyrsus lies stored up" (1386). Her verb "stored up," *anakeitai*, also means "dedicated," and it was Pentheus' word, on the verge of his doom, for his "dedication" to the god (*soi gar anakeimestha*, 934). Thus even as she would forget, her language pulls us ironically back into the Dionysiac experience from which we

[59] For the *schema Pindaricum* in 1350 see Dodds, *Bacchae* and Roux ad loc. Roux well appreciates the pathos of the line.

have emerged with her. Instead of being a maenad fused with her
god, Agave passes over into the full human knowledge and remembering effected by the tragic spectacle; but her anagnorisis is also ours.

• IX •

Her word *mnēma* in the closing wish to escape the past ("May I go
. . . where no memorial of the thyrsus is stored up," μήϑ' ὅϑι ϑύρ-
σου μνῆμα ἀνάκειται, 1386) recalls the god's "memorial of [his]
thunder-smitten mother" in the prologue (ὁρῶ δὲ μητρὸς μνῆμα τῆς
κεραυνίας / τόδ' ἐγγὺς οἴκων, 6-7). That "memorial" of a dead mother
is embedded in the remoteness of Olympian power and in the joyful
vitality of his own powers as a god of the life force of the natural
world (cf. 11-12). Agave's "memorial" of her contact with Dionysiac
power holds the unbearable grief and remorse of having murdered a
son. In both cases the *mnēma* that commemorates the power of a god
is the token of mortal suffering. The two poles of the myth in its
tragic form here confront one another: memorializing the divine power
and bearing witness to human suffering and injustice through a monument which, in the last analysis, is only the fragile art-work of the
play itself.

Agave's rejection of "the thyrsus' memorial" in order to assert and
endure the autonomy of her suffering also enacts tragedy's separation
from myth, cult, ritual, and the other social forms that provide a
closure to the problems of meaning that tragedy raises. Agave, now
fully involved in the immanence of human suffering, rejects the kind
of monument that, in her sister's case, was authorized by remote
divine will or political advantage (6-12; cf. 30-31). The surge of her
own repugnance against the *thyrsou mnēma* lays the work open to the
paradoxes of its own deconstruction, that the fixity of the work of
tragic art as an ever-renewed source of pleasure is also an experience
of ever-renewed pain. Like the god's gift of wine, the play, which in
some sense is also the god's gift and the god's memorial, brings both
oblivion of pain and the power to stir our deepest, most buried mem-
ories of suffering and guilt.

Agave's lines at the end reject a view of the play as a *mnēma* to

Dionysus. The ongoing internal dynamic of human memory in experiencing and reexperiencing suffering contrasts with the static, frozen monumentalization of suffering in Semele's tomb. Agave refuses to be another Semele, to allow her suffering to be enclosed, delimited, explained like Semele's by Dionysus' frame of vine-covered tomb and Cadmus' frame of political sanction. Agave's "monument" is itself a questioning, a rejection, of monuments.[60]

In the prologue Dionysus acknowledged that Semele's *mnēma* is also a memorial to the "immortal violence of Hera against [his] mother," ἀθάνατον Ἥρας μητέρ' εἰς ἐμὴν ὕβριν, 9).[61] But the contradictions implicit in imbedding that memorial within the city are still hidden. At the end the sufferings of a mother who has played the roles of both a Semele (victim of divine persecution) and a Hera (female agent of divine cruelty) are the focal point for a movement away from the city. Her *mnēma* commemorates the harshness of a characteristically irrational Euripidean universe where the conflicting wills of childish gods catch innocent humans in a murderous crossfire.

In her refusal of Dionysus Agave points to the power of the tragedy to rise to a vision that is more inclusive than the Dionysiac experience. In so doing, she makes the play a monument not of the remote and immortal god but of her own (and Cadmus') human pain and loss. The end of the play thus pulls sharply against the civic frame within which it is to be performed. Agave, like Cadmus, moves into a noncivic place marked by the absence of those monuments to the god of which the play itself is one. Agave is perhaps the only exile in extant Greek tragedy to exit without a specific destination either foretold or implied.

[60] For the ambiguity of monumentalizing in Euripides see Pucci (1977) 181ff. and *Violence of Pity* 186f. On *mnēma* Roux ad loc. observes, "Toute offrande non périssable consacrée aux dieux est un *mnēma*, parce qu'elle a pour objet de rappeler en permanence à la divinité la piété du dédicant." Here, however, just that contrast between the dedicant and the "imperishable offering" that the *mnēma* should be is so powerful. Grube (1935) 53 too easily dismisses this last scene as "very weak" and adding "nothing whatever to the drama."

[61] The ambiguity of the "monumentalization" of Semele in the cult of Dionysus is intensified by the possibility of construing line 9, "Hera's immortal outrage against my mother," as an appositive to the "monument of Semele" in line 6 as well as the entire action of the sentence: for the syntactical complexities see Dodds, *Bacchae* ad loc.; Sandys ad loc.; WI 18 with n. 5; Verdenius (1980) 2-3. For the stage setting of Semele's tomb see Hourmouziades 51f.

These ambiguities of the monument/memorial parallel the ambiguities of memory and forgetting in the poetics of the Greek heroic tradition on which the play reflects. Poetry that extends memory far into the future also seeks to banish the recollection of suffering by absorbing us into the oblivion brought by its involving fictional world. It makes us forget sorrow by evoking the memory of others' sorrow. In the *Odyssey* Demodocus' songs about Troy immerse Odysseus in grief and weeping but give pleasure to the Phaeacians (*Od*. 8.83ff., 521ff.).

The prologue's concrete, tangible memorial to the power of the god and to the certainty of his rightful claim to belong within Thebes is balanced by the ambiguity of his presence in the hallucinatory scenes around the palace miracle (585ff., 618ff.) and indeed in the whole mechanism of a disguised god present onstage (cf. the *double entendres* of 470-518). The role of the monument as a symbol of the traditional function of poetry as commemoration is more profoundly undercut by Agave's rejection of the *mnēma* at the end, a rejection of the god's presence in her life henceforth. The monument to divine presence at the beginning becomes the focal point for a whole series of absences at the end: the missing role of Pentheus and the exiles of Cadmus and Agave.

The monument to this ambiguous presence/absence is ultimately the play itself, which enacts simultaneously the god's nearness and distance, the tangibility and the elusiveness of his power and his being, and the difficulty of comprehending him in any of the familiar structures of human discourse or society. As both a monument to Dionysus and as a rejection of such monumentalization, the play comes up against its own ambiguous role, conveying truth about the gods and questioning the divine order and an orderly world. As this position is also exactly that of Dionysus, the play is, after all, the (ironically) appropriate monument to the god whom it both celebrates and criticizes.

In heroic epic the monument is the assurance of eternal fame, the "glory imperishable" (*kleos aphthiton*) that confers a lasting value on the hero's life and surrounds his death with meaning, nobility, and grandeur. In the second great duel of the *Iliad*, the warriors fight no longer for a beautiful woman or possessions, but only for empty armor and the glory commemorated by dedicating it in a temple or by building a mound to mark the event. Hector sets forth the terms of the contest as follows (*Iliad* 7.77-91):

> If with the thin edge of the bronze he takes my life, then
> let him strip my armour and carry it back to the hollow ships,
> but give my body to be taken home again, so that the Trojans
> and the wives of the Trojans may give me in death my rite of burning.
> But if I take his life, and Apollo grants me the glory,
> I will strip his armour and carry it to sacred Ilion
> and hang it in front of the temple of far-striking Apollo,
> but his corpse I will give back among the strong-benched vessels
> so that the flowing-haired Achaians may give him due burial
> and heap up a mound upon him beside the broad passage of Helle.
> And some day one of the men to come will say, as he sees it,
> one who in his benched ship sails on the wine-blue water:
> "This is the mound of a man who died long ago in battle,
> who was one of the bravest, and glorious Hektor killed him."
> So will he speak some day, and my glory will not be forgotten.
>
> (Lattimore's translation)

The *Bacchae*, as we have seen, provides an ironical parody of these commemorative acts. The contest that would make Pentheus "conspicuous to all" (*episēmon onta pasin*, 967, "conspicuous" coming from the same root as the far-seen tomb, *sēma*, of *Iliad* 7.86) brings only the hero's degradation, not his ennoblement. The trophies hung up on the walls to commemorate the great exploit of the play (1212-15, 1238-43) constitute a massive reversal of the entire heroic code. The memorials that late Euripidean tragedy places at the center of the city preserve not "glory imperishable" but the "immortal violence" (10). Semele's *mnēma* is the visible mark of her absence (she is the missing daughter of Cadmus, the missing sister of Agave) and of her suffering as a victim of the gods. This absence is precisely symmetrical with the presence of the gods to whose power that tomb attests. She is present only through her absence and through the appropriate symbol of absence/presence, the memorial/tomb or *mnēma*.

The *mnēma* of Agave at the end has similar ambiguities: it is not for remembering but for forgetting, forgetting the dismemberment of her son in the wild. That act nearly deprives him of a *mnēma* within the city by making the body "no easy object of search" (1139, 1216-

21). It actually does deprive him of the heroic, martial death worthy of Homeric "glory imperishable" and its monumentalization in the kind of grave described by Hector above or in the kind of song that contains that description. For Pentheus, too, this ambiguous work is the proper *mnēma*.

All the memorials of the play are in a sense empty. Semele's holds, at best, charred ashes. Pentheus' body is reconstituted for a *mnēma* in a tomb only after painful search and repulsive effort. That effort over, Agave would go where there is no *mnēma* of the god's thyrsus. The mortals who are touched by Dionysus and his arts move ambiguously between memory and forgetting, re-collection and scattering, just as the god and his gifts move ambiguously between pleasure and pain, gentleness and horror (861).

In sharp contrast to the remote memorials of Semele or Agave is the very present body of Pentheus, left bloody and still unburied in the empty orchestra after the Chorus's exit-song at 1392.[62] His suffering has neither the alleviation nor the covering of the heroic "memorial," only the ambiguous monument that is the play.

The play is both a monument to past suffering—to all the suffering possible in a world of anthropomorphic gods and a capricious world-order—and also a reflection on the futility of such monumentalization, on the emptiness of the traditional strategies of the society to explain suffering or relieve the pain of loss: cult, memorials, fame.

Agave's self-chosen exile from "the thyrsus' monument" at the end is the exact negation of the conspicuousness of the monument at the beginning. Awakened from her homicidal madness, Agave would leave her polluted house for a place she knows not where (1366). The mountain of her past revels is not sanctified ground (the proper place for a monument to a god) but just the reverse, defiled and loathsome, *miaros* (1384), and she hopes never to see it again (1383-87).

· X ·

For Agave the Dionysiac experiences wipe out the middle ground of life where a stable human happiness is possible. For Cadmus, too,

---

[62] See Kott 187 and 222 on Pentheus' unburied body.

there is an unmediated polarity of bestiality and divinity. His bestial metamorphosis is imminent, but in the future stand the Islands of the Blest, place of a godlike bliss (1330-39). The future happiness— a distant token, perhaps, of the gods' mercy, as Anne Burnett suggests—seems hardly to matter in the overwhelming ruin that closes the play (cf. 1360-61).[63] Like Pentheus finally and like Agave, he confronts his suffering neither as the serpentine monster nor as the godlike hero that he will become but as a man, on the ground of his present helplessness and mortality. For all the fairy-tale quality of Dionysus' prophecy, Cadmus, in his own version of the god's account, sees nothing but an unhappy mortal end before him (1360-67):

Κα.   οὐδὲ παύσομαι
κακῶν ὁ τλήμων, οὐδὲ τὸν καταιβάτην
'Αχέροντα πλεύσας ἥσυχος γενήσομαι.
Αγ.   ὦ πάτερ, ἐγὼ δὲ σοῦ στερεῖσα φεύξομαι.
Κα.   τί μ' ἀμφιβάλλεις χερσίν, ὦ τάλαινα παῖ,
ὄρνις ὅπως κηφῆνα πολιόχρων κύκνος;
Αγ.   ποῖ γὰρ τράπωμαι πατρίδος ἐκβεβλημένη;
Κα.   οὐκ οἶδα, τέκνον· μικρὸς ἐπίκουρος πατήρ.

Cadmus.   Nor shall I cease from woes, alas miserable that I am, nor ever shall I find rest as I sail down the steep way to Acheron.

Agave.   My father, I shall be an exile, deprived of you.

Cadmus.   My poor child, why do you throw your arms around me in embrace, as the swan protects its white-haired helpless parent?

Agave.   Where then shall I turn, cast forth from my fatherland?

Cadmus.   I do not know, my child. Your father is an ally of little help.

These are among the most moving lines in the play. As in the *Hippolytus* and the *Heracles*, the divine personages recede into the background and the two mortal survivors, their lives wrecked, cling to one

[63] Burnett (1970) 29. Lesky, *TDH* 497 cites Pindar *Ol.* 2.78 but remarks, "Weder Dionysos in seinem strafenden Schlusswort, noch Kadmos selbst in seinen Klagen berücksichtigt die schliessliche Erhöhung." See also Dodds, *Bacchae* ad 1360-62; also Rosenmeyer 109, 112.

another for the little time that remains to them, desolation all around and exile or worse ahead. The indifferent justice of the gods elicits and highlights by contrast the love, devotion, and protectiveness of these two people to one another.[64] Alone with Agave, Cadmus could effectively help her to find the way back to herself. When the god appears, his power to comfort and aid suddenly fails, and limp helplessness replaces calm wisdom and control. The embrace of father and daughter is no less poignant, but in the distance between the mortals on the ground and the god above (on the *theologeion*) futility and hopelessness once more dominate and hold to the end.[65]

Cadmus' swan simile in 1365 contrasts with the earlier comparisons of the Theban maenads, in their triumphant and destructive fury, to flocks of birds (748, 957). Description of the flock changes to focus on the single bird. Gory pollution changes to whiteness, savage bestiality to the shared feelings of a recovered humanness. The animal imagery now conveys deep human feelings. In these last lines the poetic spirit of the early odes and speeches moves from Dionysus to Cadmus and Agave. The god has grown up, as it were, and lost the youthfulness and playfulness shown in the previous odes about him. He has become as austere an Olympian as the Aphrodite of the *Hippolytus* or the Hera of the *Heracles*. The drama moves from lyrical mysticism to human suffering; and poetry moves from the mountains back to the city, from Asia to Thebes, reclaiming its age-old function of expressing and consoling the grief of men and women with whom we identify.

These gentle and reflective gestures contrast not only with the bacchants' frenzy but also with Cadmus' temporary maenadism as he "shook his hoary locks" (cf. *polios* in 185 and 324) in a Bacchic

[64] See Glover 88: "The only good things that remain undefiled at the end are the love and loyalty of human beings to each other; and how impotent these are." See also Grube, *Drama* 417f. and Conacher 71f. Kirk ad 1365, however, can find "a cynical reflection by the poet on the self-centeredness both of Agave and of her father at this point."

[65] Dionysus' appearance in his proper divine form on high at the end contrasts, of course, with his appearance in the orchestra in mortal guise in the prologue: see Hourmouziades 163 and Sansone (1978) 43 with n. 18. Note also the echoes of the prologue here (cf. 1340f. with 1f. and 53f.). In this distance, both physical and emotional, between god and mortals, as Steidle notes (38, n. 29), "kommt die göttliche Unbedingtheit ebenfalls schroff zum Ausdruck."

rejuvenation. Now he accepts his extreme old age and has displayed the wisdom and compassion appropriate to it. For all his recognition of his helplessness, Cadmus discerns the consoling element in his daughter's gesture, and he responds in similar terms, though he has to admit that the "help" he can offer is small (1367, *mikros epikouros*). At the same time the embrace by "hands" (*amphiballeis chersin*, 1364) that are still stained with kindred blood reminds us that this last touch by father and daughter, like Oedipus' embrace of his daughters at the end of Sophocles' *Oedipus Tyrannus*, occurs in the shadow of a house destroyed by the most terrible pollutions.[66]

The last lines of iambic dialogue allow us to measure the distance that we have traversed in our knowledge of the god and all that he implies, a movement from the joyful to the dark and destructive side of his power, from ecstatic bliss to misery, from group experience to isolation, from youthful energy to defeated old age, from vitality to death, from song to lamentation and silence. "I too am young" (*hēbō*, 190), Teiresias had said, as he joined Cadmus in the Bacchic dance. But when Cadmus returns with Teiresias from the mountain, it is with "the *old* Teiresias from the bacchants" (*syn tō[i] geronti Teiresiā[i] Bakchōn para*, 1224); and Cadmus feels the full weight of years on his own "white-haired" head.[67] The singing associated with the swan and also with the delight of the bacchantic ecstasy in the parode, the first stasimon, and the latter part of the second stasimon is as far as possible from lyricism. Cadmus' confident contrivances (cf. *sophismata*, 30; 180-83), voluble advice (330-32), reflective funeral eulogy (1302-26), or even protest against the god (1346, 1348) change to the three simple words of broken strength and utter futility, "I do not know, child" (*ouk oida, teknon*, 1367).

In the swan simile just before, Cadmus calls himself a "drone," *kēphēn*, a metaphor for his uselessness. The image suggests by contrast the loss of the Golden-Age abundance of the Dionysiac intensity, when honey flowed freely from the earth (cf. 142-46, 710-11). Shortly before, amid the wreckage of his house, Cadmus bitterly observed

---

[66] For the destructive force of "hands" see 969, 1136, 1207, 1209, 1237, 1247; above, Chap. 3, sections 3-4 and Chap. 7, n. 23.

[67] In 1310, too, Cadmus refers to himself as "the old man," *gerōn*, when Pentheus was alive. Cf. also 1025.

that he will no longer "sail in calm [*hēsychos*] down to steep-plum-meting Acheron" (1361-62). He is here ironically echoing the maenad Chorus's beatitudes about the "life of calm" (*hēsychia*, a key word for the happy effects of Dionysiac worship)[68] and "thoughts untossed [by the sea]" (389-92). "Happy he who has fled the sea and reached the harbor; happy he who has passed beyond toils" (*mochthōn*, 902-5): those were among the Chorus's closing generalities just before Dionysus led in the dazed Pentheus. But now those toils have been extreme (cf. 1279; 1346), and the "sailing" that lies ahead for one of the two survivors is a harsh voyage to Hades.

That ode concluded with a traditional reflection on the differences in human fortunes ("In different ways one surpasses another in wealth and power," 905-906) and the instability of hopes: "Some [hopes] end in wealth for mortals, others depart. Whoever has a life of happiness [*biotos eudaimōn*] for the day, him I bless as happy" (*makarizō*, 908-11). The shift from the blissful *makarismoi* of the parode to this conventional wisdom about the uncertainty of human happiness is a heavily underlined effect. But the gnomic generality becomes visually specific in the person of Cadmus, whose "good fortune" (*eutycheis*, 1024) introduces the news of Pentheus' miserable end. He is the instrument by whose means Agave is brought from her illusion of bliss, happiness, good fortune (*makar, eudaimōn, eutychēs*, 1232, 1242-44, 1258) to the reality of "ill fortune" (*dysdaimonia*, 1262, 1292), and finally he stands before us on the stage totally crushed and without hopes.

Agave's closing reference to "other bacchants" (1387) may suggest that the god's cult will now be firmly established in Thebes and in Greece. But the triumph appears only as part of the ruin of the lives touched by the god. It is part of the parallel between Agave and Semele that the god appeared in exactly the same way in the prologue, by the tomb that marks his mother's ruin. As in other Euripidean plays that conclude with a cultic or ritual foundation—particularly *Medea* and *Hippolytus*—the consolation offered by the memorial or commemoration (Agave's *mnēma* of 1385) is ironical or embittered,[69] and what emerges of value is not the luminous divinity estab-

---

[68] For *hēsychia* see 622, 636, 647, 790.
[69] See Pucci, *Violence of Pity* 182ff. and (1977) passim; Segal (1978/79) 139.

lished among men but the decency, loyalty, and pity of the human survivors left among the wreckage.

It is certainly not accidental that our view of the establishment of that cult comes through the eyes of Cadmus and Agave. In the case of Cadmus the establishment of the god's worship in Thebes is balanced by his expulsion from the city he founded and by his attack on holy places (1359), for those "altars" belong to other gods, and Apollo is specifically mentioned at 1336-38. We are reminded of the future cycles of disorder and chaos among both gods and men in Artemis' vengeance on some hapless devotee of Aphrodite in the *Hippolytus* (1416-22), presumably the makings of another tragic suffering.[70]

In the case of Agave, who has experienced the god to the full, the rite is a subject of personal revolt and revulsion.[71] For her, too, the establishment of Dionysus in Thebes contrasts with her exile from Thebes, a point she dwells on with pathetic insistence (*phygai, phygas, symphygades,* all terms for "exile," 1350, 1370, 1382; cf. 1366). The god's incorporation into a civic structure contrasts with the total disorientation and chaos of her life: "Where shall I turn, cast forth from my fatherland?" is her last iambic line in the play.

Her exile is also a flight from her own guilt as well as from the god and his worship; but in both cases it is a flight that exiles her from all joy in life. The erstwhile "companions of her revels" (*synkōmos,* 1172) are now the "pitiable companions of exile" (*symphygades oiktrai,* 1382; cf. 1146). For both Cadmus and Agave the flicker of civilized values in their recognition and compassion comes in the physical presence of the mutilated body of the dead king, who for all his faults is still the symbol of the civic order of Thebes. But he is also a symbol of a dismembered society whose pieces can be put together only for burial.

---

[70] Commentators suggest connections with the oracles foretelling the sack of Delphi in the Persian War: see Hdt. 9.43. The possible historical reference, however, does not change the picture of the chaotic world order. Cf. also Hdt. 5.61.

[71] Lesky, *TDH* 499 suggests that in Agave's response at the end "lebt etwas von dem Widerstande des Pentheus weiter, den der Gott zu seinen Opfer machte." We should also note the harsh contrast between Agave's jubilant triumphal entrance (1186) and her exit here, a contrast in which, as Steidle 38 suggests, "das ganze Ausmass der Katastrophe sichtbar wird."

· XI ·

The dark vision of the *Bacchae* invites comparison with the contemporary works of his fellow dramatists, Sophocles and Aristophanes. The *Oedipus at Colonus* at least partially closes the breach between divine and human justice that is so insuperable in Euripides. The outcast hero can find a place in city marked by political order and religious reverence. The quintessentially pious, civilized community of Theseus' Athens can welcome the polluted wanderer, shelter him within its own civic and sacred order, and receive in return the mysterious healing power that the aged Oedipus has to confer.

There can perhaps be no clearer contrast in the response to the social, moral, and intellectual crises at the end of the fifth century than these two plays. The sacred grove of Colonus that delimits Athens from the wild outside contrasts with the dissolution of those boundaries in the *Bacchae*.[72] A good king and a secure polis contrast with an unstable, tyrannical king and a city on the verge of disintegration. In the *Coloneus* the gods bring ultimate peace and mercy after suffering, whereas in the *Bacchae* the god is vengeful and the divine order is divided, chaotic, ambiguously just. The miracle of the *Coloneus* is a mysterious divine grace that subsumes an ancient crime into a larger order reaching beyond the grave; in the *Bacchae* the miracles are "part of the uncanny forces rising from the background to conquer man's reason and self-reliant independence."[73]

In the *Frogs* Aristophanes can send Dionysus down to Hades to recover the moral and aesthetic vitality that has disappeared from Athens with the death of its great tragic poets. Descending on a dangerous journey to recover Euripides, Dionysus finds himself involved in an endeavor of another kind, judging a contest of dramatic and poetic talent between Euripides and Aeschylus. Choosing the older, more traditional, more socially cohesive dramatist over the new, iconoclastic, radical Euripides, Dionysus recovers something of his own identity as a communal, civilizing deity, a god of the moral integrity and vitality that Athens has lost. And, in this restoration and reintegration of Dionysus as the god of the healthy civic spirit of the dra-

[72] On the grove at Colonus see Segal, *Tragedy and Civilization* 371-76, 391-92.

[73] See Wasserman (1953) 568. The whole of this brief article has a number of suggestive comparisons and contrasts between the *Bacchae* and the OC.

matic festivals, Athens too regains a lost life and energy in a world of death.[74] This, too, is a vision very different from the ambiguous, disintegrative Dionysus of the *Bacchae*.

The "most tragic" of the dramatists, as Aristotle called him, Euripides has a more rigorous, uncompromising view of Dionysus. He refuses to let us evade the basic contradiction between the god of the civic rituals and the god of the ecstasies and frenzy on the wild mountainside. Teiresias or Cadmus, after the manner of political and religious leaders and administrators, would skillfully neutralize the god so as to render his cult socially and politically useful. Theirs is a humane, philanthropic endeavor, even if marred by shallowness. But the chasm between their view of Dionysus and the Dionysus experienced without the supervision of civic magistrates or the limitation of social norms is too great, ultimately, to be bridged. Euripides insists on the radical otherness of the god, his cult, and all that the cult and the god involve. That insistence and that vision are what give the play such disturbing power and profound truth. He thereby provides a view of the essential contradictions that every culture contains: the necessity for repression and for its release; the existence of the irrational, the ecstatic and the murderous, and the necessity for their release too; the necessary interaction between "officially affirmed and officially negated patterns," between approved, normative values and marginal, suppressed anti-values in the constitution of human society and human civilization;[75] and the role of art in revealing and symbolically enacting these contradictions.

Tragedy itself, as we have seen, emerges as the natural vehicle for incorporating Dionysus into the city and into society. The vicarious reception of Dionysus into the center of the polis through the play obviates the necessity for the violent reception that the play depicts, just as the play-sacrifice of Pentheus obviates the necessity for choosing and murdering a real victim-pharmakos. Dionysus as the god of

---

[74] For this aspect of Dionysus in the *Frogs* see Segal (1961) 212ff. On the relation between the *Frogs* and the *Bacchae* see Carrière 120-24 (the *Frogs* is Aristophanes' reply to Euripides' atheistic attack on Dionysus) and Cantarella (1971) and (1974), especially 308-10 (Aristophanes' concern to demonstrate the other side of the god of tragedy).

[75] George Devereux, *From Anxiety to Method in the Behavioural Sciences* (The Hague 1967) 212. See also L. A. Montrose, "The Purpose of Playing: Reflections on a Shakespearean Anthropology," *Helios*, vol. 7, no. 2 (1979-80) 51-74, esp. 62ff.

tragedy is both the double and the surrogate of the *Bacchae*'s god of frenzy and madness: his appearance on the stage of the Athenian theater insures that that city will not suffer what the Euripidean Thebes suffers in receiving him. At the same time the image he reflects of the city and the citizens is a network of criss-crossing tensions and paradoxes. Only a form able to incorporate this god's necessary contradictions will be able to contain him within the civic space. The neutralized forms of Cadmus' or Teiresias' rationalism, flimsy constructs of *logos*, will be shown for what they are when they confront the full Dionysiac experience outside the limits of the city, in the wilds of Cithaeron.

The Dionysiac "conversion" in the play is not the shallow acceptance of the god by Cadmus and Teiresias, but, as Walther Kranz suggests,[76] the poet's own newly awakened capacity to convey in language the untrammeled energies of the god, to write "as the old servants of Dionysus felt"—but (and it is a critical "but") without obscuring the price one might pay for that intensity. Agave, Cadmus, and Pentheus are the victims of Dionysus; but they are also, in another way, the victims of the poet, the surrogates of his own inner life whom he sacrifices to his own demons. In their deaths he acts out symbolically the price he himself pays for venturing beyond the safe limits of experience and language, and for exploring the exposed, interstitial realm beyond or beneath the familiar and acceptable norms and patterns of behavior, the places in himself and in us all where the polarities between bestiality, humanity, and divinity collapse, where conflicting drives and energies meet at their most heightened and uncompromising exigency. These are the places where the Theban or civic Dionysus dissolves into the ambiguities of the Asian Dionysus, the outsider, the god "most gentle and most terrible" at the same time (861).

The suffering of the mortal characters of the play, then, is at some level the suffering of the poet who created them. It is part of the price that Dionysus, as the god of every type of illusion, exacts for the participating audience's Pentheus-like vision of the unity-in-contradiction, the coexistence of pleasure in pain, revealed through his mysterious nature. For representing and grasping this mystery, tragedy is the appropriate, the definitive form, with its masking and unmasking, its interplay of illusion and truth, surface and depth, its systematic reversals and its exploration of the identity of opposites.

---

[76] Kranz, *Stasimon* 235; see also 248–49.

By choosing as his central figure a god whose very nature is the coexistence of contraries and the crossing of boundaries, Euripides provides a summation and distillation, of a sort, of his tragic art, while also fashioning a powerful representation of an essential quality of all tragedy, the polarization of what we call reality into mutually contradictory extremes that are also coexistent with one another. Self-clarification blends with self-destruction. Madness crosses over into truth, truth into madness. Is Pentheus saner, more *sōphrōn*, when he fulminates against the maenads or when he acts on his desire to see them on the mountain? Only by fusing with his opposite and double, with the god and with the part of himself whom he resists and yet loves, who inspires both resistance and erotic fascination, can he discover what he is.

Corresponding to this chaos of the soul, this inability to bring the two sides of his identity together, is the chaos of the world-order. *Dikē*, the notion of the just distribution of prerogatives in an orderly system of exchange and worth, is lacking in both the internal balances of the king's personality and in the external constitution of the world, in both man's relation with himself and in his relation with the gods. The extension of *dikē* from microcosm to macrocosm characteristic of tragedy is also part of the multivalence of Dionysus: a divinity of the world-order governed by the gods and a power and a need within the human soul.[77]

In this gap between the justice executed by the god and the justice demanded by mortals lies another gap that refuses to be closed, one

---

[77] *Dikē*, justice, is obviously an important theme in the play. Pentheus, Dionysus, and the Chorus all have conflicting claims and views on it. Pentheus vehemently claims *dikē* in 356f., 673, 676, but his relation to *dikē* is clearly ambiguous (cf. 518, 673), and *dikē* finally turns against him: cf. 847f., 995ff., 1043, 1249, 1312, 1327f., 1344. It is interesting that Cadmus finally comes to agree, in part, with the Chorus's view, but not on the severity of the punishment; cf. 1312 with 1327f. On the other hand Pentheus defended Cadmus from *adikia* (1320ff.); and Dionysus' *dikē* has its problematical side: 1249f., 1343ff. In like manner *hybris* is the subject of claims and counterclaims between Pentheus and Dionysus. Pentheus accuses Dionysus of *hybris* in 247 and 779; the maenads so accuse Pentheus in 375 and 555; and Dionysus claims that he has been a victim of *hybris* in 1347. Yet he and his followers are also capable of *hybris* (113, 743), just as Pentheus can defend old Cadmus against *hybris* (1311). See in general WI 23-25, 143-45; Dyer 22f. We may compare the shifting values of *dikē* and its ambiguities in the *Helen* too: see Gilberte Ronnet, "Le cas de conscience de Théonoé ou Euripide et la sophistique face à l'idée de justice," *RPh* 53 (1979) 251-59. See above, Chap. 6, n. 58.

at the center of all tragedy in the classical tradition. Like Aphrodite in *Hippolytus*, Dionysus is one of the laws of existence which, if violated, brings a justice that is immediate, absolute, and for the god beyond sorrow, regret, or compassion: "What for man is guilt is for the god merely a matter of fact."[78] Early in the play Dionysus' cult promised the fusion of worshiper and divinity. Now that the god has destroyed an opponent born from mortal woman (*paidos ex emēs ge-gōs*, 1309) and made a surviving mortal "childless of male children" (*ateknos arsenōn paidōn gegōs*, 1305), his repeated expressions for divine and human birth at the end stress the impassable distance between one who is "born mortal" and one "born from a god": "Ares' daughter, Harmonia, whom you have, a mortal born" (*thnētos gegōs*, 1332); "Not born of mortal father [*ouchi thnētou patros ekgegōs*] do I speak these things, but as the son of Zeus" (1340-41); "Yes, for I suffered insult from you, I born a god" (*theos gegōs*, 1347). Dionysus' emphasis on the gap between human and divine also cancels Cadmus' earlier attempt to bring god and man together, for the greater glory of Thebes, in his lie that Semele "may seem to have given birth to a god" (*dokē[i] theon tekein*, 335).

Through these and related passages the play traces the elusiveness of Dionysus back to the conjunction and separation of mortal and immortal. In the attempt, and the ultimate failure, of mortals to encompass the eternal in their lives and in their works lies much of the impulse behind Greek tragedy, probably all tragedy. The *Bacchae* locates the source of that tragic discrepancy in the birth of Dionysus, which brings together, powerfully and enigmatically, sexuality and death, celestial and chthonic, the forces of creation and destruction in our world and ourselves.

Both the lucid rationalization of Dionysus' nature, expounded by a mortal character who stands before us with his prophetic authority, and the multiform epiphanies in and behind the stage action only refer us back to the complexities of the god's origins, to the obscurity, both moral and objective, of something that lies hidden in mystery, outside of the theatrical space and beyond the dramatized, or dramatizable, events. The privileged, suspended world of the play comes

[78] Wasserman (1929) 285; also (1953) 561f.; Grube (1935) 52, on viewing Dionysus as an elemental power, a force of nature, which, when unleashed, goes its own way regardless of the damage it may cause to human life.

into being in this gap between ordinary language, ordinary causality, and the places that hold the birth of the god. Through the failure of Thebes to incorporate Dionysus without its own dismemberment, the play also dramatizes the impossibility of closing that gap. As Dionysus is the god of the theater as well as the god of Thebes, this failure is also among the paradoxes of tragedy's artistic truth. The triumph of the god of (theatrical) illusion is also the destruction of the world his theater creates.

As both external to Thebes, a surplus added from outside to an existing whole, and as a native belonging inherently to Thebes, Dionysus' irruption into the city follows the paradoxical logic of Derrida's "supplement."[79] He is necessary to complete the whole and at the same time exposes its deficiency. In adding himself to the mortals and their world, he reveals their incompleteness to such an extent that they are destroyed. Yet in their destruction they demonstrate the god's incompleteness too. Like Zeus with Semele, Dionysus can enter and manifest his power in the mortal world only by destroying it. And like Zeus with Semele, he is a presence afterwards only through the absence, the trace, marked by the monuments left behind.

The play began with a narrative of Dionysus' birth that subsequent events reveal, dramatically, as increasingly problematical, at least for the mortals asked to believe it. The play closes with a similar problem, the gap between the visualized stage action of the present and the strange metamorphosis of Cadmus and Harmonia in the future, narrated as a prophecy by Dionysus, *ex machina*. The vividness of a dramatized present moment onstage only sets off the obscurity of past and future history. In other terms, the play not only calls attention to the gap between narration and dramatic visualization but also shows language as the necessary, and necessarily inadequate, mediator between these two forms of fictional representation. In the prologue Dionysus, narrating the tale of his own birth, held out the promise of divinity present among men: he was assuming a mortal shape to play his part in the drama. Now, defending the barrier that separates

---

[79] See Jacques Derrida, *On Grammatology*, trans. G. C. Spivak (Baltimore 1976) 144f., 280ff., 303ff., 313f.; also Vincent Descombes, *Modern French Philosophy*, trans. L. Scott-Fox and J. M. Harding (Cambridge 1980) 147f., who summarizes as follows (148): "The supplement outside stands for the missing part inside the whole. It is because the whole does not succeed in *being everything* that a supplement from without must be added, in order to compensate its defective totality."

men from gods, he speaks from the unreachable distance symbolized by the *theologeion*, an even more elusive object of knowledge than he was in the prologue.

In tragedy, unlike epic, continuous narrative marks a new stage of crisis, a new obstacle or difficulty. The essential quality of the dramatic form, dialogic exchange or lyric interaction with events, is interrupted. Instead of an interplay between word and action, speech and spectacle, there is only description, narration. Even the narrative has no meaning until we see how the principal actors respond to it.[80]

At such moments the dramatic action, *qua* drama, is revealed as unequal to the task it must perform. The thread is carried by a narrative form from which the actors are, in one sense, excluded. At such moments they are silent, absent, or included in the narration only as third-person elements in a story, not the creators of the story that they themselves, as actors, make appear before our eyes in the three-dimensional solidity of the performance.

The previous chapter tried to show how the play enacts the gap between seen and unseen (narrated) events, staged and imagined acts. No verbal explanation proves ultimately able to circumscribe the tale of Dionysus' birth, even though that event is the ultimate cause of the events now unrolling before us. The play can only testify to our distance from that primary event; it shows the fiction, and the language of the fiction, as unable to close the gap between itself and what impelled it into being. Dionysus' birth, union of mortal and divine, earth and fire, perishable and eternal substance, can only leave behind among men the ambiguous trace of its problematical origin and its equally problematical "monument" (6-9).

Dionysus' beginnings are the beginnings both of the "story" (*histoire*)—the myth as it might be told in chronological order in the handbooks—and the "plot" (*récit*), the artistic structuring of events in this play. The elusiveness of these beginnings is in part the question of whether Dionysus' arrival marks a *return to origins* and therefore a creative completion of Thebes, of the audience, of coherence at the level both of plot and of world, or whether it marks a *return of the*

---

[80] For these questions see my essay, "Literacy, Tragedy, Orality," above, n. 2. On recitation versus dramatic performance see Reiss, *Tragedy and Truth* (above, n. 2) 28.

repressed, bringing the destruction and dissolution of all of the above.[81] The parallelism between the mysterious "monument" of origin (6-9) and the centrifugal "monument" of ending maintains the meaning of Dionysus' appearance as a problem, open and unresolved for us as for Thebes.

On this monument, which is itself the play, the play inscribes the presence of the god, which is also fully an absence: his elusiveness and remoteness, the gap that he leaves in language. Hence the necessary complementation between the "monuments" of Semele and Agave. The close and tangible presence of the "monument" described by the god in the prologue, created verbally as well as visually when he takes on mortal form to associate with men (1-9), has that rejected distant monument as its inseparable other side. The literal monument of a dead mother in a city that has rejected him parallels the figurative monument of a doomed mother who has accepted him.

Even the tangible monument of Semele is ambiguous: it points back to the incompatibility of the birth of this god and a mortal constitution. For all the authority of the god's account of it here or of the mysterious fire of the palace miracle later (596-99), it only leads back to the infinite regress of his hidden origins, mysteries of birth and death, god and man, *semper cedentia retro.* The *mnēma* of both Semele and Agave memorializes the god and his origins under a paradoxically negative sign—paradoxical because it does the opposite of what a monument is expected to do. This monument only marks the inability of verbal and visual representation to encompass its most essential, most yearned-for, and most elusive reality.

Concluding his account of Pentheus' gory death, the Messenger proclaimed (1150-52): "To have good sense [*sōphronein*] and revere what belongs to the gods [*sebein ta tōn theōn*] is the noblest thing. I think this the wisest [*sophōtaton*] possession too for the mortals who enjoy it." Words like "good sense," "noblest," "wisest" have a strange ring when "what belongs to the gods," *ta tōn theōn,* inspires the insane and bloodthirsty fury that has just been described. Still closer to the event, Cadmus sums up, "If there is anyone who scorns the gods [*daimonōn hyperphronei*], let him believe in gods when he looks at this man's death" (1325-26). Cadmus' view of the gods elsewhere

---

[81] For the two kinds of "return" see Peter Brooks, "Freud's Masterplot," *Yale French Studies* 55/56 (1977) 288.

in this scene does not smooth the way to platitudinous moralizing (cf. 1249, 1346, 1348). Here he says not a word about justice: it is the death of mortals that proves the existence of the gods.[82] The monumentalizing effect of these lines again puts truth about divinity in the form of an absence, the death of the king and his necessary absence from the last act of the drama.

· XII ·

In placing the god of illusion and the tragic mask at the center of the inexplicable, the nonjustifiable, the irrational in experience, and in setting it off sharply against the rationalizing *logos* of Teiresias that would absorb it or the emotional vehemence of Pentheus that would reject it, Euripides cuts to the core of the tragic view of the world. Suffering and violence are always in some sense irrational because no explanation can ever fully account for them or ever fully remove the pain, physical or emotional, present or remembered, that they leave behind. Just because they elude logic and reasonableness they have some kinship with Dionysus and find expression in that Dionysiac form we call tragedy.

At the end of the Gilgamesh epic, the hero who returns from his quest for his dead companion, Enkidu, brings back not the magical talisman of eternal life but the tale of its loss. That is what he engraves on the tablets and builds into the walls of his city of Uruk.[83] The gap

[82] Is there just possibly an ambiguity in 1325f.? Cadmus sums up the disaster of his house thus: "If there is anyone who scorns the gods, looking at his death, let [one] believe in the gods," ἐς τόνδ' ἀθρήσας θάνατον ἡγείσθω θεούς (1326). It is admittedly torturing the syntax of 1326 a little, but not beyond the limits of Euripidean possibility, to translate, "Looking at this man's house, let him think the gods [to be] death." I am not forgetting the difficulties in the way of so construing *toude* nor the problem of the omission of *einai*. Given Euripides' play on double meanings, however, I wonder if it is not possible as a secondary meaning or *Doppelsinn*—a conceptual tool to be used most sparingly but perhaps justified here.

[83] *The Epic of Gilgamesh*, Akkadian Version, in James B. Pritchard, ed., *Ancient Near Eastern Texts Relating to the Old Testament*, 2nd ed. (Princeton 1955) 7 (tablet I.i.5-10):

The hidden he saw, laid bare the undisclosed.
He brought report of before the Flood,

between human life and immortality, between desire and reality, between passion and the laws of the universe, is thus incorporated, literally, into the city and made part of its physical barrier between culture and nature. So too the poet of Greek tragic drama, like that of Sumerian epic, does not restore order through or against the suspension of the aesthetic frame of his work. Rather, he inscribes the gap between order and disorder, justice and chaos, in his paradoxical monument to the coherence of the city and its celebration of itself. He inscribes that gap into the city at its center, its ritual forms, the language of its citizens, the houses of the parents and children that it shelters.

Whereas the mythical or folktale hero often brings back some tangible boon, magical token, symbol of power, or precious gift to be stored forever as a safe and prized possession, the tragic hero brings back from his exploit beyond the city not order, but the afterglow of an experience that questions all the familiar conceptions of order. One thinks of Aeschylus' Agamemnon or the Heracles of Euripides or of Sophocles (in the *Trachinian Women*), of Ajax or Philoctetes, or of Agave here. Through Agave's, Cadmus', and Pentheus' experience, commemorated in the tragic performance, the city inscribes at its center not a victory over chaos but a tension between order and chaos. This is the paradoxical "monument" through which the city takes Dionysus into itself. The head/mask with which Agave enters for the last scene, as we have seen, is the play's richest and most ambiguous reflection on itself and its god. What Agave brings back from her journey is not the "wisdom" (*sophia*) so tantalizingly and elusively held out to us throughout the play, but an absence, an emptiness. The "wisdom" that union with the god seemed to offer proves to be something possibly consisting not in fusion but in separation, not in epiphanic presence but in the contradictions and paradoxes of absence, in the framing and distancing of fiction, language, art.

It is perhaps necessary, if optimistic, for those engaged in the work of civilization to believe that by getting some hold—through symbolic

Achieved a long journey, weary and worn.
All his toil he engraved on a stone stela.
Of ramparted Uruk the wall he built,
Of hallowed Eanna, the pure sanctuary.

representation—on our capacity for violence, murder, the insane infliction of suffering, we can somehow control it. Myth and tragedy,
for all their apparently unreal fantasies, are one way of getting this
hold. "The legend tries to explain the inexplicable," Franz Kafka
wrote about another ancient myth, "but, since it comes from a ground
of truth, it must end once more in the inexplicable."[84]

[84] Franz Kafka, "Prometheus," in *Parables and Paradoxes*, ed. N. H. Glatzer (New
York 1961) 82: "Die Sage versucht, das Unerklärliche zu erklären. Da sie aus einem
Wahrheitsgrunde kommt, muss sie wieder im Unerklärlichen enden."

9

Dionysiac Poetics
and Euripidean Tragedy

Οὐ ξυνιᾶσιν ὄκως διαφερόμενον ἑωυτῷ
ὁμολογέει· παλίντροπος ἁρμονίη ὄκωσπερ
τόξου καὶ λύρης.

They do not understand how being drawn
apart it is in agreement with itself: a back-
stretched harmonious fitting, as of bow and
lyre.

Heraclitus

In the poetry of Homer, Hesiod, and Aeschylus the myths of the
gods are a source of order. In the poetry of Euripides the myths of
the gods, more often than not, are a source of disorder. One must
either reject "the wretched words of the poets," as the hero does at
the end of the *Heracles* (1346), or else, as the *Bacchae* does, make
the tension between order and chaos, destructive randomness and
creative meaningfulness, the mainspring of the work instead. In the
latter process the centrality of an heroic protagonist of the Aeschylean
or Sophoclean type takes second place to the shaping artistry of the
work itself. Here the checks and balances, inadequately labeled "ironic,"
maintain meaning as a dialectic of opposing forces that neither cancel
one another out nor are fully reconciled. Tragic meaning then emerges
as the interactive space between world as disorder and art as order.

The very possibility of confronting the destructive forces in the
world, in the gods, in ourselves, and then shaping a verbal structure
that can crystallize them into aesthetic form provides a counterweight

to chaos and destruction. In the *Bacchae* this essential and paradoxical quality of tragedy, its counterpoise between the creative and destructive energies of life, emerges with a unique clarity and self-consciousness.

A counterpoise of this sort is arguably a distinctive feature of all those artistic works that we call tragic. The beauty and healing power of such tragic drama lie not so much in a cathartic effect as in the very existence of the play as a work of art. Although all tragedy, and certainly all of Euripides' tragedy, shares something of this quality, it is particularly marked in his later plays. As the moral and spiritual center seems to disintegrate, the poetry becomes more beautiful. The choral odes and the poetic diction of the later plays gain an increasingly self-conscious sweetness, richness, and variety that contemporaries like Aristophanes admired (if grudgingly) and parodied (*Frogs* 1309ff.).

For the *Bacchae* we have already noticed the contrast between the mystical serenity and almost pastoral innocence of the odes in the first half of the play and the fierce vengefulness dominating those of the second half. In this contrast, as in the gap between the beauty of the language and the harshness of the world the language depicts, the poet may be performing "an ethereal dance above the abyss," as Gunther Zuntz suggests of the *Helen*.[1] Viewed one way, late Euripidean tragedy points up the fragile isolation of beauty and art in a world rent by ugly motives, base character, and irrational forces; viewed another way, it reveals the strength of the work of art as a radiant center illuminating the darkness of its surroundings. The two views are not separable but simply different perspectives on a unitary object. The two sides always coexist, as the two sides of a sheet of paper or the two poles of a magnet. In plays like *Ion, Helen, Taurian Iphigeneia* the lighter side is more visible, and the shaping strength predominates; in *Bacchae, Orestes, Iphigeneia at Aulis* the darker side is more in evidence. But in all of these works both sides are co-present.

Euripidean tragedy, like all tragic art, holds a tension between the centrifugal forces it represents—entropy, irrational and inexplicable suffering, chaos—and the centripetal, cohesive forces that lie, ultimately, in the creative, ordering, unifying energies of the work itself

---

[1] G. Zuntz, "On Euripides' *Helena*: Theology and Irony," *Entretiens, Euripide* (1960) 227.

and in the order-imposing mind behind the work. The perception and powerful presentation of the tragic events, if carried to their logical conclusion, are corrosive of life; but in the artful elaboration from which that presentation derives its power and persuasiveness lie the saving and healing that the work of art also brings. Here perhaps is one source of what Nietzsche called the metaphysical solace of tragedy.

In its Dionysiac affinities, the poet's mind has as much capacity for imagining order as for representing disorder; but the creation and the very existence of the finished work validate order, lift cohesion above dispersion. The Dionysiac forces bound and channeled into the work of art, unlike those released on Cithaeron, are always in some sense a victory of the gentle over the terrible god (861), although, as Rilke says, the beautiful is also the beginning of the terrible.

The clashes between inner and outer space, mountain and city, in the *Bacchae* and the emptiness of the public and personal monuments that attempt to incorporate into the city the meaning of the god's destructive passage are the poet's acknowledgment that what he can achieve in the ordered microcosm of his play, his world of words, may not be possible in the macrocosm outside the theater and outside the text. Euripides' "Dionysiac poetics" creates in fact an endless tension between world and text, a tension we can describe or even partially recreate figuratively but never exhaust.

The text, like Dionysus, provides a relief, a drug (*pharmakon*), from the pain of life; like Dionysus, it also provides an intensification, an almost unbearable condensation, of the pain of life. In order to grasp the interdependent relation of the two sides of Dionysus and of the tragedy we must have recourse to metaphors like that of the poles of a magnet, or the Derridean *pharmakon*, or Heraclitus' tensed bow, or Keats's "bitter-sweet" taste in the fruit of reading *King Lear* once again. In Keats's image the audience is both "consumed in the fire" and given "new Phoenix wings" that carry it upward in desire.[2]

In the worship and attributes of Dionysus Euripides found the plot-structure and symbolic forms ideally suited to depicting basic conflicts

---

[2] John Keats, "On Sitting Down to Read *King Lear* Once Again": "Once more humbly assay / The bitter-sweet of this Shakespearian fruit. / . . . But when I am consumed in the fire, / Give me new Phoenix wings to fly at my desire."

and needs in our civic and emotional life. These same elements are also particularly well suited to clarifying imagistically some of the essential qualities and problems of tragic art and dramatic representation. As art is in some sense a microcosm of life, this double function of the myth of Dionysus is not surprising. In the Dionysus of the *Bacchae* this mysterious conjunction of the creative and destructive power of art—as of emotion, passion, and religious ecstasy— reaches its fullest form. The mixture and coexistence of beauty and horror, gentleness and terror, serenity and violence in the god apply not only to the Dionysiac religion but also to the Dionysiac art form of tragedy.

The inner dynamics of the play's Dionysiac poetics resemble the taut harmony, the *palintonos harmonia*, of opposites in Heraclitus' taut bow or lyre. The double nature of the god and the play's reflectiveness on its own power of illusion and release of emotion show aesthetic form absorbing the destructiveness of its contents (the violence recounted in the plot) and simultaneously reveal the power of those contents to question and trouble the beauty and coherence of the aesthetic form.

The multiple doublings and reversals of god and hero work together in a closely complementary way to reveal that interdependent antagonism of the play's *palintonos harmonia*, its coinciding oppositions and tautly maintained paradoxes. There is a just and an unjust Pentheus, a just and unjust Dionysus, a terrible and a gentle god, a lyrically mystical and a savagely murderous Chorus of Asian bacchants, a play that calls us to the remote beauty of ecstatic worship of the life energies in the world and in ourselves and a play that makes us recoil with revulsion from the release of those energies. Both coexist simultaneously; both belong equally to the "truth" about the world and about ourselves that the play presents. The Dionysiac poetics of Euripides' tragic art makes both sides visible in their simultaneity and their inseparability. We cannot remove one or the other part of that finely calibrated interdependence without destroying the essential fabric of the work itself.

We may here redirect the difficult coexistence of opposites in the god and his worship, discussed in the first chapter, toward the paradoxes of pleasure and pain, identification and distance, affirmation and despair in tragedy and in all art. Dionysus is a god of energies that hold both destruction and creation. The ludic freedom, the playful exuberance essential to poetry and the poet may work with the god's deceptions and strategies to undermine the rigid, unplayful, life-denying, energy-repressing king. The inherent playfulness of poetic language and artistic creation is also an instrument of Dionysus. The early odes repeatedly stress the god's affinities with music, art, play, and conjoin the creative energies of song with the life energies of nature.[3] Through the poet's representation of Pentheus' defeat by the god, play and art undo the monolithic authoritarianism of an over-literalistic, over-rigid, reading of words and of life.

In the practical discourse of everyday life we demand, rightly, that words mean only one thing; and we run into trouble when they do not. In the realm of Dionysus, whether in the cult or in the theater, language is free to enter playful combinations. Language, action, and emotion too, bracketed within the liberating play-world of the theater, can explore possibilities beyond the limits of normative practicality or necessity.

The poet's probing of Dionysus in the *Bacchae* thus also probes the nature of theatrical illusion and symbolic transformation, the benefits and the dangers of substituting fiction for reality and engaging in mimicry, acting out passion and violence, playing at and playing with the serious business of life. The Dionysiac perspective questions just this division of serious and playful. What I have called the *Bacchae*'s Dionysiac poetics lies in the creation and exploration of the ludic space in which these interchanges can occur.

The spirit of ludic energy and the power of transformative play are at the heart of the richest creations of art and in Aristophanes' comedies, Rabelais' *Gargantua*, Mozart's *Magic Flute* become a theme of art itself. They are also behind the creation of the mathematical formulas and scientific theories that have changed the face of the world. But Dionysiac play, like its artistic equivalent, is jealous of practical application; it insists on the spirit of play for its own sake, on the release of energy not for an ulterior end but for the sheer pleasure of movement, dance, celebration and enjoyment of the god. The attraction of the god and his cult comes, in part, from this non-

[3] For Dionysus' affinity with music and art and his association of natural energy with artistic creation see *Bacchae* 126-34, 151-69, 409-33, 356-75; also above, Chap. 3, section 6. On Dionysus and the "ludic" spirit of art see Chapter 7, ad fin.

directed freedom of emotional and physical expression. Culture sets restrictions upon uninhibited emotional and physical freedom. Hence the advent of Dionysus will appear as a movement back to nature, as a return from *nomos* to *physis*.

At this point the relation of Dionysus to civilization and to art becomes more complex, for clearly an essential part of our humanity lies in just this imposition of norms and restraints upon "natural" impulses and instincts. Indeed, the latter are so transformed by men as to bear little resemblance to what goes on in nature. Or, from another perspective, one adopted by a contemporary of Euripides, the norms and restraints of "culture" (*nomos*) really resemble nature in creating a moral character or sensibility that seems as inseparable a part of us as our hands or eyes.[4] When Dionysus reveals to us our kinship with what of nature still survives in us, the effect, as the *Bacchae* shows, is one of shock and horror.

The Greater Dionysia at Athens contained performances of both tragedies and comedies. Dionysiac comedy enacts the beneficial side of temporarily releasing the civilizing constraints on sex, violence, and aggression. Dionysiac tragedy enacts the inevitable conflict between the rest of the world and our humanness—whether that be phrased as a conflict of culture and nature, thought and feeling, reason and emotion, divinity and mortality, duty and passion.

In writing a tragedy about Dionysus and about the liminal, Dionysiac spaces in the city and in ourselves, Euripides is, as Chapter 7 suggests, writing metatragedy, tragedy about the very nature of tragedy, the sources and the paradoxes of artistic creation and reception. The poet stands in a peculiarly paradoxical relation to Dionysus: he draws upon and celebrates the god's transformative play but simultaneously, by the very act of intellectual creation, asserts an implicit victory of culture over nature and of order over chaos. The poet does

---

[4] See Democritus 68 B 33 DK: "Nature [*physis*] and education [*didachē*] are similar. For education reshapes the man [*metarhysmoi*], and in reshaping makes nature [*physiopoiei*]." Protagoras may have speculated upon a similar "natural" quality in the *nomoi* in his "Myth" (Plato *Protag.* 322c-e) and in his analogies between the educative effects of the *nomoi* and the learning of language (*Protag.* 326e-329a), if these passages reflect genuine Protagorean and not Platonic thinking. We should note too the Chorus's reconciliation of *nomos* and *physis* in 893-96, on which see Dodds, *Bacchae*, Roux ad loc., and Conacher 77.

not exult in the free release of life energies for their own sake but sublimates those energies into the creation of his tragedy.

In this sense, as we suggested earlier, the *Bacchae* also reflects on a process by which tragedy emerges from ritual. The suffering of an individual crystallizes out from the group ecstasy of the *thiasos*. The rending of a victim in the bloody group-killing of Dionysiac sacrifice becomes the symbolic rending of the figure who stands at the center of the civic order. The exultation of the rite turns to the remorse of self-conscious guilt and sorrow: an individual reflects on past action and with tragic knowledge deliberately rejects the Dionysiac ritual. Instead of the joyful actions in the wild that use up all the participants' energies and leave behind no residue, no tension of sublimated desires or instincts, there is the ambiguous "monument" of Agave and of Semele, and there is the tragedy.

The tragedy is the *mnēma*, the memorial, the monument, not only to the suffering caused by Dionysus but also to the poet's partial refusal (or discriminating acceptance) of Dionysus. It commemorates not just the individualized tragic suffering of Agave but also the poet's individualizing and internalizing of Dionysiac life energies into his work of art. Instead of participating (symbolically) in the release of those energies in the wild, in nature (*physis*), the poet sublimates them and creates his tragedy. The monument/memorial is the mark of both accepting and rejecting the god, of both defeat by Dionysus and triumph over Dionysus. It marks the existence of the suffering involved in both the acceptance and the refusal of the god. It also marks the place where Dionysiac energies have resisted desublimation and have been transformed into an implement of civilization, into a token of personal reflection on the god and his rites. This token, or monument, replaces the ecstatic *thiasos* of the maenads at the celebration of the god in the city. Were those rites celebrated with full exuberance on the mountain and in the forest, without resistance, without reflection and hesitation, there would be no monument, no tragedy. Resistance to the god, we recall, is a fundamental part of the myths of the god. The relation of civilized humanity to Dionysus and to all that Dionysus symbolizes is necessarily ambiguous. The *Bacchae* explores that ambiguity in its tragic dimension and in its relation to tragedy; but it is an oversimplification to view the play as a statement either for or against Dionysus and his cult.

Euripides shows the liberating forces of Dionysus as destructive when they have to dissolve narrow constrictions upon life energies. Here Dionysus will act through the subversive power of play and deception, akin to the playfulness of art and the fictions of the poet. But these playful, fiction-indulging, illusion-casting roles have a concomitant positive side insofar as they also participate in the energies of creation.[5] The Dionysiac power of both god and poet establishes connections among the life forces of all living beings and taps the primitive sources of creative energies in dance, sexuality, the sheer joy of being alive. Like the god, the poet restores to us a vision of lost unity, a sense of the interrelation among all the parts of ourselves, and a glimpse of our kinship with all the parts of the world, from plant to star.

In the process, however, the play, along with Dionysus in the play, diffuses our sense of self. If through terrible suffering the individuated consciousness of Agave is eventually separated from the ecstatic madness of the Dionysiac fusion, it is only after the grippingly staged dissolution of the king's personal identity. Euripides here deliberately fragments the unitary heroic personality as we know it from earlier tragedy and from earlier Euripidean plays like *Medea*, *Hippolytus*, or *Heracles*. Going beyond even the partial fragmentation of the real and the cloud-formed heroine of the *Helen*, the *Bacchae* divides the protagonist into two. The figure of the king, focus of world order, social stability, emotional coherence, becomes a field for the systematic reversal of ritual, domestic, and civic order and heroic values. Through the shifts from active to passive, the king also becomes the field for the confusion of the basic syntax not only of language but of all reality, that system of logical correspondences through which we find, or make, coherence in our world and in our ever-changing selves.

In these reversals the role of the god becomes no less ambiguous than that of the mortal hero. This god theatrically stages his own triumph. His victorious procession as a civilizing force and as a savior

---

[5] Cedric Whitman seems to have had this positive side of the play in mind when he wrote, "The *Bacchae* impresses us as the play Euripides always meant to write, for with all its negativity and despair, it is a kind of yea-statement, a realistic grasping of the tragic essence in terms of myth.": *Sophocles. A Study of Heroic Humanism* (Cambridge, Mass. 1951) 19. Whitman seems to be echoing, perhaps subconsciously, Nietzsche's notion of tragedy's "metaphysical solace" (*Birth of Tragedy*).

from the East leaves behind as much chaos as coherence. He acts out on the stage the *hieros logos*, or holy tale, of a god defeating the enemies of order. But his adversary is, after all, no monstrous Typhoeus or powerful Giant, but a pitiable, confused young man.

If the gods themselves spread disorder, the order we need to stay alive lies elsewhere. Perhaps, Euripides suggests, it lies in the work of art that contains but does not resolve the violence. The hero of the tragedy may be in some sense the shaping power of the poet that fashions the lucid form of the play. Euripides has given this play a highly formalized, traditional structure, marked by careful articulation of the parts, striking beauty of language, intricate strength and deliberate orderliness of design. All these counterbalance the random creativeness, and destructiveness, of the smiling god.

Afterword

Dionysus and the Bacchae in the Light of Recent Scholarship

Whose Dionysus? Myth and Cult

Nearly a hundred and seventy years ago Goethe wrote of Euripides, "And what splendid plays has he made! I consider the *Bacchae* his best. Can the power of divinity be represented more excellently, the delusion of men more brilliantly than happens here?"[1] This contrast between divine power and human weakness has always held the center of attention for audiences of the *Bacchae*, but the particular nature of that divinity — that is, Dionysus — has also been the source of greatest perplexity. The fifteen years since the publication of *Dionysiac Poetics* (henceforth *DP*) have greatly enriched our understanding of Dionysus.[2] A number of scholars, led by Albert Henrichs and Richard Seaford (though in very different ways), have emphasized the great division between the savage, destructive Dionysus of myth and the far more benign Dionysus of cult practice. What is cruel and outrageous in myth often appears as mild and innocuous in ritual. In our extant records of actual cult performance, the eating

---

[1] J. W. von Goethe, Letter to C. W. Göttling, March 3, 1832: "Und was für prächtige Stücke hat er doch gemacht! Für sein schönstes halte ich die 'Bakchen.' Kann man die Macht der Gottheit vortrefflicher und die Verblendung der Menschen geistreicher darstellen, als es hier geschehen ist?" The passage is quoted in Erbse (1984) 99.

[2] For surveys of recent studies of the *Bacchae* and Dionysus see Versnel (1990) 96-99; Bierl (1991) 17-18 and 177-78 (with the literature there cited); Henrichs 1996a. For recent bibliographies see also Carpenter and Faraone (1993) 303-29 and Seaford (1996b) 267-68. The wide-ranging 1990 conference on Dionysus in the United States (published in Carpenter and Faraone 1993) was preceded by two other conferences in France and Italy, respectively, both now published: *L'Association dionysiaque dans les sociétés anciennes*, Rome 24-25, May 24-25, 1984, Collection de l'École Française de Rome 89 (1986) and *Dionysos Mito e Mistero: Atti del convegno internazionale*, Comachio, November 3-5, 1989, ed. Fede Berti (1991).

of raw flesh, the *omophagia* so vividly described in the *Bacchae*, is attested only once, in an inscription from the early third century B.C., when it seems to have become regularized as the throwing of prepared bits of raw meat by the priestess and the worshipers.[3] Maenadism, the raging on the mountains by the "mad women" possessed by the god, seems not to have been practiced in Attica itself and was doubtless something much tamer than what our play suggests even in those places, like Boeotia, where it was practiced.

In cult Dionysus is experienced as a joyful divinity, the giver of wine associated with abundance, good cheer, and festive singing and dancing. In myth he is the dangerous god at the margins of civilized life, a newcomer who brings his foreign rites to Greece and inflicts terrible punishments on those who resist, usually involving madness, killing, and mutilation within the family. The Dionysus of civic cult is a purifier, not a destroyer. He is invoked as a savior of the city, as he is in prominent passages of Sophocles' *Antigone* and *Oedipus Tyrannus*. In myth his arrival is marked by resistance from the city followed by his wrath and revenge; in cult he comes as a civilizer, bringing the life-enhancing benefits of viticulture and the drinking of wine, including its moderate use in libations and of course in banquets (see Obbink [1993] 80ff.). The iconography reveals the same contradictions: "On one level, the painters show a society of men singing, dancing, and drinking, processions of joyous revelers, or assemblies of banqueters sprawled on their couches. On the other, they transport us to a parallel universe, a world of images in which anything is possible, where the human norm is inverted, an exception proving the rule."[4] Euripides does not forget the positive side of Dionysus, especially in Teiresias' defense of the god (*Bacchae* 274-85; see *DP* 292-94, 306); yet in the play's version of the resistance myth, the god's violence and vengefulness eventually drown out these happier voices. The god's magical imaginative world of music, flowing wine, the ecstatic dance, and oneness with animal and vegetative nature shows its darker side in madness and murder.

[3] The inscription is from Miletus and is dated to 276/5 B.C.: F. Sokolowski, *Lois sacrées de l'Asie Mineure* (Paris 1955) no. 48: for discussion and bibliography see Henrichs 1978 and (1996) 480-81; Versnel (1990), 139ff., especially 145-46; Obbink (1993) 70-71; and Seaford (1994) 261 and (1996b) 37.

[4] Jean-Louis Durand, Françoise Frontisi-Ducroux, and François Lissarrague, "Wine: Human and Divine," in Bérard et al. (1989) 121

Despite the beneficent festivity of the civic Dionysus, then, interpreters are forced repeatedly to return to the god's ambiguities, contradictions, and multiplicities. Henrichs, for example, whose writings
over the past twenty years have done much to illuminate these ambiguities, admits, in a masterly survey of ancient and modern views of
Dionysus, "But when all is said and done, we are still baffled by the
enigma that is Dionysus and by the polymorphous nature with which
the Greeks so amply endowed him" (Henrichs [1993] 13). The god's
epiphanies, so vividly represented in both literature and art, exemplify the mysterious and disturbing quality of his presence among
mortals.[5] Henrichs calls attention to the elusiveness of this presence:
the closer Dionysus seems to be, the more mysterious he is.[6] In his
recent study of the cults and myths of Dionysus in various cities,
Marcel Detienne also stresses the ambiguous nature of Dionysus'
gifts. For Detienne the god's essence lies in the vital, leaping energies
of the dance, the bubbling of the new wine, the beating of the heart
in fear or ecstasy, and the spontaneous, uninhibited response of
whole peoples in what he calls "*la pulsion 'épidémique,'*" "the god's
'epidemic' drive."[7] For Jean-Pierre Vernant in his 1985 study of Dionysus as "the god of the mask," Dionysus is the civic god who nevertheless brings strangeness and otherness into the heart of the city.
He carries with him "aspects of eccentricity," that is, marginality, or
modes of life that lie outside or beyond normal civic behavior.[8] Anton
Bierl, in his useful survey of current scholarship on Dionysus, takes it
as the accepted view that this is a god who exists in tension between

---

[5] On the epiphanic quality of Dionysus in a broad perspective see Henrichs (1993)
16ff. The place of Dionysiac epiphany in the *Bacchae* (see *DP* 32, 154-57, 220-23,
228-32, 297-98) continues to be widely recognized and discussed; e.g., Oranje (1984)
120-23, 131-42 (the play is "one great epiphany of the god Dionysus," 120); Vernant
(1990) 390-400.

[6] Henrichs (1993) 21. On the other hand, elusiveness and ambiguity are not li-
cence for the claim that Dionysus "has no center" or "lacks an essence, an inherent,
unchanging nature": see Michelle Gellrich, "Interpreting Greek Tragedy: History,
Theory, and the New Philology," in *History, Tragedy, Theory*, ed. Barbara Goff (Austin, Tex. 1995) 53, apropos of the *Bacchae*; and similarly Alford (1992) 46-47. See
contra Henrichs (1993) 22: "But the true status of Dionysus is never in doubt."

[7] Detienne (1989) 63; see in general Detienne (1989) 34ff., 53ff., 60ff.

[8] Vernant (1990) 389ff., especially 402; see also Vernant's "Conclusion'" to the
1985 conference at the École Française de Rome (above, note 2), 291-303, especially 299-303.

opposites, even though the lines of division now have shifted some-what from contradictions between beauty and violence, or fertility and death, to those between myth and cult, polis and country, civic and noncivic forms of worship.[9]

The intensive study of Dionysiac myth and cult over the past two decades has brought into relief the discrepancy between the god as described in myth (tragedy and of course the *Bacchae* above all) and the god of cult, who, as Henrichs points out ([1993] 26) is much less dangerous or destructive. Given the deep ambiguities of Dionysus in the play, one can only wonder if Euripides' representation of Di-onysus would appear so anomalous if we had Aeschylus' Lycurgus and Pentheus' trilogies or some of the other lost tragedies about Di-onysus.[10] Rather than trying to even out and reduce the discrepancies between the Dionysus of cult and the Dionysus of the *Bacchae*, we should perhaps be readier to accept them as Euripides' radical con-struction of the god in a play that is a unique work of art but also has affinities with other Euripidean explorations of anthropomorphic di-vinity (see *DP* 53-54, 301-3). The remote, cruel, and vengeful Di-onysus has a place beside Aphrodite in the *Hippolytus*, Hera in the *Heracles*, Athena in the *Trojan Women*, and Apollo in the *Ion* — a point to which I shall return later.

H. S. Versnel, while recognizing the established role of Dionysus as a god of the polis, notes his potentially threatening "charismatic" side and suggests that Euripides, "fully alive to the timeless ambiguity of Dionysos," uses him to depict "the eternal tension between the routinization of religion and the craving for the immediate experi-ence of the god" (Versnel [1990] 99 and 110, respectively). On this view Dionysus is a convenient and plausible figure for what could be perceived as an invasion by the new, more mystical and emotional cults, like those of Cybele, Bendis, Cotyto, or Sabazios, into Greece, and especially into Athens, at the end of the fifth century. Pentheus, then, is not just the conventional stage-tyrant but the good bourgeois citizen defending law and order against what he perceives as a poten-

---

[9] Bierl (1991) 15-17; see also Versnel (1990) 131ff., with the references there cited.

[10] The Hypothesis to the play by Aristophanes of Byzantium reports that "the myth is found in the *Pentheus* of Aeschylus": for recent discussion see Seaford (1996) 26-28. For this and other plays on the myth of the *Bacchae* see Dodds (1960) xxviii-xxxiii and, more recently, Seaford (1994) 276 n. 186, and (1996b) 26, with n. 9.

tially anarchic foreign cult. Only a few years after the performance of the *Bacchae*, Socrates was condemned and executed on the charge (in part) of introducing new gods. Pentheus persecutes what he sees as impiety toward the polis-religion, only to be caught up in a still greater impiety as the authenticity of the new god is established (Versnel [1990] 163, 173).

Versnel's concern, however, is not with the psychology of Pentheus but with types of religious experience and with the ways in which the cult of Dionysus could be regarded as anticipating the new, marginal sects. Euripides, he suggests, "has sensed the first signs of a new religious atmosphere and projected them onto the only Greek god who could bear this burden" (ibid., 205). Some of Versnel's theories are confirmed by recent discoveries of initiatory texts — the so-called Gold Tablets, and particularly the tablets from Pelinna in Thessaly — that unmistakably link Dionysus to mystery cults assuring the initiates a better life in the hereafter.[11] These new texts, including a fascinating fifth-century B.C. inscription on a bone tablet from Olbia, also confirm the paradoxical association of the god with both life and death and thus reveal his ambiguities as a god of both the chthonic and Olympian realms. We can now take more seriously Heraclitus' puzzling fragment, "Hades and Dionysus are the same" (see *DP*, Chap. 5).[12]

The new texts also lend support to Seaford's earlier suggestion, now developed further in his recent commentary, that the *Bacchae* draws directly on such initiatory and mystic rites.[13] He suggests that

[11] On these tablets see Segal 1990a; Lloyd-Jones, "Pindar and the Afterlife: Addendum," in Lloyd-Jones (1990) 105-9; Graf (1993) 240-50; Bremmer (1994) 87-89, with further references there cited. Significant too is a red-figure Apulian volute crater by the Dareios painter, now in the Toledo Museum, which shows Dionysus in Hades with Pentheus and Actaeon: see Bažant and Berger-Doer 1994, plate no. 70 and the commentary on p. 316; also Graf (1993) 256. For a detailed discussion see J.-M. Moret, "Les départs des enfers dans l'imagerie apulienne," *Revue archéologique* (1993) 293-351, especially 293-300 (the new vase) and 330-318 (underworld associations of Dionysus and his circle); also S. I. Johnston and T. J. McNiven, "Dionysos and the Underworld in Toledo," *MH* 53 (1996) 25-36.

[12] On the Olbia bone tablets see West (1983) 17-20; Lloyd-Jones (1990) 93; Graf (1993) 242. On Dionysus and Hades see also Seaford 1996b on 1157.

[13] Seaford 1981; 1994, chap. 8; and (1996b) 40-44. The detail of the linen dress is especially interesting (see Seaford [1996b] 222, on 912-76, which is developed from [1981] 260-61). Yet he seems to me to go too far in his comments on lines 881,

Pentheus' experiences in the play reflect the "negative emotions of the initiand," but replace the metaphorical "death" of the initiation ceremony with actual ritual death.[14] And these negative emotions would "combine with the theme (characteristic of aetiological myth) of resistance to the cult, perhaps also with a historical memory of actual resistance" ([1996b] 43). This is an interesting view, and it illustrates the valuable insight that Seaford's sensitivity to ritual brings to the understanding of the *Bacchae*. Yet we must recognize how little we actually know about the content, diffusion, or organization of these mysteries in Athens, or in mainland Greece generally, in the fifth century; nor can we be sure that the Dionysiac mysteries resembled those of Eleusis as closely as Seaford suggests.

Within the structure of the play, moreover, these initiatory elements do not necessarily imply an ultimately happy resolution in the ritual and civic order or a neat, positive answer to the problem of Dionysus' responsibility for Pentheus' punishment and suffering, for they also form part of the symmetrical perversions or reversals of ritual that organize the action.[15] Just as Dionysus punishes the Theban women through the negative ritual pattern of turning the blessings of his gifts to destructive madness, so he punishes Pentheus by turning the blessings of mystic initiation to a fearful isolation and nightmarish horror. The erstwhile enemy of the god can be "initiated" only to death and suffering, not to the joy, calm, and blessedness that follows initiation (see the Homeric *Hymn to Demeter* 480). Thus the *makarismos* of 902-12, where Seaford is probably right to detect mystic language (Seaford [1996b] 221), stands in the most striking contrast with the mocking of Pentheus in the initiatory dressing scene that follows. Agave undergoes an exactly analogous reversal: the language of blessedness, joy, and blissful vision in her maenadic revel describes a sight and an experience of wrenching horror and misery (e.g., 1180, 1197-99, 1242f.). The mockery and humiliation in these

---

902-11, 935-38, 939, 972. On the fifth stasimon of Sophocles' *Antigone* and traces of the mystic Dionysus see Seaford (1994) 381-82 and Henrichs (1990) 264-69. See also Bierl (1991) 127-32; 33-34, with n. 30; and 140 n. 80.

[14] Seaford (1994) 299-301 and (1996b) 43; also (1981) 261ff. See *DP* 169-71 for the death-rebirth initiatory pattern, with a very different emphasis.

[15] This pattern of reversal was one of the main points of *DP*, e.g., Chaps. 2 and 6; see especially pp. 37-42. For the structure in a broader context see Seidensticker (1996) 391-92.

scenes, as Seaford suggests, may indeed project into mythic narrative the experience of initiatory ceremonies in which the initiand "dies" from his or her previous status to be reborn into a new life (see *DP* 169-71); but within the play's dramatized world these scenes also create a powerful impression of divine cruelty, and they show the dangerous side of a god who is "most terrible" as well as "most gentle" (861).

Mystic rites and initiation operate on another level through a close parallelism between initiatory and psychological meaning. Both tragedy and initiatory ritual use a dramatic enactment of symbolic events to bring to light a hitherto hidden reality and to lead the audience (spectator or initiand) to a knowledge or acceptance of an otherwise invisible power.[16] In the question-and-answer scene between the Stranger and Pentheus (460-518), the Stranger, acting simultaneously as god and initiating priest, reveals the hidden truths of the mystic divinity through necessarily enigmatic language. This same enigmatic language, however, also brings forth hidden dimensions of Pentheus' character, truths about himself that he refuses to know. In the dressing scene later in the play Dionysus adopts the even more blatantly initiatory strategy of robing his adversary as a devotee and leading him to the place of mystic communion with the god, which is also the place of frightful communion with his hidden and denied other self. This first interview between Pentheus and the Stranger echoes the meeting between Oedipus and Teiresias in the *Oedipus Tyrannus* (cf. *Ba.* 506-8 and *OT* 412-14; see also *DP* 229-30 and 282), and the similarities are significant for the parallelism between mystic initiation and psychological revelation. The Stranger's enigmas, like those of Teiresias, unveil hidden meanings about both the god and the self and open up the path of tragic suffering through which the "initiand" passes from ignorance to knowledge.[17] But the religious and psychological meanings also reflect ironically on one another. What is a healing, integrative vision for the initiand means disintegration and

---

[16] See Foley (1985) 243-44, with n. 52.

[17] For these parallels between initiatory and psychological meanings see my essay, "Euripides' *Bacchae*: The Language of the Self and the Language of the Mysteries," in Segal (1986) 294-312, especially 304ff. McDonald (1992) 228-29, 232-33 also suggests parallels between wine and theater as modes of revealing hidden truths.

failure in self-knowledge for the young king as he confronts his Dionysiac alter ego.[18]

DIONYSUS AND CIVIC IDEOLOGY

In the last fifteen years debate over the psychology of Pentheus has given way to discussion of issues of civic identity and civic ideology, including increasing attention to the relation between Dionysus and women.[19] As all literature must now be political, it has become fashionable to view tragedy primarily as a part of Athenian civic ideology, an expression and validation of the norms and values of the state and the society. Yet, as Richard Buxton has remarked in his recent study of Greek myth, such an approach tells "barely half the story: and the less interesting half" (Buxton [1994] 32). The *Bacchae* presents particular problems for such an ideological reading, if only because critics have had such a hard time in agreeing on what its ideology might be.

Among those whose recent work has been especially illuminating for this aspect of the play, Richard Seaford and Froma Zeitlin have almost antithetical interpretations. For Seaford, the Thebes of the play is a positive model for Athens, overturning the royal house with a god whose cult is popular and democratic (Seaford [1996b] 44-52); for Zeitlin, Thebes is the city of unsuccessful integration of self and other: it fails where Athens succeeds.[20] Thus for Seaford (apropos of the *Antigone*) Dionysus "put[s] an end to that introversion and autonomy of the family which gave rise to tragic conflict" (Seaford [1996a] 291), whereas for Zeitlin Dionysus is himself the cause and expression of that very introversion (Zeitlin [1993] 151-53). Seaford, to be sure, suggests a way of integrating Zeitlin's Athens–Thebes antithesis into his own theory. For him the city's failure to incorporate the outsider (Zeitlin's "other") brings only *temporary* disaster and eventually leads from the sacrificial crisis to a refoundation of order through public cult and specifically the cult of Dionysus as the god of the

---

[18] The psychological significance of Dionysus as the repressed, threatening side of Pentheus has been developed again in Parsons (1988) 2-8.

[19] There are, however, still observations to be made about the psychology of Pentheus: see Parsons 1988; McDonald 1992; Alford (1992) 47-48.

[20] Zeitlin 1990 and 1993. See also Goff 1995.

whole polis (see Seaford [1994] 255-56, 312-18; also [1996b] 44-52).
He redirects as ritual order what in Zeitlin is a much harsher division, cast in the terms of modern ego-psychology, between the opposing principles of self and other.

The fact that two such sensitive and knowledgeable interpreters
can be so near to and yet so far from one another suggests that we are
dealing here with a truly dialectical relationship of ideas. The *Bacchae* — and indeed tragedy in general — is perhaps "tragic" because it
brings together both order-creating and order-dissolving forces of personal and social life in a balance that is always shifting and unstable.
Hence it will be conceptualized in antithetical but complementary
ways by interpreters with agendas that favor one or the other side of
the struggle. This is the dialectical process that constitutes what I
called the "Dionysiac poetics" of the play (*DP* 330-47). Much depends on the interpreter's point of departure and interpretive meth-
odology. Seaford is interested in the *Bacchae* primarily as an instance
of the order-creating function of ritual, and especially Dionysiac ritual, in the polis; fundamental for him is Dionysus as the democratic
god of the whole polis. Zeitlin is interested especially in the psychological mechanisms of integration and rejection, and her interpretive
schema brilliantly moves between the microcosm of the individual
self and the macrocosm of society and its rituals. Each interpretation
is justifiable in its own terms, but each takes only half of Dionysus
and absolutizes it as the whole.

Both interpreters rely heavily on tragedy's reformulation of ritual,
but for Seaford tragedy is a much closer reflection of its ritual and
cultic origins than it is for Zeitlin (e.g., Seaford [1994] 385-86). Although Zeitlin looks for a "Dionysiac plot" that pervades the corpus
of tragedy (see below), she positions herself closer to the action of the
individual plays and so can give full weight to those elements of
suffering and waste that we call tragic; Seaford, positioning himself
beyond the plays in an attempt at a historical perspective on Dionysiac rituals in the polis, sees this traditionally "tragic" material as
only a small piece of a total design, whose ultimate meaning is the
happy ending of Athenian tragedy in the affirmation of polis order
through civic cult.

Each of these approaches constitutes one half of a dialectic, and
their relation is characteristic of a dynamic of response and reaction
that is especially strong in today's literary criticism, which so often

begins by arguing the opposite of its immediate predecessors. The agonistic nature of academic inquiry aside, this dialectic is probably inherent in all literary interpretation, in so far as most literary forms — even the happy-seeming serenity of pastoral — can in some way or other be viewed as order-affirming or order-subverting. Classicists need think only of the ever-unresolved debate on the "two voices" of Virgil's *Aeneid*.[21] As far as the *Bacchae* itself is concerned, my own view is that Seaford prematurely forecloses this dialectic between affirmation and subversion, or order and anti-order, because his commitment is to ritual form and its order-inducing *results*, rather than to literary form and its order-questioning *process*. Hence his Dionysus is far less ambiguous than the Dionysus of *DP* and, as I continue to believe, than the Dionysus of the *Bacchae*.

The conflict of interpretive directions in this basic conception of the function of tragedy is neatly framed by Rainer Friedrich's critique of Simon Goldhill. Goldhill views tragedy as a "transgressive force" in "subverting the dominant ideology" (Friedrich [1996] 264), whereas Friedrich, though approving of Goldhill's conception of tragedy as a civic, political, and religious institution, dismisses the negative part of Goldhill's theory as "postmodern fetishism" and "cult of subversion" (ibid., 265; see also Seaford [1994] 365). I agree with Friedrich that Goldhill probably goes somewhat too far, for to dramatize tensions and conflicts is not necessarily to subvert the ethos or discourse of the polis (Friedrich 1996, 263-68).[22] Nevertheless, it is hard to refuse at least the possibility of subversion in a play like *Medea* or to reject the importance of paradox in the age that produced the *Oedipus Tyrannus*. Paradox and subversion, fashionable though they may be, are not just postmodern fetishes. Wherever one draws the line between "tension" and "subversion," these competing views show how the conception of Greek tragedy as a civic or ideological discourse, far from resolving its interpretive problems, only shifts them to another area.

On the whole, I am closer to Goldhill in one of *DP*'s main theses, namely that Euripides uses Dionysus, among other things, to reflect

---

[21] I borrow the term from the celebrated essay of Adam Parry, "The Two Voices of Virgil's *Aeneid*," *Arion* 2, no. 4 (1963) 66-80, which concisely describes this dialectical process in the *Aeneid*.

[22] For a similar critique of Goldhill's position, with a similar one-sidedness, see Seaford (1994) 363-67.

on tragedy's function in the polis in an open, questioning vein. Tragedy does not just validate the social norms (though it obviously does so to some extent) but explores their contradictions, inconsistencies, and inadequacies, and so examines rather than suppresses the "deviant signals," to use Versnel's terminology, that normally "are not allowed to pass through our cultural filter" (Versnel [1990] 3). Similarly, Christiane Sourvinou-Inwood emphasizes the paradox that the great polis festival of the City Dionysia dramatizes "the forces of disorder and the threat of loss of control associated with Dionysos," and she remarks, "Tragedy was, among other things, very importantly a discourse of religious exploration" ([1994] 289-90). In like manner Claude Calame acknowledges the important civic function of Greek tragedy but observes that, because "it operates only through a series of mediated transpositions and deformations" (Calame [1986] 137), we cannot assume that it offers simple or positive messages about social, moral, or political behavior. Because Dionysus is so intimately connected with tragedy, his relation to the city in the *Bacchae* easily becomes a model for tragedy's role in the polis generally. And here, despite the recent important demonstrations of the positive, socially integrative functions of Dionysus in Athens and in Greece as a whole, Dionysus remains a figure in whom order and anti-order meet. Euripides' Dionysus, in contrast to the Dionysus of civic cult, remains an intentionally ambiguous figure, "most gentle and most terrible to humankind," as his human avatar explicitly says.

NIETZSCHE AND DIONYSUS

Interpretation of the *Bacchae* over the past century has had an ambivalent relation to *The Birth of Tragedy*, for the choice between a subversive or a normative play inevitably involves Nietzsche's controversial view of the god. It has been traditional in classical studies, from Wilamowitz on, to heap scorn and insult on anything having to do with Nietzsche. Yet the contemporary recognition of the contradictions and paradoxes in Dionysus is inevitably indebted to Nietzsche, even if indirectly, for Nietzsche was the first in a long line of interpreters to emphasize the connections between tragedy and the breakdown of boundaries in Dionysiac ecstasy, to discern the links between the ritual background of Dionysus and the importance of the chorus (e.g., *Birth of Tragedy*, Chap. 7), and to recognize the power of the god as a symbol of the vitality and energy of nature (hence Karl Kerényi's characterization of Dionysus as the "god of indestructible life"). Unquestionably *The Birth of Tragedy* has been a seminal work for the post-romantic poetics of tragedy and constitutes a bold new step in the perception of the relations between tragedy, the tragic, and ritual. Its value and limitations have been carefully reassessed in the useful book by Michael Silk and J. B. Stern and in a number of recent works.[23] Nietzsche, however, is not concerned with a systematic interpretation of the *Bacchae*, much as he draws on it, and the sweeping generalizations that make *The Birth of Tragedy* so stimulating as a theory of art and creativity are particularly problematic for an interpretation of the play.[24]

At least as much confusion as clarification results from Nietzsche's famous dichotomy of Apollonian and Dionysiac and its corollaries: the idealization of "nature" as the realm of truth in contrast to the "pretentious lie of civilization" ("die sich als einzige Realität gebärdende Kulturlüge"), the dithyrambic exaltation of the Dionysiac satyr-figure as the expression of the sublime and the divine in its pure and strong vitality, the linking of the Dionysiac and the spirit of (Wagnerian) music, and the joining of Euripidean and Socratic intellectualism as the destroyer of tragedy. What I owe to Nietzsche in *DP* is also what interpreters from Rohde on have learned from him, an appreciation of the god's association with the vitality and energies of growth and creation that include both the natural and human worlds. But, as Henrichs points out ([1993] 23), Nietzsche's Dionysus often dissolves into his much more elusive and mysterious "Dionysian." My concern in *DP* is the Dionysus in the text of the play rather than the Nietzschean concept of the Dionysiac. As Chap. 3

---

[23] See also McGinty (1978) 39-43, 164-69; Henrichs 1984a passim, especially 219-34; 1986 passim, and (1994) 57-58, with extensive bibliography. See also Vernant (1990) 383ff.; Barbara von Reibnitz, *Ein Kommentar zu Friedrich Nietzsche "Die Geburt der Tragödie aus dem Geiste der Musik" (Kapitel 1-12)* (Stuttgart 1992).

[24] Henrichs 1986 (especially pp. 376-85 and 391-97) points out the paradox that Nietzsche's overall view of Euripides was remarkably conventional and in fact owed a great deal to the classicizing idealism of the Schlegels' approach to Greek tragedy. Hence he could couple Euripides with Socrates as the destroyer of tragedy, even though his emphasis on the "Dionysian" emotionality and fusion in tragedy in general was a radical new departure, to prove illuminating for the interpretation of the play and, indeed, for Greek tragedy as a whole, a century later.

and 4 try to show, for example, "nature" in the *Bacchae*, far from fitting neatly into Nietzsche's post-romantic, metaphysical antithesis between a truth of instincts and the "lie of civilization," belongs to a complex of religious, political, spatial, and gender relations that help define both the human condition and the Greek polis in their physical and spiritual settings.

Although Nietzsche frequently speaks of "illusion" in connection with Dionysus and tragedy, he has in mind Schopenhauer's notions of the world as "maya," the self-deception with which human beings (with the exception of the Nietzschean philosopher) mask the emptiness and meaninglessness of their lives, and hardly the kind of theatrical, and metatheatrical, illusion of my chapter on metatragedy. Nietzsche gives a radical new direction to Aristotle's remarks on the origins of the dramatic chorus in chapter 4 of the *Poetics* and thus makes the chorus virtually a metaphysical as well as a literary and historical entity. It becomes the locus of the primitive energy of the god and the residue of the truly Dionysiac (as opposed to Apollonian) element in tragedy. But for my book the chorus has a much more specific relation to the structure and conventions of the play: it is an instrument (among other things) of Euripides' intellectual exploration of the nature of tragedy and of Dionysus' relation to the polis (*DP* 242- 47). Nietzsche's antithesis between the "Dionysiac poetry of the chorus, on the one hand, and the Apollonian dream world of the scene on the other hand" (*Birth of Tragedy*, Chap. 8) recognizes the chorus's adversarial role in the *Bacchae* but extrapolates far too broadly from the play and involves a fragmented conception of dramatic form that few readers of tragedy today could accept.[25]

Nietzsche's influence, nevertheless, continues to hover over the *Bacchae* (as it does in one way or another over all studies of Dionysus), in part because Nietzsche did recognize a fundamental aspect of the god.[26] Nietzsche remains stimulating for his incipient, if

---

[25] *The Birth of Tragedy*, Chap. 8, ad fin: "Demgemäss erkennen wir in der Tragödie einen durchgreifenden Stilgegensatz: Sprache, Farbe, Beweglichkeit, Dynamik der Rede treten in der dionysischen Lyrik des Chors und andrerseits in der apollonischen Traumwelt der Szene als völlig gesonderte Sphären des Ausdrucks auseinander."

[26] See especially Henrichs (1993) 22-26. Bierl (1991) 180-81, though generally very favorable to *DP*, on which he draws heavily for his own view of the "metatheatrical" aspect of Dionysus in tragedy, is thus suspicious of what he sees as a

occasionally idiosyncratic, insight into Dionysus as the voice of the other, that which refuses integration into the logic and orderliness of normal life of men and women in society (bourgeois society, Nietzsche would say). The *Bacchae*'s continuing appeal today is due largely to the way in which it speaks of and to those suppressed — often necessarily suppressed — voices of resistance to order and normality. Pentheus, like his counterpart in the *Hippolytus* and like Creon in Sophocles' *Antigone*, cannot tolerate challenges to the rigid order that he imposes on his world and himself. Such figures see the world from a single perspective only, especially on matters of supreme importance, and are blind to the contradictions in themselves. It is precisely to indicate this blindness, as I remarked earlier, that Dionysus/Stranger has the role of the Sophoclean Teiresias in his first encounter with Pentheus. Yet, as in Sophocles' *Oedipus Tyrannus*, this spokesman for a wider vision of reality cannot illuminate the darkness of his antagonist; thus, he sets the stage for a reversal of power and weakness, illusion and truth, with the sense of inevitability that attends nearly all encounters of mortal and divine in Greek tragedy.

DIONYSIAC PATTERNS IN GREEK TRAGEDY

Apart from the concern with the ritual and psychological meaning of Dionysus for the play, recent scholarship has taken another important new direction in perceiving patterns of Dionysiac language and action throughout the tragic corpus. Renate Schlesier has argued that even where Dionysus is not mentioned directly, the god is strongly present in allusions to maenadic or Dionysiac madness, particularly in connection with violent female emotions and their destructive effects, given the generally dangerous association of female emotion in Greek tragedy (Schlesier 1993). Dionysiac images in the description

---

Nietzschean strain in it; but he seems to have missed my explicit criticisms of a Nietzschean view, e.g., *DP* 158. In the antepenultimate paragraph of *DP*, p. 346, which Bierl cites as an instance of my unconscious or unwitting echo of Nietzsche (Bierl [1991] 181 n. 15), I was in fact intentionally using the Nietzschean language of individuation and fusion to contrast with the dialectical and self-reflexive dimension of the *Bacchae* and with what I see as its specific tragic conflict between mortals and Dionysus, as opposed to Nietzsche's generalized "Dionysian" and "Apollonian."

of female-motivated violence, Schlesier argues, should be seen not merely as figures of speech but as part of a Dionysiac pattern in those plays.[27] Seaford has also argued that such maenadic imagery reflects a Dionysiac pattern of detaching women from the patriarchal household and turning them into destroyers of the family for the eventual solidification of ties between citizens in the democratic polis (Seaford [1994] 257-62, 301-11, 326-27 and Chap. 8, passim). We may not want to go so far as Schlesier does in finding such "displaced maenadism" in Phaedra's longing to go "to the mountain" (*eis oros*), as if she is participating in a Dionysiac *oreibasia* (*Hippolytus* 215-22; Schlesier [1993] 108-10). Yet such passages remind us that the violence and destructive power of women under the influence of Dionysus in the *Bacchae* are only the most spectacular realization of a deeply rooted anxiety about women in Greek culture.

Although the maenadism of the *Bacchae* is direct and literal, there is one passage where I believe the pattern is also "displaced," namely in the motif of lamentation surrounding Agave in the last section of the play. Greek tragedy often describes intensely grieving women figuratively as bacchants;[28] but Agave is literally a wildly triumphant maenad at the moment when she should be mourning over her son. Here the metaphorical maenadism of mourning is ironically inverted in the exultant maenadism of a Dionysiac sparagmos (see Segal 1994, [1995b] 20-22). Unrestrained female mourning had long been felt as dangerous in Athens and other cities, and attempts to control it date from the time of Solon. Euripides could, therefore, draw upon a certain interchangeability between the release of intense emotion among women in Bacchic ritual and the sharing of intense emotion among women in funerary lament. In this way he characteristically explores aspects of social behavior that his culture found threatening. Both bacchantic rites and funerary lament set women apart from men in a collective and exclusively female activity. In both cases this

[27] Examples are the musical celebration of Heracles' return and Deianeira's discovery of the poisonous effects of her robe in *Trachiniae* (216-20, 701-4) or Iole's disastrous union with Heracles in *Hippolytus* 545-54 or the comparison of Hecuba and the Trojan women to bacchants in *Hecuba* 1076. On Iole see also Seaford (1993) 126-28 and (1994) 356; on Hecuba see Segal (1993a) 179-82.

[28] See Eur., *Hecuba* 684-87, *Suppliants* 1038-39, *Phoenissae* 1489-90; also Aesch., *Sept.* 835. See in general Seaford (1993) 119-20.

collective, segregated, and female activity is perceived as dangerous to the women themselves and as potentially subversive of civic order.[29]

For understanding the affinities between the extreme emotionality of female lamentation and the release of violent emotions by maenads, the work of C. Nadia Serematakis on ritual laments in the Mani is particularly suggestive. Women's laments show remarkable similarities across different cultures, and these make Serematakis's material of interest for classical Greece. As Margaret Alexiou has demonstrated at length, moreover, there are strong continuities in the lament tradition in Greece from antiquity to the present day.[30] The female laments that Serematakis describes combine intense emotion with an intense feeling of community that, like the maenadic celebration, is essential to the meaning of the ritual. The wild crying of the women, known as "screaming the dead," both separates them from normal social life and simultaneously marks their place in a new community of mourners who share a special relation with the dead and with each other (see Serematakis [1991] 101). Serematakis describes one such mourning ritual as follows (110):

> One scream, coming from the elder sister, rose above all others. It retained its peak without subsiding till the woman passed out. A little old lady passed out quietly right behind her. A male voice emerged, "Take her out!" (The young woman's husband had attempted to bring her out of her deep mourning by calling her name a couple of times during the ceremony, mentioning something about her health.) Women were standing and screaming, pulling their hair out. It was the peak. It was impossible to be fully conscious, to be an observer.

This scene illustrates how closely the sympathetic transfer of violent emotion between women caught up in the collective furor of the lament can approximate the ecstasy of the Bacchic *thiasos*.

In addition to their sharp separation from the women, the men, like Pentheus at the beginning and Cadmus at the end of the *Bacchae*, are defined as outsiders and guardians of rationality and health.

---

[29] See Loraux (1990) 33-47 and Segal (1993) 68-69, with the references there cited. Aesch., *Sept.* 230-70 is a good instance of the danger of female lament to the city. See Foley (1993) 129ff. and also 122ff. on Euripides' *Suppliants*.

[30] Alexiou (1974) 122-28, 131-205, and for cross-cultural parallels see Holst-Wahrhaft (1992) 20-29, 119-24.

Serematakis describes their fear and their readiness to intervene (110-11):

> The men, aware of the power of the emotions in that room, were alarmed and frightened. *A woman can actually impose death on herself. This is the female challenge of Death* [Serematakis's emphasis]. People are alert in ceremonies for this type of catharsis, and they are ready to catch the collapsing body of the overwhelmed mourner. The men took the women out of the room to bring them back to consciousness. They pulled them out "to give them coffee and fresh air." For men — especially young men — these acts were a "medical intervention" in a ritual process that eluded their understanding; they reduced it to physiological disorder and issues of personal health.

Such is the anxiety and puzzlement that this intense, collective female emotionality can arouse in men, even in a society that is, after all, in touch with the modern world. The male role in reviving the women who are overcome by their participation also resembles the role of Cadmus in the next scene of the *Bacchae* (1264-96). I would offer Serematakis's description of male-female relations in this emotional event as a complementary approach to what George Devereux suggested over twenty-five years ago, namely that the Cadmus–Agave scene may represent actual practice in bringing such celebrants out of their ecstasy (Devereux 1970).

In the *Bacchae* the displacement of funerary by Bacchic ritual raises the inversions of the scene to a second degree. In place of a bacchant-like lament of a bereaved mother over her son, the mother rejoices in hunting him down and dismembering his body, and is urged on by the collective intensity of the bacchantic *kômos*. And as Agave's bacchantic madness jars the expected forms of ritual structure from their usual paths, so her iambic description of her joy and success in the hunt comes at the point where the mother's funeral speech might have stood. Displaced by the bloody maenadic ecstasy, the scenes of proper lamentation will have to wait for Agave's return to sanity.

The work of Nicole Loraux on the *epitaphios* (public funeral oration), though not concerned directly with the *Bacchae*, provides another, quite different perspective on the equivalence between wild female lament and maenadism. It reminds us of the complementary

masculine and civic mode of lament, the *epitaphios*, and so suggests
how that institution too forms part of the play's field of vision. Beginning probably sometime around the middle of the fifth century, the
official funeral lament over fallen warriors in Athens is pronounced
by a leader of the city in civic space, subordinating ties of family to
the duties to and rewards from the city. It pushes far into the background the female side of procreation and the personalized, emotional character of female lament.[31] Tragedy, however, as Loraux argues, releases everything that the *epitaphios* suppresses. The result
can often be a kind of nightmarish opposite of the *epitaphios*, and
this is what happens in the *Bacchae*.

The effect of these inversions is comparable to Clytaemnestra's
speech over the body of her murdered husband in Aeschylus'
Agamemnon (1372-98), which replaces sorrow with exultation, fertility with death, the expected female modesty and restrained demeanor
with outrageous action, and also releases a highly personalized female sexuality and sexual jealousy in their most dangerous forms.[32]
The inversions of the *Bacchae* lie in the area of female lament rather
than female sexuality but are precisely analogous to those of the
Agamemnon. Here, as in Euripides' *Medea*, creative energy turns to
destruction as maternity becomes murderous. As in the *Medea*, and
Agamemnon, too, these inversions have a powerful visual enactment
on the stage. And again, as in those two plays, the male is reduced to
ineffectiveness and impotence before the unleashed power of female
emotions. Thus the funeral lament that Cadmus pronounces over
Pentheus is not only an ironic shadow of a real *epitaphios* but also
highlights Pentheus' failure to achieve a heroic, masculine death.
Both in Cadmus's speech here (especially 1305-26) and also in Di-
onysus/Stranger's words at 962-64, a eulogy is being pronounced (albeit in covert form in the latter passage) over one who has met his
end not as a hoplite battling against enemy warriors from outside the
city but as a "woman" at the hands of women from his own city and
his own household (see *DP* 210-12 and Segal 1997).

---

[31] See Loraux (1990) 27-37; Segal (1993) 68-69. See also Segal (1996) 247 nn.
11-12 for further references.

[32] On these inversions see also Arthur (1994) 86-91; on the language of Clytaem-
nestra's speech see Simon Goldhill, *Language, Sexuality, Narrative: The Oresteia*
(Cambridge 1984) 89-95. For an analogous inversion of the *epitaphios* at the end of
Sophocles' *Antigone* see Segal (1996) 118-37.

The *compositio membrorum* in which Agave performs the actual funerary ritual for Pentheus near the end of the play also continues the play's pattern of inverted rituals. At the end of the *Iliad* and at the end of the *Trojan Women* Hecuba is the archetypal *mater dolorosa*, washing, laying out, and caressing the body of a son or grandson. At the end of the *Bacchae* a mourning mother actually has to piece together her son's mutilated body. Thus this most intimate role of the mother in the last offices for a dead child takes on a grisly and horrible form, and the shock and horror are all the greater because this is a body that she herself had dismembered. The destructive Dionysiac madness, as Zeitlin suggests, emphasizes the corporeal side of experience, forcing humans and animals to confront their elemental physicality, their basic existence as bodies.[33] At the end of the *Bacchae*, however, the consolation of touch and embrace in normal funerary ritual is absorbed into the dangerous and horrible potential of Dionysiac corporeality.

Zeitlin's contrast between Athens and Thebes that I cited earlier parallels Schlesier and Seaford's attempts to find broad Dionysiac patterns in the tragic corpus. For Athens and Thebes, Zeitlin argues (1990, 1993), Dionysus poses the challenge of preserving or destroying the boundaries between self and other and the balance between stability and change. For both cities he is the outsider who at the same time belongs to the center of the polis.[34] Athens can generally achieve the successful integration of the other, whereas in Thebes the stranger (the Dionysus of the *Bacchae*) causes the fragmentation of family, self, and community. *Oedipus at Colonus* in particular shows how the tragic conflict that tears Thebes apart can be resolved in Athens. Athens here brings the stranger within the city and thus transmutes his curses into blessings (see *DP* 328). In the Thebes of the *Bacchae* and the *Oedipus Tyrannus*, the apparent stranger is really an insider, and his re-integration into the city brings destruction instead of salvation. Here too the ambiguity of the stranger's relation to his city parallels the ambiguity of his salvation of the city.

[33] Zeitlin (1991) 73-74, apropos of Eur., *Hec.* 1151-71. We may compare *Ba.* 737-47, the scene of the Theban maenads on the mountainside overcoming the heavy bodies of cows and bulls.

[34] It is interesting to compare this general view of the stranger with Seaford's view of Dionysus and Dionysiac cults as linking the center and the periphery of the polis; e.g., Seaford (1994) 244-51.

In the *Tyrannus* Oedipus seems to save the city from plague (although nothing explicit is said of the plague at the end), but at the terrible cost of discovering that he is himself the polluter rather than the savior. In the *Bacchae* the god, like Oedipus simultaneously native and foreign, brings the blessings of his cult into the city, but in such a way that the royal family is wiped out and the very process of establishing this cult demonstrates its destructive and dangerous side. In Thebes Dionysus combines destructively with Ares and Aphrodite (and sometimes with Hera) to produce murderous madness or disastrous passion; in Athens that potential danger is averted through the city's association with Athens and Demeter.

Comparison of Aristophanes' *Thesmophoriazusae* and the *Bacchae* shows how the two patterns of transgression and the two uses of the carnivalesque atmosphere complement one another (see Zeitlin [1996], 400-403). The women at Demeter's festival of the Thesmophoria at the center of the city are exactly antithetical to the threatening band of women outside the city in the Bacchic madness. Their intrusion at the Thesmophoria into the public spaces that are reserved for men celebrates marriage and fertility and so promotes the health of the city, whereas the Maenads' movement from the center of the city to the periphery dangerously usurps male roles. In both plays, however, a collectivity of powerful women ranged against men calls into question the boundary between domestic and civic space and creates a troubling dislocation of inside and outside. In the Dionysiac imagery of the Colonus ode of the *Oedipus at Colonus*, on the other hand, Athens can display Dionysus within its boundaries as a benign god of fertility, innovation, and salvation.[35]

I would like to extrapolate from one aspect of Zeitlin's Dionysiac "masterplot" to the argument of *DP*, namely the parallelism between the implosion of the city of Thebes upon itself and the *Bacchae's* motif of autochthony. Thebes, turned in upon itself, is unable to establish a positive relation either with its past (the Sown Men of Pentheus' ancestry) or with its territorial extension to all that lies outside of itself (Zeitlin [1993] 149-50). The *Bacchae* shows the equally

---

[35] On these points see Zeitlin (1993) 153ff., especially 164f.; also Schlesier (1993) 100. The Colonus ode, however, also has ominous associations of death and fertility that maintain the ambiguities of Dionysus, especially his chthonic connections. See Segal (1981) 371-76 and Bierl (1991) 221.

disastrous effects of both the spatial division between inside and out-side and the temporal rupture between past and present implied by Pentheus' descent from his mysteriously absent father, the Sown Man, Echion.[36] The closed, walled polis that constitutes Pentheus' defense against Dionysus only increases his isolation and the con-strictedness of his world. The only thing that he can summon up from the past of his autochthonous origins is the Giant-like savagery and monstrosity of the chthonic realm. Here the isolation of Pen-theus reveals its social as well as personal or psychological dimension. He is also isolated from the social memory, from the living past of the family and the community, as well as from the rituals in the city. The process is just the reverse of a "patriotic" plot like that of the *Ion*, where the Athenian protagonists are triumphantly (if still somewhat ambiguously) connected to their distant past and their autochthonous origins.

METATRAGEDY

The metatragic meaning of the play, studied in Chapter 7 of *DP*, has proven one of the most fruitful directions in recent criticism of the play, and indeed of Greek tragedy, as a spate of books and articles has shown. I first put forth this interpretation in my seminar on the *Bacchae* at the Ecole des Hautes in Paris in 1975 and then in a conference on Euripides at Duke University in 1977, the proceedings of which were not published until 1985, after *DP* had itself appeared (Segal 1985). In the meantime, in 1980, Helene Foley, quite inde-pendently, also called attention to this aspect of the play in a stimu-lating article, which is now incorporated into her *Ritual Irony* (Foley 1985). She placed particular emphasis on the ritual structure of *pompê, agôn, kômos* (procession, contest, festive revel), whose rele-vance to the *Bacchae* had been suggested long ago, but she shows how the same ritual structure belongs to the Greater Dionysia where the plays, of course, are performed (216ff.). She also called attention to the way in which Dionysus destroys Pentheus "with theatrical weapons" (Foley [1980] 113).

In a valuable pair of articles originally published in 1981 and 1985

[36] On Echion see *DP* 99-114, 136-40, 152-54, 182-85, 244.

(reprinted in Zeitlin [1996] 341-74 and 375-416), Zeitlin examined the motif of cross-dressing as an indication of theatrical self-reflexivity. She argued that the dressing of a male character as a female on the stage was itself a reflection on the mimetic procedures of tragedy, in which men dress in women's clothing to represent women. Such scenes, she suggests, focus on women as the central point of the act of mimesis, precisely because tragedy is so deeply concerned with the threat of the feminization of the male and with the threatening power of masculinized women (like Aeschylus' Clytaemnestra) or with women's transgression of traditional female roles or their usurpation of male prerogatives. Needless to say, Dionysus' dressing of Pentheus in female garb, following upon the narration of the Maenads' defeat of male warriors, distills into an overpowering visual enactment the full, threatening power of dramatic mimesis.[37]

In the past few years, particularly with the publication of Anton Bierl's *Dionysos und die griechische Tragödie*, the "metatragic" or self-reflexive consciousness in Euripides, as well as in other dramatists, has emerged with ever-increasing clarity. Bierl has shown in massive detail how pervasive in Euripides is Dionysus' association with the power of illusion on the spectator, and he has offered a detailed reading of the *Bacchae* in this perspective ([1991] 177-218). As numerous interpreters have emphasized, wisdom, *sophia*, is a major motif in the play; and Pentheus' resistance to Dionysus is also the resistance to the wisdom that the illusion of the theater can convey (ibid., 201; see also *DP* 214-15, 271). More broadly, the clash between everyday reality and the world of heroic myth is a recurrent feature of Euripides, and especially of late Euripides, often calling attention to the problem of representation and containing what one scholar has recently called "a metatheatrical dimension."[38]

[37] See Zeitlin (1996) 375-416, especially 400-403 on the complementation of the dressing scene of the *Bacchae* and the disguise of Euripides' kinsman in Aristophanes' *Thesmophoriazusae* as the comic and tragic versions of a single Dionysiac/mimetic impulse.

[38] For example, Christian Wolff, "Euripides' *Iphigenia among the Taurians*: Aetiology, Ritual, and Myth," *Classical Antiquity* 11 (1992) 308-34, especially 331-34; see Segal (1986) 263-66 and Bierl (1991) 169-72 on the *Helen*. On the *Bacchae* see also Goldhill (1986) 280 and Ieranò (1991) 50-51. For other aspects of metatheater in fifth-century drama see Segal (1995c) 18-19 on *Ajax*; Charles Segal, *Oedipus Tyrannus: Tragic Heroism and the Limits of Knowledge* (New York 1993) 148-57; Ann

In a different but closely related direction, Henrichs has shown how the chorus in Greek tragedy, as in choral lyric generally, may self-referentially describe its role as performers of its play without necessarily breaking the dramatic illusion which, as characters, they help create (Henrichs [1994/95] especially 58-59, and 1996b). In this self-reflexive mood, the chorus may raise the question, "Why then should I dance?" as it does at the end of a famous ode of the *Oedipus Tyrannus*; or it may refer explicitly to the circumstances of its staging, as it does at the end of the fifth stasimon of Sophocles' *Antigone*, where the chorus of dancers on the stage doubles with the metaphorical "chorus of fire-breathing stars" of which Dionysus himself is the chorus-leader or *chorêgos* (*Antigone* 1146-54).[39] Henrichs refers to such passages as "choral projection": that is, the chorus, while not explicitly referring to its role in the orchestra, describes a scene of ritual dancing, often in a remote or mythical setting, that is clearly a metaphorical equivalent of the performance itself.

This approach holds many implications for the *Bacchae*, where some form of "choral projection" operates in nearly every ode of the play. Choral projection is especially strong in the *Bacchae* because the action of the play itself simulates the epiphanies that are characteristic of the god. Indeed, the choral songs themselves aim at effecting such epiphanies. By its very nature the Dionysiac dance summons the god into presence and creates that projected world of participation in the mythical and the numinous. The dancers of this chorus not only worship Dionysus as celebrants of his rites but also identify with him in their dance and call for the display of his epiphanic power (e.g., 519-37, 1016-23). Thus in bringing the god himself into their presence in their dance, they are creating that Dionysiac world among themselves, or, in Henrichs's terms, "projecting" their choral dance into the mythical dances of the god. This epiphanic projection (if I may use the term) is most spectacular in the fifth stasimon of Sophocles' *Antigone*, but it is also strong in the *Bacchae's* second and fourth stasima and implicit in the parode.

The self-referentiality in these odes and in the play as a whole

Batchelder, *The Seal of Orestes: Self-Reference and Authority in Sophocles' Electra* (Lanham, MD 1995) 6ff., 35ff.; Gregory Dobrov, *Figures of Play: Greek Drama and Metafictional Poetics* (Ann Arbor, forthcoming). For a useful review of the debate on metatragedy and a defence of its validity see Bierl (1991) 111-19.

[39] See Henrichs (1994/95) 77-79; also Segal (1981) 201-6 and *DP* 14-15.

finds some broad parallels in W. R. Connor's study of the symbolic and pragmatic functions of festive rituals like processions. He has called attention to the Greeks' sensitivity to participating "in a theatricality whose rules and roles they understood and enjoy" and has emphasized the "histrionic mentality" of the archaic and classical period (Connor [1987] 46). This is a culture that took delight in all the play and pageantry of its rich ritual life and was intensely responsive to the symbolic meanings of processions, the acting out of mythic roles, and the dressing as a god or a mythic figure (ibid., 42-47). Such festivals, Connor points out, serve not just for entertainment or display but also as vehicles of social and political meaning. Connor is more directly focused on historical and social rather than literary issues per se, but his concern with the rules and conventions of role-playing and their social and political messages has many resonances in Greek drama.[40]

In this same perspective the mask is, among other things, the self-referential marker of a ritual or dramatic enactment. Its aim is not just to make characters recognizable on the stage or to serve as a kind of pretechnological megaphone for the actor's voice, but rather to call attention to the representation of the sacred or ritual context of the drama. In the fully developed phase of Greek drama, it also indicates the fictive character of a role in the theatrical performance (see Calame [1986] 127-28, 136-38). Or, in the terms of Vernant's important little book, *La mort dans les yeux: Figures de l'Autre en Grèce ancienne* (Paris 1985), it is the mark not of the same but of the other, the monstrous, the mysterious, the unknown, and ultimately death. On this view, Dionysus' relation to drama lies in part in his association with the mask as the sign of this otherness: he is the god of the otherness embodied in the mask, and he "is able to guide one out of this game of deforming mirrors" that is tragedy (Calame [1986] 141; also Vernant [1990] 394ff.).

New studies in Dionysiac and dramatic iconography have brought other confirmations of the *Bacchae*'s self-consciousness of its own theatricality. Françoise Frontisi-Ducroux (1995) has collected a wide range of iconographic evidence confirming the strong connection of

---

[40] For example, Zeitlin's two essays on cross-dressing or "playing the other" in Zeitlin (1996) 341-74 and 375-416

Dionysus with the mask.[41] Much of this material has been studied before, but she confirms, among other things, that the word *prosôpon*, which the chorus uses of Dionysus' laughing or smiling "face" (1021) and which Agave uses of the severed "head" of Pentheus (1277), can also refer to the cultic mask of the god (pp. 14-17; see also *DP* 248-49, 260-61, 265). Oliver Taplin has tempered his earlier skepticism about the theatrical reference of *prosôpon* and is now inclined to see such allusions in a number of passages of Aristophanes.[42] Frontisi-Ducroux also makes the point that the ancient masks generally included hair (p. 8, with fig. 2-4); and if such a mask were used for Pentheus it would add an additional self-reflexive dimension to Agave's entrance with the head of Pentheus, for her allusions there to hair would also be appropriate to the familiar form of the mask (*Ba.* 1185-87 and cf. 1170).

The mask itself invites self-referentiality. Thomas Carpenter, in a useful survey of visual representations of the beardless Dionysus in the fifth century, has called attention to two vases of the 470s that may hark back to plays in which the bearded Dionysus disguises himself as a mortal (Carpenter [1993] 204-6). If correct, this interpretation offers iconographic indication for that embedding of disguise in a Dionysiac story that Euripides uses in the *Bacchae*. These vases, in other words, would show "a mortal disguised as a god disguised as an adolescent" (205).

How receptive the intellectual climate of the late fifth century was to self-reflexivity in the theater emerges from Taplin's recent *Comic Angels* (1993), which collects a wealth of material from late fifth- and early fourth-century vases, largely from southern Italy, illustrating theatrical scenes. To be sure, these vases draw their illustrations primarily from comedy; yet, as Taplin argues, they reveal an intense, sophisticated, and widespread metatheatrical awareness in audiences as well as in poets and in tragedy as well as in comedy, and they date

[41] For some qualifications see Pailler 1995. For Dionysus and the mask see the recent survey by Henrichs (1993) 37-40; also Claude Bérard and Christiane Bron, "Satyric Revels," in Bérard et al. (1989) 142-43, and Frontisi-Ducroux, "In the Mirror of the Mask," ibid., 151-65.

[42] Taplin (1993) 68 n. 2 cites Aristoph. *Peace* 524, *Frogs* 912, and fragment 275; also Hermippos frag. 3, Telekleides frag. 46, and Aristomenes frag. 5. See Taplin (1986) 168-72 for his earlier, more skeptical view of metatragedy. See also Pailler (1995) 107-10.

from the time when Euripides was composing the *Bacchae* (see Taplin 1993, Chap. 7). A phlyax vase in the Fleischman Collection in New York, for example, shows a figure labeled Aegisthus, whom Taplin interprets plausibly as a representative of tragedy. Next to him stands a figure called Pyrrhias, presumably a representative of comedy, while two old men, each labeled *chorêgos*, stand nearby. Taplin suggests that this scene derives from a late fifth-century comedy entitled *Chorêgoi* — chorus leaders but also providers or patrons of dramatic choruses, or, as we might call them, producers, or, with Taplin, "angels." If Taplin is correct, these vases supply additional evidence for an interest in bringing comedy and tragedy together in a common frame as part of a self-conscious reflection on both dramatic genres (ibid., plate 9.1, with pp. 55-66 for discussion). The *chorêgoi* vase points too toward the mingling of comic and tragic elements in the *Bacchae* that many critics have found disturbing.[43]

When *DP* first appeared, the chapter on metatragedy seemed its most controversial element, and it is gratifying to see that this part of the work has become so widely accepted, even in some relatively conservative circles (e.g., Latacz [1993] 294-95, 299-300). But there have also been misunderstandings and exaggerations. The metatragic dimension of the play is not simply synonymous with Dionysus, or with his role as a god of the theater, or with the mask, important though these are. Like any aspect of meaning, metatheater unfolds from the complex working together and interlocking of many different elements in the play. Hence it develops gradually from such scenes as Dionysus' announcement of his disguise in the prologue, the Palace Miracle and its immediate aftermath in the palace, and the dressing scene; and it conveys the possibility of the interchange between spectator and participant that belongs to the Dionysiac experience.

Metatragic implications need not involve a sharp break with dra-

---

[43] See Seidensticker 1978; 1982 passim. For a possible meeting of tragedy and comedy in the figure of Dionysus, somewhat analogous to Taplin's interpretation of the *chorêgos* vase, see Anton Bierl, "Dionysus, Wine, and Tragic Poetry: A Metatheatrical Reading of *P. Köln* VI 242A = *TrGF* II F 646a," *GRBS* 31 (1990) 353-391, especially 374. For a different view of the *chorêgos* vase, see H. A. Shapiro, "Attic Comedy and the 'Comic Angels' Krater in New York," *JHS* 115 (1995) 173-75.

matic illusion.[44] As Henrichs has shown in the case of choral self-reflexivity, a surplus of meaning can accompany dramatic actions without detracting from their ritual, religious, or ethical significance (Henrichs 1994/95). Just as the metatheatrical association of chorus leader at the end of the fifth stasimon of *Antigone* (*choragos*, 1147) does not detract from the ode's meditation on the relations between humanity, divinity, and nature, so the metatheatrical implication of the Stranger's dressing of Pentheus does not detract from the horror and pathos of the helpless human victim being prepared for his sacrificial death. Indeed, the metatragic dimension of the play is essential to understanding its full impact as a presentation of the power of Dionysus as god of the mask. Through the fictionalized epiphany of Dionysus' presence on the stage, the play offers a dramatic enactment of what it means to experience that presence. It makes us feel that beneath the mask of the human actor may indeed lie the face, and not just the mask, of the god. Thus metatragedy adds to, rather than subtracts from, the religious meaning of the play as a series of epiphanies of the god.

It is important, of course, not to give the metatragic dimension a disproportionate emphasis in relation to other, more traditional approaches (historical, religious and ritual, ethical, psychological, etc.).[45] But, as one scholar has recognized, the metatheatrical dimension has helped current criticism of the play break out of the endless, ultimately sterile debate about whether Euripides was for or against Dionysus, whether he was continuing his critique of the gods or had arrived at a late "conversion" (see Latacz [1993] 299-300). In any case, I would be the last to insist on an exclusively metatragic reading, and I intended my chapter on metatragedy as only one of the play's many levels of meaning and only one of the many kinds of reading that this masterpiece invites. A metatheatrical reading of the *Bacchae* no more excludes other kinds of readings than does a metatheatrical reading of the *Oedipus Tyrannus* or *Hamlet*.

This misunderstanding of the role of metatragedy has led some to a prematurely negative judgment. Wolfgang Kullmann, for example,

---

[44]Bierl (1991) 223 answers this objection to a metatragic reading of the play.

[45]I agree with Joachim Latacz's warnings about the dangers of excess in such an approach and about the assumption that such a reading is a magical key to every aspect of the play; see Latacz (1993) 299-300.

in an essay subtitled "Does the *Bacchae* Have a 'Metatheatrical' Meaning?,'" argues that such meaning excludes deep ethical or religious seriousness (Kullmann 1993). To prove this point, he accumulates numerous parallels with Homeric situations where gods deceive mortals, as in *Odyssey* 13 or 19. Such scenes do offer analogies, but they hardly have the same effect as the Stranger's dressing of Pentheus item by item on the stage. Even granting the validity of Kullmann's Homeric background (as I am willing to do), the religious meaning of such scenes does not exclude a second level of meaning. Certainly the Homeric gods can play with mortals as part of the tragic gap between the human and the divine; and certainly Euripides is drawing on this "homerische Sichtweise" (p. 252). But the effects of such scenes are very different when they are staged as drama, particularly with such details as the dressing scene contains. When Kullmann assumes that "Dionysus alone in the drama symbolizes the theater" (p. 262), he takes far too narrow a view of the metatheatrical element.

As I emphasized above, the metatheatrical resonances stand in close relation to the motifs of delusion, epiphany, mistaken inferences, double meanings of words and phrases, etc. It is mistaken, therefore, to associate the metatragic dimension of the play with either Dionysus or Pentheus alone, for this aspect of the *Bacchae*, like so many others, depends on their interaction in conflict and complementation. If Dionysus is the center of the power of illusion, Pentheus has the major role as a quasi-theatrical "spectator," especially in the play-within-the play dressing scene that Dionysus stages (*DP* 225-26, 263-64). But their shifting and interchanging of roles are essential for the play's dynamic self-reflexivity. Dionysus becomes the spectator of Pentheus' sufferings, and Pentheus changes from being a spectator to being an actor or participant. Like many other Greek tragedies, the *Bacchae* depends on this interaction between two almost equally balanced protagonists (e.g., Sophocles' *Trachiniae* and *Antigone*; Euripides' *Alcestis, Hippolytus,* or *Ion*).[46]

The theatrical and ritual meanings inevitably overlap because all

[46] For other examples of this kind of dual or even multiple focus in Euripides we may also compare *Trojan Women* or the two *Iphigeneias*. If we include Agave's powerfully presented sufferings, the *Bacchae* even has a triple focus of tragic interest, again not unlike *Hippolytus*: cf. *Hipp.* 1403-4. On the importance of Agave's suffering in the play see March (1989) 60-63.

ritual has a theatrical aspect. There is no contradiction between Pentheus' role as a celebrant in a ritual procession that the Stranger is leading as the head of a religious delegation of sorts (1047) and his metatheatrical role as a "character" in a play "staged" by Dionysus that mirrors the play being staged by Euripides.[47] I can agree with much in Kullmann's conclusion (263) on the "religious interpretation" of the play, the shift of support to Pentheus, Agave, and Cadmus at the end, and the Homeric discrepancy between the gods' anthropomorphic egotism and their supposed concern for justice. But, again, none of this is necessarily in contradiction with a metatragic dimension of the action.

In like manner there is no contradiction between viewing the dressing scene metatheatrically and as part of the ritual transvestism of Dionysiac cult, with its sacrificial and initiatory meanings. As DP also devotes considerable attention to sacrificial and initiatory patterns (DP 37-45, 157-214, 222-25), I am in full agreement with the ritual interpretation, as far as it goes; but Seaford's strictures on metatragedy result from a confusion of ritual origins with literary function in a specific work of art.[48] Tragedy everywhere uses ritual and even imitates the effects of ritual in the highly stylized framework through which it confronts the problems of social and cosmic order and disorder. Like ritual, tragedy ultimately controls the threat of chaos, but it also allows chaos to enter the human world without the crystallized clarity or certainty of ritual. At the risk of repetition, I insist on three fundamental points: (1) the metatragic elements are not restricted to the dressing scene only; (2) self-reflexivity deeply pervades the aesthetic consciousness of late fifth-century art forms, especially tragedy and comedy; (3) references to specific Dionysiac ritual(s) are not incompatible with metatheatrical implications, for theater is itself a ver-

---

[47] On Dionysus as the pompos theôrias in 1047 see DP 41 and 79.

[48] For the importance of distinguising between ritual and theater see DP 263-66. For Seaford the recognition of the self-reflexive theatricality of the play is "not wholly mistaken" but derives from "the intellectual fashion of the 1980s," whereas in his view the play's theatricality "is primarily a feature of the Dionysiac ritual from which theatre emerged" (Seaford [1994] 272). Seaford is hardly fair to the issues of self-reflexivity and theatricality in the introduction to his commentary, where he cites only Kullmann's one-sided essay, and no other work (Seaford [1996b] 32, with n. 29), as if that settled the question.

sion (I emphasize *version*) of ritual enactment, and tragedy (like ritual) regularly contains multiple, overlapping layers of meaning.

DIONYSUS, WOMEN, AND EPHEBES

No topic in Greek tragedy has attracted more interest in the last two decades than the representation of women; and the *Bacchae* continues to be a major text, especially for the culture's anxieties about female emotionality and about the transgression of the limits set to female behavior in a male-dominated society.[49] Here too the sinister interchange of male and female roles in the play reveals the darker side of the exuberant confusion of the sexes in the carnivalesque atmosphere imagined on the Dionysiac vases and perhaps realized, far more modestly, at the god's festivals.[50] Dionysus himself, we may recall, relaxes the severe division of gender roles in this highly stratified society, for he has many feminine attributes and yet is worshipped in phallic processions "that still now remain customarily practiced in many of the cities," to which Aristotle traced the origins of comedy (*Poetics* 4.1449a).

A very problematic corpus of vases from the first half of the fifth century continues to play a large role in this question of sexual fusion. These vases, sometimes referred to as Anacreontic, show virile, bearded men engaged in music and dance who adopt such details of female dress as robe, parasol, or slippers. The scenes have features appropriate to a Dionysiac *kômos* or revel. The Dionysiac atmosphere is indicated either directly, by the god's presence or attributes (like ivy), or indirectly by the wine of which he is the god. On some vases companions have Lydian, Persian, or Scythian dress. These are occasions, as Frontisi-Ducroux and François Lissarrague suggest, on which Greek men "can make themselves other — a bit female, a bit oriental or barbarian" ([1983] 29). To engage in the *kômos*, *kôma-*

---

[49] See, e.g., Des Bouvrie (1990) 83-86, who also has an extensive bibliography; also March 1990, passim; Bremmer (1994) 79-80, with further references; Just (1989) 252-63; Zaidman and Schmitt Pantel (1992) 197-207, 218-22. See also Easterling 1987; Nicole Loraux, *The Experiences of Teiresias* (1989) trans. P. Wissig (Princeton 1995); Katz 1994; Goff 1995.

[50] For the mixing of gender roles on the vases see, for example, Claude Bérard and Christiane Bron, "Satyric Revels," in Bérard et al. (1989) 143ff.

zein, "if one believes the images [on the vases], would mean 'to play at becoming other'" (loc. cit.). Yet it is only the men who play with otherness in this way, for the women on these vases, where they occur, retain their own female attributes and do not cross over into the other gender. As flute-players or musicians, these women are only ancillary to the male game; but also, as women, they already possess the otherness "that renders them near the animal but also permits [them] to approach the god without a transformation of [their] essence" (31).

These vases, with their scenes of "playing the other" in Dionysiac surroundings, have some analogy with the theater as the Dionysiac Poetics of the *Bacchae* defines it: that is, they provide "a measured dose of alterity" (ibid., 33). The *Bacchae* brings together the areas of this alterity that are also most prominent on the vases, a fluid passage between both Greek and barbarian and male and female and a release from the control and discipline of the male citizen in an atmosphere of music, play, and art.

The presence or nonpresence of women at the dramatic performances seems finally to be receiving the intense scrutiny it deserves, with three major articles in the last seven years. This issue obviously impinges on the way in which Euripides would have conceived of the reception of the play. If women were allowed in the theater, we can think of Euripides as addressing an audience part of which would certainly be intensely involved in the sufferings of Agave as well as Pentheus and Cadmus and which would perhaps also be especially sympathetic to Dionysus' release of women from the house. On the other hand, if the audience were exclusively male, the poet could anticipate a very different response to the terrifying spectacle of collective female violence and to women defeating men as both warriors and hunters (see *DP*, Chap. 6). Unfortunately, the question remains unresolved, although scholars increasingly incline to the view that some women were in the audience for the late fifth and early fourth centuries.[51] It needs to be kept in mind, however, that even if women were allowed in the theater, the judges who awarded the prizes were exclusively male.

---

[51] Podlecki 1990, Henderson 1991, Goldhill 1994; see also Des Bouvrie (1990) 86-90. All but Goldhill are inclined to believe in female attendance (with qualifications).

To turn to another controversial area of audience composition and response, John Winkler, in a stimulating essay, has suggested that tragedy is much concerned with the ephebe (the young man between late adolescence and adulthood who performs a pre-hoplite military service), in part because the chorus may have been made up of ephebes and in part because ephebes had a major role in the events of the Greater Dionysia (Winkler [1990] 57-61). Whether they occupied a fixed block of seats in the theater is less certain (ibid., 39-40; see contra Goldhill [1994] 364-65). Unquestionably the tragedies, and certainly the *Bacchae*, often highlight issues involving ephebic education and training (Winkler [1990], 31-35; see *DP*, Chap. 6, especially 164-72, 190-204). Yet, with all due respect to the brilliance of Winkler's intriguing hypothesis, the notion of tragedy's primary address to an ephebic audience is an implausible and unnecessarily narrow view. In the *Bacchae* the grief (*penthos*) that Pentheus brings to Agave and Cadmus points to another area of the ephebe's importance to tragedy, namely his role as the link between generations and as the heir to his father's name and property. Thus not only the young men of the audience would be involved in the maturation and survival (or nonsurvival) of the ephebe in his time of trial and crisis, but also the elders as well. This is especially the case during the Peloponnesian War, when so many families lost young men (see the conclusion of Pericles' Funeral Oration, Thucydides 2.44). The last two plays of the *Oresteia*, Sophocles' *Trachiniae*, *Antigone*, and *Electra*, and Euripidean plays like *Hippolytus*, *Electra*, *Ion*, and *Iphigeneia in Tauris* probe the emotional and social challenges of emerging manhood; however, they all equally involve problems of the entire *oikos*, as well — succession in the household, the obedience of children, conflict or harmony between parents and children, the death of a son, and so on.

DIONYSUS AND THE DEMOCRATIC POLIS: A POSITIVE MODEL?

Just as it is mistaken to view the *Bacchae* as nothing but a reflection on tragedy, so it is mistaken to insist exclusively on its supposed political dimension. Unquestionably Greek tragedy is a form of civic celebration, and tragedy is concerned with political issues in indirect and sometimes even very direct ways.[52] There are probably political overtones in the first stasimon's endorsement of "what the meaner mob regards as lawful" (430) and in the disastrous consequences of the advice given the shepherds by the fast talker from the city (717f.). Interpreters have found here implicit criticisms of the radical democracy in Athens, or, alternatively, a celebration of the ultimately democratic spirit associated with Dionysus.[53] Such hints at possible contemporary circumstances, however interesting, do not really touch the essence of the play, which is certainly far more concerned with religion and ritual than with political matters in the narrow sense.[54] As the last two chapters of DP suggest, the most serious political meaning of the play has to do with the way in which the polis absorbs Dionysus and neutralizes his potential dangers. The very existence of the play as a celebration, however complex, of Dionysus marks Athens' avoidance of the fate that befalls Pentheus' Thebes.

Because Dionysus has so solid a place in the polis, we watch the arrival and acceptance of a god whose triumphant success is the very basis of the performance itself at the Dionysia, where the tragedies and comedies are in a sense offerings to Dionysus. Yet if the settled benignity of Dionysus in the city makes us feel that the Athens of the Dionysia has escaped the fate of the Bacchae's Thebes, the dramatic fiction also invites us to identify with Thebes. Athens may be the antithesis of Thebes elsewhere in tragedy (notably at the end of the Heracles and in the Oedipus at Colonus), but the dangerous power of Dionysus dramatized in the Bacchae also holds out the possibility that Athens may become Thebes, and indeed that any city may become Thebes. The appropriate model for the Bacchae, then, may not necessarily be the comforting contrast between Athens and Thebes, as in the Heracles or the Coloneus, but the more unsettling possibility of a mimetic identification of Athens with the "other" city. We may recall the exquisite eulogy of Athens in the third stasimon of the Medea (824-65), presented just months before the Spartans laid waste the land, where the daemonic vengeful power that has wrought such

---

[52] See in general Euben 1990, especially chapter 2; also Goldhill 1990 and Meier 1993.

[53] See respectively Bierl (1991) 72-73 and Seaford 1994, Chap. 8.

[54] See Alford (1992) 179-83 (especially 180) for an interesting redefinition of the political aspect of Greek tragedy in terms of a larger concern with "connectedness."

havoc in Corinth will migrate to Athens and dwell henceforth in this citadel of purity, grace, beauty, and art (*Medea* 824-45).[55]

In his stimulating and wide-ranging *Ritual and Reciprocity* (1994) Seaford argues for a pervasive polis-ideology in tragedy centered on a Dionysiac pattern wherein the dissolution of a royal family leads to a reaffirmation of the democratic polis under its democratic god, Dionysus. As Seaford puts it succinctly elsewhere apropos of *Antigone*, Dionysus "is the civic god who in tragedy after tragedy presides over the self-destruction of the ruling families of the mythical past, to the benefit of the polis."[56] The funerary ritual with which tragedies often end is analogous to communal mourning over the hero in hero-cult and perhaps over the suffering of Dionysus himself. In all these cases the polis is united in mourning for the suffering and pathetic death of the tragic hero (see Seaford 1994, Chap. 8, especially 312-18, 324-27).

On this view the democratic polis asserts the primacy of civic values over the introvertive tendencies of the individual households, and so the Dionysiac cult provides a model by which women are released from the aristocratic *oikos*. Yet the application of this model to the *Bacchae*, and to other Greek tragedies as well, seems to me highly problematic, for what the women are released *to* is not clearly beneficial to the polis or to the kind of male-centered civic order that the polis seeks to establish. The model tends to polarize institutions that the Greeks generally view as complementary rather than antithetical, for from Homer and Hesiod the health of family and city together is central to the ideal polis.[57] More broadly, Seaford's approach implies a monolithic relation between myth, cult, and tragedy; yet there is scarcely a single extant Greek tragedy that does not leave us with conflicts and questions about the gods or about the relations between gods and mortals.[58]

The destruction in the *Bacchae*, it is true, is wrought by the mad-

---

[55] See Euben (1990) 138-39 for a similar qualification of Zeitlin's Athens-Thebes dichotomy in tragedy (Zeitlin 1990 and 1993).

[56] Seaford (1996a) 291.

[57] See Hesiod, *Works and Days*, 225-47. See Friedrich (1996) 273ff., especially 275.

[58] For these difficulties with Seaford's interpretation of tragedy see my review of Seaford 1994 in Segal 1995a, especially 655-57; also Friedrich (1996) 272-77; see also *DP* 263-66.

dened women of the city who resist the god, and their leaders are the women of the royal house. It is also true that the destruction of Thebes is reflected primarily in the ruin of the royal family. But I cannot agree that the play envisages the establishment of the cult of Dionysus as an unambiguous benefit to the polis, and I cannot reconcile Seaford's reading with the somber tone of the play's ending and its concluding view of the god. In fact, Seaford's claims for the social and political usefulness of the cult of Dionysus take a position vis-à-vis the god that the play itself anticipates and criticizes (*DP* 309, 329). Of course the play foreshadows Dionysus' victory and the establishment of his cult in Thebes: that is the necessary condition of the play's human tragedy (*DP* 326-27).

Seaford's reading also seems to me to exaggerate or distort other features of the play. He argues, for example, that the opposition to Dionysus focuses exclusively on the royal family; yet the play clearly dramatizes the center of that opposition in Pentheus rather than in the royal family per se. In his resistance to the god, Pentheus is isolated from both his city and his family. In the prologue Dionysus singles him out, as Aphrodite does Hippolytus, as the one who fights against the god (*theomachei*, 45).[59] In the next scene Cadmus and Teiresias attempt in vain to check Pentheus' vehement resistance to Dionysus, and the chorus does the same in the following ode ("Holiness, do you hear these things of Pentheus?" 374). The climax of the play stresses Pentheus' isolated death ("Alone you suffer in behalf of the city, alone," 963).[60] It is also an exaggeration to claim that "it is never the polis but only the royal family that positively rejected Dionysus" (Seaford [1996b] 253, on lines 1329-30), for there are a number of strong and clear references to the responsibility of the city or "all the city" (e.g., 39-40, 195-96, 1295), and Seaford has to find various ways to explain these away.[61]

---

[59] On *theomachos* and derivatives in the play (45, 325, 1255-56) see Erbse (1984) 94-95. The word occurs here for the first time in Greek literature and within Euripides' extant work only in the *Bacchae*.

[60] For what it may be worth, the Hypotheses to the play, including that of Aristophanes of Byzantium, also emphasize the fault of Pentheus, not the royal family.

[61] See Seaford (1996b) 253, apropos of 39-40, 195-96, and 721. Of the two passages that he cites in his favor, 26-31 seems to have at least as much to do with a rationalistic or interested rejection of the god as with family solidarity. The emphasis here is not on the family as a whole but on the women of Cadmus' house, who have

Cadmus' funeral eulogy, as Seaford rightly notes, praises only Pentheus' personal interventions in his grandfather's behalf rather than his contributions to the city as a whole (Seaford [1996b] 47). But this point does not reflect the solidarity of the royal family so much as Pentheus' failure to become a mature leader (see *DP* 211-12) and the resultant collapse of the leadership of Thebes.[62] Euripides gives much more attention to the characterization of Pentheus than to the royal family as a family, a technique in keeping with his dramaturgy from *Medea* and *Hippolytus* on to *Electra* and *Orestes*. It is hard to see how even a speech by Dionysus predicting his future cult in Thebes could mitigate the destructive violence that surrounds him and his cult in the last third of the play, or how it could soften the harsh contrast between the god's remoteness and the human sufferers' pathos in the last scene. For most readers the play's final impression is well put by Foley: "In the *Bacchae* we are left uncertain whether the polis will ever absorb and domesticate Dionysos or control the proliferating and dangerous repercussions of his entry into civic life." (Foley [1985] 258).[63]

---

not granted Dionysus the recognition of his divine birth as they should have done ("the sisters of my mother, who should least have done so"); i.e., they have not allowed him the full measure of honor that he deserves. Seaford's other passage, line 45, has nothing to do with the royal family but consists of the god's accusation of Pentheus alone as a *theomachos*. On 1148-49, too, Seaford seems to me to introduce a forced and arbitrary reference to the royal household; and at 1248-49 he suggests an antithesis between the "solidarity and interests of the polis" and the royal household for which I can find no basis in the text. Cadmus is merely lamenting the cruelty of a god destroying a household into which he had been born (*oikeios gegôs*). The point has nothing to do with an alleged antithesis between *polis* and *oikos*, but is intended to depict the pathos of Cadmus' situation and is part of the criticism of the god's harshness that characterizes the closing scenes.

[62] Interpreters differ as to the meaning of *tarbos têi polei* in 1309: see *DP* 211 n. 77. Seaford takes it pejoratively, as "a terror to the city." Roux 1972 ad loc. has the opposite view: "Ce n'est pas un trait péjoratif; malgré sa jeunesse, Penthée savait se faire craindre; il mettait son autorité au service de la justice, et en cela se distinguait d'un tyran." Roux probably goes too far in the opposite direction. Dodds (1960) 233, ad 1302-29, interprets 1310 similarly to Seaford, but his overall view of the passage is actually closer to Roux's: the speech moves sympathy not just for Cadmus but also for Pentheus, "by exhibiting, belatedly, the more attractive side of the young man's nature."

[63] For similarly pessimistic readings of the play recently see Euben (1990) 159-63 and Ieranò (1991) 59-60.

Hans Oranje's careful study of the language and dramatic progression of the play (Oranje 1984) arrives at a view of the play and of Dionysus antithetical to Seaford's. He rightly observes the sharp contrast between the first three stasima of the play, with their emphasis on "the inner piety and the loveliness of the Dionysiac attitude to life," and the aggressive vengefulness of the last two odes (170).[64] While this shift might appear merely the result of the god's condign punishment of the impious, it in fact leaves us with sympathy for the victims. So too the play leaves in the background those aspects of Dionysus that belong to the god of the Athenian cult—wine, festivity, peace, and the good life—but enacts most vividly on the stage his attributes of ecstasy, madness, violence, and vengeance (101-13). The fruitful, happy, and exuberant sides of Dionysus, which the early scenes do portray, "are loaded with irony, because the mania of Dionysiac ecstasy does not in the play result in the joyful and liberating appearance of the god to men, the prospect which in the parodos the chorus had held out to Thebes, but in the terrifying revelation of Dionysus' divinity by the bloody destruction of Thebes' political heart" (168-69).

Oranje draws an interesting parallel between Dionysus' plot in the *Bacchae* and Apollo's in the *Ion*. In both cases a god's devices to attain his end backfire: Apollo's scheme nearly leads to a mother and son killing one another; Dionysus' initial attempt to establish himself at Thebes by appearing as a Lydian youth and working minor miracles in the first third of the play only reinforces Pentheus' obstinacy, so that Dionysus finally has to resort to destructive madness (75-77). Although Oranje does not push his argument to its logical conclusion, his reading makes the play as bitter an incrimination of anthropomorphic divinity as *Hippolytus, Heracles,* or *Electra.* Yet he goes

[64] Oranje's interpretation is a useful corrective to Seaford, who pays too little attention to the shift in the tone and subject matter of the choral odes in the second half of the play and the complementary shift toward increasing sympathy for Pentheus, Agave, and Cadmus at the end. Important here is the highly controversial passage 877-79 = 897-99, where Seaford ([1994] 402-4 and 1996b, ad loc.) adopts a reading that exonerates the chorus of bloody thoughts: see contra Oranje (1984) 159ff. and Segal 1997, n. 25. Seaford's interpretation of the fourth stasimon (1996b, 228, ad 977-1023) seems to me improbable, for he would explain away this bloodthirsty vengefulness of the chorus by suggesting that it here is singing "the imagined words (of Agave)"; and he further glosses over the violence by the understatement, "although the mood of the ode is less pacific than in earlier *stasima.*"

too far in suggesting that Dionysus is somehow defeated ("A god never suffered a greater defeat on the Athenian stage," 77); the god's power and triumph are never in question, and both are terrible, *deina* (861).

Oranje's reading has the merit of following the shift of sympathy in the course of the play and showing how crucial for an overall interpretation is the division of sympathy between Dionysus and Pentheus.[65] Yet he seems to miss many of the cues to Pentheus' violence in the first half of the play (e.g., in lines 239-41: see *DP* 171-74) and goes too far in defending his resistance to Dionysus as merely a common-sense response to a threat to civic order.[66]

Sympathy for Pentheus is also the basis of the interpretation by Jennifer March (1989, summarized in March [1990] 49-56), who argues from vase-painting that Euripides may have been the first to represent Pentheus' humiliation by his being dressed as a woman and his being killed by his mother. The more common depictions in vase-painting show him killed by the maenads whom he confronts armed in battle, and a well-known vase in the Boston Museum of Fine Arts gives the name Galene to one of his killers. March gives Agave's sufferings the emotional force they deserve, but unfortunately neither the literary evidence nor the vases can establish her point that the *Bacchae* is the first work to have Agave kill her own son. In many of the depictions on vases Pentheus is unarmed, though one might argue that the arms have already been stripped away. Important, however, is a red-figure hydria in the Villa Giulia, which probably predates the *Bacchae*. This vase almost certainly presents Agave as the killer, for she is symmetrically paired with Lycurgus beside an ancient statue of Dionysus; Lycurgus is identified by the double ax with

---

[65] Oranje in fact begins his study with a useful survey of how interpretations of the *Bacchae* have been determined by shifts of sympathy between Dionysus and Pentheus: Oranje (1984) 7-19. How divided these sympathies still remain is illustrated by Siegfried Jäkel, "Der Dionysus-Kult in den Bakchen des Euripides," *Grazer Beiträge* Supplementband 5 (Festschrift W. Pötscher) (1993) 93-107, especially 103ff., for whom the play shows the justified victory of Dionysus, as a god of wine and joy balanced by peace and moderation (*sophrosyne*), over the despotism and irrational violence of Pentheus.

[66] Oranje's hostility to a psychological appproach and his insistence on a rather unsystematic "audience response" lead him to read elaborate motivations into the text in a manner approaching documentary fallacy.

which he kills his son.[67] In *Medea* 1282-84, it is true, the chorus emphatically lists Ino as the only woman whom they know of as having killed her own children. But this passage is not really an *argumentum ex silentio* for the *Bacchae's* priority in the maternal killing. The mythical paradigm of Ino has a number of features that are peculiar to the *Medea*, and in any case the child-killings by Althaea and Procne were already well established in myth.[68] Within the frame of Dionysiac myth, too, are the daughters of Minyas, who kill their own children. Aeschylus' Lycurgus trilogy presumably dramatized the story of a maddened father killing his son; and his *Pentheus*, which is supposed to have influenced Euripides' *Bacchae*, presumably dramatized the story of Agave and Pentheus along the lines of the *Bacchae* (see the Hypothesis by Aristophanes of Byzantium).

Euripides frequently ends a play with an aetiological myth about the foundation of a cult. Such endings, however, generally complicate rather than resolve its moral problems and tend to incriminate rather than exonerate the deity in question (e.g., *Hippolytus*, *Electra*, *Ion*).[69] The extant portions of the *Bacchae's* finale suggest that this play was no different (e.g., 1345-51).[70] The picture of god versus mortal in the last scene is in fact close to the end of the *Hippolytus*, where the suffering of innocent victims on stage, united by funerary lament, contrasts with the foundation of a cult by a distant Olympian in the remote future.[71] Like the *Hippolytus*, too, the *Bacchae* has two

[67] J. D. Beazley, *Attic Red-Figure Vase-Painters*, 2d ed. (Oxford 1963), 1343a; for illustration and interpretation see Bažant and Berger-Doer 1994, plate 65 and p. 317.

[68] On the pecularities of *Medea* 1282ff. see my essay, "On the Fifth Stasimon of Euripides' *Medea*," *AJP* 118 (1997) 175-76. Incidentally, March (1989) 39 n. 28, seriously misrepresents my view of Pentheus' character apropos of *DP* 28, where I wrote of "two Pentheuses: a Pentheus in control of his realm as ruler and a guardian of civilization, and a Pentheus who is violent, 'savage,' destructive of civilization, an enemy of the Olympian gods." In the kind of distortion through selective quotation that is regrettably all too common, March quotes only the second half of my formulation as if that were the whole.

[69] On the complicated nature of these closing *aitia* in Euripides see *DP* 275-76; Dunn (1996) 54-57, 61-63; also below, n. 71 on *Hippolytus*.

[70] Seaford's efforts to exculpate Dionysus are not convincing: e.g., 1996b on 1165-1392 (p. 242) and on 1348-49 (p. 255). In the latter passage he acknowledges a "note of irrational finality" in the reference to Zeus but has to dismiss this, finally, as "social necessity." On this scene see *DP* 317.

[71] On the end of *Hippolytus* see Knox (1979) 227-29; Segal (1993b) 127-35, 151-53, with further bibliography; Dunn (1996) 91-97. For the end of the *Bacchae*

interrelated concerns: to explore the moral problems inherent in anthropomorphic divinities and to examine extreme emotional states in complex, conflicted, often pathological personalities. To these issues, as *DP* tries to argue, the *Bacchae* adds its particular concern with probing the relations of Dionysus to individual and collective psychology and to the nature of drama and especially dramatic illusion.

Although Seaford and I have diametrically opposite views of the ending of the play, we do agree (in part) on one aspect of its self-reflexivity, namely its concern with incorporating Dionysus into the polis through the dramatic festivals, the Greater Dionysia at which both the comedies and tragedies were presented. In contrast to Seaford, I view Dionysus' demand for worship by the whole city not just as a reflection of the democratic nature of the god but as itself part of a continuing tension between the public institutions of the polis and the "other" modes of Dionysus' activity: the religious band or *thiasos*, a collectivity that in fundamental ways stands apart from the polis and political organization and engages in secret as opposed to public rites.[72] The last chapter of *DP* suggests that Euripides views tragedy itself as the way in which the polis can incorporate Dionysus, but poses as a paradox the form and manner in which the city and its institutions contain the god (*DP* 328-30, 342-46). Tragedy thereby recognizes and uses the potential danger in the god and his cult but also benefits from their creative energies: the joy and exuberance of wine and festivity, the release and renewal that come from Dionysiac masking, disguise, and symbolic enactment of otherness in drama.

It is striking that at the end the Dionysus who has earlier laid such emphasis on his Theban origins refers to himself only as the son of the remote Olympian Zeus, not as the son of Theban Semele (*Ba.* 1340-42; see Ieranò 1992; also *DP* 332). It might be possible to interpret the omission as the god's shift away from familial to wider panhellenic connections; but the principal effect seems to be to present Dionysus as one of those remote, austere Olympians who jealously defend their honor (see *Ba.* 319-21) and are ultimately indifferent to

---

see March (1989) 64 and (1990) 61-62. Dunn (1996) 75 calls the end of the *Bacchae* "the bleakest of happy endings."

[72] See Vernant (1990) 402. On the nonpolitical or extra-political nature of Dionysiac and other mystic *thiasoi* see Burkert (1987) 30-53, especially 33ff., 44ff.

human suffering, like Aphrodite in *Hippolytus*, Hera in *Heracles*, or Athena in the *Trojan Women*.[73]

The *Bacchae* in fact offers no clear or positive voice for civic values. Unlike Sophocles' *Oedipus at Colonus*, it provides no alternative, positive model; there is no Theban democratic polis waiting in the wings, as it were, to take over from the destroyed Theban royal house. The city reflected in the *Bacchae* has no communal center, in part because there is no chorus of citizens who can speak as a community of involved fellow-citizens. Instead, the dominant collective voice is that of the barbarian followers of a beautiful but dangerous god who is even more unpitying than they. Even when the chorus does sympathize with the common woes of mortality in gnomic generalities, the contexts make its utterances problematic. The mortal sufferers at the end are driven out of their city, and this collapse of civic authority has been prefigured in the ruin of the king's palace and in Dionysus' figurative breaching of the walls of Thebes (585-603, 653f.). The survivors, in the closing moments of the play, can only comfort one another as private individuals, alone, defeated, and on the verge of exile.[74]

Elsewhere in tragedy, the chorus generally articulates civic values and speaks for a significant and representative community within the polis (see *DP* 242-43). But because the chorus of the *Bacchae* stands in such a strong adversarial relation to the civic authority, it has less interaction on the stage with the members of the polis than does the chorus in most tragedies; and even that interaction is narrowly focused on the conflict between Dionysus and Thebes. Aside from the odes, the chorus has only two short exchanges with a human character in the first two-thirds of the play, and both of these are statements

---

[73] Seaford ([1994] 256) takes a very different view of 319-21 ("You see, you take pleasure when many stand at the gates and the city magnifies the name of Pentheus: so too does he [Dionysus], I think, delight in being honored"). For Seaford the lines merely foreshadow the establishment of Dionysus' cult in Thebes as the new basis for civic order and unity after the destruction of the royal house engineered by the god: "Dionysos will by implication (319-21) now enjoy the honour once publicly bestowed by the polis on Pentheus." But the lines have a very different feeling if read, for example, alongside Aphrodite's anthropomorphic ruthlessness in defending her honor in the prologue of *Hippolytus*. For this more negative view of the passage see *DP* 279, 303.

[74] See *DP* 322-27. Here and in some of what follows I draw on Segal 1997.

of devotion to its god.[75] In the entire preserved portion of the play, the maenad chorus speaks only thirteen lines of iambic trimeter.

This meagerness of the chorus's dialogue both reflects and contributes to the gulf between itself and the Theban characters, who (with the exception of Agave in her bacchantic madness and Cadmus and Agave in the closing lines) speak in iambic trimeters. Chorus and protagonists virtually speak different languages. The chorus's language and behavior in fact reflect one of the characteristic qualities of a religious *thiasos*, namely that the bonds among its members depend on their common devotion to a god, not to the polis (see Burkert 1987, Chap. 2), although the city could try to incorporate these *thiasoi* into its religious structures.[76] Euripides has replaced the more familiar chorus of men or women of the city (as in *Hippolytus* or *Medea*) with this extra-polis group. The play's only representative of something like a democratic polis is the "wanderer around the town, well versed in words" (717), who urges the disastrous attack on the maenads.[77] One effect of this situation is to intensify the division between the chorus's world of Dionysiac cult — with its landscape of mountains, rivers, forests, and sheer animal energy — and the landscape of the city — with its walls and prisons and its repressive, authoritarian king, its hypocritical and foolish elders, and its crazed women (see *DP*, Chap. 4, especially 89ff.).

In a comedy like Aristophanes' *Frogs* (see *DP* 328-29) the positive, collective vision of Dionysus as a god of the polis is fully realized, especially in this god's ultimate preference for the civic, martial values of Aeschylean tragedy and the sturdy, oaken fighters at Marathon, over the subversive, sophistic, amoral subtleties of Euripides. The differences, of course, reflect the differences between tragic and comic outlooks; but the harsher vision of the *Bacchae* may also reflect Euripides' insights into some of the problems of the democratic polis (including the dangers inherent in its repression of female emo-

---

[75] Thus the three amoebean exchanges of the chorus with another character (576-603, 1024-29, 1168-99) are all focused narrowly on its loyalty to Dionysus: see Oranje (1984) 156. On the anomaly of the chorus's detachment from the main action in the first third of the play see Easterling (1987) 25-26.

[76] The evidence for the civic incorporation of such *thiasoi*, however, is epigraphic and mostly from the postclassical period: see, e.g., Versnel (1990) 152ff.; Zaidman and Schmitt Pantel (1992) 199.

[77] See also the chorus's reference to "the meaner masses," 430ff. and supra.

tionality) in the years after his exile from Athens and his abode at the frontiers of Greek civilization at the court of King Archelaus of Macedon.

I would like to push my observations on the chorus a little further and suggest that the dissolution of the civic center that the play enacts also implies a statement about tragedy. The calm, beatific visions and the ecstasy that appear in the first four odes of the play belong only to the Lydian maenads and are not accessible to the Thebans, who experience Dionysus only through his punitive violence and bloodshed. The play evokes a world of experience that extends beyond the polis to a wider frame of reference in which the distinction between Greek and barbarian is blurred. This is the aspect of Dionysus that appealed to the world of Alexander's conquests — a cosmopolitan deity whose power reaches far beyond the walls of any single Greek polis. This cosmopolitan Dionysus is already present in Sophocles' *Antigone* (1115-54). For Euripides, perhaps because of his distance from Greece when he wrote the *Bacchae*, the cosmopolitan Dionysus is far more vivid than the civic Dionysus of the *Antigone*. Euripides could not, of course, have guessed that his Macedonian hosts would eventually bring Dionysus to the limits of the Greek *oikoumene*; but, as Versnel has also seen, Euripides seems to have captured a facet of the god that was to have a remarkable life in the imagery of the Hellenistic and Graeco-Roman world.[78]

The *Bacchae* develops the primarily negative side of Dionysus' blurring between Greek and "barbarian"; but there may also be a hint of its positive side in the implicit recognition of the universalizing power of Dionysus in the theater and specifically in tragedy. By the end of the fifth century tragedy has become panhellenic, and this cosmopolitan appeal extends into the fourth century, as the vases and the proliferation of theaters all over the Greek world attest. The tragic Dionysus of the *Bacchae* extends beyond the confines of the individ-

---

[78] Versnel 1990, passim, especially 189-205; also Henrichs (1979) 8-11, with further references there cited. The authenticity of the remote Asian geography of Dionysus' conquests in 11-19 has been questioned by Albrecht Dihle, *Der Prolog der Bacchen und die antike Überlieferungsphase des Euripides-Textes*, Sitzungsberichte der Heidelberger Akademie der Wissenschaften, phil.-hist. Klasse, Heft 2 (1981), pp. 11-27, who regards the lines as a later interpolation; but their authenticity has been strongly maintained by Erbse (1984) 91; Diggle (1994b) 444-51; and Seaford (1996b) 149.

ual polis and reaches out to all humankind. In that respect the play has been prophetic far beyond even what its Teiresias could envision.[79]

The *Bacchae* gripped the generation coming of age in the sixties and seventies because it seemed to express the defiance of repressive authority by unbounded youthful energy. Many a lecturer on the play has tried to enliven a class by drawing analogies between Dionysiac rites and rock-concerts. Many a director has cast Euripides' Dionysiac Stranger as a rock-band leader or something similar. For audiences of the third millennium, whose historical and moral consciousness has absorbed Bosnia and Rwanda, violence rather than authority or emotional repression may emerge as the key issue of the play: the potential animality of humankind and the savage cruelty that we are capable of inflicting on one another in situations of mob violence. Here René Girard's theories of mimetic violence and Walter Burkert's concern with the relation between ritual and human aggression may prove to be the compelling interpretive models (Girard 1972 = 1977; Burkert 1972 = 1983).

The murderous violence of cultic madness that leads a mother to rip apart her living son might not have appeared so foreign to audiences familiar with the massacres at Mitylene and Melos or the effects of civil war on Corcyra, to say nothing of the panics or other irrational impulses that may seize armies and other large groups (cf. *Ba.* 302-5). The effect of Dionysus on the women of Thebes shows Euripides' understanding, after thirty years of war throughout Greece, of how murderous frenzy can overpower a large segment of otherwise normally functioning members of a society. The outbreaks of cultic violence at Jonestown (the mass suicide of the followers of Jim Jones) and in Japan and southern California more recently, though not to be simplistically assimilated to Dionysiac violence, nevertheless indicate the dangerous areas of human behavior implicated in the play. On the other hand, the government's response to David Koresh and his Branch Davidians at Waco, Texas might easily evoke comparisons with Pentheus' call to mobilize his armed forces against the cult of Dionysus (*Ba.* 778-86, 796, 809, 845-6; see also *DP* 194-96).

The triangular relations between Dionysus as god of wine, festivity,

[79] On the cosmopolitanism of Dionysus in relation to the expanding, panhellenic audiences of tragedy see Segal (1995b) 22-25.

and ecstatic ritual within the polis, Dionysus as god of emotional release and possible madness, and Dionysus as god of the mask and dramatic illusion give the *Bacchae* a unique power and complexity. All three aspects of Dionysus are still powerful forces among us, and the balance between them can never be sure or stable. It is obviously important not to conflate the Dionysus who has specific cultic and social functions in the polis, with the "Dionysiac" (with or without Nietzsche) that tends to accrue to itself only the dangerous side of the god in myth as opposed to polis ritual. Yet if we completely eliminate the "Dionysiac" from the *Bacchae* or insist only on the social and civic functioning of the Dionysiac in fifth-century Athens, we amputate a large segment of the *Bacchae*'s meaning. As much as the play is about the cult of Dionysus, it is also about different kinds of influences that Dionysus can exert on different personalities. The play, therefore, is also about those darker potentialities and susceptibilities of the psyche that make Dionysus "most terrible" as well as "most gentle." Particularly if we extend the realm of Dionysus to include the contemporary reaches of his power — drugs, the exhilaration of rock music and its derivatives, the hypnotic effect of film and television, and the powerful effect of mimetic violence on sociopathic or antisocial individuals — then the *Bacchae* and its god will continue to have a life of their own into the new millennium, and the play will continue to enthrall, horrify, and divide its readers and viewers as energetically as it has done in the past.

Selected Bibliography

Arrowsmith, W. A. (1959). "The Criticism of Greek Tragedy," *Tulane Drama Review* 33: 31-57.

Arthur, Marylin B. (1972). "The Choral Odes of the *Bacchae* of Euripides," YCS 22: 145-79.

——. (1977). "The Curse of Civilization: The Choral Odes of the *Phoenissae*," HSCP 81: 163-85.

Barlow, Shirley A. (1971). *The Imagery of Euripides*. London.

Barthes, Roland. (1973). *Le plaisir du texte*. Paris.

Benedetto, Vincenzo di. (1971). *Euripide: Teatro e società*. Turin.

Bérard, Claude, (1974). *Anodoi, Essai sur l'imagerie des passages chthoniens*. Institut Suisse de Rome, vol. 13. Neuchâtel.

Bogner, Hans. (1947). *Der tragische Gegensatz*. Heidelberg.

Brelich, Angelo. (1969). *Paides e Parthenoi*. Incunabula Graeca 36. Rome.

Bremer, J. M. (1976). "De interpretatie van Euripides' Bacchen," *Lampas* 9: 2-7.

Bremmer, Jan. (1978). "Heroes, Rituals, and the Trojan War," *Studi Storico-Religiosi* 2:5-38.

Broadhead, H. D. (1968). *Tragica: Elucidations of Passages in Greek Tragedy*. Christchurch, New Zealand.

Burkert, Walter. (1972). *Homo Necans: Interpretationen altgriechischer Opferriten und Mythen*. Berlin and New York.

——. (1977). *Griechische Religion der archaischen und klassischen Epochen*. Stuttgart. (Cited as Burkert, *Gr. Rel.*)

——. (1979). *Structure and History in Greek Mythology and Ritual*. Sather Classical Lectures 47. Berkeley and Los Angeles.

Burnett, Anne Pippin. (1970). "Pentheus and Dionysus: Host and Guest," *CP* 65: 15-29.

Calame, Claude. (1977). *Les choeurs de jeunes filles en Grèce archaïque* 2 vols. Rome.

——, ed. (1977). *Rito e poesia corale in Grecia: Guida storica e critica*. Rome and Bari.

Cantarella, Raffaele. (1971). "Il Dioniso delle *Baccanti* e la teoria aristotelica sulle origini del dramma," in *Studi in onore di Vittorio De Falco*, 123-32. Naples.

———. (1974). "Dioniso, fra *Baccanti* e *Rane*," in *Serta Turyniana*, edited by J. L. Heller and J. K. Newman, 291-310. Urbana, Ill.

Carrière, Jean. (1966). "Sur le message des Bacchantes," AC 35: 118-39.

Coche de la Ferté, Étienne. (1980). "Penthée et Dionysos: Nouvel essai d'interprétation des 'Bacchantes' d'Euripide," in *Recherches sur les religions de l'antiquité classique*, edited by Raymond Bloch, 105-257. Geneva and Paris.

Conacher, D. J. (1967). *Euripidean Drama: Myth, Theme and Structure*. Toronto.

Cook, Albert. (1971). *Enactment: Greek Tragedy*. Chicago.

Darkaki, Maria. (1980). "Aspects du sacrifice dionysiaque," *Revue de l'Histoire des Religions* 197: 131-57.

Deichgräber, Karl. (1935). "Die Kadmos-Teiresiasszene in Euripides' Bakchen," *Hermes* 70: 322-49.

Detienne, Marcel. (1972). *Les jardins d'Adonis*. Paris.

———. (1967, repr. 1973). *Les maîtres de vérité dans la Grèce archaïque*. Paris.

———. (1977). *Dionysos mis à mort*. Paris.

——— and Vernant, Jean-Pierre. (1979). *La cuisine du sacrifice en pays grec*. Paris.

Devereux, George. (1970). "The Psychotherapy Scene in Euripides' *Bacchae*," *JHS* 90: 35-48.

———. (1974). "Trance and Orgasm in Euripides: *Bakchae*," in *Parapsychology and Anthropology*, edited by A. Angoff and D. Barth, 36-51; discussion: 52-58. New York.

Diller, Hans. (1955). "Die Bakchen und ihre Stellung im Spätwerk des Euripides," *Akademie der Wissenschaften und der Literatur in Mainz, Abhandlungen der Geistes- und Sozialwissenschaftl. Klasse.* 5: 453-71. (Cited from Schwinge, *Euripides* [*infra*] 469-92.)

———. (1960). "Umwelt und Masse als dramatische Faktoren bei Euripides," in *Entretiens, Euripide* (infra), 81-105; discussion: 106-21.

Dodds, E. R. (1940). "Maenadism in the *Bacchae*," *HThR* 33: 155-76.

———. (1951). *The Greeks and the Irrational.* Sather Classical Lectures 25. Berkeley and Los Angeles.

———. (1960). *Euripides' Bacchae.* Edited with an Introduction and Commentary. 2nd ed. Oxford.

Dyer, Robert R. (1964). "Image and Symbol: The Link between the Two Worlds of the 'Bacchae,'" *AUMLA* 21: 15-26.

Entretiens sur l'antiquité classique, 6, *Euripide*, edited by O. Reverdin. (1960). Fondation Hardt. Vandoeuvres-Geneva. (Cited as *Entretiens, Euripide.*)

Farnell, Lewis R. (1895-1909). *The Cults of the Greek States.* 5 vols. Oxford.

Feldman, Thalia Phillies. (1965). "Gorgo and the Origins of Fear," *Arion* 4: 484-94.

Festugière, A. J. (1956). "La signification religieuse de la Parodos des Bacchantes," *Eranos* 54: 72-86.

———. (1957). "Euripide dans les 'Bacchantes,'" *Eranos* 55: 127-44.

Foley, Helene P. (1980). "The Masque of Dionysus," *TAPA* 110: 107-33.

Fontenrose, Joseph. (1959). *Python: A Study of the Delphic Myth and its Origins.* Berkeley and Los Angeles.

———. (1980). *Orion: The Myth of the Hunter and the Huntress.* University of California Publications in Classical Studies, vol. 23. Berkeley and Los Angeles.

Frazer, Sir James George. (1921). *Apollodorus, The Library*, with an English translation. 2 vols. Loeb Classical Library. London and Cambridge, Mass.

Gallini, Clara. (1963). "Il travestismo rituale di Penteo," *SMSR* 34: 211-28.

Gantz, Timothy N. (1980). "The Aeschylean Tetralogy: Attested and Conjectured Groups," *AJP* 101: 133-64.

Gernet, Louis. (1953). "Dionysos et la religion dionysiaque: Éléments hérités et traits originaux," *REG* 66: 375-95.

Girard, René. (1972). *La violence et le sacré.* Paris. English translation, *Violence and the Sacred*, trans. P. Gregory (Baltimore 1977).

Glover, M. R. (1929). "The Bacchae," *JHS* 49: 82-88.

Gold, Barbara K. (1977). "*Eukosmia* in Euripides' *Bacchae*," *AJP* 98: 3-15.

Green, André. (1969). *Un oeil en trop: Le complexe d'Oedipe dans la tragédie.* Paris.

Grube, G.M.A. (1935). "Dionysus in the *Bacchae*," *TAPA* 66: 37-54.

————. (1941, repr. 1961). *The Drama of Euripides.* London.

Guépin, Jean-Pierre. (1968). *The Tragic Paradox.* Amsterdam.

Guthrie, W.K.C. (1950). *The Greeks and Their Gods.* London.

————. (1969). *A History of Greek Philosophy,* 3, *The Fifth-Century Enlightenment.* Cambridge.

Hamilton, Richard. (1974). "*Bacchae* 49-52: Dionysus' Plan," *TAPA* 104: 139-49.

Harrison, Jane Ellen. (1927, repr. 1962). *Themis.* Cleveland.

Henrichs, Albert. (1978). "Greek Maenadism from Olympias to Messalina," *HSCP* 82: 121-60.

————. (1979). "Greek and Roman Glimpses of Dionysos," in *Dionysos and his Circle: Ancient Through Modern,* edited by Caroline Houser, 1-11. Cambridge, Mass.

Hillman, James. (1972, repr. 1978). *The Myth of Analysis.* New York.

Hourmourziades, Nicolaos C. (1965). *Production and Imagination in Euripides.* Athens.

Huizinga, Johan. (1950, repr. 1955). *Homo Ludens: A Study of the Play Element in Culture.* Boston.

Jeanmaire, Henri. (1951). *Dionysos, Histoire du culte de Bacchus.* Paris.

Kamerbeek, J. C. (1948). "On the Conception of *Theomachos* in Relation with Greek Tragedy," *Mnemosyne,* series 4, 1: 271-83.

————. (1960). "Mythe et réalité dans l'oeuvre d'Euripide," in *Entretiens, Euripide* (supra), 1-25.

Kerényi, C. (1976). *Dionysos: Archetypal Image of Indestructible Life,* trans. Ralph Manheim. Princeton and London.

Kirk, Geoffrey S. (1970). *The Bacchae by Euripides: A Translation with Commentary.* Englewood Cliffs, N.J.

Knox, Bernard M. W. (1979). *Word and Action: Essays on the Ancient Theater.* Baltimore.

Kott, Jan. (1973). *The Eating of the Gods: An Interpretation of Greek Tragedy.* New York.

Kranz, Walther. (1933). *Stasimon*. Berlin.

Kristeva, Julia (1969, repr. 1978). *Sēmeiōtikē: Recherches pour une sémanalyse*. Paris.

Leach, Edmund. (1976). *Culture and Communication*. Cambridge.

Lesky, Albin. (1972). *Die tragische Dichtung der Hellenen*. 3rd ed. Göttingen. (Cited as Lesky, *TDH*.)

Loraux, Nicole. (1979). "L'autochtonie: une topique Athénienne," *Annales E.S.C.* 34: 3-26. Revised version in *Les enfants d' Athéna* (Paris 1981) 35-73.

McDonald, Marianne. (1978). *Terms for Happiness in Euripides*. *Hypomnemata* 54. Göttingen.

McNally, Sheila. (1978). "The Maenad in Early Greek Art," *Arethusa* 11: 101-35.

Murray, Gilbert. (1913). *Euripides and His Age*. London.

Musurillo, Herbert, S. J. (1966). "Euripides and the Dionysiac Piety (*Bacchae* 370-433)," *TAPA* 97: 299-309.

Nagy, Gregory. (1979). *The Best of the Achaeans: Concepts of the Hero in Archaic Greek Poetry*. Baltimore.

Nestle, Wilhelm. (1901). *Euripides. Der Dichter der griechischen Aufklärung*. Stuttgart.

―――. (1942). *Vom Mythos zum Logos*. Stuttgart.

Neumann, Erich. (1954). *The Origins and History of Consciousness*, trans. R.F.C. Hull. Princeton.

Nietzsche, Friedrich. (1956). *The Birth of Tragedy and the Genealogy of Morals*, trans. Francis Golffing. Garden City, N.Y.

Nilsson, Martin P. (1935). "Early Orphism and Kindred Religious Movements," *HThR* 28: 181-230.

―――. (1955). *Geschichte der griechischen Religion*. Vol. 1, 2nd ed. Munich. (Cited as Nilsson, *GGR*.)

Norwood, Gilbert. (1908). *The Riddle of the Bacchae*. Manchester.

―――. (1954). *Essays in Euripidean Drama*. Berkeley and Los Angeles.

Ogibenin, Boris L. (1975). "Mask in the Light of Semiotics—A Functional Approach," *Semiotica* 13: 1-9.

Oranje, Hans. (1979). "*De Bacchae van Euripides: het stuk en de toeschouwers*." Dissertation. Amsterdam.

Otto, Walter F. (1965). *Dionysus, Myth and Cult*, trans. R. B. Palmer. Bloomington, Ind.

Parke, H. W. (1977). *Festivals of the Athenians*. Ithaca, N.Y., and London.

Parry, Hugh. (1978). *The Lyric Poems of Greek Tragedy*. Toronto and Sarasota.

Philippart, Hubert. (1930). "Iconographie des 'Bacchantes' d'Euripide," *Revue Belge de Philologie et d'Histoire* 9: 5-72.

Podlecki, Anthony J. (1974). "Individual and Group in Euripides' *Bacchae*," AC 43: 143-65.

Pucci, Pietro. (1977). "Euripides: The Monument and the Sacrifice," *Arethusa* 10: 165-95.

————. (1980). *The Violence of Pity in Euripides' Medea*. Cornell Studies in Classical Philology, vol. 41. Ithaca, N.Y., and London.

Ramnoux, Clémence. (1962). *Mythologie ou la famille olympienne*. Paris.

Ricoeur, Paul. (1967). *The Symbolism of Evil*, trans. Emerson Buchanan. New York, Evanston, and London.

Ridley, R. T. (1979). "The Hoplite as Citizen," AC 48: 508-48.

Roberts, Patrick. (1975). *The Psychology of Tragic Drama*. Boston and London.

Rohde, Erwin. (1925). *Psyche*, trans. W. B. Hillis. 8th ed. London.

Rohdich, Hermann. (1968). *Die Euripideische Tragödie*. Heidelberg.

Romilly, Jacqueline de. (1963). "Le thème du bonheur dans les *Bacchantes*," REG 76: 361-80.

Rosenmeyer, Thomas G. (1963). *The Masks of Tragedy*. Austin, Tex.

Roux, Jeanne. (1970, 1972). *Euripide, Les Bacchantes*. 2 vols. Paris.

Rudberg, Gunnar. (1933). "Euripides' Naturgefühl," SO 12: 39-51.

Sale, William. (1972). "The Psychoanalysis of Pentheus in the *Bacchae* of Euripides," YCS 22: 63-82.

————. (1977). *Existentialism and Euripides*. Ramus Monographs. Melbourne, Australia.

Sandys, J. E. (1900). *The Bacchae of Euripides*. Cambridge.

Sansone, David. (1978). "The *Bacchae* as Satyr-Play?" ICS 3: 40-46.

Schnapp, Alain. (1979). "Pratiche e immagini di caccia nella Grecia antica," *Dialoghi di Archeologia* 1: 35-59.

Schwinge, Ernst-Richard, ed. (1968). *Euripides*. Wege der Forschung, vol. 89. Darmstadt.

Scott, William C. (1975). "Two Suns over Thebes: Imagery and Stage Effects in the *Bacchae*," TAPA 105: 333-46.

Seaford, Richard. (1981). "Dionysiac Drama and the Dionysiac Mysteries," *CQ*, n.s. 31: 252-75.

Segal, Charles P. (1961). "The Character and Cults of Dionysus and the Unity of the *Frogs*," *HSCP* 65: 207-42.

———. (1962). "Gorgias and the Psychology of the *Logos*," *HSCP* 66: 99-155.

———. (1965). "The Tragedy of the *Hippolytus*: The Waters of Ocean and the Untouched Meadow," *HSCP* 70: 117-69.

———. (1971). "The Two Worlds of Euripides' *Helen*, *TAPA* 102: 553-614.

———. (1973/74). "The Raw and the Cooked in Greek Literature: Structure, Metaphor, Values," *CJ* 69: 289-308.

———. (1975). "Mariage et sacrifice dans les *Trachiniennes* de Sophocle," *AC* 44: 30-53.

———. (1976). "Bacchylides Reconsidered: The Dynamics of Lyric Narrative," *QUCC* 22: 99-130.

———. (1977). "Euripides' *Bacchae*: Conflict and Mediation," *Ramus* 6: 103-20.

———. (1978). "The Menace of Dionysus: Sex Roles and Reversals in Euripides' *Bacchae*," *Arethusa* 11: 185-202.

———. (1978b). "The Magic of Orpheus and the Ambiguities of Language," *Ramus* 7: 106-42.

———. (1978/79). "Pentheus and Hippolytus on the Couch and on the Grid: Psychoanalytic and Structuralist Readings of Greek Tragedy," *CW* 72: 129-48.

———. (1979). "Solar Imagery and Tragic Heroism in Euripides' *Hippolytus*," in *Arktouros, Hellenic Studies Presented to B.M.W. Knox on the Occasion of his 65th Birthday*, edited by G. W. Bowersock, Walter Burkert, and M.C.J. Putnam, 151-61. Berlin and New York.

———. (1980/81). "Visual Symbolism and Visual Effects in Sophocles," *CW* 74: 125-42.

———. (1981). *Tragedy and Civilization: An Interpretation of Sophocles*. Martin Classical Lectures 26. Cambridge, Mass.

———. (1982). "Etymologies and Double Meanings in Euripides' *Bacchae*," *Glotta* 60 (1982).

Seidensticker, Bernd. (1972). "Pentheus," *Poetica* 5: 35-63.

———. (1978). "Comic Elements in Euripides' *Bacchae*," *AJP* 99: 303-20.

————. (1979). "Sacrificial Ritual in the *Bacchae*," in *Arktouros, Knox Studies* (supra), 181-190.

Simon, Bennett, M.D. (1978). *Mind and Madness in Ancient Greece.* Ithaca, N.Y., and London.

Slater, Philip. (1968). *The Glory of Hera.* Boston.

Steidle, Wolf. (1968). *Studien zum antiken Drama.* Munich.

Taplin, Oliver. (1978). *Greek Tragedy in Action.* Berkeley and Los Angeles.

Thomson, George. (1979). "The Problem of the *Bacchae*," *Epistēmonikē Epetēris tēs Philosophikēs Scholēs tou Aristoteleiou Panepistēmiou Thessalonikēs* 18: 424-46.

Toporov, V. N. (1978). "On Dostoevsky's Poetics and Archaic Patterns of Mythical Thought," trans. Susan Knight, *New Literary History* 9: 333-52.

Tschiedel, H.-J. (1977). "Natur und Mensch in den 'Bakchen' des Euripides," *Antike und Abendland* 23: 64-76.

Turato, Fabio. (1979). *La crisi della città e l'ideologia del selvaggio nell' Atene del V secolo a. C.* Rome.

Turner, Victor. (1973). *The Forest of Symbols.* Ithaca, N.Y., and London.

————. (1974). *Dramas, Fields, and Metaphors.* Ithaca, N.Y., and London.

————. (1974b). "Metaphors of Anti-Structure in Religious Culture," in *Changing Perspectives in the Scientific Study of Religion,* edited by Alan W. Eister, 63-84. New York.

Van Looy, Herman. (1973). "Παρετυμολογεῖ ὁ Εὐριπίδης," in *Zetesis,* Festschrift for Emile de Strijcker, 345-66. Antwerp and Utrecht.

Verdenius, W. J. (1962). "Notes on Euripides' *Bacchae*," *Mnemosyne,* ser. 4, vol. 15: 337-63.

————. (1980). "Notes on the Prologue of Euripides' *Bacchae*," *Mnemosyne* ser. 4, vol. 33: 1-16.

Vernant, Jean-Pierre. (1969, repr. 1974). *Mythe et pensée chez les Grecs.* 2 vols. Paris.

————. (1974). *Mythe et société en Grèce ancienne.* Paris.

———— and Vidal-Naquet, Pierre. (1972). *Mythe et tragédie.* Paris. See also Detienne, supra.

Verrall, A. W. (1910). *The Bacchants of Euripides and Other Essays.* Cambridge.

Vian, Francis. (1963). *Les origines de Thèbes: Cadmos et les Spartes.* Paris.

Vicaire, Paul. (1968). "Place et figure de Dionysos dans l'*Antigone* de Sophocle," *REG* 81: 351-73.

Vidal-Naquet, Pierre. (1968). "The Black Hunter and the Origin of the Athenian Ephebia," *PCPS* n.s. 14: 49-64. Revised French version in *Le chasseur noir*, infra, 151-74.

———. (1972). "Chasse et sacrifice dans l'*Orestie* d'Eschyle," in *Mythe et tragédie* (supra) 135-58.

———. (1978). "Plato's Myth of the Statesman, the Ambiguities of the Golden Age and of History," *JHS* 98: 132-41. Revised French version in *Le chasseur noir*, 361-80.

———. (1981). *Le chasseur noir: Formes de pensée et formes de société dans le monde grec.* Paris.

Wassermann, Felix. (1929). "Die Bakchantinnen des Euripides," *NJbb* 5: 272-86.

———. (1953). "Man and God in the *Bacchae* and in the *Oedipus at Colonus*," in *Studies Presented to David M. Robinson*, edited by G. E. Mylonas and D. Raymond, 2: 559-69. St. Louis.

Webster, T.B.L. (1967). *The Tragedies of Euripides.* London.

Whitman, Cedric H. (1974). *Euripides and the Full Circle of Myth.* Cambridge, Mass.

Willink, C. W. (1966). "Some Problems of Text and Interpretation in the *Bacchae*," 1, *CR* n.s. 16: 27-50; 2, ibid. 220-242.

Winnington-Ingram, R.P. (1948). *Euripides and Dionysus: An Interpretation of the Bacchae.* Cambridge. (Cited as WI.)

———. (1960). "*Hippolytus*: A Study in Causation," in *Entretiens, Euripide* (supra), 171-97.

———. (1966). "Euripides, *Bacchae* 877-881 = 897-901," *BICS* 13: 34-37.

———. (1969). "Euripides: *Poiētēs Sophos*," *Arethusa* 2: 129-42.

Wohlberg, J. (1968). "The Palace-Hero Equation in Euripides," *Acta Antiqua Academiae Scientiarum Hungaricae* 16: 149-55.

Zeitlin, Froma I. (1980). "The Closet of Masks: Role-Playing and Myth-Making in the *Orestes* of Euripides," *Ramus* 9: 62-77.

Zielinski, Th. (1923). "L'évolution religieuse d'Euripide," *REG* 36: 459-79.

Bibliographical Addenda (1997)

For abbreviations see above, pages xvii-xviii; for most items prior to 1982, see pages 395-403.

Alexiou, Margaret. (1974). *The Ritual Lament in Greek Tradition.* Cambridge.

Alford, C. Fred. (1992). *The Psychoanalytic Theory of Greek Tragedy.* New Haven.

Bažant, Jan, and Gratia Berger-Doer. (1994). "Pentheus," *Lexicon Iconographiae Mythologiae Classicae.* Zurich and Munich. Vol. 7, part 1, 306-17, and vol. 7, part 2, 250-65 (plates).

Bérard, Claude, et al. [1984] (1989). *A City of Images: Iconography and Society in Ancient Greece,* trans. D. Lyons. Princeton.

Bierl, Anton F. H. (1991). *Dionysos und die griechische Tragödie.* Tübingen.

Bremmer, Jan N. (1984). "Greek Maenadism Reconsidered," ZPE 55: 267-86.

———. (1994). *Greek Religion.* Greece and Rome: New Surveys in the Classics, vol. 24. Oxford.

Burkert, Walter. [1972] (1983). *Homo Necans,* trans. P. Bing. Berkeley and Los Angeles.

———. (1987). *Ancient Mystery Cults.* Cambridge, Mass.

Buxton, Richard. (1989). "The Messenger and the Maenads: A Speech from Euripides' Bacchae (1043-1152)," *Acta Antiqua Academiae Scientiarum Hungaricae* 32: 225-34.

———. (1991). "News from Cithaeron: Narrators and Narratives in the *Bacchae,*" *Pallas* 37: 39-48.

———. (1994). *Imaginary Greece.* Cambridge.

Calame, Claude. (1986). "Facing Othernesss: The Tragic Mask in Ancient Greece," *History of Religions* 28: 125-42.

Carpenter, Thomas H. (1993). "On the Beardless Dionysus," in Carpenter and Faraone 1993. 185-206.

——— and Christopher A. Faraone, eds. (1993). *Masks of Dionysus.* Ithaca, N.Y.

Connor, W. R. (1987). "Tribes, Festivals and Processions; Civic Ceremonial and Political Manipulation in Archaic Greece," *JHS* 107: 40-50.

Des Bouvrie, Synnøve. (1990). *Women in Greek Tragedy. Symbolae Osloenses*, supplement 27. Oxford.

Detienne, Marcel. [1986] (1989). *Dionysus at Large*, trans. A. Goldhammer. Cambridge, Mass.

Diggle, James, ed. (1994a). *Euripidis Fabulae*, vol. 3. Oxford Classical Texts. Oxford.

――――. (1994b). *Euripidea: Collected Essays*. Oxford.

Dunn, Francis M. (1996). *Tragedy's End: Closure and Innovation in Euripidean Drama*. Oxford.

Easterling, P. E. (1987). "Women in Tragic Space," *BICS* 34: 15-26.

Erbse, Hartmut. (1984). *Studien zum Prolog der euripideischen Tragödie*. Berlin. (See especially 89-100.)

Euben, Peter. (1990). *The Tragedy of Political Theory*. Princeton. (See especially "Membership and 'Dismembership' in the *Bacchae*," 130-63.)

Fisher, Raymond K. (1992). "Palace Miracles in Euripides' *Bacchae*," *AJP* 113: 179-88.

Fitzgerald, Gerald. (1992/93). "Textual Practices and Euripidean Productions," *Theatre Survey* 33: 5-22.

Foley, Helene. (1985). *Ritual Irony: Poetry and Sacrifice in Euripides*. Ithaca, N.Y.

――――. (1993). "The Politics of Lamentation," in *Tragedy, Comedy and the Polis, Papers from the Greek Drama Conference, Nottingham, 18-20 July 1990*, ed. A. H. Sommerstein, S. Halliwell, J. Henderson, and B. Zimmermann. Bari. 101-43

Friedrich, Rainer. (1996). "Everything to Do with Dionysus? Ritualism, the Dionysiac, and the Tragic," in Silk 1996. 257-83.

Frontisi-Ducroux, Françoise. (1995). *Du masque au visage*. Paris.

―――― and François Lissarrague. (1983). *"De l'ambiguïté à l'ambivalence: un parcours dionysiaque,"* *Annali del Istituto Orientale di Napoli* 5: 11-32.

Gasparri, Carlo, et al. (1986). "Dionysos," "Dionysos/Fufluns," "Dionysos/Bacchus," etc., *Lexicon Iconographiae Mythologiae Classicae*. Zurich and Munich. Vol. 3, part 1, 414-566, and vol. 3, part 2, 296-456 (plates).

Goff, Barbara. (1995). "The Women of Thebes," *CJ* 90: 353-65.

Goldhill, Simon. (1986). *Reading Greek Tragedy*. Cambridge.

———. (1988). "Doubling and Recognition in the *Bacchae*," *Metis* 3: 137-56.

———. (1990). "The Great Dionysia and Civic Ideology," in Winkler and Zeitlin 1990. 97-129. Originally published in *JHS* 107 (1987) 58-76.

———. (1994). "Representing Democracy: Women at the Great Dionysia," in *Ritual, Finance, Politics: Athenian Democratic Accounts Presented to David Lewis*, ed. Robin Osborne and Simon Hornblower. Oxford. 347-69.

Graf, Fritz. (1993). "Dionysian and Orphic Eschatology: New Texts and Old Questions," in Carpenter and Faraone 1993. 239-58.

Gregory, Justina. (1985). "Some Aspects of Seeing in Euripides' *Bacchae*," *G&R* 32: 23-31.

Henderson, Jeffrey. (1991). "Women and the Athenian Dramatic Festivals," *TAPA* 121: 133-47.

Henrichs, Albert. (1982). "Changing Dionysiac Identities," in *Jewish and Christian Self-Definition*, ed. Ben F. Meyer and E. P. Sanders. London. 137-60, 213-36.

———. (1984a). "Loss of Self, Suffering, Violence: The Modern View of Dionysus from Nietzsche to Girard," *HSCP* 88: 205-40.

———. (1984b). "Male Intruders among the Maenads: The So-called Male Celebrant," in *Mnemai: Classical Studies in Memory of Karl K. Hulley*, ed. Harold J. Evjen. Chico, Calif. 69-91.

———. (1986). "The Last of the Detractors: Friedrich Nietzsche's Condemnation of Euripides," *GRBS* 27: 369-97.

———. (1990). "Between Country and City: Cultic Dimensions of Dionysus in Athens and Attica," in *Cabinet of the Muses* (Festschrift T. G. Rosenmeyer), ed. M. Griffith and D. J. Mastronarde. Atlanta. 257-77.

———. (1993). "'He Has a God in Him,': Human and Divine in the Modern Perception of Dionysus," in Carpenter and Faraone 1993. 13-43.

———. (1994). "Der Rasende Gott: Zur Psychologie des Dionysos und des Dionysischen in Mythos und Literatur," *Antike und Abendland* 40: 31-58.

———. (1994/95). "'Why Should I Dance?': Choral Self-Referentiality in Greek Tragedy," *Arion*, 3d series 3.1: 56-111.

————. (1996a). "Dionysus," entry in *Oxford Classical Dictionary*, 3d ed., ed. Simon Hornblower and Anthony Spawforth. Oxford. 479-82.

————. (1996b). "Dancing in Athens, Dancing on Delos: Some Patterns of Choral Projection in Euripides," *Philologus* 140: 48-62.

Holst-Wahrhaft, Gail. (1992). *Dangerous Voices: Women's Laments and Greek Literature*. Ithaca, N.Y.

Ieranò, Giorgio. (1991). "Forme della necessità nelle Baccanti di Euripide," *Dioniso* 61: 45-60.

————. (1992). "Zeus e Dioniso: in margine a Eur. *Bacch.* 1349," *Rivista di Filologie e Istruzione Classica* 120: 286-91.

Just, Roger. (1989). *Women in Athenian Law and Life*. London and New York.

Katz, Marylin A. (1994). "The Character of Tragedy: Women and the Greek Imagination," *Arethusa* 27: 81-103.

Kovaks, David. (1991). "Notes on the *Bacchae*," *CQ* 41: 340-45.

Kullmann, Wolfgang. (1993). "Die 'Rolle' des euripideischen Pentheus: Haben die *Bakchen* eine 'metatheatralische' Bedeutung?" in *Philanthropia kai Eusebeia: Festschrift für Albrecht Dihle zum 70. Geburtstag*, ed. G. W. Most, Hubert Petersmann, and A. M. Ritter. Göttingen. 248-63.

Latacz, Joachim. (1993). *Einführung in die griechische Tragödie*. Göttingen.

Leineiks, Valdis. (1996). *The City of Dionysus: A Study of Euripides' Bakchai*. Stuttgart. (Appeared too late to be considered in the Afterword.)

Lloyd-Jones, Sir Hugh. (1990). *Greek Epic, Lyric and Tragedy: The Academic Papers of Sir Hugh Lloyd-Jones*. Oxford.

Loraux, Nicole. [1985] (1987). *Tragic Ways of Killing a Woman*, trans. A. Forster. Cambridge, Mass.

————. (1990). *Les mères en deuil*. Paris.

McDonald, Marianne. (1992). "L'extase de Penthée: Ivressse et réprésentation dans les *Bacchantes* d'Euripide," *Pallas* 38: 227-37.

McGinty, Park. (1978). *Interpretation and Dionysus*. The Hague.

March, Jennifer. (1989). "Euripides' *Bakchai*: A Reconsideration in the Light of the Vase-Painting," *BICS* 36: 33-65.

————. (1990). "Euripides the Misogynist," in *Euripides, Women, and Sexuality*, ed. Anton Powell. New York and London. 32-75.

Meier, Christian [1988] (1993). *The Political Art of Greek Tragedy*, trans. A. Webber. Baltimore.

Obbink, Dirk. (1993). "Dionysus Poured Out: Ancient and Modern Theories of Sacrifice and Cultural Formation," in Carpenter and Faraone 1993. 65-86.

Oranje, Hans. (1984). *Euripides' Bacchae: The Play and Its Audience*. Mnemosyne supplement 78. Leiden.

Pailler, Jean-Marie. (1995). "Dionysos avec ou sans masque," *Pallas* 42: 105-112.

Parsons, Michael. (1988). "Self-Knowledge Refused and Accepted: A Psychoanalytic Perspective on the *Bacchae* and the *Oedipus at Colonus*," *BICS* 35: 1-14.

Podlecki, Anthony J. (1990). "Could Women Attend the Theatre in Ancient Athens? A Collection of Testimonia," *Ancient World* 21: 27-43.

Schlesier, Renate. (1993). "Mixtures of Masks: Maenads as Tragic Models," in Carpenter and Faraone 1993. 89-114.

Seaford, Richard. (1993). "Dionysus as Destroyer of the Household: Homer, Tragedy, and the Polis," in Carpenter and Faraone 1993. 115-46.

———. (1994). *Reciprocity and Ritual*. Oxford.

———. (1996a). "Something to Do with Dionysus—Tragedy and the Dionysiac: Response to Friedrich," in Silk 1996. 284-94.

———, ed. and trans. (1996b). *Euripides, Bacchae*. Warminster.

Segal, Charles. (1982). *Dionysiac Poetics and Euripides' Bacchae*. Princeton.

———. (1985). "The *Bacchae* as Metatragedy," in *Directions in Euripidean Criticism*, ed. Peter Burian. Durham, N.C. 154-71.

———. (1986). *Interpreting Greek Tragedy: Myth, Poetry Text*. Ithaca, N.Y.

———. (1990a). "Dionysus in the Golden Tablets from Pelinna," *GRBS* 31: 411-19.

———. (1993). *Euripides and the Poetics of Sorrow: Art, Gender, and Commemoration in Alcestis, Hippolytus, and Hecuba*. Durham, N.C.

———. (1993a). "Violence and the Other: Greek, Female, and Barbarian in Euripides' *Hecuba*," = Segal 1993, 170-90. Originally published in *TAPA* 120 (1990): 109-31.

———. (1993b). "Theater, Ritual, and Commemoration in Euripides' *Hippolytus*," in Segal 1993. 110-35. Originally published in *Ramus* 17 (1988): 52-74

———. (1994). "Female Mourning and Dionysiac Lament in Euripides' *Bacchae*," in *Drama, Mythos, Bühne: Festschrift für Helmut Flashar*, ed. Anton Bierl and Peter Möllendorf. Stuttgart and Leipzig. 12-18.

———. (1995a). Review of Seaford 1994, *Bryn Mawr Classical Review* 6: 651-657.

———. (1995b). "Classics, Ecumenicism, and Greek Tragedy," *TAPA* 125: 1-26.

———. (1995c). *Sophocles' Tragic World: Divinity, Nature, Society*. Cambridge, Mass.

———. (1996). "Catharsis, Audience, and Closure in Greek Tragedy," in Silk 1996. 149-172.

———. (1997). "Chorus and Community in Euripides' *Bacchae*," in *Poet, Public, and Performance in Ancient Greece*, ed. Lowell Edmunds and Robert W. Wallace. Baltimore. 65-86, 149-53.

Seidensticker, Bernd. (1982). *Palintonos Harmonia: Studien zu komischen Elementen in der griechischen Tragödie*. Hypomnemata 72. Göttingen.

———. (1996). "Peripeteia and Tragic Dialectic in Euripidean Tragedy," in Silk 1996. 377-96.

Serematakis, C. Nadia. (1991). *The Last Word: Women, Death, and Divination in Inner Mani*. Chicago.

Silk, Michael S., ed. (1996). *Tragedy and the Tragic*. Oxford.

Sourvinou-Inwood, Christiane. (1994). "Something to Do with Athens: Tragedy and Ritual," in *Ritual, Finance, Politics: Athenian Democratic Accounts Presented to David Lewis*, ed. Robin Osborne and Simon Hornblower. Oxford. 269-90.

Taplin, Oliver. (1986). "Fifth-Century Tragedy and Comedy: A *Synkrisis*," *JHS* 106: 163-74.

———. (1993). *Comic Angels and Other Approaches to Greek Drama through Vase-Paintings*. Oxford.

Vernant, Jean-Pierre. [1985] (1990). "The Masked Dionysus of Euripides' *Bacchae*," in *Myth and Tragedy in Ancient Greece*, ed. Jean-Pierre Vernant and Pierre Vidal-Naquet; trans. J. Lloyd. New York. 381-412.

Versnel, H. S. (1990). *Inconsistencies in Greek and Roman Religion I: Ter Unus*. Leiden. 96-205.

West, Martin L. (1983). *The Orphic Poems*. Oxford.

Winkler, John J. (1990). "The Ephebes' Song: *Tragôidia* and *Polis*," in Winker and Zeitlin 1990. 20-62.

———— and Froma I. Zeitlin, eds. (1990). *Nothing to Do with Dionysus?* Princeton.

Zaidman, Louise Bruit, and Pauline Schmitt Pantel. [1989] (1992). *Religion in the Ancient City*, trans. P. Cartledge. Cambridge.

Zeitlin, Froma I. (1990). "Thebes: Theater of Self and Society in Athenian Drama," in Winkler and Zeitlin 1990. 130-67.

————. (1991). "Euripides' Hekabe and the Somatics of Dionysiac Drama," *Ramus* 20: 53-94 = Zeitlin 1996, 172-216.

————. (1993). "Staging Dionysus between Thebes and Athens," in Carpenter and Faraone 1993. 147-82.

———— (1996). *Playing the Other: Gender and Society in Classical Greek Literature*. Chicago.

Index